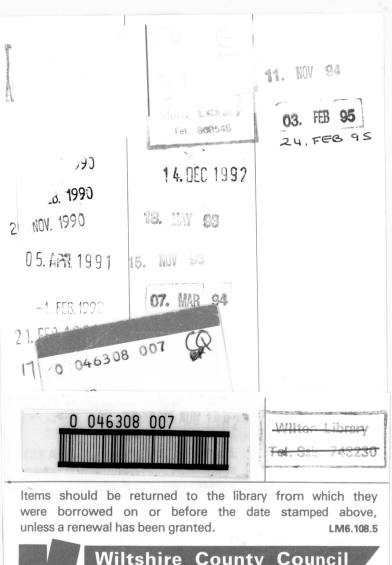

THE GENIUS OF BRITISH PAINTING

EDITOR DAVID PIPER

WEIDENFELD AND NICOLSON LONDON

Series design by Trevor Vincent
Layout by Rod Josey
for George Weidenfeld and Nicolson Limited,
11 St John's Hill, London SW11

Filmset by Keyspools Ltd, Golborne, Lancs
Printed in Italy

ISBN 0 297 76866 2

CONTENTS

INTRODUCTION

Forty years ago, the vast exhibition of British Art, 1000–1860, at the Royal Academy provoked inevitably ruminations on the essentially British quality of the country's art, all the more as it followed a famous and majestic sequence of winter exhibitions of Flemish, Dutch, Italian, Persian and French art. The opening was saluted by *The Times* with a leader, and by a long article by the art critic. (Also, splendidly in the best Academy tradition by a piece, not much shorter than that by the art critic, headed – 'The Private View – Some of the Dresses'.) Both leader and art critic happily found cause for satisfaction, but undeniably the tenor of both articles was of apologia. 'In most other countries – in Italy and France in particular – the forms of expression proceeding from general artistic sensibility are more clearly differentiated – or, to put it another way, the stream of general artistic sensibility is more definitely canalized according to the logic of the particular senses. There seems indeed to be a constitutional difference in the very act of seeing between English and Continental – or at any rate Latin – people. . . . The Italian or the French visual artist is, as nearly as may be, purely visual, whereas the English artist as often paints what he hears or feels – or tastes or smells – as what he sees, which leads the unthinking to attribute to confusion of aim what is really due to mixed inspiration.' An ingenious, if not entirely happy skip in the argument leads then to the equation of British art with 'aesthetic "muddling through",' but thereafter the writer descends more solidly to specifics – notably, the long-agreed notion that this art is 'graphic rather than plastic', and that its subject matter is 'people and things' rather than 'forms and colours'.

The defensive note is intelligible, for British art had by then been long under fire. Taine had diagnosed the lack of plasticity seventy years before, and had even (confronted by the Pre-Raphaelites in their polychrome prime) anticipated in rather more forceful form *The Times*'s suggestion, that the English see differently, by stating bluntly that there must beyond doubt be something wrong with the English retina. Later, in the 1880s, Henry James noted more than once the lack of a true plastic sense in British painting – and, 'I may frankly observe that English painting interests me chiefly, not as painting, but as English. It throws little light, on the whole, on the art of Titian and of Rembrandt, but it throws a light which is to me always fresh, always abundant, always fortunate, on the turn of the English mind.' Ruskin, though of course unlike Taine an ardent supporter of the Pre-Raphaelites, had strict reservations about the scope of ability of English art; in his second Slade lecture, at Oxford in 1870, he suggested the English abjure design, and ideal or theological art, their strength being in portraiture, domestic drama, animal painting and especially landscape. In 1934, when it fell to Roger Fry to deliver some lectures in connection with the Academy exhibition, it was the lack of plasticity again that offended the critic, irrespective of the particular branch of painting in which the lack occurred. But in general, Roger Fry mounted a briskly murderous campaign on British art; still very good reading today, even if some of the concepts he slaughtered had, for many people, died years before he attacked them. 'A minor art' said Fry to his rather old-fashioned audience; 'an ominous preponderance of portraits.' It was the destructive side that really appealed to Fry ('thoroughly enjoyed myself', he wrote in a letter about his audience's disapproval), but coming down to positive basics, he was not the first to categorise the quality of British art as 'primarily linear, descriptive, and non-plastic'.

Since then there have been two extensive attempts to indentify those elements in British art that make it specifically British. The first, by Dagobert Frey, in German, appeared in the curious context of Stuttgart in 1942; that is, at a point in time when the German-speaking peoples were dedicated to the extinction of Britain by force of arms. But, far from being an attack on British art, the book is sympathetic and sensitive – and very well informed – and agrees in the main points of its analysis very closely with the conclusions offered later (1956) by Sir Nikolaus Pevsner in his *Englishness of English Art*.

Any account of the Englishness of English art must begin with geography, with the obvious fact that Britain is an island; thence it is only logical to expect that its art is likely to be insular. Detached, floating off the western sea-board of Europe, Britain has always been the receptacle for the overspill of the Continent, both of ideas and of people, the latter till 1066 mostly violent in the form of invasion and thereafter peaceful, generally peace-seeking – refugees from religious or political persecution, or simply people seeking work or a livelihood. The art of Roman Britain was predominantly provincial Roman, but even so – as it is to be remembered that 'Roman Britain' lasted some four hundred years, approximately an equal time-span to that of post-Renaissance art in England – native insular accents have been convincingly diagnosed in some sculpture of the period, most forcefully perhaps in the famous 'Gloucester' head, with its tendency to abstraction of form combined with an intense emotionalism. But the first resonant statements, in painting, that have survived are later, from the seventh to ninth centuries, the Book of Durrow to the Book of Kells, and are also masterpieces of their kind that have never been surpassed. Here, the linear and the abstracting qualities are displayed in dazzlingly inventive yet highly controlled profusion: the style however can be claimed with reason (even though it flourished notably in Northumbria) to be too purely Irish to be classified as British, far less so as English. Its transposition into English develops into something of a compromise, at its best achieving a most finely balanced marriage of abstract decorative design with recognisably (though of course far from naturalistic) figurative representation. It is, though, an art which most people would judge, in post-Renaissance terms, to be more akin to drawing than to painting, and, as Jonathan Alexander stresses, it is very noticeable that 'colour wash drawings of wonderful quality occur in English manuscripts of all periods'.

This in turn implies from the beginnings that the English genius in painting does not conceive instinctively in terms of three-dimensional painting, or in terms of mass and volume in space. Here geography may well be partly responsible: the English climate, even when seeming crystal-clear to the natives, appears slightly hazy to those coming from, say, Italy. Mediterranean light has an extraordinary faculty of seeming to order, in the onlooker's eye, its component elements into interrelationships that have a visual logic, and inevitability, that is rarely glimpsed in England. And when Continental originals in art, imported into Britain, are copied, or used as source for inspiration, their painterly and monumental qualities tend to be transposed into linear values. Yet for the medieval period, as Dr Alexander again stressed, the diagnosis of differences, and of the significance of any such differences, of art this side of the Channel from the Continental main tradition, is a very delicate task, for the similarities of English art, with particularly North European art as a whole, are 'more striking than the dissimilarities'. At that point of time it is perhaps more meaningful to talk of Christian church art rather than of European art, for the Church, as patron and supplier of subject matter almost to the point of monopoly, overrode all racial, political and geographical boundaries in Europe. All the same there was an insular individuality and the vitality of illumination in England seems to have flourished or faded in relation to the vitality of that individuality: up to the mid-fifteenth century the insular style was able, for the most part, to take what it wanted from influences coming from the Continent, to adapt and digest them into forms that might then be shipped back across the Channel to inspire new trends there. Only with the invasion of the naturalistic style that developed from the Van Eycks, does the insular vitality in art seem to have succumbed, so that most late fifteenth and early sixteenth-century English art, in painting, glass or illumination, becomes a mere, weak, provincial exercise in the Netherlandish manner. It is almost as though the native · genius had consciously decided that this imitative art was not for them (Michelangelo was to do much the same even if for other reasons and with very different results) – and turned their endeavour to other things, notably of course the unique – and uniquely English – achievement in the final flowering of Gothic architecture.

Stylistically, in the medieval period certain traits are strongly emphasised that recur throughout the subsequent history of English art. The linear emphasis tends to provide, seemingly inevitably, a fascination for vertical emphasis and often for attenuation: this occurs in the enduring tradition for whole-length standing figure, though in very varying forms, ranging from society portraiture to the visionary wraiths of Blake. The implication that the English worked, in painting, most happily to a relatively small scale, is also apparent; monumental paintings, such as those of the two kinds in the sedilia in Westminster Abbey of the early fourteenth century, are witness that work of that scale, of high quality, did occur in England, but the rarity of survivors of that standard compared with the fairly crude level of wall-paintings that still lurk in churches throughout the country, suggests that it was indeed in manuscript illumination that the medieval painters excelled. And there were to be no worthy rivals in England ever to the great fresco painters and mural decorators of Italy. The English climate is here again partly to blame, for the island's persistent damp is noxious to large-scale painting, whether fresco or stretched on vast canvases, but even so the ablest of the English-born large-scale operators, Thornhill, seems but diligently laborious compared with the aerial inspiration of the great Venetian or south German decorators, or for that matter with Rubens' superbly vigorous ceiling in Whitehall. In terms of subject matter, a significant English innovation in illumination was that brisk and lively fascination – which might seem contradictory to the native compulsion towards abstraction – in quirks and oddities, realised in the grotesqueries that frolic in the margins of so many manuscripts of the thirteenth and fourteenth centuries.

The history of post-Renaissance English art seems to carry on, as far as native-born artists are concerned, the native reluctance to come to terms with the major consequences of the formal discoveries of Continental art, but it also bears overwhelming evidence that English patronage was very much interested in the results of these discoveries. The patrons tended not to buy British – even at home. Throughout the sixteenth and seventeenth centuries the outstanding, and most successful artists working in England were not English-born, nor were many of the more important secondary ones. Holbein – Swiss-German; Van Dyck – Flemish; Lely – Dutch; Kneller – German; and all came as immigrants with their style fully-fledged in Continental modes.

The flowering of a true native-born English school in the eighteenth century diminished the foreign impact, though considerable painters from abroad happily continued to settle here – Gravelot, Canaletto, Zoffany, de Loutherbourg, Fuseli, amongst them; the American, West, even became the second President of the Royal Academy, and then, late in the nineteenth century, arrived the American expatriates, Whistler and Sargent. So Sickert was perhaps not exaggerating all that wildly when – delighted to cause maximum embarrassment in the Guards' mess where he was dining one night near the end of the first world war – he claimed loudly: 'And no one could be more English than I am – born in Munich in 1860, of pure Danish descent.'

Such a levity would not have amused Hogarth. As research over recent years into earlier history of English painting has intensified, Hogarth's title, once often used, as the 'Father of British Painting' has become somewhat qualified, and indeed it cannot be claimed that, as painter, he was the fountain-head of an enduring and developing style (though his influence on caricature has never failed). But psychologically, in his continuing battle for the rights of native artists and the prestige of English art, in his belligerent, sometimes chauvinistic nationalism, he signalled a new independence. In his work some of the abiding English characteristics can be diagnosed, especially the linear quality, with his very explicit emphasis on the S line of beauty. This is an undulating line that might be thought to be, and indeed is, an element of the international baroque style, or, in a quicker, more broken, rhythm, of the rococo, but as practised by Hogarth, it is much more of an arabesque across a relatively shallow plane. It is also used to describe subject-matter that was much more down to earth than elsewhere, at the time, in Europe. His interest in quirks and oddities of human nature may recall the English illuminations of the middle ages, but is co-ordinated into a comic version of a grand design. Hogarth was of course the interpreter of the rising middle-classes of the first half of the eighteenth century. 'Comedy presents persons of inferior rank, and consequently of inferior manners' – 'it presents the ludicrous instead of the sublime, and life everywhere furnishes an accurate observer with the ridiculous.' (That is the novelist Fielding, not Hogarth, and the overt cross-referencing between painter and writer emphasises on several occasions their common roots in ordinary life.) Comedy is the other side of the medal from tragedy, and none the less serious – it can indeed, as Shakespeare had long ago demonstrated, embrace tragedy, as in *The Rake's Progress* or *Mariage à la Mode*.

Hogarth's 'straight' portraiture, while relying generally on well-established formulae, realised them with a new and direct robustness, while in his conversation pieces, of which he was the first major master, portraiture is extended to reflect a whole way of life – the family in its domestic setting, with furniture and possessions portrayed with the same literalness as their owners – a form that flourished in England as nowhere else, in a comfortable confidence of enduring stability. Other artists – Devis, Zoffany, and, most superbly, George Stubbs – extended it to embrace the mansion, park, animals – especially horses. Some of their paintings might almost be read as portrayals of the reclamation of the Garden of Eden by man – a garden now satisfactorily developed into respectable civilisation, even if, say, Hogarth's own figures, in his portraits, are a little grossly swelling in their charming complacency, or rather knobbly in the articulation of their limbs. The next generation removed any hint of possible gaucherie; one may regret the lack of any major follow-up of Hogarth's forthrightly bourgeois style of portraiture, but Reynolds and Gainsborough between them, in their very different ways, were to lift the normally limited genre of society portraiture into the category of high art. Different indeed as were the two men, their visions were both rooted in the particular, while from the individual idiosyncracies of appearance with which their sitters presented them, both produced images of a much more general validity. Reynolds, drawing on a widely eclectic knowledge of the old masters, and applying this to the production of his characters, endowed them, and English portraiture, with the formal depth and richness of history or religious painting. If Reynolds could range all the way between the domestically intimate and the heroically sublime, Gainsborough relied on sheer quality of paint and draughtsmanship, in his last years achieving at his best a lyric felicity which invests his long-dead sitters with the immediate freshness of a dream. Often inspired by Van Dyck, his genius is yet essentially English in its high key, its linear quality.

In portraiture, Reynolds's and Gainsborough's subject matter was the English men and women who sat for them. For the first genius of English landscape painting, Constable, the subject matter was the English countryside, the local weather moving across known fields and woods; his art was in a real sense portraiture again, the capturing of the likeness of the countryside, not of course in a dryly topographical sense, but in a stubborn quest to capture nature live – and always English nature. Turner, on the other hand, though in his person a splendid example of English eccentricity, sought his subject matter through Western Europe. Sky and sea, incandescent with light, fascinated him more and more, rather than the solidity of the earth itself, yet even so wherever he was, it was the vaporous opalescence of atmosphere, rather than the Claudeian azure serenity of classical landscape, that visually caught his interest. It was an English eye, grown to maturity in a misty climate, that seized moments in Venice very unlike the crystal clarity of Canaletto's vision of the city. And then, William Blake, seeming to operate in a theatre of art that had no connection at all with the work of his great English predecessors or contemporaries, but who was perhaps the most English of them all, the master of 'the flaming line'.

The English achievement between 1750 and 1850 was indeed of such quality, originality and variety that its failure to develop in Victorian times seems difficult to explain. However, the Victorian and Edwardian achievement has been underestimated owing to the acceptance of the idea that the formal discoveries – from Courbet through the Impressionists and Post-Impressionists – exploited especially in France, drained all value from any other kind of art. Clearly, the English were at this point insular, and even frequently bigoted in their conservatism, but that did not prevent them from painting some enchanting pictures. Now that the heady waves of movement on movement on the Continent have receded in time, the perseverance of English painters according to their own traditional lights appears at times almost heroic (even if, in the current boom of Victoriana, far too much is praised); they were in fact working in a perfectly honourable alternative tradition, and with its tools and techniques they here and there enlarged that tradition meaningfully – as did the Pre-Raphaelites and even some of the most academic of Academicians, like Leighton. Certainly, the English vices, especially that of literary painting in the bad sense – anecdotal and sentimental trivia – flourished exceeding, but solid achievement, as Mr Bowness makes clear, was not rare.

In the 1970s the English picture-loving public – though not always the artists (especially, understandably, the young ones) – has a remarkably wide tolerance of taste. This has of course its dangers, and springs partly from accidental factors, especially that of the inflationary boom of monetary value of anything at all that has merely technical quality or facility. But on the whole it means that more and more people are deriving pleasure from more and more worthwhile sources – long considered as purely English eccentricities, digestible only by English eyes – and that this art is now exported for the wonder of America, Europe and Japan. Two English painters of today, Nicholson and Bacon, rate very high in international categories of major living artists, and both, in the swift merging of national individualities in the 'international styles' of the second half of the twentieth century, remain very strongly rooted in England. In Ben Nicholson's famous white reliefs of the thirties he produced work that was of major importance in art-historical terms, and which also eluded any attempt at national definition as 'English' in precise terms. Yet in the later reliefs – as also in drawings produced throughout his long career – there is again that linear accent combined with a moody weather that seems a recurrent English theme. One commentator has suggested that the reaction to the white reliefs or the later textured ones depended on personal taste – whether one liked, it was suggested, one's martini's dry or with rather more vermouth. In this case I would plump for the latter mixture: an equation of pure form with atmospheric, locally inspired, overtones that seems a magical solution of the English dilemna.

DAVID PIPER

1

THE MIDDLE AGES

Jonathan Alexander

The material available to the student of medieval art is only a small fraction of what once existed. The surviving works of art are not necessarily representative or typical; it is likely that a number of others have not yet come to light. This is particularly so of book illumination, but even in mural painting new discoveries of the greatest importance have been made in the last few years. We can form some idea of what is lost from medieval descriptions and inventories. Wars, fires and other disasters, the collapse and replacement of buildings, all resulted in the loss of works of art during the Middle Ages. The intentional and catastrophic destruction of the Reformation period, greater than any other single cause, is too well known for comment; but time, neglect, accidents and restorations have destroyed much else since then.

In this country, very little mural painting survives compared with Italy, or stained glass compared with France. The monumental painting is all fragmentary and mostly in a very poor state: the climate and the technique used were against its survival. Throughout the Middle Ages earlier cycles were painted over or destroyed and replaced with new ones. We have a few detailed descriptions of cycles which do not survive, such as the titles for the paintings in the Chapter House at Worcester or the description of the paintings in the choir stalls at Peterborough.

In illuminated manuscripts we are much richer and, moreover, the surviving works are, as the mural painting is not, unrestored and often in pristine condition. They tended to be produced in the great artistic centres and it is often through them alone that we can trace a continuing tradition of creativity in these centres. Winchester is a case in point. Nor should they be considered simply as a reflection of more important works of monumental art. Undoubtedly some of the greatest achievements were in book painting, especially in the earlier Middle Ages.

With manuscripts, too, inventories and library catalogues show us how little survives. For example, Dr N.R.Ker in his *Medieval Libraries of Great Britain* lists about 300 identifiable surviving books from the library of Christ Church cathedral priory,

Canterbury. The catalogue drawn up under Prior Eastry (1284–1331), as printed by M.R.James, contains 1,831 items. These do not include the Mass books kept on the altar or in the sacristy, which would be the most highly illuminated. At St Paul's Cathedral a catalogue of books of 1255 gives unusually detailed descriptions, including notes of the illuminations, of 123 books. None of these can be identified today. More than 170 medieval manuscripts survived into the seventeenth century, but all except three were destroyed in the Fire of London in 1666. The losses have continued; the fire at Ashburnham House, in 1731, which destroyed many of the books rescued by the antiquary Sir Robert Cotton (1571–1631), is just one example. More recently there have been disastrous losses in the two World Wars, for example the magnificent, early-fourteenth-century, East Anglian Psalter preserved at Douai, which was buried for safety in 1914, only to be recovered severely damaged by damp.

The art of the Middle Ages was predominantly a literary art, that is to say based on written texts. There was much decorative ornament, of course, painted and carved decoration on buildings, carpet pages in Insular books, arabesque initials in Romanesque manuscripts, or marginal grotesques in Gothic manuscripts. But where there are figures they are almost always illustrating or in some way dependent on a text.

Throughout the period under discussion the major part of the surviving works is religious. Secular works increase in proportion and in importance as the Middle Ages decline. The same is true of patronage and of the artists. Until about 1200 the artists whose names we know tend to be in religious orders, many of them monks, and their task was to produce works of art for the Church. Even where the patron was a king or a great nobleman the work often had the same purpose. From the twelfth century onwards lay craftsmen predominate and the secular patron has a more important part to play. The bourgeoisie as well as the nobility commission and own works of art.

In Christian theology, from the earliest times, there had been controversy over the function of images: the destruction of the Reformation was only the last of a series of iconoclastic movements of which St Bernard's denunciation of useless ornament in the twelfth century, or the Byzantine iconoclastic controversy, which was discussed also at the court of Charlemagne, are earlier examples. The opposing party's main defence was discussed by Pope Gregory the Great (590–604), who said that the Bible stories were to be portrayed for the poor who could not read. A supplementary justification lay in making the Church on earth a reflection of the heavenly Jerusalem, as Abbot Suger emphasises in his account of his rebuilding of the church of St Denis, outside Paris, an account which seems to be intended as a reply to St Bernard's strictures.

Secular art also very often had a didactic aim in glorifying a ruler or his house. It too usually depends on a text, for example the chivalrous histories and romances. But it is not always possible to make a clearcut distinction between religious and secular art, and there is a world which spans both, including allegorical, didactic and moralising material, such as the illustrations to the bestiary. Scenes of very varied character could be portrayed in the same building, as at Longthorpe near Peterborough.

The religious, political, social and economic conditions of the Middle Ages inevitably affected the art of the period. We can observe such factors dictating the nature and the content of that art. It is harder to explain the genesis and the development of styles in these terms, however. With certain reservations we can say of English art that the Norman Conquest introduced the Romanesque style into England. But the style already existed and there can be no simple explanation of its creation. A growth in population, monastic reform, increasing economic prosperity and a certain stability after the upheavals of the Norman invasions of the tenth century, may all have combined to create the right conditions. But they still do not adequately explain the qualities which typify Romanesque art.

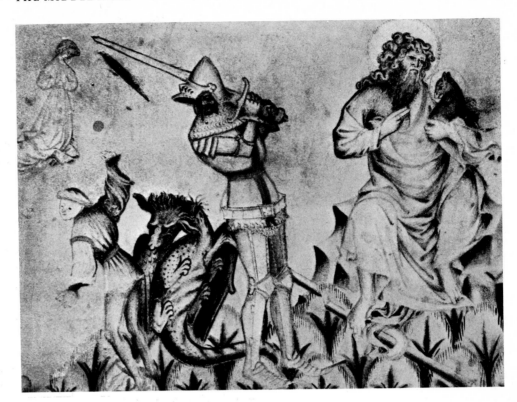

Page from a sketchbook showing St George and
St John the Baptist. Late fourteenth century.
Pepysian MS 1916, folio 16.
By permission of the Master and Fellows of
Magdalene College, Cambridge.

In recent years it has been the tendency to emphasise the importance of the patron
who commissioned the work of art. Certainly his willingness to provide resources or
money is a basic necessity, for medieval art was always expensive to produce, apart
from the labour involved, because of the cost of the materials. The costliness itself
was considered an important feature of a work of art and is constantly singled out
for praise by the chroniclers. But we must not go too far in attributing a sort of
vicarious creativeness to the patron. There is an obvious temptation to do this from
the fact that we know so much more about the patrons than we do about the artists,
who were humbler men.

The question of an artist's originality is at all times a difficult one to assess. In the
Middle Ages artistic freedom was always limited. In general terms we see it increase
as the Middle Ages decline. Many factors have to be borne in mind, such as the
artist's mobility, the accessibility of works of art for him to see, and the availability
of materials. The apparent reluctance of the medieval artists to sign their work is
certainly significant, both for their own view of their function, and for their place
in society. At the same time we must remember that one of the consequences of the
losses already mentioned is that many works referred to in literary records and
accounts giving the artists' names can no longer be identified. Similarly documents
have no doubt been lost which could have given us information about works
which do survive.

The medieval artist's dependence on models is well known and a large part of art
historians' attention is concentrated on reconstructing such sources. For example,
cycles of illustrations created in the classical or late antique periods continue to be
copied in the Middle Ages and these enable us to reconstruct lost works, as well as
to study the alterations made to them. We must not indeed underestimate the medieval artist's ability to alter his model. He did this often by small but effective modifications. He could also combine different models or create new scenes by analogy
with ones which already existed. We know little of how the models were transmitted
in the early Middle Ages, but in the later period we have a number of sketchbooks
surviving. These contain notes of compositions for use when required, or, often,

single figures, studies of drapery, animals, birds, architecture, or ornament, which could be combined to form very different pictures (see p. 15). In many medieval works of art we find the same types of figure recurring in different scenes, and this use of a *modulus*, as it is called, is especially noticeable from the thirteenth century onwards. From about 1200 there is a notable enlargement and enrichment of pictorial cycles for both old and new texts. This enrichment applies also to both stained glass and to mural painting.

Though the importance of the model is cardinal in medieval art, medieval artists could and did invent new illustrations. Even where they copied a composition they rarely reproduced the style of their model. This can be illustrated by a famous example from English art – the copies made in the eleventh and twelfth centuries of an illustrated Psalter made at Rheims in the second quarter of the ninth century. Known as the Utrecht Psalter, from its present home, this manuscript came to England at an uncertain date, probably in the second half of the tenth century. The technique of line drawing in the Carolingian manuscript, and its dynamic style, with shivering calligraphic outlines, evoked a remarkable response from Anglo-Saxon artists, and the effects on Anglo-Saxon painting of the tenth and eleventh centuries were far-reaching. The first of the three surviving copies (London, British Library, Harley 603) was begun about AD 1000 at Canterbury. It is extraordinarily faithful to the style of the original even though certain important modifications were made, such as the introduction of various coloured inks to supplement the brown of the original. Though closest in style, this copy, which is unfinished, is least faithful iconographically, even inserting scenes not found in the Utrecht Psalter, as if the artists (for there are different hands and the work continued into the twelfth century) felt so sure of themselves that they could abandon their model. The second copy (Cambridge, Trinity College, MS. R. 17.1) was written by the scribe Eadwine, whose portrait it contains, in the mid twelfth century, perhaps about 1147, since a comet which appeared in that year is mentioned. Here again there are different artists. In the earlier Psalms, additions were made to the Utrecht Psalter scenes, some, like the portrayal of Absalom caught up in the tree by his hair, depending on biblical exegesis. These additions were soon abandoned, however, and the remainder of the scenes are copied accurately. In spite of the close iconographic dependence on the model the style has now altered greatly. The figures are outlined by a continuous emphatic contour and their drapery is divided into contrasting areas, with coloured bands of red, blue and green. The scenes are contained in frames, not for any illusionistic purpose of representing a view as if seen through a window, for they overlap the frame slightly, but to anchor them, so to speak, by providing a fixed boundary. The artists do not feel the need to fill every space with incident, but leave blank areas of open space to contrast with the areas of activity.

Later still in the century, perhaps about 1180, a third copy was made (Paris, Bibliothèque Nationale, latin 8846). This is also incomplete, additions having been made by a Catalan artist in Spain in the fourteenth century. The artist of this third version seems either to have had both the Utrecht and the Eadwine Psalter before him or to have used another copy which does not survive. If we look at the same illustration to Psalm 20, we find an even greater contrast than before. The miniatures are fully painted in rich colours with highly burnished gold leaf backgrounds. The most obvious alteration is in the increased size of figures relative to setting, and to achieve this the artist, in many scenes, has sacrificed a number of the figures. In the particular miniature illustrated the artist has rearranged the lower right-hand corner. The horses, figures and chariots tumble as if from the sky, where before they were shown on the ground. We might think that the artist has made the alteration in order to fill an awkward space, were it not that there is a striking resemblance between the group and the pagan composition of the Fall of Phaethon from the chariot of the

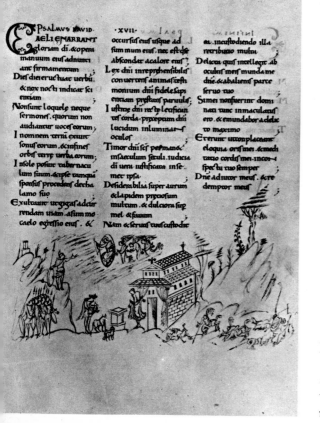

Illustration to Psalm 20 (Vulgate XIX).
'Some trust in chariots and some in horses.'
Psalter, Canterbury, c. 1000.
Harley 603, folio 11.
British Library, London.

16

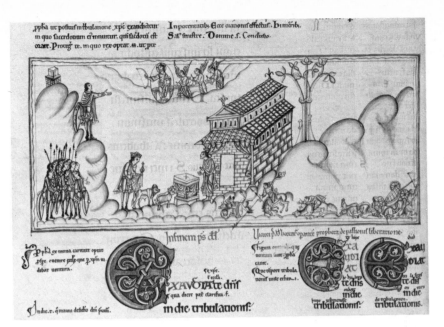

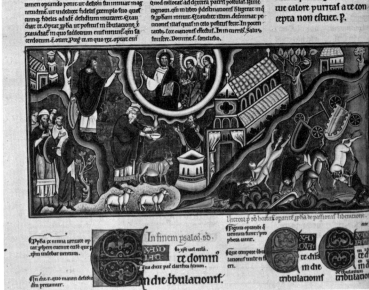

Above, Illustration to Psalm 20.
Eadwine Psalter, Canterbury, *c.* 1147.
MS R.17.1, folio 33ᵛ.
Trinity College, Cambridge.
Above right, Illustration to Psalm 20.
Psalter. Canterbury (?), late twelfth century.
Latin 8846, folio 33ᵛ.
Bibliothèque Nationale, Paris.

Sun, as it is represented on a number of classical sarcophagi. I think it is almost certain that the artist had this scene in mind. This is a high point of classicism in western art which gives real meaning to the concept of a twelfth-century Renaissance. In all three copies of the Utrecht Psalter, therefore, modifications in style or in iconography are made and none of the artists is a slavish copyist; each made his own significant alterations.

Another fact about the medieval artist which should be emphasised is that he was a very skilled craftsman. Many artists certainly practised metalwork and other techniques besides painting. We have a number of treatises on the technical aspects of medieval art and from these and study of the originals we can learn much of the methods and materials used. There can be no doubt that then, as now, reading a manual was no substitute for training in a craft with a man who was already master of it.

This is another reason, then, for rejecting excessive claims made for the importance of the patron. He might put models before an artist or enable him to travel, he might dictate the form a work of art was to take, he might choose one artist and reject another, though even here caution is necessary when we consider what very different works of art a patron like the Duke of Bedford owned or commissioned. But the craft was passed on from artist to artist, and this training and the tradition within which he worked remains fundamental for the artist's style as well as for the content of his art, together with his own gifts. It is this tradition which needs emphasis and which explains why it is that in the history of English medieval art the same places reappear again and again at different dates, Winchester, Canterbury, Westminster, St Albans, Durham, Peterborough, for example.

In what follows we must remain content to try to trace the stylistic changes, realising that almost everything remains to be discovered about their causes. Three things are worth saying. First, the great artist both reflects and sums up his age in a particularly intimate way. He is both leader and follower. He may seem to anticipate trends which only become obvious to the historian in a wider context later. At the same time he is the most typical product of his age, crystallizing its qualities in his art. Secondly, it is common in art-historical enquiry to find the same tendency, whether in iconography or in style, occurring in widely separated areas at about the same time. Of course it may be our ignorance of all the facts which prevents us from seeing some connection which may have existed. On the other hand it may be that in a mysterious way different people in different places may feel the need independently to express themselves in a similar way at the same moment. Thirdly, earlier works of art may be perfectly accessible to artists without catching their attention. For example, classical monuments and classical sculpture survived into the Middle Ages even in England. But it was only at certain periods and selectively that artists were able to profit from them by adopting their style and their forms.

Throughout the Middle Ages English art was intimately connected with European art. The main stylistic changes occur as they do on the Continent and there are numerous points of contact. It is impossible to consider English art in isolation. On the other hand one asks, how is it that we can say at all of works that they are English? Are there specific qualities which we find at certain times or even throughout the Middle Ages in English art, which are not present, or not to the same extent, in European art? Certain scholars have tackled this problem and certain qualities have been singled out by Adolf Goldschmidt, Professor Pevsner and others. In the enormous variety of medieval art it might seem possible, to some extent, to document almost any set of supposed characteristics. Nevertheless, with caution, we may observe certain trends to which English medieval art is particularly susceptible. It will be seen, for example, that colour-wash drawings of wonderful quality occur in English manuscripts of all periods. The manuscripts are equally notable for an ability to unify the design of different elements on a page into a rich and varied pattern. This implies an interest in two-dimensional design which tends to abstraction. We can find many examples of imported monumental three-dimensional forms being gradually replaced by two-dimensional abstract patterns. In the iconography of their pictures, that is the types of figure and the various ways of representing certain scenes, English artists were often inventive, even eccentric. Another characteristic which has been noted is a tendency to caricature, to represent the grotesque and the ugly. Nevertheless the similarities at any given moment to European art, particularly in North France and Flanders with which there were strong political and trade ties, are more striking than the dissimilarities, at least from the twelfth century onwards. The importance of the Church as an organization transcending national boundaries should also be emphasized.

The earliest painting of the Middle Ages in Britain which survives dates from the end of the seventh century. The conversion of England had been begun a century earlier by St Augustine, apostle of the English, who was sent by Pope Gregory the Great and landed in Kent in 597. A Gospel Book which has pictures of events from the Life of Christ, and one surviving Evangelist portrait was, by tradition, brought over by St Augustine to this country (Cambridge, Corpus Christi College, MS. 286). Certainly it was written in Italy in the sixth century and was at St Augustine's, Canterbury, in the Middle Ages. In the twelfth century the arrangement of the small scenes of Christ's life, set twelve to a page in squares within a frame, was twice copied, once in the Paris Psalter just mentioned and once in some detached leaves which may once have belonged to the Eadwine Psalter. This illustrates the important point that there were preserved in England ancient cycles from the Mediterranean lands made in the late antique period, which were copied, and so in some cases preserved, when the originals had disappeared. We know also from Bede that Augustine brought pictures of the Last Judgement to represent the terrors of Hell to his pagan audience.

At the same time Irish missionaries had begun the conversion of Northumbria. The result was the extraordinarily fruitful conjunction which produced what are probably the works of medieval British painting best known to the general public, the Books of Lindisfarne and Kells, the former made at Lindisfarne just before 700, the latter perhaps at Iona around 800. Though scholars differ on the relative importance of the Irish and Northumbrian contributions to these works, their extraordinary creativeness is not in doubt, and some at least of their sources are clear. On the one hand are Mediterranean models. These existed most obviously for the figures and

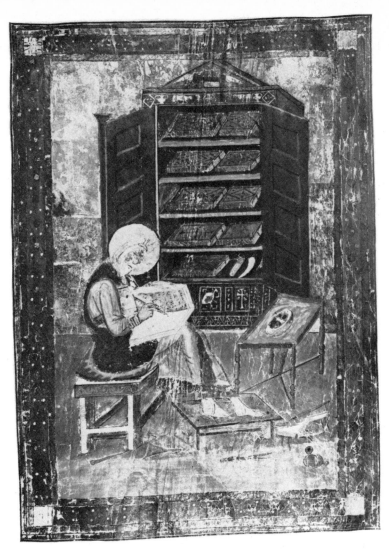

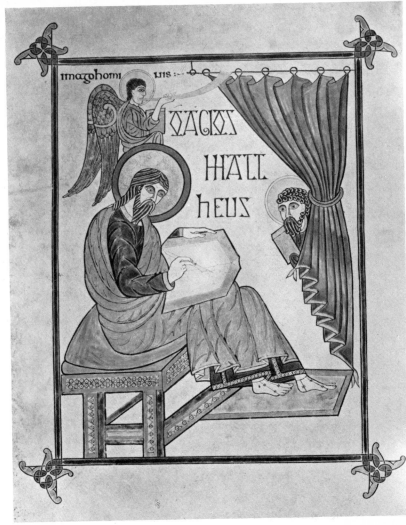

Above, The prophet Ezra. Frontispiece to a Bible (Codex Amiatinus I). Monkwearmouth/Jarrow, before 716. Codex Amiatinus I, folio v^v. Biblioteca Laurenziana, Florence.
Above right, St Matthew, from a Gospel Book (the Lindisfarne Gospels). Lindisfarne, c.698. Cotton Nero D. IV, folio 25^v. British Library, London.

we can see the Insular artists' use of them in two famous manuscripts. The first is a giant Bible (Florence, Biblioteca Laurenziana, Cod. Amiatinus 1), one of three identical copies made at Monkwearmouth/Jarrow in the late seventh century and taken from there to Italy in 716 as a present to the Pope by Abbot Ceolfrith (690–716). Ceolfrith had been in Italy before and had evidently brought back a Bible which had been made in south Italy under the direction of Cassiodorus (*c.* 485–*c.* 580) at his monastery of Vivarium. This was accurately copied by the Anglo-Saxon monks, including its illustrations, which comprised an author portrait of the prophet Ezra who, like Cassiodorus, made an attempt to edit the Bible text, a page of Christ in Majesty, and a series of diagrams. Ezra is shown in three-quarter profile, writing. Behind him is a cupboard with seven volumes in it bearing the names of the books of the Bible contained in each. There can be no doubt that this is a substantially accurate copy of the late sixth-century model. There exists another version of the figure, however, which has been considerably modified. This is the portrait of St Matthew in the Lindisfarne Gospels (London, British Library, Cotton Nero D. IV). This copies the Cassiodoran original not the Amiatinus portrait. Though the outline of the figure is very nearly the same, the setting is omitted, being replaced by a curtain from which a figure with a book looks out. Above St Matthew is his symbol, the angel, clearly an addition inserted in the corner, and labelled 'imago hominis', image of a man. The other inscription is in Greek transliterated 'O Agios Mattheus', Saint Matthew.

The broad frame of the Ezra portrait encloses a scene in which objects are related to each other in a space, which, even though the perspective is not accurate, is continuous and merely curtailed by the frame. The frame of the Matthew portrait on the other hand is a narrow band, which has the function of defining a space to be filled rather than inviting the eye to penetrate through to an imaginary space. Within this defined space objects are arranged to balance in the most subtle way. If one mentally removes an object in the Ezra portrait, the ink bottle on the floor or one of the volumes in the cupboard, it would make scarcely any difference to the picture. Every detail in the Matthew portrait counts, the lettering, the small pattern of circles running along the stool and then on the hem of St Matthew's tunic, and above all the series of overlappings which relate the figures and the objects, St Matthew's halo over the angel, the trumpet over the curtain, the curtain's lower corner behind the foot-stool on which the saint's feet rest. This, then, is already a two-dimensional design in which overlapping plays a vital part. Insular artists could go much further in reducing the figure to abstract pattern, but the point which emerges even here and which is important, is that a classical type of space construction is rejected. We shall see that medieval artists continued to copy models with classically derived, illusionistic space and at the same time that they continued to experiment with alternative methods of organizing figures and objects in relation to each other.

In addition to the Evangelist portraits the Lindisfarne Gospels contains initial pages and carpet pages. It seems likely that these, as well as the portraits, are the work of the scribe Eadfrith, bishop of Lindisfarne 698–721. Many of the carpet pages in Hiberno-Saxon manuscripts, some of the earliest being in the Book of Durrow of *c.* 680 made perhaps at Iona, contain cross motifs. Crosses are also found prefacing Eastern Gospel Books from Syria, Armenia and Egypt which though later in date no doubt copy earlier models. Such models from the boundaries of the classical world may already have shown a linear abstract style opposed to classical illusionism, and this no doubt partly explains their attraction for insular artists. Here again, however, the artist of the Lindisfarne Gospels has made very great modifications in his model. His crosses are outlined by a thin continuous band, but they are set on a writhing mass of interlacing lacertine beasts and birds. The background and the main object, the pattern and the intervals have equal importance.

Thirdly there are the initials. Already in the Psalter of St Columba of the sixth century (Dublin, Royal Irish Academy) possibly written by St Columba himself, who died in 597, the small initials in the text are decorated with rhythmic calligraphic motifs. The initial is as it were phased into the text by a series of letters, decreasing in size from the initial to the ordinary text script. This same principle is applied in the initial pages of the Gospel Books and as the opening letter or monogram of each Gospel Book increases in size and ornamentation, more decorated initials are needed to bring us down to the scale of the script (illustration opposite left). The sources of the patterns are complex, some being Celtic, others deriving from Anglo-Saxon metalwork as seen in the Sutton Hoo burial objects, for instance. But the idea of the initial emphasized in this way seems to come from Ireland, and the intricate balancing of shapes and curves is found in Celtic metalwork.

For the history of medieval art it is the abstract decorative aspects of Insular art which are most important and in particular the emphasis on the initial. Not only did the Insular artists increase the initial's size and importance, they also took the further step of using it as a frame to enclose a scene, for example in a Psalter made probably at Canterbury in the second quarter of the eighth century (London, British Library, Cotton Vespasian A.I.). Known as the historiated initial, this combination of letter and picture, script and illumination, continued in use by artists throughout Europe until the end of the Middle Ages.

The Book of Kells (Dublin, Trinity College, MS. A.i.6) which is the culmination of this series of manuscripts, was made perhaps in Iona about a hundred years later than the Lindisfarne Gospels. In addition to its decorated Canon Tables, Evangelist

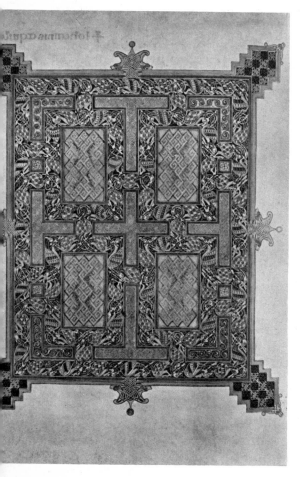

Cross-carpet page from the Lindisfarne Gospels.
Lindisfarne, *c.*698.
Cotton Nero C. IV, folio 210ᵛ.
British Library, London.

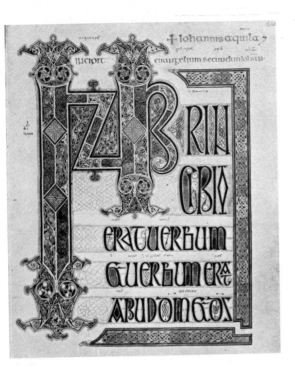

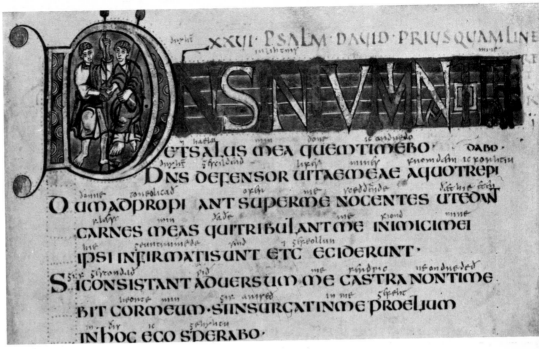

portraits and initial and carpet pages, it has a number of extra miniatures such as the Virgin and Child, the Temptation and the Arrest of Christ, whose iconographical sources are probably Eastern. Its ornament is overwhelming in its incredible profusion and the minute delicacy of its calligraphic skill. In addition to the manuscripts made in Northern England and in Ireland, there were active scriptoria in southern England, and, as a result of the missions of Willibrord and Boniface in the Netherlands and in Germany, the Insular style was transferred to the Continent. Some of the books still at such centres as St Gall were imported by Irish monks, but others were made abroad in centres such as Echternach near Trier, founded by Willibrord in 698.

The succeeding century, the ninth, is largely a blank for English painting due to the chaos in the country produced by the Norse invasions, which began in 835. At the same time there may, at this stage, have been some reluctance on the part of Insular artists to accept the classical style revived under the Emperor Charlemagne (742–814) and his successors. Insular art on the other hand was extremely influential on the Continent, partly since books were already at such centres as Bobbio, St Gall, Salzburg and Echternach, and partly due to the presence at the court of Englishmen and Irishmen, such as Alcuin of York (*c.* 735–804).

When, at the end of the ninth century, Alfred the Great (reigned 871–99) succeeded in restoring some stability to the kingdom, the debt could be repaid with the introduction of continental manuscripts which were used as models by English artists. For example, King Athelstan (reigned 925–39), Alfred's grandson, gave one such manuscript still surviving (British Library, Cotton Tiberius A.II) to the monks of Christ Church, Canterbury. This is a Gospels made in the early tenth century at the monastery of Lobbes in Belgium, which Athelstan seems to have received as a present from Otto the Great, later Emperor, who had married one of his sisters. A contemporary English artist used one of its Evangelist portraits as a model when he wanted to embellish a Gospels which had no portraits (Oxford, St John's College, MS. 194).

Another continental manuscript produced probably in the same area at about the same date was given by Athelstan to the Old Minster, Winchester, according to a later but probably reliable tradition. It is a small Psalter (British Library, Cotton

21

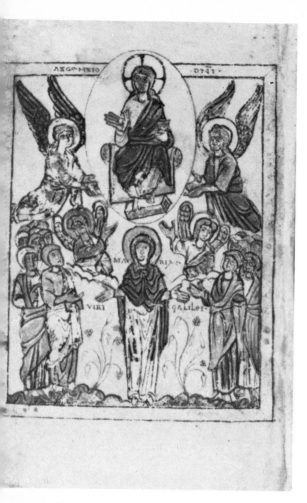

The Ascension. Miniature added to a Psalter (Athelstan Psalter). Winchester, second quarter of tenth century.
Cotton Galba A. xviii, folio 120ᵛ.
British Library, London.

Galba A. XVIII) with gold interlace initials, to which Anglo-Saxon artists added miniatures and a calendar with zodiac signs and small standing saints. Two of the surviving miniatures, those which precede and follow the calendar, show the saints adoring Christ. A third, which preceded Psalm 1 (now detached, Oxford, Bodleian Library, MS. Rawlinson B. 484, fol. 85) shows the Nativity and a fourth preceding Psalm 101, the Ascension of Christ. Another miniature, perhaps the Crucifixion, as Professor Wormald has suggested, may have preceded Psalm 51, marking the division of the Psalter into three equal parts, as was common in Ireland and England.

The sources of these miniatures are not yet established, but it seems quite possible that they lie in early Christian art of the sixth or seventh centuries rather than in Carolingian works. The miniature of the Ascension, for example, is of a type found in Eastern works, such as murals in Egypt and the Syrian Rabbula Gospels of 586, as well as in later Byzantine manuscripts. Christ is enthroned above, in a mandorla, supported by angels, whilst the Virgin stands below, in the centre, with the Apostles on either side. The style, on the other hand, suggests Western sources and as origin of such a combination Ravenna seems one possibility, especially as the bands of saints adoring the Christ in the two All Saints miniatures bring to mind the sixth-century mosaics there. Such an Italian model could already have reached England by the seventh or eighth centuries.

Another example of an Anglo-Saxon copy of a Carolingian model is a manuscript of Rhabanus Maurus' *de laude sanctae crucis* (Cambridge, Trinity College, MS. B. 16.3). The text, which was written at Fulda in the early ninth century, contains illustrations and diagrams which are an integral part of it. The style of the copy is close to that both of the Athelstan Psalter and of another manuscript, a Bede, Life of St Cuthbert, which was presented by the King to the Canons of St Cuthbert about 935 (Cambridge, Corpus Christi College, MS. 183).

One of the most important additions to our knowledge of medieval English painting made in recent years was the discovery in 1966 of a small fragment of what must have been a large mural found in the excavations at Winchester. The archaeological evidence gives a date of before 903, that is during the reign of Alfred's son, Edward the Elder. The style of the three heads which, together with a fragment of a border of pelta pattern, are all that remain, is quite close to that of the manuscripts connected with Athelstan just discussed. The new find suggests that the origins of this style go back further than might have been supposed, though the embroideries, made between 909 and 916 at the order of Queen Aelfreda, Edward's second wife, (now at Durham) are an intermediate stage.

Royal patronage was one important reason for the revival of learning and the arts in tenth-century England. Alfred had already seen this as part of his task in rebuilding the country. Equally important was the monastic revival of which three men, St

Fragment of wall painting. Before *c.* 903.
Winchester City Museum, by permission of the Winchester Excavations Committee.

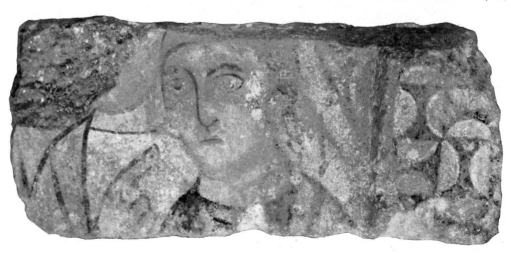

Dunstan, Abbot of Glastonbury, *c.* 943–57, Archbishop of Canterbury 961–88, St Ethelwold, monk at Glastonbury under Dunstan, Abbot of Abingdon, Bishop of Winchester 963–84, and St Oswald, Bishop of Worcester, 961, Archbishop of York, 972–92, were the leaders. Both Dunstan and Oswald visited the Continent, the former being in exile in Ghent, the latter visiting the monastery of St Benoît-sur-Loire (Fleury) near Orléans. The document known as the *Regularis concordia*, drawn up about 970, perhaps by Ethelwold himself, with the support of King Edgar (died 975), aimed to introduce greater discipline and uniformity into the English houses, and was based on continental customs. Thus the reformed monasticism of the Carolingian period, as instituted originally by St Benedict of Aniane was introduced into England, and this context of Benedictine monasticism is fundamental to the painting produced over the next two and a half centuries.

The most important illuminated manuscript of this period, a Benedictional (formerly Chatsworth, library of the Duke of Devonshire, now British Library, Additional 49598) was written, as its scribe, Godeman, tells us, for St Ethelwold himself.

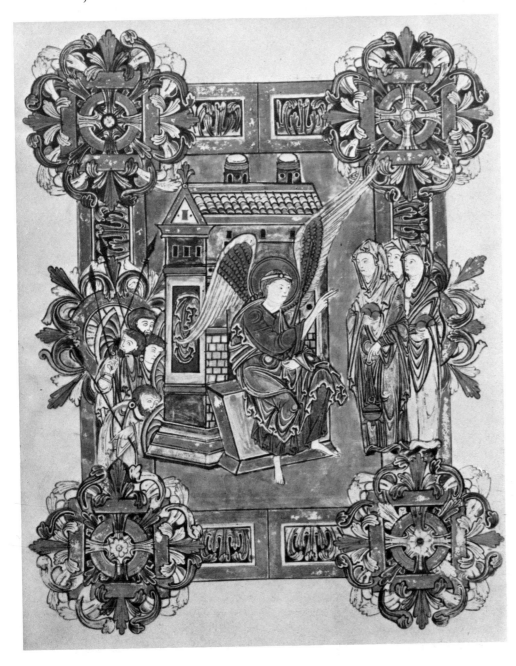

The three Maries at the sepulchre.
Benedictional of St Ethelwold. Winchester, *c.* 971–80. Additional 49598, folio 51ᵛ.
British Library, London.

23

It contains no less than twenty-eight full-page miniatures (three others are missing) as well as two historiated initials and nineteen pages decorated with frames. The date is probably shortly after the Translation of the relics of St Swithun in 971, and almost certainly the manuscript was written at the Old Minster, Winchester. It is a manifesto of the new movement. Both in iconography and in style it depends to a very large extent on Carolingian models. Homburger demonstrated the close similarities of certain scenes, particularly the Baptism, the Annunciation, the Presentation in the Temple and the Adoration of the Magi, to ivory carvings, reliquary caskets and book covers of the school active at Metz in the second half of the ninth century. There are also hints of other models in the iconography, perhaps post-iconoclastic Byzantine sources of the tenth century, or contemporary Ottonian works from Germany. There is also a special emphasis on the ceremony of coronation and the crown which is explained by King Edgar's close connection with the reform movement. The style also demonstrates a debt to Carolingian works, both the ivories already mentioned, and a series of sumptuous Gospel Books connected with Charlemagne himself, at the turn of the eighth–ninth century. These last have similar richly varied drapery patterns. Their colouring is rather more sombre. Notable in the Benedictional is the use of white, both mixed with other colours and as an outline of the garment folds. It also occurs in the wavy bands representing the sky. A similar effect in the sky and similar colouring can be found to some extent in later Carolingian manuscripts, particularly those connected with the Emperor Charles the Bald (823–77). The Anglo-Saxon artist has used his colours with very great richness and he has aimed to achieve an all-over effect of pattern and movement.

In his explanatory poem Godeman refers to the 'circos multos', the many frames. These are indeed the most striking aspect of the pages. They are of two kinds, arches in which acanthus leaves fill the imposts and capitals and even at times the arches themselves, and square frames with corner or side rosettes and acanthus leaves filling the bars of the frame. We are reminded of the carpet pages of Insular manuscripts as we look at all this profusion of ornament and observe how it invades the space of the miniatures and interlaces with the feet of the actors, rather than marking off an imaginary space as the classical frame had done.

Nevertheless, the main feature of Insular ornament, the interlace patterns, hardly appear at all, and where they are found, are transmitted via Carolingian art. The artist is trying to emulate Carolingian *de luxe* manuscripts, especially those of the Metz school, which provide certain precedents for the forms the ornament takes. The plant ornament used in these borders, with three-dimensional leaves and flowers, is not found in Carolingian art, however, and its introduction is one of the most far-reaching innovations of Anglo-Saxon art. The turning scrolls occur already in the embroideries made at the order of Queen Aelfreda mentioned above, and are further developed in various manuscripts associated with Athelstan. Their origin is Eastern and they may have been transmitted by textiles or possibly metalwork. The scroll is also used to form initials and is later taken up with great enthusiasm on the Continent. It is a notable feature of the Benedictional that such initials are rejected in favour of plain gold capitals and this again suggests a rejection of Insular art in favour of the more classical, plain Roman capitals which had been revived by Carolingian scribes. Similarly the minuscule script is copied from Carolingian minuscule rather than using the native type of script.

Another manuscript connected with Bishop Ethelwold contains a charter of King Edgar to the New Minster, Winchester, granted in 966 (British Library, Cotton Vespasian A. VIII). The New Minster had been refounded as a Benedictine community by Ethelwold in 964. Though not necessarily made in 966, there seems every reason to suppose that this rather exceptional document, which is written in gold script in codex form, was made not long after, and so precedes the Benedictional in date. The miniature on folio 2ᵛ (see p. 49) is painted on parchment stained purple, now faded to pink. This was a practice of late antique *de luxe* manuscripts, copied in Carolingian and Ottonian manuscripts. In the border the acanthus scroll grows out in the form of branches from central bosses on either side. The leaves twine round the bars of the frame like a living plant and on the outer side further fruits and flowers grow out on stalks. The miniature shows King Edgar seen from behind holding up the codex to Christ who is enthroned above and surrounded by four angels. The King is flanked by St Peter and a female saint, probably the Virgin.

Here we have an example of a further step made by medieval artists. This is not a representation of some event which took place or was supposed to have taken place, as narrated in some text or observed by the artist himself. It is a symbolic rendering, not only of the King's action in making his gift and having it duly recorded, but also of his intention of making a gift to God for the benefit of his immortal soul. Since there was no precedent for this scene, the artist adapted the scene of the Ascension, where Christ is enthroned above with a group of figures below. This is an example of the process of creation by analogy mentioned earlier.

The figure style is transitional between the Athelstan style as seen in the Psalter and the Benedictional with features of each. The facial types, with almond eyes, and the contained form of the female figure, for example, recall the earlier manuscript. The patterned drapery outlined in white and the active figure of the King seen from behind (a similar figure occurs in the miniature of the Entry to Jerusalem in the Benedictional) anticipate the style of the later manuscript.

Somewhat earlier is a drawing with a portrait of St Dunstan (p. 26 right) added to a miscellany of grammatical texts of ninth-century date, which was at Glastonbury in the later Middle Ages. It bears an inscription in the first person asking for Christ's mercy on St Dunstan, in a contemporary script which could be Dunstan's own. Since the anonymous life tells us that Dunstan was skilled in the art of painting, this drawing could be, as a much later inscription suggests, by Dunstan himself.

The figure of Christ is very monumental and by showing him in three-quarter length, the artist has emphasized both his supernatural existence and the insignificance of the little figure prostrated before him. Christ is portrayed as a type of Holy Wisdom with a sceptre. The style of the drawing is close to that of Carolingian art of the early ninth century. Since no Carolingian drawings survive in this style, it is likely that the artist was transposing from a different medium, that of ivory carving. At any rate this is one of the earliest examples of what became an English speciality, and we shall see a number of later examples of the technique. The drawing is not an unfinished miniature and clearly the Anglo-Saxon artists considered their drawings as in no way inferior to painted miniatures.

As a second example we may consider the drawing of the Crucifixion (p. 26 left) prefixed to a Psalter perhaps made for Ramsey Abbey (London, British Library, Harley 2904). The manuscript is of the late tenth century and was probably written at Winchester. The drawing is mainly in reddish-brown ink, but there is also some use of blue. The figures are again set against a plain background, but there is a simple rectangular frame. The Christ – as with the earlier drawing – is larger in scale than the other figures, the more important actor being magnified, as was often done in medieval art. As so often with Anglo-Saxon miniatures the composition is centripetal, the whole being organized around a central point. The flanking figures are raised, to leave balancing spaces on each side and at top and bottom.

So close in style that they might well be by the same artist, are the miniatures in a Gospels from St Bertin (Boulogne-sur-Mer, Bibliothèque Municipale, MS. 11). The manuscript was certainly written at St Bertin and the script and some of the initials are close to manuscripts made under Abbot Otbert of St Bertin around the year 1000. We can be sure, therefore, that the Anglo-Saxon artist travelled to St Bertin. Other

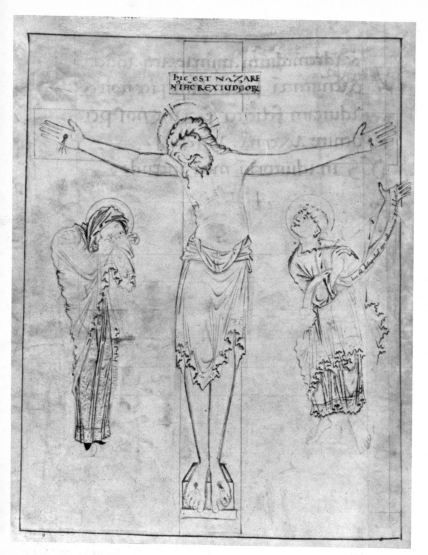

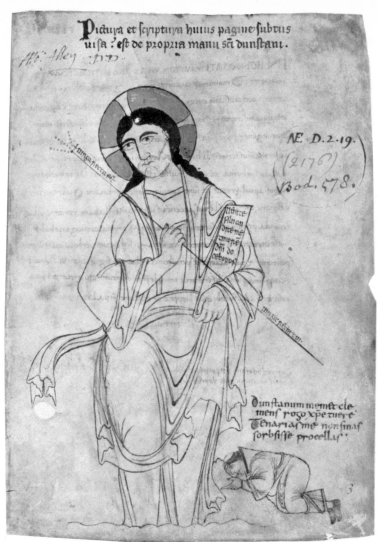

Above, The Crucifixion. Psalter, made possibly
at Winchester, late tenth century.
Harley 2904, folio 3ᵛ.
British Library, London.
Above right, St Dunstan adoring Christ Wisdom.
Frontispiece to St Dunstan's classbook.
Glastonbury, mid tenth century.
MS Auct. F.4.32, folio 1.
Bodleian Library, Oxford.

illustrations by him in a Gregory the Great, Homilies on Ezekiel (Orléans, Bibliothèque Municipale, MS. 175), and an Aratus manuscript with constellation pictures
(London, British Library, Harley 2506), both manuscripts coming probably from
Fleury, suggest that he was on his way to or from Fleury. Be that as it may, these
manuscripts show that by the late tenth century, English art was being imported to
the Continent. Apart from the Anglo-Saxon illumination which survives and can be
shown to have arrived on the Continent early, we have many copies by French,
Flemish and German artists of the eleventh and twelfth centuries. France had suffered
the sort of upheavals from foreign invasions and internal dissensions that had struck
England in the ninth century. So that when the monasteries of North France,
Flanders and Normandy began to produce illuminated manuscripts again in the late
tenth century, it was natural that they should look to England for models.

The Boulogne manuscript is a Gospel Book containing illuminated Canon Tables
(the tables which showed the passages common to the various Gospels), four
Evangelist portraits, a miniature of Christ in Majesty, and another of the Ancestors
of Christ which succeeds the portrait of St Matthew in whose Gospel they are
enumerated. There are also initials to each Gospel combined with scenes of the
Annunciation, the Nativity, and the Annunciation of the Angel to Zacharias. The
miniatures are painted with colour washes of delicate shades of green, blue, pink,
orange and violet. Though the miniatures have rather more restrained frames than
in the Benedictional, there is the same purpose in the colouring of unifying the page
through alternations and juxtapositions of colours. The difference in technique, in

fact, makes no difference to the artist's purpose. The combination of Gospel scenes with the portraits shows that the artist had a wide range of models at his disposal and even in the standard portraits he has introduced novelties. For example the bird perched on St John's shoulder must be based on the iconography of Pope Gregory the Great, who received inspiration from the Holy Dove. The usual symbol of St John, the eagle, has been moved to the right and an altar placed below to fill the space. The Carolingian author portraits, which were, in turn, modifications of classical representations of philosophers or teachers, are now also receiving accretions.

Another English manuscript which came to the Continent and had an effect on artists there, is a Sacramentary given by the Norman, Robert of Jumièges to his old

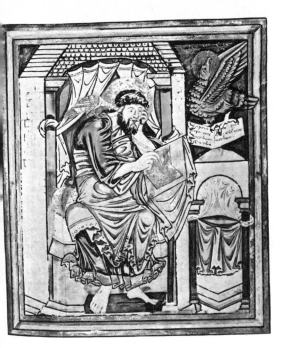

Above, St John the Evangelist, from a Gospel Book written at St Bertin, *c.* 1000. MS 11, folio 107. Bibliothèque Municipale, Boulogne-sur-Mer. *Right, The Ascension.* Sacramentary of Robert of Jumièges. Canterbury (?), second quarter of eleventh century. MS Y.6 (274), folio 81ᵛ. Bibliothèque Municipale, Rouen.

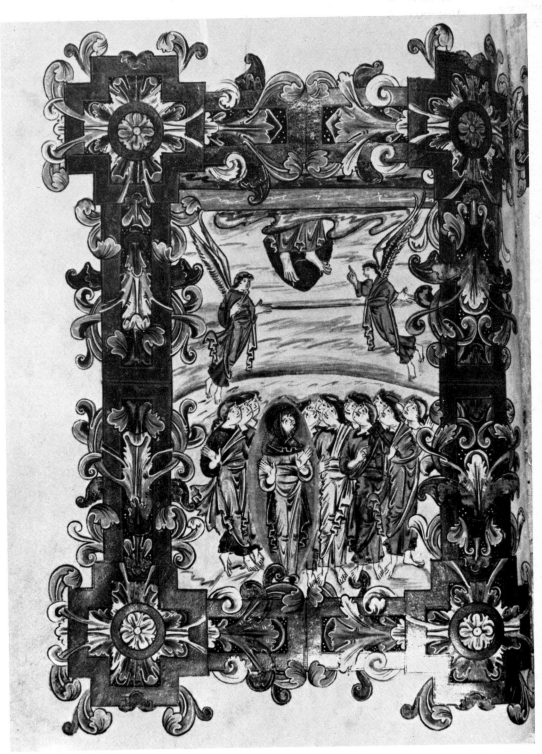

monastery (Rouen, Bibliothèque Municipale, MS. Y.6). King Edward the Confessor had made him Bishop of London in 1044, and in 1051 Archbishop of Canterbury. But in 1052 he had to flee the country and returned to Normandy. The manuscript cannot have been made for him since it was probably written *c.* 1020–30. It is not known where it was illuminated, though stylistic similarities with a Psalter from Canterbury (London, British Library, Arundel MS. 155) and a Gospels written and signed by a Christ Church scribe, Eadwi Basan, also an early import to the Continent, where it later formed part of the Guelph treasure (Hanover, Kestner Museum), suggest Canterbury. The Sacramentary contains thirteen miniatures and several others are now missing. The scenes are framed in arches and leaf scroll frames as are the miniatures in the Benedictional of St Ethelwold. Again the composition is centripetal and the figures are, as it were, interlaced with the frame. The Apostles on the right are overlapped by the scroll, but below, their feet are on top of it. Both the figures and the ground are painted in strips of colour of varying tone. The effect is extraordinarily restless, a sort of painted equivalent of the Utrecht Psalter style. At the same time this striping had the seeds of later development in it, for it could be turned into sharp corrugated folds with pointed outlines. This development is seen more especially in certain eleventh-century continental manuscripts from Cologne, Liège and St Bertin, perhaps influenced by English art, and in two English manuscripts, perhaps from Hereford (London, British Library, Cotton Caligula A. XIV, and Cambridge, Pembroke College, MS. 302). It was still used in English illumination and mural painting in the twelfth century, for example in the Eadwine Psalter and in the churches at Hardham and Clayton, Sussex.

Other surviving Anglo-Saxon illuminated manuscripts which reached the Continent in the eleventh century are the two Gospel Books which belonged to Judith, daughter of Baldwin of Flanders, who married Earl Tostig (New York, Morgan Library, M. 708 and M. 709). Judith must have taken them with her when she and her husband fled from England in 1064. After Tostig's death at the battle of Stamford Bridge in 1066, she married, in 1071, Guelph IV, Duke of Bavaria, and bequeathed these and other manuscripts to the abbey of Weingarten at her death in 1094. Both manuscripts have Evangelist portraits and the second, in addition, a miniature of the Crucifixion with a small kneeling figure of a woman clasping the base of the cross. Though no inscription indicates her identity the likelihood is that this is Judith herself, and in that case the painting was probably made after her marriage to Tostig in 1051.

The richness and variety of Anglo-Saxon illumination is amazing. The large numbers of miniatures inserted in liturgical books are a new development, for there is nothing surviving on this scale from the Carolingian period, though contemporary artists in Germany were doing the same thing. We have seen examples of additions to the normal illustrations of the Gospel Books and others could be quoted. In addition there are illustrated Psalters including the earliest example with a prefatory series of Christological scenes (London, British Library, Cotton Tiberius C. VI) which comes from Winchester, and another with a whole series of marginal scenes (Vatican, Biblioteca Apostolica, Reginensis lat. 12), later at Bury St Edmunds but probably made at Canterbury. There are also Herbals, sets of calendar pictures with Occupations of the Months, and illustrations to the Marvels of the East. Finally two Biblical manuscripts should not be passed over, the famous so-called Caedmon manuscript (Oxford, Bodleian Library, MS. Junius 11), an Anglo-Saxon version of Genesis, etc., with drawings in two styles, and the illustrated copy of Aelfric's paraphrase of the Pentateuch and Joshua with painted miniatures (London, British Library, Cotton Claudius B. IV). Both manuscripts are unfinished and in both there are indications of much earlier cycles of pictures which lie behind the miniatures. For example, in the miniature of Cain and Abel in the Caedmon manuscript the

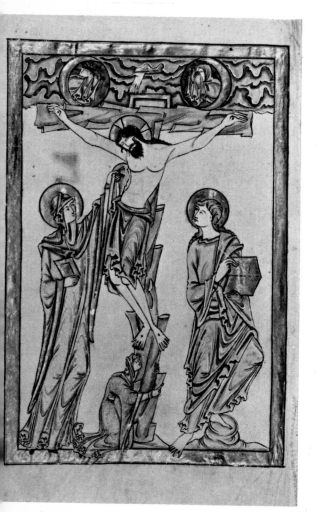

Crucifixion with Judith of Flanders kneeling below the Cross. Gospel Book. Mid eleventh century. M. 709, folio 1ᵛ. Pierpont Morgan Library, New York.

narrative is like a strip cartoon with different episodes succeeding each other but unified within a single landscape. The same system is found in one of the earliest surviving illustrated Old Testament manuscripts, a Greek Genesis of the sixth century now in Vienna (Nationalbibliothek, Theol. Gr. 31). It is likely that there was an intermediary of the time of Athelstan between the Junius manuscript and the late classical model or models. The style suggests this, and another small clue is provided by the figures of Cain and Abel making their offerings, which are repeated in the Athelstan Psalter mentioned above.

Though the Norman scriptoria in the first half of the eleventh century had been strongly influenced by Anglo-Saxon art as known to them by the importation of works like Robert of Jumièges' Sacramentary, they soon made important modifications. The centripetal compositions of Anglo-Saxon art were rejected and the figures and objects are brought down to and anchored on the base line of the miniature. At the same time the frame was simplified and a new organization of the picture in terms of planes of background and foreground was introduced. In many Anglo-Saxon miniatures the fluid space of classical art survived vestigially. In Romanesque art it is finally rejected. The Norman Conquest of 1066 thus served to introduce features of the new Romanesque style as it was being developed on the Continent, even though the native tradition was so strong that it survived in certain centres into the twelfth century, as Professor Wormald has shown.

If the scene or figure is not to be seen in space as though through a window frame, but rather as if projected against a backcloth, then the form of the backcloth is immaterial as long as the figure can be attached to it. Its shape need not be regular. This is the explanation of the way Romanesque artists transferred figures and whole scenes to the initials introducing texts in manuscripts. The historiated initial becomes the characteristic form in Romanesque illumination and it provided, like the capital for Romanesque sculptors, the vehicle for countless brilliant inventions. We can see this, for example, in a series of great Bibles, in one or two volumes. The Winchester Bible, still in the library of the Cathedral, illuminated by various artists in the second half of the twelfth century and never finished, so that we have drawings as well as paintings, and paintings by different artists over the drawings of their predecessors, contains both miniatures and initials. As an example of a narrative scene fitted into an initial we may look at the 'P' introducing the second Book of Kings (overleaf). The bowl of round letters, 'O', 'D', and, as here, 'P', was suitable to enclose a scene, and we see above the messenger of King Ahaziah being addressed by the prophet Elijah. The second episode, Elijah being taken up to Heaven in the fiery chariot and, below, his mantle falling to his disciple Elisha, is combined with the stem of the letter in such a way that the upward movement of the chariot is thereby increased.

The initial letter here forms a setting for the scene and the figure of Elisha is comparable to a columnar statue on a contemporary portal. The shape of the 'P' has dictated the bent figures of the messengers and the upright of Elijah. At the same time the rhythmical curves of the figures are most skilfully balanced in relation to each other and are echoed internally by their drapery, either emphasizing the figure's movement, as does the cloak of Elisha, or contrasting with it, as does the cloak of the first of the King's messengers. This rhythmic interlacing is also found in Romanesque sculpture and is a second important distinguishing characteristic of Romanesque art.

The curved folds of the drapery, particularly noticeable in the works of this artist, who has been aptly named by Dr Oakeshott 'the Master of the Leaping Figures', derive ultimately from classical Greek sculpture of the fifth century BC onwards. There drapery is used to emphasize rather than conceal the forms of the body, being pulled tight over rounded parts and gathered into folds between. Because the material is made in this way to look as if it is wet, the convention is known as the 'damp fold' style. This Hellenistic style was to a large extent preserved in the Greek

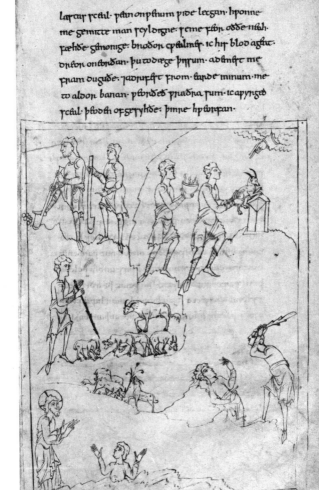

The story of Cain and Abel. Old English Genesis (Caedmon manuscript). Canterbury (?), *c.* 1000. MS Junius 11, p. 49. Bodleian Library, Oxford.

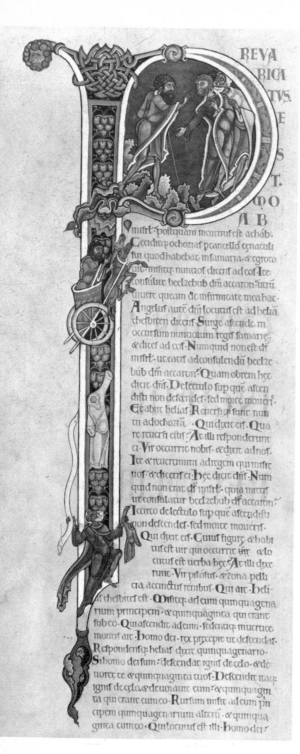

Initial 'P'. *Elijah meeting the messengers of King Ahaziah. Elisha receiving the mantle of Elijah.* Winchester, mid twelfth century. Winchester Bible, folio 120ᵛ.
By permission of the Dean and Chapter of Winchester Cathedral.

East and this form of drapery, when it begins to appear in the early twelfth century, is certainly the result of contact with Byzantine art.

Western artists had been influenced by Byzantine art already in the second half of the tenth century, not to speak of earlier contacts. Especially in Germany, the Ottonian rulers tried to emulate the Eastern Emperors, and in 972 the Emperor Otto II married a Byzantine princess, Theophanu. Stimulated by these contacts Ottonian artists, in a series of illuminated Gospel and Pericope Books and also in monumental paintings as at Reichenau Oberzell on Lake Constance, began to experiment with a new system of spatial organization, according to a series of overlapping planes which replaced illusionistic perspective. These experiments were of the greatest importance for the development of Romanesque art in the eleventh and twelfth centuries. The combination of Anglo-Saxon art with its dynamism and its interlacing forms and Ottonian art with its planar space and new system of colouring is central to the genesis of the Romanesque style.

There were, however, other channels by which Byzantine art became known in the West. First it should not be forgotten that many pilgrims made their way to Jerusalem, even before the crusades and the establishment of the Latin Kingdom. After the Conquest of Constantinople in the fourth crusade in 1204, pillaged works of art were brought back in quantity to Europe. In the eleventh and twelfth centuries both Eastern Europe and Southern Italy and Sicily were in contact with the Byzantine Empire. South Italy had remained part of the Byzantine Empire until its conquest by the Normans. The doors of the great pilgrimage church at Monte St Angelo in Apulia were made in Constantinople as late as 1076. Desiderio, Abbot of the mother house of Benedictine monasticism at Monte Cassino, brought artists from Constantinople to work for him in the abbey church, consecrated in 1071. The late eleventh-century murals at St Angelo in Formis, nearby, and a series of illuminated manuscripts remain to demonstrate the closeness of contacts with Greek art. In the twelfth century the Norman kings of Sicily began to build the churches at Cefalù, Palermo and Monreale, containing cycles of mosaics in Byzantine style.

Thus, in the late eleventh century, Western artists who had already received a glimmering of tenth-century Byzantine style, began to be conscious of later phases of Byzantine art. In so far as this style of the late eleventh and early twelfth centuries was less classical and more abstract, it could be more easily assimilated.

The earliest dateable English manuscript to show these trends is a Psalter made at St Albans *c.* 1120 (Hildesheim, Church of St Godehard). It has a prefatory series of miniatures and historiated initials to the Psalms and Canticles. There are also pictures of the life of St Alexis accompanying the French prose life which is of great linguistic interest. In the iconography of the miniatures the main artist, the 'Alexis Master', combines a knowledge of native Anglo-Saxon sources with Byzantine models received via Ottonian art and apparently known at first-hand from a visit to South Italy. He also makes his own contributions. For example, in the scene of Christ in the Garden of Gethsemane (opposite) it seems that he is the first to illustrate the words 'Lord, if it be thy will, take away this cup from my lips', with a chalice before the kneeling figure of Christ, an innovation which is to remain a standard part of the scene for the rest of the Middle Ages.

Signs of the influence of eleventh-century Byzantine style received via South Italy are the incipient 'damp fold' drapery with its network of small white lines and the elongated proportions of the figures. The master also adapts from Ottonian illumination a system of colour background panels which serve to throw forward the figures, as we have already seen, and which are also used in a subtle way to suggest dramatic relationships between figures and movement by means of overlapping.

About fiteen years later, in the abbey of Bury St Edmunds, another outstanding artist illuminated a Bible (Cambridge, Corpus Christi College, MS. 2). Documentary sources speak of a Bible illuminated at this date by a certain magister Hugo, and M.R.James was the first to show that this is the work in question. Hugo was also a craftsman in metal and in ivory and it seems likely that he was a layman, not a monk. The miniatures of the Bible are painted on separate pieces of parchment and stuck in. The documents tell us, in fact, that Hugo sent away for parchment of specially fine quality. Certain of them have unfortunately been removed and others have been defaced by later scribblings. Master Hugo is already using the damp fold technique in its fully developed form, as we saw it in the Winchester Bible. He tends to use grounds of a deep blue which throw forward his figures, coloured in rich reds, greens and purples. The colour range of the St Albans Psalter had already broken decisively with that of Anglo-Saxon art. Colour is used conceptually not naturalistically and by juxtapositions and alternations emphasizes the different balancing parts of the picture surface.

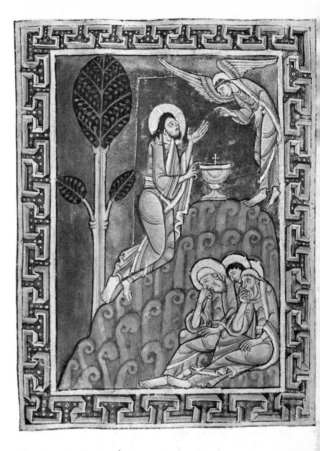

The Agony in the Garden.
St Alban's Psalter, p. 39. St Alban's, *c.* 1120.
Church of St Godehard, Hildesheim.

The twelfth century was a great age of Biblical studies, with the compilation of the glosses which sought to expound the significance of the whole Bible, using the exegesis of the early fathers and, where necessary, supplementing it. Efforts were also made to standardize the text. Miss Beryl Smalley has drawn attention to an example of the literal exegesis of the text, as practised by Hugh of St Victor, influencing the iconography of biblical representation. This is the miniature in the Bury Bible showing Elcana giving presents to his two wives. The text does not specify what the presents were, but Hugh, following a ninth-century commentator, explains that they were robes and this is what master Hugo shows in his miniature.

The damp fold style was used all over England. At Canterbury, another Bible (Lambeth Palace, MS. 3) shows an extreme treatment in which the folds become like a grid of lines (see p. 32). The English artist has reduced the classical convention to a linear pattern. A Gospel Book written at Liessies in north France in 1146 (formerly Metz, Bibliothèque Municipale, MS. 1151, destroyed in World War II, two detached leaves surviving at Avesnes, Société Archéologique) was also illuminated by him and shows that he travelled in north France, where his style influenced local artists, at Anchin for example. This may also indicate that he was a layman and not a monk.

From the twelfth century we have the first considerable remains of wall-paintings in this country. Those in the small churches of Hardham and Clayton in Sussex and of Kempley in Gloucestershire are the best preserved and most complete. Their style is related to that of contemporary Anglo-Norman illumination of the first half of the twelfth century, with the draperies in bands as in the Eadwine Psalter; but the colour is more restricted, browns and yellows being predominant. In all three churches the emphasis is on the heavenly Jerusalem and the last Judgement, showing Christ in Majesty above the altar in the chancel accompanied by the Apostles. A wall painting at Copford, Essex, of the healing of Jairus's daughter may be mentioned, since it shows the influence of the Alexis Master's style as practised at nearby Bury St Edmunds. In these small churches the paintings probably survive because of their relative isolation. The two outstanding surviving monuments, however, are at great creative centres, Canterbury and Winchester. St Gabriel's chapel at Canterbury contains a whole apse with Christ in Majesty and various Gospel scenes painted in the second quarter of the twelfth century. Even more impressive is the small fragment in St Anselm's chapel showing St Paul stung by the viper in Cyprus (see p. 32). This is an unusual scene, presumably part of a larger cycle, and demonstrates how difficult it is, using only the chance survivals of medieval art, to generalize about which subjects were commonly represented. Again the remarkable blue background (blue was a particularly expensive colour) serves to project the figure and the drapery is in the damp fold style.

At Winchester cathedral the paintings revealed in the Chapel of the Holy Sepulchre are the most important new work of English medieval painting to come to light in

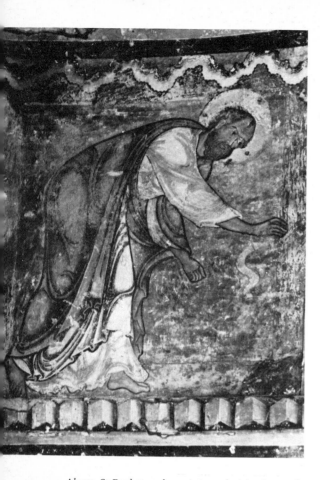

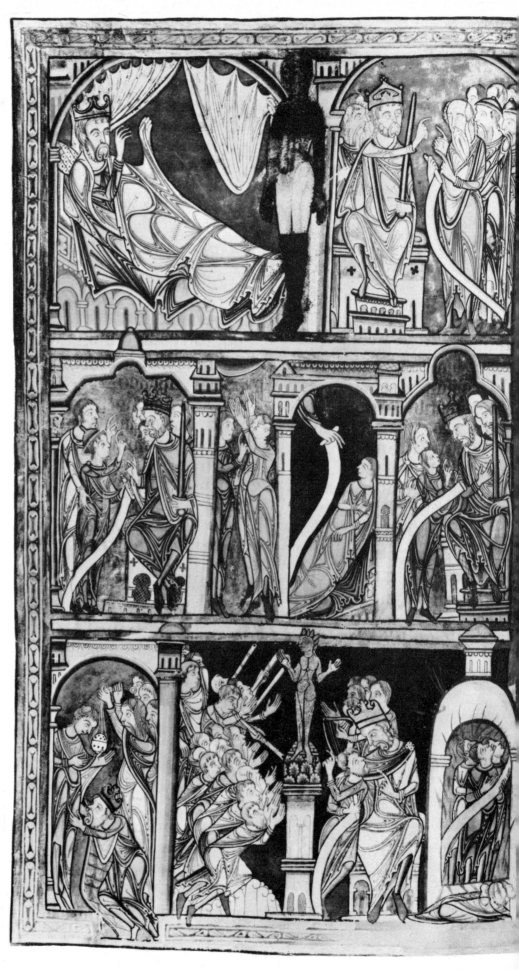

Above, St Paul stung by a viper on the island of Cyprus. St Anselm's Chapel, Canterbury Cathedral, mid twelfth century.
By permission of the Dean and Chapter of Canterbury Cathedral.
Right, Nebuchadnezzar's dream from the Lambeth Bible. Canterbury, mid twelfth century.
MS 3, folio 285^v.
By permission of the Archbishop of Canterbury and the Trustees of Lambeth Palace Library.

Opposite, Deposition and Entombment. Chapel of the Holy Sepulchre, Winchester Cathedral, late twelfth century.
By permission of the Dean and Chapter of Winchester Cathedral.

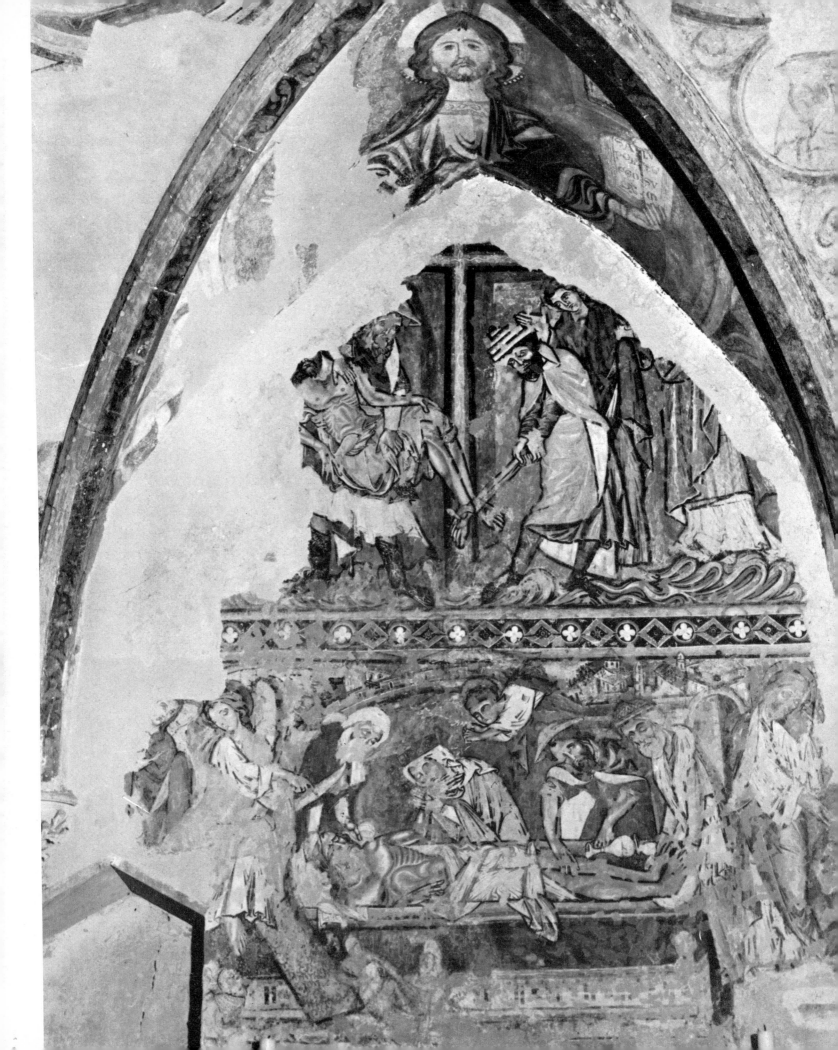

recent years (see p. 33). They were painted over in the thirteenth century and though the earlier cycle was long ago suspected to be underneath, only in 1965 did modern techniques enable the two layers to be separated and the older painting to be revealed. The scenes shown are, above, the Deposition from the Cross and, below, the Entombment combined with the three Marys meeting the Angel at the Grave, the standard early medieval representation of the mystery of the Resurrection.

The style is very close to that of some of the later artists of the Winchester Bible, the so-called 'Master of the Genesis initial' and the 'Master of the Morgan leaf'. This suggests that the same artists may have worked both at monumental art and at book illumination. The remarkable monumental qualities of many Romanesque miniatures, which are capable of great enlargement when projected from slides on a screen for instance, tend to the same conclusion. A third series of wall paintings of even more considerable extent and of the highest possible quality were tragically damaged by fire in 1936. These were the paintings in the chapter house at Sigena (founded 1183) in northern Spain. The fragments have been restored and are on view in the Museum in Barcelona, but the colour is, for the most part, gone. Fortunately, good photographs were taken before the fire. The similarities of style with the work of the Winchester artist named, after a detached leaf intended for insertion in the Winchester Bible (New York, Morgan Library, M. 619), the 'Master of the Morgan leaf', have been analysed by Professor Pächt and Dr Oakeshott and are reinforced by iconographic evidence. There can be no doubt that English artists travelled to Spain to execute these paintings.

With these works we reach the last years of the twelfth century and the beginnings of Gothic art. The style of a group of works executed before and after 1200 has been labelled 'Transitional', meaning to emphasize its position between Romanesque and Gothic art. Recent studies and a memorable exhibition in New York at the Metropolitan Museum in 1970 have begun to examine the problem of whether such works can be said to have a style of their own, rather than as the term 'Transitional' implies, partaking more or less of Gothic style. At present the origin and trends of the style and the crucial questions of dating the monuments are still under discussion. In the late twelfth century we see a further understanding of the principles of classical art which leads far away from the mannerisms of the damp fold style. This classicism is particularly notable in the works of goldsmiths and sculptors in the area of the Meuse and the lower Rhine, for example in the reliquary shrines of Nicholas of Verdun, and culminates in the west portal sculptures at Rheims cathedral of c. 1220–30, which have been compared to classical Roman sculpture.

In England such classicism appears in a number of late twelfth-century works of which we have already seen examples from Canterbury and Winchester. A group of books made for Abbot Simon of St Albans and therefore datable before his death in 1183, are also important in this connection. One artist who appears in these also worked in a Psalter for St Bertin (Cambridge, St John's College, MS. C. 18) and in a Bible (Paris, Bibliothèque Nationale, latin 16743–6) mainly illuminated by a French artist. Another instance of similarity of English and French illumination at this time is in the painted initials found particularly in glossed books of the Bible. This is seen in a group of books given to Christ Church, Canterbury, by St Thomas Becket and so made before his martyrdom in 1170, though certainly written during his exile in France. Whatever its origins, this type of initial spread quickly to most of Western Europe. The characteristic figure style of the Transitional period can be seen in a Psalter of unknown provenance (Copenhagen, Royal Library, Thott 143.2⁰) in which the static and monumental figures contrast with the agitated and interlacing figures of the mid-century, even if patterning is still to some extent apparent, particularly in the drapery.

In painting the Gothic style appears some 70–80 years after its introduction in

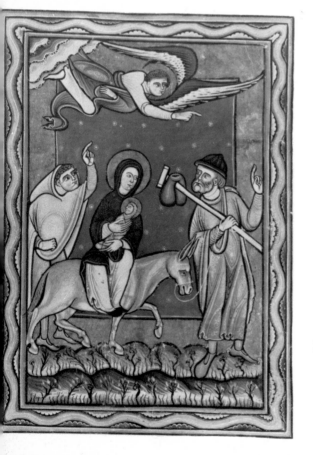

The Flight into Egypt, from a prefatory cycle of miniatures to a Psalter.
c. 1170–80. MS Thott 143.2⁰, folio 12.
Royal Library, Copenhagen.

architecture at St Denis in the choir built by Abbot Suger (d. 1151). Professor Jantzen has sought to analyse gothic architecture in terms of what he has described as 'diaphanous space' and this is the key to Gothic art in general. Art forms which come to mind as typical of the period are window tracery, stained glass, wrought-iron metal grilles, and stone and wooden carved stalls and screens.

As an example of early Gothic style we may look at a Psalter probably made at Peterborough for Abbot Robert de Lindseye (d. 1222) (Cambridge, Fitzwilliam Museum, MS. 12). The blessing figure of Christ seated on a throne is set in a quatrefoil and silhouetted against a gold ground. The quatrefoil overlaps the throne and encloses the figure, who is not projected towards us as a Romanesque Majestas figure would be. The quatrefoil is set inside an initial 'D' whose thin shape is outlined on a darker ground in a paler colour. Within the bowl of the letter is a restrained symmetrical scroll which forms a grille so that we are conscious of the background through it. The ground is emphasized by the groups of little white dots which, with an enormous variety of lozenge and diaper patterns, are a typical feature of Gothic backgrounds.

In Transitional works, as noted above, a high point of classical, and therefore to some extent naturalistic, drapery is reached. Very quickly this was transformed into abstract pattern in a series of loops in the so-called 'hairpin bend' convention. In the Peterborough figure we see again how the drapery takes on a diaphanous texture so that we see the arm beneath it. Where classical art used transparency to reveal the solid forms beneath, however, the Gothic artist has used it to emphasize the incorporeality of the supernatural figure. This is no longer naturalistic, and English artists soon transformed the style into even more abstract patterns.

The way in which the new French style was taken over and developed is clearly seen in the work of Matthew Paris, a monk of St Albans, who died in 1259 and was born probably in the late 1190s. Matthew is best known for his historical writings, but he was also an artist, and according to a later chronicler of his own abbey, one without peer. His only signed work shows him at the feet of the Virgin and Child (London, British Library, Royal 14 C. VII) recalling the miniature of St Dunstan discussed earlier. The substitution of the enthroned Virgin for the Christ is symptomatic of later medieval piety in which the cult of the Virgin played an increasing part. Like many of the works connected with Matthew this is a drawing tinted with pale colours, green, red, or yellow, and thus returns to the Anglo-Saxon tradition. The Royal manuscript contains the third part of Matthew's *Chronica Majora* and is mostly written in his own hand. This, and the first two parts (Cambridge, Corpus Christi College, MSS. 26 and 16) contain marginal drawings, some executed by Matthew himself, others, for example a drawing of him on his death bed, by assistants. The marginal scenes show that he was able to invent pictures to illustrate his narrative. He also wrote in French the Lives of St Alban, St Edmund, St Edward the Confessor, and St Thomas. Of these the original manuscript of the Life of St Alban with Matthew's own illustration survives (Dublin, Trinity College, MS. E.i.40), whilst we have copies of the illustrated lives of St Edward and St Thomas in similar style and format to the Alban and no doubt copying Matthew's originals. The influence of Matthew was therefore certainly considerable. How far he was an originator and what part was played by the monastery of St Albans in forming the art of this period is more difficult to evaluate. One of his manuscripts contains a single leaf inserted with a drawing of the Apocalyptic Christ (London, British Library, Cotton Nero D.I, the *Liber additamentorum*) stated to be by Brother William the Franciscan (p. 36). This is certainly in a more advanced style than Matthew's own work, which by his death was decidedly old-fashioned. A note on the back gives instructions that the back is to be left blank because the drawing can be seen better if held up to the light, a striking instance of transparency as a positive stylistic feature of Gothic art.

The early Gothic period is a time in which large picture cycles were developed and

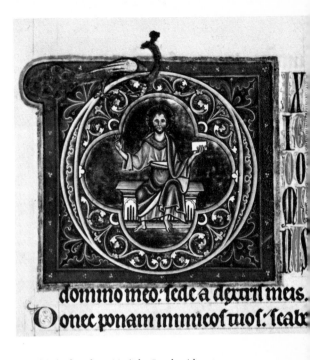

Initial 'D' of Psalm 109, 'The Lord said unto my Lord'. Christ enthroned.
Psalter of Robert de Lindseye, Abbot of Peterborough, d. 1222.
MS 12, folio 159.
Reproduced by permission of the Syndics of the Fitzwilliam Museum, Cambridge.

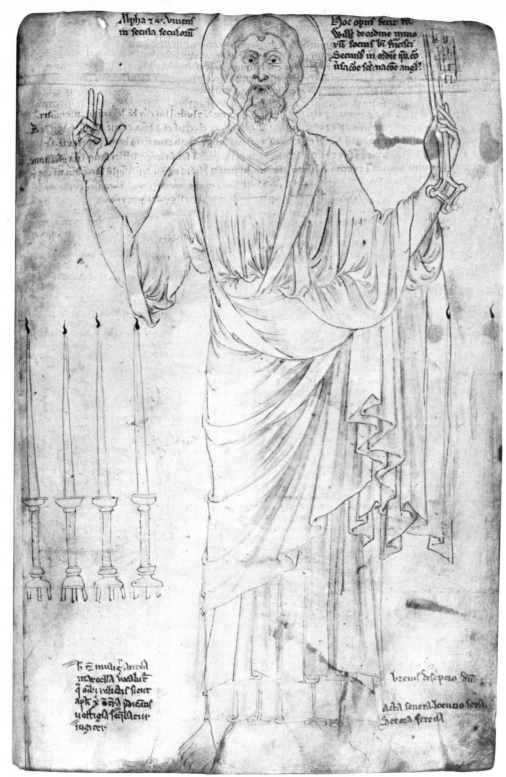

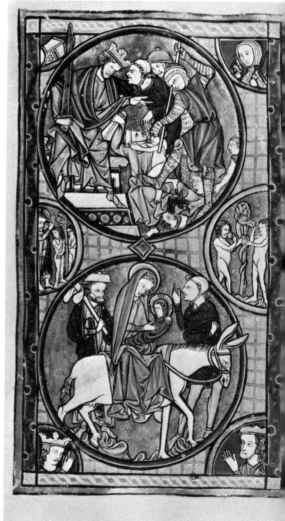

Left, Apocalyptic Christ, drawn by
Brother William, O.F.M., and inserted in
Matthew Paris's *Liber Additamentorum*.
Mid thirteenth century.
Cotton Nero D.1, folio 156.
British Library, London.
*Right, Sailors anchor their ship to
a sleeping whale*. Bestiary. *c.* 1220.
MS Ii.4.26, folio 54ᵛ.
University Library, Cambridge.

*Below, The Slaughter of the Innocents and
the Flight into Egypt*. Prefatory cycle
to the Oscott Psalter. *c.* 1260–70.
Additional 50000, folio 13.
British Library, London.
Below right, The Crucifixion with a kneeling
abbot. The Evesham Psalter. *c.* 1250–60.
Additional 44874, folio 6.
British Library, London.

many were copied over and over again. Two texts, of which larger numbers of fine illuminated manuscripts survive than for other countries are the Bestiary and the Apocalypse. One of the earlier examples of the former (Cambridge, University Library, MS. Ii.4.26) is illustrated with drawings, many of which are set in circles. The same artist illustrated a Life of St Guthlac (London, British Library, Harleian Roll Y.6). He is, therefore, a predecessor of Matthew Paris in two important respects, reviving the tinted drawing style and also the narrative illustration of saints' lives, a type of illustration which first becomes widespread in the eleventh century. This should make us beware of overrating Matthew's importance as an innovator.

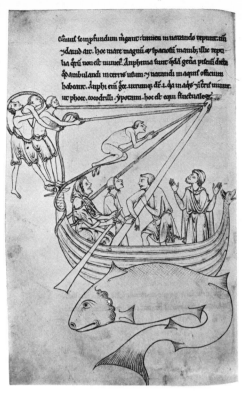

Matthew Paris was in close touch with the court and knew many of the notable people of his day, among them King Henry III (1216–72). It is possible that St Albans fulfilled, to some extent, the function of a court scriptorium. At any rate a similar style was practised at the court, as is shown by a small fragment of painting, a head of a king, surviving in the cloister of St George's Chapel, Windsor.

Matthew as a monastic artist is probably exceptional by this date and can be contrasted with another contemporary artist who signed his works, William de Brailes. Though de Brailes portrays himself with a tonsure he can only have been in minor orders since he was married and owned property in Catte Street, Oxford. Presumably he worked largely on commissions for members of the new university.

In de Brailes' work and the drawing by Brother William we see a more angular type of fold making its appearance. In the second half of the century the figures become taller and the drapery falls in sharper folds, as if in heavier material, reacting to the loops and rounded forms of Matthew Paris's style. The particularly angular manneristic folds and the contorted poses which reach a climax in the Crucifixion page of a Psalter, executed for an abbot of Evesham after 1246, probably *c.* 1250–60 (London, British Library, Additional 44874) are simplified in the Oscott Psalter of *c.* 1270 (London, British Library, Additional 50000). In the latter and in the Douce Apocalypse of about the same date, the exaggeration is restrained, and balance and rhythm are restored, as opposed to angularity, juxtaposition and contrast. This more elegant, swaying style has a counterpart in contemporary French painting, though, as so often, the priority is not fully established. It seems likely, as has been generally thought, that French art influenced English. The prefatory miniatures in the Oscott Psalter show the twelve Apostles and scenes from the Nativity and the Passion of Christ. The latter are placed in large roundels, here, the Slaughter of the Innocents and the Flight into Egypt, combined with scenes from the Creation in the subsidiary half roundels, here, God addressing Adam and Eve, and the Fall. This arrangement of roundels enclosing the scenes set on coloured rectangles is particularly common in Parisian manuscripts of this date, and, as has often been observed, recalls stained glass window design. Here again this is not a case of influence of one art form on another but of both subserving the same stylistic needs.

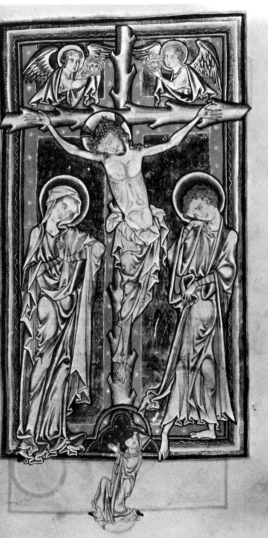

The Douce Apocalypse (Oxford, Bodleian Library, MS. Douce 180) bears the arms of England with a label and of Castile and must therefore have been made for Edward I before his accession in 1272 and after his marriage to Eleanor of Castile in 1254 (p. 39). The text is both in Latin and in French, with a commentary, the use of French in this as in many other illustrated Apocalypses being an indication of the lay patrons for whom they were intended. The cycle of miniatures consists of ninety-seven pictures, beginning with St John lying asleep on the island of Patmos and ending with Revelation XXII, vv. 16–21, the angel testifying. The sources and the interrelationships of these illustrated Apocalypses, of which a great many survive from the thirteenth and fourteenth centuries are still not clear. Benedict Biscop, who founded Monkwearmouth/Jarrow *c.* 674–82, brought back Apocalypse pictures from Italy, and there are three ninth-century surviving manuscripts, of which one, at Valenciennes, may reflect Benedict Biscop's cycle. There are also a series of Spanish manuscripts and another cycle in the *Liber Floridus*, an encyclopaedic compilation made in the twelfth century by Lambert, a canon of St Omer. The thirteenth-century Apocalypses are a good example of the process of medieval creativity described earlier. They are a new departure from an existing tradition.

The Douce Apocalypse illustrations were never finished and because the miniatures were left in various stages of completion we can see how the artist proceeded. The composition was drawn in pencil first and then inked over. These drawings are of exquisite quality but in the completed miniatures they are totally obscured. The next stage was to apply the pure gold leaf on a ground and then to burnish it. Next colour was applied in flat washes over which the shadows and lights to model the forms were applied. Finally the outlines of the figures and the drapery were put in again. Sometimes the final outline of the painting seems to have been done by a less sensitive hand and to obscure the quality of the original drawing. Even so one cannot be sure that it was a different hand that did this. A good example is provided by another Apocalypse, one of the earliest of the thirteenth-century, where over-drawing in dark black ink and underdrawing in brown ink are both still visible (Cambridge, Trinity College, MS. R. 16.2).

The miniatures of the Douce Apocalypse still partake of early Gothic 'diaphanous space'. The intervals of the blank parchment between the figures, which is never, in any of the miniatures, coloured, have a positive value in the compositions. The actors are interwoven with each other, the landscape details and even the frame to form a grille pattern. There is no depth or real spatial relationship. The colouring is of great richness and intensity, wine-reds, mauves, buffs, and blue-greens being used. But it is not used naturalistically. Rather it emphasizes alternations and intervals.

In the history of European painting developments in the late thirteenth and early fourteenth centuries in Italy mark a watershed. The works of Cavallini in Rome and of Cimabue and Giotto in Florence, Assisi and Padua, were bound eventually to affect the rest of Europe. Nevertheless the monumental art of Giotto with its totally dif-ferent aesthetic could not easily or quickly be assimilated by Gothic art. This was, of course, particularly so in book illumination where there were obvious difficulties in the introduction both of spatial illusion by vanishing point perspective and of Giotto's new type of monumental narrative. Northern artists were much more in-fluenced by the works of somewhat later Italian masters, particularly Simone Martini and the Sienese school, whose style was more Gothic, less plastic and monumental. After the exile of the Popes to Avignon there was a bridgehead of Italian art in France. The comparatively small, panel paintings of Tuscan artists were exported too. A third source of Italian influence existed in the law books from the great law school of the University of Bologna. Copies of the canon and civil law with the glosses of the Bologna Masters reached all parts of Europe.

Two features of the new Italian painting which could be taken up by northern artists were the plastic, modelled drapery with light and shade, and a new interest in physiognomy, which resulted in types having a certain sense of character without being yet individual portraits. Both these features can be found in French painting, for instance in the works of the outstanding illuminator of the late thirteenth century, working in Paris for King Philippe le Bel (1268–1314), Maître Honoré. They are not necessarily due to Italian influence, but possibly rather a parallel development. Similar tendencies are apparent in Parisian sculpture.

Both features can be seen in the painting on wood known as the Westminster Retable, which may have been, in fact, the antependium of the main altar of the Abbey (p. 50). There are other signs of Italian influence, in particular the small cameo heads of very classical type on the frame. The Retable, though damaged and frag-mentary, is of the highest quality. It is divided into compartments and even the main figure of Christ in the centre flanked by the Virgin and St John, is quite small. The refinement and detail, for instance the landscape in the globe carried by the Christ, remind one of illumination. This is also so with the quatrefoils containing scenes of the miracles of Christ. Unfortunately there are no documents which can certainly be con-nected with the painting, so that the dating depends on comparisons with other works, none of which are of such high quality.

There are further paintings in Westminster Abbey of the late thirteenth and early fourteenth centuries, which may be connected with the name of master Walter of Durham, the king's painter, known from documents, who died in 1308. Other con-siderable cycles in the king's palaces are known from the accounts. Those in the

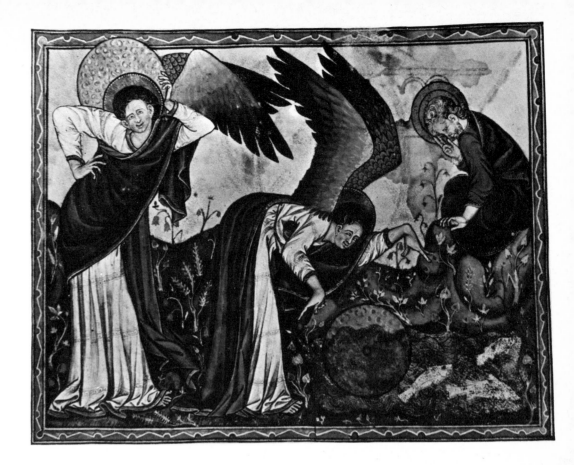

The Angel casting a great millstone into the sea (Revelations XVIII, v. 21). Westminster (?), before 1272. MS Douce 180, page 77. Bodleian Library, Oxford.

Palace of Westminster were destroyed by fire in 1834 but we have copies made a little earlier giving the subjects and some idea of the style.

From the early years of the fourteenth century a series of quite exceptional manuscripts, mostly Psalters, survive. A number of these were produced for lay magnates, many of them of East Anglian families, often on the occasion of a marriage. We thus see the circle of patronage widening from the great churches and their prelates, and the royal family, to the nobility. The term East Anglian school has been widely used, for the manuscripts are connected by style as well as by their provenance. It seems likely that some of them were produced at Norwich, which was at this time one of the largest and wealthiest cities in the country, and perhaps also at the Fenland monasteries, particularly Peterborough and Ramsey.

Some of the Psalters continue the tradition of prefatory cycles of miniatures, for instance the De Lisle, Ramsey, Peterborough and so-called 'Queen Mary' Psalters. In others, such as the Ormesby, Tickhill, Gorleston and Luttrell Psalters, the decoration consists of historiated initials with borders of great richness and inventiveness.

As an example, we may consider the page with the introduction to Psalm 109 in the Ormesby Psalter (Oxford, Bodleian Library, MS. Douce 366). The very complicated history of the illumination of this manuscript, which was executed with various alterations of plan in at least four different stages between the late thirteenth century and *c.* 1330, was elucidated by S.C. Cockerell in a model publication for the Roxburghe Club in 1926. The Psalter receives its name from its last owner, Robert of Ormesby, who gave it to Norwich Cathedral, where he was a monk. Portraits of him, and of the bishop of Norwich were inserted about 1320–30. Originally the manuscripts may have been intended for the abbey of Bury St Edmunds, and later, about 1310, portraits of a man and woman with the arms respectively of Bardolf and Foliot were added. No marriage of this date is recorded, however. The page reproduced here was illuminated at about this time.

At the top of the page we see a monkey riding a greyhound and pursuing an owl sitting on a rabbit. The monkey is equipped as a falconer with pouche, gloves and a

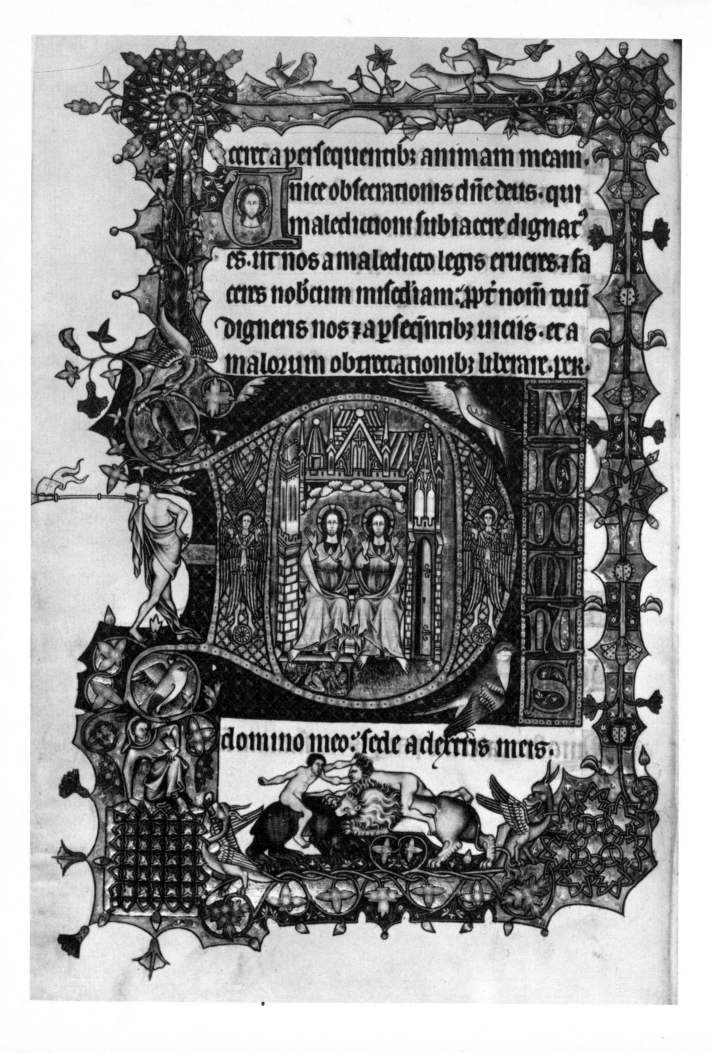

lure. He is swinging the lure with his left hand in a vain attempt to recapture the owl which apparently replaces the falcon and which seems to be escaping on the rabbit's back. In the lower margin two naked ruffians fight pig-a-back on a bear and a lion. In the border to the left is a trumpeter and to the right bees and ladybirds alternate. In addition there are real birds as well as imaginary dragons with long ears.

This is a typical example of the humorous marginal drollery, one of the most delightful products of the Gothic imagination. In the marginal borders the artists felt free to introduce all sorts of grotesque or ribald scenes which could never have been tolerated in the main miniatures or initials. Here, for example, the initial encloses a devotional picture, two Persons of the Trinity flanked by Cherubim, illustrating, as was usual in Psalters, the words: 'The Lord said unto my Lord sit thou upon my right hand until I make my enemies thy footstool' (Psalm 109, v.1).

The question of the meaning of the marginal drollery is a difficult one. Often interpretation is clear either as part of the *monde renversé* type of commentary, a parody of a serious scene, or as a symbolic representation. Many scenes can be explained with reference to the stories or *exempla* with which the Friar preachers enlivened their sermons. But often we do not know if the scenes have some meaning concealed from us, or if they are just put in to amuse the patron.

The origin of such marginal drolleries can be traced back to the end of the Romanesque period. Romanesque initials commonly included grotesque figures, beasts and birds often in combat, hunting scenes, and other subjects later found in the marginal scenes. In the early thirteenth century they begin to be released as it were from the plant scroll which had formerly enmeshed them, and they go free in the borders. Some of the earliest examples of the fully developed marginal drolleries appear in England, in the Rutland Psalter for instance (Belvoir Castle, library of the Duke of Rutland). They were also common in manuscripts made in north France and Flanders, in such centres as Arras, Thérouanne, Cambrai, St Omer and Ghent.

The borders of Gothic manuscripts from the earlier thirteenth century onwards again illustrate the principle of diaphanous space or texture. For example the border illustrated is not rectilinear but a series of curves, so that the space enclosed is of varied irregular shape and thus has a positive value in the design of the whole page. Leaves and flowers project on either side to emphasize this. The solid panels of blue, pink and gold of the border are overlaid by a mesh of fine scroll in white. At the four corners are complicated knot rosettes set like grilles on a gold ground. Even the gold interior of the initial letter is patterned with tiny punched dots. The whole page is a network of interpenetrating layers.

In the initial, the two Persons of the Trinity are framed by a building consisting of an open door, windows, and a complicated superstructure of pinnacles and roofs. There is some elementary foreshortening in the tower on the left and in the footstool. Here then is the beginning of an attempt to represent an interior realistically. This is an indication of the influence, felt indirectly no doubt, of Italian Trecento painting, and this is startlingly confirmed by the extraordinary, half-naked, twisting figure, blowing a trumpet with his left hand and placing his right hand on his hip. For this figure is a classical *tubicinarius* figure, shown in a pose which can be paralleled on a classical sarcophagus. Since the two wrestling figures can be compared with a marginal scene in a Bolognese late-thirteenth-century Bible (collection of the late Major J.R. Abbey, J.A. 7345, formerly Dyson Perrins MS. 51) no doubt the *tubicinarius* was also transmitted by some similar intermediary.

Another instance of Italian influence which like the *tubicinarius* was pointed out by Professor Pächt, occurs in the Gorleston Psalter (London, British Library, Additional 49622). This manuscript contains an entry in the calendar of the parish church of Gorleston in Suffolk. Like the Ormesby Psalter with which it is probably contemporary, the Gorleston Psalter was later at Norwich. It also contains historiated

Initial 'D', Psalm 109, with the Trinity.
Psalter of Robert of Ormesby.
Norwich (?), c. 1310.
MS Douce 366, folio 147ᵛ.
Bodleian Library, Oxford.

Opposite, Tree of Jesse. David killing the lion.
Psalter written by Prior John Tickhill of
Worksop. *c.* 1303–14.
Spencer MS 26, folio 6ᵛ.
The New York Public Library, Spencer
Collection, Astor, Lenox and Tilden Foundations.

Virgin and Child. De Lisle Psalter, *c.*1310.
Arundel 83, folio 131ᵛ.
British Library, London.

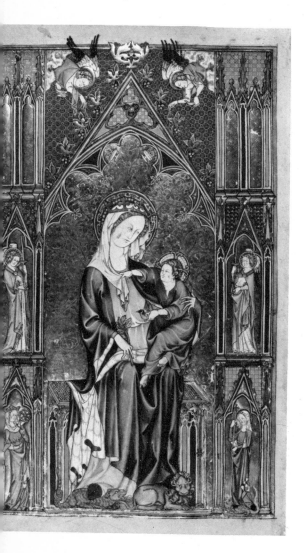

initials and in addition a full-page miniature of the Crucifixion (p. 51), inserted later perhaps when the manuscript had reached Norwich. In this, the medallions with bust heads suggest Italian models, but even more striking is the figure of Mary Magdalen embracing the cross, which is very nearly identical to that in a small panel by Simone Martini (Antwerp, Musée des Beaux-Arts). The high cross and the narrow platform of fissured ground are further features borrowed from the Italian model.

There are certainly important links between English early-fourteenth-century illumination and contemporary French work which remain to be worked out in detail. The group of which the so-called 'Queen Mary Psalter' (London, British Library, Royal 2.B. VII) is leader has always been considered the closest to contemporary French work. The 'Queen Mary Psalter' receives its name from the fact that it was confiscated by a customs officer as it was about to leave England in 1553 and presented to the Queen. The Psalter contains both tinted drawings and painted miniatures. The drawing technique is used for a long series of Old Testament miniatures at the beginning of the manuscript and for numerous marginal scenes at the bottom of the pages of the Psalter. The *bas-de-page* scenes include fables and bestiary scenes, illustrations of saints' lives, and a series of combats between grotesque creatures. There is a large group of manuscripts related to the Psalter in style, which suggests an important workshop, perhaps located in London, since Breviaries were made for Chertsey and Hyde Abbeys and a Psalter for Canterbury. The borders in this group are much more restrained than in the East Anglian manuscripts and the range of colour is more restricted.

Another series of miniatures with calendar but no text no doubt also originally preceded a Psalter (London, British Library, Arundel 83, folios 117–35). An inscription in the calendar states that the book was given in 1339 by Robert de Lisle to his daughter Audrey, a nun in the convent of Chicksands, Bedfordshire. Two artists worked on the surviving miniatures, one, illustrated here, in a style of *c.* 1310, the other in a later style influenced by Parisian miniature painting of the 1330s. The earlier style is connected with the paintings in the sedilia at Westminster Abbey.

The Tickhill Psalter (New York, Public Library, Spencer MS. 26) also contains, like the 'Queen Mary Psalter', *bas-de-page* scenes, mostly of Old Testament subjects. It receives its name from the colophon which states that it was written by John Tickhill, prior of Worksop, Nottinghamshire. Another group of manuscripts including Psalters in Oxford (Bodleian Library, MS. Barlow 22) and Brussels (Bibliothèque Royale, MS. 9961–2) suggests that there was an atelier in the Fens working for Peterborough Abbey.

Altogether the production of this period, of which only a part and not even all the first-rate manuscripts have been mentioned, is astonishing in its profusion and quality. The last of this series which we shall mention here is probably the best known, again principally for its enchanting *bas-de-page* scenes, the Luttrell Psalter (London, British Library, Additional 42130), made for Sir Geoffrey Luttrell (died 1345) who is portrayed with his wife and daughter-in-law on folio 202 verso. He is shown in full armour on his charger, a personification of medieval chivalry. Heraldic art has always been practised with great skill in England since its beginnings. There are fine coats-of-arms painted by Matthew Paris in his manuscripts for instance. Partly, perhaps, this reflects a continuing English preoccupation with genealogy. But this is also an art of stylization in which balance and counterpoise have a large part to play and three-dimensional representation little if any. Sir Geoffrey Luttrell is almost a cardboard silhouette and the main emphasis is on his arms and armour.

From this period we have what has been described as the most important domestic mural paintings of the medieval period in England. These are the wall-paintings in the fortified manor house of Longthorpe near Peterborough. The subjects of the paintings are a mixture of secular, religious and moralizing themes. They include the

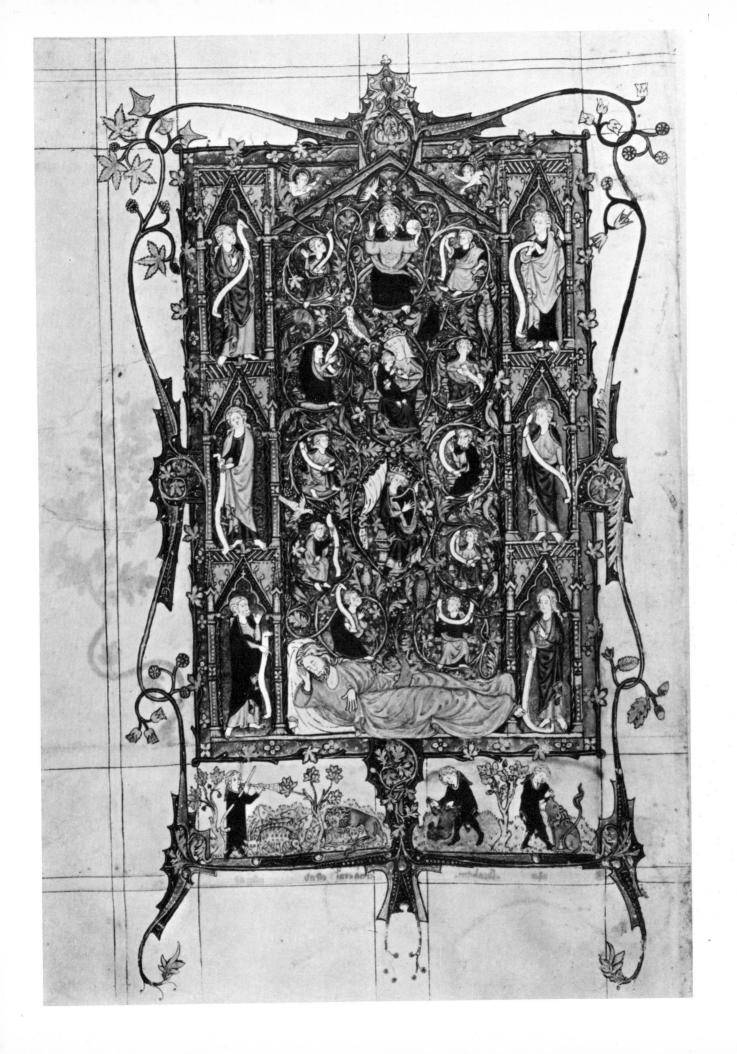

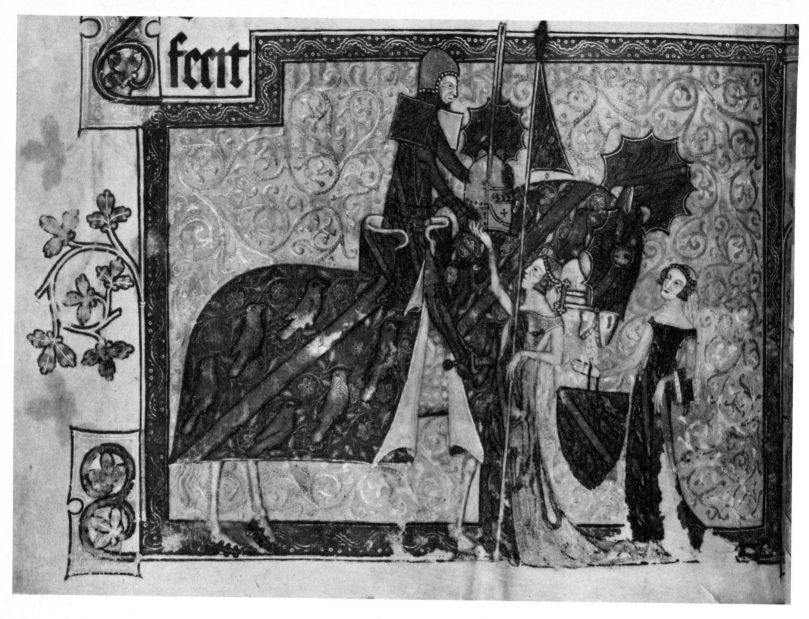

Apostles with large scrolls recalling the Tickhill Psalter (a linear device always common in English art), the Labours of the months, the Nativity of Christ, an enthroned king, perhaps Edward II or Edward III, the meeting of the Three Living with the Three Dead (a *memento mori* which becomes common in the later Middle Ages), and a strange representation of a king holding a wheel with animals on the circumference which seem to represent the five senses. The style is related to that of the group of Peterborough manuscripts mentioned above.

Also of this period are two retables, one in the Cluny Museum, Paris, the other in the church of Thornham Parva, Suffolk (p. 46). The Cluny panel shows the Nativity of Christ, the Death of the Virgin, the Adoration of the Magi and the Virgin being taught by her mother to read. The Thornham Parva panel shows the Crucifixion flanked by SS Peter and Paul. The tall swaying figures are set on richly patterned and punched grounds which serve to emphasize their curving silhouettes. In spite of the increased modelling of the hair and of the interior folds of the drapery if compared with the 'Queen Mary Psalter' there is still a Gothic emphasis on the silhouette and its relation to the background, as opposed to an attempt to set the figures in space.

In 1348–9 the Black Death carried off a large part of the population. Though English illumination of the second half of the century is not so prolific or of such

Above, Sir Geoffrey Luttrell (d. 1345) *with his wife and daughter-in-law.* Psalter. East Anglia, *c.* 1340. Additional 42130, folio 202ᵛ. British Library, London.

Right, The north wall of the Great Chamber, Longthorpe Tower, near Peterborough, showing the Seven Ages of Man, the Nativity, Apostles with scrolls of the Creed, birds, etc. *c.* 1330–40.

44

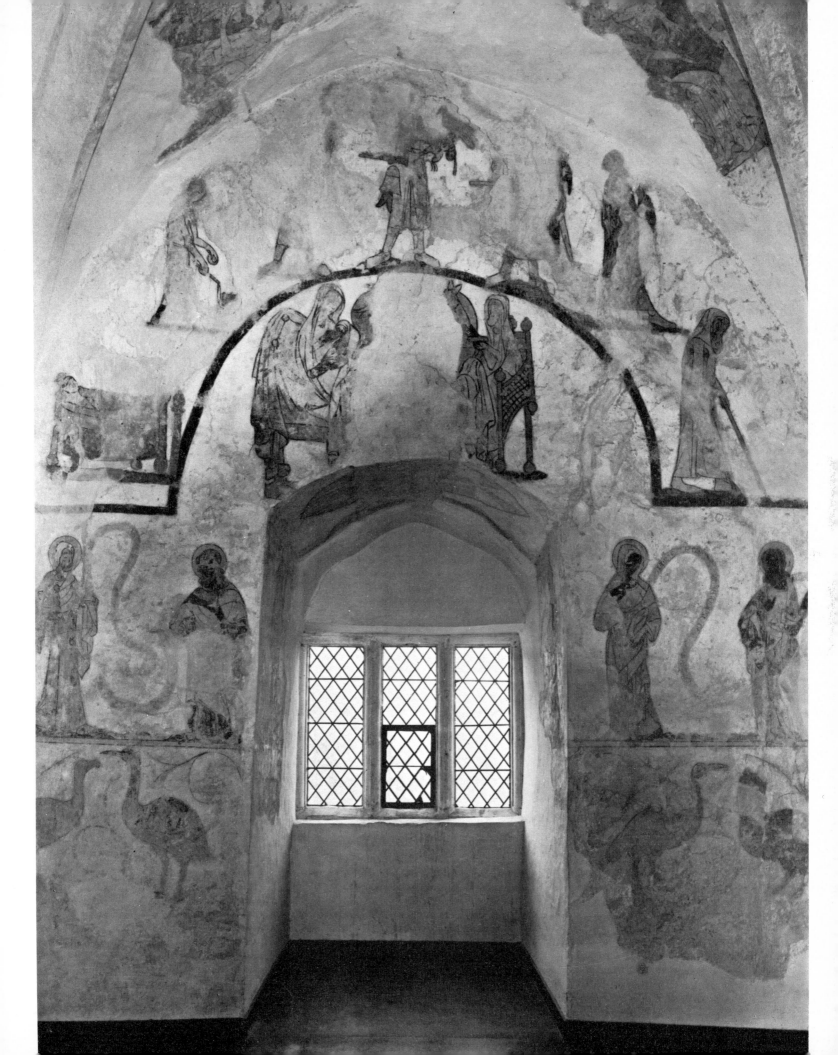

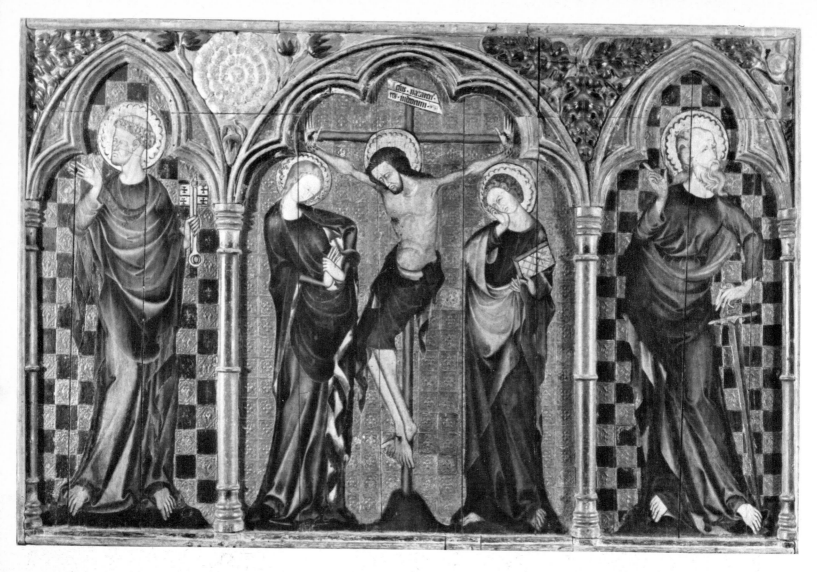

Retable. *The Crucifixion, the Virgin and St John flanked by St Peter and Paul.*
East Anglia, *c.* 1340.
By permission of the rector, Thornham Parva church, Suffolk.

outstanding inventiveness, it would be a mistake to suppose that there was a complete break with the earlier production. A group of manuscripts of the third quarter of the fourteenth century, centering on the Fitzwarin Psalter in Paris (Bibliothèque Nationale, latin 765) emphasize certain expressionistic trends already seen in the Luttrell Psalter. The figures are contorted in angular poses and their faces are often grotesque. Again we are witnessing a reaction to the style of the preceding years, a reaction which occurs also in France and even in Italy. The use of complicated architectural canopies as a decorative frame rather than a spatial setting, is a feature in contemporary carving, stained glass and embroideries. Embroidery is a form of painting but because, like stained glass, it tends to stylization and cannot, by its context, be illusionistic, it was an art at which the English excelled. The fourteenth-century production of *Opus anglicanum*, English work, as it was called, had tremendous prestige and was exported to all parts of Europe.

Slightly later than the Fitzwarin group are a number of *de luxe* manuscripts all connected with the Bohun family. Of these a Psalter in Oxford (Bodleian Library, MS. Auct. D. 4.4) was begun for Humfrey de Bohun, Earl of Hereford (d. 1372), since his name is included in the prayers, and finished for his daughter, Mary, first wife of Henry of Lancaster (Henry IV). She is portrayed in the manuscript with her patron saint, St Mary Magdalen, presenting her to the Virgin and Child. The earliest manuscript with the Bohun arms (Oxford, Bodleian Library, MS. Dep. Astor A.1) is linked stylistically with the Fitzwarin Psalter. The later manuscripts are in a different style. The most obvious feature is the small scale of the illumination. The numerous scenes

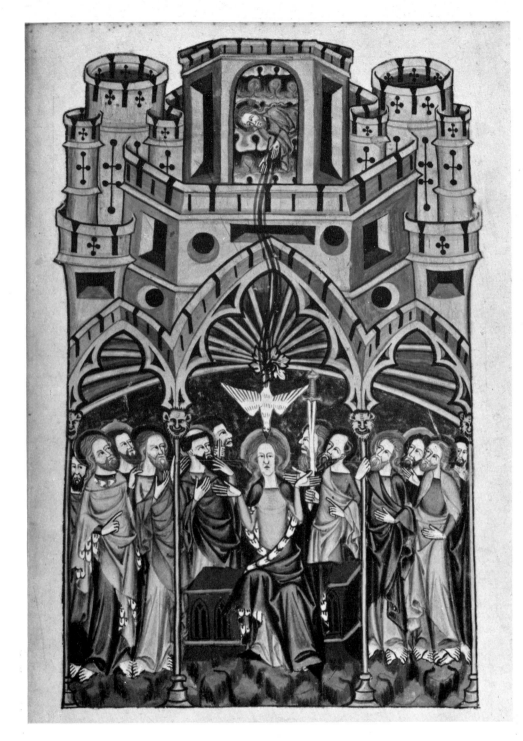

Left, Pentecost. Fitzwarin Psalter.
Third quarter of fourteenth century.
Latin 765, folio 20.
Bibliothèque Nationale, Paris.
Below, Temptation and expulsion of Adam and Eve.
Bohun Psalter. *c.* 1370–80.
MS Auct.D.4.4, folio 24ᵛ.
Bodleian Library, Oxford.

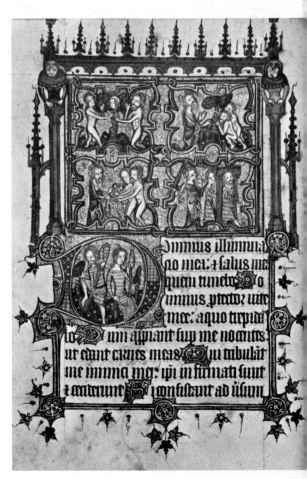

are usually enclosed in quatrefoils or historiated initials and even where a miniature fills a whole page the figures are still small. This scale recalls the Psalter of the St Omer family (London, British Library, Additional 39810) and there are connections between the border motifs of these earlier East Anglian manuscripts and the Bohun group. There are also foreign influences. Humfrey went to Milan in 1368 for the marriage of Lionel, duke of Clarence, to Violanta Visconti, and the influence of Milanese illuminators, such as Giovanni Benedetto da Como, is apparent in colouring and in facial types, for example in the miniature of the raising of Lazarus in the Bodleian Manuscript; and in iconography, for example the winged Evangelists in the Exeter College, Oxford, Psalter (MS. 47). Other parallels can be drawn with contemporary French illumination in the landscape conventions and the use of restrained colours and tinted grisaille.

At the end of the fourteenth century the *'Weiche'* or 'Soft style' makes its appearance all over Europe. Other names given to it, the 'Courtly style' or the 'International style', draw attention to other of its aspects. The similarity of works produced in different parts of Europe at this time is a phenomenon which makes it difficult to comment on possible influences of one country on another. Not only were works of art extensively exported, partly as a result of linked networks of patronage, but artists themselves travelled widely, for example Hermann Scheerre discussed below. There are still works of considerable importance for whose origin no agreement has been reached. In fact it is always easier to date a work of this period than to place it.

In England foreign influence is apparent through various channels. In 1382 Richard II married Anne of Bohemia (d. 1394) and one might expect some influence from a school of painting and illumination which was of great importance at the time. The large portrait of the King, today in Westminster Abbey, has been seen as one instance of this. Comparisons can also be made between Bohemian illumination and a large group of manuscripts of the 1380s of which the Lytlington Missal (p. 53) made for the abbot of Westminster in 1383–4 and the *Liber Regalis* (both still at Westminster Abbey) are the finest examples.

For contemporary French influence we have the later evidence of Froissart that André Beauneveu, court sculptor and painter of the Duc de Berry, worked in England. A Book of Hours in Cambridge (Fitzwilliam Museum, MS. 48), made for a marriage of the Carew and Poyntz families, contains miniatures of seated saints (p. 53) whose rich convoluted draperies and imposing thrones can be compared with figures of prophets and apostles in a Psalter illuminated by Beauneveu for the Duc de Berry (Paris, Bibliothèque Nationale, fr. 13091). The Hours also contains perspective interiors which suggest Italian sources transmitted via French art, since comparisons can be made with work of the 'Parement Master' working in Paris in the 1380s.

Italian influence has been seen in the most famous work of English painting of the period, the Wilton Diptych (London, National Gallery) (pp. 54–5). Both inconographic and stylistic comparisons can be made with works commissioned by the Visconti, dukes of Milan. Though the English origin of the diptych is now generally accepted, the date remains a subject of controversy, chiefly because, as so often where this is so, there is no other English panel comparable to it and little comparative material at all.

The fourth source of influence on English art is the art of the lower Rhine and of the Netherlands. A very large Missal made for the Carmelites in London (London, British Library, Additional 29704–5) survives in fragments (p. 53), having been cut up as a scrapbook for children in the nineteenth century! It was illuminated with historiated initials and borders in three main styles. Two of these are English, being related to styles found in the Lytlington Missal. The third style at its finest is, as Professor Rickert showed in her publication of the Missal, that of a foreign illuminator working in England. The closest resemblances are with Dutch illumination, such as that in the Gelders Arms Book (Brussels, Bibliothèque Royale, MS. 15652–56) of the late fourteenth century. There is a new realism both in landscape and architectural details and also in facial types.

A second foreign artist, Herman Scheerre, signed a Book of Prayers (London, British Library, Additional 16998). Hermann is very probably the Hermann of Cologne who is known from accounts to have worked for the Duke of Gelders in Cologne in 1388–9 and for the Duke of Burgundy in Dijon in 1401–3. In 1419 he was working for Isabeau de Bavière in Paris. A group of manuscripts by different overlapping hands suggests that between these dates he headed an atelier at work in England. Such shops or 'ateliers' were now reaching considerable size and complexity, with specialist assistants doing different parts of the work.

King Edgar presents the charter of the New Minster, Winchester, to Christ.
Winchester, after 966.
Cotton Vespasian A. VIII, folio 2.
British Library, London.

48

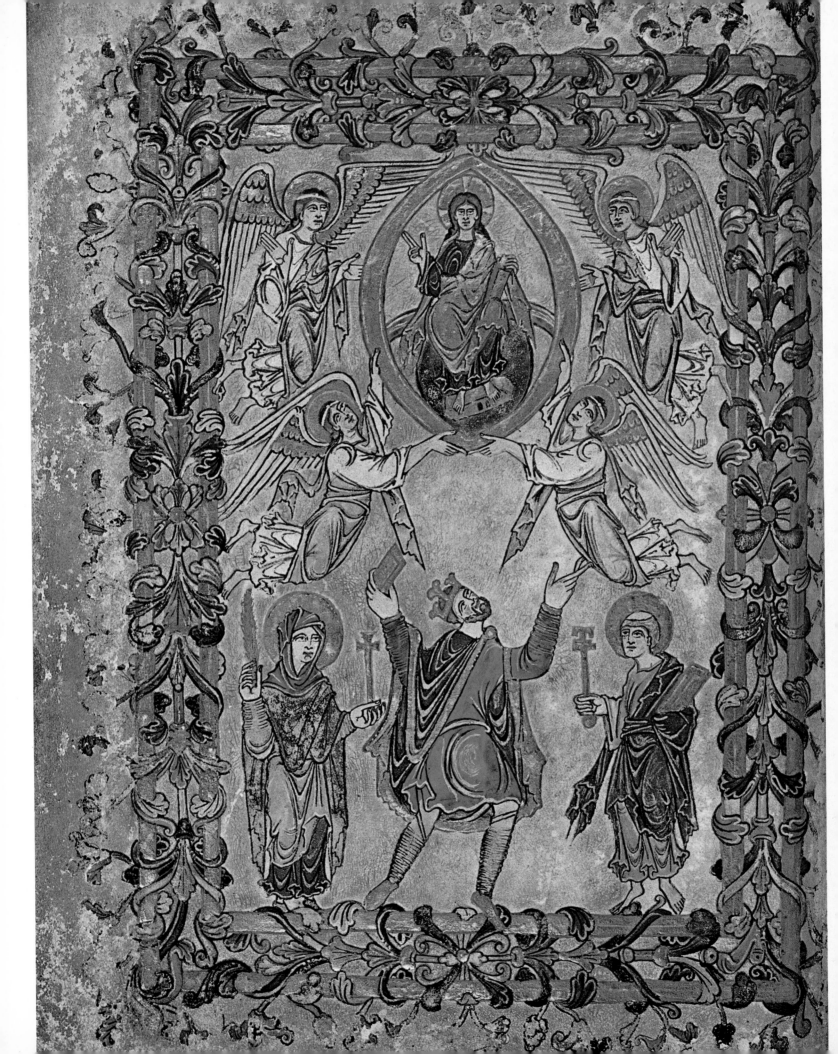

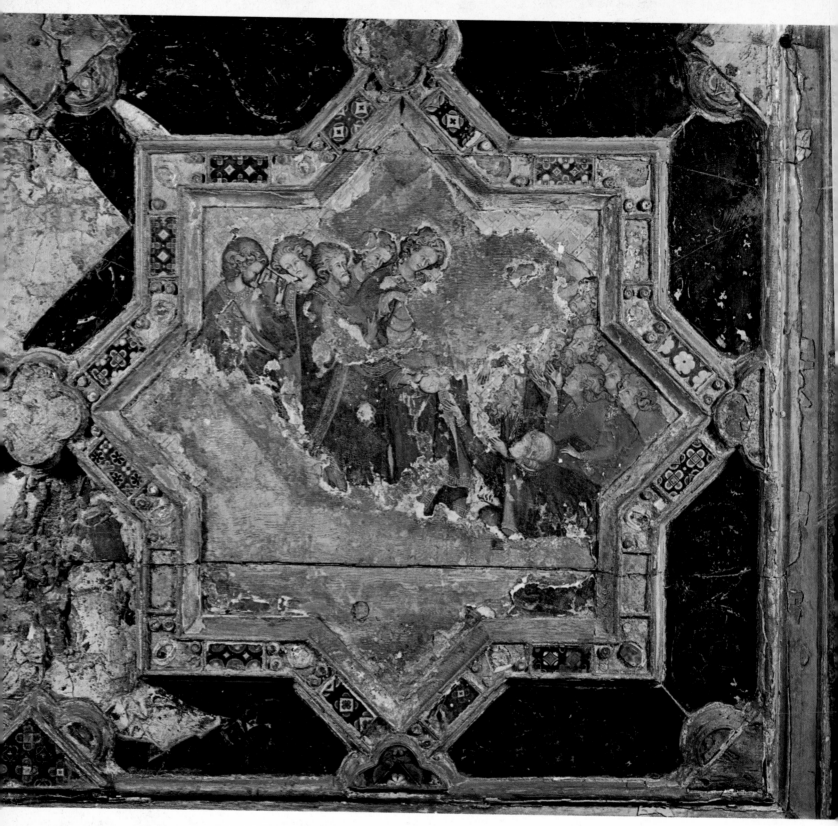

Retable (detail). *The feeding of the five thousand.* Westminster, *c.* 1275.
By permission of the Dean and Chapter of Westminster, London.

Scheerre's style, which is closely related to that of Cologne painters such as the so-called Veronica Master, is more refined and elegant than is that of the Master of the Carmelite Missal. The outstanding miniature in this style is an Annunciation (p. 52), in which the Angel Gabriel kneels before the Virgin in a small polygonal tower, outside which the owner and his wife kneel on either side at a prie-dieu. There is no clue to the owner's identity but on the prie-dieu, to the left, there may have been a coat-of-arms and if it is ever possible to penetrate the overpainting of this, the identity

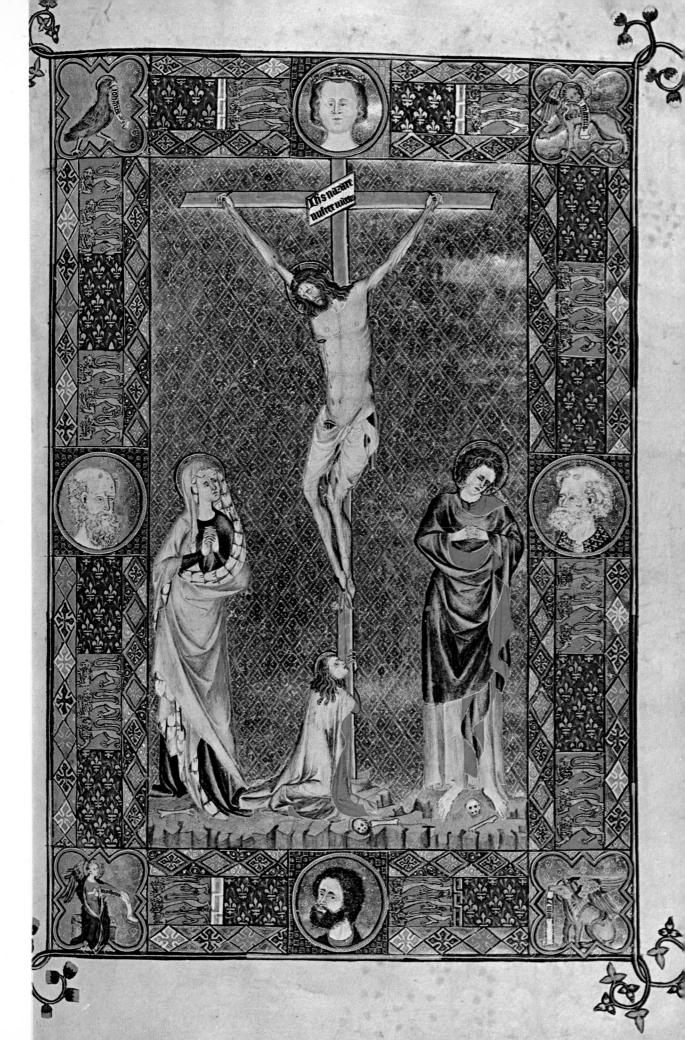

The Crucifixion: added
to a Psalter made for
Gorleston Church, near
Yarmouth, Norfolk.
East Anglia, *c.* 1325.
Additional 49622,
folio 7.
British Library, London.

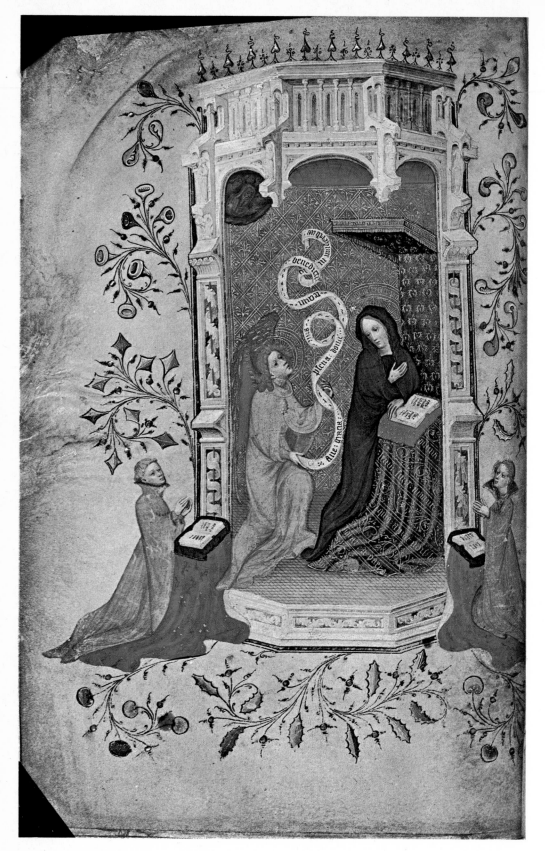

Right, The Crucifixion from the Missal
of Abbot Lytlington of Westminster Abbey,
written *c.* 1383–4. MS 37, folio 157ᵛ.
By permission of the Dean and Chapter of
Westminster, London.
Far right, St Andrew. Carew Poyntz Hours.
Late fourteenth century. MS 48, folio 47.
By permission of the Syndics of the
Fitzwilliam Museum, Cambridge.
Below right, The Birth of Christ.
Missal for the Carmelites in London, *c.* 1393–8.
Additional 29704, folio 3.
British Library, London.

Above, Annunciation with kneeling donors,
inserted in a Book of Hours. Signed 'de Daer'.
Early fifteenth century.
Royal 2. A. XVIII, folio 23ᵛ.
British Library, London.

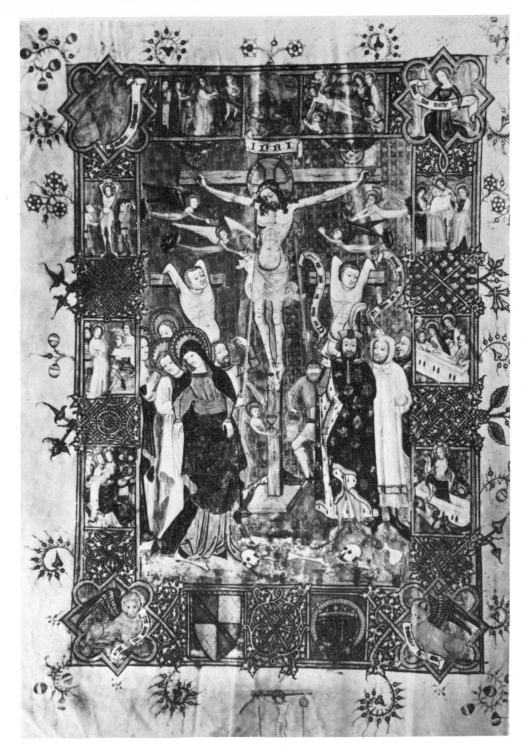

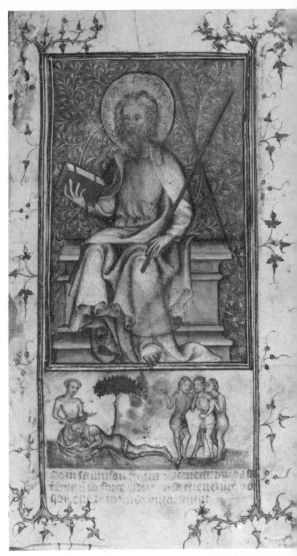

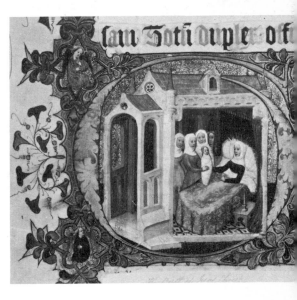

could be revealed. This and other miniatures originally belonged to a Psalter now in Rennes, and were some time later prefixed to a Book of Hours which belonged to Margaret Beaufort (London, British Library, Royal 2 A. XVIII).

On the Virgin's prie-dieu in gold letters is the motto *'Omnia sunt levia amanti'* which occurs in the manuscript signed by Scheerre and in other works of the atelier. Nevertheless it does not seem possible to attribute the miniature to Scheerre himself. The other words on the prie-dieu *'de Daer'* may conceal the identity of the artist. The 'S'-shaped pose of the angel, the undulating draperies and the curving scroll are all marks of the International style. The refinement extends to the colouring which is mostly of pale shades, with reds and pinks, blues and greens overlapping and emphasizing the sinuous movement of the composition. This miniature provides in

Overleaf, The Wilton Diptych. Richard II with his patron saints, St Edmund, St Edward the Confessor and St John the Baptist kneeling before the Virgin and Child. *c.*1413. National Gallery, London.

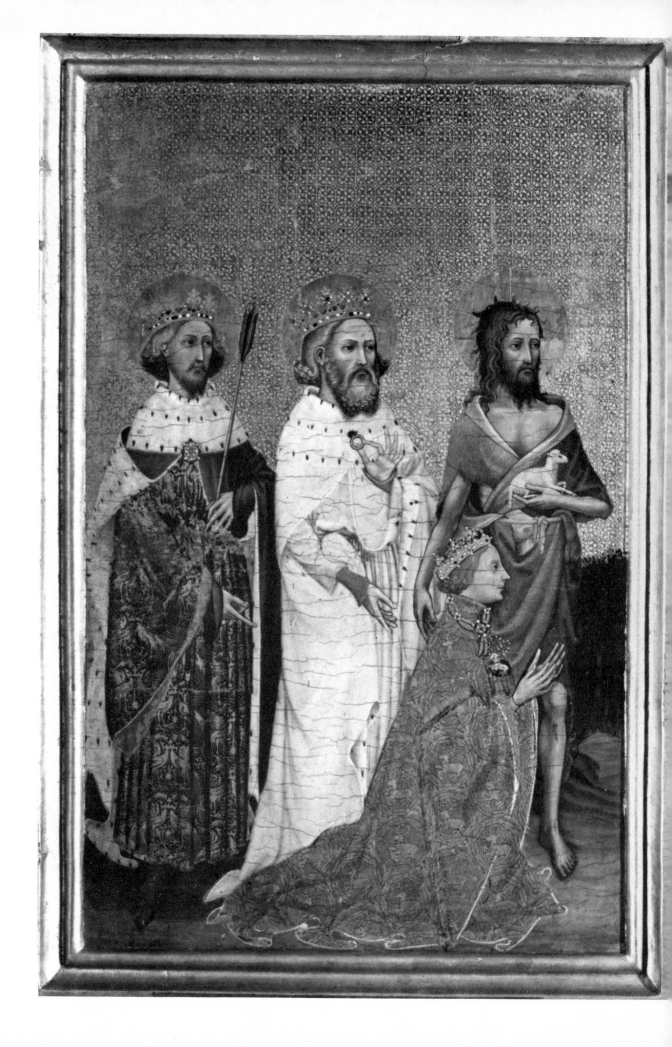

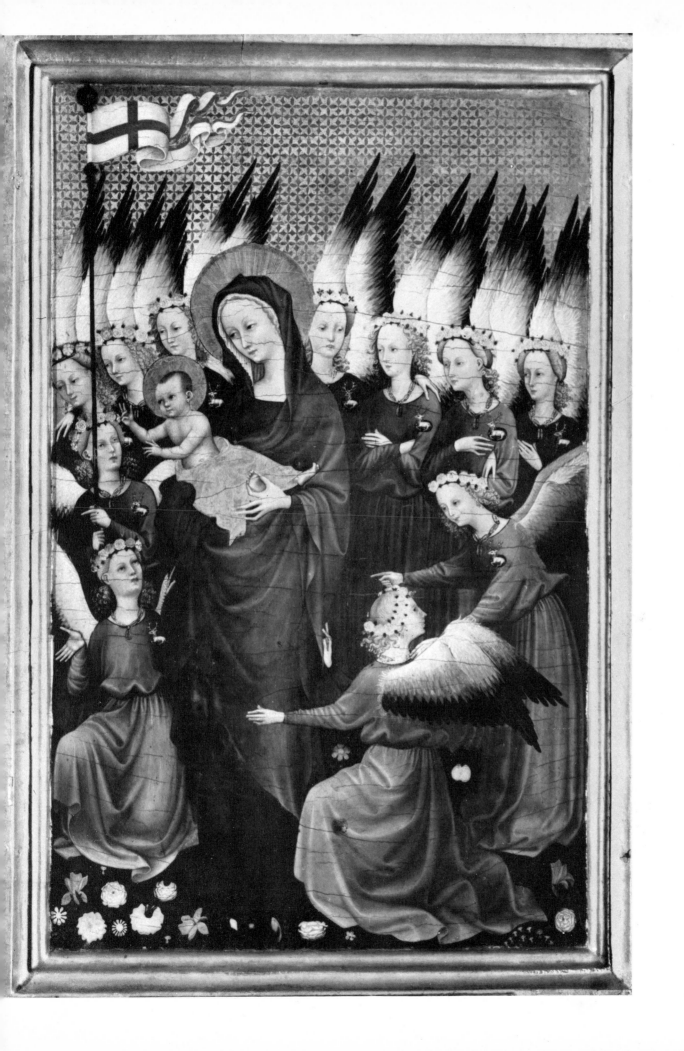

style and quality the closest point of comparison extant to the Wilton Diptych. This suggests, as Professor Wormald has demonstrated, that the latter is a posthumous portrait of Richard II, perhaps executed in connection with his reburial in Westminster Abbey in 1413 by order of Henry V.

Two other artists of this period are also known by name. They are John Siferwas who executed the Missal made for Sherborne Abbey, Dorset (Alnwick Castle, Northumberland, library of the Duke of Northumberland) and the Lovell Lectionary (London, British Library, Harley 7026). The latter contains a presentation scene of Siferwas giving his book to Lord Lovell. Portraits in the sense of recognizable likenesses first begin to appear at this date and a little earlier, sculpture leading painting in this development. We have already mentioned the Westminster Abbey portrait of Richard II. Though these and other representations are idealized to some degree, they are nevertheless important for a new interest in natural appearances. Another sign of this in the Sherborne Missal is the large number of realistic birds portrayed. There are also some naturalistic plants, though in general border leaf ornament remains stylized. In the Magdalene College pattern book (p. 15), several pages are filled with accurate sketches of birds, early nature studies, for which striking parallels have been cited in North Italian pattern books, such as that of Giovanni dei Grassi at Bergamo.

From the same period we have likenesses of Henry V (d. 1422) and of Geoffrey Chaucer (d. 1400). A miniature preceding Chaucer's *Troilus and Cressida* (Cambridge, Corpus Christi College, MS. 61), shows Chaucer reading at the court of Richard II. On the basis of the border decoration it can be dated to the second quarter of the fifteenth century, but there are signs that it depends on an earlier miniature, which must have been painted by one of the Limbourg brothers who worked for the Duc de Berry. Not only individual figures, the group in the lower right-hand corner, for example, but the architecture in the background and the whole composition in which the zig-zag path is used to lead the eye inwards in depth recall the Limbourgs' most famous work, the *Très Riches Heures*, left unfinished at their death in 1416 (Chantilly, Musée Condé). At this time many manuscripts from the French royal library were in England since John, Duke of Bedford, regent for Henry VI, had purchased the library in Paris and removed it first to Rouen and then to England.

The third artist who signed an example of his work was named Johannes. The signed miniature, again gold lettering on a piece of drapery, is in the copy of Marco Polo's *Livre du Grand Caam*, now in Oxford (Bodleian Library, MS. Bodley 264). There are a number of miniatures in the manuscript besides the signed one, of varying style and quality, but Johannes certainly executed the most important miniature, the frontispiece showing the departure of the travellers from Venice (p. 58). Here again there is a remarkable portrait quality. We can recognize San Marco with the Golden Horses, the Doge's Palace and the columns with the statues of the lion of St Mark and St George. The sources of this remarkable miniature have never been explained. The earliest example of naturalistic townscape is, after all, Ambrogio Lorenzetti's view of Siena, painted in the Palazzo Publico in 1338–40, so an ultimate source in Italy seems likely. It is symptomatic of the International style that the earliest surviving topographical view of Venice should be in an English manuscript.

The International style continues in English illumination until early in the third decade of the fifteenth century. Another outstanding manuscript, a Psalter and Book of Hours bearing the arms of John, Duke of Bedford, contains the signature of Hermann Scheerre in the line endings (London, British Library, Additional 42131). It also contains work by an assistant of Scheerre who is remarkable for the portrait quality of his heads. Also of this late phase is the Hours which belonged later to Queen Elizabeth, wife of Henry VII, in which the main part of the work is by Johannes (London, British Library, Additional 50001). Johannes' style is more important for the future than is that of Scheerre because certain of its features,

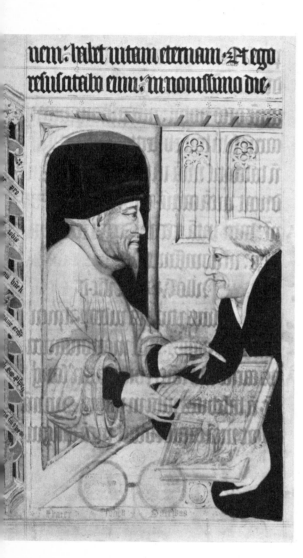

Lectionary for Salisbury Cathedral.
John Siferwas, the artist, presents the book to John, 5th Lord Lovell, d. 1408.
Harley 7026, folio 4ᵛ.
British Library, London.

Opposite, Chaucer reading his 'Troilus and Cressida' to the court. c. 1420–30.
MS 61, folio 1ᵛ.
By permission of the Master and Fellows of Corpus Christi College, Cambridge.

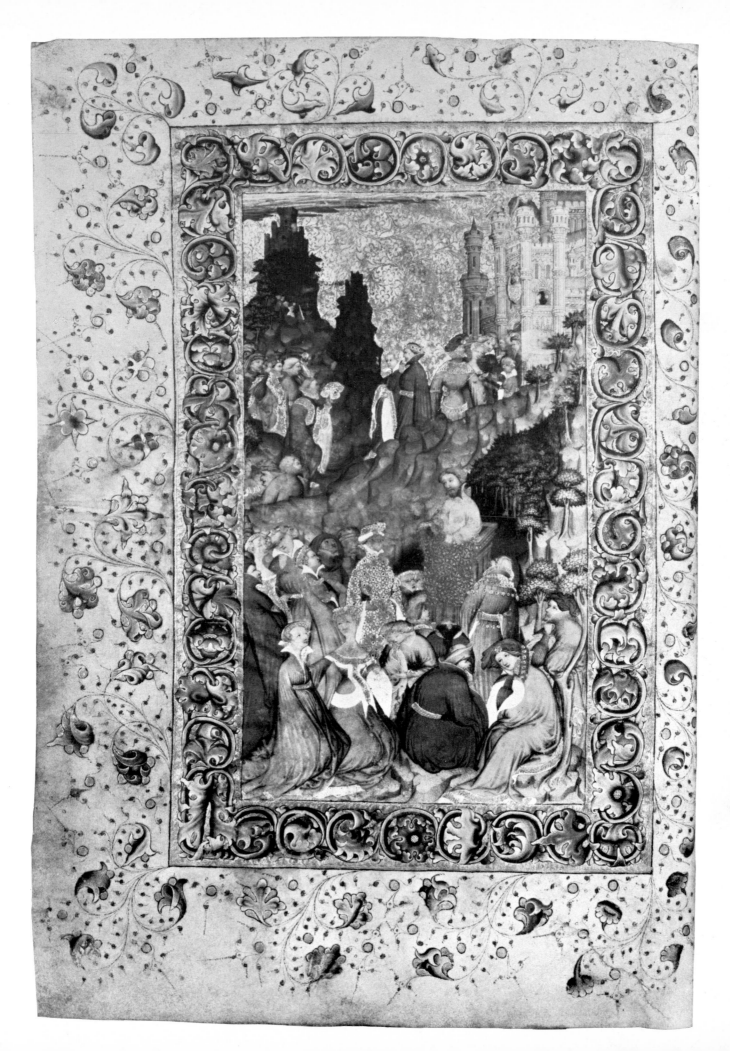

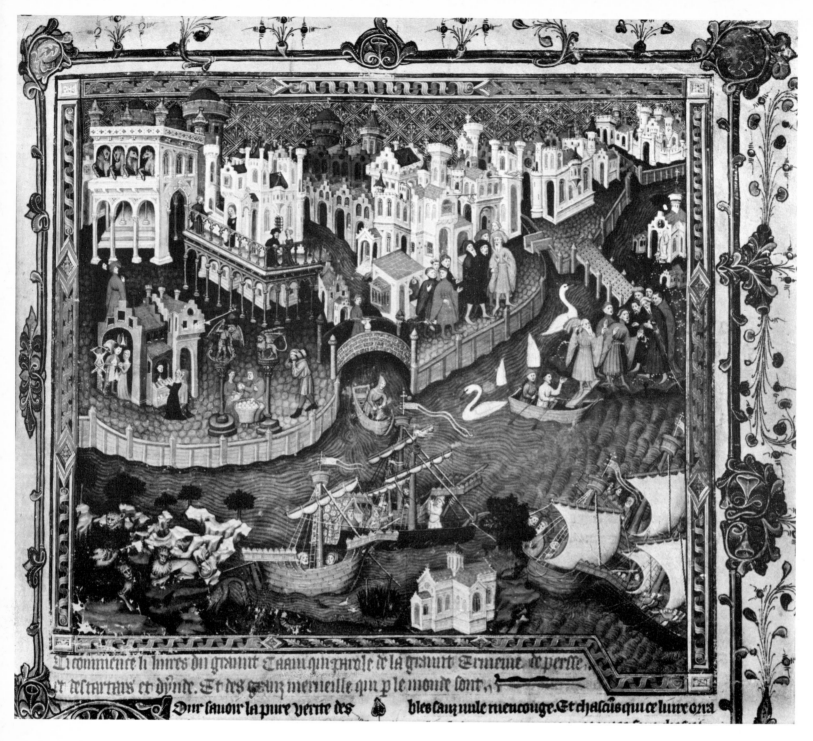

Niccoló and Maffeo Polo setting out from Venice.
Marco Polo, *Le Livre du Gran Caam. c.* 1400–10.
By the artist Johannes.
MS Bodley 264, folio 218.
Bodleian Library, Oxford.

notably the fantastic costumes and certain grotesque facial types, were taken up by later artists beginning to react to the International Gothic style.

In the second quarter of the fifteenth century the flowing line begins to be replaced by broken forms, curves by angles and the subtle delicate shades by opposing primary colours. English artists do not seem to have found acceptable either the new naturalism of Dutch and Flemish painting with its more painterly style, or the new experiments in three-dimensional vanishing-point perspective made in Italy. Like certain artists in Germany they introduce a style which depends for its effect on qualities which can best be described as heraldic – balance, counterpoise and linear stylization of forms which become recognizable by a convention.

The decline in the number of important works of painting in fifteenth-century England seems to me explicable at least as much in these terms, that is because of English artists' inability to accept the latest developments of European painting, as because of the disruption of the Wars of the Roses. The argument can be reinforced by the observation that stained glass, which for precisely the same reasons is not a major art form at this date in the Netherlands or Italy, continued to be made in England and is of high quality, for example at York, Malvern, Oxford and in East Anglia. Secondly, where England can show works of the highest quality is in a group of manuscripts containing pen drawings. The outstanding examples are an illustrated copy of a work by Thomas Chaundler concerning the compassion of God to Man (Cambridge, Trinity College, MS. R.14.5), and the so-called 'Beauchamp Pageants' (London, British Library, Cotton Julius E. IV). Here the new style becomes acceptable because it is transformed into a linear framework. Chaundler composed his work whilst he was Chancellor of Oxford University between 1457 and 1461, and he dedicated it to Bishop Thomas Beckington of Wells. Since both men belonged to the group of English humanists and were in contact with Italy, here if anywhere one might expect to find vanishing-point perspective. However, the floor tiles are shown as a grid without any foreshortening and the drapery recalls Flemish far more than Italian sources. Such facts lead one to distrust arguments attributing too great importance to the patron.

The artist of the 'Beauchamp Pageants' is closer still to Flemish and Dutch style and may even be a foreigner. The miniatures show episodes in the life of Richard Beauchamp, Earl of Warwick, 1389–1439, glorifying him as the type of chivalrous knight (p. 60). They were probably executed in the late 1480s. Here also, though there is much observation of detail and skill in the narrative, there is no attempt to relate actors and settings to each other in relative proportion. The artist's designs remind one more of tapestries, for which indeed they have sometimes been supposed to be cartoons.

The most important remaining piece of fifteenth-century mural painting belongs to the end of the century and also shows very close ties with Flemish art. We know from documents that the paintings in the chapel at Eton College were executed by Gilbert and by William Baker in the years 1478–9–80 and 1487–8. The paintings, which are almost entirely monochromatic, are on a large scale and show scenes of the Miracles of the Virgin with standing Apostles and female saints set in niches under canopies as if carved statues between the different episodes (p. 61). The work on the north side shows a greater ability to render interior space and more interest in light and shade, and is in the so-called 'long line' style of Flemish painters of the '60s and '70s such as Dirk Bouts and Hugo van der Goes. Close comparisons can be made with books illuminated for Edward IV in Bruges and Ghent in the 1480s. The paintings on the south side, though similar in technique, show the figures crowded at the front of the picture plane, not set in space. Perhaps these are by William Baker, an Englishman, and the others by Gilbert, who was possibly a Flemish artist.

In so brief a survey it has hardly been possible to do more than attempt to sketch an outline of the stylistic development of painting in Britain in the Middle Ages. In spite of all the destruction the original material remaining is still very extensive and the plates can give no idea of the richness of the subject matter of medieval painting, nor of the varying ways in which the same subject was treated at different periods. Nevertheless we can observe certain significant changes over the period even in so limited a selection of material.

If we compare the representation of St Dunstan prostrating himself before the Lord (p. 26) with the Annunciation miniature of some 450 years later (p. 52), we can see a change which is reflected throughout medieval art. In the earlier miniature the abbot is of minute size if compared to the Christ, and, as the inscription makes clear, it is *'timor domini'*, 'fear of the Lord', which is necessary to salvation. In the later minia-

Death striking down Man. Thomas Chaundler, *Liber Apologeticus. c.* 1457–61.
MS R.14.5, folio 8.
Trinity College, Cambridge.

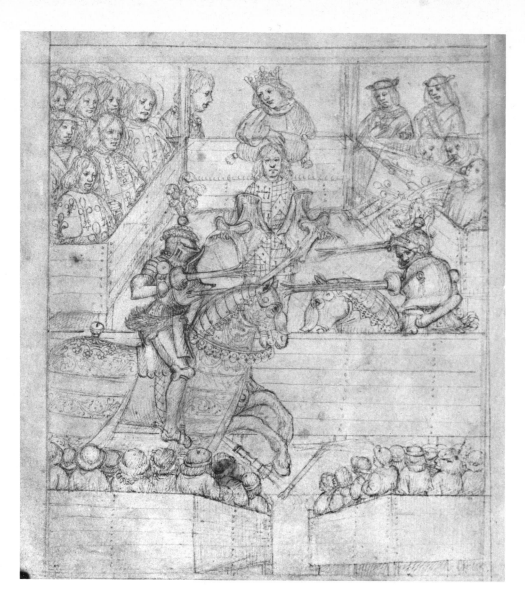

*Richard Beauchamp, Earl of Warwick, jousting
against Sir Hugh Lawney.*
'Beauchamp Pageants', *c.* 1470–80.
Cotton Julius E. IV, folio 15ᵛ.
British Library, London.

ture the two donors are almost on the same scale as the archangel Gabriel and the
Virgin. There is an ambiguity in their relationship as to whether they are kneeling
before a picture of the event or actually assisting at it. But the Creator's mercy in the
Redemption of the world through the Conception of the Christ is the subject of the
miniature. The kneeling figures pray for the intercession of the Virgin as the inscription on her halo makes clear, '*Sancta Virgo intercede pro nobis*', in confidence and
humility, but not in fear.

The earlier scene is abstracted from all reality and is purely a devotional picture.
The later shows the scene, at least to some extent, as a contemporary could imagine
it happening in his lifetime. The further step of representing it as it might have happened in history, is not taken yet, of course. But this illustrates the change in late
medieval piety which aimed to excite the devotion of the faithful by urging them to
imagine themselves as present at the events of the Gospel narrative. This was clearly
best done by dressing the scene in contemporary clothes. The late medieval types of
emotive image such as the Christ as Man of Sorrows, wounded, and wearing the
Crown of Thorns, and surrounded by the instruments of the Passion, are found in
England as elsewhere, though not illustrated here. Even in these strictly devotional
images realism is a necessary ingredient if they are to be effective.

Christian art, therefore, which, in the fourth century, after the Peace of the Church,
was first provided with scenes for the Gospel events emphasizing their narrative
content and to some extent realistically portrayed, gradually abstracts the narrative

60

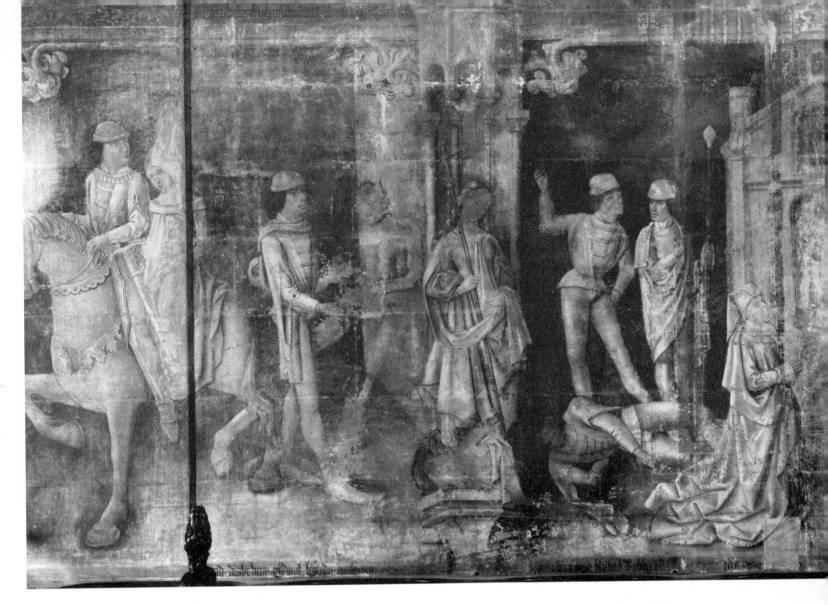

The Miracle of the Wounded Image.
Painting on the north wall of Eton Chapel.
Late 15th century.
The Provost and Fellows of
Eton College, Windsor.

and realistic elements and turns the pictures into devotional images without reference to time and space. Gradually the scenes are reinterpreted with reference to contemporary life with increasing naturalism, at first in details, but later in the whole interpretation of the scene. At the same time a secular, non-religious art gains ground.

Thus we saw that the portrait of Ezra, deriving from a late antique model, is almost a genre scene. He sits surrounded by the tools of his trade as scribe and author with his books in the cupboard behind him (p. 19). By about the year 1000 an Anglo-Saxon artist represented the Evangelist John (p. 27) as a scribe symbolically, by pen and lectern, but without showing the objects in any spatial relationship, so that his mode of work could scarcely be imagined or reconstructed from them. His status and supernatural inspiration, on the other hand, are clearly emphasized. By about 1400, however, we see the artist John Siferwas portraying himself and his patron in an interior space (p. 56) with the intention of evoking an event which no doubt actually took place. Thus in a sense even the subjects of religious art were being represented in secular terms by the fifteenth century. Both the drawings in the 'Beauchamp Pageants' (opposite) and the scenes of the Miracles of the Virgin (above) take place in the same sort of setting amongst the same actors, members of the court and their retainers. The effect of the Reformation could not be, therefore, to alter the *language* of art, however disastrous the removal of so much patronage might be. What was needed was a new artistic stimulus and, as so often before, this had to come from outside.

2

TUDOR AND EARLY STUART PAINTING

David Piper

The sixteenth century in England is a watershed in the history of politics as of religion. It is the century of the Tudors, a dynasty established by right of might rather than of law by Henry VII's victory at Bosworth, 1485, yet the dynasty that consolidated England, through its ups and downs, into a nation-state of law, of monarchic order, and of economic and military power of major international consequence. It is also the age of the reform of religion, the break from Rome and the establishment of the Anglican Church, the head of which – representative of God on earth – was also the head of the nation-state. That this period should gestate at its close the greatest English-born genius of the human imagination – Shakespeare, rooted so deeply in the insular English soil yet of such unparalleled and enduring universal relevance – seems entirely proper. But when one looks for his English counterpart in the visual arts, one looks in vain: there is only Hilliard to match the mood and exquisite contrivance of the comedies; the equivalent of the sombre profundities of the tragedies was to be provided not by an Englishman, but a Dutchman, Rembrandt, who was ten years old when Shakespeare died. There is, with the exception of Holbein and Hilliard, a glaring discrepancy between the literary and the visual achievement, but this has meant also that, until very recently, the history of painting, especially in the sixteenth century, has been over-neglected and underestimated; its achievement, if at one extreme peculiar and at odds, even, with the European post-Renaissance mainstream, is real, individual and still fascinating in its own right.

The basic themes of the period are revolutionary: the acclimatisation, if belated, of the easel painting as the dominant form of painting, accompanied by the virtual withering away of its predecessors, the art of the illuminators, of the glass-painters, and of the large-scale wall-painters. The latter was the inevitable consequence of the Reformation, which cut off abruptly both the main traditional source of patronage and the subject-matter; though the secularization of painting, as is stressed in the preceding chapter, had gained a greater momentum in the fifteenth century than is generally realized, its framework nevertheless had remained essentially a religious one. From the 1530s on, religious images were at first suspect, and then, rapidly, taboo; the Church, as patron, was extinct, and the habit of a new kind of patronage developed only slowly, with the gradual consolidation of the courtier class in splendid new mansions that called for decoration as once the churches had done. The fashion of having pictures as wall-furniture (though often they were covered with curtains) spreads slowly into the next century, and towards the end of the period focuses in some individual patrons – not yet very many – in the more specialized form of collections, and discrimination on grounds both of aesthetic and of financial value begins to appear: paintings begin to be treasured as works of art, as an essential part of a civilized person's furniture, as evidence of wealth and status. What is conspicuously absent in England throughout is a lead in patronage from the Crown itself; Henry VIII is the arguable exception, but his inventories read in terms of the old concept of the *Schatzkammer*, the treasure-store of jewels, plate, curiosities, not of an art-collection in the modern sense. And while he certainly set up as patron in rivalry to Francis I of France, and imported artists from abroad, his entire aim was to create a setting for the Crown. He failed also to attract the major artists, with the important exception of Holbein, and there is no evidence that he had much aesthetic sensibility nor any special feeling for pictures.

The emergence of a national style in the new form of painting was a tentative process, and its major aesthetic triumph came in the English pre-eminence in what, elsewhere, was always thought to be a minor variant, the art of miniature portraiture. If the adoption of the main form, the easel-painting, was belated, so too was full acceptance of the styles current on the Continent: the Renaissance principle of perspective and the realistic illusionism that went with it never, in this period, were wholeheartedly, universally, and enduringly adopted. The yielding to Italian *motifs*, so general throughout the rest of Europe, was slow and generally superficial. Tudor painting as we now know it, was in fact but one, probably subsidiary, expression of even the most important artists' activity; it was born on a flood of elaborately designed, expensive, pageantry – revels, triumphal processions, tilts, masques, entertainments – which were entirely ephemeral but were of enormous and lavish splendour (and sometimes, as Holbein's drawing for the triumphal arch for Anne Boleyn bears witness, must have been of great quality).

In these entertainments much of the spirit of medieval chivalry persisted, and even continued to influence the forms. The expression of the Gothic tradition in painting, in the last fifty years of its active survival, *c.* 1485–*c.* 1535, though what remains is mostly fragmentary or damaged, reads now as a real decay: the characteristic *Dooms* that still loom faintly, recovered from under layers of whitewash, from quite a few church walls (as at St Thomas's, Salisbury), are more or less coarse exercises in the fifteenth-century Flemish manner. There are no surviving followers to the Eton Chapel *grisailles*, finished in 1485/86, of comparable quality, and the painted church-screens, beloved prey of antiquaries, are mostly of gauche provincial quality – of archaeological rather than aesthetic interest – though they do indicate that there were local strains of provincial painting with pronounced, sometimes robust characteristics of their own, if all within a debased Gothic Netherlandish tradition. Their diversity may be gauged by comparison of the forceful, if crude, figures in one of the splendid Devon screens, at Ashton, *c.* 1510, with the more sophisticated, suave saints of 1507 (?) at Aylsham in Norfolk (see overleaf). St George's, Windsor, retains several interestingly various examples, including the Oxenbridge chantry that has scenes from the Life of St John the Baptist, 1522, with the earliest painting (other than in MSS) to show Italian Renaissance ornament, and a series of retrospective whole-length portraits of kings treated like a stained glass design (South Choir Aisle). These last are characteristic of a recurring theme in Tudor painting; sets of portraits, sometimes

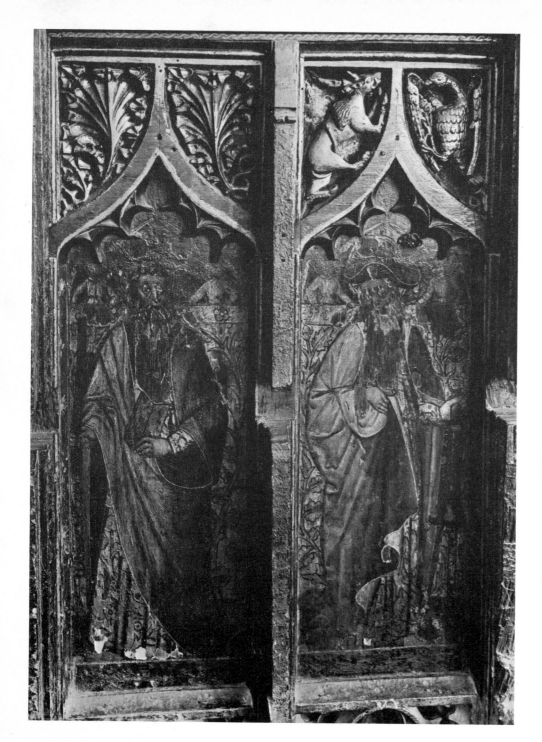

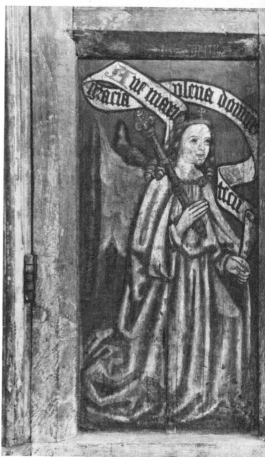

Above, Screen to the north choir aisle at
Ashton Church, Devon, *c.* 1510.
Left, Screen to the chancel, Aylsham Church,
Norfolk, *c.* 1507.
Right, Figure of a king, late fifteenth century.
Society of Antiquaries of London.

entirely imaginary, of kings of England were in production all through the sixteenth
century. Chance survivors, of exceptional quality, are the late fifteenth-century
fragments in the Society of Antiquaries, but the characteristic format, to be repeated
in varying sets or editions *en masse* (late in the sixteenth century they were obtainable
from a shop in the Strand) is a rather modest little head-and-shoulders, pale and linear,
muted reflection of the Flemish tradition that goes back to the Van Eycks.

The very few portraits of sitters other than royal that are known are likewise
variants in this modest tradition, which persists even as late as the 1530s in some
types of portraits of Henry VIII (as in the National Portrait Gallery, no. 3638):
in contrast with Holbein they are very two-dimensional and archaic, and although
in oil or tempera, and often using gold leaf, they have the appearance of line drawings
with colour-wash. As far as painting is concerned, the lack of sophistication in the
patronage of Henry VIII in the first twenty years of his reign, and, perhaps more

64

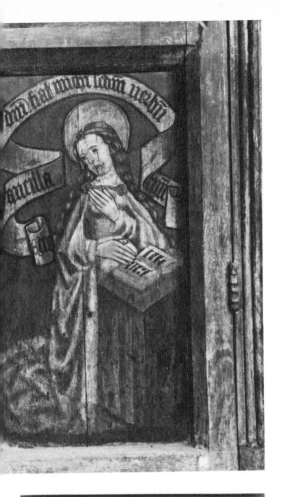

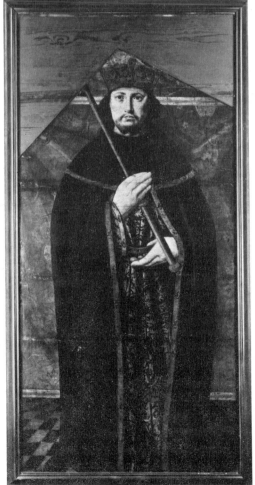

unexpectedly, in that of the great international prince-cardinal Wolsey, is striking. Wolsey's sumptuous way of life became legendary, and some sculpture of fine quality, in the full High Renaissance tradition, was carried out by not insignificant Italian artists under his aegis (the imperial roundels by G. da Maiano at Hampton Court, for example). All that survives of paintings connected with him are a series, of not very high quality, in Wolsey's Closet at Hampton Court. But these may be as late as the 1540s, well after the royal takeover of the Palace. They are scenes from the Passion, derived from Italian and German (Dürer) sources, and perhaps their main interest is that they are evidence of what may have been a general type of decoration by paintings in the palaces, as friezes above the panelling. Henry VIII was employing some Italians from early on: Vincent Vulpe, a Neapolitan, emerges in some detail from documents but not from surviving works, and he and his colleagues were mainly employed in the now entirely vanished decorations of Henry's palace building projects and on the essentially ephemeral, if very lavish, pageant spectacles, such as the famous Field of Cloth of Gold in 1520. A type of painting which occupied them a great deal in the 1520s was the 'plat', or big, pseudo-bird's-eye perspective views of towns, battles or other historic occasions. These were fairly archaic in conception, though Holbein's first employment for the Crown, in 1528, seems to have been in collaboration on one of them, the *Plat of Tirwan*; their effect can be gauged from four paintings still at Hampton Court, including one of the Field of Cloth of Gold, which, it has recently been convincingly suggested, are likely to be Elizabethan copies of originals executed by Corvus (alias John Reff), with the aid of some fifty assistants, at Whitehall *c.* 1530.

Of early patronage other than royal the evidence is thin and scattered. At Chichester, around 1530, there was a local workshop headed by Lambert Barnard patronized by Bishop Sherborne (d. 1536), an interesting if isolated example of early English Renaissance painting. Some quite elegant and accomplished decorative painting survives from this shop in the Bishop's Palace and at Boxgrove Priory Church nearby; but the most important monuments are two enormous paintings in the Cathedral itself. Both bear on the characteristic themes of ancestral piety and legitimacy, as it were illustrations to a personal and local version of the Tree of Jesse, including series both of roundel imaginary portraits of the Bishop's predecessors, from St Wilfrid onwards, and of early English kings. The major section, showing Henry VIII confirming his royal favour on the See (overleaf), makes a pious use of Renaissance decoration, even if the spatial organization of the composition is still medieval. Of other patrons we know very little. Brian Tuke seems to have had something almost approaching a collection of pictures, including works by Antonio da Solario, who very likely visited England, if briefly and with no impact on the native style, about 1514 (his dated portrait of the merchant donor Withypol is in Bristol Art Gallery). Tuke however, like Sir Thomas More, was one of Holbein's first English patrons, and the Humanist group centring on More was probably the most aware in England of artistic developments in Europe.

Sir Thomas More, in that haven of enlightenment and learning that was his house at Chelsea, was ready-prepared ground for the acclimatization of High Renaissance art when it arrived at last, not in embryonic seed form, but as transplant in full flower, in the shape of Hans Holbein. Holbein arrived late in 1526, via Antwerp from Basle; he was still under thirty but already in full maturity. His earlier work is outside the scope of this essay, but the nature of the equipment with which he was already armed on arrival must be indicated. He is celebrated as the great synthesizer of Northern and of Italian Renaissance art, blending Italian classic monumentality with Northern linear particularity – above all in his portraits. In Basle, besides his prolific output of spectacular illusionistic façades, of designs for glass-painting, of portraits and religious paintings, he had been deeply involved in drawings for

65

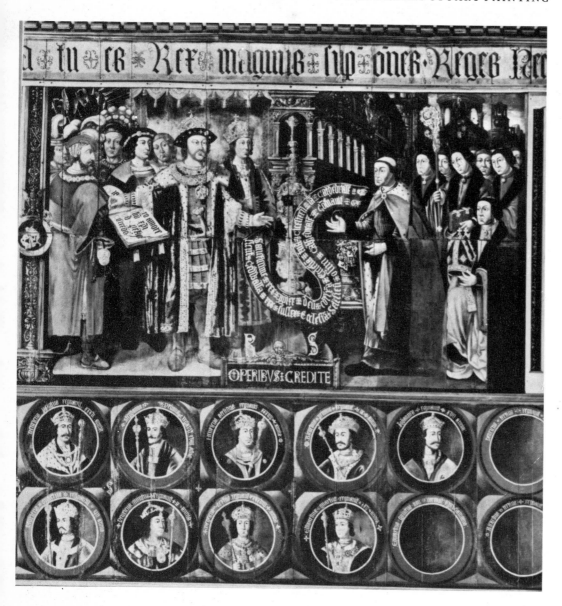

LAMBERT BARNARD, *Henry VIII presenting a charter to the Pope*, plus portraits of royalty. Before 1536. South transept, Chichester cathedral.
By permission of the Dean of Chichester Cathedral.
Right, HANS HOLBEIN, *Sir Thomas More*, 1527. Copyright The Frick Collection, New York.

engravings, in the service of the new printing industry of which Basle was a major European centre. There he was in close contact with the exalted Humanist circle, including the printer Froben, but above all Erasmus himself. Though the personality of Holbein is opaque and elusive, those very qualities may speak of his affinity with Erasmus – a core of detachment, perhaps not untinged with irony. His translation from Basle to London seems to have been due to the withering of patronage as the Swiss reformed religion accelerated its iconoclastic course, and he came with introductions from Erasmus to the latter's closest and dearest English friend, More, and his firmest English patron, Warham, Archbishop of Canterbury: his portraits of these two are doubtless the first works that he made in England.

The *Thomas More* is, happily, one of his masterpieces: a rare match of genius in both artist and sitter. If more eloquent of the sitter as future Lord Chancellor of England than as the Humanist, wit, author of Utopia (and, ultimately, martyr), it is nevertheless both human and humane, while a monumental rendering of *gravitas*. As Horace Walpole observed, it is More 'in the rigour of his sense, not in the sweetness of his pleasantry'. In a European context, it sustains comparisons with any High Renaissance portrait – of the calibre of, say, Raphael's *Castiglione* or the young Titian's so-called *Ariosto*. In an English insular context, it ought, one feels, to have staggered

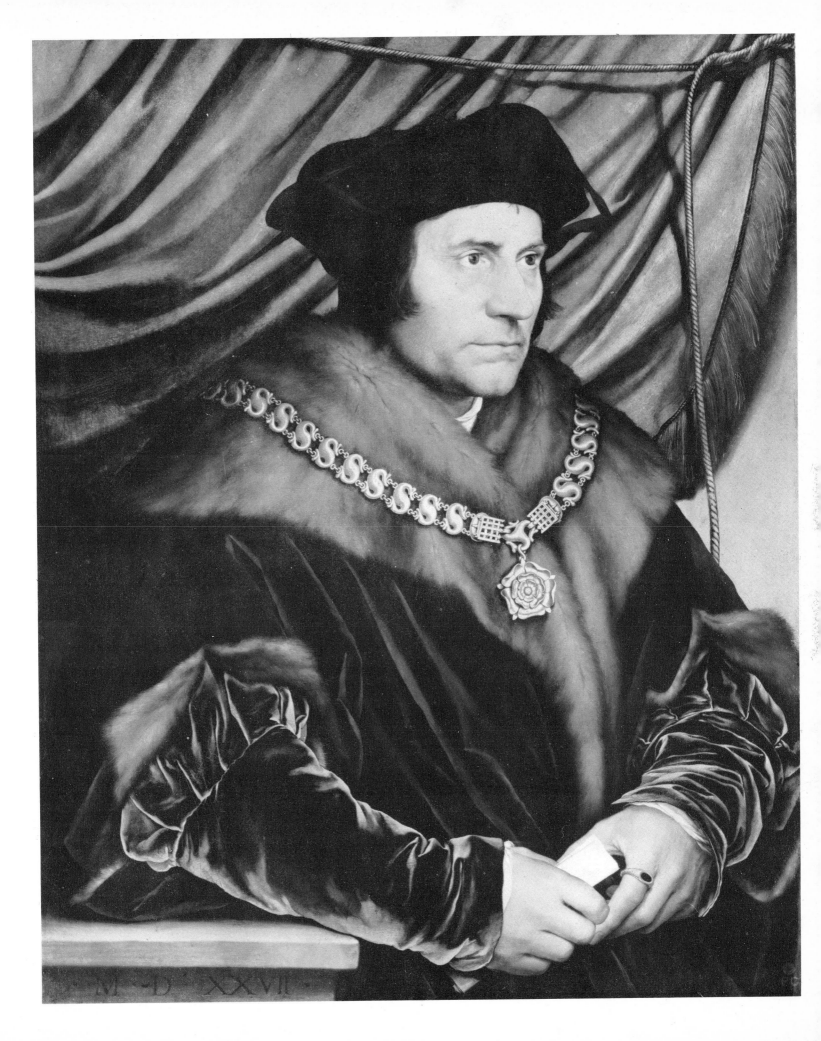

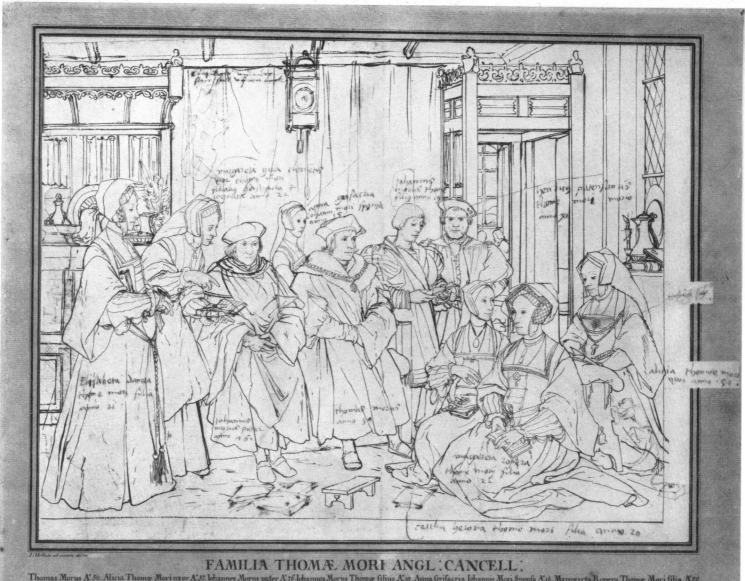

FAMILIA THOMÆ MORI ANGL : CANCELL :

Thomas Morus Æ. 50. Alicia Thomæ Mori uxor Æ. 57. Iohannes Morus pater Æ. 76. Iohannes Morus Thomæ filius Æ. 19. Anna Grisacria Iohannis Mori Spensa Æ. 15. Margareta Ropera Thomæ Mori filia Æ. 22.
Elisabeta Damen Thomæ Mori filia Æ. 21. Cæcilia Heroina Thomæ Mori filia Æ. 20. Margareta Giga Clementis uxor Mori filiabus Condiscipula et cognata Æ. 22. Henricus Patensonus Thomæ Mori morio Æ. 40.

its beholders with the force of a revelation. As far as we know, nothing remotely comparable had been seen here, in the first place in terms of sheer virtuosity of technique and of the vivid illusionism that this produced: in the clarity, and final inevitability of the image combined with the sense of actuality, the sitter's presence. A monumental serenity absorbs even the distinguished sitter's indifferent but scrupulously observed shave. Yet there are, on close scrutiny, internal discrepancies that would be inconceivable in a Raphael: the inconsistency of the lighting (the shadow of the rope on the curtain), or the exaggerated foreshortening in the daring drawing of the right eye. They are characteristic of Holbein, and, married with conviction into the overall composition, serve in a curious way both to stress the classic unity of the form and to enhance its vivid, stereoscopic quality. This fascination with what, in lesser hands, might seem optical gimmicks, is typical and oft-recurring in his work: like Dürer before him, he was much concerned with optical mechanics, and almost certainly used some elementary apparatus when making his preparatory studies from life. His usual method was to work from preparatory drawings, and a famous series of these of his English sitters has miraculously survived (Windsor): that for More is pricked for transfer. More, however, evidently moved (one can almost see him doing it) in the course of the drawing, after the contour of the head had been

Above, HANS HOLBEIN, *Sir Thomas More and his Family*, 1526. Pen-drawing. Kupferstichkabinett der Öffentlichen Kunstsammlung, Basel.
Right, HANS HOLBEIN, *Henry VIII*, 1537. Thyssen Collection, Castagnola, Switzerland.

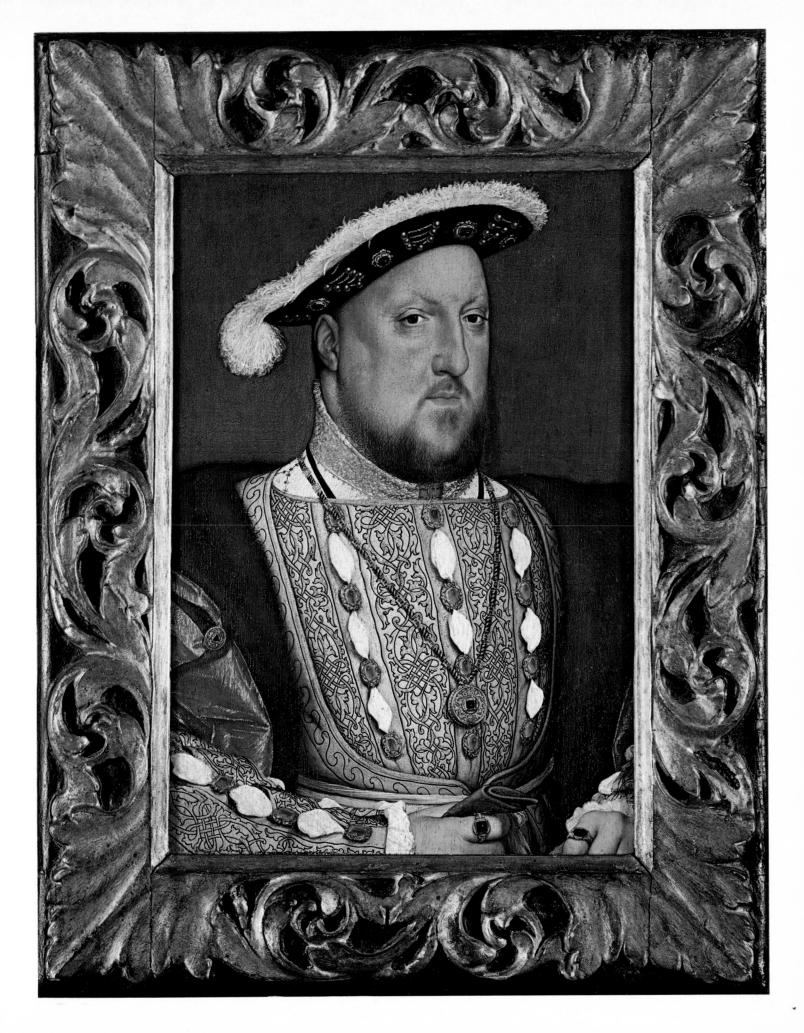

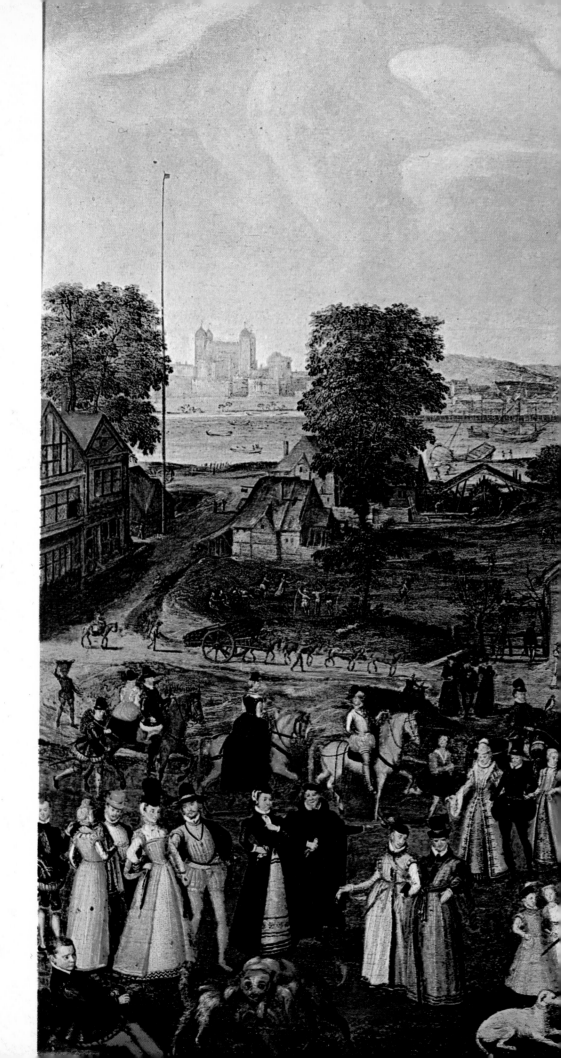

JORIS HOEFNAGEL, *A Marriage Feast at
Bermondsey, c.* 1570.
Hatfield House.
By courtesy of the Marquess of Salisbury.

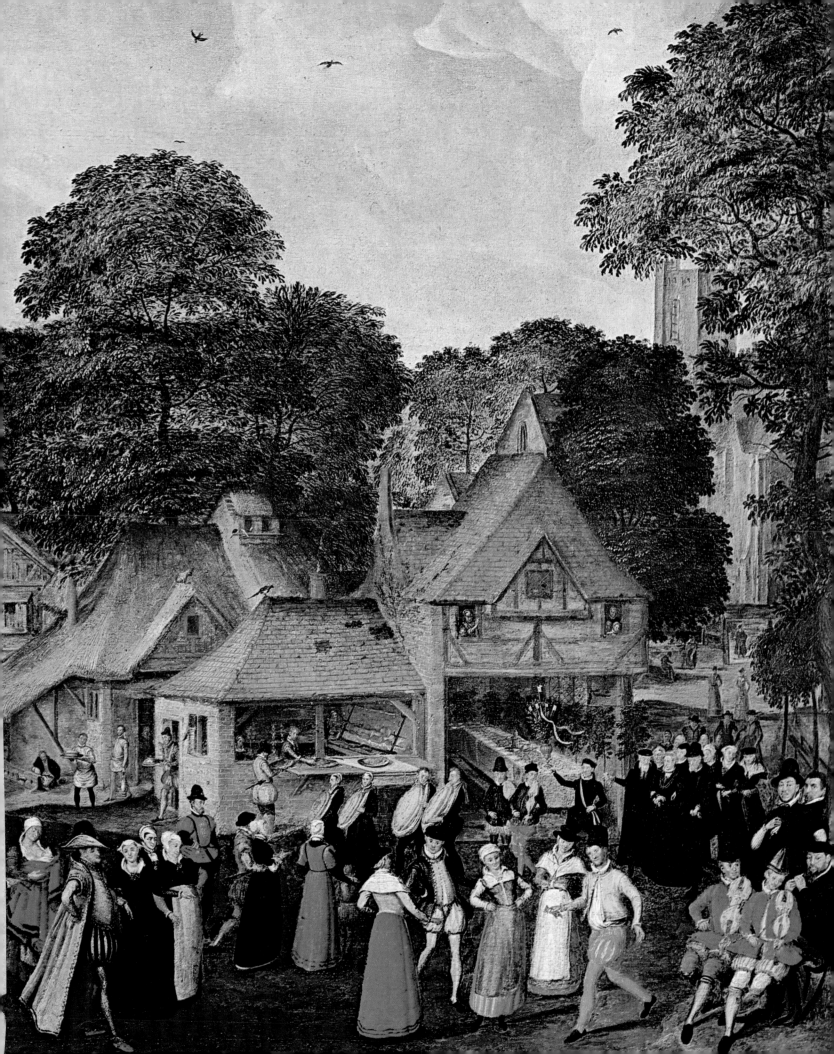

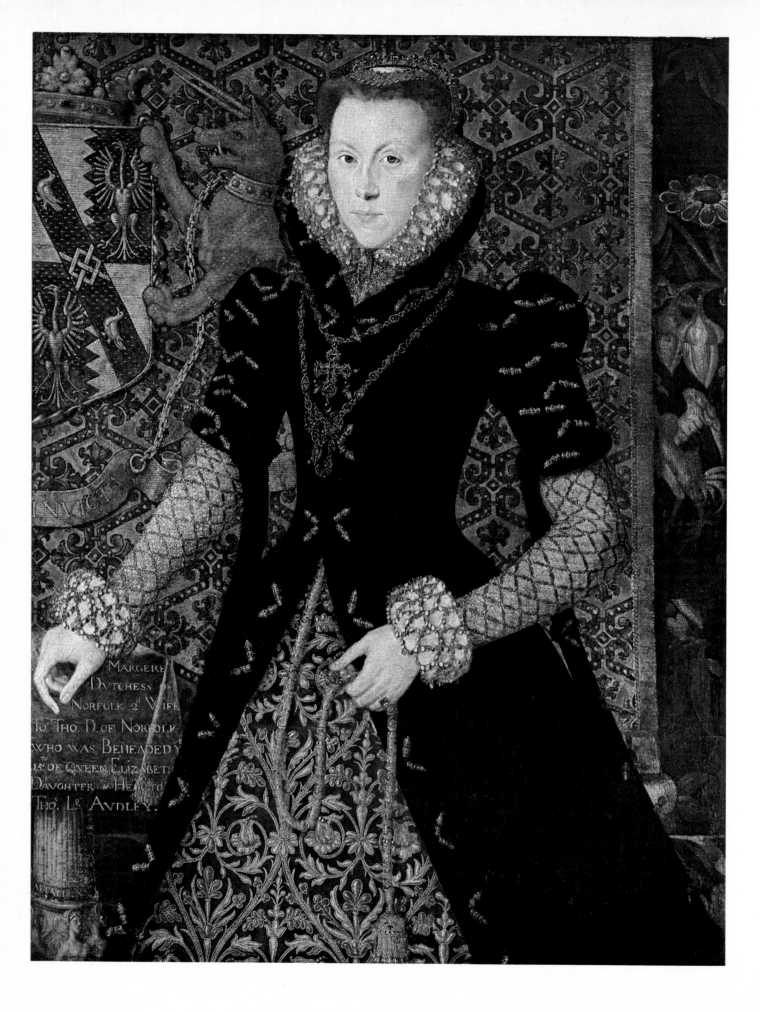

established, but before Holbein had drawn in his right eye, and this is consequently misplaced. The correction (as is confirmed by X-ray of the painting) only took place after the painting itself was well on its way.

Holbein's second portrait of More was still more astonishing, the great life-size family group, long lost but known from Holbein's pen drawing of it that More sent to Erasmus (p. 68), and later copies by Lockey (p. 97). A precedent for this, which Holbein may have known, is Mantegna's group in the Palazzo del Te at Mantua, but in England it had none, and though it is the first essay into what was to be one of the most characteristic and original contributions by English painting, the 'conversation piece', it had no immediate followers. In it, More, though officially gowned and be-chained, is shown (in comparison with the single portrait) much more in his Utopian character, as the centre of his family in the rich and civilized setting of his home. As usual, it was preceded by drawings of the individual sitters' heads, and then very possibly by cut-out cartoons of their whole individual figures, which were then assembled in a collage (as was later the Whitehall cartoon) to be transferred by pricking to the canvas (the Basle drawing appears to be, not a compositional study, but rather a record perhaps of the cartoon in a transitional stage, as the final painting was somewhat altered from it). Perhaps something of the quality of informal ritual of the group is due to this technique, its air of posed yet serenely content contrivance, but the composition is also typical of Holbein's approach to a problem that grew out of the increasing secularization of painting. The Italian masters had long developed a whole series of solutions to the problem of representing groups of figures, and Holbein's solutions, here as in the Whitehall group, are adaptations of these religious formulae to secular subjects. Thus, while the true subject of this group – a family in its material and spiritual togetherness – is formally somewhat diffusely rendered, if a small infant were set central in the foreground, the whole would cohere instantly, a variation on a traditional Adoration design.

Apart from the More portraits, only about half a dozen originals from Holbein's first English period (only two years) are known. The *Archbishop Warham* (Louvre), while very solidly realized, is also conceived as a religious icon, the old man most ceremonial in fur-trimmed velvet, with open Bible, mitre, and ceremonial crucifix, and its hieratic nature is stressed by the use of gold leaf in parts. The others all show, though in varying scales, the sitters turned slightly to one side, generally not looking directly at the spectator; the settings vary greatly, but there are no landscape backgrounds and the recession is fairly shallow, though the figures, in their illusion of three-dimensional substance, are very solid. The accessories that will repeat later are already there; the vine tendril in arabesque against a blue background, the curtain, the pilaster; also the habit of inscribing the date and/or the sitter's age, defining the moment fixed in time, that was to become commonplace in Tudor portraiture and that seems to answer an urge stronger in England than elsewhere. These inscriptions could be on a *trompe-l'oeil* label, representing a paper held to the picture by blobs of sealing-wax, but later were more satisfactorily worked into the design in the form of lapidary lettering in gold on the background. Holbein's sitters included *Sir Henry Guldeford*, 1527 (Windsor) shown as Controller of the Royal Household and wearing the collar of the Garter given him after the siege of Thérouanne (this supports the speculation that the 'Master Hans' paid for help in the painting of a pageant battle-piece, the '*Plat of Tirwan*' in 1527, was indeed Holbein). Other sitters were two members of the *Godsalve* family, officials of the court; Henry VIII's astronomer, and compatriot of Holbein, *Kratzer*, 1528 (Louvre), and perhaps of the same date *Sir Brian Tuke*, whom we have glimpsed as collector but who also, in 1528, became Treasurer to the King. Though there was clearly patronage from the highest ranks of the Court, there is no evidence yet of any direct contact with the King.

By summer 1528, Holbein was on his way back to Basle, somewhat enriched (he

HANS EWORTH, *Margaret Audley, Duchess of Norfolk*, 1562.
Audley End, Essex.
By courtesy of Hon. R.H.C. Neville.

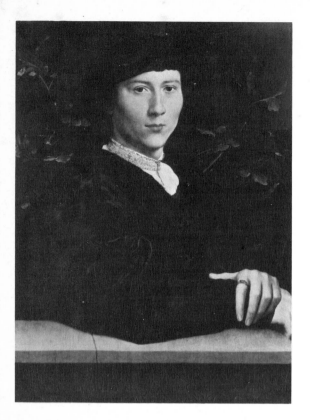

HANS HOLBEIN, *Derick Born*, 1533.
Windsor Castle. By gracious permission of
Her Majesty the Queen.

bought a house on his arrival home). In Basle he painted two of his major master-pieces – the Darmstadt Altarpiece and the portrait of his wife and two sons (this again a secularization of a religious, Madonna, theme). But, by now, the extremist, icono-clastic, wing of the Swiss reformers was in full cry. Holbein's own religious creed is obscure, but was probably somewhat Erasmian – he subscribed to the reformed church, but without extremist enthusiasm. His return to England, in late 1532, was perhaps prompted by a specific commission from a German community in London, the Hanseatic merchants of the Steelyard. For them he executed two large, ambitious Triumph paintings, the *Triumphs of Riches and of Poverty*, both long vanished but known from small later copies: in near-monochrome, simulating reliefs, they must have been notable contributions to the tradition of such decorations, associated above all with that master with whom Holbein had such sympathy, Mantegna. They seem to have caused no stir in England, and had no progeny, but the earliest portraits of his second stay were of several members of the Steelyard. Their interest was very probably sparked by the brilliant, highly elaborate portrait of *George Gisze of Dantzig* (Berlin); while none of the half-dozen or so surviving Steelyard portraits are as ambitious as that, they are, in their highly individual variations on the half-length theme, amongst Holbein's finest works. In some of them he presents now the formid-ably forthright full frontal approach, but the most successful, serenely relaxed yet entirely classical, is the *Derick Born* of 1533 (Windsor).

In the same year, Holbein's main preoccupation must have been the extraordinary virtuoso composition known as *The Ambassadors* (National Gallery, London); it shows two life-size subjects standing each side of a table laden with a remarkable still-life representing the arts and sciences. This combines naturalistic portraiture of high order with the *Vanitas* theme, the splendid richness of sitters and attributes contradicted by the distorted skull that hovers, a monstrous riddle, in the fore-ground and which only coheres in the eye of the beholder when seen from an acute angle from the lower left-hand side of the painting, or – as has recently been plausibly argued – when seen with one eye, through the stem of a glass tube. Here, in this ambiguousness or positive contradiction of forms within the picture, Holbein is, of course, far from classical, but it is the extreme example of his interest in the play of perspective, and no doubt makes implicit comment that in death things will be seen in another mode. From 1534 comes an important, though sadly damaged, portrait of *Thomas Cromwell* (Frick Collection, New York), with a curiously tense, almost clenched, composition that seems an apt extension of the sitter's character. It was through Cromwell that Holbein probably came to paint Henry VIII, apparently not before about 1536.

It is from this time – that is, during the last seven years of his life, that historians tend to trace an increasing rigidity, a linear and hierarchic quality. Certainly the setting of the figure against a plain background, with a consequent emphasis on its silhouette strengthened by the use of a cast shadow, and an even more concentrated stillness with gloss of finish, do become much more marked: the figures dominate the picture-space even more, while the artist seems to have stepped back in his utter detachment. Yet this does not mean that the quality of his best (and best preserved) late works is low, and the not-infrequent accusation of a decline in quality is perhaps due in part to the fact that a number of late works, included in a canon that badly needs revision, are not by him. His most hieratic manner seems to have been reserved for his royal sitters, as in the *Jane Seymour*, with its frozen, rather than still, poise; its intricate detailing of the dress – its severity heightened by the close tightness of the features. Holbein's only surviving original painting of *Henry VIII* himself (p. 69) is equally splendid and equally chill, but alleviated by its small scale. A more humane note enters though with both the infant *Edward VI* of 1539 and the famous whole-length of *Christina of Milan*, based on a three-hour study made in Brussels in 1538 (p.

74

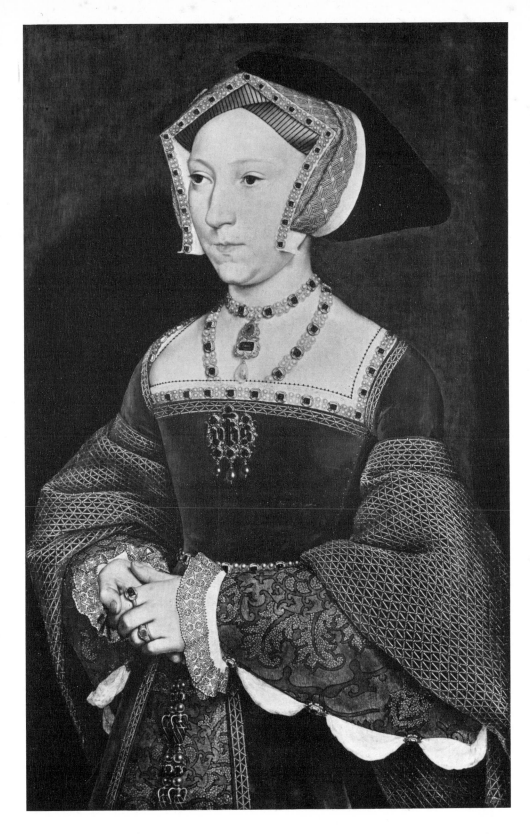

76). The *Edward VI* retains remarkably a childlike charm in the image of the heir-
apparent, saluted by the Latin inscription below, and the infant seems, with his right
hand to be dispensing blessings (a prophecy not to be fulfilled by his short reign)
with the natural divinity of a Christ-Child. In *Christina*, as recovered by its recent
cleaning, sheer and dark against the brilliant blue background, there is again a
magisterial merger of two qualities that might seem contradictory: on the one hand,
the dignity of the precocious widow in her weeds, in the erect sacrificial purity of a

pawn for gambit in the international game of state marriage; on the other hand, a mere individual in the expression caught in the features, the watching eyes over the half-smile – a girl of only 16 or 17, yet one who is said to have remarked, of the proposal that Henry might marry her, that if only she had two heads, she would be happy to put one of them at his Majesty's disposal.

Holbein's major large-scale work in England is now only imperfectly known from copies and from a cartoon for part of it: the famous wall-painting of the Tudor dynasty painted in 1536/7 in the King's Privy Chamber at Whitehall, and burned there with the rest of the palace in 1698. It showed four figures, of rather more than life-scale; central the founder, Henry VII and his queen, Elizabeth of York; left and right, and slightly below them, Henry VIII and Jane Seymour, Henry VIII in the straddling, uncompromisingly frontal aggression in which, in this image, Holbein fixed him for posterity. The composition is once again a secularization of a standard Italian Renaissance composition, this time of four saints about a central Madonna and Child. We no longer know what in fact was at the centre of Holbein's design: it may have been a real window in the Privy Chamber (as, in the Stanze, Raphael had lapped his designs round windows), but the most faithful-seeming copy, despite being very small in scale, shows something like an altar or obelisk, with inscription. The siting of the painting is also speculative, but it was almost certainly above eye-level, over a panelling and with its illusionistic background architecture at the top marrying into the real architecture of the Privy Chamber. Its focus, in real life, may well have been the gross and splendid flesh and blood of the King himself, enthroned below under a cloth of state at the physical inner heart of his power. The background of the painting, with its feralesque frieze of mermen and the startling illusion of depth above, is a literal import from the Italian High Renaissance, for it is based fairly closely on an engraving ascribed to Bramante. The part of the cartoon that survives, for Henry VIII and Henry VII, still conveys something of the formidable quality that the painting must have had. The cartoon is a collage, the figures being silhouetted and pasted on the background, and is pricked for transfer. It shows also that Henry VIII was originally meant to be shown three-quarter and not full face. Painted versions of the portrait of the King are numerous; some are of high quality but none universally agreed as from Holbein's own hand. A later design, which may be Holbein's, shows the King frontal again but in a surcoat, now with a very linear, icon-(amost idol-)like rigidity: the best version is at Castle Howard. But in Holbein's last version of the King, though known now only from imperfect witness (he did not finish it, and it is best gauged by the restored cartoon in the Royal College of Surgeons), Henry really does become very like an idol, or an Oriental or Byzantine potentate; this is a group of the *Barber-Surgeons' Company receiving their charter from the King*, who, thus seated in robes, and on a slightly larger scale than his supplicant audience, seems indeed to embody absolute power, both spiritual and divine. The figure is a re-statement of the medieval majesty-figure, and the group, artlessly crowded, is as a whole likewise reminiscent of treatments of the bounty of majesty, often repeated in charter headings.

Holbein's activity was not confined to portraiture, and his drawings for jewellery, plate, dagger sheaths, and even architectural detail, in a decorative style of copious cursive Renaissance arabesque and complexity contrast sharply with the rigour of his state portraits. If he did little for the engravers, that was no doubt due to the undeveloped state of the printing industry, but one of his designs, for the title page of the 1536 translation of the Bible, must have been widely broadcast through the sixteenth century, and incorporates Henry enthroned with Sword and Book, a patently reforming image of the King as arbiter of temporal and of spiritual power.

A most significant development, however, was Holbein's work on the miniature portrait in watercolour. This was a new form of art: the exact stages of its inception

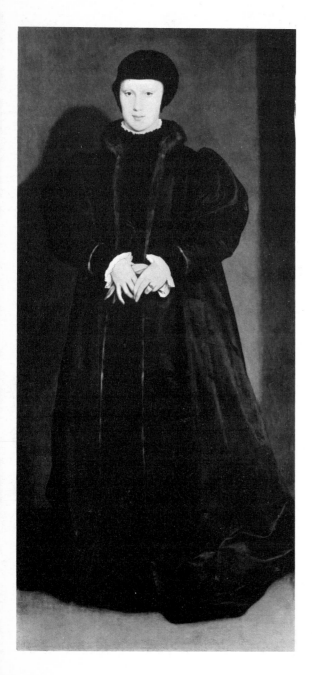

HANS HOLBEIN, *Christina of Milan*, 1538. National Gallery, London.

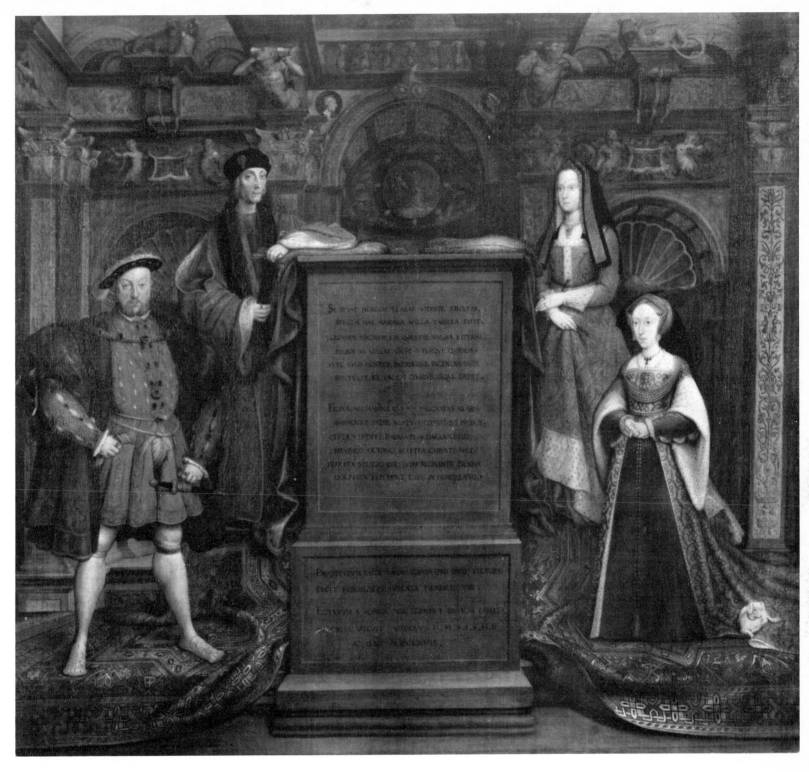

Copy by Leemput of Holbein's Privy Chamber
fresco, 1536–7, of Henry VII, Elizabeth of York,
Henry VIII and Jane Seymour.
Royal Collection.
By gracious permission of
Her Majesty the Queen.

are still argued, but it clearly relates in form to the medallist's art and in technique
to the illuminator's craft. The earliest examples are a series of portraits of Francis I's
generals by Jean Clouet, in a manuscript of 1519; vivid head and shoulders against a
blue background. They are still incorporated on the manuscript page, but if cut out
and framed they would be entirely practicable as independent portraits. Two miniature portraits are known to have been sent from France by Madame d'Alençon to
Henry VIII in 1526, and these – though we do not know what they were – may well
have been seminal, for the first miniature painting in England that is firmly datable
is from the same year. It is of *Henry VIII*, aged thirty-five, one of a handful of closely
comparable miniatures of very high quality associated with the name of Luke

Horenbout. The decorative border is strongly reminiscent of the illuminator's tradition and the technique is watercolour on vellum, laid down on card; in the other miniatures of this group, however, there is no border, and the initial format of the English miniature is established. The Horenbouts, or Hornebolts, were a distinguished family of illuminators from the Ghent-Bruges school who came to England probably about 1525. Luke was retained (by 1531 he was described as 'the King's painter') until his death, in 1544, at a higher salary than Holbein ever received, and the attribution of this group of miniatures to him makes perfect sense, though that of a group of life-scale portraits is much more speculative. According to early tradition, Holbein learned the miniature technique from 'Master Luke', and indeed his own follow closely on the early ones. Only a dozen survive, all dating from his second English period, after 1532. Holbein, as has emerged already, was fairly indifferent to scale; he seems to have been able to formulate the image in its naked essential clarity, usually in a drawing, and thence project, as if from a lantern slide, on a screen of any size. The only differences between his *Mrs Pemberton* and the larger portraits is that it is indeed small (about two inches diameter) and in a different technique, watercolour on vellum – yet it is as dense and monumental in characterization as the noblest of his large portraits. The *Anne of Cleves* is a miniature variant of the three-quarter length (itself on a small scale, and painted on vellum) of 1539/40 in the Louvre, and is brilliant proof of how aptly the patterning of the court-portrait could marry into the miniature form, an example that Hilliard would later take still further. Its effect is at once highly formal yet elusively intimate, and it is in this most intimate form of portraiture that the English, with Hilliard and again with Cooper and then with Cosway and his eighteenth-century colleagues, were to establish a unique supremacy. The earliest miniatures were probably mostly enshrined, like little reliquaries, in ivory boxes, as *Anne of Cleves* still is. The development of the locket form comes later, and *Mrs Pemberton's* present framing is a slightly later embellishment.

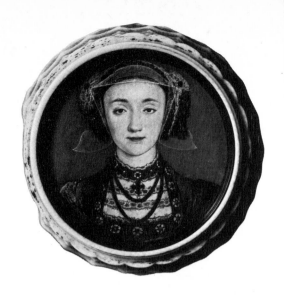

The majesty of Holbein's achievement has largely obliterated even the memory of other artists, of major repute in their day, working in England at the same time. In fact, very little of their work has survived or is yet recognized. The Horenbouts must have been the leading practitioners of the Netherlandish tradition here, though a portrait of *Bishop Frere* by Corvus, 1522, seems prophetic in its severe, bleak angularity of later English developments. But there were also the Italians: Bartolommeo Penni, Florentine brother of two pupils of Raphael, is recorded from 1530 to 1554, and Antonio Toto del Nunziata, former pupil of Ridolfo Ghirlandaio, between 1519 and 1554; the latter was made Serjeant-Painter in 1544. He certainly produced some lost easel pictures, but probably, with Penni, was mainly absorbed in decorative pageant activities. Of later arrivals, Girolamo da Treviso, here between *c.* 1538 and 1544, a distinguished name, is known only, as far as his English pictures are concerned, for one not very distinguished *grisaille* painting. It is a propaganda, reformist painting of the stoning of the Pope (Hampton Court). His talents were mainly exercised by Henry VIII in the realm of military engineering. Nicholas da Modena (or Bellini) was certainly of greater contemporary consequence. He came, in 1537, from working at Fontainebleau, and was probably the leading figure in the development of a version of the Fontainebleau style, particularly in Henry VIII's hasty building of his new palace at Nonsuch from 1538. The fragmentary evidence of this long demolished building indicates a modish and extravagant setting for the monarch, if in an apparently relatively restrained version of the Fontainebleau manner, very different from the classicism of Holbein's Privy Chamber. A lost drawing ascribed to da Modena is a design for an interior, but apart from that his work can only be guessed at; the only actual surviving paintings plausibly associated with Nonsuch are of an older manner, a series of decorative panels (Loseley Park) that seem to reflect very

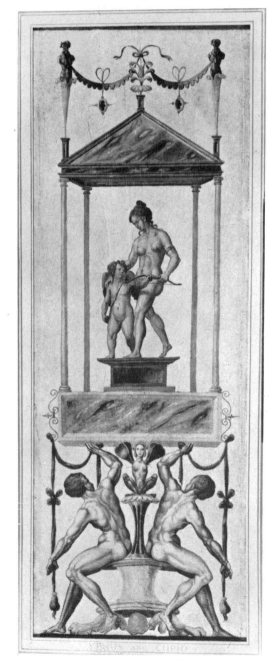

Left, HANS HOLBEIN, *Anne of Cleves,* miniature.
Victoria and Albert Museum, London.

Below, left and right, TOTO DEL NUNZIATA (?),
Raphaelesque grotesque panels, probably
from Nonsuch Palace. *c.* 1538.
Loseley Park, Guildford.

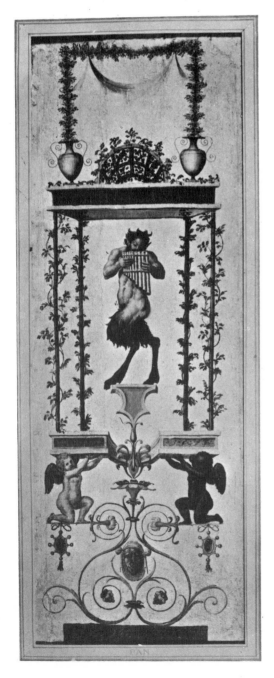

directly the grotesques from Raphael's workshop in the Vatican, and which, other
things being equal, it would seem more logical to associate with Toto or Penni rather
than da Modena. Holbein is not recorded as working on Nonsuch, but while its style
would not seem to be sympathetic to him, there was plenty of room in England for
co-existence of the two different manners.

Holbein died in London, in October 1543, victim of an outbreak of the plague; he
was only forty-six. Four years later, Henry VIII, decayed now into an obese hulk,
was laid in brief if splendid state under the more enduring image in which Holbein
had crystallized him and the Tudor dynasty in his Privy Chamber at Whitehall.

With Henry's death, the dour progress of the Reformed Religion accelerated its
tempo, with – from many aspects – literally devastating results for the visual arts in
England. Understandably, for it is a depressing subject, the history of the iconoclastic movements in Britain has yet to be written in detail, and when it is chronicled
it cannot but reveal a quantity of loss so thorough that the surviving fragments are
not really representative enough to convey witness of the nature of the major quality;
even in manuscripts, as the preceding chapter makes clear, the loss was formidable.
Most of what survived the sixteenth-century smash succumbed to the fury of the
second wave of destruction by the Puritans between 1640 and 1660. The breaking of
images, as official national policy, was introduced modestly in 1538 by the suppression of images that were focuses for pilgrimage. Only on Henry's death was this
mandate extended, by a Council order early in 1548, ordering 'that all the images
remaining in any church or chapel within your diocese be removed and taken away'.
The restitution of the old faith under Mary I, between 1553 and 1558, was too brief
to nourish a revival, and the Puritan reaction on the Catholic queen's death was so
violent and widespread, an indiscriminate breaking of all images, even tomb effigies,
that Elizabeth had to issue a proclamation, in 1560, condemning the breaking and
defacing of tombs.

This attitude of mind, the fear and hatred of all images that might be construed as
idolatrous, was negative not only in its ruthless destruction of the heritage of the
past, but also in its constriction of present possibilities, both in patronage and range
of subject matter. The great traditional patrons of the arts had been the Church and
the Court, the latter very often for the adornment of the former. The subject matter
for painters, as anywhere in medieval Europe, had been predominantly religious;
painting had been an act of faith, to the glory of God, His Church and its saints and
martyrs. The only substitute was man himself; perhaps inadequate, but Henry VIII
had added an extra dimension to his projection of himself in the rich guise of European
Renaissance Prince, being not only within his realm the supreme temporal authority
but also the supreme spiritual one. The possibilities of such a theme had been magis-
terially indicated by Holbein not only in the Privy Chamber but also in the Barber
Surgeons group; its wider application was to take time to develop, until the glorification of Elizabeth by her painters, in the last two decades of her reign, as virtual
goddess, might seem to substantiate the fears of certain extreme reformers who
refused to sanction portraits of themselves, as this might lead to idolatrous practices.

The nourishment for forms of art other than portraiture was thin: the concept of
art collections, as we understand them today, was barely embryonic until the beginning of the seventeenth century. Contact with Italy, the prime source of Renaissance
art, was cut off for religious reasons, and its art wholly suspect – thus an Elizabethan
was to note the skill of the natives when in Italy, but with utter scorn – 'and no
wonder' – as their main concern was with 'amours' and other frivolities.

The suppression of the monasteries had severed the tradition of the illuminated
manuscripts with one mortal stroke, and the craft of the illuminators survived,
generally at a fairly low level, mostly in the headings and initials of official documents, patents, charters and so on, and in the service of heraldry and genealogy. The

centuries-old tradition of mural painting in churches also simply ceased, and though the grander houses continued to be decorated with wall paintings, ranging from simple abstract patterns through complex strap-work designs, even to copies of Raphaelesque origin (as the *Cupid and Psyche* series at Hill Hall in Essex), the quality was very rarely at all sophisticated, though some of the painted plaster reliefs have considerable charm. As for easel paintings – even including portraits – the concept of their being standard components of a well-to-do house's furnishing was very far from being established, as contemporary inventories demonstrate. Only, perhaps, with the fashion for building long galleries in the larger houses, beginning in the 1560s, did paintings start to take up residence in quantity, and then only slowly: mainly portraits, with life-scale images equally slowly becoming the standard scale. In part the slow rate of development was due to economic causes: Henry VIII's magnificence had been achieved at a cost that brought the nation close to bankruptcy.

Nevertheless the habit of painted portraiture did take root, to expand through succeeding centuries into what has even been described as the national vice in painting. In its beginnings, it had been provided with a standard of quality, by Holbein, which it was rarely to match and perhaps never to surpass. Holbein was, however, illustrative of one curious fact about British painting that was to remain constant for nearly two centuries: that the most skilled and successful recorders of the English image were, with few exceptions such as Hilliard and Dobson, to be immigrant foreigners. The stylistic history of the period is concerned mainly not with the development of a national school, but with the modulation of imported mature styles from the Continent under the impact of the English temperament and condition – one might almost say, of the English weather. But if the clients were to find best satisfaction in the services of foreigners, the urge that drove them to use these painters sprang from an inherent and already long, native tradition. It had expressed itself earlier in sculpture – the tradition of the memorial effigy, with its strange and touching blending of personal vanity and familial piety. In the memorial effigy pride of appearance is matched with profound melancholy, with awareness of the vanity of life – most dramatically in those tombs that contrast the subject in full panoply of wealth and rank above with the naked, worm-riddled, cadaver below; on it, the inscription, with its tale of personal achievement and virtue, may be set in context with a heraldic and genealogical statement, in the quartering of the arms, of the individual's subordinate role, merely a stage in the growth of the family tree. These characteristics all enter into the composition of a great proportion of English sixteenth-century portraits, so that I have elsewhere described them as 'domesticated effigies'. To this memorial habit of mind, something of the characteristic rigour of early English portraiture is doubtless due. Only towards the end of the century do some portraits seem concerned with the psychological atmospherics of the sitters. More generally, they read like effigies before the event, as inventories rather than analyses.

The basic pictorial formula upon which variations of the theme were embroidered became virtually standardized through the 1560s and 1570s: the standing, three-quarter length, the sitter seen from just above the knees, turned slightly to left or right. The format is vertical in character, narrower than the 50 × 40 inch painting that was to become standard in the seventeenth century for three-quarter lengths, thus both heightening the sense of impassive aloofness, of aristocratic *hauteur* of the sitter, and constricting the three-dimensional space. This is, in fact, the international formula of most European court portraiture of the sixteenth century, brought to high perfection on the one hand in Italy, by Bronzino, and on the other in the Netherlands by Antonio Mor. What was to become the characteristically English development has its roots in Mor and the Antwerp School, for obvious reasons, political, religious and geographical, but was constantly reconditioned by reference back to its sources, both by the arrival of new painters from Northern Europe and by travel by the native artists abroad – most notably that of Hilliard in France. And again and again, there is reference back, often difficult to diagnose specifically, but undeniable, to Holbein.

But it is a formula, with its overriding emphasis on the hierarchic grandeur of the sitter, that leads to impersonality of style. In the conflict, which goes on inevitably in all portraiture, between the personality of the artist and that of his sitter, in this type of portraiture the odds are heavily in favour of the sitter. At this point in time in England, the artist was hardly allowed a personality in the intellectual and professional context of contemporary society: he was simply a humble artisan. Somewhere in the 1580s, Stowe wrote that painting was 'a meer mestier of an Artificer and handy Craftsman' – then a backward view perhaps, for in 1579, in a forthright self-portrait, the English-born painter, George Gower had set out, with verbal inscription and symbols, his claim that gentle birth and the profession of the painter were compatible. But the substantiation of that claim, and its development to the concept of the artist as genius, needed the glamour of the 'artist-prince' Van Dyck, before it became generally accepted, and before his time the artist tends to evaporate from the polished and glorious carapace of his sitter. In fact, for almost three centuries the Tudor painters, apart from Holbein, all but vanished from history, and in the great English family collections, portraits of the period were generally ascribed to two painters only: if apparently dating from before 1550, to Holbein (whose death date was long believed to be much later than 1543); if after, then to the Italian Federico Zuccaro, whose actual sojourn in England had in fact been only a matter of months, in 1575. Other names, Lucas de Heere, Gheeraerts, and others – lurked obscurely in the pages of Horace Walpole's *Anecdotes of English Painting*, first published in the 1760s. Only since 1900 have the Tudor painters begun to take shape as individual artistic personalities, cohering gradually in the photographic archives of the National Portrait Gallery. And only since 1945 has the concentrated research of scholars such as Graham Reynolds, Dr Erna Auerbach, and Roy Strong succeeded in marrying together with some conviction a significant number of actual paintings with the artists' names that surface haphazardly in surviving records of the time. Yet even so, what might seem a crass insensitivity of earlier generations, is not really such, for to all but the most trained specialist eyes, Tudor, or at least Elizabethan, painting must still read primarily as the work of a school or a period, rather than as a sequence of individual masters: what they have in common is far stronger than what differentiates them. Thus the factors which have enabled them to be separated out one from another are not generally those of individual style and handling: part of the break-through which enabled Roy Strong to establish what will surely be, for many years, the standing corpus of work by individual masters (*The English Icon*) sprang from the realization that several of the most important painters used a form of inscription peculiar to themselves, and clearly identifiable. Once the groupings of paintings bearing a common form of inscription are established, the character of the painter becomes clear – especially in the very important case of Gheeraerts the Younger – yet it is also true that many uninscribed paintings, subsequently associated with the painter purely on grounds of style and handling alone, remain as very tentative and uncertain attributions indeed, and that one painter occasionally seems to merge into another. Contributory factors to possible confusion include the non-existence of any notion of artistic copyright, so that the same portrait pattern might be used by any painter, and portraits not only of the monarch, but also of the great patron-statesmen, such as Burghley and Leicester, were clearly reproduced by many workshops. Late in the period, there was also the close family inter-relationship of some of the leading painters – de Critzes, Gheeraerts, Olivers – who may well have worked in some degree of collaboration, conceivably even to the extent of a common workshop. The problem of attributions is also bedevilled by the crucial question of condition: the use of canvas as support for oil-painting is very rare indeed until the 1580s, and only wholly supplanted the wood panel in the second quarter of the next century; wood, unhappily, is particularly vulnerable to the whims of English humidity, constantly expanding, contracting and even splitting so that the brittle film of paint, which cannot move with it, tends inevitably to flake off. Very few Tudor paintings are in anything approaching pristine condition, and most have been restored not once but many times. An over-eager student could easily find that a new master he had thought to have identified was in fact the hand of a common restorer.

The identification of the work of painters other than in Holbein, in the last years of his life, through the 1540s and into the 1550s, remains a very vexed problem. Almost nothing seems to remain from the hand of any of the resident Italian painters; an attempt to single out a number of works by Luke Horenbout, who was working until 1544, and who was paid apparently at a higher rate than Holbein, remains speculative. Of Holbein's workshop, and his pupils and assistants if any, there is no documentary evidence, yet there are several paintings long attributed to him, and of very high quality, which are now often doubted as being his hand, though they clearly relate very closely to his work. These include a number of early versions of what are certainly his designs – such as the very fine and well-preserved three-quarter length of *Henry VIII* in Rome, or the Duke of Buccleuch's magnificent *Sir Nicholas Carew*, in which the head repeats Holbein's drawing of this sitter at Windsor – and various other designs that are not certainly his but which reflect his vision very clearly – for example, the late three-quarter length, very iconic and frontal, of *Henry VIII* at Castle Howard; the roundel profile of Edward VI at Washington; the massive frontal and straddling three-quarter length known as Lord de la Warr. These bear eloquent witness that there were hands of great competence working alongside Holbein and in the decade after his death. But the generally fairly shadowy figures that are actually identifiable seem, on surviving evidence, to have been, for the most part, of somewhat lesser ability. Closest to Holbein's is the work of one known as 'Master John'; the *Mary I* as princess, dated 1544, in the National Portrait Gallery, is believed to be identical with that recorded in a payment of November 1544 'to one John that drue her grace in a table, v.li.'; the whole-length of Lady Jane Grey, of a year or so later, also in the Portrait Gallery, is clearly by the same hand, and is a highly formalized variation of Holbein's *Christina* design. Style and technique here suggest an actual collaborator of Holbein's, as they do also in the work of John Bettes I; he is documented as active between 1531 and about 1570, but the work thus far recognized, centring round a rare, signed and dated *Unknown Man* of 1545 (Tate Gallery), and including the *1st Baron Wentworth* (National Portrait Gallery) and *Sir William Cavendish* (Hardwick Hall) all are of the period 1545–50. They are obviously very closely dependent on Holbein's vision, but more individual and livelier in treatment than 'Master John's' work.

Holbein's successor as King's Painter came to England only after Holbein's death: William Scrots (or Streetes), a Netherlander and formerly Mary of Hungary's court painter, arrived in late 1545, and remained (at a remarkably high yearly salary of £62 10s.) until his death, probably in 1554. It is certain that he was responsible for the production of the state portraits of *Edward VI* (though these were repeated by other hands), and a payment to him survives, of March 1551–2, for 'three great tables', two of the King and one of the *Earl of Surrey*. Three early versions of the latter are known, the most spectacular being that at Arundel Castle, a whole-length leaning on a broken column, a design that goes back to Moretto, but set in a rounded archway copiously garlanded with allegorical figures in the Fontainebleau manner of Primaticcio. The *Edward VI*, of which a fine version once in the Lumley Collection is at Hampton Court but which was produced in some quantity, also for export to foreign princes, shows on the one hand an elegant acknowledgment of Holbein's

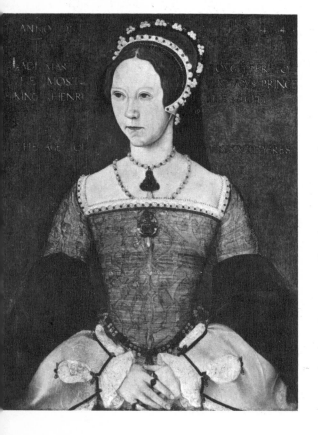

MASTER JOHN (?), *Mary I*, 1544.
National Portrait Gallery, London.

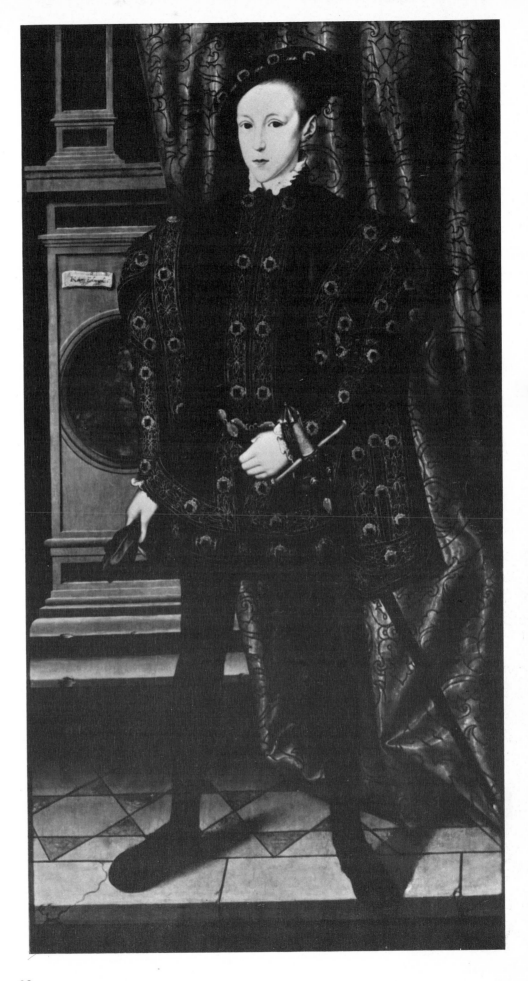

WILLIAM SCROTS, *Edward VI*.
Hampton Court.
By gracious permission of
Her Majesty the Queen.

authoritative realization of monarchy in the *Henry VIII* in the Whitehall Privy Chamber – the stance is repeated almost literally – and on the other a clear reflection of the tradition of whole-length international court-portraiture developing from Seisenegger's work for the Imperial Court of Charles V. Though whole-lengths were to remain rare, except in the case of royalty, until the 1580s, in the *Edward VI* there are present many of the qualities and motifs that were to recur constantly in characteristic Tudor three-quarter lengths to the end of the century: the vertical emphasis and sharp silhouetting of the figure, the shallow and constricted space; the pallor of the flesh; the accessories of plinth and column or pilaster; the brocaded curtain; the linear emphasis, especially in the faithful tracing of elaborate costume. The essential quality of Scrot's original work remains enigmatic, however, owing to the uncertainty as to which are from his own hand, and which are repetitions or copies; thus two earlier works, both at Windsor Castle and recently associated with his name, the three-quarter length *Edward VI* of c. 1545 and the *Princess Elizabeth* of c. 1546 do not seem, at least not to all who have studied them side by side, to be by the same hand nor, necessarily, either by the Scrots responsible for the later *Edward VI* whole-length at Hampton Court.

Two artists do emerge with a more specific individuality, aided by a rare but happy habit of signing their works. The first is Gerlach Flicke, active in England from c. 1545 till his death in 1558, though interrupted perhaps by a period abroad and certainly by a spell of imprisonment apparently for involvement in Wyatt's rebellion in 1554. Only a handful of works survives, the characteristic masterpieces being his *Cranmer*, signed and dated 1546 (N.P.G.) and the three-quarter length known as '*Lord Grey de Wilton*', 1547 (Marquess of Lothian, Newbattle Abbey). Though influenced by Holbein's English style, Flicke seems to have remained very German (he came from Osnabrück), with a formidably forthright, even brutal, power of characterization. In the beautifully preserved *Cranmer*, the acknowledgment to Holbein is very explicit – understandably, as this was painted perhaps even as a pendant to Holbein's *Warham*, and hung with it at Lambeth Palace for many years. If, compared with Holbein's archbishop, Flicke's is almost blatantly lacking in subtlety, and cramped and crowded into the picture space, the portrait retains, nevertheless, a vital and vivid actuality. But the *Lord Grey de Wilton* is far more purely Teutonic, and very closely comparable to good, standard portrait work of the period in Germany, aggressive interpretations of feudal power.

The second painter who obligingly signed was of greater consequence, and is, amongst other things, the real bridge between Holbein and the full-blown late Elizabethan 'costume-piece': Hans Eworth, whose name is recorded in a bewildering variety of spellings, but who signed, almost always, with a firm monogram of HE. He came apparently from Antwerp, and is recorded in England between 1549 and 1571 by many documentary references and some thirty-odd certain works, mostly signed and dated. He seems to have had Catholic connections, and certainly purveyed a number of variations on the image of Mary I which may account for an apparent lack of court favour under Elizabeth until very late in his career. The paintings of the first decade of his activity in England, 1549–59, demonstrate an eclectic talent with a delicately sensitive approach to the variety of human character. His early variety is indeed remarkable, starting with an almost miniature panel of the *Grand Turk* on horseback, with a formidable turban (derived from a print by Coecke van Elst), and then in the following year, two outstanding portraits of English sitters, both of which are unique of their very different kind. The *Thomas Wyndham*, while echoing in its pose Holbein's *Sieur de Morette*, is a precociously actual image of a serving soldier (referring probably to the sitter's action in the Scottish campaign of 1547); here the military accessories are not used as ornaments of rank and chivalry, but convey, aided by the taut, bleak modelling of the face and the massive power of the hands,

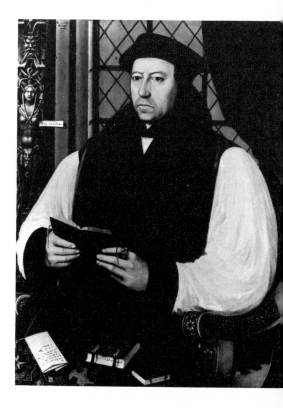

GERLACH FLICKE, *Cranmer*, 1546. National Portrait Gallery, London.

one thumb tucked in the belt, a convincing aura of the fighting soldier. The crowded but constricted treatment of the background indicates some uncertainty in the painter when confronted with a composition full of incident. Eworth did not often attempt such, but the *Sir John Luttrell* (p. 86) is even more complex: it shows a rare awareness of the Mannerist fashions of Fontainebleau, but its mixture of realistic portraiture, in the head and naked body of Luttrell, wading in the sea in which he was drowned that year, with a vividly detailed shipwreck beyond, and of allegorical figuration (the goddess leaning from the clouds to take his upraised arm) together with a larding of inscription, scarcely adds up to visual coherence. Yet, in a way, it looks forward to many paintings of the end of the century, with their inscriptions, emblems, symbolic allusions and indifference to a visual coherence according to the rules of Renaissance congruity of perspective. More characteristic of the main line Eworth's work was to take is the admirably subtle and simple three-quarter length (unsigned, about 1550 or a little later) of an *Unknown Lady* in the Fitzwilliam Museum. The conception goes back to Holbein, and the still but tense image of *Jane Seymour*; and the use of the cast shadow, which recurs again from time to time through Eworth's work, also comes from Holbein. The effect of the whole, however, is less monumental than Holbein's and in a sense more humane, if less final: there is a tenderness in the character shown, almost a demureness, a hesitancy of mood that vitalizes the serene composition so beautifully ordered in the picture space. Note the hesitation of the hands – Eworth's hands are almost always nervously eloquent. The modelling of the flesh, set against the subdued lustre of the blacks, is pale, translucent and closely akin to that of Jan van Scorel.

A number of paintings of *Mary I*, from 1554 on, are witness of court patronage of Eworth. They range in scale from an oil miniature, some two inches in diameter (Duke of Buccleuch) to the hieratic three-quarter length in the Society of Antiquaries, posed as is the Fitzwilliam Museum lady, but with full detailing of the magnificently brocaded gown, and set against a background panelled off in rectangles. A three-quarter length of *Baroness Dacre*, about 1555 (National Gallery of Canada) pays specific homage to Holbein by reproducing his portrait of her dead husband in the background. But in its somewhat unresolved treatment of the many accessories, reveals again Eworth's relative weakness at complex compositions, while, in the face of the stout and heavy-lidded widow, there shows a tendency, to become more marked later, of the flesh of his sitters to seem almost inflated. What is perhaps Eworth's masterpiece, however, is perhaps later than this, the small-scale panel, signed and dated 1559, of the *Duchess of Suffolk*, aged thirty-six, but looking every substantial inch of a rapacious fifty, with her second husband, Adrian Stokes aged twenty-one. The impression of a husband-eating spider is superb, but so too is the detailing of crisp and gaudy magnificence of costume, the strut and swagger of the young popinjay's pose, as confidently brash as a twentieth-century pop singer. But through the 1560s, Eworth tends towards much more iconic treatment of sitters, and also, most often, to a life-size, or near life-size, scale – the standard mode of representation of the later Tudor 'society portrait', whence the atmospherics of individual characterization tend to evaporate from the image of the sitter, set in the context of society, rank, family and wealth. To the end he remained capable of individual characterizations of a haunting subtlety in simplicity, but generally the image becomes much more rigid. In the pair of portraits of the *Duchess of Norfolk*, 1562 (p. 72), and the *Duke of Norfolk*, 1565, much of the character of the Elizabethan 'costume-piece' is established. The two figures, she notably like a doll in richly encrusted rigour of dress, are set against a formally patterned brocade background that is common to both pictures, likewise their coats of arms are divided between the two.

Though at the end of his career Eworth seems (from his recorded employment for revels 1571–3) to have recovered some court patronage, most of his later sitters are

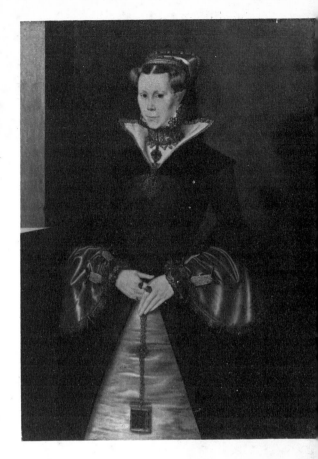

HANS EWORTH, *Unknown Lady*, called Mary I, *c.* 1550–55. Fitzwilliam Museum, Cambridge.

Overleaf,
HANS EWORTH, *Sir John Luttrell*, 1550. The Courtauld Institute of Art.

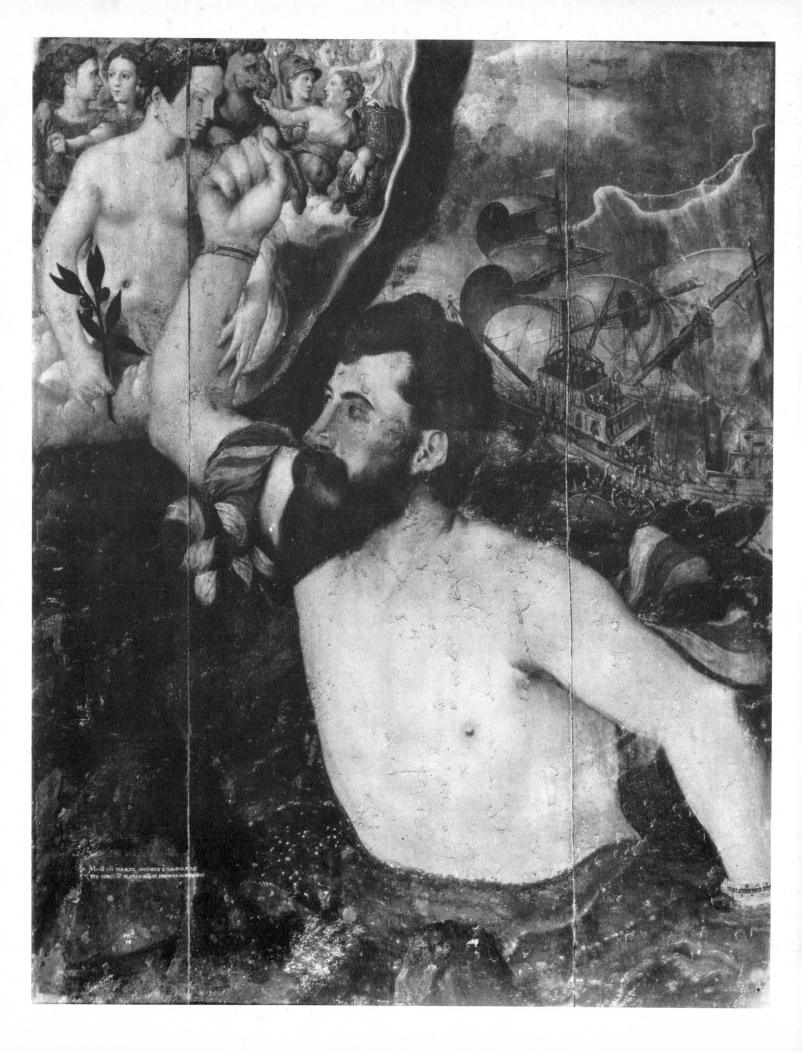

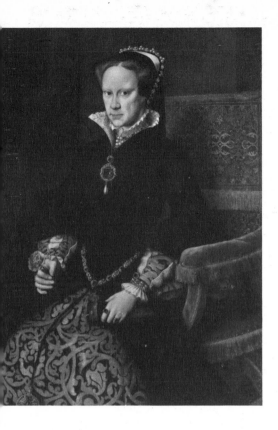

Above, ANTONIO MOR, *Mary I,* 1554.
Castle Ashby. By permission of Earl Compton.

Below, STEVEN VAN DER MEULEN,
Sir William Petre, 1567.
National Portrait Gallery, London.

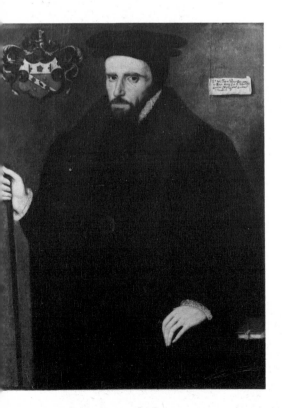

relatively obscure figures; his last dated work, of 1570, at Copenhagen, is *An Allegory of the Wise and Foolish Virgins,* reverting back almost to the manner of the Luttrell portrait of 1550. As far as the court was concerned, its standard seems to have been set for the first decade of Elizabeth's reign, 1563–73, by Steven van der Meulen, who came from Antwerp to London about 1560. Though recorded with unique approbation in the 1590 Lumley Inventory as 'the famous paynter Steven', identification of his work is still at a highly speculative stage. The three documented works known are a pair, of *Lord and Lady Lumley,* 1563 (Earl of Scarborough), and a whole-length of *Eric XIV of Sweden,* 1561 (Gripsholm Castle). The first two are in very worn condition, and have little now in common with the third; the attributions of other paintings that have been grouped round them have in common, most markedly, a mere reflection of the style of Mor, as it were an Antwerpian anonymity, though some of them seem closer to Eworth than to the direct Mor tradition. That Antonio Mor himself visited England in 1554 seems to be attested by his seated three-quarter length of *Mary I,* of which three versions are known (that reproduced here from the collection of Earl Compton), and his reputation as court painter was supreme in Northern Europe. Van der Meulen repeats the stance and *hauteur* of Mor's sitters but has, as far as we are able to assess his work, little of Mor's forcefully vivid particularity. The *Sir William Petre,* 1567, whether rightly given to him or not, is typical of the mode – the life-size three-quarter length, rather inert, though angled against a plain background more sharply than was Eworth's wont, and also depending more on the use of shadow (and often a rather lowering expression) for characterizing the features. Eworth's sitters, in contrast, seem to have faces scrutinized under the shadowless stare of limelight. The attribution amongst them of the gorgeous whole-length of the *Countess of Sussex, c.* 1565, (p. 88) to Steven seems somewhat exceptional but it has points in common with the *Eric XIV.* Like Eworth's pair of Norfolk's portraits, it is also, but now on whole-length scale, a notable step towards the uniquely English variant of international court portraiture at the close of the century: a votive image (though not specifically painted as foundress of Sidney Sussex College which dates only from 1596), the human being almost abstracted into the decorative pattern of the ermined gown with its regal studding of rosettes, of the tented baldaquin and the gold-encrusted cushion of the chair of state (the portrait has been cut down, probably on all sides).

There were certainly, in the 1560s, other hands at work, in a style varying between those of Eworth and Steven, and of a vivid, if relatively gauche competence. One of them was the master of two potent portraits of one of the great blue-stocking ladies of the age, *Mildred, Lady Burghley,* at Hatfield (though these are still given by some to Eworth); and another is the engagingly clear, direct hand responsible for the visual inventory of *Lord Cobham and his Family,* itemizing with dispassionate, alert scrutiny adults, children, costume, dishes, food and parrot (p. 89). Very different from this naive venture towards the conversation piece is a celebrated painting of highly sophisticated competence at Hampton Court, signed HE and dated 1569, and long given to Eworth until Roy Strong demonstrated convincingly that this is a different monogram. It is tempting to ascribe it – *Elizabeth I and the Three Goddesses* (p. 88) – to the Fleming, Lucas de Heere, who was in London as a religious refugee from *c.* 1568 to 1577, and by whom no certain works in England have survived. It is, anyway, a transplant (into the grounds of Windsor Castle) of the full-blown Flemish Mannerist style, deriving from such painters as Floris, and blooming for the greater glory of the Virgin Queen: Elizabeth is shown in the place of Paris in his choosing, but routing the three female candidates for selection by the dazzle of her own beauty and lyrically retaining the apple (in the shape of the orb) for herself.

Lucas de Heere, celebrated in his time both as poet and painter, was but one of many Netherlandish refugees from the persecutions of the Duke of Alva: there was, from the 1570s, an artistic Flemish circle in London centring perhaps on the person of the distinguished historian Emanuel van Meteren, and including the founding fathers of two family dynasties that were to become fully anglicized and celebrated in the next generation – the Gheeraerts and the de Critzes. Marcus Gheeraerts the Elder's work is so far almost entirely unrecognized, apart from an admirable small-scale whole-length, *c.* 1580, of Elizabeth and a spectacular, large etching of the *Procession of the Knights of the Garter*. Traces of a re-injection of Netherlandish influence, or at least any permeation of it are curiously rare: examples such as the *Elizabeth I and the Three Goddesses* stand out as exotics. Another one is Joris Hoefnagel's genre painting called *A Marriage Feast at Bermondsey* of *c.* 1570 (pp. 70–71); Hoefnagel, from Antwerp, seems to have been in England from 1569 to 1571, and this is an historically uniquely valuable recording of English costume of the period.

There were also, in the 1570s, two other passing visitors, of greater international stature and very different character. Cornelius Ketel, from Gouda, was here for a fairly extended period (*c.* 1573–81) and worked under the exalted patronage of Sir Christopher Hatton and the Earl of Oxford, but less than half a dozen works are certainly of his English period. The most striking, the *Sir Martin Frobisher*, 1577 (p. 90), and the *William Gresham*, 1579 (Major R. H. G. Leveson-Gower) have a lively, forceful naturalism that is the antithesis of the mode of English court portraiture of the 1580s. It represents, however, the extreme of one abiding concern of portraiture – the desire for a breathing literal likeness of the sitter – which Gheeraerts the Younger was later to attempt, in his best work, to modulate into the rigorous patterns of court portraiture. The *Frobisher* in particular has a swagger and movement, aptly for its sitter's thrusting quest into exploration of the New World, that presages the important part that Ketel was later to play in the early foundation of the Baroque style in Holland. This is apparent too in the very fine portrait of *Elizabeth* at Siena (p. 90); the attribution of this to Ketel rather than to Zuccaro seems at present reasonably convincing. This, while sensitive to the peculiar requirements of the Queen as subject, and replete with symbolic allusion (the sieve, the mottos, the reliefs on the column) to demonstrate her as Vestal Virgin, has in the background in counterpoint to the stillness of Elizabeth's figure, a strenuously swirled movement of her courtiers' approach, reminiscent of the vast life-size Guild portrait groups Ketel was later to do in

Above, Frances Sidney, Countess of Sussex,
attributed to STEVEN VAN DER MEULEN,
c. 1565. Sidney Sussex College, Cambridge.
Right, Monogrammist HE,
Elizabeth I and the Three Goddesses, 1569,
Hampton Court.
By gracious permission of
Her Majesty the Queen.

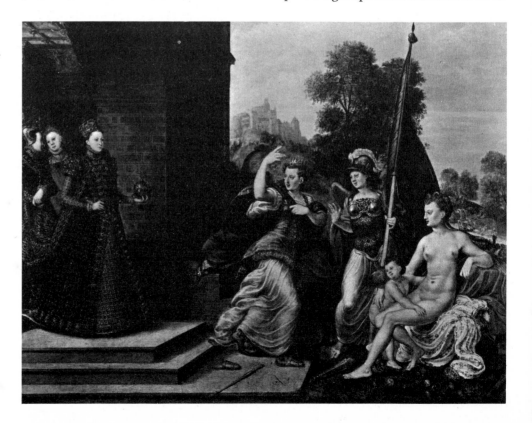

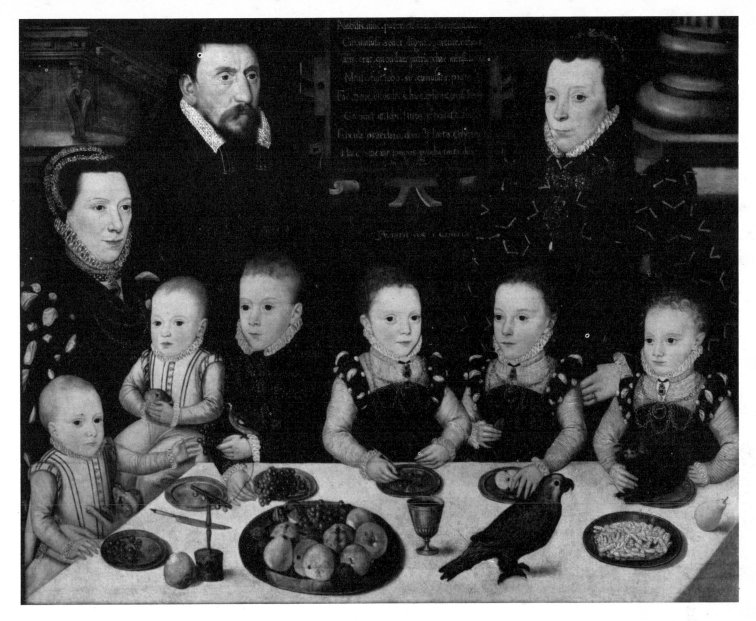

MASTER OF THE COUNTESS OF WARWICK,
*William Brooke, 10th Lord Cobham,
and his Family*, 1567.
By permission of the Marquess of Bath.

Amsterdam. The other major visitor was Federigo Zuccaro, who was in London only for six months at the most, in 1575; he came under the Earl of Leicester's patronage, and painted certainly only two portraits – whole-lengths of *Leicester* and of *Elizabeth*, both vanished, but known from drawings for them in the British Museum. The English workshops do not seem to have been touched by this brief impact of Roman mannerism, though the Elizabethan design is interesting in its incorporation again of symbolic characterization of the Queen's virtues (the column with snake, ermine and dog), while the Leicester, with its strewing of shells of armour may have influenced Hilliard's whole-length miniatures such as the *Anthony Mildmay* in Cleveland.

More important than these Italian and Netherlandish visitations, in terms of the creation of the finer English court portraiture of the time, was the increase of sympathy between France, the court of the Valois, and England. An awareness of the French style – the work of Clouet the Younger especially (though the Clouets too were of Flemish origin) – is perhaps first apparent in the earliest known work of George Gower, but is even clearer in some of the work of the 1570s by the most famous English painter of the sixteenth century, Nicholas Hilliard. Both Gower and Hilliard, the leading resident painters between 1570 and 1590, were English born, and both interestingly made specific reference to the claims of painting to be considered not as a mere craftsman's trade but as a liberal art, the practice of which was

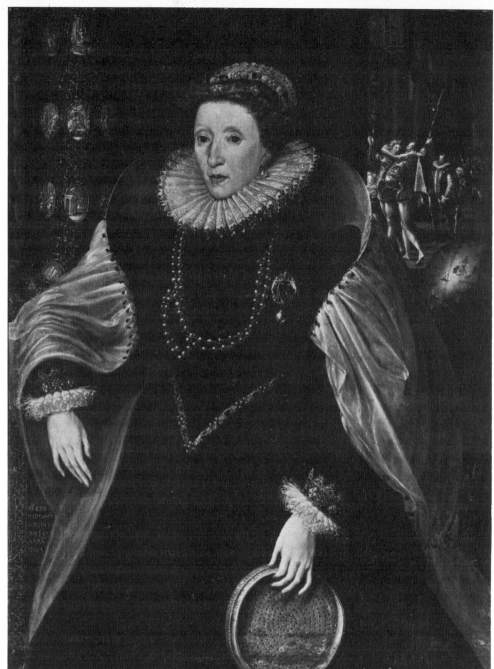

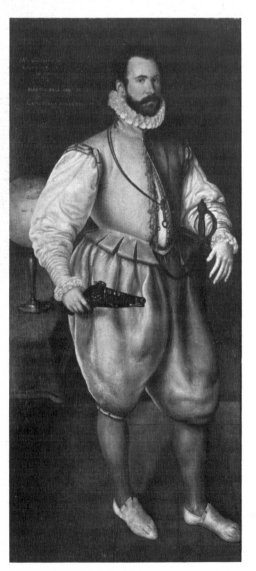

Right, CORNELIUS KETEL, *Elizabeth I.*
Pinacoteca Nazionale, Siena.
Below, CORNELIUS KETEL, *Sir Martin Frobisher,*
1577. By permission of the Curators of
the Bodleian Library, Oxford.

entirely becoming for those of gentle birth – indeed, by implication, perhaps only susceptible of reaching its perfection in the hands of men of birth and high culture. Thus Gower, grandson of a knight, shows in his self-portrait, mentioned earlier, his palette in hand, and a balance with the painter's compasses in one scale outweighing his family arms in the other. Hilliard, in his famous *Treatise* (written between 1597 and 1603, though unpublished in his lifetime), devotes considerable space to the civilized qualities inherent in painting, but describes especially limning, or miniature painting, as 'fittest for gentlemen'.

Gower, probably the elder of the two, was certainly in good practice in London by about 1570, and in 1581 was appointed Serjeant-Painter to the Queen; he died in 1596. His association with Hilliard was probably closer than that of mere professional colleague, for in 1584 the two of them made a joint attempt to secure a monopoly in production of portraits of the Queen. His earliest certain portraits, the pair of Sir Thomas and Lady Kytson (both Tate Gallery), documented as 1573, head and shoulders clearly silhouetted in strong even light, have something of the alert clarity of characterization of French court portraiture. There is a markedly sculptural quality modelled by line, light and tone, not shadow, as it were a divination of the underlying bone structure, especially in the male face, that also refers back to the Holbein tradition rather than the immigrant Netherlandish one. Though only three surely documented works are known so far, about a score of works can be attributed with some certainty. The three-quarter lengths (especially female) show an increasing abstraction of the naturalistic figure into silhouette, and ornate, sometimes near two-dimensional treatment, of the splendid decoration of court costume. The problem of Gower's portraits of Elizabeth has still to be resolved (he must have produced them). Thus the 'Cobham' portrait of her *c.* 1576 (p. 92), one of the simplest yet most serenely noble of the Queen, has points in common with him, yet is more as if Zuccaro had yielded to the Elizabethan vision to modulate the manner of Florentine or Roman court portraiture into an English mode, the luminous flush almost silvery over the drawing of the face. But the attribution of the hieratic, flat, design of the 'Armada' portrait, at Woburn Abbey, seems fairly convincing (p. 93): Elizabeth is now resolved into pure icon, her anatomy lost in the formal upholstery of pearls and brocaded satins; the face (for which the same ideal pattern is used as by Hilliard in his late miniatures of the Queen) palely radiant in the geometric halo of the ruff. The fingers of her left hand are each rigid as a sceptre, and the right hand rests proprietorially on the globe of the world; the imperial crown is faithfully drawn in, and above, left and right, her culminating triumph over the Spanish Armada. As a regal image, the full formal compendium of majesty, this, in the logic of its rigour, was not to be surpassed by anyone in the last fifteen years of the Queen's life, and is a most ambitious example of the strange, late Elizabethan style as applied to the regal theme, so far removed from the Renaissance principle.

With Hilliard we revert to the story of the portrait miniature. Surviving evidence of the art is very rare indeed between Holbein's death and 1570, although one artist, Levina Teerlinc (daughter of a famous Flemish illuminator, Simon Benninck) is recorded as enjoying unusually lucrative patronage almost till her death in 1576; a *Young Girl* of 1549 (Victoria and Albert Museum) may be by her. Nicholas Hilliard, though attested as early as 1560 by two precocious, minute, roundel self-portraits (at the age of 13), really launches into his career about 1570. Son of an Exeter goldsmith, he was apprenticed in 1562 to a leading London goldsmith, and his background and training in their craft had a lasting effect on his work; his early style as a painter points also to instruction from a craftsman used to illuminating patents and charters, the main medium in which the practice of illumination persisted after the Reformation, though not generally at a very high level; one of his early works (*c.* 1569(?)), a minute rectangular image of Elizabeth in robes of state (Duke of Portland, Welbeck Abbey), complete with an inset diamond, might seem cut from some singularly lavish charter, but is, in fact, painted on the back of a playing card, a vehicle Hilliard was to use frequently, sometimes with allusive intent (as on the ace of hearts). The early, round miniatures also indicate an enduring inspiration which Hilliard later specified in his *Treatise*: 'Holbeans maner of Limning I have ever Imitated, and howld it for the best'. Yet there is also an evident knowledge of French art of his own time; a rectangular miniature of an *Unknown Man* aged twenty-four, dated 1572 (Victoria and Albert Museum) might be based on a Clouet drawing, though its exquisitely flourished and calligraphic inscription is peculiarly Hilliard's. Already, by this date, he was in high court favour, and it is assumed that a miniature of Elizabeth, 1572, which is certainly *ad vivum*, is the first such that he made of her, and also the one to which he refers in a famous passage from the *Treatise*. During the sittings, in an open garden in an even, unforced light, sitter and artist agreed on the undesirability of modelling by shadow – 'for beauty and good favour is like cleare truth, which is not shamed with the light, nor neede to bee observed'.

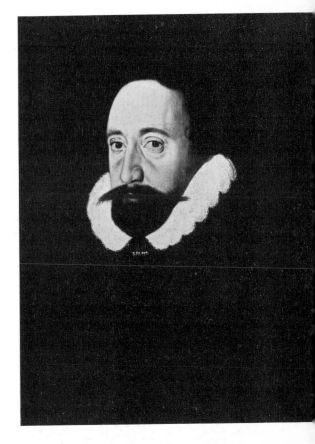

GEORGE GOWER, *Sir Thomas Kytson*, 1573. The Tate Gallery, London.

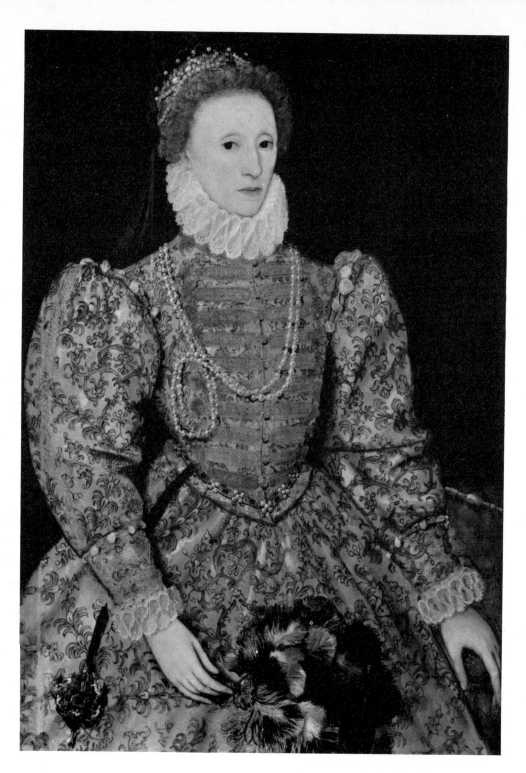

Elizabeth I (Cobham portrait), *c.* 1576.
National Portrait Gallery, London.

Here Hilliard is in tune with continental Mannerist theory, with its demand for modelling by colour and tone, but the total effect of the finished miniature has no parallel in Mannerist art: it conveys at once the conviction of a lively likeness, married, by its placing within the azure of the oval and by the delicate response of gold calligraphy to the ornament of dress and hair, into a decorative unity that becomes literally jewel.

Between 1576 and 1578 Hilliard was actually working in France, and the *Self-portrait* of 1577 (p. 105) was presumably painted there. Some miniatures of this time reflect perhaps a direct French influence, as in the placing of the figure almost to fill the picture space, reminiscent of Germaine Pilon's medals. The *Self-portrait* again incorporates the elegant calligraphy in gold, and more important is superb witness

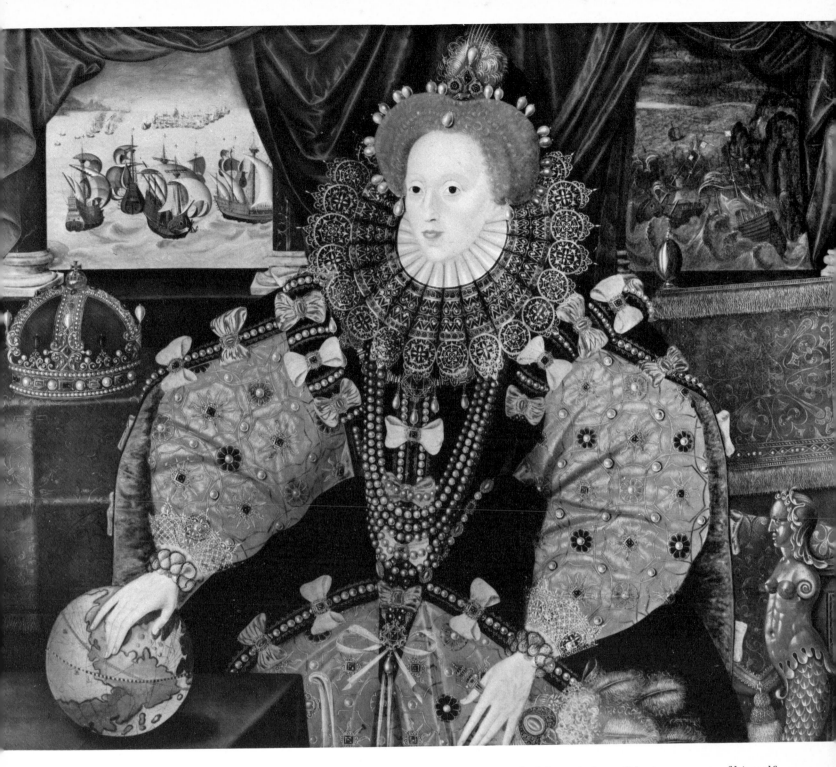

GEORGE GOWER, *Elizabeth I*
(Armada portrait) *c.* 1588. Woburn Abbey.
By permission of the Duke of Bedford.

both of a flawless skill and technique and of the artist's confident awareness of himself as a brilliant creature of status and fashion: clearly not one interested in the 'meer mestier of an Artificer and handy Craftsman', even though one who, in fact, in artifice and craftsmanship of his chosen kind was supreme in England in his time. In the twenty-five years from his return from France in 1578, he became clearly acknowledged as such: his prime patron was the Queen herself, and he produced a quantity of miniatures of her, even if one may suspect her patronage consisted more in allowing others to pay Hilliard for her portrait than to dispense cash herself. But Hilliard was also responsible for the designs of her Great Seals, and further is recorded as having painted her on a life-scale. The problem of Hilliard's work 'in large' in oils is still controversial; there is general acceptance of the attribution to him of two

93

exquisitely detailed and highly finished bust panels of the Queen (the 'Pelican' portrait, Walker Art Gallery, Liverpool, and the 'Phoenix' portrait, N.P.G.) on stylistic grounds; these, while clearly by the same hand, are both early, of *c.* 1575, and later portraits sometimes associated with him are very different in handling from these, ranging from the Woburn Abbey portrait, already mentioned as perhaps by Gower, and the fine 'Ermine' portrait of 1585 at Hatfield, which seems most likely to be the masterpiece of a Hilliard follower, Sir William Segar. Whatever the final solution may prove to be, it is clear that none of these works in large, splendid though some are, rivals the best of the miniatures in quality, as though the concentrations of scale were a vital ingredient to weld Hilliard's style into perfect harmony, a distillation of the visual character of the sitter into a gem-like decorative unity. The manner depends on a very subtle harmony of the most delicately fine yet highly tensile line drawing (and often calligraphy) with the modulation of clear lucent colour. Famous for the human liveliness of his likenesses, Hilliard, by abstracting them in little from rivalry with their life-size originals of flesh and blood, was able to reconcile them perfectly with the formal requirements of his design, and also to incorporate with them his calligraphic inscriptions in gold: often, too, even the highly artificial symbolic or emblematic allusions, as in the *Young Man against a Background of Flames*. On a life-scale the method tends to become diluted, and the tension between the contour line and the areas of colour difficult to sustain, while the figures, large as life, consort with far less ease, visually, with the arbitrary impositions of inscriptions, coats of arms, and inset emblematic devices that all became commonplace in the last decades of Elizabeth's reign.

Through the 1580s Hilliard settled fairly consistently for the oval format for his bust miniatures, the shape that responded best to their function often as lockets, personal jewels, sometimes indeed worn as jewellery and sometimes incorporated into magnificently intricate lockets of goldsmiths' work. They are indeed the most personally intimate form of portraiture: their littleness, worn or held in the hand, providing an ambiguous sense of ownership of the subject yet also of forlorn remoteness from him or her, and so ideal symbols of the baffling conflict of identities in love – '*O God! from you that I could private be! Give me myself and take yourself again ...*'

A new development in form, apparently in the second half of the 1580s, was the whole-length miniature. Hilliard's supreme masterpiece in fact is in this form, though its shaping into an oval is unique for a whole-length, the famous *Young Man amongst Roses* of *c.* 1588 (p. 105). If the Elizabethans failed signally to produce a visual art to match the spiritual profundity, the naked passion, of the Shakespeare of the tragedies, in Hilliard's *Young Man* there is nevertheless summoned up an archetypal lovelorn hero of the comedies, exquisite in the sharply melancholic tangle of the wild rose. The haunting enigma of his identity has provoked many interpretations, but the only one so far with at least a ghost of factual evidence is that he is the Earl of Essex, in the full conceit of youth and beauty snared by love for the Tudor rose. The other whole-lengths, mostly rather larger, some ten inches high, follow essentially the patterns of life-scale court portraiture then established throughout Europe, from Rome to the Netherlands, and are paintings in small, not personal jewellery, though they still could be part of a nobleman's travelling furniture in a peripatetic age. Only some six or seven survive, but these include masterpieces, such as the brilliantly decorative evocations of Elizabethan pageantry in the *Earl of Cumberland* (National Maritime Museum) and *Sir Anthony Mildmay* (Cleveland); most original is the recumbent whole-length, almost certainly of that deviously enigmatic Elizabethan character, *The 9th Earl of Northumberland*, known as the 'Wizard Earl' (p. 95) – shown here melancholic in a surreal setting of emblematic device.

The esteem for Hilliard is shown not only by the status of his sitters – who include

NICHOLAS HILLIARD, *Elizabeth I* (Pelican portrait), *c.* 1575. Walker Art Gallery, Liverpool.

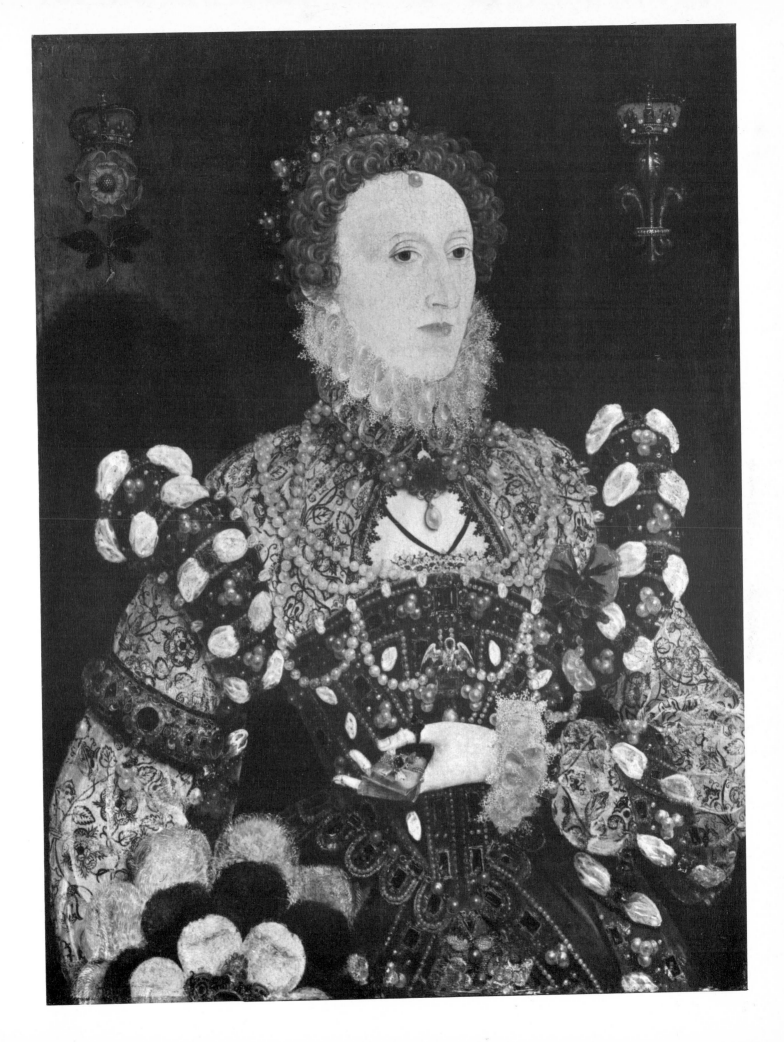

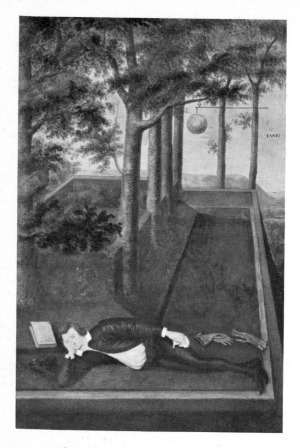

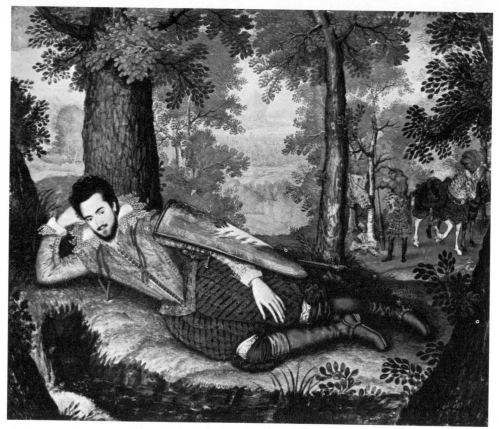

Above, NICHOLAS HILLIARD,
The 9th Earl of Northumberland (miniature).
Rotterdam.
By permission of Dr M. E. Kronenberg.
Above right, ISAAC OLIVER, *Lord Herbert of
Cherbury* (miniature), *c.* 1610–15.
By permission of The Earl of Powis.

Opposite left, R. LOCKEY,
More Family Group, 1593.
National Portrait Gallery, London.

Bacon, Raleigh, Drake, Leicester, Essex, Burghley, Mary Queen of Scots (he surely knew also Philip Sidney, and was supported by the Cecils) – but in the hitherto unprecedented quantity of contemporary references to him. There are several eulogies other than Donne's famous *'a hand, or eye / By Hilliard drawne, is worth an history, / By a worse painter made . . .'* and in the occasional listings of painters that now (witness of a growing acknowledgment of their art) begin to appear, Hilliard is always given pre-eminence. Nevertheless he perhaps outlived both his full fame and the early vitality of his vision; after the accession of James I in 1603 he continued under direct royal patronage, and repeated whole series of the new monarch and his family, but his images tend to be drier, more mechanical and pale in comparison with his earlier work, and he was probably overshadowed as miniaturist in the eyes of up-to-date fashion by Isaac Oliver, who was once Hilliard's pupil but developed on a fundamentally different line.

In miniature, Hilliard had hardly any successors of any quality; his son Laurence (1582–*c.* 1647) was of some prosaic competence, but Rowland Lockey (fl. 1582–1616), who started as Nicholas's apprentice, was a livelier talent. Almost his only certain works are three versions, of which two are 'revisions' of Holbein's *Thomas More* family group; the 'revisions' repeat Holbein's painting on the left and add in, on the right, More's descendants of Lockey's own time; one version is in miniature, and the other, in life-scale, conveys perhaps more of the quality of Holbein's original than the known copies (including Lockey's own third one, at Nostell Priory). The closest of other painters to Hilliard are John Bettes II and Sir William Segar. Both are known by only one surely proven painting, but in each case a group can be established with fair confidence around them. Bettes's one certainty, an *Unknown Girl,* 1587 (St Olave's Grammar School), while far short of Hilliard's skill, takes his delight in the linear filigree and arabesque of lace and costume still closer to abstract pattern, and a group of three portraits of *Elizabeth,* attributed to him (e.g. N.P.G. no. 2471) are impressive demonstrations of iconic majesty in almost geometric terms. Segar's one certain painting – his three-quarter length of *Essex,* 1590 – was once Lord Lumley's and

96

1635, his patronage seems to have come mainly from more modest social and academic sources.

De Critz's work is still remarkably elusive: his *Walsingham* of *c.* 1585 (N.P.G.) is strongly and vividly modelled in a searching light somewhat reminiscent of Gower, but is predominantly like contemporary Flemish work, able but fairly stereotyped. Later such individuality of handling as he had seems to have evaporated; he was author of the standard portrait of the Earl of Salisbury, in production from about 1595 (e.g. N.P.G. no. 107) of which perhaps a score of workshop repetitions exist, and later for a likewise oft-repeated portrait of James I. The *Salisbury* is a standard three-quarter length, essentially the design that had been repeated from Van der Meulen in the 1560s onwards. The portrait of Shakespeare's patron, *Southampton*, 1603, reasonably attributed to him, commemorating the sitter's imprisonment, is refreshingly engaging, with its rather sinister, self-conscious cat, inscriptions, and inset view of the Tower. But its 'programme' was doubtless specified by the sitter and the handling is inert (the cupped, but void, left hand is characteristic). The other two painters are much more individual. Oliver indeed was near-equal to Hilliard in sheer skill. He starts with a Hilliardesque manner, but already with a pronouncedly

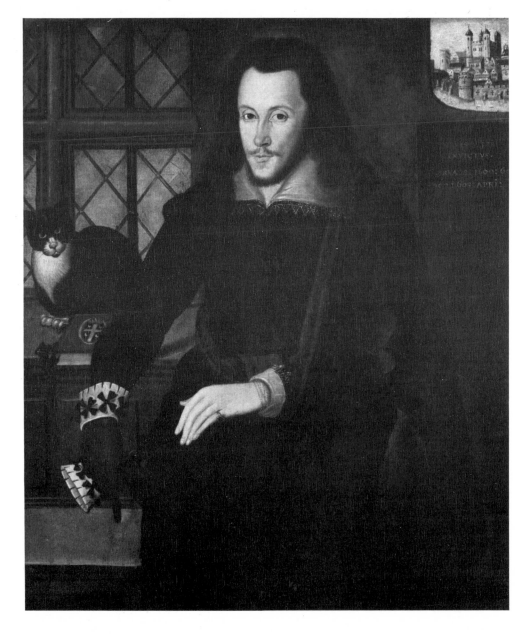

JOHN DE CRITZ. *Henry Wriothesley, 3rd Earl of Southampton,* 1603. By permission of the Duke of Buccleuch.

Flemish accent in the modelling; a very splendid whole-length *c.* 1590, of a melancholy man reclining against a tree-trunk (at Windsor; long, but wrongly, known as Sidney) is in essence a small Flemish painting, while the contrast of the recumbent *Herbert of Cherbury* (p. 96) with Hilliard's likewise recumbent *Northumberland* illuminates the distance between the two artists. In the Oliver, the theme is still of melancholy and there is even still an inscription – *Magica Sympathia* – but the more naturalistic relaxation of the figure, the realization of space in the very Flemish landscape, are entirely different. The Italian influence also appears in Oliver's work after 1596, most nakedly in numerous, very accomplished Parmigianinesque drawings, and an occasional religious miniature, such as the *Prodigal Son* at Welbeck Abbey, but also in some of his finest portrait miniatures, such as the *Lucy Harrington, Countess of Bedford* (Fitzwilliam Museum) absorbed into the service of the portrait in brilliant, swirling design. His royal portraits also show interesting developments – classical profiles of *Anne of Denmark* and *Prince Henry*, and in one type of *Prince Henry* a *morbidezza*, a sweetness of soft modelling that is Italian rather than Flemish. Like Hilliard, he too is recorded as a painter of life-scale portraits, but certain identification is even more problematic than with Hilliard. Although sometimes he reverts to a very Hilliardesque conception in miniatures, as in one type of *Anne of Denmark* (e.g. N.P.G. no. 4010) of a gem-like linear delicacy and clarity, his later work, in small, is very close to the life-size characterizations in bust portraits by Gheeraerts, or even Cornelius Johnson (to one of whose children he was godfather), in everything except scale. It is a primarily naturalistic rendering, depending on modelling by shadow to a degree that would have been unacceptable to court taste of the 1570s and '80s, and enlivened, in Oliver, by his idiosyncratic trick of a minute movement upwards at the corners of the sitter's mouth, giving the ambiguity of a half-smile.

A comparable concern for the lively likeness of the features in this new mode is evident in the work of Gheeraerts, who seems to have taken Gower's place as the chief fashionable portrait painter in the 1590s. Some forty paintings have now been firmly ascribed to him, up to some five years before his death in 1635. In pose and presentation his three-quarter lengths repeat the standard formulae, but tend to be softer, more atmospheric in treatment, and with a more three-dimensional quality. His whole-lengths tend to be much more strikingly new, and suggest that the painter probably visited the Netherlands early in his career. In some (the *Essex*, Woburn Abbey, *c.* 1596, or the *Thomas Lee*, 1594, on loan to the Tate Gallery) there is the earliest attempt to set the figure in the weather of outdoor landscape, while in his great masterpiece, the 'Ditchley' portrait of *Elizabeth*, *c.* 1592 (N.P.G.), he achieved a remarkable solution to the problem of revealing the essence of enduring, ideal, majesty in the ageing woman of flesh and blood in whom it resided (p. 107). The answer of Hilliard and Gower was to abstract into purely formal idealization: the 'mask of Youth' that is repeated in all Hilliard's royal miniatures of the 1590s, as in the life-size 'Armada' portrait, shows no stain or wrinkle of age, but shines perfect, pale and dispassionate as the full moon. But in Gheeraerts' face of the Queen, the hollowing sockets of the eyes, the carving by time of the flesh upon the bone, is focussed with, one guesses, little softening of flattery, into high, bleak authority as of an eagle. This forthright vision (very close to, perhaps related to, a famous unfinished miniature by Oliver in the Victoria and Albert Museum) is married with improbable but very real success into an historic allegorical decorative icon of majesty that uses all the apparatus of traditional Elizabethan Court portraiture; and the face becomes the living figurehead of a galleon of state full set in sail of satin studded with gold and rigged with ropes of pearl; she moves on a tapestry of England through the seas, out of lightning-shot storm clouds into the clearing skies of peace; bedecked with mottoes, and indeed a whole sonnet, though it is, the sense of depth and space is coherent. If the 'Armada' portrait distils majesty into an almost abstract still-life in terms of line

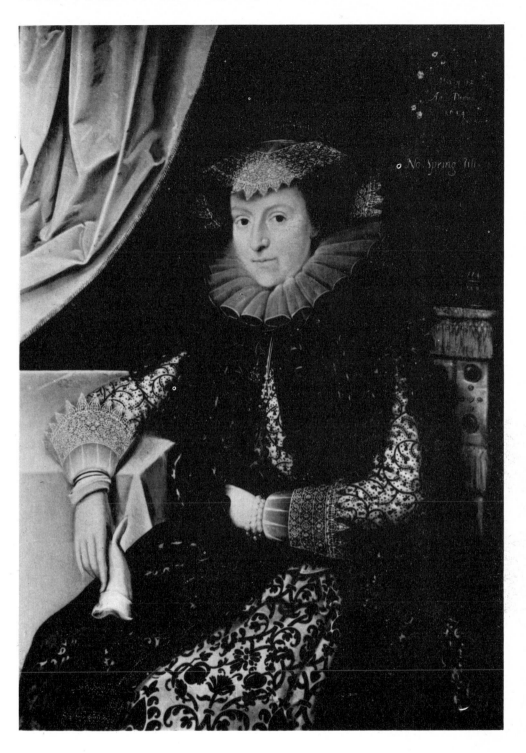

Marcus Gheeraerts II, *Lady Scudamore*,
1614–15.
National Portrait Gallery, London.

and heraldic colour, the 'Ditchley' painting manages, in contrast, to quicken with
life the frozen pageantry of a *tableau vivant* on a stage.

Sensitive to sitter and occasion, Gheeraerts' subsequent work is of some diversity.
The *Duke of Wurtemburg*, dated 1608, is signed *'gerardi Brugiense'* and is indeed very
close, though gentler in handling, to international court formulae as found in, for
example, Pourbus. The *Lady Scudamore* of 1614–15 has the brilliant translucent
decorative clarity of the 'English' costume-piece (it is in unusually pristine condition).
The *Sir John Kennedy* of the same date stands somewhere between the two, magnificent in costume, with a sharp, steep diagonal recession in space. At this time he was
much employed by Anne of Denmark and her court (an official portrait of her, e.g. a

101

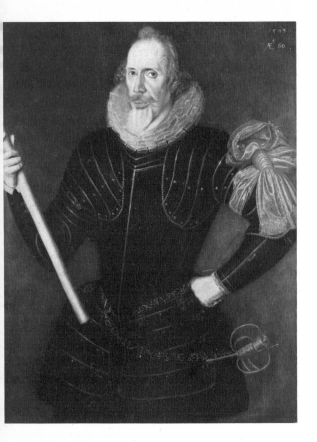

Above, ROBERT PEAKE, *A Military Commander,* 1593.
By permission of Lord Rootes.

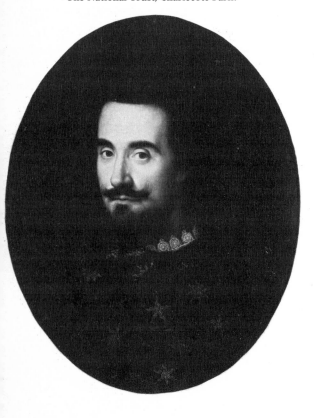

Below, WILLIAM LARKIN, *Lord Herbert of Cherbury,* 1609–10.
The National Trust, Charlecote Park.

three-quarter length at Windsor Castle, exists in many versions), but even before her death in 1619 he seems to have faded from high fashionable favour as it yielded to the more up-to-date immigrants from the Netherlands – Van Somer, Blijemborch and then Mytens.

His colleagues or rivals included, besides de Critz and Oliver, the Englishman Robert Peake, principal painter to Prince Henry, and, from 1607, joint Serjeant-Painter with de Critz. A prolific but uninspiringly unindividual painter, he is certainly known only by two paintings – *A Military Commander,* signed and dated 1593, which has a lively forceful characterization that evaporates from his later work, and a whole-length, *Charles I as Prince of Wales,* 1612–13 (Old Schools, University of Cambridge), which is a pale and bloodless official record. The recent identification by Roy Strong of over twenty more works was possible from the use, in them, of a common form of inscription rather than from any marked common individuality of style. The style is a weakening continuation, in fact, of the Hilliard/Segar tradition. More impressive is a strange, exotic, part reversal to the vision of Hilliard and Gower, in contrast to that of Gheeraerts in the decade 1610–20; this group of paintings is associated by Roy Strong with William Larkin, known from documentary references and from a pair of oval head-and-shoulders, in 'antique' costume and painted on copper, c. 1609–10, at Charlecote: *Lord Herbert of Cherbury* and *Sir Thomas Lucy;* these have the air of Oliver miniatures, enlarged (Larkin is known also to have worked in miniature). The works associated with these are a brilliant series especially of whole-lengths, the most impressive surviving set being that from Redlynch. The figures are shown stiff, forcefully lit from above, lavish costume largely copied in minute detail; pose and accessories go back to the standard Clouet designs: curtain, chair or table, the figure turned slightly to one side, one foot forward (p. 106). The accessories, however, both tend to repeat literally from picture to picture and are very highly standardized – notably the Turkey carpet (one pattern recurs in eight paintings) and curious tubular, almost plastic-seeming, folds of embowering curtain; in their brilliant precision, *en masse,* they are reminiscent of old-style, municipal park flowerbeds. How far the attribution to Larkin can be sustained is still open to argument; they do not all seem to be by the same hand, and one carpet design is first found in a Gheeraerts, but this problem must remain until more is known about their production and the Jacobean workshops' organization. As a belated culmination of the Elizabethan 'costume piece', costume taking on a transcendental quality and becoming vestment in the service of high social ritual, they are a remarkable achievement – but a very archaic one, their brief fashion dispelled by 1620 by the invasion of new movement from the Netherlands.

The pattern seems to repeat, and the history of Tudor painting is one of recurring injections direct from the Continental mainstream, offset by the English tendency to abstract from each development of the more-or-less naturalistic new modes a more generalized silhouette in terms of line and clear colour. Though the desire for a lively individual likeness was always there – Hilliard writes even of capturing 'these lovely graces, wittye smilings, and thesse stolne glances which sudainely, like lightning passe and another countenance taketh place' – and was presumably achieved to the client's satisfaction, now to the onlooker gazing back through the centuries, the individual impression tends to be less strong than the overall one of rank, costume and formal design: the face can seem but a pale differencing as in a coat-of-arms. The concern that provoked this stylization, pushed to a further extreme than in any continental variant of Mannerist formal portraiture, was no doubt the urgent wish of a society actually in fairly violent flux to stabilize and define their position. The *leitmotif,* a uniquely English one, of Elizabethan portraiture, proves to be stated in the evolving portraits of the Queen herself; and its trend is precociously announced by Elizabeth, still almost a child, in a message to her brother Edward VI, accompany-

102

ing a portrait of herself: 'For the face I grant I might well blush to offer, but the mind I shall never be ashamed to present'. From very early in the reign onwards, the quality and nature of portraits available of her was a subject of official concern. In 1563 there was a move to establish an approved master-image by 'some speciall person', from which all others could be copied – the first glimpse of the still prevalent practice of the official state portrait; as late as 1596 there was a purge, apparently an actual holocaust by fire, of unworthy portraits. The earliest portrait of her, c. 1546 – very possibly that alluded to in the letter to Edward VI – we have already mentioned, and it is by far the most distinguished until well on in her reign. Between 1558 and 1575 portraits are relatively few, and even the best of them unremarkable exercises in the current manner. The Hilliard miniature of 1572 and the 'Cobham' portrait of c. 1575 are at once of an entirely superior order of quality and the first and almost last convincing impressions of their subject as a woman of flesh and blood who is also a queen: thereafter the emphasis would be on her majesty. At this point she was moving into her early forties – no longer young, as is indeed movingly manifest in the taut pallor of the 'Cobham' portrait. The problem confronting her painters was to produce a convincing equivalent of a woman who was no longer young yet who was also the unfading embodiment of majesty, head not only of State but of Church; not only the immaculate apex of the social pyramid, but the lively focus, living myth, both sun and moon, of an actual court and an extraordinary court culture of adulation, expressed not only in poetry and the normal ritual of majesty, but in the constant staging of pageant entertainments both in London and her palaces and in the course of her famous 'progresses' about the country. Through the 1570s and 1580s it became clear that she would not marry, but remain the Virgin Queen; this accentuated even more her isolation, while the splendour of her position strengthened steadily in the consolidating economic and commercial prosperity of her country, and was crowned by spectacular martial victory with the defeat of the Spanish Armada in 1588.

The solutions produced by the painters varied naturally according to their style and talent. Hilliard moved from the decorative naturalism of the 1572 miniature to the jewel of the 1590 miniatures, the unblemished ideal face like a pearl in its filigree setting of curls crisp as finest gold wire and the white calyx of the ruff; the Gower-like vision of the 'Armada' portrait is perhaps most reminiscent of the formal ordering of heraldic painting in its clear colour and formalized design; Gheeraerts' 'Ditchley' portrait is the perfect evocation of the Queen as star of pageantry, and may even have been part of the props of Sir Henry Lee's complex entertainment for her, in 1592, at his house at Ditchley (it was painted for her, and in it she stands on Ditchley on the map). The 'Sieve' portrait at Siena shows her still and melancholy, but with a movement in the drawing, and very emphatically in the scene of courtiers in the background, that is already eloquent of the proto-baroque style Ketel was to develop fully on his return to Holland. But the 'make-up' has much in common besides the central individuality of the sitter. A major factor is the fantastic stiff elaboration of costume – the ruff, the vast hoops of the farthingale, the profusion of jewels – that developed in the last twenty years of the century. In extremes, this could be drawn out as most purely in engravings, as William Rogers's *Eliza Triumfans*, though the paintings associated with Bettes II go far in that direction, almost as a geometric diagram. Each colour had its symbolic significance, now almost entirely lost. Then there are the extraneous elements, the use of visual symbols in the service of allegorical demonstration of dominant qualities or a mood. They include the usual attributes of majesty, of course, orb, sceptre, sword and crown (though often the latter is the imperial rather than the English crown, indicating universal majesty in accordance with the apologists of the descent of the royal line), and chair and cloth of state – but also coats-of-arms, mottoes, whole poems; objects and animals mythically associated with

103

specific activities – the ermine for chastity, olive for peace, pelican for piety, sieve both for the chastity of the Vestal Virgin, Tuccia, and for its literal qualities. These appear first imported in Zuccaro's drawing of 1575 (pillar for constant Fortitude; serpent for Prudence; doves for Fidelity, and ermine), and were the stock-in-trade of Mannerist, and even High Renaissance, portraiture; in Elizabeth's portraits they are, however, used in most complex profusion and in disregard of continental Renaissance principles of perspective. Elizabeth is set up, in short, as a votive image with attributes, and not always this side idolatry: the tide of emotion that found constant expression in the late Middle Ages through Mariolatry now turned, cut off from its old objective by the Reformation, to the Virgin Mother of the nation – 'In earth the first, in Heaven the second Maid'.

Around the Queen, the courtiers emerge in constellations of ever increasing magnificence – the women sometimes as only slightly less gorgeous versions of her, the men blossoming from the 1570s in brilliant panoply of costume from the earlier plain, often black sobriety. The exchange of portraits between royalty, as tokens of courtesy, or often as proxies in marriage negotiations, was already established practice, but from about 1570 onwards it became more general within the court. In the great new 'prodigy houses' the collections began to build up: though the only survivor that gives any reliable indication of how they once looked is Bess of Hardwick's at Hardwick Hall, a few surviving inventories are witness of a once vast profusion. Lord Lumley owned, by about 1600, some two hundred portraits; Bess of Hardwick's inventory of 1601 lists seventy-odd, and in 1583 the great Earl of Leicester had thirty-seven at Kenilworth alone. The natural habitat for them, especially with the increasing fashion for whole-lengths from the 1590s was that characteristic Elizabethan feature, the Long Gallery; in 1609 Viscount Howard of Bindon is furnishing, and asks for Robert Cecil, Lord Salisbury's portrait – 'to be placed in the gallery I lately made for the pictures of sundry of my honourable friends, whose presentation thereby to behold will greatly delight me to walk often in that place where I may see so comfortable a sight'. From much earlier on the Cecils, Burghley and then Salisbury, had been lavish in distribution of their portraits to friends and supporters, and even abroad. Something of the mechanical nature of much Elizabethan portraiture is due to this reduplication, for, although a great many portraits of Burghley survive, they are almost all variants of only two originals, though by varying workshops. But they too witness the rapidly spreading habit of portraiture: we have lost probably far more than we guess, even if most of it was of indifferent quality. It is striking, though, that the musician Thomas Whythorne, even if, as author of the first English autobiography he may be thought to be of precocious and unusual introvert sensibility, had himself painted three times between the early dates of 1550 and 1569.

In portraits, the hieratic element of the memorial effigy persists. Examples even survive of works painted for use as memorials in churches: one is the big triptych of three members of the Cornewall family in Burford Church, signed and dated by the very obscure Melchior Salabossh, 1588, a crude but impressive transposition of the themes of funeral sculpture – arms, shrouded corpse – into painting (p. 109). A charming version of the Tree of Jesse theme, 1578 (p. 108), shows Sir Nicholas Bacon with his two wives and progeny, a vivid witness of the close alliance of portraiture with genealogy and heraldry. So, throughout the period, the ordinary family portraits tend ever to the quality of domestic effigy or mute chantry. They are assertions of individual vanity within the frame of family and of society: coats-of-arms feature frequently, with inscriptions of sitter's (but very rarely artist's) name, age and the date. Elementary aids to characterization or a special occasion are emblematic devices, especially towards the end of the century, as well as mottos, and the melancholy, inherent in the pure memorial, tends to give way to a more specific melancholy, of love. Love, and melancholic love, was the dominant poetic humour and mood, and

104

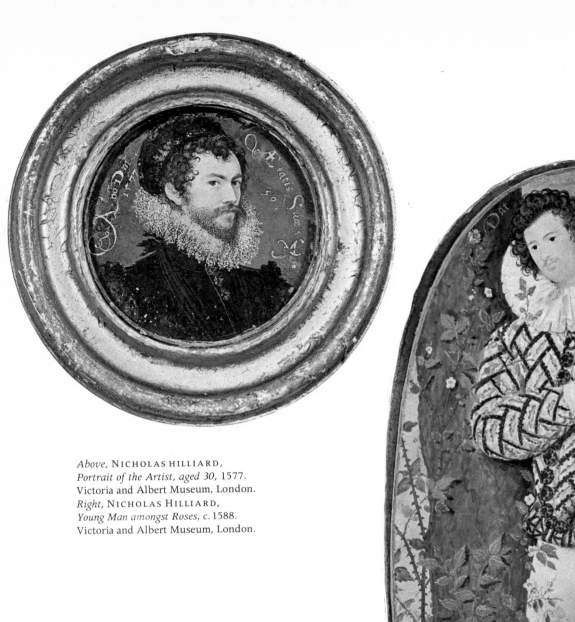

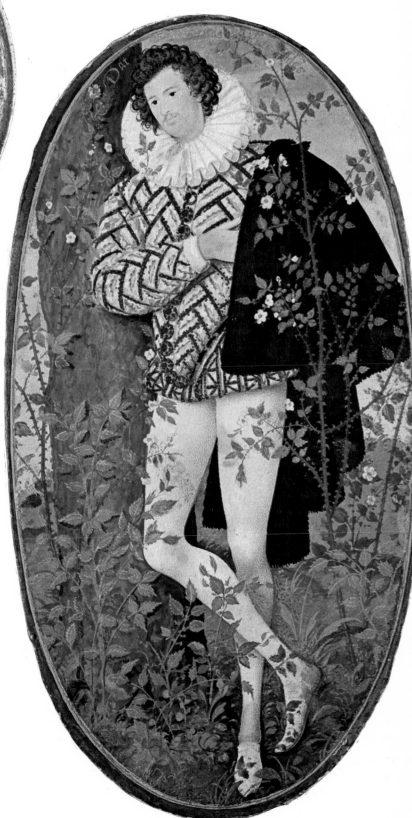

Above, NICHOLAS HILLIARD,
Portrait of the Artist, aged 30, 1577.
Victoria and Albert Museum, London.
Right, NICHOLAS HILLIARD,
Young Man amongst Roses, c. 1588.
Victoria and Albert Museum, London.

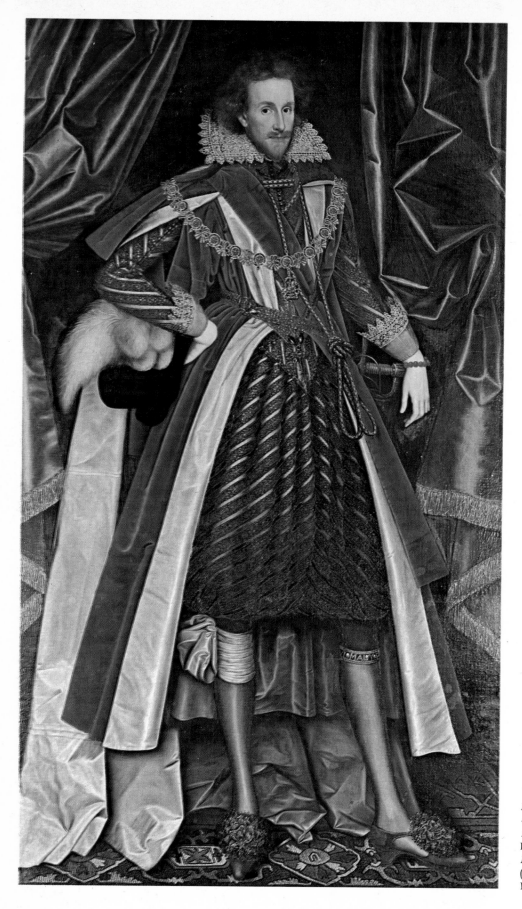

Left, WILLIAM LARKIN, *Philip Herbert,*
4th Earl of Pembroke, c. 1615.
Audley End, Essex.
By courtesy of Hon. R. H. C. Neville.
Right, MARCUS GHEERAERTS II, *Elizabeth I*
(Ditchley portrait), *c.* 1592.
National Portrait Gallery, London.

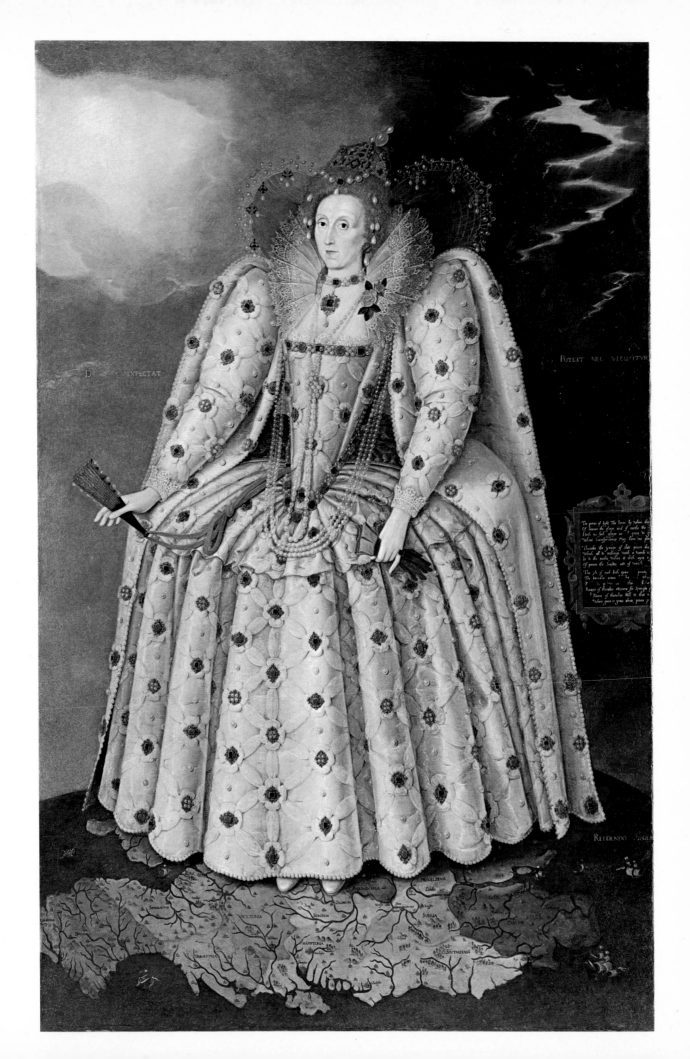

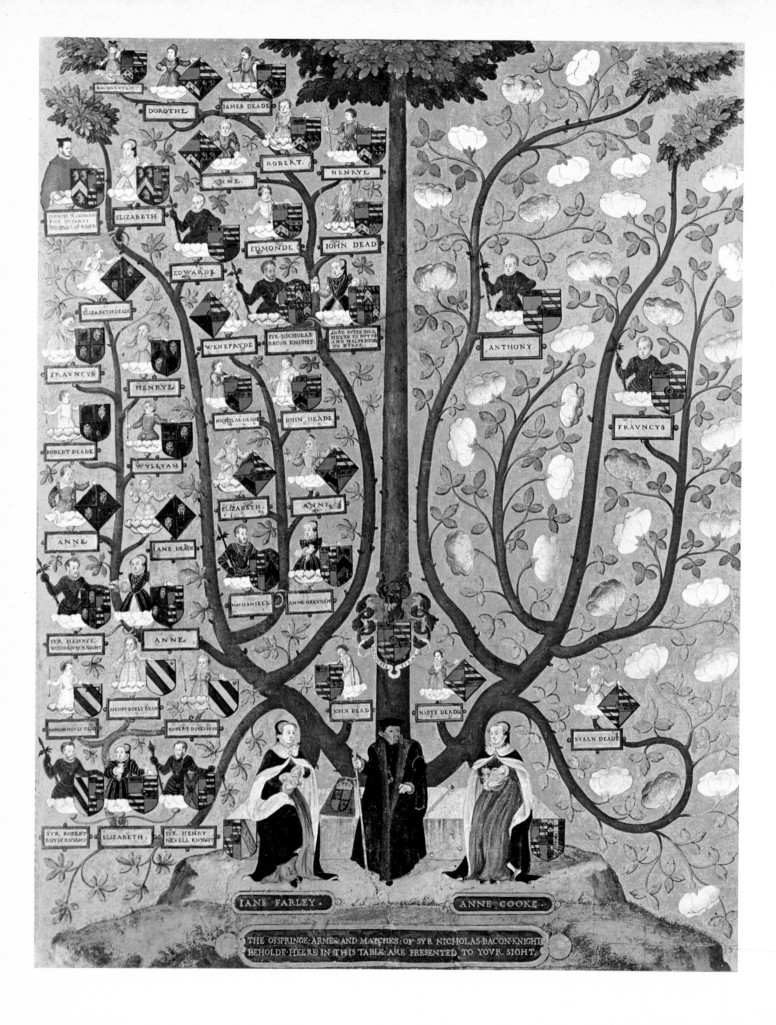

THE·OFSPRINGE·ARMES·AND·MATCHES·OF·SYR·NICHOLAS·BACON·KNIGHT
BEHOLDE·HEERE·IN·THIS·TABLE·ARE·PRESENTED·TO·YOVR·SIGHT

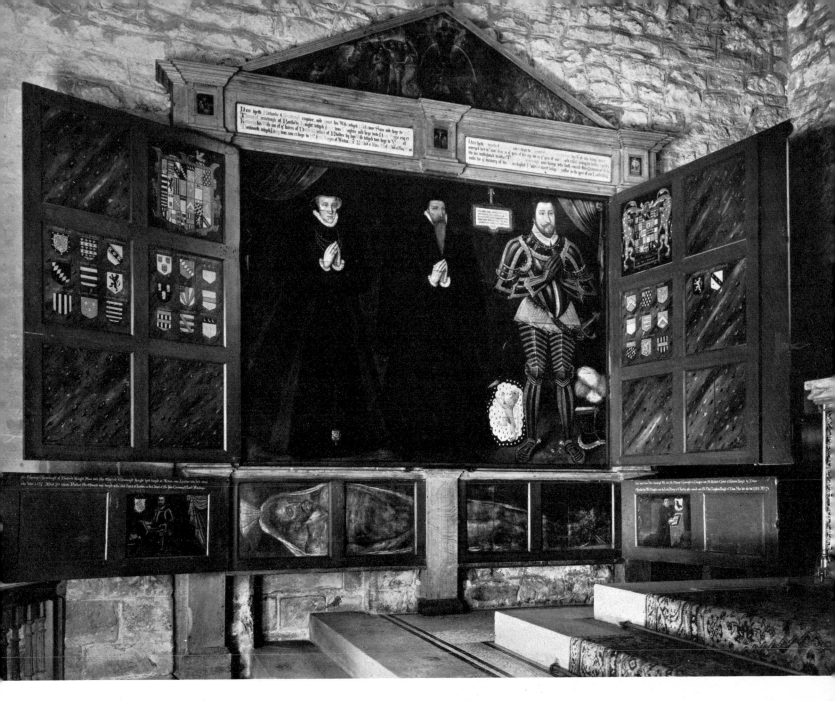

Above, MELCHIOR SALABOSSH, *Cornewall Monument,* Burford Church, 1588. By permission of Burford Church Council, Worcestershire.

is analysed at length as such in Burton's classic *Anatomy of Melancholy* in 1621. It pervades Hilliard's miniatures, and sets into classic poses – head on hand – many life-scale portraits: thus in the portrait of *John Donne* the poet appears appositely shadowed by his best black hat, and the mood is pointed by an inscription.

Apart from portraiture, subject pictures remain very rare through the second half of the sixteenth century. A number surely still lurk in country houses with generic labels as Flemish or Dutch School, but specifically English survivors of any quality are very few. They repeat mostly pietistic themes, such as the Seven Ages of Man, and an outstanding one of high quality is the *Allegory of Man, c.* 1570 at Fawns Manor (overleaf). But by about 1600 there is various evidence of increased concern for painting as painting. Hilliard's *Treatise* is eloquent on this, and likewise are Haydock's translation, of 1598, of Lommazo's influential work and the publication of Sidney's *Defense of Poesie*, 1595, with its often explicit parallel between poetry and painting. The connoisseur and collector is, in the modern sense, in sight too: that various virtuoso, Sir Henry Wotton, in Venice; in London the mysterious merchant Andreas de Loo collecting Holbeins; or, in a more down-to-earth English manner with

Left, Artist unknown, *The Tree of Jesse. Sir Nicholas Bacon and family,* 1578. Raveningham Hall, Norfolk. By permission of Sir Edmund Bacon.

109

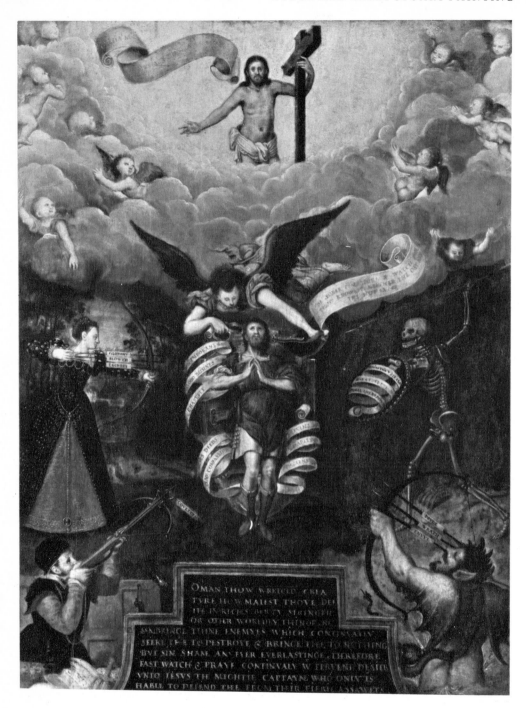

Artist unknown, *Allegory of Man*, c. 1570.
Reproduced by permission of Mr Derek Sherborn.

a hard sense of values, Robert Sidney (Earl of Leicester) shipping home, in 1591, from
Holland, wines, blankets, and lastly 'certain pictures which I pray God may come
well to Penshurst, for they have cost me a good deal of money. There is one of Adam
and Eve, another of the birth of Christ, a St Gerome and the picture of Ernestus . . .'.
The first great collector, Arundel, was already busy, and the element that had been
so sadly lacking through Elizabeth's reign, that of direct, informed, sensitive and
spending patronage from the monarchy, was introduced by the brilliant brief-lived
Prince Henry and taken up *in excelsis* by his brother Charles I.

3

PAINTING UNDER THE STUARTS

Oliver Millar

On 25 November 1620 Tobie Mathew, who was living in exile in Flanders, and was in regular touch with Rubens, wrote from Antwerp to Sir Dudley Carleton, Ambassador at The Hague: 'Your Lordship will have heard how Van Dike his famous Allievo is gone into England, and that the Kinge hath given him a Pension of £100 per annum.' Four months earlier the Earl of Arundel, 'father of vertu in England', had received a letter from Antwerp in which the writer had described the progress Rubens was making on a portrait of the Countess with her suite. In a postscript he added that Van Dyck, a young man of one and twenty, whose parents were people of substance in the city, was constantly in the company of Rubens and was producing pictures which were 'scarcely less esteemed than those of his master'. If the Earl was hoping to persuade the young man to remove to London, his correspondent concluded, he would find it difficult, as Van Dyck was impressed by the fortune Rubens was amassing in Antwerp.

Van Dyck, nevertheless, was induced to spend the winter of 1620–1 in London: long enough to receive, in February 1621, a payment of £100 for special services performed for James I. In the same month he was granted, as the King's servant, leave to travel for eight months: leave of absence which the painter himself arbitrarily extended to eleven years. The time Van Dyck ultimately spent at the court of Charles I, from the early spring of 1632 until his death on 9 December 1641 on the eve of the Civil War, was to bring about a revolution in the development of painting in this country as dramatic as any other upheaval in that turbulent period in our history. His visits to London, although we know tantalisingly little of what he was doing at James I's court, must also be seen in the wider context of the rapid growth in connoisseurship and taste in court circles under the early Stuarts: a phenomenon which makes this perhaps the most spectacular phase in the staccato history of taste in England. Very broadly speaking the Reformation and the religious strife of the sixteenth century, coupled with Elizabeth I's parsimony, had cut England off from a full understanding of the main developments in the visual arts of Europe. Very little was known of the works of the great painters of the *seicento* and almost the only foreign painters to work in England, for any length of time, after the death of Holbein in 1543, were those who fled from religious persecution in France and the Low Countries to settle in London. But in the reign of James I, blest with 'the uninterrupted pleasures and plenty of twenty-two years peace' to which Lord Clarendon looked back many years later, an interest in the arts was fostered within the so-called 'Whitehall group' of connoisseurs and collectors. James I's consort, Anne of Denmark, and his dashing elder son, Henry, Prince of Wales, built up important collections of works of art which passed at their deaths into the possession of the younger son, the future Charles I. The royal favourites, the Earl of Somerset, the Pembrokes, and the 1st Duke of Buckingham, showed a taste for works of art characteristically opulent and flamboyant and were prepared to spend large sums on their collections. The grave and more scholarly Arundel filled the galleries and gardens of Arundel House in the Strand with pictures and statuary. Collections only slightly less magnificent were formed by the Feilding family and the Hamiltons. Perhaps the most remarkable tribute to the civilized atmosphere of the English court was paid by no less a connoisseur than Rubens, who wrote to Pierre Dupuy from London on 8 August 1629: 'This island, for example, seems to me to be a spectacle worthy of the interest of every gentleman ... not only for the splendour of the outward culture, which seems to be extreme ... but also for the incredible quantity of excellent pictures, statues, and ancient inscriptions which are to be found in this Court.'

No less important – and more important for the future of the arts in England – were the efforts made by these Jacobean and Caroline *cognoscenti* to attract foreign artists and craftsmen, regardless of their religion, to work in London and inevitably to raise the level of artistic excellence, albeit at the expense of the artists already established. Diplomats accredited to the capitals of the Continent, as well as special envoys and agents, were encouraged to visit the studios of painters and to invite painters to try their fortune in London. As early as 1611, for example, in the year after Prince Henry had received a gift of pictures from the States-General, we find Sir Edward Conway negotiating on the Prince's behalf with Miereveld, regarded then as 'the most excellent Painter of all the Low-Countries', and almost persuading him to enter the Prince's service. Although this particular project failed, Daniel Mytens, a no less distinguished Dutch portrait-painter, was working for Arundel by 1618 and a number of Dutch painters came for short periods to work in England: Hendrick Gerritsz. Pot, Lievens, Ter Borch, Vroom, Poelenburgh and Honthorst, for example. Contacts, no less fruitful, were established with painters in France, Italy and Spain where, as a young man in 1623, Charles I sat to Velazquez: a moment in the history of the English royal portrait almost as dramatic as the later commission to Bernini to carve his bust in marble. The King's interest, up to the Civil War, in distinguished artists from overseas sprang principally from his desire to find a painter for his personal service – Mytens, Honthorst, Rubens or, pre-eminently, Van Dyck – who could hold his own with any other court painter in Europe and satisfy the sophisticated tastes of a sovereign who had built up, by the time the halcyon years of his personal rule came to an end, a collection of contemporary, classical and renaissance works of art which is unsurpassed in the annals of English taste. Perhaps, if the Caroline court and its delicate culture had not been shattered by the Civil War, and if the court collections, and in particular the King's, had not been dispersed in the War and during the Interregnum, native English painting would have been seen to benefit dramatically from the King's patronage of the illustrious foreign painter. Only Samuel Cooper (1609–72) and William Dobson (1611–46) had the ability to absorb something of Van Dyck's sense of rhythm and movement; Dobson was perhaps the only English painter of importance who can be seen, in his technique, to have benefited from seeing something of the King's collection, especially his marvellous Venetian pictures. Royal patronage also put firmly into the hands of foreigners the most important commissions. The official likenesses of the early Stuarts, their consorts and children, the likenesses which were painted and repeated for presentation purposes, were made by foreigners. This set the precedent for the royal patronage given later, after the return of the Stuarts at the Restoration, to Lely, Wissing and Kneller: a practice which ultimately provoked the chauvinistic insistence by Lord Halifax, in the reign of George I, that an important royal commission should be given to an Englishman, Sir James Thornhill, and not to the Venetian, Sebastiano Ricci, a more accomplished artist whose claims were put forward by a much-travelled magnifico, the Duke of Shrewsbury. During the Stuart period the English-born painter worked, in the main, under the shadow of, and often in open rivalry with, the well-placed and highly favoured exotic from abroad.

If his *The Continence of Scipio* at Christ Church is the picture ('one Great Piece being Scipio') which Van Dyck painted for Buckingham during that obscure first visit to the English court in the time of James I, it could, with its flowing rhythms and odd, melancholy air, only have been comprehended and appreciated within a limited circle. Its subtle evocation of Rubens and Veronese shows a sophistication far beyond the powers of the painters whom Van Dyck would have encountered in London. Nor was there, in the Protestant capital, and in a country where the walls of houses were still on the whole small or hung with tapestry, any demand for history pieces and religious subjects of the kind Van Dyck had been producing in Antwerp under Rubens's eye. It is indeed tempting to suggest that James I required Van Dyck, experienced in producing designs for tapestry, to supply patterns for his new tapestry factory at Mortlake. It was, however, the painting of portraits that was – and remained – in all its aspects, the principal task facing painters in England during the Stuart period. Peter Lely (1618–80), arriving from Holland in the 1640s, received the sympathy of his friend William Lovelace for English patrons' obsession with 'their own dull counterfeits' and their lack of interest in the higher genres or in the small mythological subjects which Lely had painted with no apparent success.

In scale, the seventeenth-century portrait ranged from the miniature – a tiny,

SIR ANTHONY VAN DYCK, *The Continence of Scipio*, c. 1620–1.
By permission of the Governing Body of Christ Church, Oxford.

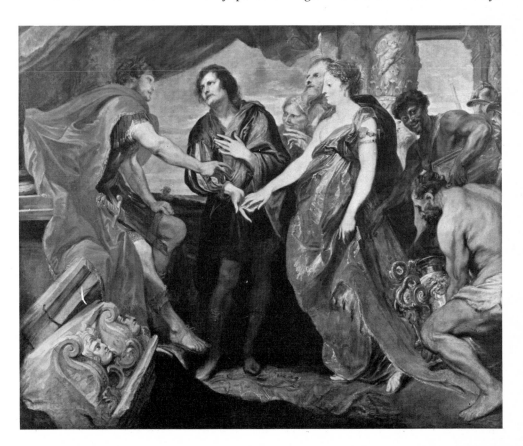

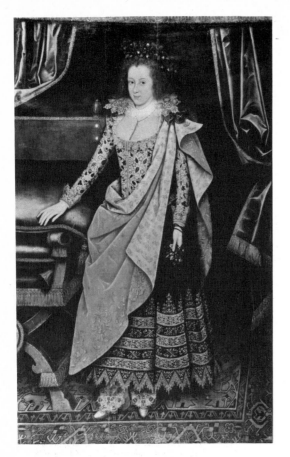

personal and very special image – to the great presentations in family groups, equestrian portraits or on the walls and ceilings of royal palaces or the houses of the richer nobility: presentations that displayed the power of a family or dynasty in a theatrical baroque fashion. There was also, throughout the period, a steadily increasing demand for straightforward portraits: for family collections, for the formation of historical and family portrait-galleries, for fraternities of all kinds, for City Companies and for University Colleges. With this increased demand came a new professional approach by the most successful and business-like portrait-painters, who organized a form of production-line which could incorporate the help of a band of studio assistants and, by the increasing standardization of the actual size of canvas – the head-and-shoulders, the half-length or the full-length – would in turn have helped the makers and stretchers of canvases, and the makers of frames, to increase their output.

Under the early Stuart painters at court seem to have become bound to the service of particular patrons. The younger Marcus Gheeraerts (fl. 1590–1635) brought over to London by his father from Bruges in 1568, was painting official royal portraits between 1609 and 1618 and, perhaps until his position was challenged by Paul van Somer (c. 1576–1621/2), was Queen Anne of Denmark's favourite painter. He was a more sensitive artist than his rivals; even his most elaborate portraits, such as the full-length, painted in 1611, of the Duchess of Richmond, are more sensitive than the elaborately ornate full-lengths of the Jacobean period, with their hard, opaque texture and rigid composition. The splendidly decorative quality of such pieces, of which the finest may have been produced by William Larkin (fl. 1610–20) or in his studio, should be seen perhaps as an essential element in the decoration of a lavish Jacobean interior: the series produced for the 1st Earl of Suffolk would have been entirely suitable for the embellishment of Suffolk House at Charing Cross or his huge new palace at Audley End. Gheeraerts's portraits are consistent throughout in their delicacy: a delicacy of touch as well as of tone and characterization. Details of costume and accessories, and a particularly attractive and distinctive form of inscription, are painted with a no less delicate attention. There is an innate modesty which was inherited by Cornelius Johnson and may have unfitted Gheeraerts temperamentally for sustaining his position at court. From the end of 1616 until his death, very early in 1622, the Fleming, Van Somer, was a serious rival. He almost certainly usurped Gheeraerts's place as the Queen's painter. His full-length of her, painted in 1617 (opposite), is broader and more vigorous in handling, and stronger in tone, than Gheeraerts's slightly earlier portraits of her (versions are in the royal collection and at Woburn) which looks immediately old-fashioned by contrast. It is on a big scale; it is an elaborate statement of the Queen's taste in building, her position in society and her love of the chase; and the figure is set more convincingly in its landscape setting than are Gheeraerts's sitters. The portrait marks, indeed, an important stage in the development in England of the portrait in a pastoral setting. Although he survived Van Somer by many years and died indeed four years after Van Dyck had settled in London, Gheeraerts never regained court patronage. He seems to have found his later patrons among country gentlemen and scholars such as William Camden. His later portraits show no loss in their quality and carry an archaic, and by now provincial, charm into the age of Van Dyck. The career of Robert Peake seems to have followed the same course. The favoured painter of Prince Henry, he produced ambitious portraits for his patron (p. 116) but his later works, which are recorded as late as 1635, remain untouched by Van Dyck's influence and perpetuate an element of an almost Elizabethan style down to the eve of the Civil War.

Daniel Mytens (c. 1590–d. 1647) was far the most distinguished portrait-painter working in London before Van Dyck arrived for the second time. Trained in The Hague, probably the protégé in England of the Earl of Arundel, he painted James I, was taken up by Buckingham and the already perceptive Prince Charles, and painted

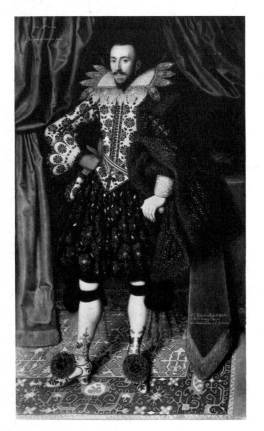

Above, MARCUS GHEERAERTS II, *Frances, Duchess of Richmond,* 1611.
By permission of Viscount Cowdray.
Below, Attributed to WILLIAM LARKIN, *Richard Sackville, 3rd Earl of Dorset,* 1613.
The Greater London Council
Ranger's House, Blackheath.

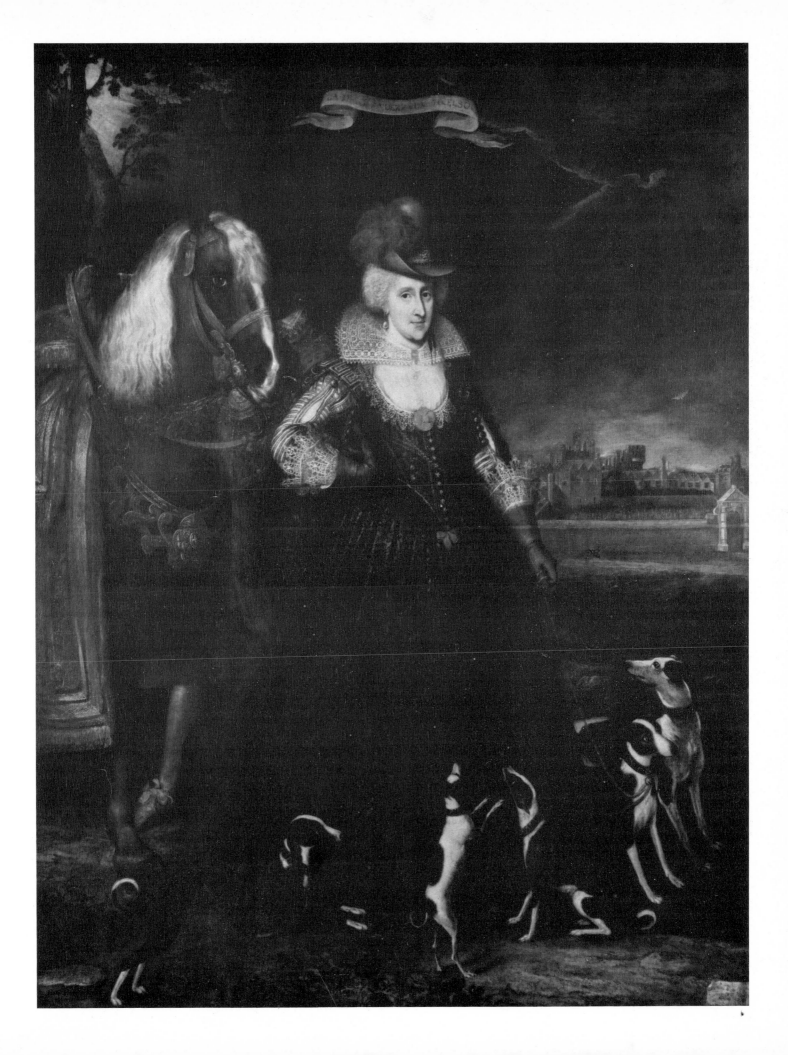

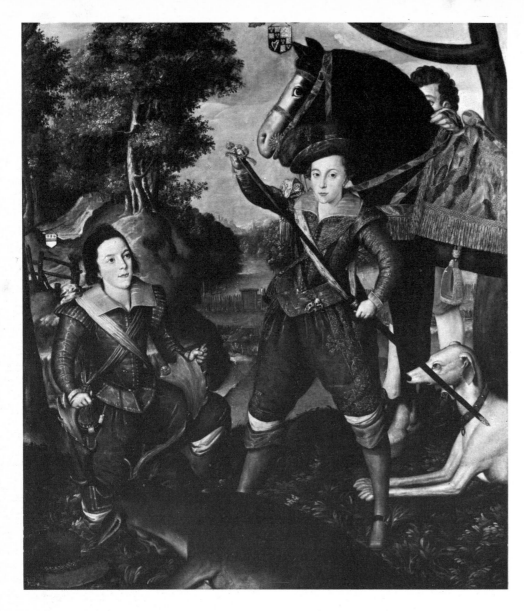

ROBERT PEAKE,
Henry, Prince of Wales, in the Hunting Field,
c. 1606–7.
Royal Collection.
By gracious permission of
Her Majesty the Queen.

the official royal portraits for him until he was in turn superseded by Van Dyck. The earliest portraits which Mytens painted in London show a certain confusion in the handling of the space between the sitter and the background, but in his mature portraits the sitters stand with assurance against a lucidly constructed, and often very simple, background, and enveloped in a tangible atmosphere more real than the cold and airless light of the full-blown Jacobean portraits. His handling of paint, which one can study clearly in his smaller pieces, is direct and sensitive and the texture of the paint is full and creamy: evidence of his training in the neighbourhood of a painter such as Ravesteyn in The Hague. His nature remained essentially Dutch, but no Dutch portrait-painter, and no court painter with the exception of Velazquez, was painting in the 1620s full-lengths of such grave and reticent distinction.

Mytens had the humiliation of seeing at least one of his important pieces painted on commission from the King revamped – and conceivably overpainted – by Van Dyck in 1632. There is almost no trace of Van Dyckian influence on his work, although occasionally a sitter such as the Earl of Holland (N.P.G. and Drayton House) will turn away from the spectator. Cornelius Johnson, on the other hand, attempted to ape Van Dyck's elegance in one or two full-lengths painted in the 1630s and, after his departure for Holland in 1643, imparted a not very congenial, Van Dyckian elegance to his solid Dutch sitters. Although he was one of the King's 'Picture Drawers' and had painted Charles I, Johnson's most accomplished portraits were

Previous page, PAUL VAN SOMER,
Anne of Denmark in the Hunting Field, 1617.
Royal Collection.
By gracious permission of
Her Majesty the Queen.

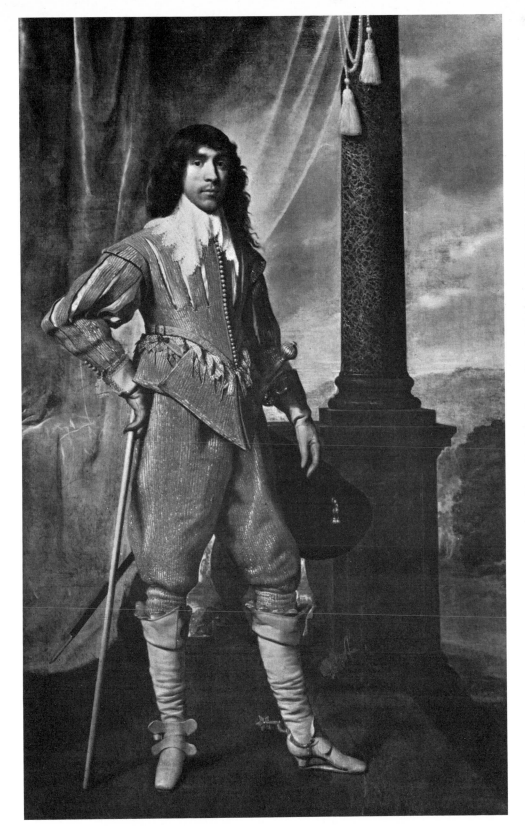

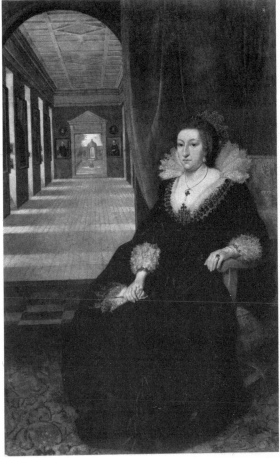

Above, DANIEL MYTENS,
Aletheia, Countess of Arundel, 1618.
By permission of
the Duke of Norfolk.

Left, DANIEL MYTENS, *James, 1st Duke of Hamilton,* 1629.
By permission of the Duke of Hamilton.

painted for patrons outside the court circle. A less robust painter than Mytens, he produced a succession of charming portraits, many set within the painted oval, which are reminiscent of Gheeraerts in mood and even in style; but they are stronger in design and more accomplished in handling. His earliest portraits are opaque in texture (and often painted on panel); but his later works are soft and atmospheric and show a lovely range of sensitive and silvery colour (p. 118). In the quiet charm and consistent integrity of Johnson's portraits one is often reminded of these qualities in Allan Ramsay a hundred years later; and it is not fanciful to see in

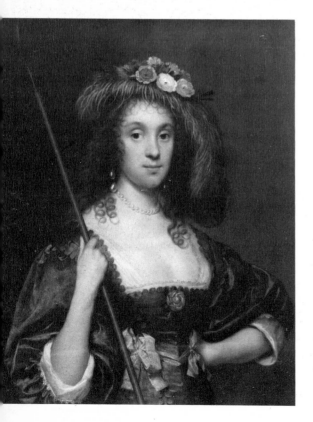

Above, CORNELIUS JOHNSON,
Sir Alexander Temple, 1620.
Collection of Mr and Mrs Paul Mellon.

Below, CORNELIUS JOHNSON,
Anne Uvedale, Mrs Henslowe, 1635.
Collection Ralph Verney.

Johnson's portraits of the 1630s a reflection of the lives of the quiet country families which we read of in the Verney or Oxenden letters.

Although they were foreigners by birth, Gheeraerts and Cornelius Johnson reveal or develop qualities in their work which can be described as English: a certain fragility, restraint and amateurishness which are in contrast with the assurance of Mytens and the consummate ease and grandeur of Van Dyck. Other, less familiar, painters worked in the same Anglo-Netherlandish style: the style in which an increasingly English spirit pervades formal designs which are Netherlandish in origin. The rare portraits of Abraham van Blijemborch and the monogrammist VM are at times close, respectively, to Van Somer and Johnson. A Flemish, but Scottish-born painter called Adam de Colone is beginning to emerge as an artist with a fashionable practice in Scotland and London, who painted an important likeness of the King in 1623 and whose portraits, painted (at the present moment of knowledge) between 1622 and 1628, are like rather boney Scottish reinterpretations of Van Somer. Portraits by John Eycke are related in pattern to Mytens and Johnson. The almost equally rare Johann Priwitzer painted a set of portraits of the Russell children which are close in format to Johnson. George Geldorp's early portraits, such as the full-length of the 2nd Earl of Salisbury, are very near to Mytens, but in his later years he was to be associated successively with Van Dyck and Lely.

Van Dyck, on his return to London in 1632, was warmly welcomed by the King. He was established in a house at Blackfriars and granted an annual pension of £200. As an elegant and accomplished gentleman and an artist of wide experience he would have claimed the social standing that had been accorded to Rubens, who had been warmly welcomed by the King in London on a short diplomatic visit three years earlier. By comparison with the portrait-painters whom he found working in London, with their predominantly Dutch and Protestant backgrounds, Van Dyck had spent a long time in Italy and had worked for princes of the Church and for the Genoese nobility. Between leaving Italy and coming to London he had produced, in addition to a succession of great portraits, a number of religious and mythological subjects, many of them on a large scale. With the incalculable advantage of a training in Rubens's studio, he had then soaked himself in contemporary and sixteenth-century Italian painting and had a particular admiration for the work of Titian, the painter for whom Charles I had had a special love since his youth and, in particular, since his visit to Spain in 1623 had enabled him to see a great collection of his works. In Van Dyck the King would have felt that at last he had at his command a painter who was the equal of any court painter in Europe, and who was steeped in the artistic traditions which by now particularly appealed to him.

As a painter Van Dyck was in a different world from that of Mytens or Johnson. He had learnt as a boy to design on a scale on which they had never been expected to work. The big groups, of the royal family in 1632 or the Pembrokes a few years later (p. 120), are magnificent theatrical statements of dynastic greatness, which can still, in the case of the Pembroke group, extend and enrich an architectural space in the full baroque manner; they were, in fact, planned carefully by the artist and patron to fill an actual space in the design of an interior from which they could command attention. Van Dyck was, moreover, the master of a superb technique and a most sophisticated palette. His touch could be nervous and refined, sometimes with the delicacy of watercolour, if the subject required it, or bold and richly Venetian. His range of tone, with its lovely harmonies of silvery greys and blues, whites, pinks and greens, his lustrous blacks and occasional glowing golden brown is, to a considerable extent, influenced by the great Venetians; yet both his handling and colour – and so often the mood of the portrait – foreshadow such Rococo painters as Watteau and Gainsborough. Even more revolutionary, perhaps, seen in the context of contemporary painting in England, was the flowing movement he gives to his figures which,

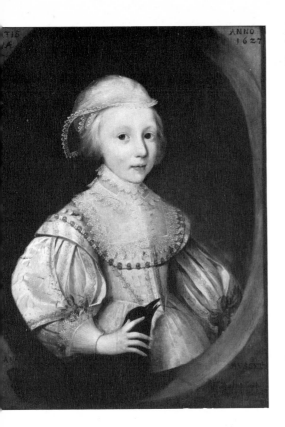

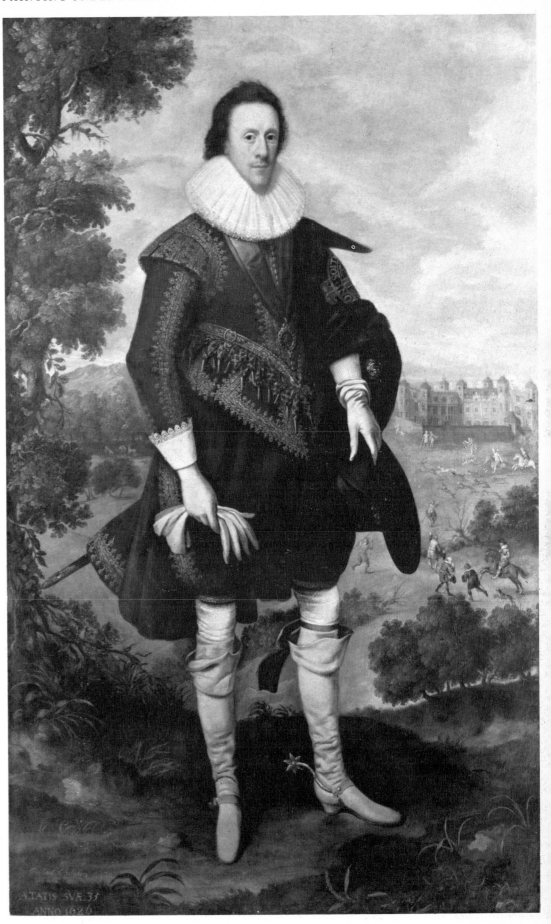

Above, JOHANN PRIWITZER,
Lady Diana Russell, 1627.
Woburn Abbey.
By permission of the Duke of Bedford.
Right, GEORGE GELDORP,
William, 2nd Earl of Salisbury, 1626.
Hatfield House.
By courtesy of the Marquess of Salisbury.

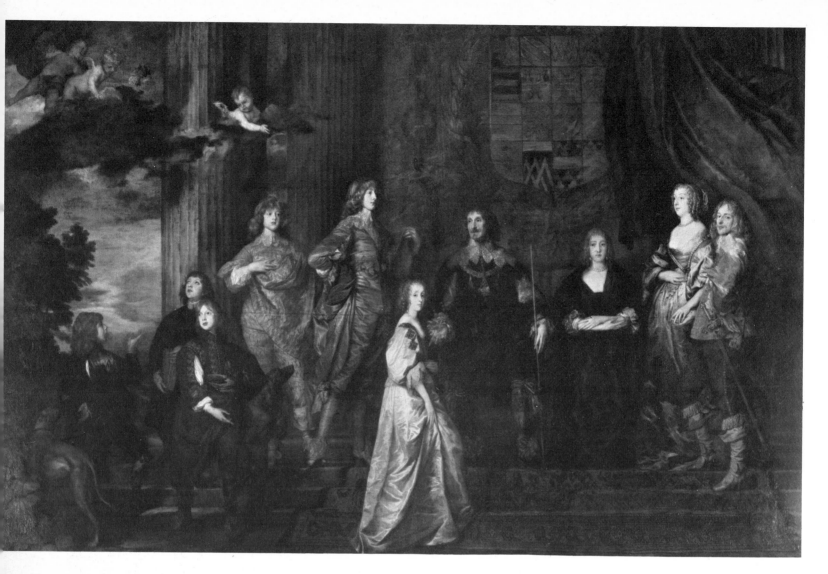

SIR ANTHONY VAN DYCK, *The Family of Philip, 4th Earl of Pembroke, c.* 1634–5.
Wilton House.
Collection of the Earl of Pembroke.

with his rich and shimmering surface and his ennobling and romantic treatment of his subjects, transformed the appearance of the men and women who had earlier sat to Mytens or Johnson. In Mytens's portraits there is never (with, as we have seen, possible exceptions at the end of his career in England when he would have been influenced by Van Dyck) any movement down the line of the figure away from the standard angle at which it is placed in relation to the surface. The Countess of Monmouth, for instance, in Mytens's portrait of her *c.* 1620, is a solid, very Dutch, but convincing figure, set firmly in space; in Van Dyck's full-length she glides imperceptibly across the canvas, against a lovely, Gainsborough-like, backcloth of foliage and hanging curtain. Even more complete is the metamorphosis between Johnson's quiet portrait of Sir Thomas Hanmer and Van Dyck's wonderful creation, which seems to be a bridge between Titian and Gainsborough (p. 122).

Van Dyck's greatness as a designer on a large scale, and his skill in combining elements from his own experience and training with the predilections of his royal patron and the traditional demands on a painter in court service, appears most impressively in the two large equestrian portraits of the King, riding out of a wood in the National Gallery and through a triumphal arch in the royal collection, and in the portrait of the King in the hunting-field, in the Louvre (p. 125). The transfiguring power of Van Dyck's imagination and his sensitivity towards the King's personality and taste create an apparently new and infinitely grand image which is, in fact, subtly distilled from earlier elements in English royal portraiture: from equestrian images in engravings or on the Great Seal, from earlier essays in the outdoor sporting portrait, from the painter's own knowledge, from his years of study and travel and, afresh, from the pictures, principally those by Titian, which he saw in the new English collections, and from the stimulus of his patron's cultivated mind: the whole expressive perhaps, though this can be overlaboured, of the ideals of courtly love, heroic behaviour and romantic melancholy which coloured some aspects of civilization of the Caroline court.

The statement by painters of the ideals which affected Charles I's attitude to the arts reached its most sumptuous form in the canvases painted by Rubens for the ceiling of the Banqueting House at Whitehall. The commission had been in the minds of the painter and his royal patrons as early as 1621; but the iconography of the ceiling may not have been worked out in detail until Rubens actually met the King in London in 1629. The dynastic achievements of the early Stuarts, the benefits which flowed from their rule, and their position as God's vicegerents on earth are proclaimed in magnificent neo-Venetian terms by Rubens. The ceiling is the climax of Inigo Jones's superb interior and an integral part of a great early English Baroque achievement in which the minds of architect, painter, carver and gilder work in harmony. To compare the ceilings of Rubens at Whitehall and (for the Duke of Buckingham) at York House, and the ceilings painted for the King and Queen by Orazio Gentileschi and Simon Vouet, with the monochrome repetitive patterned decoration produced in royal palaces by the Serjeant-Painter John de Critz, or with Rowland Buckett's work for the 1st Earl of Salisbury at Hatfield, is to experience the same shock as in comparing Van Dyck with Gheeraerts: to realize how the course of artistic development in England was being transformed by the enlightened, cosmopolitan patronage of Charles I and his fellow connoisseurs.

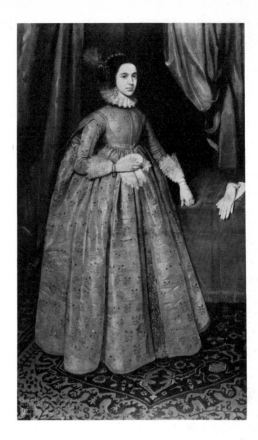

Above, DANIEL MYTENS, *Martha, Countess of Monmouth, c.* 1620.
By permission of Lord Sackville.
Below, SIR ANTHONY VAN DYCK,
Martha, Countess of Monmouth, c. 1635.
Private collection.

The break-up of the court, with the King's departure from London early in 1642, the Civil War, and the dispersal of the great Caroline collections, destroyed the world in which Inigo Jones and Van Dyck had worked. Without the stimulus of the visiting artists from overseas or the demands of patrons who had travelled on the Continent and the educative influence of collections of Renaissance and contemporary European works of art, painters in England seem, during these years, inevitably provincial. The significance of Edward Pierce's very bad ceiling in the Double Cube Room at Wilton is that the part allotted to painting in the design of the whole is influenced by what the Earl of Pembroke, a renegade Lord Chamberlain, had seen of the decorative schemes carried out for the King and Queen by Jones, Rubens and Gentileschi and of the very important scheme projected on the eve of the Civil War at Greenwich, where the Queen's House was to be enriched with a series of canvases by Jordaens and Rubens. Van Dyck's influence on painting in England was immediate. Distinguished painters, who had originally worked in the Anglo-Netherlandish manner, immediately tried to recapture his rhythms and movement. Adriaen Hanneman (*c.* 1601–d. 1671), for example, fell completely under his spell and, having at first painted rather quiet, essentially Dutch portraits of his English patrons, produced portraits which are often of an exaggeratedly Van Dyckian elegance. But it is interesting to note that a number of lesser painters, many of them still irretrievably anonymous, continued to work in the old-fashioned provincial vernacular: in the country, for the Inns of Court and the City Companies, and in the Universities. Such circles were largely untouched by the influence of the court, and, indeed, painters could gain employment there who had strongly resented the success of the distinguished foreign artists who were so much encouraged at court. The portraits of Gilbert Jackson (fl. 1622–40), for example, who painted portraits of scholars, writers and country gentlemen (p. 122), or Edward Bower (d. 1666/7), 'the famous painter at Temple Barr', have a naive quality which shows nothing of Van Dyck's influence; even the portraits which Bower painted in the 1640s only ape Van Dyck's mannerisms on occasion and in a very clumsy fashion. The same could be said of more obscure

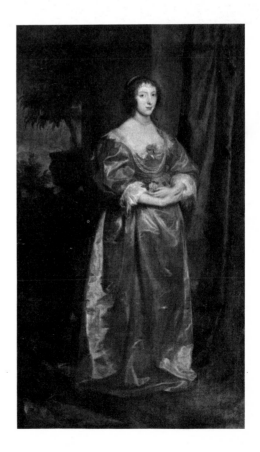

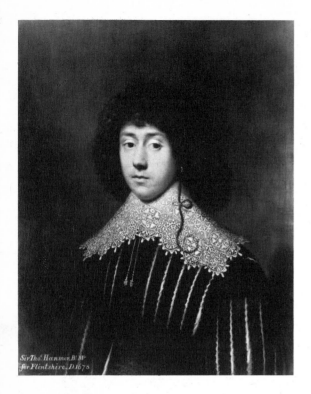

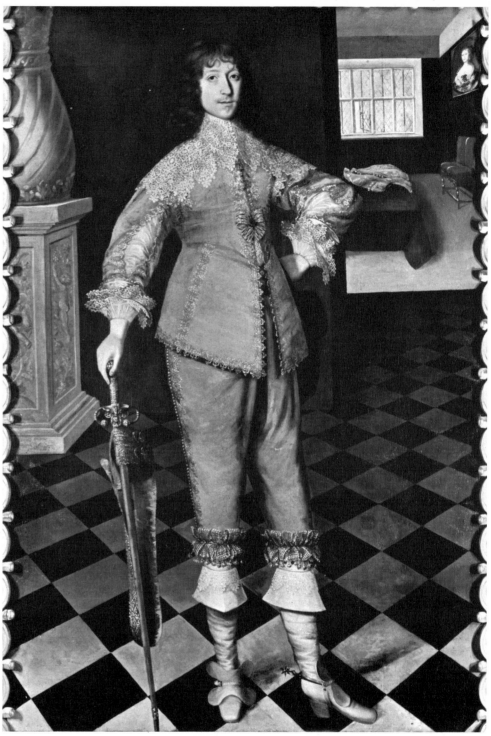

Above, CORNELIUS JOHNSON,
Sir Thomas Hanmer, 1631.
National Museum of Wales, Cardiff.
Right, GILBERT JACKSON,
John, Lord Belasyse (identity uncertain), 1636.
Scottish National Portrait Gallery, Edinburgh.
By permission of the Duke of Hamilton.
Below, SIR ANTHONY VAN DYCK,
Sir Thomas Hanmer, 1638(?).
Collection of the Earl of Bradford.

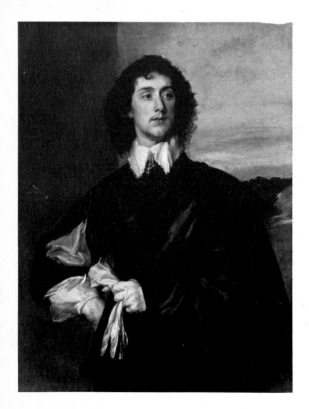

painters with local connections in the provinces: men like John Souch of Chester whose record of the death of Lady Aston, in 1635, is one of the rare and fascinating accounts, on a large scale, of English life at this period. Gradually the personality of these provincial painters is becoming clearer. John Parker, for example, was painting, in the 1630s, portraits of the Evelyn and Petre families, in an archaic manner. Peter Trovell (fl. 1636–41) was painting portraits of the Ottley family at the same period, but in a rather softer style. Edward Bellin (fl. 1630), Thomas Leigh (fl. 1643) and the monogrammists I.W. and J.H. also had connections in the provinces. During the 1640s there was an increasing tendency among painters to ape Van Dyck and to take

122

JOHN SOUCH, *Sir Thomas Aston at the Deathbed of his Wife,* 1635–6. Manchester City Art Gallery.

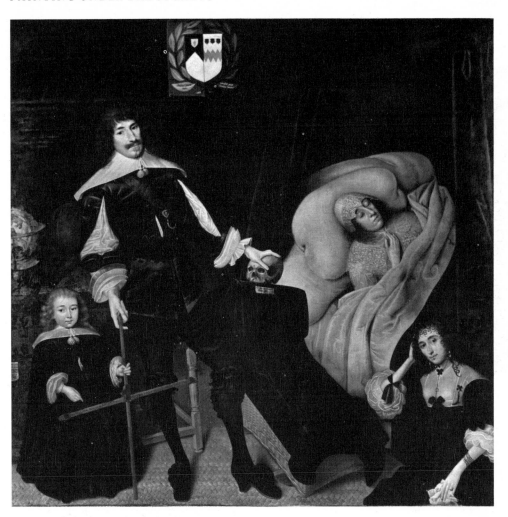

advantage of the rich repertory of patterns he had bequeathed to his successors. Paradoxically, Robert Walker (d. 1658), the painter most favoured by the parliamentarians, used Van Dyck's designs for his rather clumsy portraits of such men as Cromwell, Ireton, Lambert and Colonel John Hutchinson.

Van Dyck's influence was felt no less strongly, but was more subtly absorbed, in the development of painting in miniature. Charles I was almost certainly the first collector of miniatures in the modern sense. He assembled at Whitehall nearly eighty 'lim'd peeces' in cupboards in the Cabinet Room at Whitehall; by the end of the Stuart period the collection of miniatures, which is still at Welbeck Abbey, was being put together by the Duke of Newcastle and Lord Oxford. The miniature was, however, still conceived primarily as a small portable portrait: as an official present which could be sent as a token of esteem to foreign sovereigns and ambassadors, as were portraits 'in large', or as a little portrait which could be kept in a private cabinet, or worn as a token of a warmer affection. There are a number of portraits of widows – among them the Duchesses of Richmond and Buckingham – in which limnings of their dead lords are seen fastened over the heart. It is significant that when John Evelyn, in 1646, wished to present to his young wife an especially tender and meaningful portrait, he only turned to Walker for a portrait 'in large' because none of the miniaturists whom he wished to employ was available.

In the Stuart period the English miniature reached the second great peak in its development. The finest and most sensitive native-born portrait-painter in the period was a miniaturist, Samuel Cooper. At the court of James I the most successful miniaturist was Isaac Oliver whose brilliant surfaces, superb technique, meticulously

123

elaborate backgrounds, and vigorous characterization (p. 126) overshadow the quieter mood – and the odd lack of confidence – which one sees in Nicholas Hilliard's last miniatures. When Oliver predeceased Hilliard by two years in 1619, Hilliard had for some years been in financial difficulty. Oliver's sitters are often painted in masquing costume and his portraits have something of the brassy confidence that we see in the most elaborate of the Jacobean full-lengths. Cornelius Johnson, who was a close relation, painted miniatures in oil, and there are affinities between the work of Johnson 'in large' on the one hand and the miniatures of Peter Oliver (c. 1594–1647) and John Hoskins (c. 1593–d. 1665) on the other; just as Hilliard's delicate perception of character and fragile sense of design are reflected as much in the portraits of such native painters as Robert Peake as in miniatures by Hilliard's own son Laurence.

Peter Oliver's miniatures are gentler in mood than his father's, more painterly and suffused in a richer atmosphere (p. 127). In the placing of the figure and the treatment of the background there is an advance towards naturalism. He was commissioned by Charles I to paint for his Cabinet Room miniature copies of some of his finest Italian pictures. John Hoskins, the first important English-born Stuart miniaturist, whose earliest miniatures are very close in feeling to Cornelius Johnson or Gheeraerts, was employed, by the King and other patrons, to produce copies in miniature, often for distribution to friends, of Van Dyck's most popular or important portraits, to which he often gave backgrounds of his own designing. His later portraits, though they lack the weight and sheer technical mastery of Cooper, who was Hoskins's nephew and pupil, have a psychological penetration which can often remind one of the younger man's vision (p. 126).

Whether or not he painted under his uncle's eye the lively miniature of the Queen in masquing costume, Samuel Cooper revealed at an early age a technical assurance and a marvellous sense of colour, which place him in the first rank of English miniaturists. His portrait of Van Dyck's mistress, Margaret Lemon (p. 127), shows in its understanding of Baroque movement, a feeling for the air moving round the sitter, and, in its painterly touch, the extent to which Cooper had absorbed much from Van Dyck's example. Throughout his long career, moreover, Cooper never failed to present an individual, and often deeply moving, image of his sitter's character; he gives us, with a consistency attained by no other painter of his time, a searching commentary on what it was like to be an ordinary man or woman in that troubled age. His later portraits, which are sometimes larger in scale, show even greater technical ability, as well as a gain in psychological understanding. In some of his larger works, such as the magnificent set of unfinished heads in the royal collection, Cooper's touch has a nervous brilliance which can make one think of Gainsborough or Van Dyck. It is not surprising that he enjoyed during his lifetime a high reputation: 'in the highest degree of estimation, both in and out of the kingdom'.

Although in the history of taste and patronage in this country the Civil War and Interregnum may seem a watershed between the age of Van Dyck and the Restoration, it was an active and interesting period in the history of painting. From such sources as Sir William Sanderson's *Graphice*, published in 1658, or the notes made by the antiquary Richard Symonds in London in the early 1650s, it is clear that a considerable number of painters were active in the capital. The period saw, for instance, the emergence of Lely as the heir to Van Dyck, much of Cooper's finest work and the whole short career of the most interesting of English seventeenth-century painters, William Dobson.

Very little is known of Dobson's training, although in at least one picture, a copy of a painting by Matthias Stomer, he is seen to have been influenced, perhaps through the teaching of Francis Cleyn, by the Caravaggesque painters of Utrecht: painters whose works were well represented in the Whitehall collections. Van Dyck's

SIR ANTHONY VAN DYCK, *Charles I*, c. 1635. The Louvre, Paris.

124

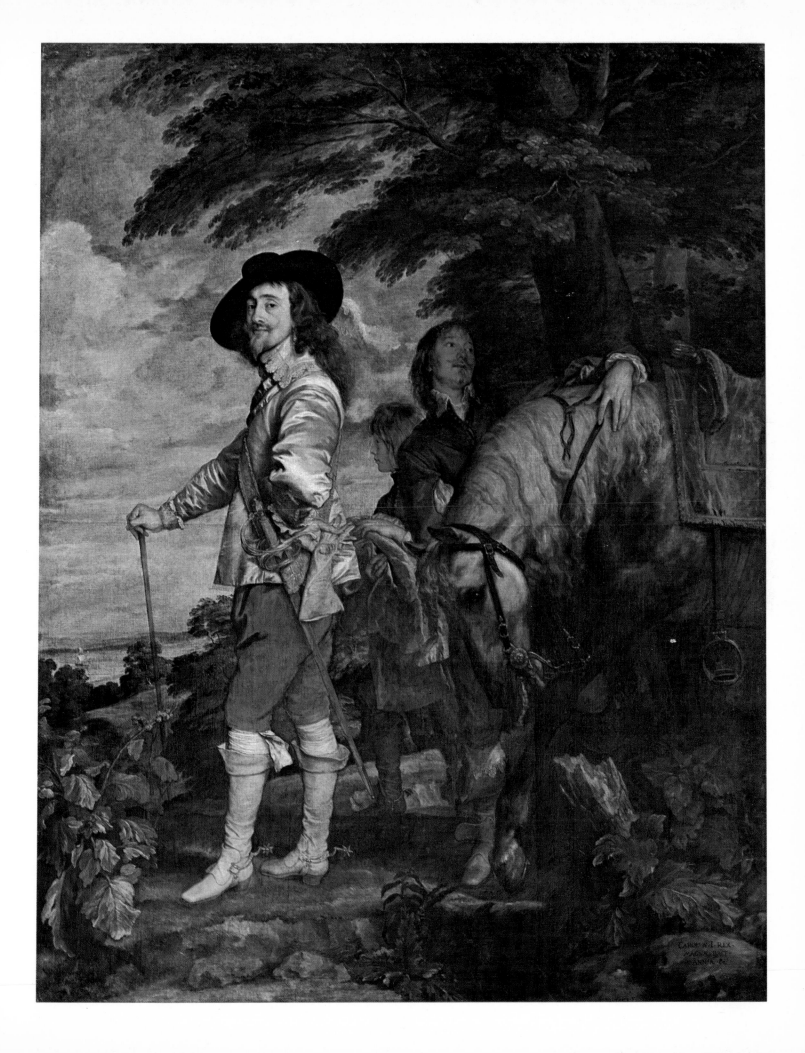

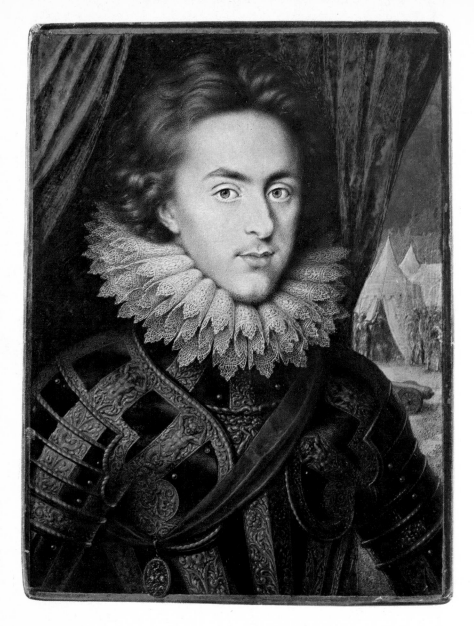

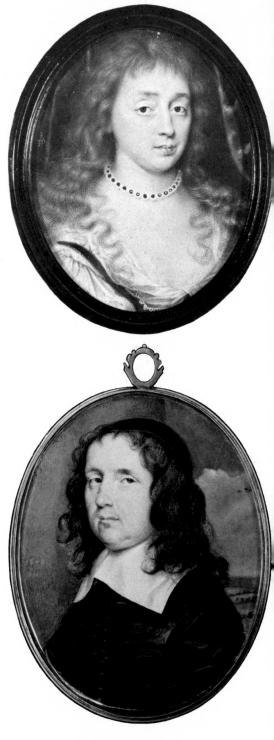

influence seems to have counted for less than the lessons Dobson could have absorbed at Whitehall from the King's collections, from friendship with his Surveyor of Pictures and from other members of the court circle. Of his working life we still know nothing before 1642, when he is found to be attached to the royalist wartime court at Oxford (where he painted the King, his eldest sons and a number of their adherents), and his death in poverty, in London, soon after the surrender of Oxford by the royalists. Dobson's earliest dated work (1642) is completely mature; his latest (1645) is thinner and less vigorous, as if the painter had been starved, in the unstable wartime conditions in which he worked, of fruitful outside influences; but Dobson's later works influenced such provincial painters as John Taylor and Robert Fisher. His approach to character is direct and honest; his paint is strong, rich and often ruddy in tone, rather dry in texture. In contrast with the elegant rhythms of Van Dyck, Dobson fills his canvases with accessories which point, in a rather self-consciously learned way, to the pursuits and inclinations of his sitter. The pattern of his well-known portrait of Endymion Porter (p. 129) is based on one of the Roman Emperors, by Titian, which Porter would have known well and Dobson may have seen, at St James's Palace in happier times; the gun, dog, dead hare and little page show Endymion as the country squire; the bust is almost certainly a head of Apollo and, with the frieze representing the visual arts, commemorates Porter's interest in literature and the arts. In two

Above left, ISAAC OLIVER,
Henry, Prince of Wales, c. 1612.
Royal Collection.
By gracious permission of
Her Majesty the Queen.
Top, JOHN HOSKINS,
Unknown Woman. Collection of
the Duke of Portland.
Above, JOHN HOSKINS,
Sir William Montague, 1656.
Collection of the Duke of Rutland.

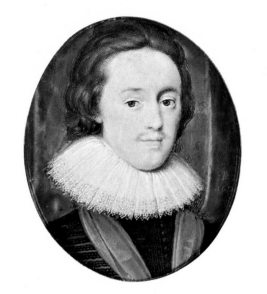

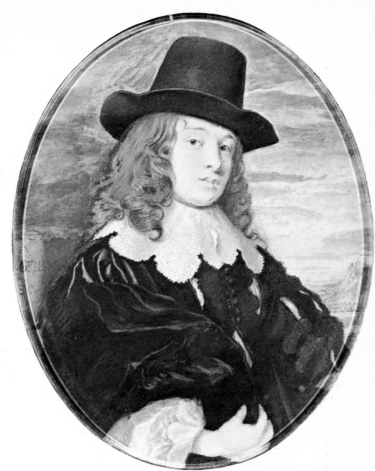

SAMUEL COOPER, *Thomas, Lord Clifford*
1672. Collection of Lord Clifford.

clumsily composed groups, both enigmatic in content, Dobson produced the first
English conversation-pieces on the scale of life (p. 133); the sombre and arresting *Sir
William Compton* (p. 134) is possibly the most accomplished full-length painting by an
Englishman before the advent of Hogarth. This obviously English spirit in portraiture
is felt in the earliest portraits by John Hayls (d. 1650), who was painting portraits, at
about this period, of both royalists and parliamentarians; but in Hayls there seems a
more definitely Van Dyckian element in handling and in design, and in his later work
there is likewise evidence that he had been influenced by Lely.

The return of the court in 1660 ushered in a revival of the cosmopolitan and
Catholic influences, which, in the earlier court, had so profoundly affected the arts.
Charles II and many of his chief courtiers encouraged painters from abroad; and their
admiration of France, in particular, fostered an exotic style at Whitehall. Very bad
painters like Simon Verelst, Henri Gascars or Philippe and Claude Vignon did far
better than they deserved because they were pushed by such patrons as the Duke of
Buckingham, the King's sister the Duchess of Orléans, or his mistress the Duchess of
Portsmouth. The more accomplished Flemish painter Jacob Huysmans (*c.* 1633–d.
1696) owed his original success to the support of the new Queen, Catherine of
Braganza. The affectations of these painters, their passion for crowding their designs
with accessories, the foppishness of their gestures, even, briefly, influenced Peter Lely.

In October 1661, when Van Dyck's annual pension was resuscitated for his benefit,
Lely had been in England for nearly twenty years. His family owned property in
The Hague; he himself had been trained in Haarlem. By 1647 he was well-established
in London, although, if we interpret aright the sympathetic verses of his friend
Lovelace, he had found no buyers for the little subject-pictures (p. 135), which he
painted in a style which is clearly Dutch but has something of the neo-Venetian, Van
Dyckian qualities which we find in the pictures painted slightly earlier in England by

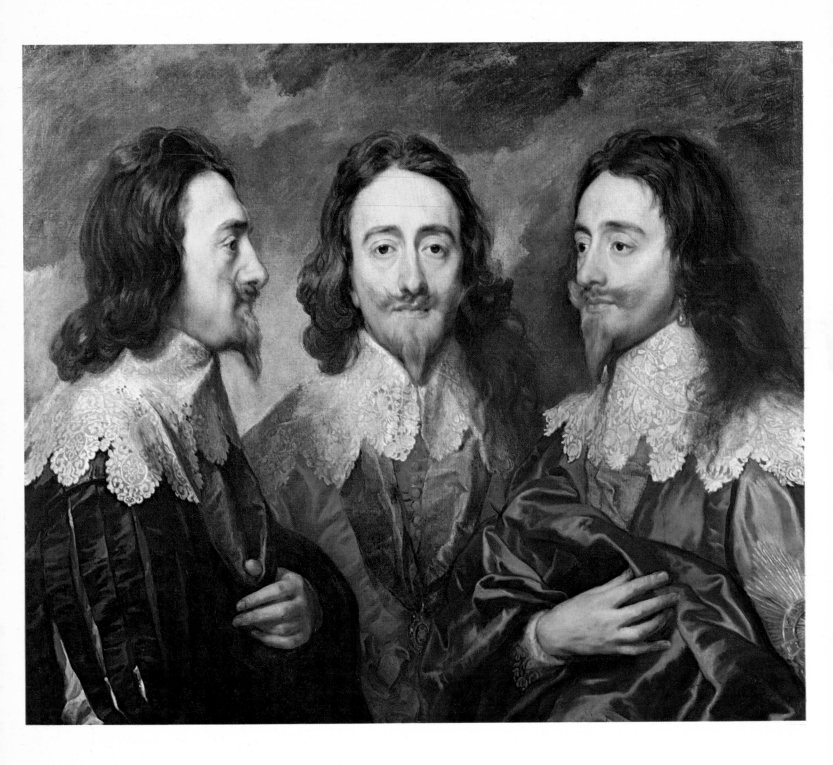

Above, SIR ANTHONY VAN DYCK,
Charles I in Three Positions, 1635–6.
Royal Collection.
By gracious permission of
Her Majesty the Queen.
Right, WILLIAM DOBSON, *Endymion Porter*,
c. 1643.
The Tate Gallery, London.

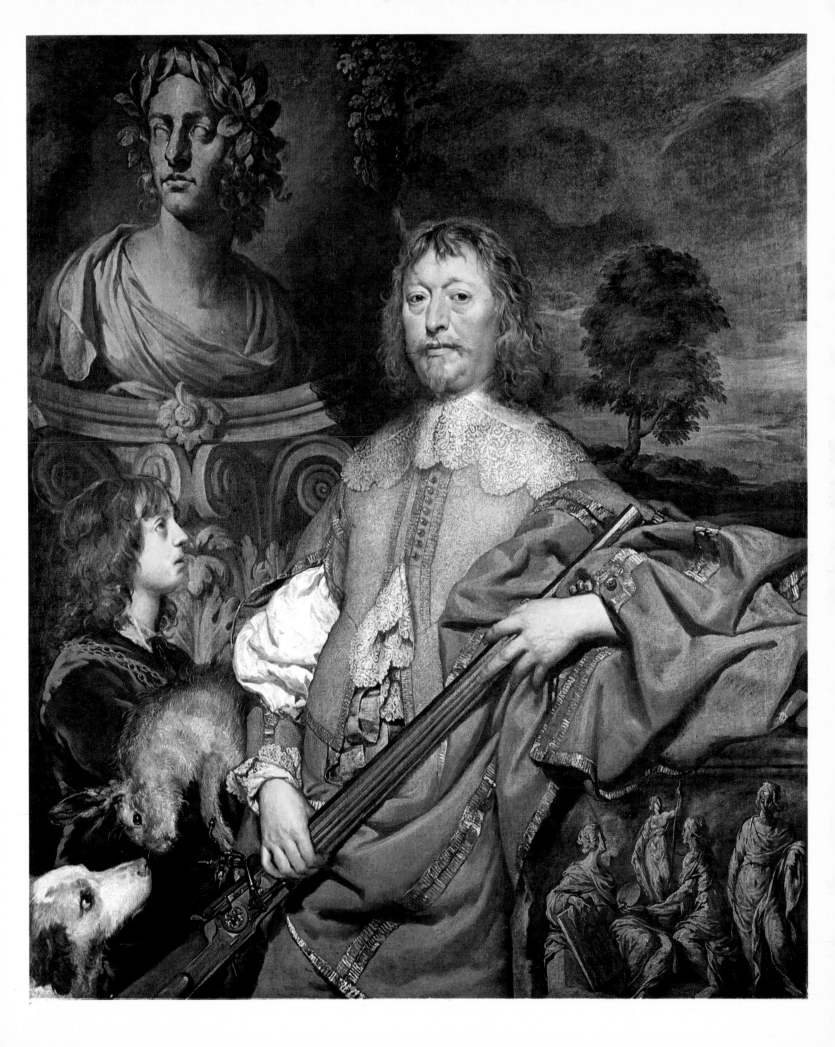

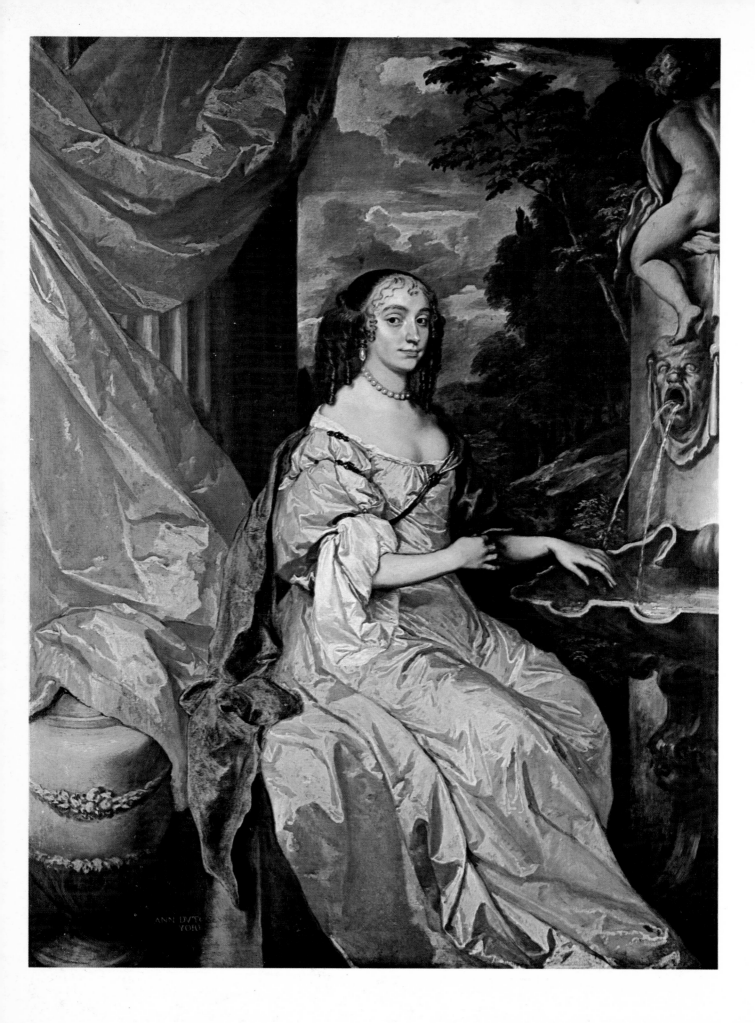

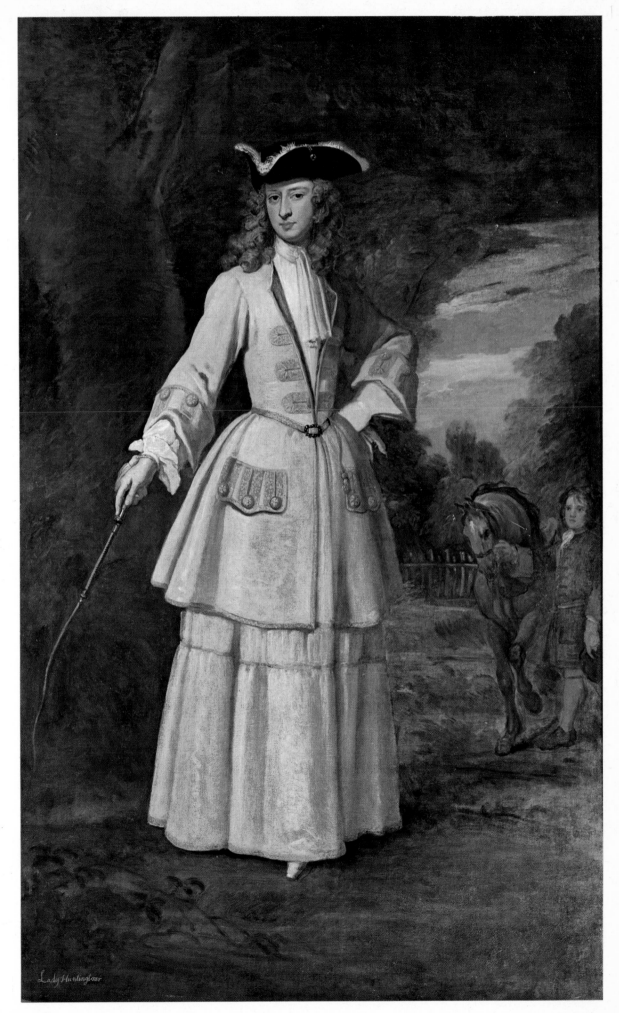

Left, SIR PETER LELY,
Anne Hyde, Duchess of York, c. 1660.
The Scottish National
Portrait Gallery,
Edinburgh.
Right, SIR GODFREY KNELLER,
Henrietta Cavendish,
Lady Huntingtower.
Ham House, Property of
the National Trust.

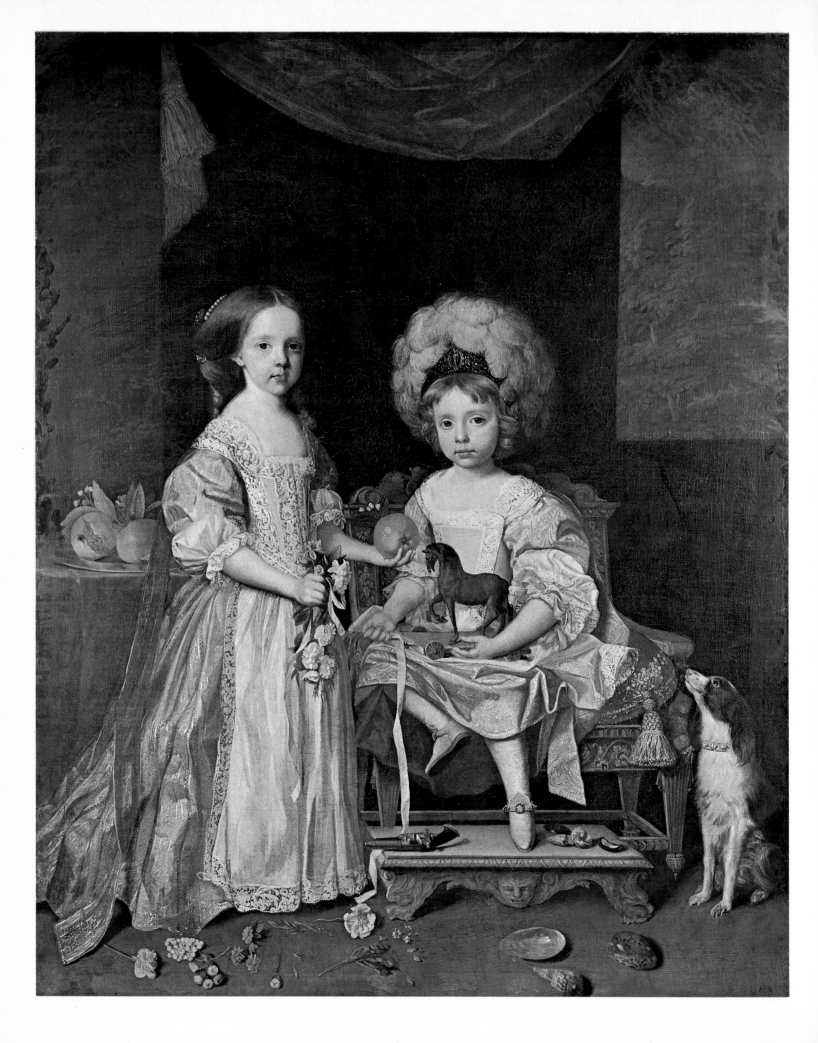

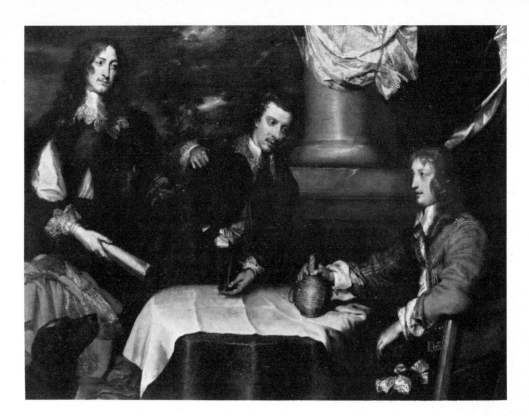

Left, JOHN MICHAEL WRIGHT,
*James, 4th Earl of Salisbury,
and his sister, Lady Catherine Cecil, c.* 1668–9.
Hatfield House.
By courtesy of the Marquess of Salisbury.
Right, WILLIAM DOBSON, *Prince Rupert with
Colonel William Murray and Colonel John Russell,
c.* 1644.
Private collection.

Frans Wouters. There is, in a group of portraits which may belong to his early years in England, a delightful freshness of vision which disappears from his later work. He was fortunate, by contrast with Dobson, who had been isolated at Oxford, to secure the patronage of a group of rich noblemen who had remained in London during the conflict and had been, in happier times, among the patrons of Van Dyck. Lely was very slow to mature, but by the mid-1650s proved himself to be a superb handler of paint and a sound draughtsman; his colour has a resonance that no other painter of the century in England can rival; and he ultimately succeeded in fusing Van Dyckian elegance with an innately Dutch sense of weight so as to produce portraits of rare splendour, or of an overbearing Van Dyckian ease. Hard-headed and practical, Lely lived in great state and organized a large studio practice which could cope with the enormous demands upon him. He frequently relied on his assistants to paint the costume, background and accessories in his portraits; there are portraits, principally in the 1660s and 1670s, where it is easy to detect the join between Lely's own painting of the head and a studio hand's completion of the rest of the figure; but what Lely painted himself was always assured and sensitive. His colours became increasingly muted, and his pigments thinner, towards the end of his life. His later portraits on a large scale, moreover, established the main conventions of fashionable portraiture almost to the end of the century. One sees in the *Duchess of Cleveland* at Goodwood (p. 135), for instance, how stereotyped the Van Dyckian manner has become: the flowing rhythms of the figure almost reduced to a two-dimensional and stagey image placed against a conventional backcloth made up of the accessories which Van Dyck had used so subtly.

Lely's personality dominated the Restoration scene almost as completely as Van Dyck's had done in the 1630s. Of his pupils the most interesting was perhaps the English John Greenhill. The portraits he painted before he came under Lely's auspices have a gentle reserve (p. 136) which lingers even in the portraits which he cast, in his later years, into a wholly Lelyesque mould. Greenhill came to an untimely end in 1676, and Lely's fashionable practice, and most of his patronage from the Crown, passed after his death into the hands of his fellow Dutchman Willem Wissing, whose own early death in 1687 helped to advance Godfrey Kneller (1646–1723) already, by

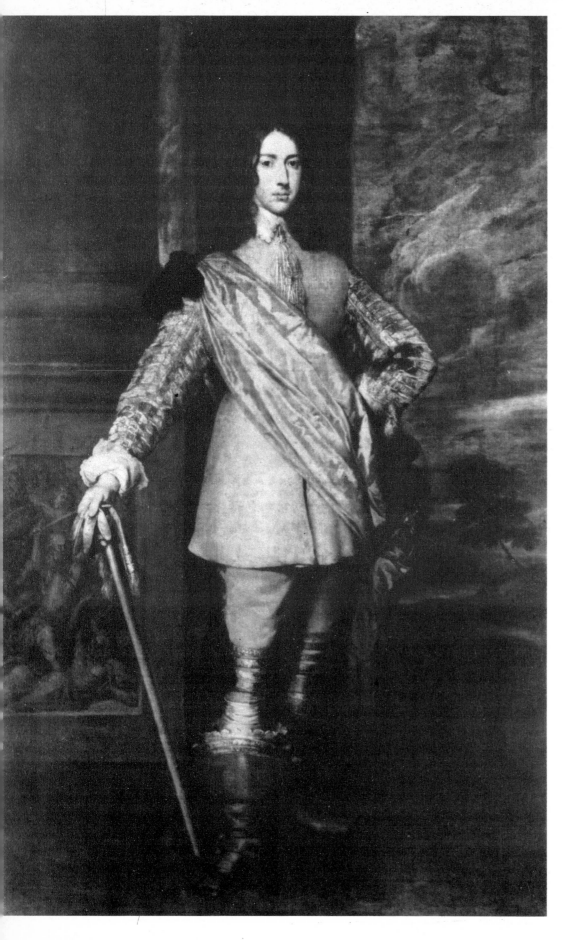

Left, WILLIAM DOBSON, *Sir William Compton,*
c. 1644.
Collection of the Marquess of Northampton.

134

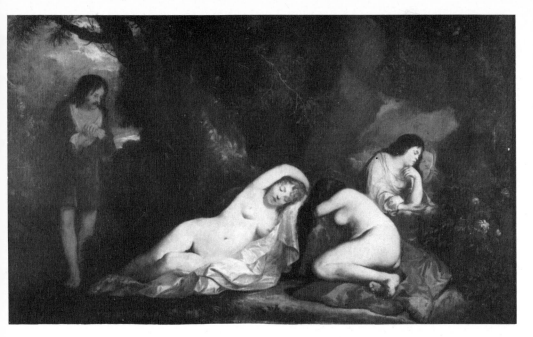

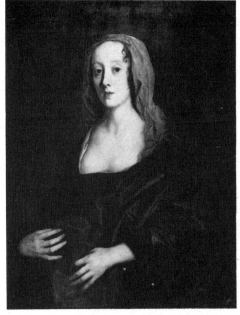

now, a formidable rival. Wissing's portraits are competently designed essays in Lely's late fashionable manner, close in all but a certain stridency of colour to John Riley (1646–91) and Kneller at the same period. Riley's heads, on the other hand, are perhaps the most truly English portraits of this period, as delicate in handling and perceptive in character as Cornelius Johnson's fifty years earlier, but the rest of the design is often stiffly put together, without the facility of Wissing or Kneller. This may partly have been owing to Riley's collaboration with John Closterman (fl. 1681–2) who, after Riley's death in 1691, produced some of the most ambitious large-scale Baroque portraits of the period. Among them are the large equestrian portrait (Chelsea Hospital) of the Duke of Marlborough, which was obviously influenced by the portrait of the 1st Duke of Buckingham by Rubens; classical portraits in the style of Carlo Maratti for the 3rd Earl of Shaftesbury; and the group of the Duchess of Marlborough and her children (p. 136), which is clearly influenced by Van Dyck's Pembroke family group. Riley's combination of sensitive portraiture with uncertainty over the broader problems of design was inherited by Thomas Murray (1663–1735) and Jonathan Richardson (1665–1745), whose portraits (p. 136) are firmly in the tradition that was to produce Hogarth and Reynolds. The two most important painters to stand rather outside the principal line of development between the emergence of Lely and the end of the century were the Dutchman, Gerard Soest (d. 1681), and the Scot, Michael Wright (1617–c. 1700). Soest was probably settled in London by 1650. He never gained fashionable applause and had nothing of Lely's social and professional ease; his portraits, with their odd mannerisms in colour, idiosyncratic feeling for personality and in the disposition of draperies, are never without a sombre and often touching seriousness (p. 136). He is perhaps the least conventional painter of the age. One finds the same unvarying honesty in the portraits of Michael Wright, who had been in Italy and the Low Countries during the Interregnum and enjoyed royal patronage after the Restoration. There is always, in Wright's portraits, something of the amateur. The charm of his likenesses is enhanced, for us, by the awkward two-dimensional quality of his designs – in comparison with Lely's supple ease – and the gaiety of his colour. His sitters often wear gay contemporary dress in contrast with the generalized draperies used by his more fashionable rivals. Wright probably lacked the toughness of temperament to be a successful painter and after 1688 his Catholicism would have been a grave liability. Among his more ambitious portraits are the spectacular full-lengths of Scottish and Irish chieftains (p. 137) in native garb.

Above left, SIR PETER LELY,
Cymon and Iphigenia, c. 1650.
By permission of Lord Sackville.
Above, SIR PETER LELY,
Portrait of a Lady, c. 1647.
Collection of Lady Aberconway.

Below, SIR PETER LELY, *Barbara, Duchess of Cleveland, c.* 1670.
Goodwood House, by courtesy of the Trustees.

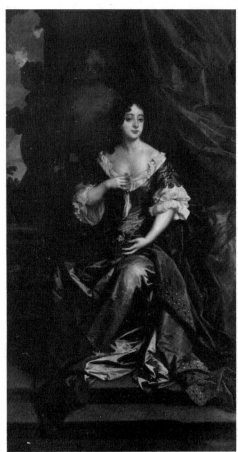

135

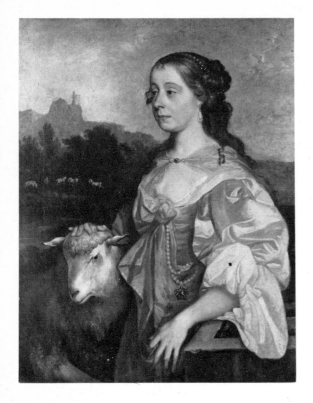

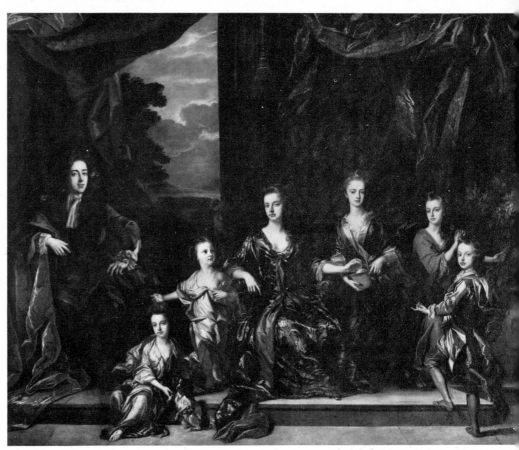

Above, JOHN GREENHILL, *Ann Cartwright with a Lamb, c.* 1665.
By permission of the Governors of Dulwich College.

Below, JONATHAN RICHARDSON, *Sir William Daines, c.* 1710.
Collection of Lord Barrington.

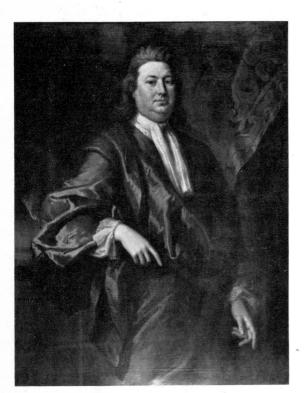

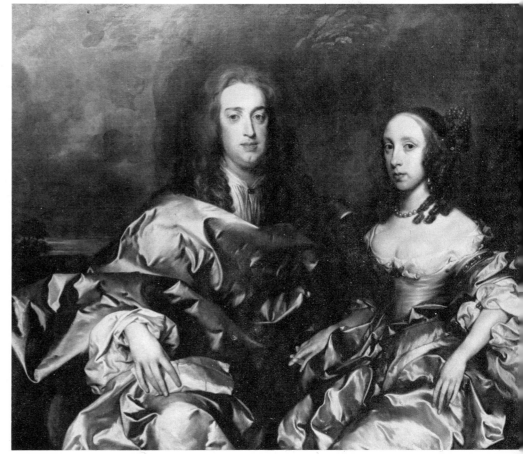

Left, JOHN CLOSTERMAN,
The Family of the 1st Duke of Marlborough, c. 1696.
By permission of the Duke of Marlborough.
Right, JOHN MICHAEL WRIGHT, *Sir Neil O'Neill,* 1680.
The Tate Gallery, London.

Left, GERARD SOEST, *Portrait of a Man, probably Sir Charles Waldegrave, and his Wife, c.* 1658.
By permission of Earl Waldegrave.

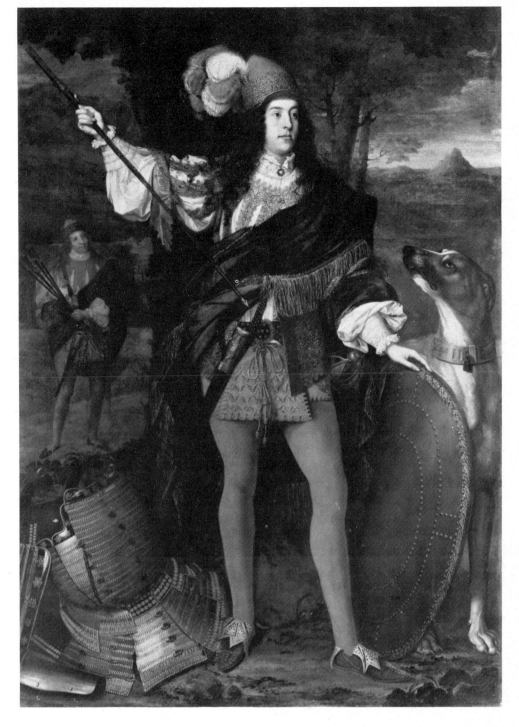

By 1680, the year of Lely's death and the year in which Wright signed his Irish chieftain with the title 'Pictor Regius', the young German portrait-painter, Godfrey Kneller, was already well placed in fashionable circles. Born in Lübeck, he had travelled and worked in Holland, Italy and Germany before coming to London in 1676. It is significant that a young painter from abroad seems to have come to England at this stage in the century under the auspices, not of a royal patron or a member of the court circle, but of merchants with connections in Hamburg. Kneller was reported to have had a 'longing' to see the works of Van Dyck in England, and an appreciation of pictures and the ability to buy great works of art and support young painters were now no longer the monopoly of the King and the court. Within a short time of his arrival, however, certainly by 1677, Kneller had made valuable

137

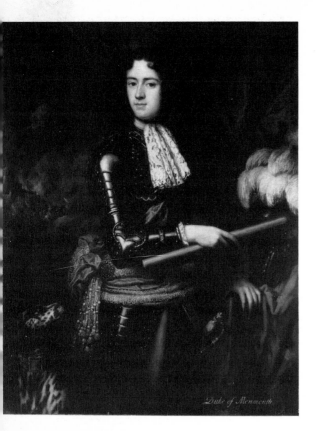

Above, SIR GODFREY KNELLER,
James, Duke of Monmouth, 1678.
By permission of the Duke of
Buccleuch and Queensberry.
Below, SIR GODFREY KNELLER, *Matthew
Prior,* 1700.
Trinity College, Cambridge.

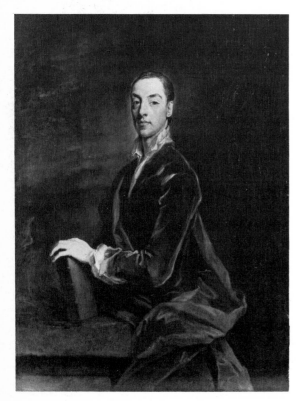

contacts at court. He painted thereafter every Sovereign from Charles II to George II and had almost a monopoly in the official state portrait between the reigns of James II and George I; he was sent abroad by Charles II to paint Louis XIV; he painted visiting ambassadors and heads of state; he was knighted by William III and made a baronet in 1715; he was a Knight of the Holy Roman Empire, received many other honours, lived in state in a country house at Whitton and was buried in Westminster Abbey. Confident and overbearing, he was, in a worldly sense, as grand a man as Van Dyck and he carried even further than Van Dyck and Lely the efficient organization of a large studio so as to produce a vast number of portraits.

The first portraits he painted in England are, like those he painted in Germany before coming to London, rather Dutch in texture and diffident in design. They have an unpretentious quality which would have seemed refreshing to those used to the mannerisms of Lely and his rivals. His earliest court portraits, such as the *Monmouth* of 1678, which marked a turning-point in his career, has the rather Frenchified affectations of his fashionable contemporaries. By the mid-1680s he was a mature and successful painter. Much of his work thereafter was uninspired, but he was at his best a brilliant craftsman: a superb draughtsman, a distinguished colourist and the master of a swift and vigorous brush. Many of his patterns are repetitive, but he also produced a series of arrestingly original designs – many of them at full-length – which break new ground in the history of the English portrait: direct, spontaneous, varied in mood, often free of tiresome fashionable conventions. They reveal an approach to character which anticipates the Augustan simplicity of Reynolds or the rough vigour of Hogarth. The extraordinary *Matthew Prior*, painted in 1700, is one of the most electrifyingly brilliant portraits of the Stuart period; and even Kneller's most tedious portraits have a certain distinction of manner. His chief rival, the Swedish Michael Dahl, was never at ease with the conventional mannerisms of pose and gesture; but in his more serious vein he produced portraits of distinction and integrity. His tone is lighter than Kneller's and his handling crisper and less fluent; but both painters paint in their later years with a Rococo lightness of touch and in a silvery Rococo key which belong wholly to the eighteenth century.

Although the history of painting in England in the Stuart period is to so great an extent the history of the portrait, the other genres of painting were also developed. The seventeenth century saw on the Continent, in Flanders, France and Italy, the climax of Baroque wall-painting on a large scale, for the decoration of churches, palaces and private houses. The influence of Continental decorative painting in England provides an interesting commentary on the nature of English patronage. Charles I had employed such distinguished foreign painters (and Roman Catholics) as Rubens and Gentileschi to decorate walls and ceilings in the Baroque style; and after the Restoration, when the same cosmopolitan atmosphere prevailed, a succession of decorative painters flourished again in this country. The Englishmen among them, such as Isaac Fuller (1606?–d. 1672), Robert Streeter (1624?–1679) and Robert Robinson (fl. 1674), were occupied mainly, as their predecessors had been, with painting scenery for the stage and decorating wainscot panels in small interiors; but Fuller's *Last Judgment*, the altarpiece in the chapel at All Souls, and the huge ceiling which was painted by Streeter for the Sheldonian were, although very clumsy by continental standards, ambitious essays on a big scale and, like Pierce's ceiling at Wilton, in the full Baroque tradition. This tradition culminates, at the end of the Stuart period, in the work of an Englishman, Sir James Thornhill (1675/6–1734). Until then the most successful decorative painters under the later Stuarts had been French and Italian. Antonio Verrio (1639?–1707), a native of Lecce, who had worked in Naples and Paris, where he had attracted the notice of the English ambassador, was put in charge of the painted decorations at Windsor, where Charles II, influenced by what his cousin Louis XIV was creating at Versailles, had set a team of artists and craftsmen to work in the creation of a series of State Apartments. Verrio had seen some of the *Grands Appartements* at Versailles completed, but his style retains an Italian gaiety of tone. The work at Windsor, in which the painter collaborated with the King's architect, Hugh May, and the carver Grinling Gibbons, represents an important stage in the history of English Baroque. In Verrio's most ambitious decorative schemes, at Windsor and at Burghley, where he was in the service of the 5th Earl of Exeter after the Revolution of 1688, he displayed the full range of Baroque decorative devices for extending the space of an interior; painting comparatively restricted areas within limits marked off by carved, painted and gilded decoration (a method one sees in the Duchess's Bedroom at Ham House); painting the entire area above the cornice with a fanciful feigned architectural and sculptural design which is opened to the heavens (a good example is in Charles II's Dining-Room at Windsor); or painting the entire area of wall and ceiling in a huge room, such as St George's Hall at Windsor, the Great Staircase and Queen's Drawing-Room at Hampton Court or the Heaven Room at Burghley, with a wholly feigned architectural and decorative design as a setting for a riot of figures. Rex Whistler's famous room at Plas Newyd is a nostalgic essay in this manner. Verrio's figure-drawing is often almost ludicrously clumsy, but the decorative elements, the feigned reliefs and gilding, the still-life and the painted architecture, carried out by specialized members of his team, are gay and lively; and the iconography in his work at Windsor – the glorification of the Order of the Garter, the Stuart dynasty and the Catholic Church – are of intense interest to the historian of ideas and link Stuart royal patronage very closely to Catholic monarchs and the Catholic Church.

Louis Laguerre (1663–1731), who was actually a pupil of Le Brun and was more thoroughly trained in the *Style Louis XIV*, painted in a more sombre but wholly French style: less gay in colour and design, he was, however, much more experienced than Verrio in varying the combination of painting – both direct and feigning decoration – with surrounding carved and gilded decoration. His ceilings for the 1st Duke of Devonshire at Chatsworth are worthy of a place in the *Grands Appartements* at Versailles; and his masterpiece, the huge Saloon at Blenheim is based on an illusionist scheme which he had derived from Le Brun's *Escalier des Ambassadeurs*.

In contrast with the academic competence of Laguerre is the sparklingly brilliant decorative style which was imported from Venice by the English ambassador, the Duke of Manchester, in 1708. Giovanni Antonio Pellegrini, Marco Ricci and his uncle Sebastiano (who joined Marco in England a few years later) painted a series of decorative schemes, principally for Whig patrons at Kimbolton, Castle Howard, Burlington House, Chelsea Hospital and Bulstrode, in which a Venetian sparkle enlivens the interiors of Vanbrugh and Wren (p. 140). In a continental context the work in England of Pellegrini and the elder Ricci marks a stage in the development of the full Venetian Rococo style, which in Venice reaches its culmination in Tiepolo and is based to a great extent on a return to the lively colour and painterly execution of Veronese. This pretty, sun-washed style certainly influenced Thornhill, although he was a bitter rival of the Venetians. His early work, such as the Sabine Room at Chatsworth, is still in the tradition of Laguerre; but Thornhill's grasp of architectural detail is stronger than the Frenchman's and his figures are always more painterly and Rococo. His drawings for the work at Chatsworth are already delightfully free. He became ultimately a more ambitious designer than Laguerre and a sounder painter than Verrio. Thornhill's achievement, and indeed the story of painted decoration in this country on the full Baroque and early Rococo scale, culminate on the ceilings and walls in the Painted Hall at Greenwich, and in the Upper Hall beyond: a symposium, vast in scale, competent and slightly monotonous, of the motives and iconographical ideas which had been developed by decorative painters in England from Rubens onwards. Thornhill's charm as a painter is perhaps more easily appreciated in the

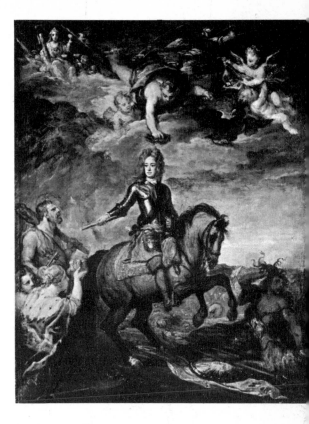

SIR GODFREY KNELLER,
*James Churchill, 1st Duke
of Marlborough, c.* 1706.
National Portrait Gallery, London.

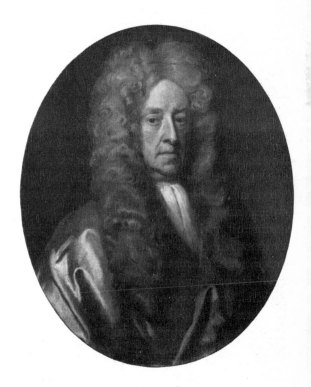

MICHAEL DAHL, *Francis, 1st Earl of Bradford,
c.* 1700.
Weston Park.
Collection of the Earl of Bradford.

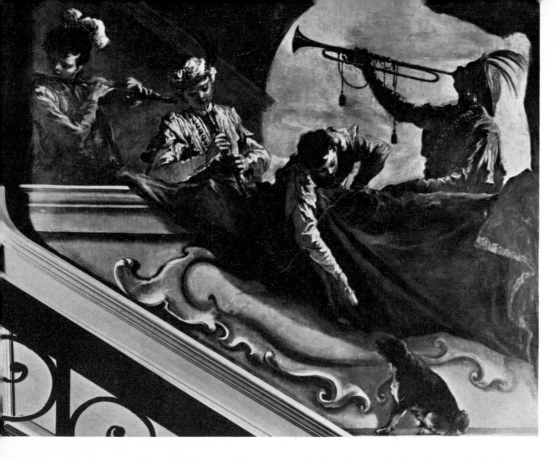

Left, G. A. PELLEGRINI, *The Musicians'
Balcony*, on the main staircase of
Kimbolton Castle, *c*. 1710.
Kimbolton School, Huntingdonshire.
Right above, FRANCIS PLACE, *Bridlington Quay*.
British Library, London.
Right below, JAN SIBERECHTS, *Longleat*, 1675.
By permission of the Marquess of Bath.

enormous number of light and charming oil-sketches and drawings which he produced. Many of the drawings bear annotations which reveal his mind at work on the
problems involved in designing a decorative scheme. They are often reminiscent in
their scope of the designs by Inigo Jones for the masques at the early Stuart court.
Thornhill is also the only painter of the Stuart period who repeatedly used the oil-
sketch as Rubens had done in preparing a modello for a projected scheme.

In the reign of Charles I, and under his patronage, there can also be detected the
beginnings of landscape painting. Painters from the Low Countries, such as Stalbempt,
Keirincx and Poelenburgh painted landscapes in the Romano-Flemish style. Landscapes by Rubens himself were in the collection of the Duke of Buckingham. During
his years in England Van Dyck painted a handful of landscape drawings in which the
use of wash has an almost eighteenth-century fluency. In their attitude to landscape
painting, English patrons show the same concern for topography as for portraits of
their family. Van Dyck's drawings include studies of Rye. Keirincx's work for Charles
I included views of the King's Scottish properties. Even the great *Landscape with St
George* which Rubens painted or began in England, in 1629–30, contains in the background a nostalgic evocation of the Thames at Southwark and Lambeth. Itinerant
Dutchmen, such as Claude De Jongh and Cornelis Bol, painted views of the Thames
at London. Special landscape scenes were commissioned, such as Boscobel House
with the escaping Charles II perched in the oak tree. The finest topographical drawings produced in England are perhaps those done by Esselens, Schellinks and Doomer
in the 1660s. The topographical tradition was carried on by a number of artists
working in pen, ink and wash; the most indefatigable was the Bohemian, Wenceslaus
Hollar, who was brought to England by the Earl of Arundel in 1636, but the most
attractive English landscape painter in watercolour was probably his follower,
Francis Place, whose work always retains something of the amateur's freshness
of vision and touch. In Hollar's and Place's output there was a close link between
the drawing and the print: a connection which culminates in Johannes Kip's engraving, for the volumes of *Britannia Illustrata* (1707–8), of a large number of Leonard
Knyff's careful bird's-eyes of English palaces and houses. The finest views of

140

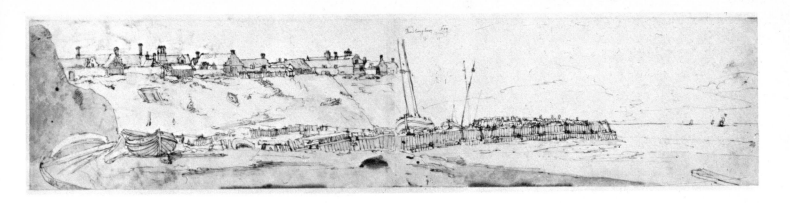

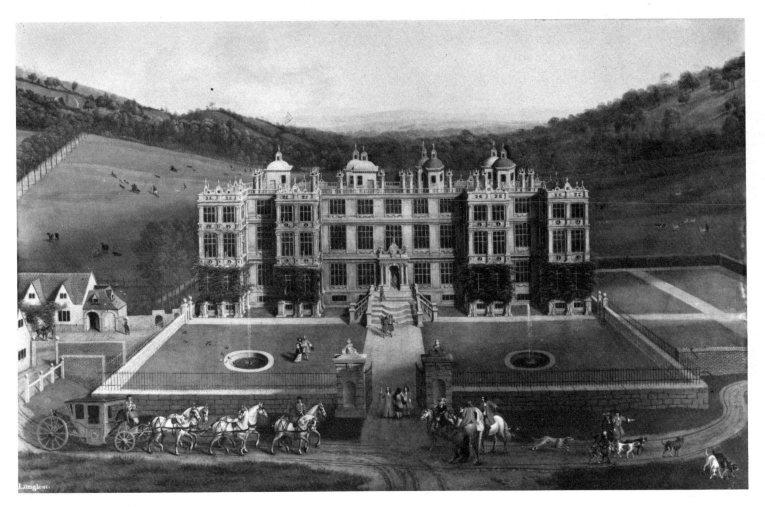

English houses are those by the Fleming, Jan Siberechts (1627–c. 1700). They provide a charming picture of the life on a great estate and sometimes give us rare and informal glances at the English countryside, a church, house or town: in backgrounds to groups of peasants and their flocks or to a coach splashing through a stream. The topographical tradition, especially when it was developed by the draughtsman, is of course fundamental to the future of landscape painting in England; and although much of it, especially when designed for the engraver, is contrived, one surely sees in watercolours by Place and Siberechts instances of the artist working out of doors to record the more informal and fleeting aspects of nature.

Landscapes were often commissioned as part of the design of an interior: to be set in a carved surround over a fireplace or over a door and in these fields the landscape could be romantic or classical in mood. The Dutchman Hendrick Danckerts (c. 1630–after 1679), for example, produced a number of large, rather empty, scenes remotely

141

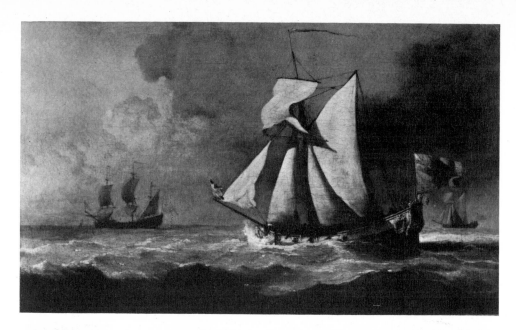

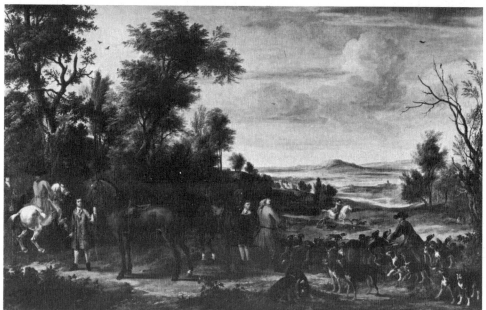

in the manner of Claude, for the royal palaces; in 1669 Pepys commissioned from him four views of royal palaces for the panels in his dining-room. The classical landscapes of Jacques Rousseau (there are good examples at Hampton Court) and the flower pieces by Jean Baptiste Monnoyer (1636–99), who had both been brought over from France by Ralph Montagu, were often designed for the same utilitarian purpose. The most instructive set of pictures in the lesser genres, painted as overdoors and over-mantels, is to be found in the rooms decorated by the Duke and Duchess of Lauderdale at Ham House in the 1670s. They were among the first to patronize the two marine painters, Willem van de Velde (1633–1707), father and son, after their arrival in London; and both painters remained in England, producing for English flag officers big set pieces of naval battles, huge sombre storms or less formal and brilliant painterly studies of smaller boats crashing through the waves in a stiff breeze and under a broken sky. The Lauderdales commissioned a battle-piece by land for the Duke's Closet from the Dutch Jan Wyck, who painted engagements of all kinds in a lively style which is a rather mannered variation of Wouwermans. His hunting-pieces are the most accomplished seventeenth-century impressions of life in the English countryside and, with his straightforward portraits of horses, directly foreshadow the work of his pupil, John Wootton, which is, indeed, at one period almost indistinguishable from his master's. The emergence of Wootton (1686?–1764) as the first important English sporting artist is evidence of the significance of the work of the immigrant artists under the later Stuarts in developing forms of painting which their English followers were to develop in the eighteenth century: the work of Monamy and Brooking in the early Georgian period is, for instance, unintelligible without an awareness of the younger Van de Velde's achievements; the subjects painted by De Jongh and Bol are important as foreshadowing Scott and Canaletto; and in the field of genre painting the satirical subjects of Egbert van Heemskerck in the manner of Ostade or Steen are among the premonitions of Hogarth. Even the small-scale conversation piece, which we also associate with Hogarth in the early Georgian period, is not unknown in the Stuart period. The most engaging English painter of animals and birds was Francis Barlow (1626?–1704), whose gauche designs are marked by an affectionate, painstaking study of the animals and birds he fitted into his designs; his work has none of the stagey fluency of such animal painters as Abraham Hondius, who worked in an extremely mannered style which was ultimately based on Snyders.

So short an account of painting under the Stuarts can only give inevitably a broad view of the chief trends. Although the principal lines of development are probably correctly charted, there is still an immense amount that we do not know. There are gaps in our knowledge of the careers even of the leading painters. We do not know, for example, how Van Dyck organized his studio; we do not know what Dobson was painting before 1642; we do not know precisely when Lely arrived in London. When we look at the lesser figures and at the copyists and journeymen, such questions can be multiplied almost indefinitely. There are an enormous number of pictures painted in the Stuart period to which a name cannot safely be given. This is particularly true of the painters working in the provinces, or painters based on the capital but with contacts out of London, of whose work we still know so little. Many of these anonymous pictures and sets of portraits possess distinction as well as rare charm; it is extraordinary, for instance, that the most celebrated puzzle of all, posed by the set of Tradescant portraits in the Ashmolean Museum, remains unsolved. At the same

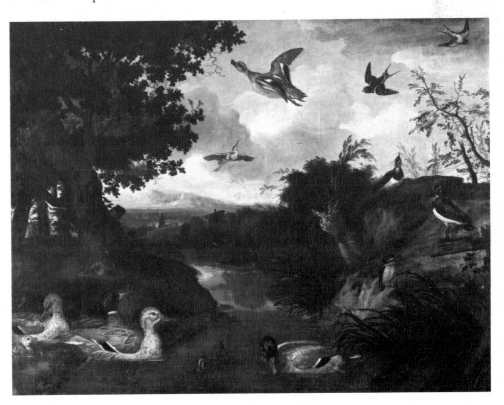

FRANCIS BARLOW, *Ducks and other Birds about a Stream in an Italianate Landscape,* 1671.
Collection of Paul Mellon.

time we know from documentary sources – the official returns of aliens living in London or the records of the Painter Stainers Company, for example, to say nothing of private accounts – the names of a large number of 'picture-drawers' to whom we cannot, in the present state of knowledge, safely attribute a single picture.

The Stuart period saw considerable advances in what one may loosely call the state of the arts. At the beginning of the period it was essential for a painter, if he was to achieve success, to capture the patronage of the court. It was the King and the grandees of the day who commissioned pictures and built up collections. By the end of the century, with the spread of wealth, a large number of collections, many of them admittedly small, had been formed, often on an iconographical and historical rather than a purely aesthetic basis, without reference to the taste of the court. Patronage also was provided from a much broader basis. By the end of the century the great equestrian portrait of the Duke of Buckingham, the quintessence of the early Baroque splendour of the Caroline court, belonged to Sir Francis Child, son of a Wiltshire clothier who epitomizes the growth of the financial interests in the City of London; and we have seen that Kneller owed the first step in his career in this country to the good offices of a Hamburg merchant. The taste for pictures was also fostered by an increasingly vast production of reproductive engravings which, after the invention of the mezzotint, could provide collectors with reproductions which were fine objects in themselves and recorded the tonal values as well as the lines of the originals.

Changes in taste were, therefore, after the Civil War, no longer principally dependent on the taste of the court. The influence of foreign travel, the steady flow of pictures into England, the exposure of pictures for sale and the increasing number of auctions gave a wider public a chance to decide for itself what sort of pictures it most liked. The interplay of foreign influences in the arts in Stuart England became also more complex as the century advanced, from the early years when the sophisticated synthesis exploited by Van Dyck can be seen in contrast to the varying English or Netherlandish strains in his lesser contemporaries. By the end of the century the French taste, epitomized in the patrons who employed Ralph Montagu's team of painters from Versailles, would have competed with successive waves of painters from Holland, whose subject-matter delighted collectors of a waggish frame of mind and whose technical virtuosity fascinated Samuel Pepys. These qualities, however, would in turn have disgusted men of serious classical tastes, such as the 3rd Earl of Shaftesbury or Jonathan Richardson, whose ideals were expressed in their writings but were to gain their most lucidly practical expression in Reynolds's *Discourses*.

The arrival of Van Dyck had indeed marked a turning-point in the history of English painting: a moment that explains the stylistic changes that separate a portrait by Gheeraerts from Kneller's *Matthew Prior*. In a period so soaked in foreign influences and so dominated by the immigrant painter one searches for a native spirit in British painting. In the portraits of Dobson, Mary Beale, and Hayls, in the miniatures of Hoskins and Cooper, in the portrait-drawings of Greenhill, Loggan and Robert White, in Barlow's drawings of animals and birds or Place's freely drawn watercolours one finds that combination of honest vision and lively touch with a charming vein of amateurishness. It is the vein one detects in Hilliard or the young Gainsborough, and which one senses to be English.

4

THE EIGHTEENTH CENTURY

Mary Webster

An *Artists' Club in London*, 1735, a small picture by Gawen Hamilton (1698–1737), shows us the successfully established and fashionable artists of its day (p. 146) – among the painters are Dahl, Wootton and Hamilton himself, Kent who counts as both painter and architect, the engravers George Vertue and Baron, Rysbrack the sculptor, and perhaps best known of all, James Gibbs the architect. Grouped together in a formal Baroque setting these little portraits, painted with humour and individuality, reveal much of the state of the arts at the beginning of the period covered in this chapter. The very Baroque setting with statues set into niches in a heavily architectural wall, the high coved ceiling and curtain draped at the right, the dark rich colours, sum up the work of the generation depicted, all of whom were born in the previous century. The small-scale of the figures and the intended spontaneity and informality of their poses introduce us to the dawning changes in English art.

By this time English artists had already made one or two attempts to break through the difficulties that cramped their activity. The Augustan age had been a great age of collecting, but English connoisseurs preferred to buy the great masters of the Italian sixteenth century and the Roman Baroque, or, if their taste were less noble, paintings of the Dutch school. The great nobility, who were the most important patrons of the day, despised English artists, preferring to employ Italians and Frenchmen. An English artist could only really hope for commissions in one genre – portraiture – and even in portraiture the visit of a foreigner, such as Van Loo, might sweep the patronage of the town. Unlike France, where Louis XIV had reared a magnificent structure of art education and patronage, the English state did not provide any form of training for artists, and Thornhill's decorations in St Paul's and Greenwich were the last important public commissions before the reign of George III. In Paris French artists could learn the rudiments of their art by drawing either from casts of the antique or from the life at the Académie Royale. English artists were deprived of the training in correct drawing and noble style which were considered

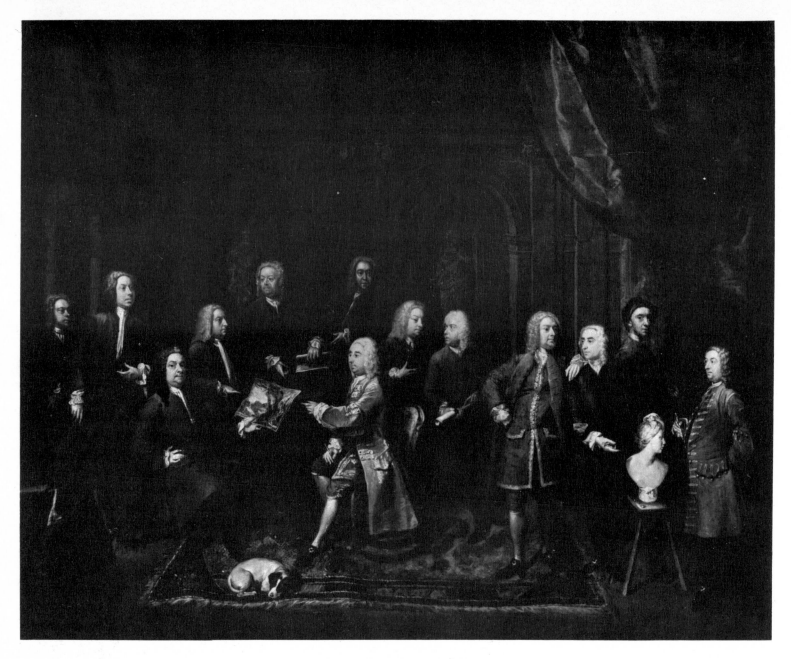

GAWEN HAMILTON, *An Artists' Club
in London*, 1735.
National Portrait Gallery, London.

essential in the loftiest of all genres, history painting. If we remember that the masterpieces of the past, from which artists then hoped to learn by assiduous copying, were dispersed throughout England in the great houses of the nobility and gentry, and were often difficult or impossible to see, it becomes evident that those students who could not afford the considerable expense of a trip to Paris or Italy were deprived of the means of improvement. The history of eighteenth-century art is partly the history of a struggle by English artists to end this humiliating and confining situation, and to obtain general recognition of their despised art of painting as a liberal and learned profession.

The first real blow was struck against the connoisseurs by the greatest figure of the age: William Hogarth (1697–1764). Hogarth was no crusader for official academic education, but he thought that English connoisseurs ought to patronize living English artists and buy modern English pictures, instead of squandering large sums on the worthless copies and school paintings to which great names had been attached by crafty dealers. In spite of the lack of enlightened patronage which militated against the development in England, by English artists, of every genre other than portraiture, Vertue, whose notebooks record contemporary happenings in the art

146

world, remarked in 1732 that 'Art flourished more in London now than probably it has done 50 or 60 years before', and certainly some of the foreign artists who were attracted to London by this state of affairs were richly rewarded by the immensely wealthy, if artistically ignorant society they painted. For, whether English or foreign, successful 'face-painters' were able to command high prices. But those artists who were ambitious to do more than paint portraits, which were classified by the theorists of Franco-Roman classicism, the orthodox artistic creed of the day, as a much inferior genre to history painting, were far from content.

Another of the many difficulties facing the English painter was the lack of any place for the public exhibition of his work. To sell pictures that had not been painted to commission the artist had to have recourse to the public auction rooms. There, as the work of a living painter, they fetched perhaps a tenth of the price of the holed and time-smoked old masters admired by the connoisseurs. Hogarth's inventive satires still vividly convey the indignation at such prejudice and folly. It was only in the 1740s, after the establishment in London of the Foundling Hospital for

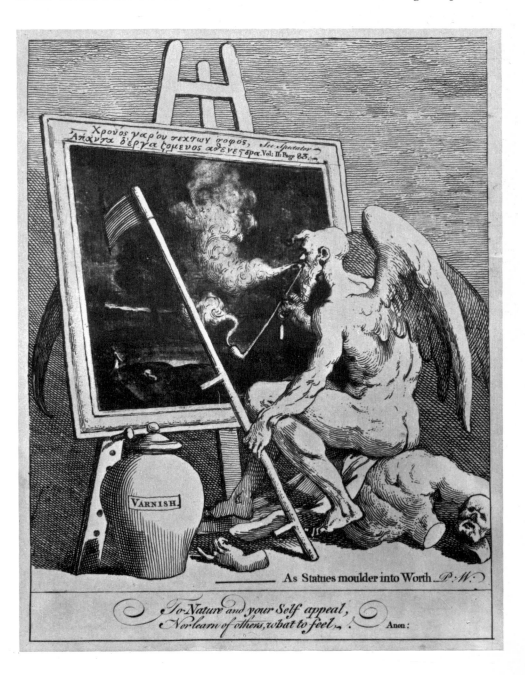

WILLIAM HOGARTH, *Time smoking a picture* (engraving).
British Library, London.

deserted children, that pictures by a group of living English artists were exhibited to the public gaze. The charity, founded by a former sea captain, Thomas Coram, was from the first patronized by many of the nobility and by prominent citizens. One of its most enthusiastic supporters was Coram's friend Hogarth, who was elected to the governing board. In 1740 Hogarth presented to the Hospital his life-size portrait of *Captain Coram* (p. 151), and, in order to decorate the Hospital without expense to the charity, a number of artists followed Hogarth's example and gave paintings to it. From the beginning the Hospital was a meeting place for fashionable London. Handel gave performances there of the *Messiah*, and its attractions were increased by the collection of works of art which formed the first gallery of British pictures to which the public had the right of admission. A number of the pictures presented were of subjects symbolic of the aims of the Hospital, others were landscapes or seascapes. There was an altarpiece for the Chapel, and of course portraits of those connected with the charity.

At the outset of our period engravings were the means whereby the work of modern foreign artists became known in England and the importation into this country of foreign engravings was a flourishing business. The introduction of the French Rococo style received added impetus from Hubert Gravelot (1699–1773), who came from Paris to London in 1733. His designs and engravings for books published in England from the mid-1730s diffused, in a hitherto unknown lightness of touch, the sparkling elegance and grace of French eighteenth-century art. Rococo gaiety began to show very quickly: it is already present in the new, small-scale figures of Hamilton's *Artists' Club in London*, and soon the light, bright colours of the French taste were enlivening the new genre of little group portraits or conversation pieces, as they were called.

One of the first painters to practise the French manner in England was the Berlin-born, French Huguenot, Philip Mercier (1689–1760), who came to London about 1716, bringing with him the ability to imitate and translate Watteau into English terms, shown in the group of *Frederick, Prince of Wales and his Sisters* making music in the park before the Dutch House at Kew. Although he stayed in England for most of the remainder of his life, producing portraits and Frenchified subject pictures of a domestic and sentimental nature, Mercier was soon overtaken by his English contemporaries.

Until the mid-1730s there were only two print shops in London and they sold

Right, ALLAN RAMSAY, *The Painter's Wife,* 1754–5.
National Gallery of Scotland, Edinburgh.

Below left, HUBERT GRAVELOT, Illustration to George Bickham's *The Musical Entertainer* (engraving).
British Library, London.
Below, P. MERCIER, *Frederick, Prince of Wales, and his Sisters: a Music Party,* 1733.
National Portrait Gallery, London.

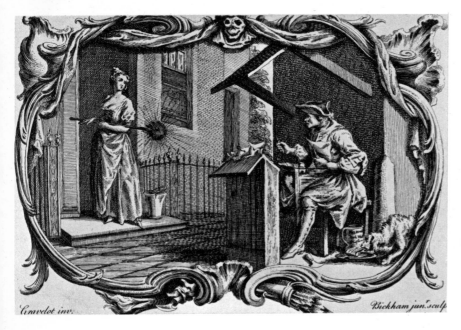

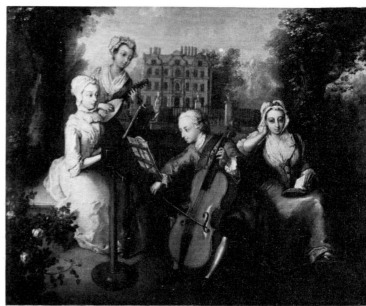

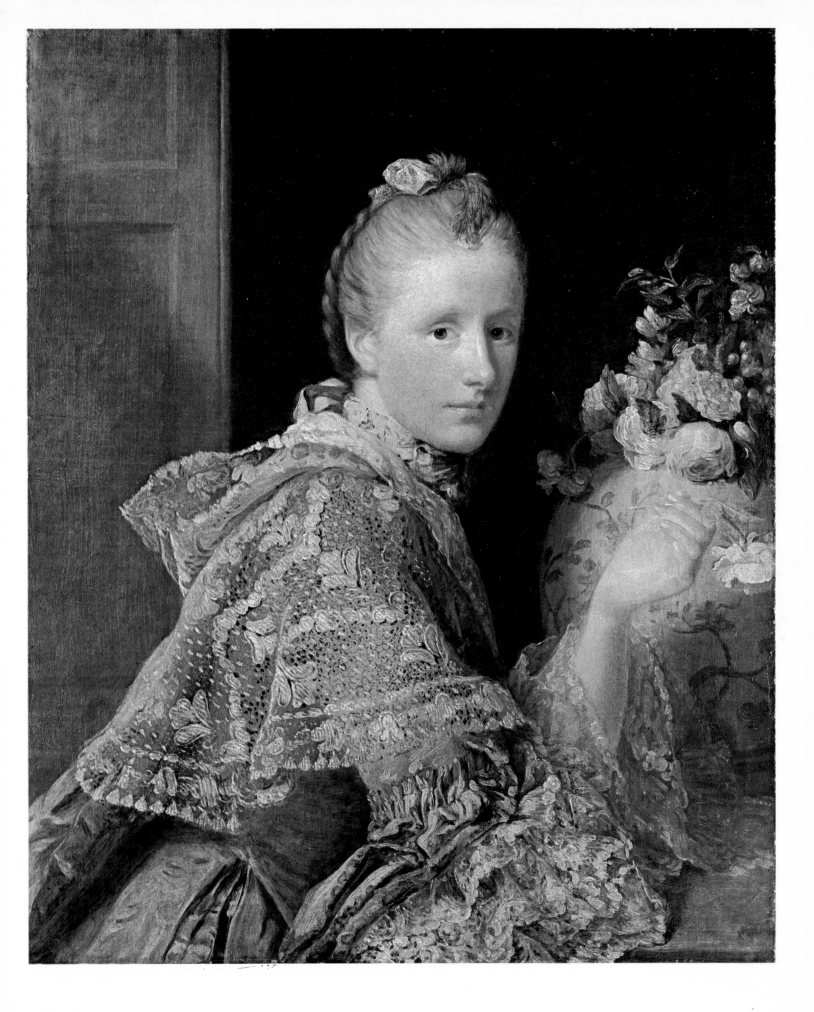

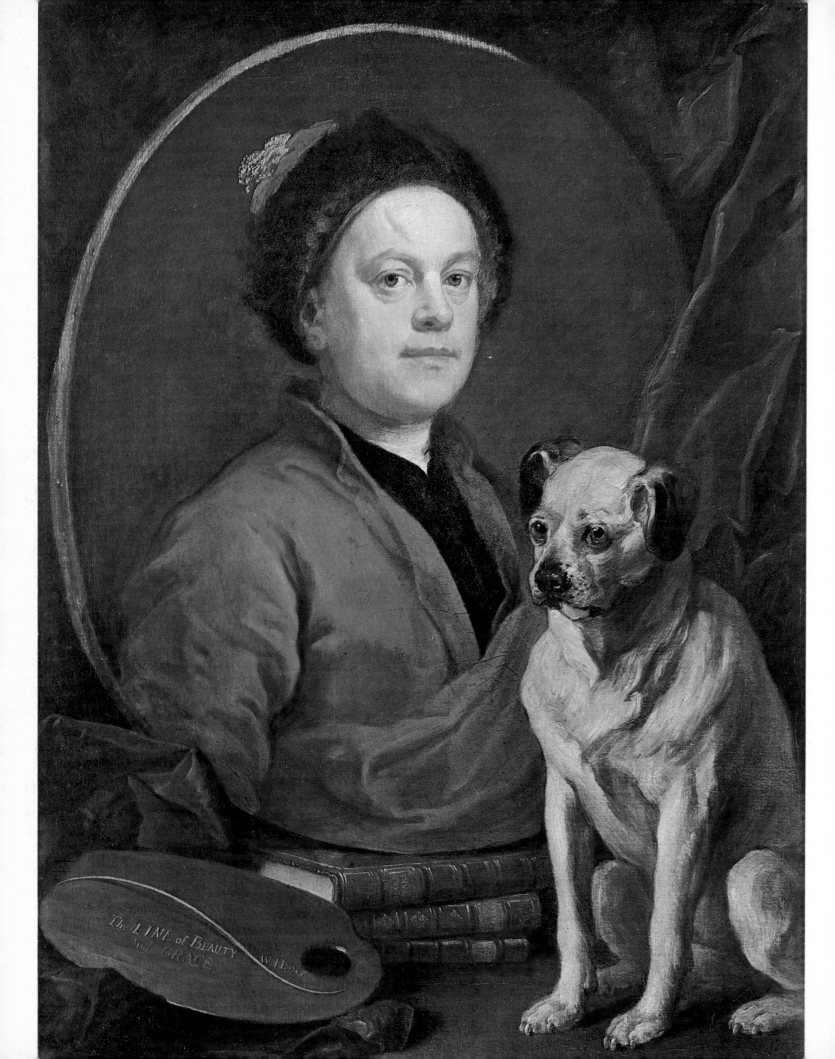

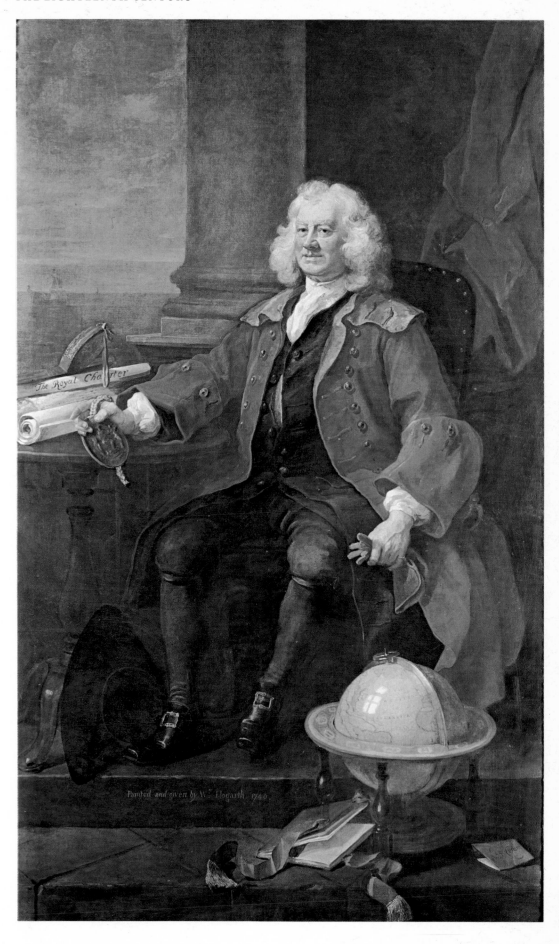

Left, WILLIAM HOGARTH, *Self-portrait,* 1745.
The Tate Gallery, London.
Right, WILLIAM HOGARTH, *Captain Coram,*
1740.
By kind permission of the Governors of
the Thomas Coram Foundation for
Children, London.

151

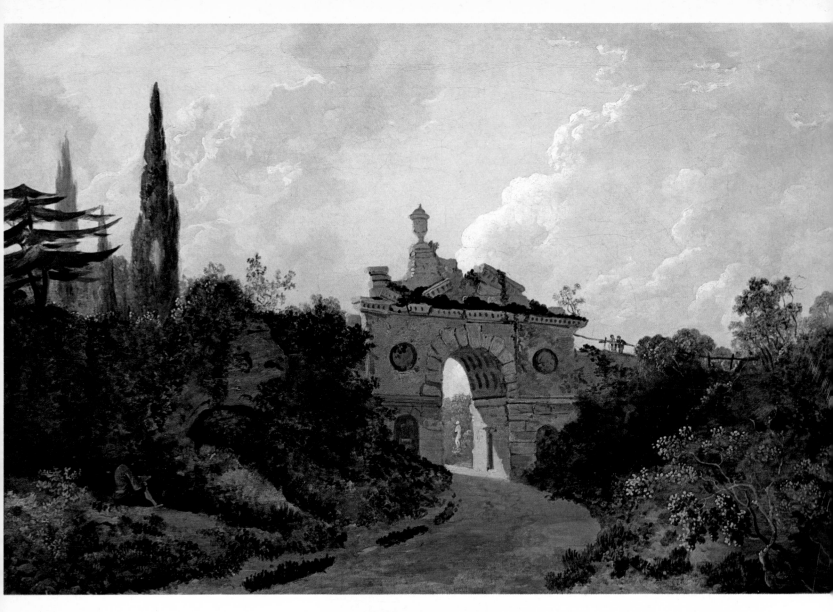

Above, RICHARD WILSON, *Ruined Arch at Kew*.
By permission of Mr Brinsley Ford.
Right, RICHARD WILSON,
Apollo and the Seasons, c. 1775–9.
Fitzwilliam Museum, Cambridge.

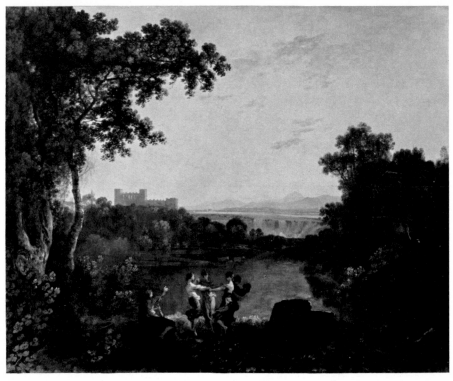

only foreign prints and engravings after English portraits. Early in the 1720s the young Hogarth, leaving behind him the purely ornamental engraving on silver plate in which he had served a long apprenticeship, branched out into engraving illustrations to books, such as the mock-heroic *Hudibras*, and began his scathing visual comments on the social scene. Finding that his designs were being pirated, Hogarth was successful in obtaining a copyright act in 1735 which secured to the designer the right in his own design, and resulted in the opening of more print shops, thus beginning the diffusion of a taste for art at social levels below the aristocracy.

Modernity is the essence of Hogarth's art. His earliest works in oil were in the newly fashionable genre of small conversation pieces. He added to the repertoire of family pieces and group portraits by painting theatrical conversations, scenes from plays, with actors performing in front of an audience. Hogarth has transferred the gaiety and vivacity of the extremely successful Newgate pastoral *The Beggars' Opera* (Tate Gallery), which was playing to crowded houses in 1728, to a permanent life on canvas. He excelled this picture only in *Children playing the 'Indian Emperor' before an audience*, in 1731–2 (p. 155); where, presenting the stage obliquely, he combined a lively group of spectators with a sympathetic presentation of the performing children. In spite of the reputation he gained from these pictures and from a number of small family groups which were commended for their likenesses, Hogarth's commissions for paintings did not bring him sufficient financial reward to maintain his household, enlarged since his runaway marriage in 1729 to Thornhill's daughter Jane. In spite of his professed chauvinism, Dutch and above all French influences manifest themselves in Hogarth's style. Both composition and colouring reveal the influences of foreign prints and of his visits to France in the 1740s.

With bold commercial enterprise Hogarth conceived and carried out the invention of depicting modern moral subjects in sets of prints that related to a story. The plot, created by Hogarth, was intended both to entertain and to improve the mind; it was, through the medium of engraving, to be open, like the theatre, to all. In style, these moral paintings develop from the stage groups. The first series he painted was *The Harlot's Progress* (about 1731, destroyed), whose success he followed up in 1735, shortly before his copyright bill became law, with *The Rake's Progress* (p. 156). Although serious paintings in their own right, the eight pictures of this series range from the liveliest to the perfunctory; their unevenness of quality is probably due to the fact that Hogarth painted them primarily as subjects for engraving. By publishing prints Hogarth began the emancipation of artists from the whims of connoisseurs and individual patrons: it was not to them but to a much wider public that he looked for his profits from these social and moral satires. The engravings swept the country, but Hogarth had the greatest difficulty in disposing of his canvasses. He brought these series of moral tales in paint to a culmination in *Marriage à la Mode* (National Gallery) painted between 1743 and 1745. He advertised his intention to represent 'a Variety of *Modern Occurences* in *High-Life*' which, despite the basic banality of the story – marriage for money and vanity followed by boredom and immorality, disease and violent death – are a series of brilliantly inventive comments, superbly executed, on the follies and vices of high society.

The portrait Hogarth painted of himself in 1745 (p. 150) is a matter of fact, English expression of the informality which the eighteenth century substituted for the solemnity and pomp of the Baroque age. The flowing wig and gestures of the Grand Manner are abolished in favour of a more down to earth accompaniment. His clear blue eyes look out from a round, open and firmly set face, framed by a fur cap. With him are the works of Shakespeare, Milton and Swift – a satirist whose fierceness was like Hogarth's own – his palette, on which is drawn the 'line of beauty and of grace' which was to occupy so much of his attention in the future, and his favourite dog, Trump. This black-nosed animal sitting foursquare at the front of the picture reminds

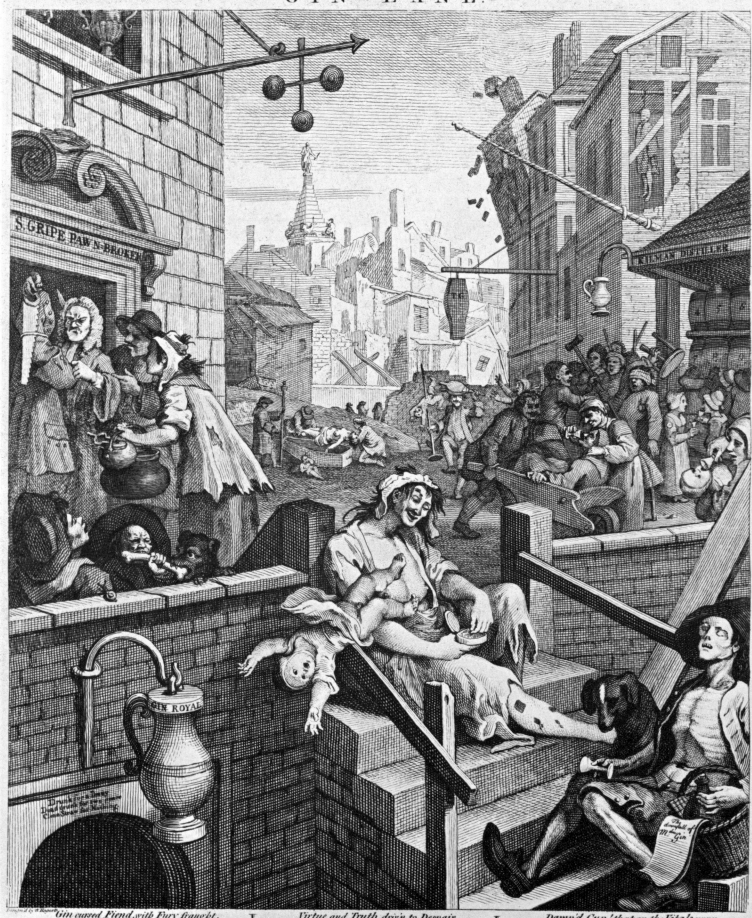

GIN LANE.

S. GRIPE PAWN BROKER

KILMAN DISTILLER

GIN ROYAL

Design'd by W. Hogarth

Publish'd according to Act of Parliam. Feb.1. 1751.

Price 1s

Gin cursed Fiend, with Fury fraught,
Makes human Race a Prey.
It enters by a deadly Draught,
And steals our Life away.

Virtue and Truth, driv'n to Despair,
It's Rage compells to fly.
But cherishes, with hellish Care,
Theft, Murder, Perjury.

Damn'd Cup! that on the Vitals preys,
That liquid Fire contains,
Which Madness to the Heart conveys,
And rolls it thro' the Veins.

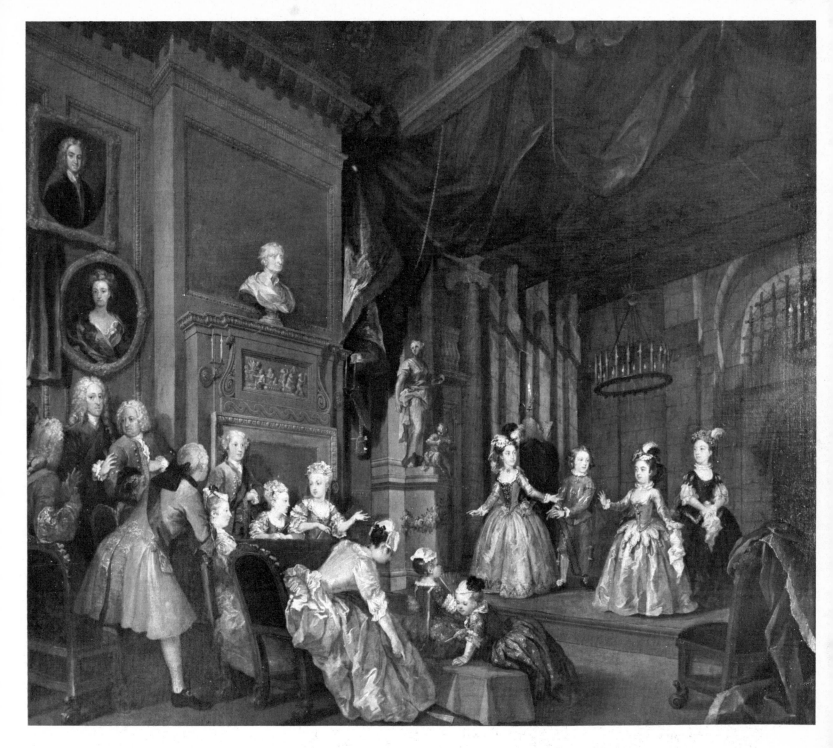

Left, WILLIAM HOGARTH, *Gin Lane*
(engraving), 1751.
British Library, London.
Above, WILLIAM HOGARTH, *Children playing
the 'Indian Emperor' before an audience*, 1731–2.
Collection of the Viscountess Galway.

us that his master, too, was well able to bark and bite. Here is the same honesty as in
the portraits of Captain Coram. This veracity and freshness is even more apparent in
the freely painted portrait heads of his six servants (Tate Gallery), which, unlike
Captain Coram and the self-portrait, is a private picture, without any message.

As well as painting savage commentaries on the social conditions of his time,
conditions also described in the novels of his friends Fielding and Richardson with
the same philanthropic intention, Hogarth aspired to become a theorist of art and a
history painter. *The Analysis of Beauty*, published in 1753, was a controversial theoretical work in which Hogarth advocated his famous waving *line of beauty*, the
serpentine line that was a cardinal principle of Rococo design.

From Sir Richard Grosvenor, Hogarth received a commission to paint a history
picture, the subject to be Hogarth's choice and the payment whatever he demanded.

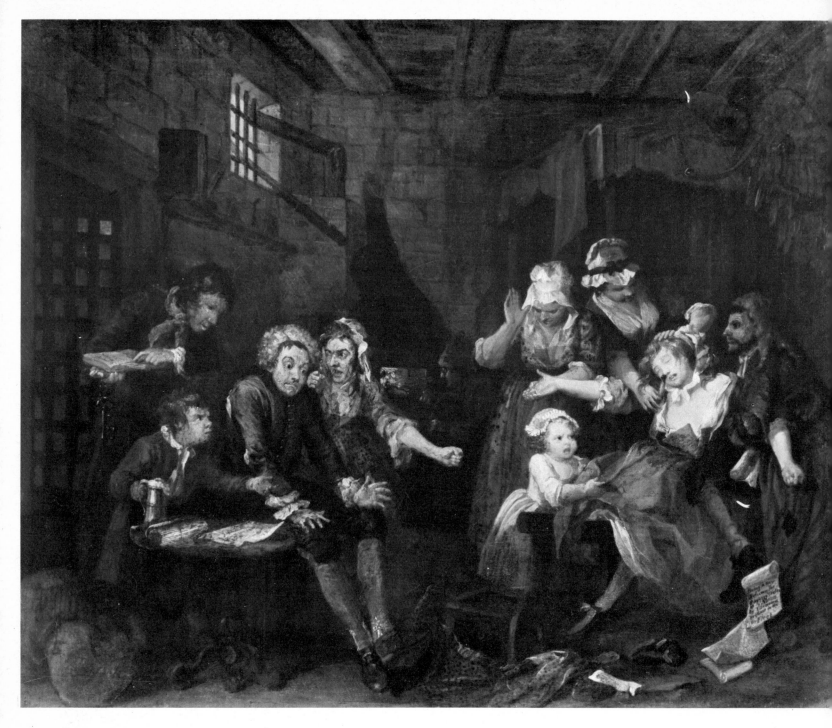

WILLIAM HOGARTH, *The Rake's Progress VII –*
Scene in the Fleet Prison, London, 1735.
By permission of the Trustees of
Sir John Soane's Museum, London.

He determined to exercise his powers of expression by painting the figure of
Sigismunda (1759) weeping over the heart of her lover. In describing his purpose
Hogarth wrote: 'My object was dramatic, and my aim to draw tears from the spectator; an effect I have often witnessed at a tragedy; and it therefore struck me that
it was worth trying, if a painter could not produce the same effect, and touch the
heart through the eye, as the player does through the ear.' His conception of history
painting, then, was that of the Baroque classicists, who had defined its theory and
compositional rules by analogy with the theory and rules of classical drama. His
patron, however, felt that this modern rival of a Bolognese old master was not to his
taste, and the picture was left on Hogarth's hands; he was to receive much abuse
about it.

Hogarth was appointed Serjeant-Painter to the King in 1757. He had a wide knowledge of painting of the European schools and his own work was greatly admired

156

on the Continent, especially in Germany. Although Hogarth left no school and no immediate followers, by the end of his life modern English painting had become more respected. The genre of moral subjects began to flourish. In France, where Hogarth's engravings were well known, Greuze sentimentalized the genre in the compositions which were later in the century to become so influential in England.

Amongst Hogarth's contemporaries were a number of artists who painted the newly fashionable small portraits and conversation pieces; Bartholomew Dandridge (1691–1755?) who painted in light, gay colours; Joseph Francis Nollekens (1702–48) 'Old Nollekens' the father of the sculptor; Marcellus Laroon (1679–1772) who produced more imaginative and fanciful pictures in a lively technique; Charles Philips (1708–47); Gawen Hamilton (1698–1737) and the best known of all Arthur Devis (1711–87). Born in Preston, the son of a Town Councillor, by 1742 Devis was established in London as a painter of small portraits. He succeeded most with the class from which he sprang, painting for them small-scale portraits to fit the small rooms of Georgian houses, and for the next twenty-five years was occupied in literal renderings of middle class and professional families. The figures and drapery are usually well lit and carefully painted, and their setting is also carefully indicated, either a rather dark and sparsely furnished Georgian interior, or a spreading park-like background, often ornamented with a bridge or pavilion. The undoubted charm of updated primitiveness that these pictures possess in their reflection of long-drawn-out English afternoons may appeal to our taste (p. 158), but Devis was never a fashionable artist. In spite of becoming President of the Free Society of Artists in 1768 – the year in which most successful and socially ambitious artists were to become Royal Academicians – Devis spent the later years of his life experimenting with glass painting and as a restorer. A few years before his death he was employed to clean and repair Thornhill's decorative paintings in the Hall of Greenwich Hospital, for which he received payment of one thousand pounds.

The art of Henry Robert Morland (1730–97) derives from paintings such as Mercier's life-size genre figures. Morland, father of the celebrated George, painted

WILLIAM HOGARTH, *Sigismunda mourning over the Heart of Guiscardo*, 1759. The Tate Gallery, London.

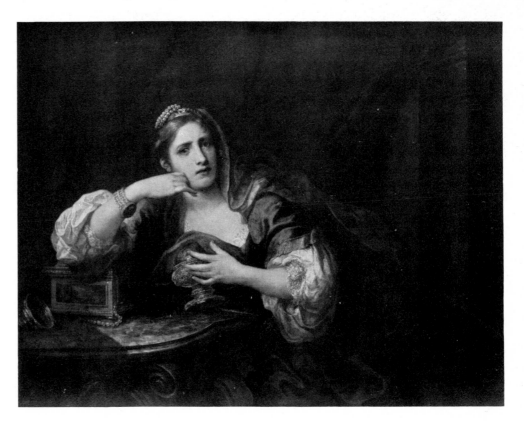

portraits and genre scenes, often with candlelight effect. Little has been identified of his prolific and frequently repetitive output; what we do know appears rather flatly painted in low-keyed colours.

Joseph Highmore (1692–1780), originally trained for the law, began painting in 1715. His early work as a portrait painter was followed in 1743–4 by twelve paintings illustrating *Pamela*, which were published as engravings in 1745. *Pamela* was the first contemporary novel to inspire a series of paintings that were not intended as book-illustrations. It was not the literary charms of the novel but its invaluable moral lessons that Highmore, following Hogarth's precedent, was proposing in pictorial form to a public which Richardson's book had taken by storm. The Rococo manner and light gay colours reveal the influence of Gravelot, whose lightness of touch also had a notable effect on Hayman and Gainsborough as well as Highmore. Highmore was well known in his lifetime for conversation groups, but his identified work principally consists of rather softly modelled, life-size portraits of a certain informality, in which the character of the sitter is sympathetically caught (*Mr Oldham and his friends*, Tate Gallery).

Vauxhall Gardens, perhaps the most famous of eighteenth-century London pleasure gardens, was the setting for an extensive scheme of Rococo decoration. Surrounding the Grove, the centre of the Gardens, were fifty supper boxes, all decorated

ARTHUR DEVIS, *Mr and Mrs William Atherton*, 1745–7.
Walker Art Gallery, Liverpool.

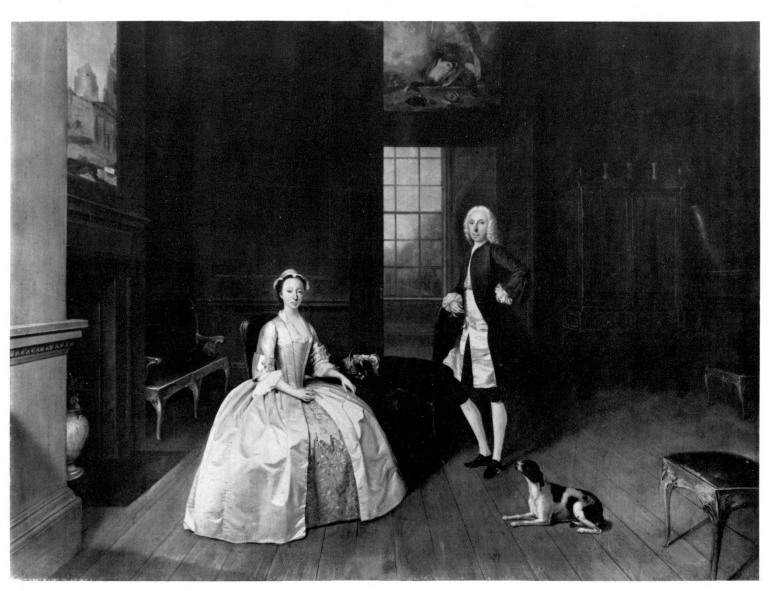

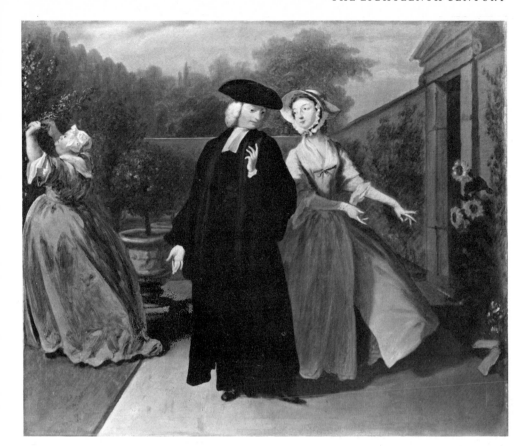

JOSEPH HIGHMORE, *Pamela shows Mr Williams
her Hiding Place for Letters*, 1743–4,
an illustration to Samuel Richardson's *Pamela*.
Fitzwilliam Museum, Cambridge.

with large pictures, mainly of rustic scenes, pastimes, scenes from common life and
novels (p. 160). In other parts of the grounds hung huge canvasses: some formed part
of movable scenery, others triumphal arches or *trompe l'oeil* vistas, and yet others
were historical scenes. Contemporary descriptions give a vivid impression of the
many kinds of occasional painting that were to be seen, not only at these pleasure
Gardens, but, on occasions of public rejoicing, in other parts of the capital. To such
commissions many well-known artists were glad to turn their hands. A lease of the
Vauxhall Gardens was taken in 1728 by Jonathan Tyers who, four years later, produced his famous Ridotto al fresco. It was Hogarth who suggested this form of
entertainment and in 1729 he presented Tyers with his picture of *Henry VIII and
Anne Boleyn* which was hung in the Rotunda. Hogarth made further contributions
including a picture of *Fairies dancing on the Green by Moonlight*. But most of the
decorations for the Gardens were executed by Francis Hayman (1708–76) and his
assistants, with, in some cases, the collaboration of Gravelot, between the early
1730s and 1761, when Hayman painted 'four glorious transactions of the late war'.

Hayman, much celebrated in his day, was early employed as a scene painter at
Drury Lane and earned the reputation of being 'unquestionably the best historical
painter in the kingdom, before the arrival of Cipriani' (1755). He too contributed to
the Foundling Hospital, presenting his picture of *The Finding of the Infant Moses in
the Bulrushes* in 1746. Hayman is best remembered today as the portrait painter who
comes midway between Hogarth and the early Gainsborough, but his stiff little
figures posed against a backdrop rather than a background are often amongst his
least successful works. The drawings he made to be engraved as book illustrations
certainly confirm Hayman as the successor to Gravelot. The two artists had collaborated on the illustrations for the 1742 edition of *Pamela* and Hanmer's *Shakespeare*
of 1743–4. After Gravelot's return to France in 1746 Hayman, whose reputation had
been made at Vauxhall, was greatly in demand to continue the now fashionable,

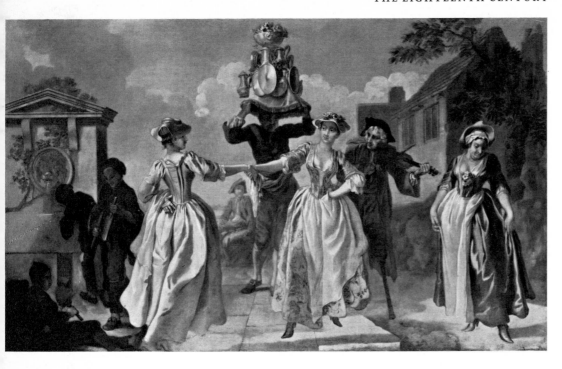

FRANCIS HAYMAN, *Mayday*.
Victoria and Albert Museum, London.

light Rococo book illustrations in which landscape played an important part. His illustrations to Smollett's translation of *Don Quixote* of 1755 and to Moore's *Fables for the Female Sex* of 1766 blend a spontaneity of action and light descriptive line into a well integrated background. Hayman succeeded Lambert as President of the Society of Artists in 1765, and after the foundation of the Royal Academy became its Librarian.

Early in the eighteenth century a number of artists made efforts to set up an academy – by academy was meant a place where a model was available to practising artists for drawing and studying from the life. Official academies of art had been founded in the major cities of Italy by the end of the sixteenth century, and in Paris, in 1648, the Académie Royale de Peinture et de Sculpture had begun its imperious career. In London nothing along any of these lines existed until 1711, when a private academy, of which Kneller became Governor, was set up by artists. It was not long before dissensions resulted in two rival establishments, one run by Vanderbank (1694?–1739) and the other by Sir James Thornhill (1675/6–1734). Neither flourished greatly, but after the death of Thornhill a small society, chiefly of foreign artists under George Michael Moser (1704–83) met regularly to draw from the living model. It was joined about 1735 by Hogarth, who had inherited the furnishings and effects from his father-in-law's academy. The academy which then set up in Peter Court, St Martin's Lane, where thirty to forty people could draw and model, prospered until the opening of the Royal Academy Schools in 1769.

Royal patronage for artists was forthcoming only from Frederick, Prince of Wales, who also discussed with Vertue in 1749 the setting up of an academy for drawing and painting which was to have included drawing schools in Oxford and Cambridge as well as London. The death of the Prince in 1751 put an end to that proposal. Two years later the artists from the St Martin's Lane academy met to revive the project, and later opened negotiations with the Society of Dilettanti for their financial support for a scheme which embraced an annual exhibition. This too came to nothing.

Meanwhile, young students were taught by drawing masters. One of the best known was William Shipley (1715–1803) the founder, in 1754, of the Society for the Encouragement of Arts, Manufactures and Commerce. By a system of prizes the Society offered encouragement to young artists, as well as to other young craftsmen.

160

Studying from the old masters and from antique sculpture, of which there was very little in England until the second half of the century, was only possible on payment of the exorbitant fees demanded by servants for showing visitors round private collections. The sole exception was the collection of the learned and enlightened Dr Mead, who from 1732 until his death in 1754, opened his gallery freely in the mornings to artists. Mead's example was followed in 1758 by the Duke of Richmond, who for a few years opened his gallery of casts of antique and modern sculptures from Florence and Rome to students. Wilton (1722-1803) and Cipriani (1727–85) attended the gallery once a week to correct the drawings and models and to give instruction.

The annual dinner of the artist Governors of the Foundling Hospital instituted in 1746, had expanded in ten years to an occasion attended by over 150 artists. At the dinner of 1759 a resolution was drawn up for a future meeting to consider a proposal 'for the honour and advancement of the Arts' by founding a 'great Museum' or an academy, where the works of those present could be on view to the public. At this and at subsequent meetings held at the Turk's Head Tavern in Soho, under the chairmanship of Hayman, plans were made to hold an annual exhibition of works of every painter, sculptor, architect, engraver, chaser, seal cutter and medallist who wished to show his performances; no copies were to be admitted. The first exhibition was held at the Society of Arts for two weeks in April and May 1760. It is estimated that between 17,000 and 20,000 people saw the exhibition, which comprised 130 works; 6,582 catalogues were sold. However, difficulties soon arose between the Society of Arts and the artists; the latter wished to impose an admission charge in order to obtain an income and to ensure the selectness of visitors. As a result the more important artists moved away in the following year to hold their exhibition in Spring Gardens. Calling themselves the Society of Artists, they were granted a Royal Charter in 1765. A number of artists remained to exhibit at the Society of Arts, moving in 1765 to Maiden Lane and subsequently elsewhere. This Free Society of Artists continued until 1783, devoting the profits from its exhibitions to the charitable support of artists in need. Meanwhile, dissension broke the Society of Artists, for the quarrels of rival factions for power within the ranks of the more than two hundred artists who belonged to the Society ended in the ousting of some and the resignation of the remaining original directors. In November 1768 a Memorial was presented to George III by a group of artists, led by William Chambers and including West, Cotes, Moser, Cipriani, Angelica Kauffmann, Wilton and Sandby, amongst them former directors of the Society of Artists, to solicit His Majesty's assistance, patronage and protection in establishing a Society for promoting the Arts of Design, by setting up a school or academy of design and by holding an annual exhibition. On 10 December 1768 George III gave his approval to the foundation of a Royal Academy of forty Academicians, to be governed by an annually elected President and eight members in Council. The Academicians were to be drawn from painters, sculptors and architects – engravers were not included – vacancies were to be filled by election from amongst the exhibitors. The schools were to be attended by Visitors, elected annually, Professors of perspective, anatomy and painting were appointed and rules laid down for the annual exhibition 'open to all Artists of distinguished merit'. Reynolds was unanimously elected the first President. The Royal Academy opened in Pall Mall, moving in 1771 to Somerset House. Thus the ground was cut from beneath the feet of the 'turbulent gentlemen' of the Society of Artists, which dwindled towards the end of the 1770s and held its last exhibition in 1791. The newly established Academy had before it a number of important tasks, and its success may be measured according to their degree of achievement. By its very foundation as a Royal Academy and the knighthood bestowed on its President, the Academicians at least could describe themselves as practitioners of a liberal profession. Besides establishing the social

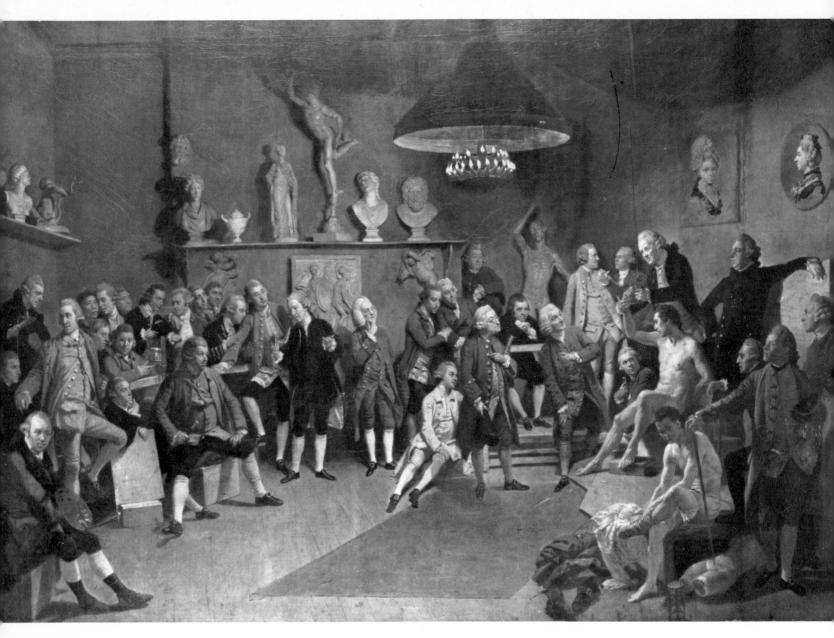

standing of the artist on a level with that of the lawyer, the poet, the clergyman, the Academy had to teach the rudiments of classical life drawing and to inspire young artists with the aspiration to realize the loftiest possibilities of their art. In his *Discourses* to the Academy students Reynolds triumphantly succeeded in the last of these tasks, firing indeed more enthusiasm for history painting than humdrum English patrons were willing to support.

One artist who never showed his pictures at a public exhibition, but who played a most important part in bringing the informal, light, Rococo portrait into vogue in the place of set Baroque patterns was Allan Ramsay (1713–84). He received his formative training in 1736–8, in Rome and Naples, under Imperiali and Solimena. He spent much of his time drawing at the French Academy in Rome and this early acquired habit of drawing remained with him throughout his working life. Indeed, in the number of drawings and studies he made for his portraits, especially of drapery and hands, he is unique amongst British portrait painters. On returning to England, rather than going back to his native Edinburgh, Ramsay set up in practice as a portrait painter in London. He was immediately successful and was able to write to a friend early in 1740: 'I have put all your Vanlois and Soldis and Roscos to flight, and now play first fiddle myself.' These and other foreign artists who had brought a

JOHANN ZOFFANY, *The Academicians of the Royal Academy*, 1772.
Royal Collection.
By gracious permission of
Her Majesty the Queen.

162

stylish, if superficial, manner to portrait painting were henceforth to find competition from native talent far from negligible.

The elegance and lightness of touch of Ramsay's paint, combined with his gift of characterization, were immediately apparent. His technique, learnt in Italy, of using a vermilion underpaint to model the sitter's head has given his portraits an enduring freshness and a gaiety of colour; the unusual steps he took to provide Van Aken, his drapery painter, with drawings for drapery ensured that the overworn stock patterns were discarded. In 1747 Ramsay presented his portrait of *Dr Mead* to the Foundling Hospital. One of his new full-length portraits, it marks the moment of transition from the Baroque to the new classicizing grand manner, first apparent in *Norman MacLeod of MacLeod* (p. 165) which he painted in the following year.

Ramsay's two essays, *On Ridicule* and *On Taste*, of the early 1750s, follow on Hogarth's *Analysis of Beauty* and commend naturalism in art. At this time Ramsay's portraits become more natural, catching overtones from such French portraitists as Subleyras and Aved. The death of Van Aken in 1749, and the appearance of Reynolds in London in 1753, materially affected Ramsay's hitherto unrivalled position, and in 1754 he returned for three years further study in Italy. During this time he painted a portrait of his second wife (p. 149), perhaps the most exquisitely tender and unaffected portrayal of the century. In Rome Ramsay was a member of the Adam circle, so active in the development of Neo-classicism, and its ideas left their influence on his later work. Royal patronage of Ramsay began in 1757 with a whole-length portrait of George III as Prince of Wales, followed by commissions for other official portraits, including those of King George III and Queen Charlotte for the coronation. Ramsay made his fortune from the replicas that were painted of these royal portraits, and after continuing in practice during the 1760s, when he executed sophisticated and entrancingly delicate portraits, including one of Rousseau, he gave up painting, about 1770, in favour of writing essays, mostly on political subjects.

The central figure in this chapter is Sir Joshua Reynolds (1723–92) of whom his friend Goldsmith wrote:

> Here Reynolds is laid, and to tell you my mind,
> He has left not a better or wiser behind!
> His pencil was striking, resistless and grand,
> His manners were gentle, complying and bland.
> Still born to improve us in every part,
> His pencil our faces, his manners our heart;
> To coxcombs averse, yet most civilly steering;
> When they judged without skill, he was still hard of hearing;
> When they talked of their Raphael's, Correggio's and Stuff,
> He shifted his trumpet, and only took snuff.
>
> *(Retaliation)*

The friend of Burke, Dr Johnson, and the great actor David Garrick, Reynolds played an important part as a theorist, discussing in his fifteen *Discourses* the theory and practice of painting. As a painter it was Reynolds' achievement to restore the Grand Manner of the Renaissance and the Baroque in portraiture. This had, in fact, deep roots in England, where Van Dyck had introduced a tradition of large-scale, glamorous portraiture which exercised as much fascination in the eighteenth century as in the more loudly and nostalgically Romantic nineteenth. In designing a pose and setting for each sitter, whom he endowed with real or imaginary characteristics of a learned nature, and whom he placed in a related setting to produce an integrated picture, Reynolds called again and again upon the Old Masters. From his Italian sketchbooks we know that he studied the paintings of the Italian, Dutch and Flemish schools, in particular of Michelangelo, Titian, the Carracci and the other Bolognese,

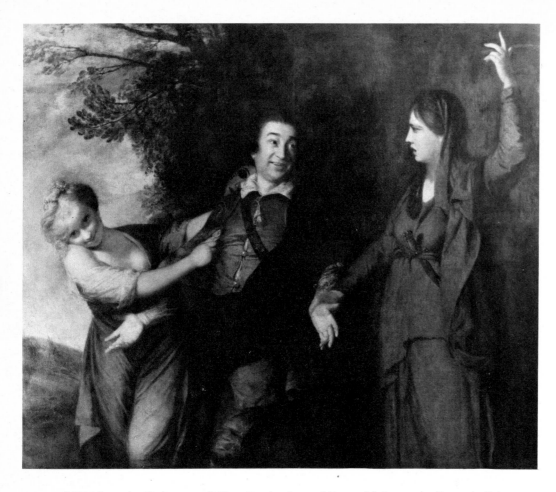

JOSHUA REYNOLDS, *Garrick between Tragedy and Comedy,* 1762. Private collection.

of Rembrandt, Rubens and Van Dyck. One of Reynolds' outstanding qualities was his ability to compose his pictures. His sitters, however improbable some may seem to us – and no doubt did when they were painted – are engaged with imposing manner in playing the role in which Reynolds chose to cast them.

Within the limited range of the portrait Reynolds was constantly experimenting, both in composition and in technique. Gainsborough recognized this inventiveness in his famous exclamation: 'Damn him, how various he is!' Something of this variousness is to be attributed to Reynolds' awareness of the Old Masters, which made him conscious of the great variety of possible solutions to the problems of portraiture that had already been discovered. In this sense he was an honest believer in the eclecticism of Baroque classicism and in his art strove conscientiously to unite what were believed to be the excellencies of the various schools – the sculptural majesty of form of Michelangelo and the colour of the Venetians, particularly Titian. Titian, indeed, exercised a fascination over Reynolds and his school, since his technique of colour was the foundation of so much in Baroque technique to which classicizing artists like Reynolds looked back across the intervening prettiness of the Rococo.

From his native Devonshire Reynolds came to London in 1740 to serve his apprenticeship to Thomas Hudson (1701–79), a fashionable, old-style society portrait painter, with whom he stayed for two and a half years. Reynolds then practised as a portrait painter, mainly in London and Devonshire, until 1749, when he set sail for Italy with his friend Commodore Keppel. After two years in Rome, Reynolds visited Florence, Parma, Bologna, Venice and Paris on his return journey to London, where he established himself in 1753. With his portrait of Keppel, Reynolds showed how he had profited by his study in Italy. This portrait secured his reputation and with it the triumph of the new style. In it classical elements are fused into the figure which is united with a seascape, illustrating an incident in the career of the sitter, to

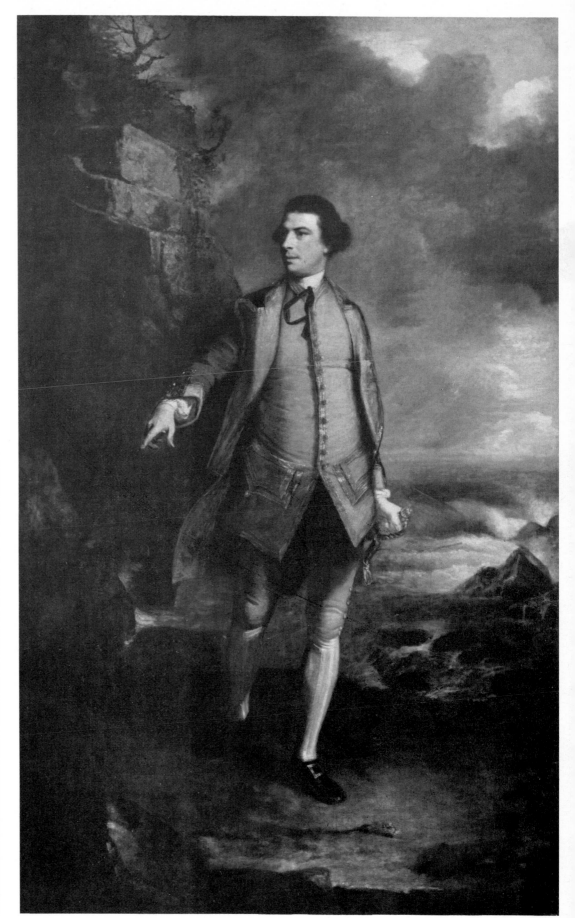

Right, JOSHUA REYNOLDS, *Commodore Keppel*,
1753–4.
The National Maritime Museum, Greenwich.
Below, ALLAN RAMSAY, *Norman MacLeod of
MacLeod*, 1748.
Dunvegan Castle.
Collection of Mr John MacLeod of MacLeod.

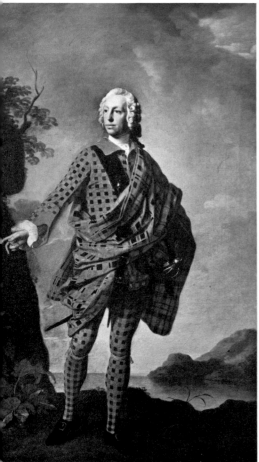

165

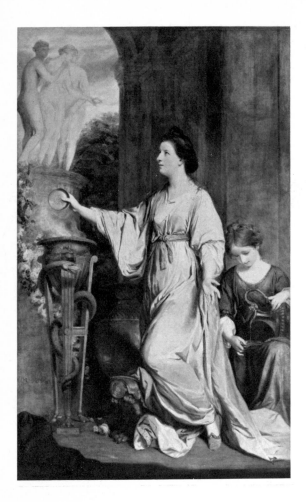

produce a precisely evocative and vital image. The fresh presentation which Reynolds gave to his sitters brought him the patronage of the town and he committed himself, in the early 1760s, to a style of stately portraits replete with learned and pictorial allusions. Its success was such that other artists of the 1760s used it momentarily for certain paintings, and Reynolds' only serious rival, Francis Cotes (1726–70), very successfully adopted classicizing drapery in a similar way for the last few years of his life.

Reynolds' prestige led him to be unanimously elected first President of the Royal Academy in 1768 in spite of the fact that 'The King and Queen could not endure the presence of him; he was poison to their sight'. During his first years as President Reynolds further extended his earlier inventions of dressing his portraits in a classicizing guise by adapting poses from Bolognese art. The paintings that Reynolds produced in accordance with these ideas appeared to some artists of the day, less committed to the theory of eclecticism, as plagiarisms. The scandal that surrounded Nathaniel Hone's (1718–84) *The Conjuror* was in part due to its attack on Reynolds' borrowings. Not only did Hone use one of Reynolds' favourite models for the figure of his Conjuror, but in the prints after the Old Masters to which he points, Hone was charging Reynolds with plagiarism. He entitled his picture *The Pictorial Conjuror, displaying the Whole Art of Optical Deception*. It was rejected from the Royal Academy of 1775, ostensibly on the ground that it contained a now painted-over figure of Angelica Kauffmann in the nude. With the advent of Gainsborough on to the London scene, in 1774, Reynolds added to his display of allegory and learning in order to enhance the strikingness of his portraits at the Academy exhibitions. After a journey to Flanders and Holland, in 1781, his portrait style acquired a greater naturalness, no doubt learned from Rubens. He used a lighter palette at this time, and even when he retained his classicizing allusions – *Mrs Siddons as the Tragic Muse* (p. 170), perhaps his masterpiece – there is a new directness and freshness.

Above, JOSHUA REYNOLDS, *Lady Sarah Bunbury sacrificing to the Graces*, 1765.
By courtesy of The Art Institute of Chicago.
Right, NATHANIEL HONE, *The Conjuror*, 1775.
National Gallery of Ireland, Dublin.

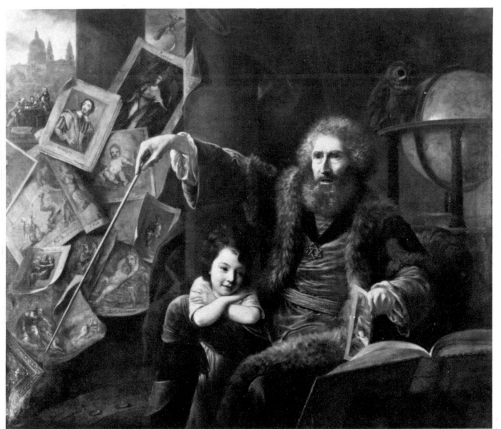

To modern taste Reynolds' intimate portraits such as those of Dr Johnson and Baretti, with their honest and penetrating confrontation of the physical appearance and the moral nature of the sitter, appeal far more than the artificial mechanisms of his portraits in the Grand Manner. The key of eighteenth-century paintings is too bright to sustain the acreage of unvaried and insensitively painted drapery which seventeenth-century art, with its darker key and dramatic composition in chiaroscuro, was able to absorb. Reynolds' paintings are no exception to this law and he has suffered besides because his constant experimenting with pigments was unfortunate in its results. There were complaints even in his lifetime that colours had begun to fade or even vanish, and in his awareness of the need for dark colours he experimented fatally with bitumen. In paintings which escaped this treatment one can see that he was a brilliant colourist with a warm palette.

In his later years Reynolds was much criticized for justifying his own practice by the theory of the 'historical portrait', in which he sought to reconcile the unpleasant fact that portraiture was the only paying genre with the duty of every artist to aspire to the highest branch of art. The artistic atmosphere of the 1770s and 1780s, when many artists believed that the foundation of the Academy would lead to the triumph of imaginative art – that is historical painting – in England, and the self-denial of James Barry (of which more later) shamed or encouraged Reynolds into producing three or four history paintings such as *The Infant Hercules strangling serpents* for Catherine the Great and *Cupid and Psyche*. Even in his own day these were received with mixed appreciation, and if Reynolds, in spite of his variousness, has suffered posthumously, like all portrait painters, from the monotony of his subject matter, it is possible that in avoiding history painting he recognized his own limitations. Yet in *Mrs Siddons as the Tragic Muse* (p. 170) Reynolds has achieved the fusion of a portrait with an allegorical character in a manner that triumphantly justifies his own theory while anticipating the imaginative sympathy of Neo-classicism with the daemonic elements of antiquity.

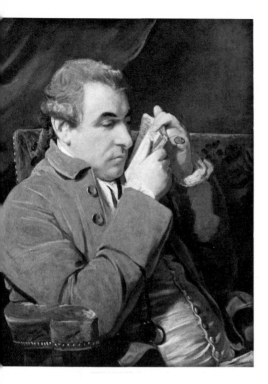

JOSHUA REYNOLDS, *Joseph Baretti*. Collection of the Viscountess Galway.

The portraits of Thomas Gainsborough (1727–88) are in antithesis to those of Reynolds. Rhythmical, gay and light, they become aerial and almost impressionistic in his later years. Unlike that of Reynolds, Gainsborough's work is technically impeccable. In 1788 Reynolds devoted his *Discourse* to the students of the Royal Academy to Gainsborough, with whom he had never been on terms. Making an exemplar of his devotion to his art, Reynolds mentioned Gainsborough's custom of painting by night: 'By candlelight, not only objects appear more beautiful, but from their being in a greater breadth of light and shadow, as well as having a greater breadth and uniformity of colour, nature appears in a higher style; and even the flesh seems to take a higher and richer tone of colour'.

As a schoolboy Gainsborough essayed landscape, and before coming to London for his training he taught himself by copying Dutch landscapes. In London he worked with Gravelot, assisting him in engravings, and so learned design from an exponent of the French Rococo style. Gravelot taught drawing at the St Martin's Lane Academy, and introduced Gainsborough there. From his early association with Gravelot, who taught drawing from dressed-up dolls, and from Hayman who taught painting at the St Martin's Lane Academy, Gainsborough's early artificiality of style derives.

An early portrait, possibly of the artist and his wife, with whom he made a runaway marriage in 1746 (p. 168), and probably dating from that year, has all the French Rococo gaiety. The ease and informality with which Gainsborough composes his sitters, eventually fusing them with the landscape in which they are set, instead of using it as a form of backdrop, developed during the period he spent in Suffolk immediately after his London training (*Mr and Mrs Andrews*, London, National Gallery). Gainsborough had settled in Ipswich by 1750 and he remained there for ten years. Inevitably his practice was in potraiture. In the life-size, half-length

167

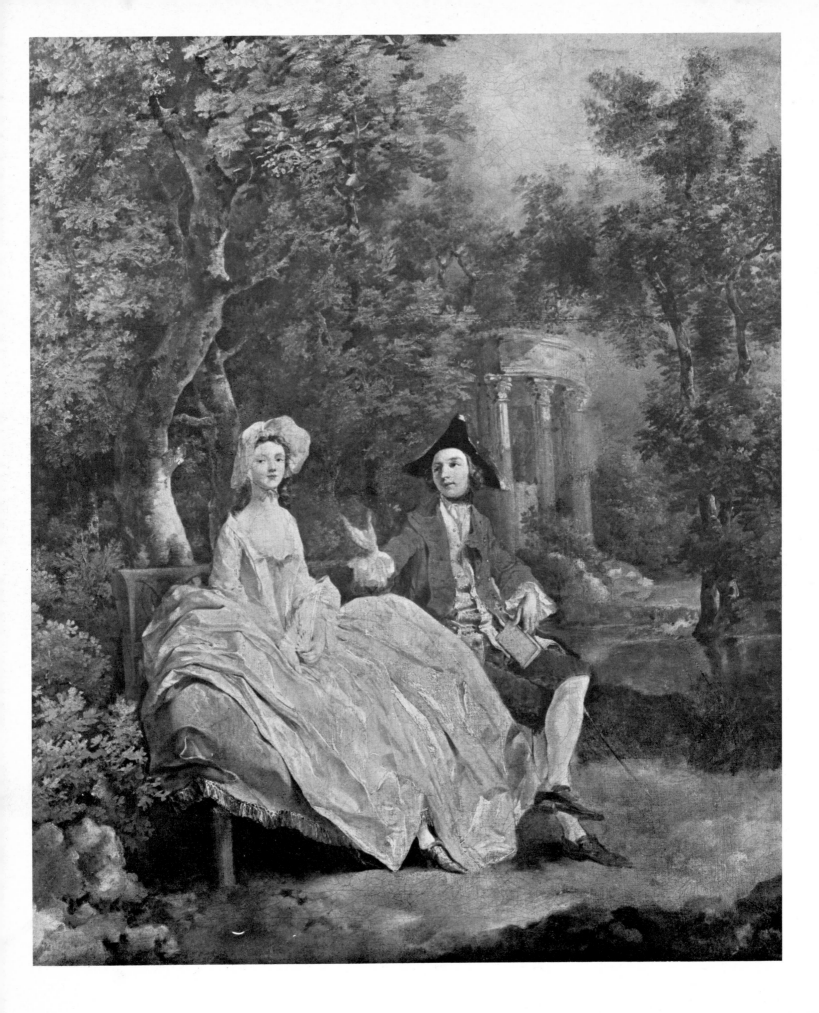

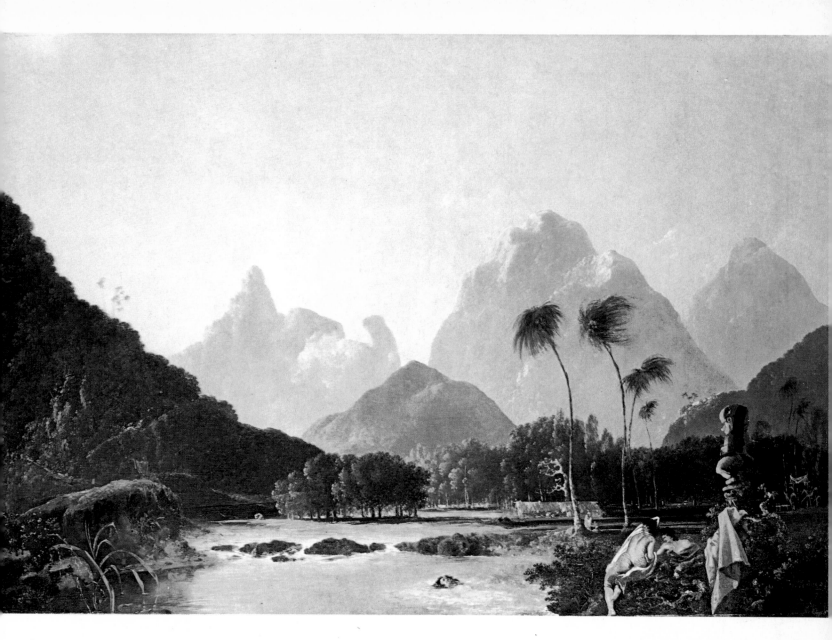

Above, W. HODGES, *Tahiti Revisited.*
National Maritime Museum, Greenwich, on loan
from the Ministry of Defence (Navy).

portraits of this period we can discern his progress from initial stiffness to the freedom he was able to exercise in his whole-length portraits after he had removed to
the wider prospects offered by fashionable Bath. In Bath, where he remained until
1774, he was more occupied with portraiture than at any other period of his life.
The relaxed and increasingly elegant figures of this period (*James Quin*, Dublin,
National Gallery) owe some of their refinement to Gainsborough's study of the old
masters, particularly Van Dyck (*Jonathan Buttal, The Blue Boy,* Huntingdon).
Gainsborough's interest in light and the shimmer and reflections of silks and satins
developed quickly at this time (*Mary, Countess Howe,* Kenwood (p. 171)). His gifts as a
draughtsman enabled him to express movement in a sensuous way which is heightened by his brilliantly fluid use of colour. Although he exhibited over a dozen of such
full-length portraits at the Society of Artists from 1761 to 1768, Gainsborough did
not adapt his style from one which required sympathetic hanging and careful lighting
to one with the bolder definitions needed for public exhibitions. Indeed, Gainsborough's relations with the Royal Academy were to founder on this very problem.

In 1774 Gainsborough moved to London, where he soon gained royal patronage.
His full-length portraits of the Duke and Duchess of Cumberland were shown at the
Royal Academy in 1777; the lively and individual manner of these state portraits was
repeated in the full-lengths of the King and Queen exhibited in 1781. The series of

Left, THOMAS GAINSBOROUGH,
*Gainsborough and his Wife
(Conversation in a Park),* c. 1746.
The Louvre, Paris.

169

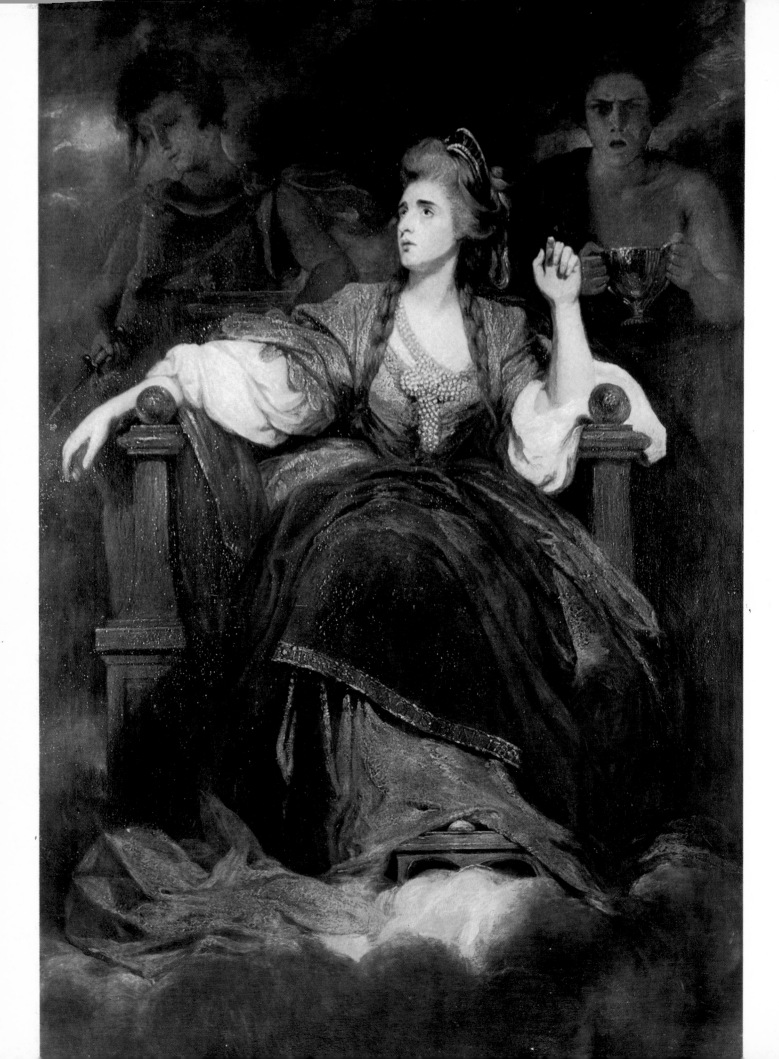

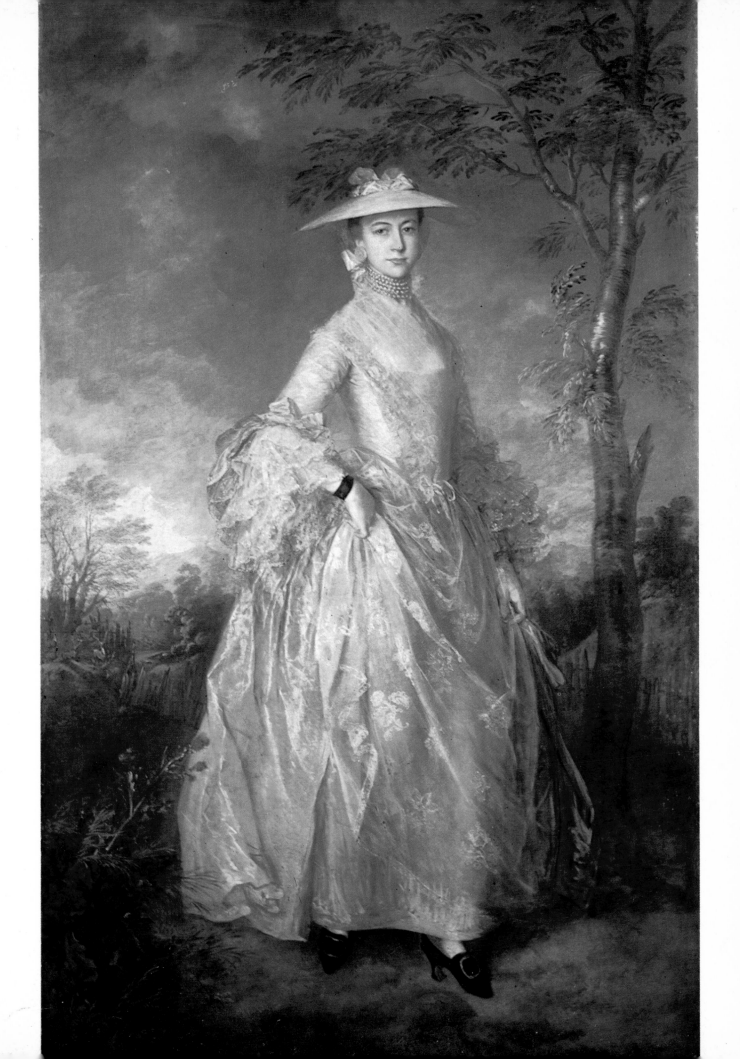

Previous page, left, JOSHUA REYNOLDS,
Mrs Siddons as the Tragic Muse, 1789.
Henry E. Huntington Library and
Art Gallery, San Marino, California.
Previous page, right, THOMAS GAINSBOROUGH,
Mary Countess of Howe, c. 1765.
By permission of the Greater London Council
as Trustees of the Iveagh Bequest, Kenwood.

Right, THOMAS GAINSBOROUGH,
Margaret and Mary Gainsborough, c. 1750.
Victoria and Albert Museum, London.

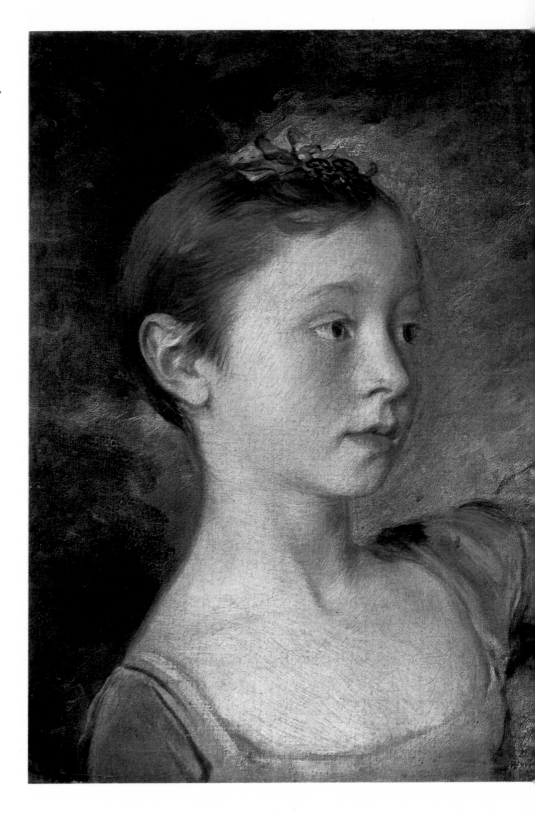

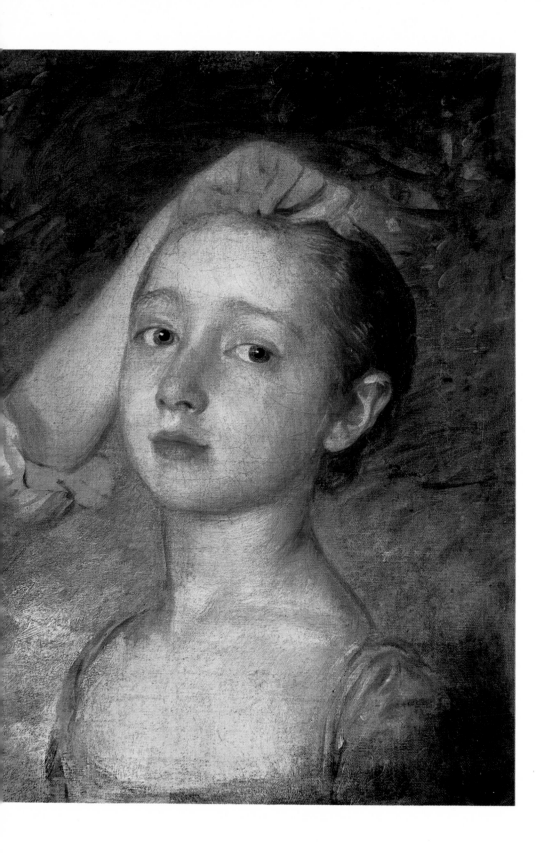

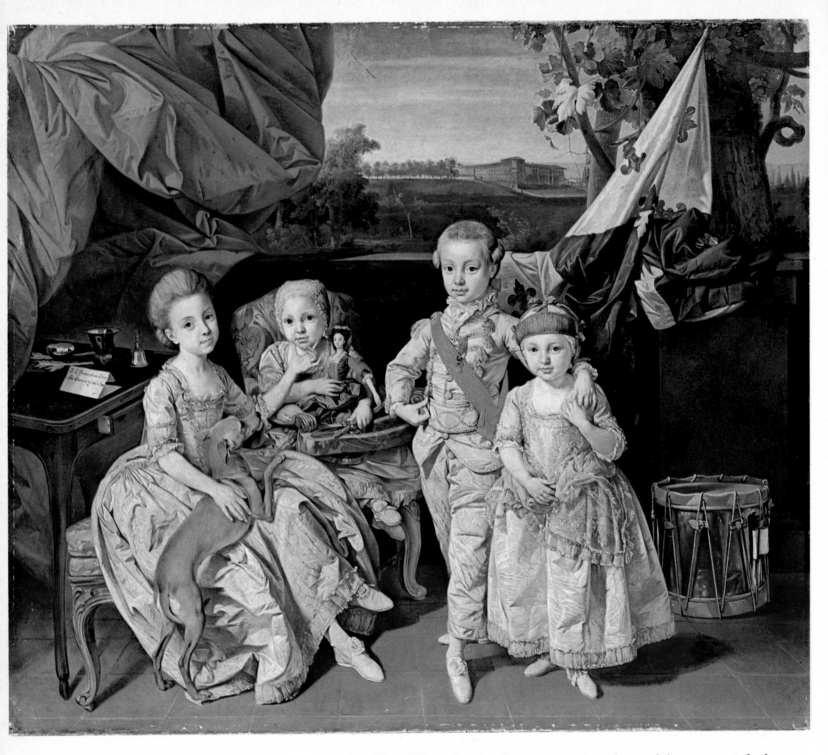

JOHANN ZOFFANY, *The Four Grandchildren of Maria Theresa*, 1778.
Kunsthistorisches Museum, Vienna.

royal children followed and at the same time Gainsborough began to satisfy the more perceptive taste of the Prince of Wales by painting portraits of the Prince and of his friends. The Prince also ordered two landscapes from Gainsborough and bought his sketch of *Diana and Actaeon* (H.M. the Queen) at the sale of pictures which belonged to Gainsborough's widow. Amongst Gainsborough's late portraits is the ethereal group of the three eldest princesses, painted for the Saloon of Carlton House, where the Prince of Wales intended to hang portraits of his family. It shows an imaginative fusion of Gainsborough's native informality and delicate style of pencilling with the European grand manner. This picture, reduced to its present dimensions in the mid-nineteenth century, was the cause of Gainsborough's second and final quarrel with the Royal Academy. He planned to exhibit it in 1784 and asked the Hanging Committee if they would waive the regulations governing the hanging of full-lengths,

174

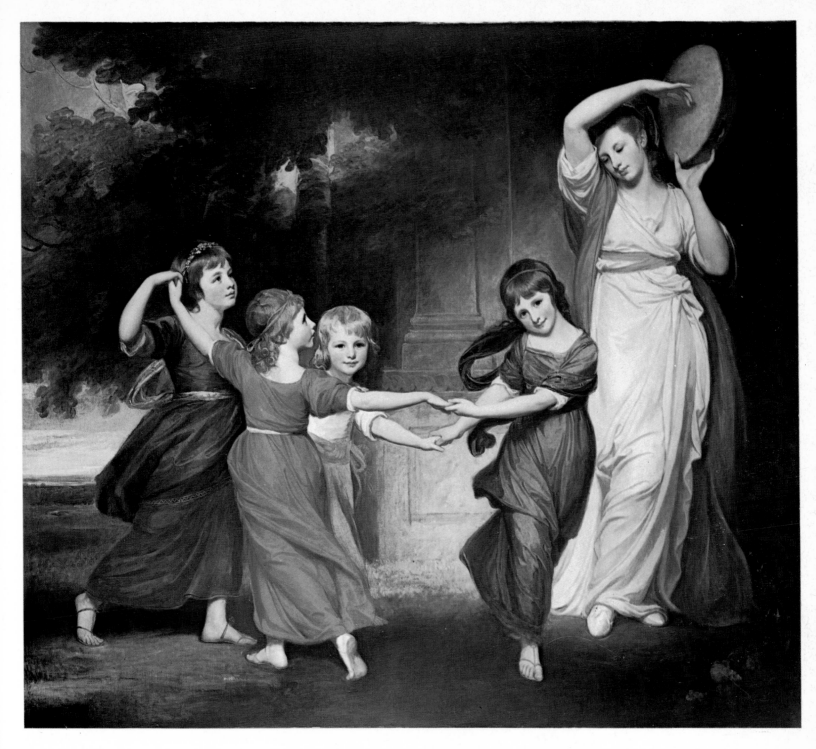

GEORGE ROMNEY, *The Leveson-Gower Children*, 1776–7.
Abbot Hall Art Gallery, Kendal.

since the picture had been painted in so tender a light that to hang it higher than five and a half feet from the ground would make the likenesses and touch invisible. His request was refused and Gainsborough withdrew all his works from the exhibition, showing them at his own house in Pall Mall later in the year.

It was not until the 1770s that English newspapers carried much comment on matters artistic. Reviews of the Royal Academy and other artistic exhibitions were an innovation of the Rev. Henry Bate, editor and part founder, in 1772, of the *Morning Post*. To Bate's friendship and support of Gainsborough we owe much information about the artist's life in London, and after 1780, when Bate founded the *Morning Herald*, he printed in it a full record of the artist he championed.

With Reynolds and Gainsborough, whose success he divided, George Romney (1734–1802) is the best known of English eighteenth-century portrait painters on a

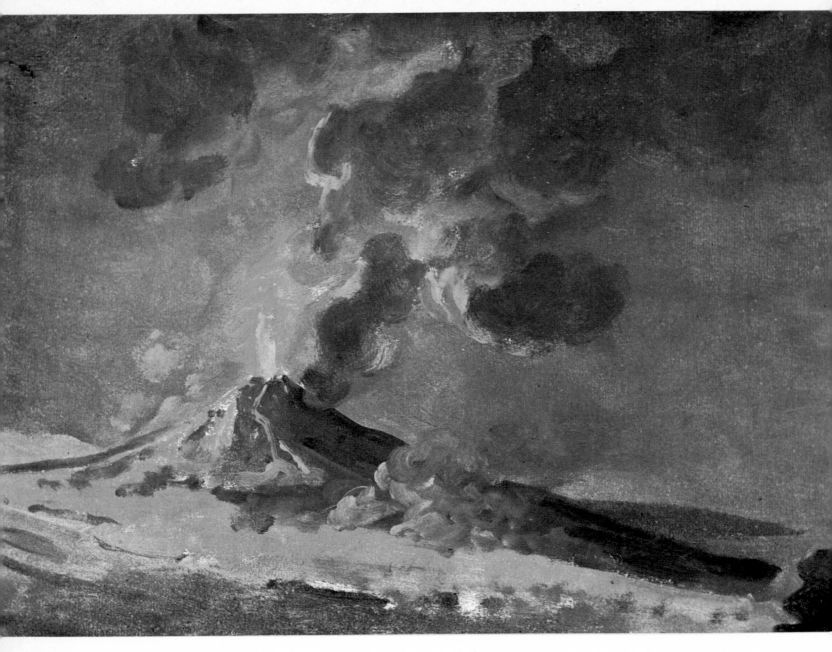

JOSEPH WRIGHT, *Vesuvius in Eruption*, 1774.
Derby Museum and Art Gallery.

large scale. Born and trained in north-west England, where he first practised, Romney came to London in 1762. Unlike many English painters who made their living from it, Romney loved portraiture, but he too had aspirations towards history painting. Although he received an award from the Society of Arts for his *Death of Wolfe* in 1763, Romney seems largely to have resolved his dilemma by making great numbers of drawings of historical and ideal subjects, many boldly drawn with a brush. Romney's life-long interest in antique sculpture, of which he owned a number of fine casts, may have been confirmed by the classicizing manner of French seventeenth-century painting, which he saw on a brief visit to Paris in 1764. Presumably, too, he drew from such classical sculptures and casts as were available in London, but it was after his visit to Italy of 1773–5, where he studied principally in Rome and Venice, that the influence of antique art became a very marked feature of his portraits (p. 175). His sense of design, modelling and colour were freer and simpler than those of his contemporaries, and the freshness and spontaneity of his many un-finished works and sketches reveal where his true interest lay. From 1781, fascinated by her power of striking plastic and expressive poses, Romney was emotionally involved with the notorious and beautiful Emma, Lady Hamilton, whom he painted

176

in countless classical and allegorical guises for the next ten years. Introspective and unsociable, Romney shrank from contacts with the world at large and only during his first few years in London did he exhibit his work publicly. In 1786 Romney's interests in literary and historical composition made him, with his friend the poet Hayley, one of the chief promoters of Alderman Boydell's Shakespeare Gallery. Romney is now best remembered as a portraitist. He responded more intimately and poetically to beauty in women than either Reynolds or Gainsborough. Reynolds was responsive only to their archness or dignity, Gainsborough to their elegance, but Romney had that sort of cult for women which regards them as divine creatures. For men, not surprisingly, he had nothing of this intuitive sympathy, though his power of clear and immediate presentation rarely deserts him. In spite of his enormous output, both of finished and unfinished portraits, during a long working life, Romney is one of the most difficult of English artists to study, since his paintings are even more widely dispersed among museums and private collections than those of his contemporaries.

George Stubbs (1724–1806) stands out from the artistic coteries of London, a forceful individualist. At the age of fifteen, he quarrelled with his master, whom he left, saying that 'Henceforward he would look into Nature for himself, and consult and study her only'. In these words Stubbs was emphasizing one of the twin tenets of classicism, the imitation of nature, at the expense of the other, the imitation of the Old Masters. By his anatomical studies of the horse he was to found his art on the same direct investigation of nature as Michelangelo in his studies of the human body. He early practised as a portrait painter in the north of England, particularly in York, the northern capital, where he began those anatomical studies which have also earned him a place among the great natural scientists. Stubbs went to Italy in 1754 to make sure that his conviction that Nature is greater than all art, whether Greek or Roman, Renaissance or contemporary, was correct. Satisfied on this point he left Rome and returned to England to pursue his studies of anatomy and his portraiture. At a lonely farmhouse at Horkstow in Lincolnshire, with the company only of Miss Mary Spencer his common-law wife, Stubbs began the work which culminated some ten years later with the publication in 1766 of *The Anatomy of the Horse including a particular Description of the Bones, Cartilages, Muscles, Fascias, Ligaments, Nerves, Arteries, Veins and Glands* for which Stubbs had gradually stripped down the carcases of horses, recording each stage in accurate scientific drawings. For this pioneering work Stubbs engraved the plates himself. Towards the end of his life in the mid-1790s he prepared dissections for another work – *A Comparative Anatomical Exposition of the Human Body with that of a Tiger and a Common Fowl* – which began to appear in 1804 and 1805, but which was unfinished at the time of his death.

None of his early portraits has been identified and our first impression of Stubbs' work in oils is therefore that of a mature artist. When he came to London, about 1760, the prevalent feeling among artists was, as we have seen, one of optimism at the prospect of enlarged horizons. The 1760s were certainly a decade of optimism for Stubbs, whose powers of invention and indefatigable productiveness – he employed no assistants – were at their height. For the Duke of Richmond, who was probably Stubbs' first patron in the south, he painted three large canvasses. That of the Duke's racehorses at exercise in Goodwood Park combines in one open landscape, stretching away to the English Channel, riders, horses and dogs in movement and repose, while the group at the right, grooming a horse, foreshadows, in its classic simplicity, Stubbs' groups of the 1780s and 1790s of labourers at work or stable boys holding horses, executed without a trace of the sentimentality that inspired many scenes of rural life painted for the escapist town dweller. Stubbs' exact physical knowledge enabled him to paint innumerable classic studies of mares and foals, of which one, without a background, painted in 1762 for the Marquess of Rockingham,

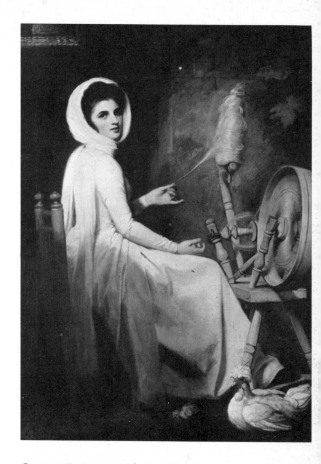

GEORGE ROMNEY, *Lady Hamilton at the Spinning Wheel*, 1782–6.
By permission of the Greater London Council as Trustees of the Iveagh Bequest, Kenwood.

177

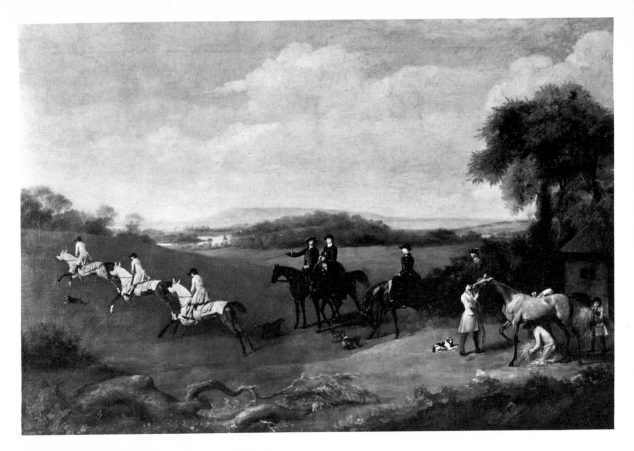

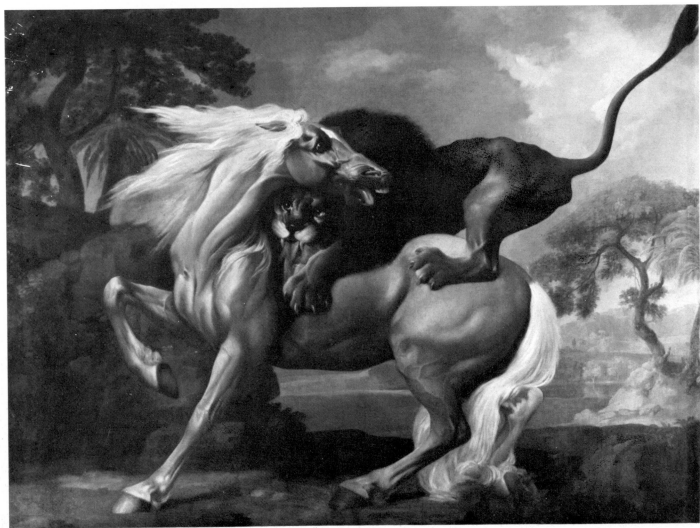

contrasts in grandeur with the huge picture of a *Lion attacking a Horse* done for the same patron. Stubbs studied other wild animals – leopards, tigers, cheetahs, a zebra, monkeys and exotic birds, in addition to domestic sheep and cattle and of course dogs. The large picture of a *Cheetah with two Indians and a Stag* (Manchester City Art Gallery) of about 1765 is an early approach to a subject he was to perfect in the 1780s, in his engravings of lions, tigers and cheetahs, done in so masterly a technique that they seem to be of warm soft sleek fur, inviting to the touch. Early in the 1770s Stubbs was experimenting with painting in enamel on copper and some ten years later Wedgwood made for him large china plaques suitable for the same medium. The smooth gloss and depth of enamel and its brilliant colours make it perfectly adapted to rendering the texture of animal fur. Stubbs' interest in the medium shows his primary concern was with truth of rendering.

In spite of his many formal compositions, his conversation pieces and subject pictures, Stubbs became known as a horse painter and sporting or horse painters were not highly thought of at the end of the eighteenth century. He quarrelled with the Royal Academy in 1781, refusing to send a picture to be deposited before being received as Academician because of having had his pictures skied at the exhibition. The feeling of detached precision communicated by Stubbs' work is even more extremely realized in the scenes of country labourers he produced in the 1780s. It is similarly present in a *Lady and Gentleman in a Carriage* (National Gallery) and a *Phaeton with Cream Ponies and a Stable-lad*, where the elegant carriage and, above all, the beautiful sleek animals are silhouetted against the dark trees. In 1790 Stubbs received a commission from *The Turf Review* to paint a series of portraits of celebrated

Opposite above, GEORGE STUBBS, *The Duke of Richmond's Racehorses at Exercise.* By courtesy of the Trustees of Goodwood House. *Opposite below,* GEORGE STUBBS, *Lion attacking a Horse,* 1762. Collection of Mr and Mrs Paul Mellon.

Below, GEORGE STUBBS, *Phaeton with Cream Ponies and a Stable-lad, c.*1785. Collection of Mr and Mrs Paul Mellon.

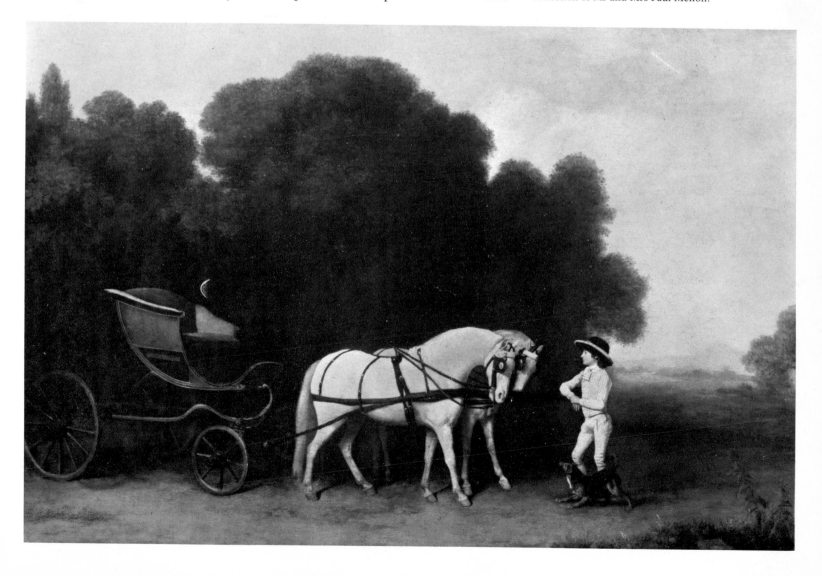

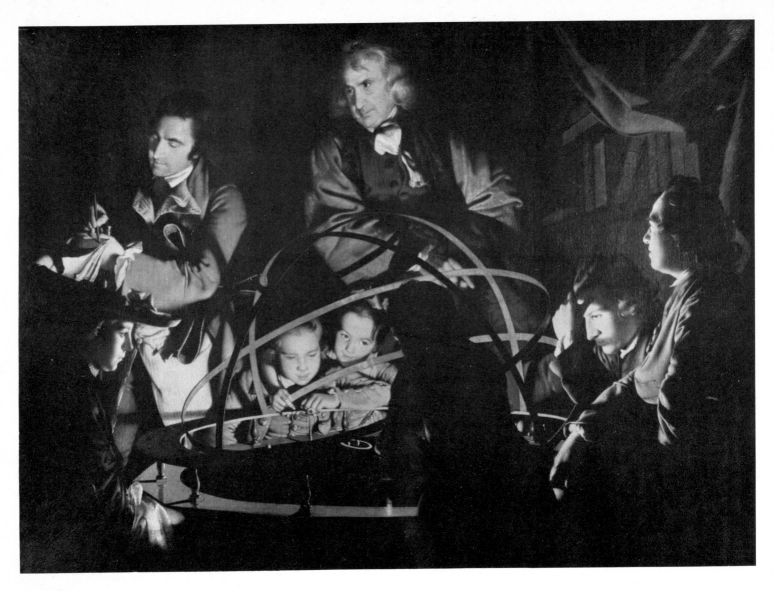

racers, which would be exhibited and then engraved and published; he completed sixteen pictures of such famous horses as Eclipse, Pumpkin, Gimcrack, and Mambrino, but the enterprise was ruined by the outbreak of the Napoleonic wars.

Joseph Wright of Derby (1734–97) started his career with a conventional training under Hudson and began as a portrait painter. It was early in the 1760s that Wright's fascination with candlelight effects of a sort that had not been painted since the early seventeenth century in the Low Countries appeared. Wright's most famous picture, *A Philosopher giving a Lecture on the Orrery*, painted about 1764–6, is certainly one of the more remarkable compositions of its age. The rapt attention given to the wonders of modern science is highlighted with a stillness of concentrated light. *An Experiment on a Bird in an Air Pump* (Tate Gallery), painted a year or two later, reflects not only the increasing interest in the Midlands in scientific experiments and the new sensibility but provides a dramatic view of the tense moment of success or failure of the experiment, resulting in the life or death of the bird. Wright's interest in these candlelight effects, outmoded though much admired in other countries, is indicative of the insistent revivalist classicism of English eighteenth-century art, and of its ambition to rival the Old Masters on their own ground.

Wright went to Rome early in 1774: there he spent his time studying the antiquities and the works of Michelangelo in the Vatican. He began to paint landscape, as might be expected, in the Italo-Dutch tradition, producing moonlights, grottoes, with their opportunities for chiaroscuro, and La Girandola, the Roman firework festival. A visit to Naples in the following year to see Vesuvius erupting resulted in dramatic pictures of the volcano demonstrating Wright's powerful effects of light and shade (p. 176).

On his return Wright continued as a portrait and landscape painter. After an unsuccessful period in Bath he returned to Derby in 1779, where, in spite of ill-health he had a large practice particularly amongst the professional men and industrialists of the Midlands, such as Arkwright and Josiah Wedgwood. His contacts were particularly close with the literary circle of Lichfield and the Lunar Society, centred on Birmingham. Some of these patrons, amongst them Wedgwood, were more sympathetic to the higher ambitions of the eighteenth-century artist than aristocratic society, and commissioned history paintings and subject pictures from Wright, rather as in the nineteenth century their successors were attracted by the imaginative art of the pre-Raphaelites. The aspirations of Wright's circle towards a better political and social order are reflected in the portrait of Sir Brooke Boothby in a pastoral setting, reclining among the simple beauties of nature, holding the manuscript of Rousseau's *Confessions* (Tate Gallery).

John Hamilton Mortimer (1741–79), apprenticed to Hudson, soon became something of a prodigy, carrying off prizes for drawing at the St Martin's Lane Academy, the Duke of Richmond's Gallery and, in 1763 and 1764, for historical paintings submitted to the Society of Arts. *St Paul preaching to the Britons* which won a first prize, was, however, one of Mortimer's last history pictures until the following decade. Meanwhile he painted portraits and conversation groups, typical of their time. Some are rather static and contrived, but they developed into a satisfactory, if staid, resolution of the problems involved, especially in interior settings, as in the *Drake Family of Shardeloes*, painted almost at the end of his life.

At about the age of thirty Mortimer's subject matter changed. He began to paint small-scale subjects, historical, biblical, moralizing genre subjects and above all *banditti*, inspired by Salvator Rosa. Elected Vice-President of the Society of Artists

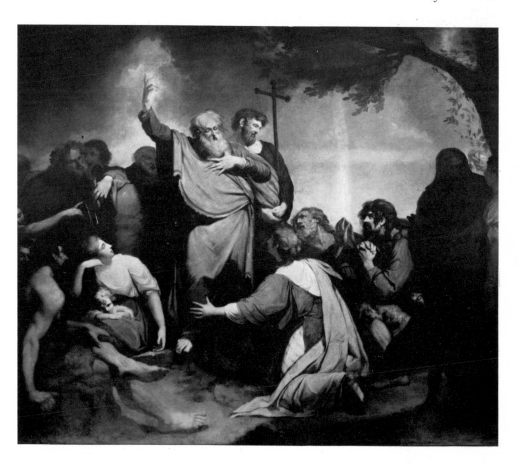

J.H. MORTIMER, *St Paul preaching to the Britons, c.* 1770.
High Wycombe Public Art Gallery and Museum.

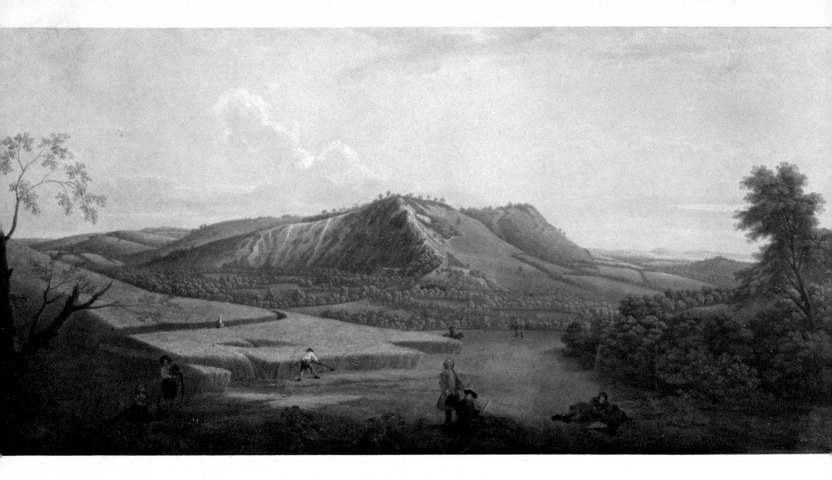

in 1770 and President four years later, Mortimer occupied a leading place in a group of artists which, if abandoned by most of the fashionable painters, was not yet completely overshadowed by the Royal Academy. At this period Mortimer's reputation was at its height, his imagination and his hand kept pace with one another. The tight and wiry drawings produced with great rapidity are transformed into scenes of painted energy, keeping all their immediacy in the process. In spite of his early death Mortimer was always regarded by his own and the next generation as an important figure in eighteenth-century art, perhaps because his subject matter had a variety and a wide imaginative range that encouraged later artists, particularly in designing for the print.

Landscape painting in the eighteenth century grew from a rather prosaic, in some cases almost diagrammatic, rendering, often of the grounds of a stately house as seen by the eye of a passing bird, into the expression of a classic vision on the one hand, and of a poetical imagination on the other. The most significant early landscape painter was John Wootton (d. 1756) who worked in both the Anglo-Dutch topographical tradition, producing sporting conversation pieces and hunting scenes, and in the manner of Claude and Gaspard, introducing overtones of Arcady. The next step away from the perspective or purely topographical view may be seen in the work of George Lambert (1700–65). Although at first an imitator of Wootton, his *Hilly Landscape with a Cornfield* of 1733 has a new and attractive simplicity and freshness. In its use of bright yellow and green it illustrates the imposition of Rococo colours on a landscape tradition derived from seventeenth-century Netherlandish formulae, which will remain characteristic of the Rococo landscape in England. Rococo too is the preference for broad daylight, rather than for morning or evening, the times preferred for landscape subjects by Baroque classical landscape artists, because they lend themselves to chiaroscuro composition and effect. During his lifetime Lambert was well known for the scenery he designed and painted for Lincoln's Inn Fields Theatre and later at Covent Garden. Active in the professional affairs of artists,

GEORGE LAMBERT, *A Hilly Landscape with a Cornfield*, 1733.
The Tate Gallery, London.

182

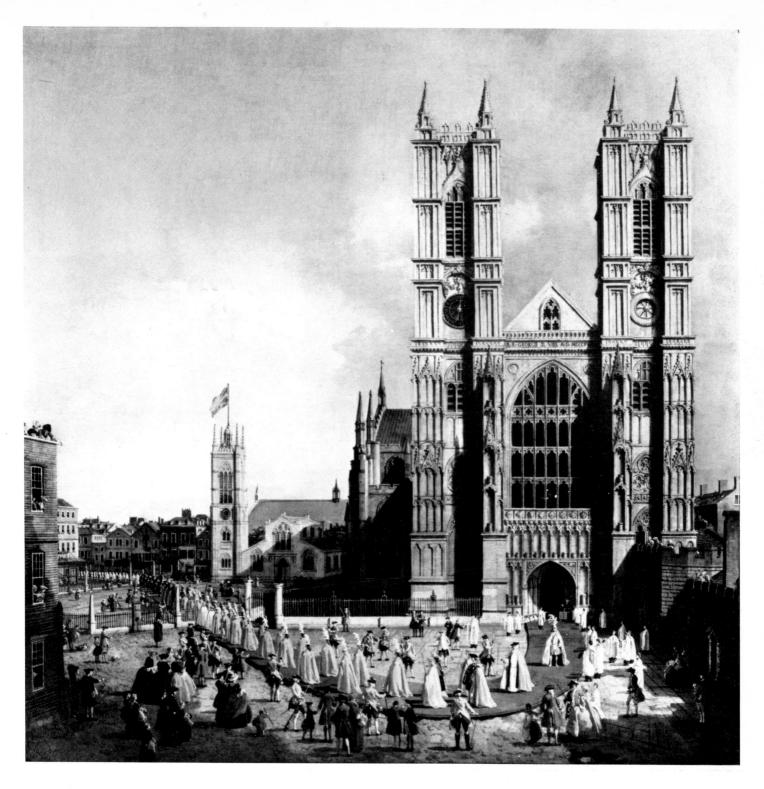

CANALETTO, *Procession of the Order of the Bath,* 1749.
By courtesy of the Dean and Chapter of Westminster.

Lambert was chairman of the Society of Artists and in 1761, shortly before he died, became its first President.

The topographical tradition received a fresh impetus in 1746, when Canaletto (1697–1768) arrived, to spend almost nine years infusing a sparkling Venetian light into the muddy waters of the Thames. His luminous paint bestowed a new and immediate gaiety on the *Procession of the Order of the Bath* and captured the poetry of Alnwick Castle, of Eton and above all of London. After looking carefully at one of these views in which the crystalline atmosphere preserves for ever the immediacy of the scene, it is a shock to turn away and find the prospect different. As a topographer Canaletto had no equal, but he inspired a successful follower in Samuel

183

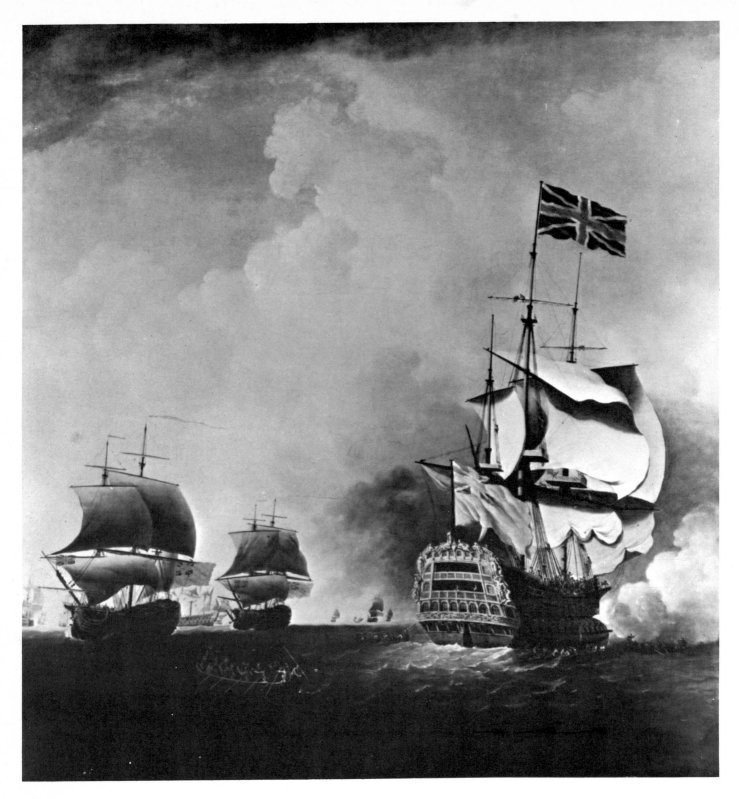

Scott (1702–72) an able marine painter in the Van de Velde tradition. Scott painted the, perhaps more typical, damp-laden atmosphere of the English waterscape, adding to the topographical element the lessons he had already learned as a marine painter.

While Canaletto and Scott were prospering Richard Wilson (1713–82) and Thomas Gainsborough, whose work was to constitute the basis of the great English landscape school, were producing their first landscapes. Wilson, who had come to London from Wales, set up as a portrait painter, making his first known excursus into landscape with the two small views he presented to the Foundling Hospital in 1746. In 1750 he went to Italy where, after a short time in Venice, he journeyed on to Rome and there

184

devoted himself entirely to landscape. In Rome he absorbed the styles of Claude and Gaspard, fusing them with the classic landscape and pure light into elegiac interpretations of the Campagna, recalling not only the form of the valleys and hills but the great figures of Republican and Augustan Rome who once moved among them. Wilson's Italian landscapes, many of which he painted after his return to London – which probably took place in 1757 – from sketches made on the spot, met with little encouragement from the collectors of the great seventeenth-century Dutch and Franco-Italian masters of landscape. Nor did they fare any better with the Grand Tourists who might have been expected to wish for some permanent reminder of the landscapes through which they had passed: but unlike Patch's picture postcard views of the Arno in Florence which had the appeal of international *vedutismo*, Wilson's poetic interpretations were alien to the taste that admired the pretty flickerings of Rococo paint. During the 1760s Wilson painted landscapes in the grand manner, peopling them with mythological figures. These too failed to please most English collectors, or even English critics. The *Niobe* (destroyed) was severely censured by Reynolds in a famous passage of the *Discourse* he delivered after Wilson's death. Wilson, like Claude, was much weaker in his figures than in his landscapes. He had greater success in developing the topographical tradition, in his distant views of great houses such as Wilton and Sion, or of prospects stretching to a distantly discerned horizon. Into the moisture-laden atmosphere of the English or Welsh landscape Wilson introduced clarity of form and colour (p. 186), and in his shadows conveys the chill of an island summer, even in so Italianate a composition as the *Ruined Arch at Kew* (p. 152). For the remainder of his life Wilson continued to paint these classic landscapes, too intellectual and austere to bring him a decent living. Perhaps the early opinion of his young pupil Thomas Jones was too widely shared: 'The characteristick Beauties of this great Master I was quite blind to – And I looked upon his pictures as coarse unfinished sketches.' Professionally Wilson was both liked and esteemed. He played an active part in forwarding the cause of artists and was a founder member of the Royal Academy, being elected its Librarian in 1776.

At this point we ought to notice briefly two currents of artistic sensibility whose fullest expression appears in Romantic art, but which exercised so considerable an influence over the Pre-Romantic period that they cannot be passed over in any discussion of later eighteenth-century landscape. The first of these was the theory of the sublime propounded by Edmund Burke in *A Philosophical Enquiry into the origin of our ideas of the Sublime and Beautiful*, 1756, in which Burke distinguishes our notions of beauty from our notions of the sublime, defining the sublime not in terms of actual physical conformation of nature or of the acts of man, but in terms of the experience of thrilling fear and amazement. The theory of the picturesque, whose most influential proponent was the Reverend William Gilpin, was, in some respects, contrary to Burke, one of whose canons for the recognition of beauty was the presence of smoothness and regularity of outline, for the advocates of the picturesque admired the rough and irregular in nature. In practice the two theories became complementary and fused at last in the Romantic sensibility. The cult of the picturesque landscape accompanied that of the sublime landscape, and was combined in the work of P.J.de Loutherbourg (1740–1812), whose scenes of violence and of grandeur – shipwrecks and *banditti*, mountain storms and avalanches – were exhibited at the Royal Academy at the same time as paintings from which the series of aquatints *The Romantic and Picturesque Scenery of England and Wales* were published in 1805. For these compositions Loutherbourg worked in the accepted tradition of sketching from Nature and working up his compositions in the studio into the sublime or picturesque mode. The only important painter of pure landscape of the second half of the eighteenth century inspired by Burke was the isolated water-colourist John Robert Cozens, who worked for that exceptional patron William Beckford.

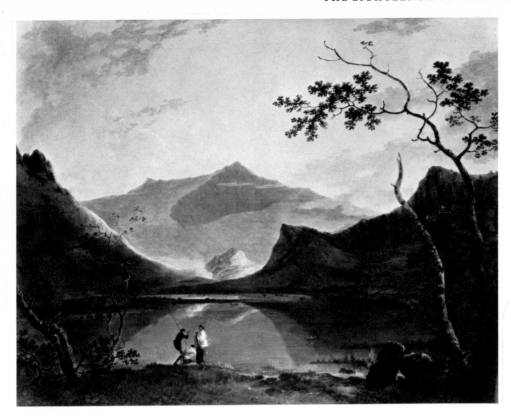

RICHARD WILSON, *Snowdon from
Llyn Nantlle, c.* 1774.
Walker Art Gallery, Liverpool.

The style and mood of Gainsborough's landscapes is in antithesis to those of
Wilson. His mature landscapes transmute into softer and deeper harmonies of greens
and browns seventeenth-century Netherlandish formulae, infusing their solemn
realities with an idyllic pastoralism whose elegant artifice corresponds to the literary
visions of the eighteenth-century man of sensibility, rather than to the literal truths
of English rural life and scenery. It was some decades before Gainsborough attained
this manner. His early studies of Dutch seventeenth-century landscapes and his
training with Gravelot, the French Rococo designer, are evident in his first commissions obtained in Ipswich. There he had a successful, if small, line in decorative
landscapes peopled with pastoral figures. Commissioned as chimney pieces they are
spontaneous and have a natural grace; they may be described as anglicized interpretations of Boucher's artificial pastorals. But Gainsborough also painted landscapes
more naturalistically at this time: *Sandy Pit by a Sandy Road* is a fresh and enchanting
picture in the Dutch tradition. Gainsborough's landscapes are imaginative compositions. It should always be remembered when looking at an eighteenth-century
landscape that *plein-air* painting was an invention of the nineteenth century and that
even the freshest of eighteenth-century country scenes was devised and executed in
the studio, using pencil sketches from nature. The intention of the artist was not to
recreate the appearance or even the feeling of an actual scene, but to use it as a
foundation on which his art could work. Unlike the nineteenth century the eighteenth
century applied the classical theory of ideal beauty to Nature thoroughly and sin-
cerely. It was the duty of the artist to put together from the elements she supplied a
composition which would include only her beauties. Obviously in interpreting this
doctrine a whole range of styles was possible, from the more or less naturalistic to
the highly artificial. Gainsborough, we know, preferred the highly artificial, using
compositions of moss and stone which he built up himself as models for his paintings.
We know from Reynolds' descriptions that 'from the fields he brought into his
painting room, stumps of trees, weeds and animals of various kinds; and designed
them not from memory, but immediately from the objects. He even framed a kind of

THOMAS GAINSBOROUGH, *A View in Suffolk:
Sandy Pit by a Sandy Road*.
National Gallery of Ireland, Dublin.

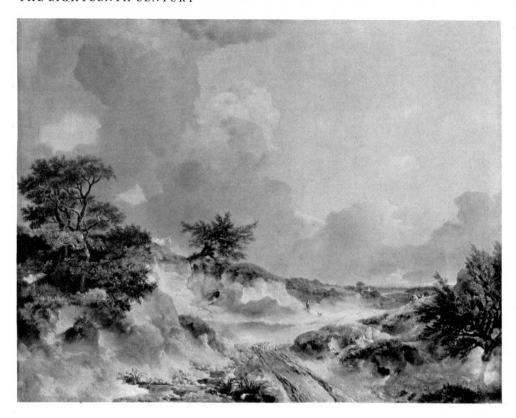

model of landscapes on his table; composed of broken stones, dried herbs, and pieces of looking glass, which he magnified and improved into rocks, trees, and water.' After Gainsborough's move to Bath, in 1759, his landscape compositions became more massive and the figures are no longer treated as accessories, lending grace and animation to the scene, as orthodox doctrine and practice prescribed, but play a vital part in communicating its mood. His landscape style changed after Gainsborough's move to London in 1774, becoming broader – as in a number of fresh seascapes – and at the end of his life, like his portraits, it was almost impressionistic (p. 188).

The influence of the picturesque is perhaps most vividly recorded in eighteenth-century oil painting in the response of British artists to the exotic landscapes of India and the South Seas. William Hodges (1744–97), a pupil and, in his early years, an imitator of Wilson, accompanied Captain Cook on his second voyage to the South Pacific, in 1772–5, as official draughtsman. His ability to convey the strangeness of a remote world of what were then believed to be noble savages, in the formal language of eighteenth-century classical landscape, is shown in the views that he painted on this occasion for the Admiralty (p. 176). He displayed the same qualities during a subsequent visit to India in 1780–4, where he was patronized by Warren Hastings. Hodges was criticized for paying too little attention to the objects he represented, an instance of how much more interested most of his countrymen were in authenticity than in art. After his return he attempted to introduce a didactic genre of landscape, and held an exhibition of twenty-five of his pictures. Two of these, entitled the *Effects of Peace* and the *Consequences of War*, were heavily criticized for their execution and content, which according to the Duke of York 'might tend to impress the mind of the inferior classes of society with sentiments not suited to the public tranquillity.'

Two other pupils of Wilson, William Marlow (1740–1813) and Thomas Jones (1743–1803) both visited Italy and thereafter produced Italianate views. Another, Joseph Farington (1747–1821) is better known today for the diary he kept from the 1790s, in which he recorded much of Royal Academy politics and artistic gossip, than for his landscapes.

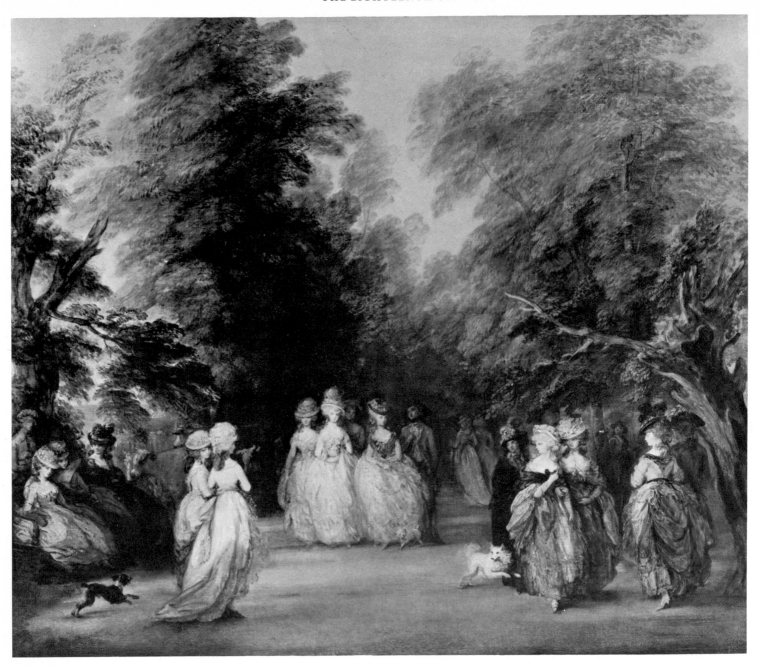

THOMAS GAINSBOROUGH, *The Mall in
St James's Park.*
Copyright The Frick Collection, New York.

Decorative painting was not a native genre. One of its chief exponents was
Cipriani (1727–85), a Florentine who came to England in 1755. Well-trained in the
Italian academic tradition, he was an able designer. Many of his graceful, decorative
compositions, which show a great facility of mythological and allegorical invention,
for instance that of the Diploma of the Royal Academy, were engraved by his country-
man Francesco Bartolozzi (1727–1815), whose attractive stipple engravings widely
disseminated the style. Cipriani was appointed to teach at the short-lived Duke of
Richmond's Gallery, in 1758, and on the establishment of the Royal Academy, ten
years later, he was elected Visitor, to attend the Royal Academy schools, set the
figures for life drawing, and advise and instruct the students.

Two artists from the Imperial lands worked in England during the 1760s and
1770s. Angelica Kauffmann (1741–1807) was trained in the tradition of the German
Rococo, which she later modified in Rome under the influence of Mengs. Technically
accomplished and highly cultured, Angelica, as a woman, was not allowed by the

188

rigid proprieties of the eighteenth century to draw from the living model, and was therefore obliged to depend even more than most eighteenth-century artists on copying from old masters. Inevitably this weakened her figure style, which seems, in any case, to have been naturally soft, and made her more than usually susceptible to the influence of any powerful artistic personality whom she encountered. In her English period, which alone concerns us here, her portrait style is dominated by that of Reynolds, from whom she quickly adopted the fashionable historical portraiture. Nevertheless it is unfair to depreciate Angelica as an artist, as so many writers on English art have done, partly because of a reluctance to accept eighteenth-century art on its own terms. Angelica was a more than ordinarily talented portraitist, especially, like Reynolds, when she felt interest or respect for her sitter. Because of the decorative quality of many of her historical and literary paintings it is all too easy to underestimate her enterprise and originality in the choice of subject. She not only painted the traditional themes from classical history and mythology (p. 190), but chose subjects from English literature, presaging in the mildest of keys some of the great themes of Romantic art. The influence of her designs for prints of decorative, literary and historical subjects was felt until the end of the century. A foundation member of the Royal Academy, Angelica painted four allegorical panels to decorate its ceiling. It is in her sketches that her German version of the Venetian Rococo style is most apparent. In pictures painted after her visit to Rome the finer contours and smooth sobriety of Mengs dominate. In her subject compositions the colouring is cool, pale and distinguished, rather like Angelica herself.

Johann Zoffany (1733–1810) was trained at an early age at Regensburg in the German late-Baroque manner. He then went to Rome where he studied with Masucci and later under Mengs. Zoffany worked briefly for the Elector of Trier as a decorative and historical painter but came to England in 1760, bringing with him a sound European training. German eighteenth-century art was highly eclectic, reflecting the country's sense of cultural inferiority which was to last until the age of Goethe and Schiller. Like most German artists of his generation, Zoffany was influenced by contemporary French art, especially, it seems, by Boucher, from whose compositions he is known to have borrowed. He nevertheless retained the preference for a relatively darker colouring typical of German taste.

On his first arrival in England Zoffany found it difficult to establish himself, but was rescued by the patronage of David Garrick, with mutual benefit to both artist and actor, for Garrick was the first actor to realize the publicity value of having his portrait painted in different roles (p. 191). These theatrical conversations, as they became known, had a wide circulation from the engravings made after them. If Zoffany's theatrical scenes are compared to the Commedia dell'Arte scenes of Watteau, the English preference for realism, even for humorous or lightly grotesque realism, in a genre that lends itself to fantasy and illusion, becomes at once apparent. In the many small portraits and conversation pieces which Zoffany painted, he chose the intimate domestic approach of Dutch and English tradition in preference to the Grand Manner. His choice was sensible because it allowed him to demonstrate his real gifts for the representation of drapery and interiors and of lively small-scale figures, and to conceal his sometimes faulty perspective in the gay verisimilitude of his details. Although these small groups are always pleasing and lively, Zoffany is not invariably successful in producing an integrated composition. His skill in domestic portraiture brought him to the notice of George III and Queen Charlotte, for whom he painted some of his most successful groups. In 1772 he was commissioned by the Queen to execute a picture of *The Tribuna of the Uffizi* in Florence (p. 192). This, the heart of the great Medici collection, where its most precious pictures and works of art were housed, was the admiration of all Europe: Zoffany was allowed special privileges in order to complete his vivid picture. He spent seven years abroad, mostly in Florence,

189

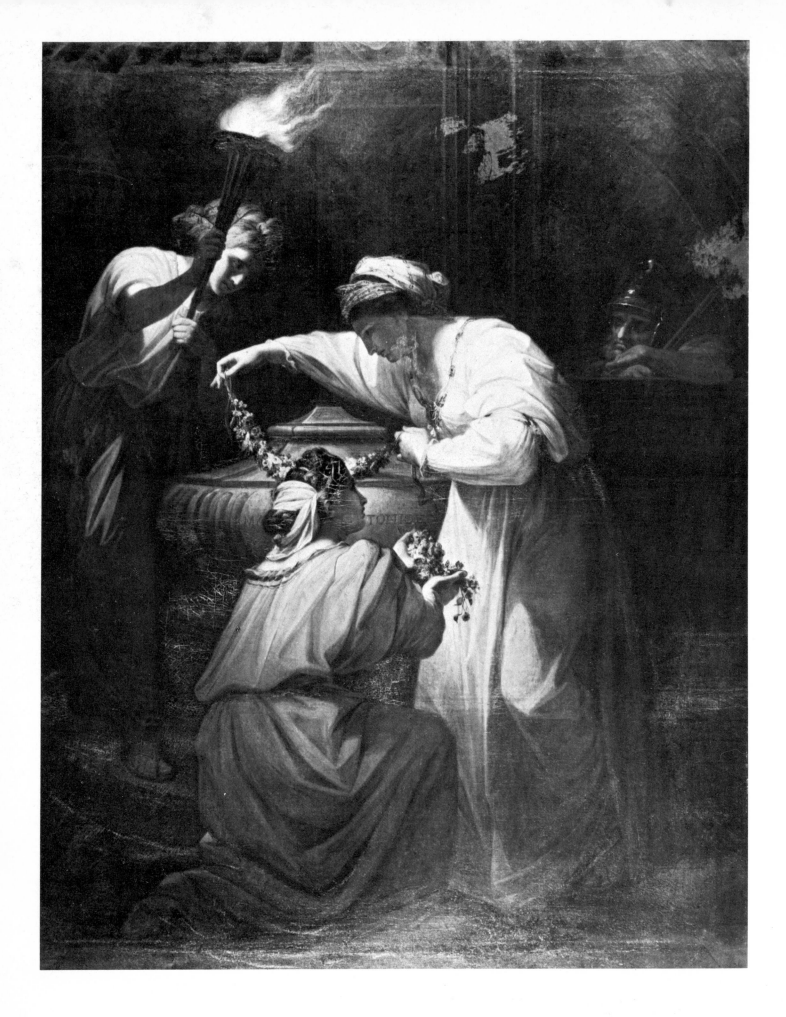

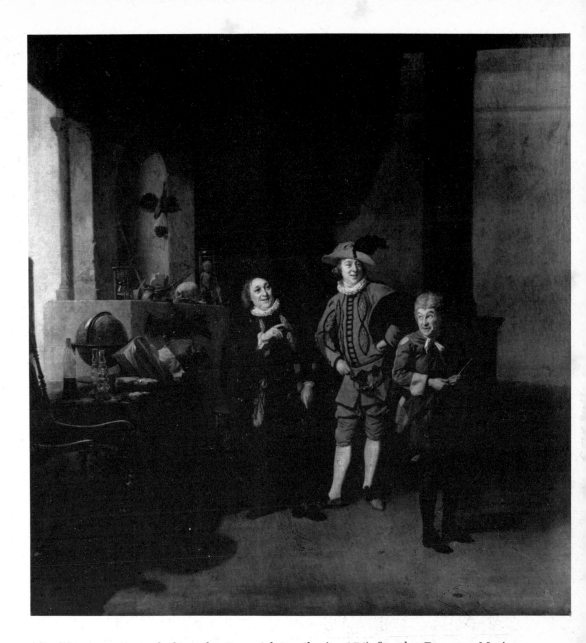

Left, ANGELICA KAUFFMANN, *Cleopatra decorating the Tomb of Mark Antony.* Burghley House.
Collection of the Marquess of Exeter.
Right, JOHANN ZOFFANY, *Garrick as Abel Drugger* in Ben Jonson's *The Alchemist.* From the Castle Howard Collection.

painting portraits including the Imperial Family (p. 174) for the Empress Maria Theresa, who made him a baron of the Holy Roman Empire when he visited Vienna in 1776. Zoffany returned to England at the end of 1779, but found himself out of favour for having remained abroad so long, and for having introduced figures of connoisseurs and travellers into *The Tribuna.* In 1781–2 he painted the *Library of Charles Towneley in Park Street.* One of the key documents of English Neo-classical taste, this famous picture is executed in cool blues, greens and reds.

Failing to re-establish himself as a portrait painter with the capricious world of fashion, Zoffany sailed for India in 1783 in the deliberate intention of making a fortune. He settled in Bengal and received many commissions, both at the rich court of Oudh and from members of the East India Company. Besides portraits and conversation pieces, he painted scenes of Anglo-Indian and Indian life. Bad health compelled his return to England in 1789.

In the 1790s Zoffany, who seems to have been the typical polished sceptic and reformer of the *ancien régime,* was shaken by the French Revolution into opposite convictions, and not only executed one or two altar-pieces for Anglican churches, but also *The Plundering of the King's Cellar* which was intended as an attack on the French Revolution. This painting was exceptional in its day, as in the early 1790s almost all English artists, contrary to modern belief, were convinced radicals.

191

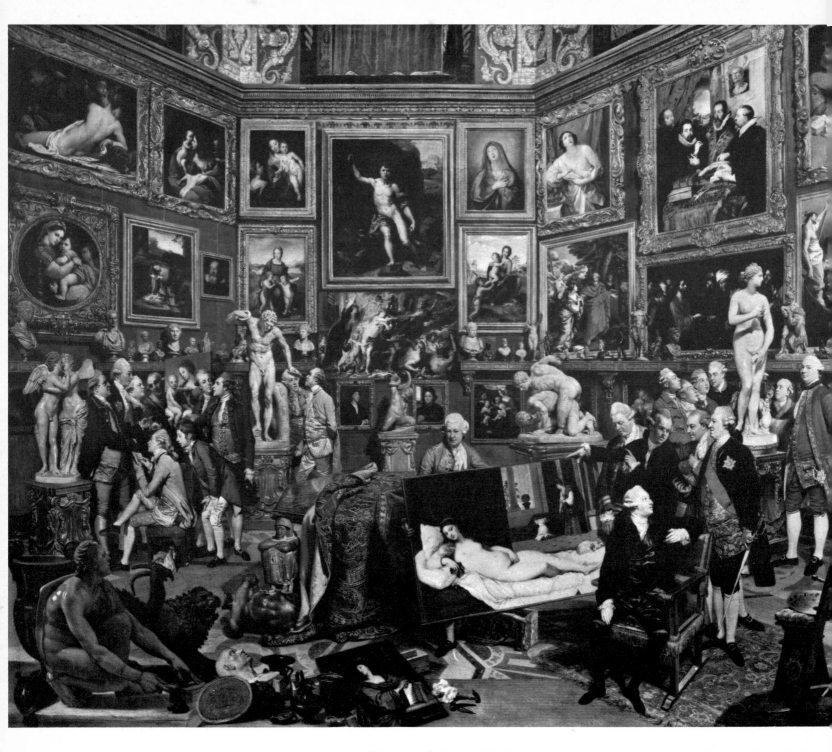

JOHANN ZOFFANY, *The Tribuna of
the Uffizi*, 1772.
Royal Collection.
By gracious permission of
Her Majesty the Queen.

The dilemma of the English history painter in aspiring to produce works which
would be as sublime in effect as those of Michelangelo and Raphael appears at its
acutest in the last four decades of the eighteenth century. The great Italian artists he
sought to rival had learned as boys in the studios of other artists all the secrets and
the skill of hand of a long artistic past, and were able to graft on to a living tradition
new lessons from the antique or from the study of nature. The English artist, if
trained at all, was trained perfunctorily in a provincial country, usually through
copying the works of an artist who himself had perhaps never mastered more than
the art of painting a face and shining draperies, in a manner, moreover, which was
not the severe, semi-sculptural manner of the High Renaissance and classical Baroque,
but the soft and colouristic manner of the Rococo. From this unlearned education he
had to strive by single-handed and single-minded study in Rome during one, two or

192

three years, to master the grand manner of antique sculpture and of Michelangelo and Raphael. It is not surprising if the result was often a series of noble failures in which the grandeur of the artists' aspirations found inadequate formal expression. In fairness it should be said that Neo-classicism in other European countries with a stronger studio tradition posed some of the same problems and foreign artists were sometimes as unsuccessful in overcoming them.

In spite of his advocacy of history painting Reynolds was careful to keep to his lucrative profession as a portrait painter, and by some of the younger generation was bitterly censured for his hypocrisy in not practising what he preached. A number of English artists like James Northcote (1746–1831), one of Reynolds' pupils, had high hopes of earning fame and wealth from history painting, but soon discovered that the indifference of eighteenth-century patrons to the grand style made success impossible and were obliged to descend to portrait painting for their livelihood.

One artist, James Barry (1741–1806) (p. 194), stubbornly refused to bend to necessity and continued throughout a long and bitter and increasingly eccentric life to fight for the superior claims of history painting. Barry, born in Cork, was discovered by Edmund Burke and was taken up by him as a genius. In 1766 the Burkes sent him to Italy where Barry spent five years in Rome, not learning the technical part of his art as Burke had intended, but attempting to master the secrets of the style of Michelangelo, Raphael and the antique. He was one of the first British artists to feel that visionary sense of the grandeur of classical art which is one of the constituents of Neo-classicism. The consequence was that if Barry's manner has an imaginative grandeur not equalled by other English artists of the eighteenth century, it is not always supported by his technique. This is evident in his most remarkable and ambitious work, the series of canvasses for the Great Room of the Society of Arts in the Adelphi. Made desperate by his failure to attract patronage on his return from Italy, he revived in 1777 an earlier joint proposal to decorate the room with historical and allegorical pictures, offering to work without payment or assistance. Barry's theme was the development of civilization, from primitive to modern times, ending with Elyzium, in which the great and good of all ages are brought together (p. 195). By a sad irony Barry's three or four portraits in the historical style are more completely successful works of art. In them he has solved the difficulty of transfiguring the sitter by a background and trappings of powerful imaginative symbolism without bombast and without the courtly insincerity of Reynolds. In his portrait of *George, Prince of Wales as St George*, for example, one is not uneasily aware, as in so many eighteenth-century portraits, of the discrepancy between the all too eighteenth-century features of the sitter and the grandeur of the mythological or historical role in which they are cast by the painter. Barry was the first painter working in England to practise resolutely a Neo-classical style and his importance in this respect has not yet been properly recognized.

The art of Benjamin West (1738–1820) is more traditional in its classicism than Barry's, for, although West strenuously denied it, the influence of French classical Baroque, particularly of Le Sueur and Poussin, is paramount in his pictures. In West's art the dichotomy between imaginative power and power of execution becomes almost grotesque. Looked at in photographs many of his designs seem impressive, even visionary; seen in the original the feebleness of figure style and the dullness and monotony of colouring are painful. These defects were not unnoticed by West's contemporaries, but for many years George III, who seems to have thought that he had discovered in West the Michelangelo of his day, unswervingly supported and patronized him. To West he entrusted the major decorative commission of the second half of the eighteenth century, a series of canvasses illustrating the history of revealed religion, in St George's Chapel, Windsor; it was never completed. Like other English historical painters West was unable to work on the monumental scale demanded by this sort of commission, and it is significant that his smaller works are

193

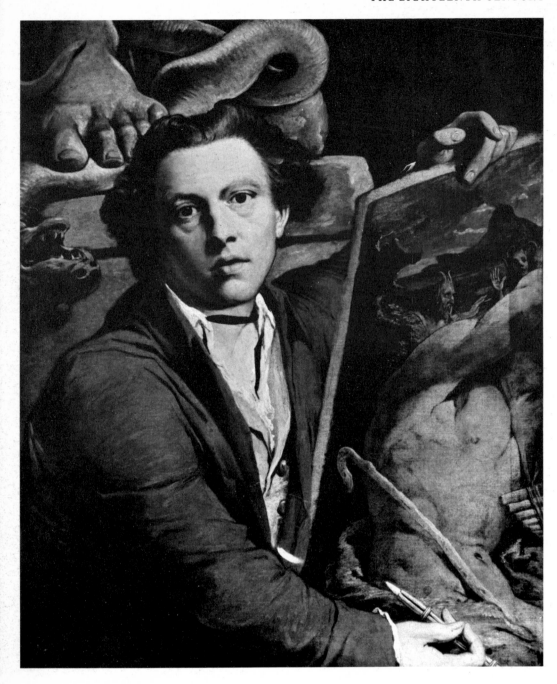

JAMES BARRY, *Self-portrait*.
National Gallery of Ireland, Dublin.

usually more successful and pleasing. Much has been made of West's having painted, in 1771, *The Death of Captain Wolfe* (p. 196), one of his most effective, medium-sized compositions, in modern dress, contrary to the rules of history painting which laid down that such a subject ought to be ennobled by classicizing costume. West's innovation had, however, been anticipated by Romney, whose painting of the same subject in 1763 would have won the prize at the Society of Arts had there not been so much criticism of the modern costume he had given to his figures. It would be truer to say that the *Death of Wolfe* vanquished the prejudice and made it possible for artists to dress their heroes in modern dress without feeling that they had deprived their subject of its dignity.

The failure of the Academy to establish a place for history painting in English culture led Alderman Boydell to try what commerce could do. His scheme of a Shakespeare Gallery, begun in 1786, was intended to give patronage to the artists through commissions for paintings of subjects from the great national dramatist, to

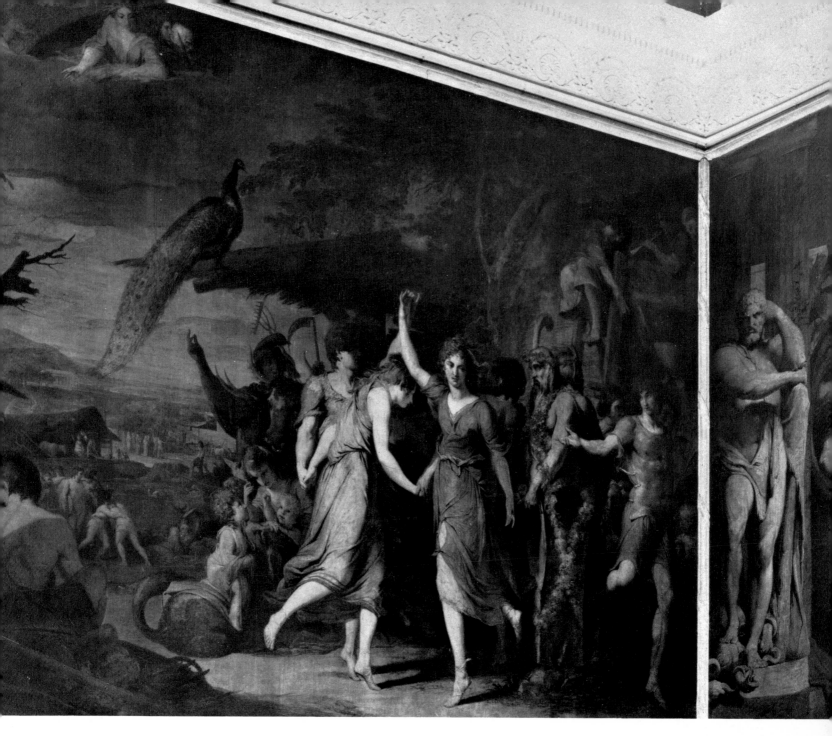

JAMES BARRY, *Commerce or the Triumph of the Thames*.
By courtesy of the Royal Society of Arts, London.

diffuse a taste among the public for history painting by showing the commissioned paintings together in a specially built gallery, and to bring profit to the Alderman, both from the admission fees to the Shakespeare Gallery and from the engravings published after the pictures. The project started encouragingly with an exhibition of over thirty pictures, in 1789, and as many more again in the following year, when the first engravings were published. Although a number of these compositions were no more than costume or fancy pictures in another guise, many were sincere and successful attempts to produce high art. The Poet's Gallery, the Milton Gallery, Macklin's Bible, and a project to illustrate Hume's *History of England* were started on similar lines. All continued into the first years of the nineteenth century, but since their financial viability depended on selling engravings abroad as well as at home the Napoleonic wars were fatal to them.

During the 1760s and 1770s the ideals of honest benevolence and philanthropy which had found expression in the novels of Fielding were supplanted in many

195

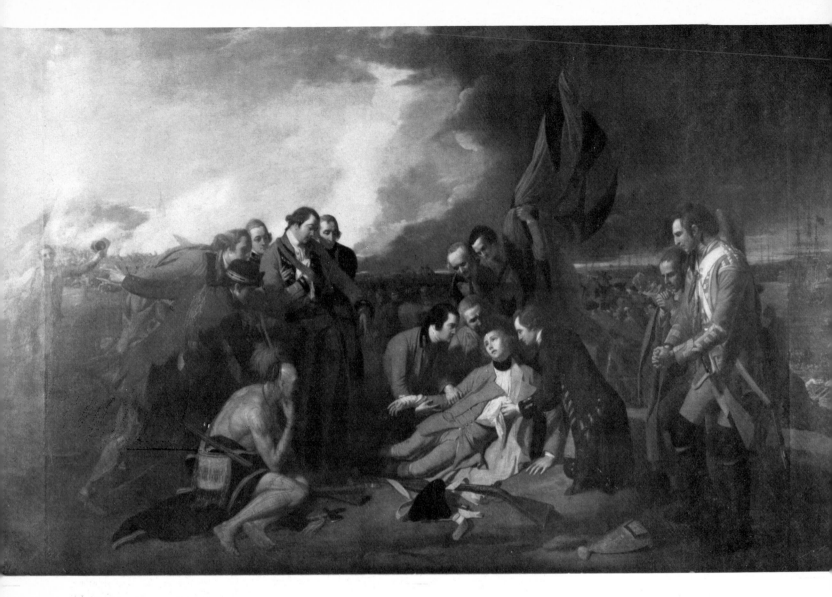

circles by the more hectic enthusiasms of the cult of sensibility, largely under the influence of Sterne and Rousseau. Sensibility found various artistic expressions. One of its most cherished illusions was that purity of manners and morals still survived in the sweet simplicity and innocence of rural life. This belief was responsible for the very popular scenes which sometimes represented acts of charity from the middle class to the distressed peasantry, adapted to English manners from Greuze, and sometimes scenes of pastoral innocence and virtue. Reynolds and Wilson were not of a temperament to be influenced by this movement, but Gainsborough was a believer in the natural virtues of the heart, who prided himself on the quicksilver enthusiasm of his feelings. It is in his art, therefore, that the new sentiment was first expressed, in *Charity relieving Distress* (1784). Another new genre first called into being to please sensibility was the fancy picture. The term fancy picture seems to have been loosely used even in the eighteenth century, but it is probably most exactly applied to genre paintings of a sentimental realism. The artist whose work is most representative of the genre is Francis Wheatley (1747–1801), an associate of Mortimer. Hitherto Wheatley had shown himself an able portrait painter, producing clearly defined and attractive small-scale likenesses, and large groups recording contemporary events. After his return from Ireland in 1783 Wheatley was prolific in designing scenes of virtue aided or relieved, and of the rural scene as conceived by a sentimental but not foolish public. A contemporary critic acutely noted 'Whenever Mr Wheatley presents us with a rural Nymph whom he wishes to be peculiarly

BENJAMIN WEST, *The Death of General Wolfe,* 1771. Royal Collection. By gracious permission of Her Majesty the Queen.

FRANCIS WHEATLEY, *A Woodman
returning Home*.
By courtesy of Eleanor MacCracken and
The Leger Galleries Ltd.

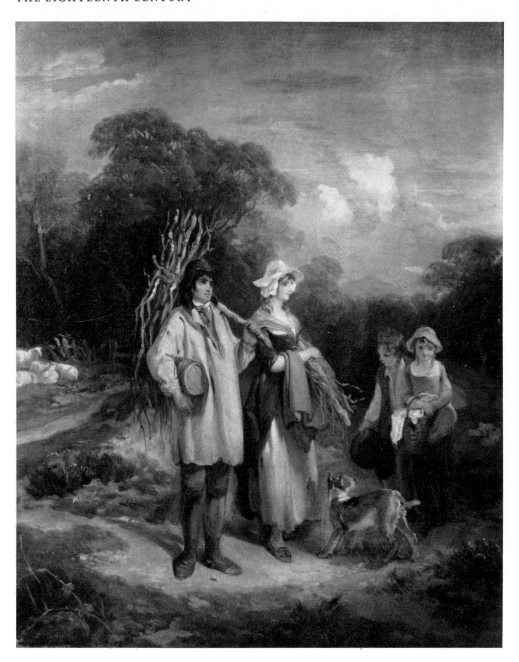

impressive, he decorates her head with a profusion of party coloured ribbands, like
a maniac in Coventry, which play in the breeze, offensive to thought and propriety.
As this is not the character of our village Daphnes, why make them so prodigiously
fine at the expense of truth?' But although this unreality was censured by the well
informed, the general public admired Wheatley's work. It is a sign of the new taste
that many of Wheatley's designs were primarily intended to be engraved as prints,
and Wheatley's prolific output is indicative of the widespread demand for furniture prints of this kind. An almost exact contemporary, William Hamilton (1751–
1801) is now best remembered for his landscapes with pastoral figures and graceful
rural scenes, while W.R.Bigg (1755–1828) produced simpler, slightly more honest
rustic figures.

5

THE ROMANTICS

Alan Bird

To attempt to chart a firm course through Romantic painting in Britain between the years 1790 and 1840 is to venture in to a quicksand on which many a reckless critic has foundered. Few statements about Romantic painting can be made with any certainty, but it can be said that it had its roots (like those of literature) in the eighteenth century, that its development cannot be seen as a single thread, and that its diversity seems unbounded. A few decades ago it was enough to mention the names of Constable and Turner, Lawrence and Blake, as being the pantheon of British Romanticism, but in recent years we have realized that there were numerous other painters who also made a valuable contribution; and it is certain that we have not yet tracked down all the lesser artists who have since fallen into obscurity, nor adequately assessed the impact made by British Romantic painters on the development of European culture.

Roger Fry once reflected that in 1815, as far as art was concerned, 'never before, in all our history, had we such a splendid array of talent. There was Raeburn, Geddes, Wilkie, Crome, Cotman, Girtin, Turner, Constable, and . . . Lawrence. . . . England seemed to be ready for a new Renaissance, and then, by 1850, scarcely anything was left of this glorious promise; British art had sunk to a level of trivial ineptitude'. Even if we accept that Fry claimed too much for Geddes and that he seemed to have forgotten that Girtin had prematurely departed the scene some thirteen years previously, this statement remains basically indisputable. In fact, the situation in painting was not dissimilar to that in literature, for as early as 1830 Keats, Shelley and Byron were dead, and the poetic fire in Coleridge and Wordsworth had long since died. The decay of Wordsworth's genius (but not his industry) after a single decade and the placid prosperity of his later years are mirrored in the lives of many artists between 1790 and 1840. Why was it that so few painters fulfilled their early promise and that so many – deliberately in some cases – drifted into that detailed and narrational sentimentality frequently and vaguely labelled 'Victorian'? No account of Romantic painting has explained this fading of the vision; nor is it possible to do so although a few reasons may be hesitatingly suggested.

198

There can be no doubt that artists were affected by the social, political and economic conditions of the day. Blake was not alone in welcoming the successful rebellion of the Colonists in North America or the Fall of the Bastille in 1789 as opening up an era of social reform and brotherly love; nor was he alone when he afterwards concealed these vanquished hopes behind the rhapsodic ambiguities of his prophetic poems. During the long wars against the Republic and the Empire all such hopes were blighted; and after the peace of 1815 there was no sign of any honour among nations. Limitless as had been the enthusiasm of the Romantics for the transformation of society promised by the French Revolution, and even by Napoleon, their despair was equally limitless when the bloody acts of revolution were unveiled and when the counter-revolutionary forces moved into repressive action.

With the passing of the Reform Bill of 1832 they breathed more easily, only to find they had lost the indifferent and occasional patronage of the landowning aristocracy and were now faced with aggressive philistinism from the brash, self-opinionated and uncultivated Bounderbys of the Victorian age. Inhibited by poverty and dependent on patronage and the few exhibiting societies of his profession, the artist was eventually too afraid to experiment, to try out new techniques or venture to fresh subject matter.

This state of affairs had been common in England for some decades. 'The Enquiry in England,' wrote Blake in the margin of Sir Joshua Reynolds' *Discourses*, 'is not whether a Man has Talents and Genius, But whether he is Passive and Polite and a Virtuous Ass and obedient to Noblemen's Opinions in Art and Science. If he is, he is a Good Man. If Not, he must be starved.' The inception of the Royal Academy and its schools in 1768 had seemed to offer security to British artists. William Collins (1788–1847), purveyor of insipid pastorals and seascapes which Constable described as 'a coast scene with fish as usual, and a landscape like a large cow-turd', remarked that it was only the Academy which prevented artists being 'treated like journeymen'.

By unnecessarily and somewhat feebly insisting on the supremacy of historical painting, the Academy (and other agencies which attempted to imitate it) actually thwarted the careers of artists and increased their financial precariousness. For the British public remained steadfast in its refusal to buy history paintings.

From the foundation of the Academy down to competitions for decorating the new Houses of Parliament (1841–3) with scenes illustrating the more glorious pages of British history, there were many futile attempts by artists to band together in the wish to influence and command public taste. The annual exhibitions held at the Academy, as well as those at The Old Water-colour Society founded in 1804, the British Institution, 1805, the Society of British Artists, 1823, the Society of Painters in Oil and Water-colour and the Art-Union provided areas in which painters might sell their works. None of these was especially successful. Artists who arranged their own exhibitions fared no better, as witness Blake's showing of 'poetical and historical inventions' at his brother's shop in 1809, and Benjamin Robert Haydon's exhibitions at the Egyptian Hall in 1832. These failures undoubtedly influenced the careers and practices of many of the most important and aspiring artists. Some, like James Barry in the eighteenth century, and Haydon in the nineteenth, felt themselves to be the victims of a narrow and oppressive patronage (when they were not absolutely neglected), while others fairly rapidly adopted a style which we recognize as essentially sentimental and narrative.

Haydon fared badly and would have starved had he not provided *The Sabbath Evening of a Christian* or *Punch and Judy* (p. 200); Calcott (1779–1844) and Leslie (1794–1859) cut history and literature down to size with their costume pieces; and while Wilkie's *Chelsea Pensioners receiving the Gazette announcing the Battle of Waterloo* (1822) was described as the most popular picture ever exhibited at the Royal

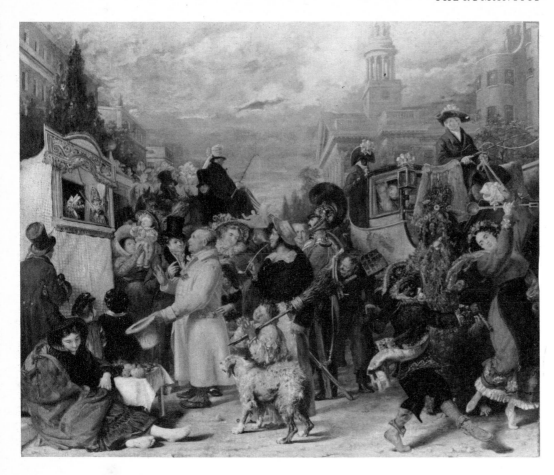

BENJAMIN ROBERT HAYDON,
Punch and Judy, 1829.
The Tate Gallery, London.

Academy, the impressively serious canvases at which he laboured after his studies in
Spain and Italy were received with indifference. Turner (who made his fortune with
his topographical works) was expected to provide annual merriment at the Academy
with his outrageous concoctions of 'whitewash and soapsuds' while Constable (with
considerable private means) struggled against abuse and contempt. In 1825 a critic
was so bemused by two pictures 'by a Mr Palmer' that he thought the painter should
have exhibited himself alongside, at a shilling a look. Crome (1768–1821) and
Cotman (1782–1842) eked out threadbare lives in the provinces; J.R.Cozens (1752–
1799) died insane and poor; and others put an end to their own lives. Is it any wonder
that a current of pessimism runs through Romantic painting or that painters so
frequently presented visions of ruin and disaster?

It is important to consider what were the tastes of picture collectors during this
period. As far as home products were concerned they disliked history painting
(despite the pretensions of the Academy) and did not care for landscape; but they
did like having their portraits painted. And during the years of isolation created by
the Revolutionary and Napoleonic wars British painters provided substitutes for the
Old Master paintings which were then unobtainable.

Morland (1763–1804) and Wheatley (1747–1801) proved in their able ways that
English peasants could be as prettily picturesque as any of Salvator Rosa's *banditti*.
But this demand ceased after 1815 when the art market was flooded with paintings
dispersed from continental collections and the wealthier aristocrats began rebuilding their galleries. For various reasons – the distaste for French Rococo art, the
apparent decay of the Italian artistic genius and the expensiveness of the Old
Masters – the British turned to Dutch seventeenth-century painting. Here were
innocuous scenes of nostalgic bucolic charm which compensated for the increasing
devastation of the surrounding countryside being brought about by the new

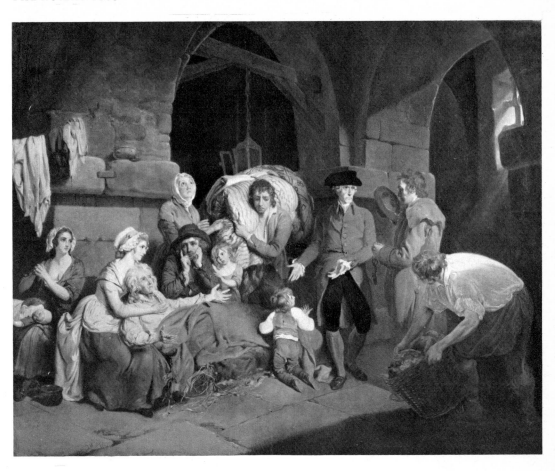

FRANCIS WHEATLEY, *Mr Howard offering Relief to Prisoners*, 1787.
By courtesy of the Earl of Harrowby.

intensive methods of farming, the enclosure of common ground and the sprawling industrial towns of the Midlands and North.

From about 1818 the Prince Regent and Sir Robert Peel were among the keenest buyers of Dutch genre scenes and landscapes. But whilst the French and Italian aristocracy were apt to ruin themselves by gambling, dissipation and unwise speculation, the Dutch burghers remained comfortably in possession of their fine objects and paintings, which thus rarely appeared on the market. To satisfy the demand for these genre scenes (which were themselves essentially artificial since they were the creation of a people without landscape), Opie (1761–1807), Wilkie (1785–1841) and Mulready (1786–1863) produced their amusing episodes of village life, and other artists such as Ibbetson (1759–1817) produced copies or pastiches of Dutch originals. This love of Dutch art was not without its beneficial aspects, for many artists, including Constable, Crome, Gainsborough and Turner, gained from the detailed calm and honest observation of the sea, the low horizons and the great expanses of sky which are so marked in the landscapes of seventeenth-century painters in the Low Countries. When Palmer noted his reverence for Cuyp, Potter, Hobbema and Ruysdael he spoke for his contemporaries.

Artistic taste was, above all, dominated by the cult of the Old Master, which had grown during the eighteenth century. England's wealth had attracted Italian pictures throughout previous centuries but the upheavals in Europe which followed the French Revolution created a situation which was new to the artist. For either in the superlative exhibitions arranged by Vivant Denon in the Louvre or in the collections which the British aristocratic landowners and newly rich industrialists made accessible to the public he was able to see a variety of styles and manners and subjects such as had never before been available to him. Small wonder that all the leading Romantic painters – and not only those in Britain – were essentially eclectic.

JOHN OPIE, *The Peasant's Family, c.* 1783–5.
The Tate Gallery, London.

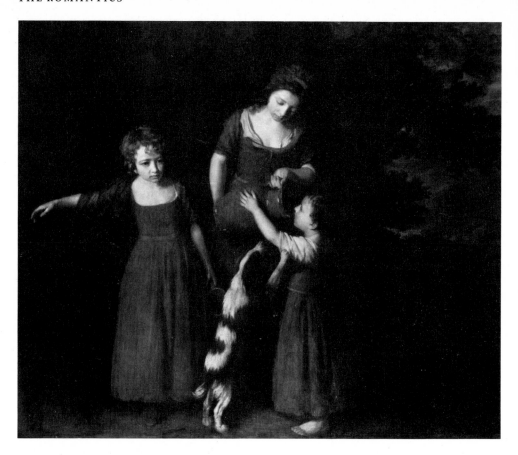

Turner, for instance, was acquainted quite early in his career with works by the Dutch masters and the masterpieces by Claude which Beckford had bought from the Alfieri Palace in Rome, and visits to the Louvre where he studied Titian and the Venetians showed in an increased vividness of tonality.

A major influence was that of Rubens, whose borrowings from other artists, as well as his own sensitivity to the natural landscape, were to be mirrored in the work of numerous Romantic artists. The exaggerated respect paid to the Old Masters had less beneficial results when, as Hogarth remarked, it called for smoked pictures. Sir George Beaumont, leading art critic and connoisseur of the day, had not a moment's hesitation in declaring that the dominant tone of a picture should be that of a Cremona violin. Too frequently the insistence of such collectors on the dark shades and amber tints which they associated with old paintings brought about the employment by contemporary artists of bitumen or megilp varnish, which gave a fugitive but agreeable depth to their pictures but which rapidly ruined the surfaces. This was the aptly named Dead Sea Pitch which is now the bane of owners of Romantic paintings and from the ravages of which it is practically impossible to retrieve works by Wilkie and his associates.

It is said that Constable replied to Beaumont's dictum by taking a violin outside and laying it on the green turf. Nevertheless, he said himself that his paintings 'should have chiaroscuro, if they had nothing else'; and he was generally concerned with the overall balance of light and dark rather than with colour sensations. It is easy to see that the bright tonality of Turner, and Constable's use of white in localized tonal contexts must have affronted connoisseurs, collectors and dealers for whom darkness was synonymous with quality.

Whatever the style of the picture the public demanded one thing of it – that it should have a subject. In 1824 Constable bemoaned 'the seeming plausible arguments that subject makes the picture', arguments which carried the authority of Sir Thomas

Lawrence, President of the Royal Academy. This emphasis on the readability of the picture was to be expected in the Regency period which saw Romanticism at its height, for it was above all a time of great literary distinction, when Chaucer, Milton, Spenser and Shakespeare were rediscovered and an immense amount of new writing was produced. In fact, Romanticism was primarily and most importantly a literary movement. Elements which we may term Romantic are certainly to be found in the music, art and literature of the past centuries and also in the lives of certain outstanding individuals; but the seeds of the Romantic movement of the late eighteenth and early nineteenth century were sown by Rousseau (and by Burke in his *Enquiry into the Sublime and Beautiful*, 1757) and given bones, blood and flesh by the Romantic poets and, to a lesser extent, by other contemporary writers.

Turner wrote poems to accompany his pictures and Constable was singularly expressive in his letters and comments. The age abounds in memoirs of artists written by artists whose use of the pen was frequently abler than their employment of the paintbrush – which they confusingly refer to as the 'pencil'. In addition to the personal synthesis of art and literature which many artists were able to effect for themselves, there was also a radical investigation of European literature. A great many foreign books became available in translation. Thus Dante, Goethe, Shakespeare, the Elizabethan playwrights, Ossian, Gray and Milton received the attention of the Romantic artists. William Blake and Francis Danby were inspired by the magnificent images of the Book of Revelations; while Milton inspired not only Blake and Barry but also William Dyce and John Martin. Flaxman prepared the way for an appreciation of Homer and Aeschylus; Romney illustrated Euripides; Runciman shared Flaxman's interest in Aeschylus; and West was inspired by Tacitus and Ovid.

There were few artists of the Romantic period who did not turn their attention to the illustration of literature or who did not give vent to their personal and emotional reactions to certain pages of literature in sketches drawn with violent abruptness. Some of these painters turned their hands to theatrical scenery, which in the first decades of the nineteenth century was to become both historically accurate and theatrically effective, particularly when painted by De Loutherbourg or Clarkson Stanfield. The great popularity of the stage (and especially Romantic opera and ballet) meant that art patrons expected from painters those exaggerated gestures and angular poses which we find more than extraordinary but which were commonplace in the vast theatres of the time. Any degree of stylistic improbability was acceptable in a picture, provided the story – or subject – was obvious enough. And yet it must be admitted that it is to the most literary of pictures, to the last products of a dying Romanticism, to the works of Chalon, Grant, Hook, Landseer, Cattermole and Leslie – of 'varied merits, essentially new' as Baudelaire (in a tribute to Gautier's pioneer appreciation of these British artists) once cried – that we are returning with a pleasure from which embarrassment is conspicuously absent.

As for the diversity of Romantic painting in Britain three subjects only are ostensibly lacking: religion, sex and politics, all of which seem to have been equally abhorrent to picture buyers and, less probably, to artists. There was simply no demand (or place) for religious pictures, so that the comparative success of *Christ Crowned with Thorns* (1825) by James Hilton (1786–1839) was the subject of much comment. Apart from a few caricaturists, of whom Gillray is the great example, no artist dared to venture on to politics. We should not forget that the secret police were active in London during the struggle with Napoleon and that Blake who, like Shelley and Wordsworth, had owned to republican and revolutionary sympathies, went in terror of their investigations. When the Greeks began their struggle for independence the event went unrecorded in Britain – not so in France, where Delacroix celebrated the event in his *Scenes of the Massacres at Chios* and *Greece*

Expiring Amid the Ruins of Missolonghi. It was in the latter, dreary town that Byron expired, a voluntary exile from his native land, whose tolerance in matters political and social he had, like other Romantic figures since, sadly misjudged. If he had thought that contemporary writers and artists would also take an interest in the fight for liberty and national freedom which was spreading throughout Europe he was also sadly mistaken.

That there was an undercurrent of sexuality in Romantic painting is obvious and not least in the portraits of Lawrence and the miniatures of Cosway, but overt sexuality found no public acceptance. Etty's odalisques seemed altogether too French and, by that same token, too erotic to find a place on the drawing-room wall. In spite of these difficulties there was a vast production of pictures. The energy of the Romantic artist was equal to the materials and sources of inspiration made available to him; and a sense of tremendous physical elation is widely apparent in his creations however much they may fail to measure up to the tests of time.

Definitions of Romanticism abound without any one receiving general agreement. In a moment of exasperation Goethe once rapped out, 'I call what is healthy the Classical and what is unhealthy the Romantic'. It would seem that behind Goethe's dictum was the belief that the momentary, the evanescent and the sickly were to be diagnosed as Romantic, whereas all that endured and successfully passed the strains and trials of history should be rewarded with the term Classical. But it should remind us that Romanticism and Classicism have always existed as opposing elements in the history of culture and that one or the other comes to the surface whenever circumstances favour its resurgence and return to dominance. In fact, it is reasonable to argue that at certain periods in the history of culture, as for instance during the late eighteenth century, the Classic and Romantic can co-exist, can draw sustenance one from the other, and can act as the manifestations of some deeper, still more complex force.

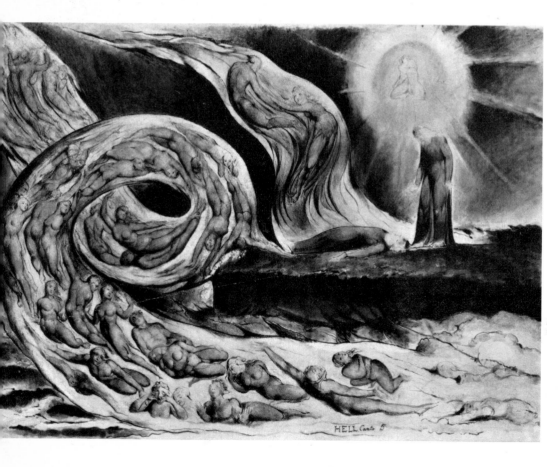

WILLIAM BLAKE, *The Whirlwind of Lovers*, *c.* 1784 (pen, ink and watercolour). Birmingham City Art Gallery.

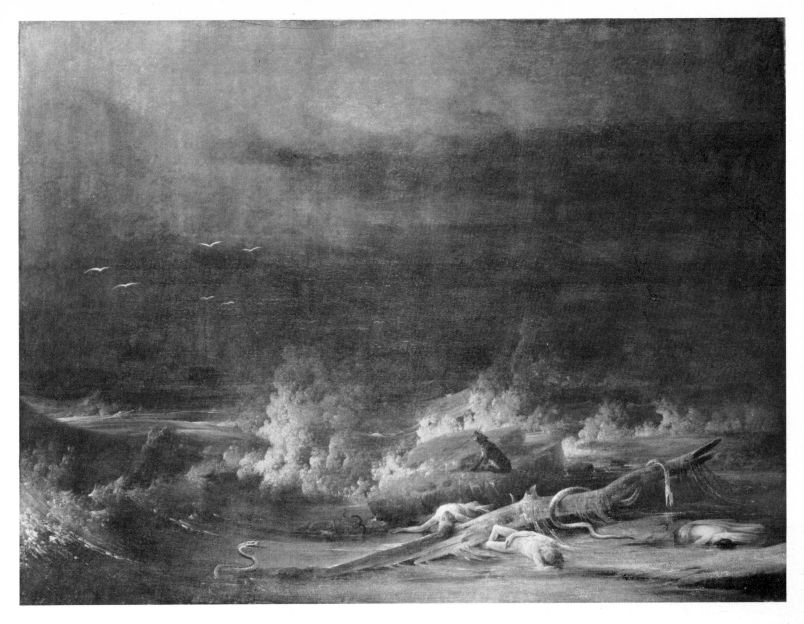

JOSHUA SHAW, *The Deluge*, 1804.
The Metropolitan Museum of Art, New York.
Gift of William Merritt Chase, 1909.

And yet there is a grain of truth in Goethe's charge of unhealthiness, for exciting as the movement undoubtedly was there were tendencies towards excess, exaggeration and the exploitation of private fantasies, nightmarish visions and oppressive dreams – not always, considering the plight of the artist in that age, without reason. The pictorial element in Romantic painting is rarely an end in itself, rather a means of playing on those aspects of our sensibility which are not entirely rational. It may be that this was the inevitable result of the newly awakened love of nature. Central to any concept of Romanticism, it supplied the place occupied in the eighteenth century by rationalism, reason and common sense; and proved itself a double-headed deity at once benevolent and implacably ireful. It was to be open to countless interpretations, and to have as many meanings and aspects. It could represent liberty and freedom and solitude but also violence, change, power, destruction and decay. Thus it is that so pervasive a part is played by dreams and horrifying collisions of natural forces whether the eruption of a volcano or the savage encounter of a horse and lion. Natural life is revealed as red in tooth and claw.

The investigation of the crushing, malevolent powers of the cosmos as manifested in storms, deluges, earthquakes and shipwrecks was continued into aspects of human behaviour and personality. This is especially true of sketches by Brown, Fuseli and Romney; and even in the portraits of Lawrence the nobility of England

205

seems strangely frozen in a state of glamorous youth while the dourest of Raeburn's sitters are threatened by the strength of light which invades the canvas. Many painters resorted to the most bizarre and imaginative pages of European literature and legend; and part of the strangeness of Blake's illustrations derives from our comparative unfamiliarity with his own writings and literary sources.

But in this liberation on to paper and canvas of the most personal emotions, and in this bursting of the shackles of reason, is there not a beneficial cleansing – a wholesome purgation of the artist's deepest emotions which we respect as distinctly healthy? Blake believed that wisdom came through excess, damned braces and blessed relaxes. Fuseli asked why 'the immediate avenues of the mind' should be shut only to the artist and proclaimed to the Academy, that every artist 'has or ought to have, a character or system of his own . . .' and that if 'you judge him by your own packed notions, or arraign him at the tribunal of schools which he does not recognize – you degrade the dignity of art, and add another fool to the herd of Dilettanti.'

At first view Constable (1776–1837), probably the most beloved of British landscapists, appears to be an obvious exception to strictures such as those of Goethe, for a potent ingredient of his landscape, that of carefully remembered and observed facts set down on canvas with an entirely honest and open love, is surely absolutely healthy in character. But Constable said that for him feeling was only another word for painting and that the purpose of art was to unite nature with imagination. Together with other landscapists he seems to provide an intensely wide-eyed and particular description of natural facts infused with an intense degree of private feeling so that hills, lakes, rivers, streams and endlessly shifting clouds become, as in the poetry of the Romantic poets, symbols of personal freedom. To some extent Constable's art is defined by Baudelaire's comment that Romanticism was precisely situated neither in choice of subjects nor in exact truth, but in a mode of feeling.

It is often suggested that landscape was the invention of British Romanticism. But this is only partially true. Constable and Turner – and many of the lesser lights – were indebted to earlier Dutch landscapists for certain valuable skills: how to organize a composition, how to use contrasts of light and shade and how to distribute tone values. To this the British added gifts entirely their own: an emphasis on light and colour, a heart-felt response to the transitoriness of natural life, and, to use Constable's own words, the union of nature with imagination.

These words of Constable are often forgotten. He was only too well acquainted with the styles of Gainsborough and Ruysdael, Claude Lorrain and Nicholas Poussin and anxious to show himself a worthy successor. He tended, perhaps deliberately, to see the scenery of the Lake District through the eyes of Gaspar Poussin. He knew, too, the prevailing artistic tenet which, as enunciated by Fuseli, was absolutely scornful of 'that kind of landscape which is entirely occupied with the tame delineation of a given spot; an enumeration of hill and dale, clumps of trees, shrubs, water meadows, cottages and houses, what is commonly called Views.' Despite Fuseli's sardonic comment on seeing one of Constable's landscapes, that it was unfortunate he had forgotten his umbrella, the English painter never aimed solely at a prosaic description of landscape; he detested the 'imitation of nature'. As a result, time and time again, his art moves from specific observation towards a generalization which is intended to be poetic and thus establish a relationship with the art of past masters. Yet it was just this careful transmutation of observed vision into acceptable and traditional pictorial form which Ruskin dismissed as 'blotting and blundering'.

But Constable has for long rightly been considered a man whose personal integrity and love of natural scenery are reflected in his paintings, conduct and writings. Having decided to create landscape pictures he scrutinized nature conscientiously and, without misusing the term, scientifically. He selected with care and with love from the things he had seen in his 'careless boyhood'. Describing them, he said,

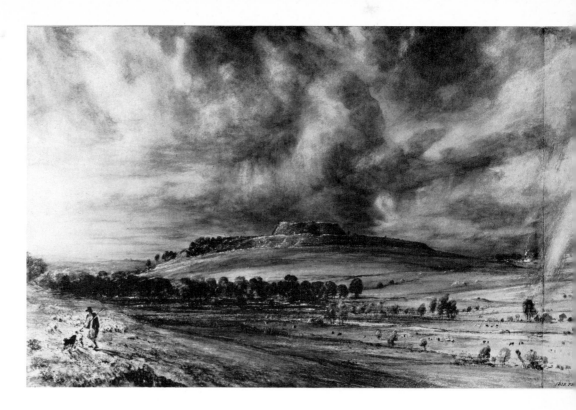

JOHN CONSTABLE, *Old Sarum*, 1834
(watercolour).
Victoria and Albert Museum, London.

'These things made me a painter, and I am grateful – that is, I had often thought of pictures of them before I ever touched a pencil. . . .'

Constable's art is one of continual rediscovery, even of the newest memories – not only of the scenes of childhood but also of the freshness of a dewy morning, of an evening sky as well as a stormy sea – and also a search for a lost innocence, for a countryside unspoiled by industrialization, for an Eden uncontaminated by man. This is why we prefer his rapid sketches, made in all humility directly before nature, though even in these we are sometimes conscious of a fussy, pedantically accurate style. Constable rarely succeeded in overcoming the discrepancy between his aims and his actual works, which is why, in front of the over-painting and over-elaboration in his large works, we see that they are never entirely worthy of his genius.

Constable was an excellent writer whose briefest notes and jottings have an artless aptness which delights his admirers: his contemporary, Turner (1775–1851), almost his opposite in character and career, was secretive, taciturn and, despite poetic ambitions, so inarticulate that he left a will which defied clarification. But he did read widely among the poets and writers of his own and previous ages. His annotated copy of Eastlake's translation (1840) of Goethe's *Theory of Colours* betrays his constant desire to learn more of his craft, although it is doubtful whether he could have gained more knowledge of colour in these final years of his career.

Constable and Turner, the greatest contrast, or so it seems, within Romantic landscape painting! And yet, how like they were in many ways! Constable could be malicious and obstinate, awkward and jealous when occasion offered, as could Turner, although less frequently. Turner was certainly very fond of money; and Constable, who was far from poor, worried too much about it. Both could be generous and simple, especially with children. Of the two Constable's was perhaps the more complex nature. After the death of his wife, whom he had married after a long and troubled courtship, the gloom began to close in on him. He cried out that every gleam of happiness was blighted for him and that tempest after tempest rolled on him. There was about him a vein of prudishness which should have endeared his memory to the Victorians; when he learnt of the death of Byron he said that the world was well rid of him although the deadly slime of his touch still remained.

Turner was never a saint; and never claimed to be one. He did make claims as a poet, affixing extracts from his *The Fallacies of Hope* to several of his pictures. The title was appropriate, for he was fascinated by disaster, and possessed of a temperament which was fundamentally pessimistic. Both Constable and Turner were deeply struck by the diversity of Nature and by the power of light, and, in their different ways, anticipated the experiments of the Impressionists. And, if we are absolutely frank, we have to confess that the larger, finished pictures of both artists are more than a trifle boring. We lack sympathy with these strivings after the masterpieces which would rival Claude and Poussin, and prefer the quick sketches, notes and studies made while impressions and feelings were still at full strength.

Throughout his life Turner was something of a showman. At the age of thirty-four he was described as resembling a prosperous master-carpenter, with his 'lobster-red face, twinkling, staring grey eyes, white tie, blue coat with brass buttons ...' and turned-up boots, large hat and enormous umbrella. This singular figure would turn up at dawn on Varnishing Days at the Academy and work for hours transforming the skeleton of his picture into a glorious rhapsody like 'a magician performing his incantations in public'.

Obviously on these occasions there was no reference to Nature but directly to his

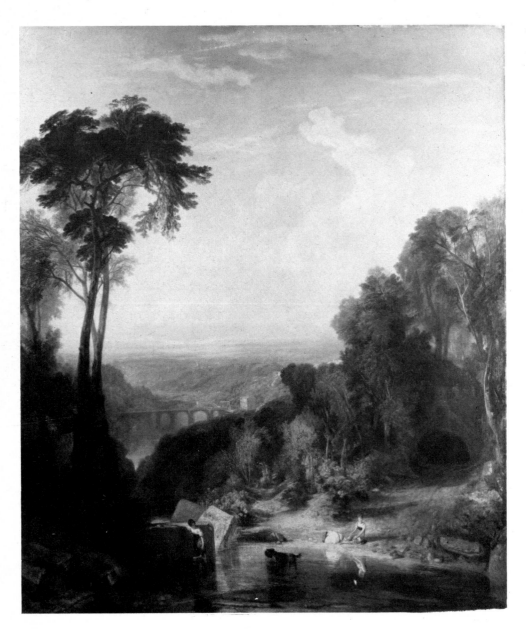

JOSEPH MALLORD WILLIAM TURNER,
Crossing the Brook, 1815.
The Tate Gallery, London.

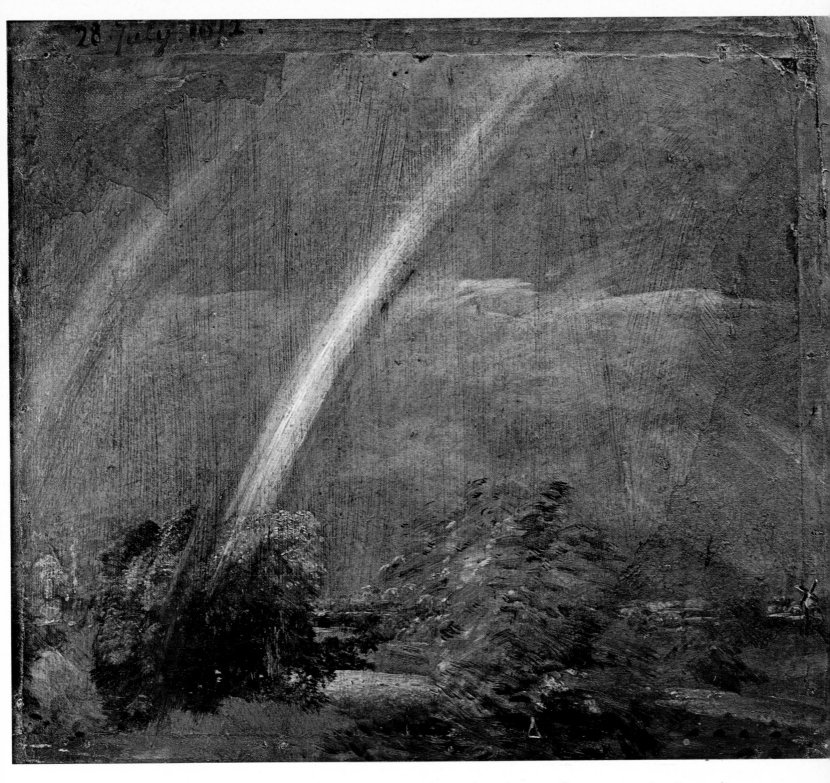

JOHN CONSTABLE, *Landscape and Double Rainbow*, 1812.
Victoria and Albert Museum, London.

own emotional states and the tonality of surrounding canvases. In a Romantic age of virtuosi, of Liszt and Paganini, Turner was the master-conjuror in the world of painting. Behind this supremacy, which was not achieved without relentless effort and unremitting industry, was the yearning of a sensitive young man to escape from that sordid little court off Maiden Lane where he was born into shabby poverty. From the age of thirteen he served an apprenticeship to topographical draughtsmen, engravers and architects which ensured an affectionate familiarity with the fundamental technique of his craft as a landscapist. It also meant that he never acquired any command of form, for he rarely painted the human figure with any degree of veracity and most of his forms were so singularly ugly that they earned comparison

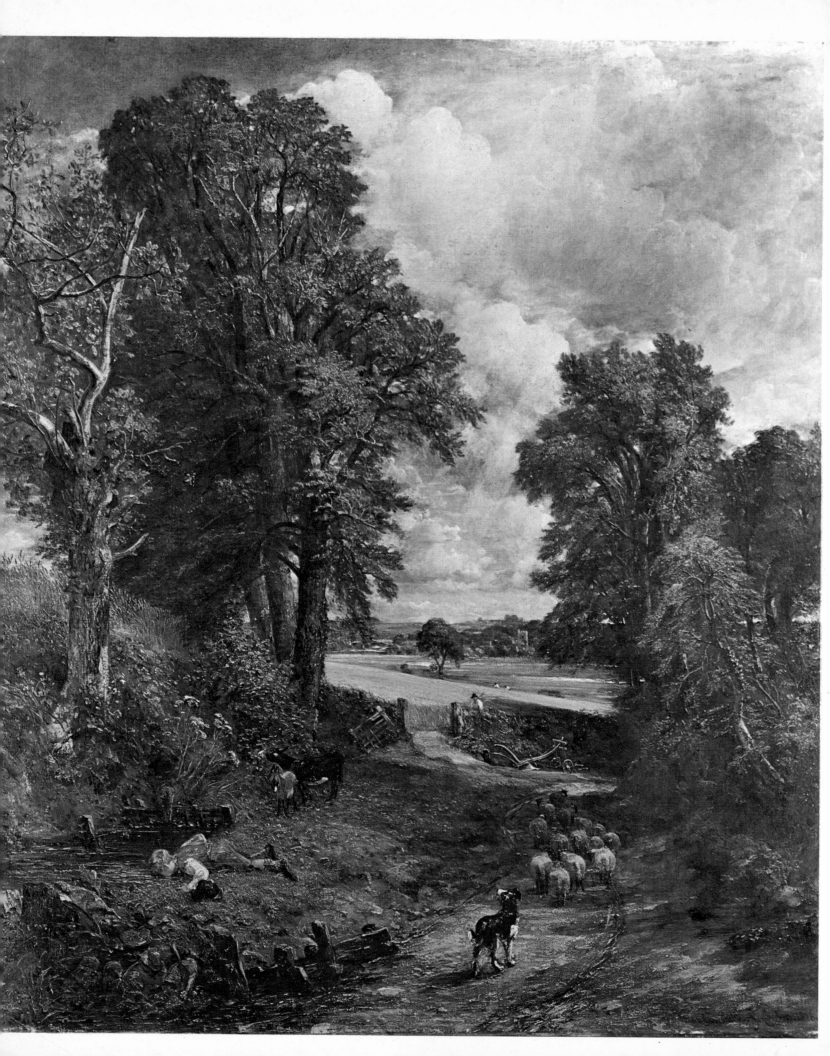

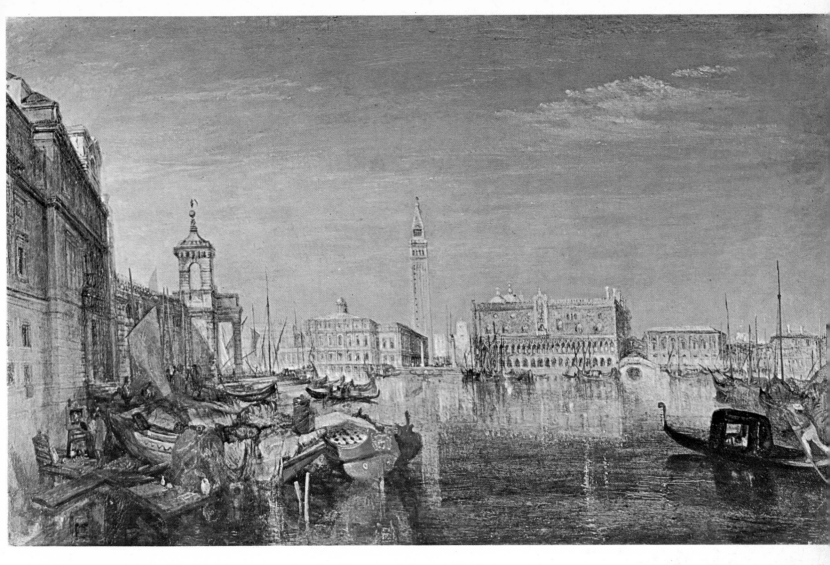

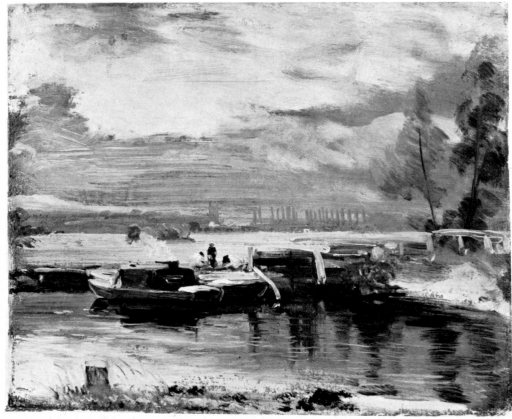

Above, JOSEPH MALLORD TURNER, *Venice,*
1833. The Tate Gallery, London.
Left, JOHN CONSTABLE, *Barges on the Stour.*
Victoria and Albert Museum, London.
Opposite, JOHN CONSTABLE, *The Cornfield,*
1826. National Gallery, London.

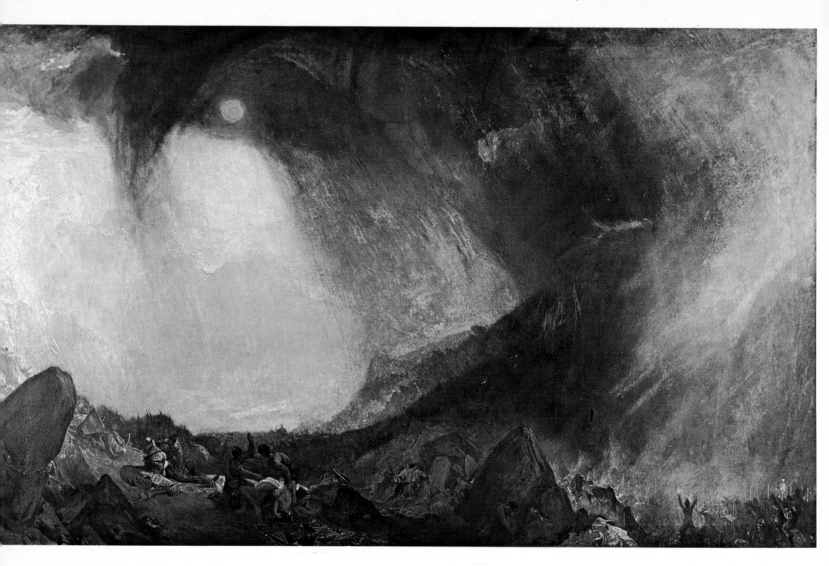

JOSEPH MALLORD TURNER, *Snowstorm: Hannibal crossing the Alps*, 1812. The Tate Gallery, London.

with a plate of poached eggs and fried sausages, a failing which was of minor significance, for Turner became and has remained the greatest master of watercolour and of the use of colour in landscape.

Turner's mother was said to have ended 'insane and in confinement'; and throughout his life any suggestions that his work showed signs of madness enraged him. But we may surmise that behind this indignation lay the fact that he knew he was in bondage to his own emotional obsessions with certain aspects of landscape, notably the sea, Venice and the Alps. He was first inspired to visit Switzerland, in 1802, by the romantic landscapes of De Loutherbourg (whom he emulated in a number of works dating from that time), the watercolours of Cozens, and Thomson's poetry; and he went to Italy, in 1819, on the advice of Lawrence, who described him as 'indisputably the finest landscape painter in Europe'. Turner returned to Italy a number of times, particularly to Venice of which he painted brilliantly opalescent sketches; and from the age of sixty-five began to make annual pilgrimages to the Alps in which he recognized a force as enigmatic and as universal as that of the sea. Sometimes his paintings were accurate depictions; more often they were emotional rhapsodies, exultant hymns of praise or wild screams of horror as the mountains unleashed their destructive fury in devastating avalanches. Like his admirer, Ruskin, it might be said that he was more than a trifle dotty about the Alps.

He seems never to have been optimistic about the human condition and whilst he could appreciate the heroic struggle of Hannibal and his men in crossing the Alps (a subject borrowed from Girtin but which fitted in well with his own experiences), his deepest feelings went to the elemental forces of Nature which threatened and over-

212

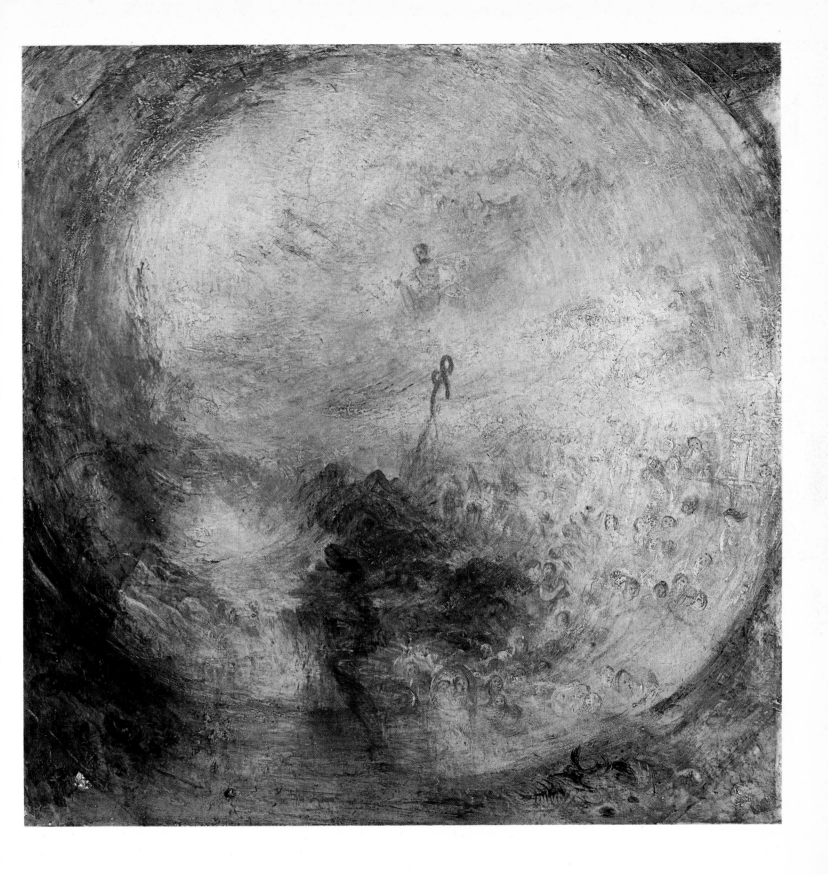

JOSEPH MALLORD TURNER,
Light and Colour (Goethe's Theory): Moses
writing the Book of Genesis, The Morning after
the Deluge, 1843.
The Tate Gallery, London.

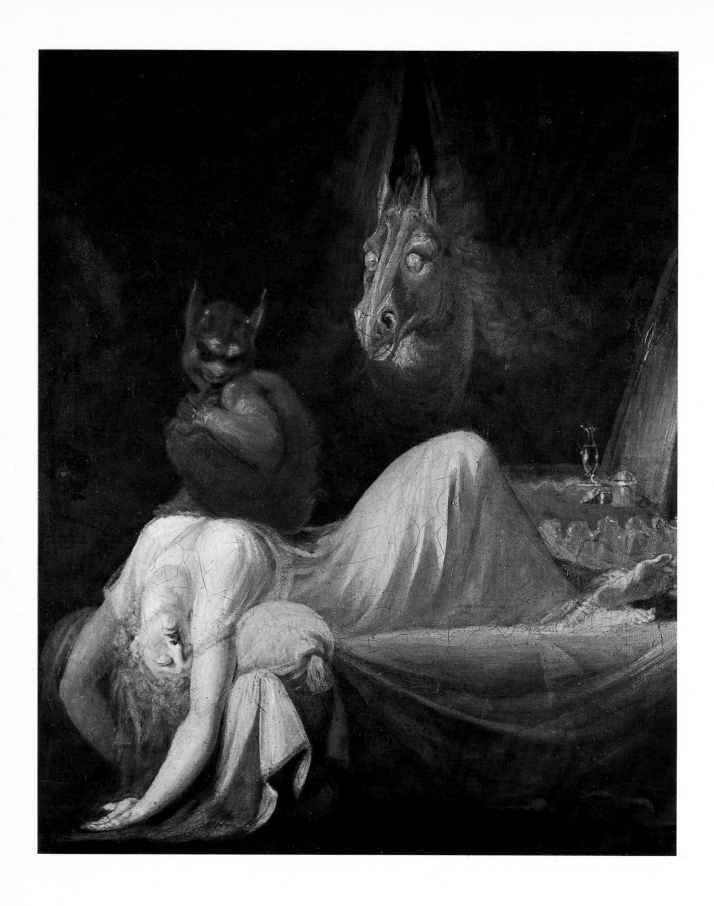

J.H. FUSELI, *The Nightmare*, 1782.
Goethe Museum, Frankfurt.

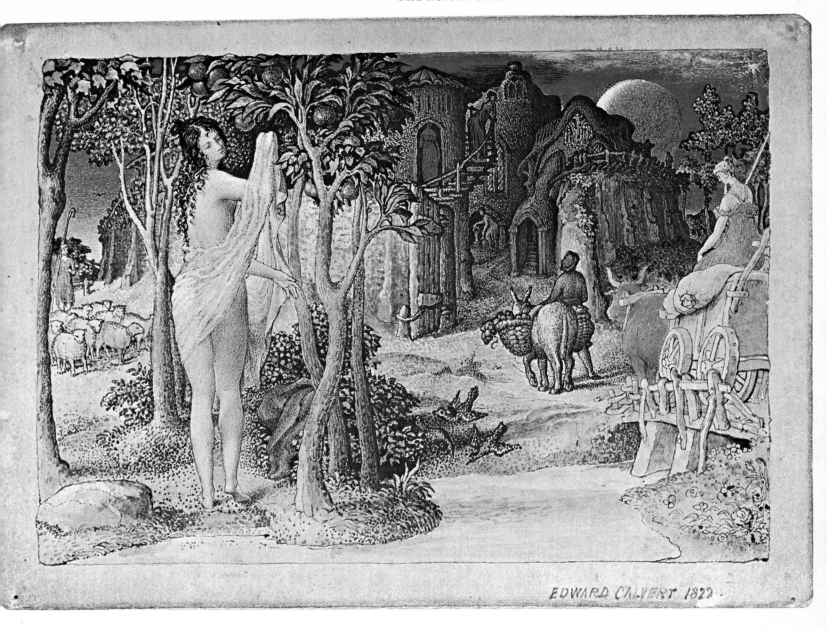

EDWARD CALVERT, *The Primitive City*, 1822
(watercolour).
British Library, London.

whelmed all human achievements. This applied to his own art, for while he left one of his compositions to the National Gallery on the understanding that it was to be hung side by side with a Claude, many of his pictures were left to rot in a ruinous house in Queen Anne Street, while he lived obscurely at 119 Cheyne Walk.

Turner's apparent fondness for low life, the ridicule showered on his verse and his alleged illiteracy have hidden the range of his emotional strength and the keenness of his intellectual faculties – which, as Ruskin pointed out, were of a high order. The titles and subjects of his pictures demonstrate the variety and width of his reading. A title such as *Light and Colour (Goethe's Theory) – The Morning after the Deluge – Moses Writing the Book of Genesis* suggests an immense degree of preliminary planning but contemporary accounts tell us that Turner simply obeyed the impulses of his senses when painting such a colour-composition and added an appropriate title afterwards.

In fact, these rapturous works may be said to exist for the sake of colour alone and considered from the point of 'subject' it was inappropriate for Ruskin to discuss their content so seriously and at such excessive length when he was cheerfully content to dismiss similar works by other painters as nonsense. In later pictures of Venice, Petworth and Norham Castle Turner retained only the slightest elements of

215

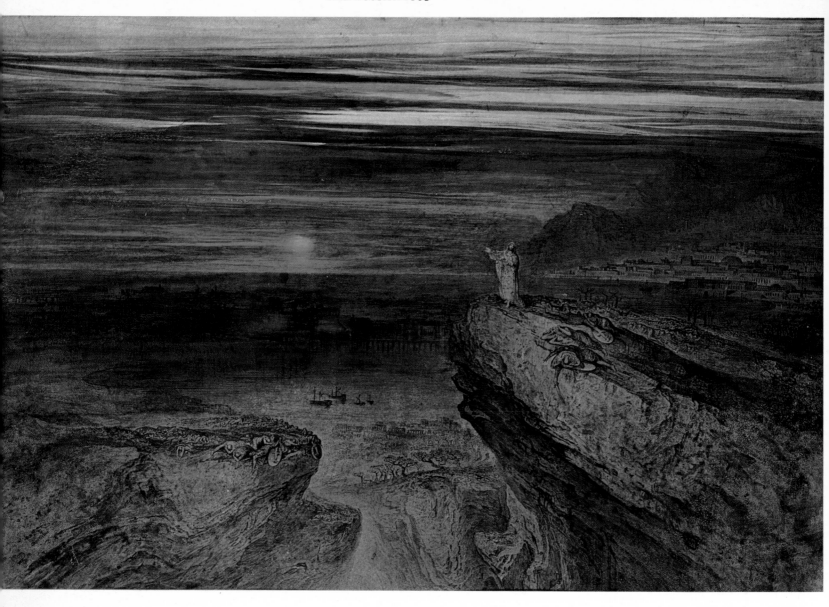

JOHN MARTIN, *The Last Man*, 1833
(watercolour).
Laing Art Gallery, Newcastle-upon-Tyne.

the scene, presenting an alliance of thought, sensibility and imagination in terms of transitions of tones and films and mists of colour. As he lay dying he is said to have pronounced, 'The sun is God'. What is certain is that he died at ten o'clock on a dull and gloomy morning; but just before nine, as his physician recalled, 'the sun burst forth and shone direct on him with that brilliancy he loved to gaze on and transfer the likeness to his pictures'.

There is some truth in Constable's description of his rival's pictures as 'airy visions, painted with tinted steam'. In his early twenties Turner had reached the top of his profession by turning out topographical scenes, illustrations and landscapes, even of countries he had never visited, much in the style of Claude and Poussin. But the greater part of his life was spent in an investigation of the nature of light, whether glittering on the domes of Rome or shimmering hazily on the Venetian lagoons or reflected in the placid waters of an Essex river. In 1779 he told Joseph Farington that he had no 'settled process' but 'drove the colours about till he had expressed the idea in his mind', a statement which anticipates almost every development in painting since his day. Yet we should beware of judging him as if he were an abstract artist – the vast range of his *oeuvre* should warn us against over-facile statements – and there is ample evidence of the preparatory sketches of land, sea and air that went into his

216

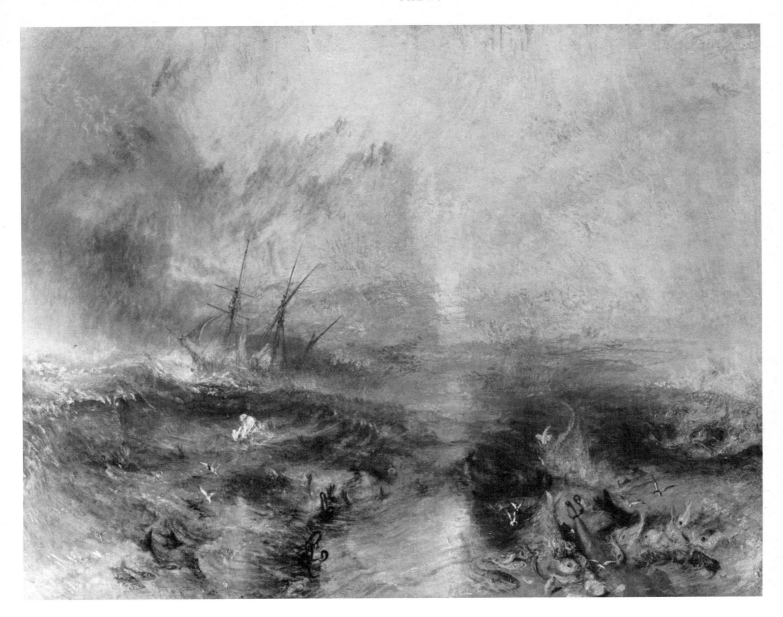

big canvases. On the other hand, his colour notes of social life at Petworth prove that long before Rimbaud and the symbolists he had found colour equivalents for sensations, objects and incidents. Face to face with the blindly hostile and destructive forces of Nature he grappled obsessively with stains of yellow, pink and blue which he encrusted with whites, finally drawing over them iridescent veils of colour.

Whether or not we care for Turner's paintings, the inherent Romanticism of his mind is undeniable. Ruskin saw that one of its innate characteristics was a profound pessimism which expressed itself in visions of horrific catastrophes, and as proof we might refer to *The Eruption of the Island of St Vincent* or *A Fire at Sea* or *The Slave Ship* in which man's inhumanity to man seems minor compared to the unsubduable hostility of Nature. It is true that the glorious strains of colour in these fireworks partly conceal the underlying message of man's impotence in the face of unleashed cosmic forces, but the pessimism is never diminished. Other painters from Joseph Wright of Derby and De Loutherbourg to Washington Allston, Benjamin West and Stanfield share this sense of awe before Nature and the age was exposed to a host of shipwrecks, sea battles, storms and volcanic eruptions.

It is remarkable that pessimism was so constant an element of Romanticism, particularly when allied to a deliberate attempt to thrill the spectator. The melodramatic

JOSEPH MALLORD WILLIAM TURNER, *The Slave Ship*, 1840.
Courtesy the Museum of Fine Arts, Boston, Henry Lillie Pierce Fund.

217

theatrical fare of the age bears this out, as does the taste for Gothic literature satirized by Jane Austen in *Northanger Abbey*. In the Academy of 1813 a picture by George Dawe of *A Child Rescued by its Mother from an Eagle's Nest*, a singularly dramatic piece on a theme also attempted by William Blake, was described by a critic as 'tamely conceived' which suggests that a taste for terror was very strong indeed.

The same love of disaster and drama often found expression in landscape painting, which underwent a singular metamorphosis at this time. From the seventeenth century, from Claude, Poussin and Salvator Rosa, there had evolved a kind of landscape decorated with a few figures of a historical or poetical character. Sometimes their significance was literary, sometimes historical, sometimes allegorical; and the basic intention was to raise the status of landscape in the same way as Reynolds had elevated portraiture by exploitation of the same non-pictorial trappings. The sketching club founded by Girtin and his friends in 1799 had as its aim the establishment of 'a school of Historick Landscape, the subjects being original designs from poetick passages.' Many of Turner's early works belong to this category, as, for instance, *The Fifth Plague of Egypt* (1800), *The Tenth Plague of Egypt* (1802), *The Destruction of Sodom* (1805) and *Snowstorm: Hannibal Crossing the Alps* (1812), for which he supplied one of the passages of poetry which he continued to compose until the end of his life and which have been too frequently dismissed as meaningless and fustian rubbish. But in these works the tranquil arcadian scenes of the Old Masters gave way to frenzied vistas of mass destruction. Four years after this last-named work of Turner's, at the age of twenty-seven, John Martin (1789–1854) exhibited his monstrous *Joshua Commanding the Sun to Stand Still* and began his triumphant career as a purveyor of *frissons*, a career which ended when, in an unusual stroke of poetic correctness, he was seized with paralysis as he sat before his *The Meeting of Jacob and Esau*.

Martin was fascinated by exotic and grandiose architecture, so that monstrous ziggurats and pyramids are to be seen in the backgrounds of his biblical works; these elaborate architectural fantasies, which probably influenced Turner and may also have inspired Nash's long terraces and vistas, are lit so luridly and dramatically that one feels Martin must have had in the back of his mind the vast mills and factories of the industrial north which were notorious for their use of night labour. Scale fascinated him, scale which defined but also blurred and intensified the unfathomable gulfs which swallowed up mankind, the waves which rolled on humanity, the heavens which split open and ejected blinding flashes of lightning, and the immense perspectives which stretched on indefinitely. David Wilkie announced that *Belshazzar's Feast* was a truly phenomenal work, while Bulwer Lytton declared that Martin was comparable only with Raphael and Michelangelo and was at the same time 'more original, more self-dependent'. Other critics thought that Francis Danby (1793–1861) whose *The Upas Tree* terrified visitors to the Academy in 1820 was a finer artist and that *The Delivery of Israel out of Egypt* and *An Attempt to illustrate the Opening of the Sixth Seal* were superior in horror to anything contrived by Martin. This view was shared by the archetypal Romantic William Beckford, who put aside the miserly habits of his old age and added the *Attempt* to his collection.

While Martin and Danby (and others such as Washington Allston (1779–1843)) were successful in imposing their visions, synthetic as they may now seem to us, on a receptive public, those artists who expressed their own private fantasies fared less well. Earliest and strangest of these was J.H.Fuseli (1741–1825), the Swiss-German scholar and painter who made England his home and exerted a widespread influence on the artists of the day. Fuseli was an art-historian of novel tastes who pioneered the rediscovery of the Italian 'primitives' but who is more appreciated for his wash drawings and sketches of nightmares (p. 214) than for his carefully finished illustrations to Shakespeare and Milton (p. 220). Fuseli had contacts with important

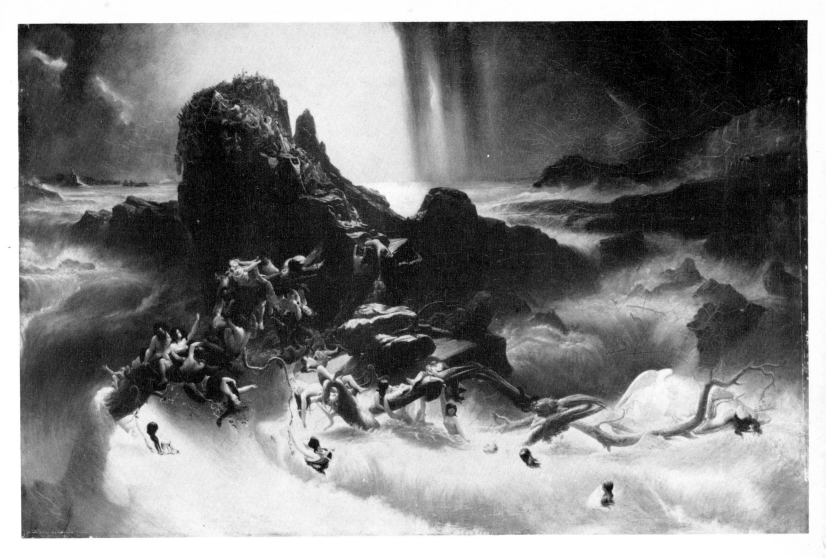

FRANCIS DANBY, *The Deluge*, 1840.
The Tate Gallery, London.

and influential personalities in the world of art all over Europe. He was at one time associated with Johann Jakob Bodmer, one of the personalities behind early German Romanticism. During his years of study in Rome he gave free rein to the development of his own personality and laid the foundations of his art by a study not only of Michelangelo and Shakespeare but also of the more imaginative and fantastic pages of Western literature and legend, from Homer, Dante and Milton to the *Niebelungenlied* and the *Chanson de Roland*.

In art, he learned both from the early Italians and the archaeological discoveries on show at Naples. He deliberately turned his back on the calm commonsense of the eighteenth century and set out to explore the world of the irrationally bizarre and fantastically macabre. He rejected seventeenth-century Italian painting, denied the validity of Neo-classicism, with its pretence at disciplined rigour, opposed all that was French and sought instead the extravagantly heroic and sublime elements of the Italian Renaissance. He selected such elements as fitted his own original and eclectic genius from the *terribilità* of Michelangelo, the sinuous grace of Parmigianino, the sinister violence of Salvator Rosa and the apparently unsophisticated mannerisms and compositions of the Italian 'primitives'. To these Italian sources he added qualities which were peculiarly northern: a sense of the demonic, of the fantastic, of the tempestuous and of the darkly terrifying. Benjamin Robert Haydon once spent five hours with him during which they talked their way through Homer, Virgil, Dante and Milton.

At one point, Haydon wrote, 'I thought I saw the stone suddenly leap and roll and rush down the hill again, while Sisyphus in despair again began his labours . . . I

219

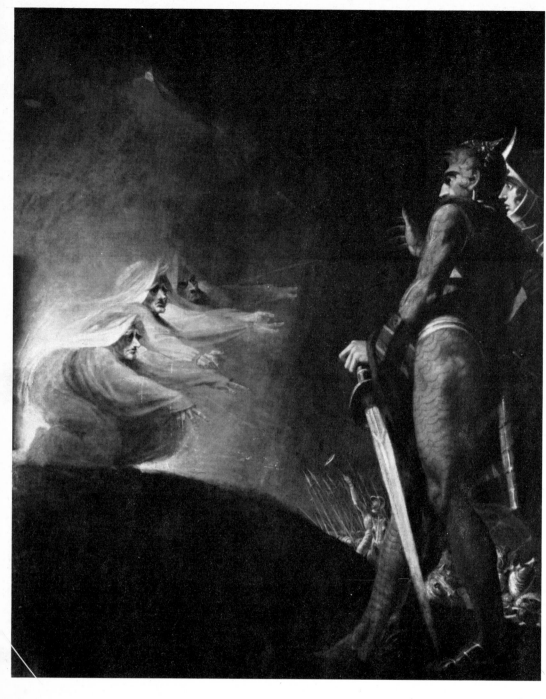

J.H. FUSELI, *Macbeth and the Witches,*
*c.*1793–4.
Petworth House, The National Trust.

never leave Fuseli without a greater delight for my art, without being more full of grand ideas, without being instructed by some observation or delighted by a flash of wit.' What Haydon also knew was that Fuseli possessed a macabre vein of diabolic eroticism which earned him the nickname of 'Principal Hobgoblin Painter to the Devil'. His contemporaries apparently recognized the Gothic elements in his art – the contrast between heavily armoured men and girls in the flimsiest of clothing, the unexpected appearances of ghosts and demons. There are strange correspondences with Goya's nightmarish musings. Fuseli's women are at once frail and monstrous, less humans than insects, decorated the more viciously to attract their prey.

Fuseli had a great admirer: William Blake (1757–1827), who said he was fonder of him than of any other man on earth. We also know that Fuseli found his friend 'damned good to steal from' without altogether sharing his views or eccentricities. When Blake told him that the Virgin Mary had appeared to him and praised one of his pictures as 'very fine' the Swiss artist, who was rarely at a loss for a word, com-

220

mented that 'her Ladyship was not possessed of an immaculate taste'. But Blake himself was not devoid of a sense of humour and, one wonders, how often and how far did he, the most cheerful and lively of men, pull his contemporaries' legs during those conversations which they recorded with the utmost seriousness.

It has been objected that Blake can hardly be classed among the Romantics since he seems never to have cared for the natural landscape; and on first consideration this is borne out by his statement that, 'The world of Imagination is the world of Eternity . . . whereas the World of Generation, or Vegetation, is Finite and Temporal'. But in addition to all their loving study of landscape did not Turner and Constable bring to it an imaginative understanding of 'the Permanent Realities of Every Thing which we see reflected in this Vegetable Glass. . . .'? Blake's landscape was that of the mind, a landscape of infinite range and variety. Like Turner he was a Londoner and whereas Turner spent the little free time of his boyhood staring at the masts and rigging of the shipping in the Thames and laboured at copying the works of the popular topographers, Blake was put to work drawing the Gothic remains in Westminster Abbey.

These memories remained with him all his life, mingling freely with recollections of Flaxman's designs and studies of Michelangelo. His pictorial genius flourished within definite channels, within the restraints of line of which he made a virtue. He was well aware of this: 'Gothic is Living Form . . . Living Form is external Existence', and 'Nature has no outline, but Imagination has'. In the *Descriptive Catalogue* which he wrote for the exhibition of his tempera paintings he wrote a defence of line: 'The great and golden rule of art, as well as of life, is this, That the more distinct, sharp and wiry the bounding line, the more perfect the work of art. . . .' Neither water-colour nor oils are suited to linear work; and it is significant that Blake experimented with tempera, which calls for a linear technique (and of which Michelangelo, object of his wild enthusiasm, was master), and with colour printing, by methods of his own devising.

In fact, Blake is a great illustrator, perhaps the greatest, in a supremely British tradition which goes back to the Middle Ages. He has never been equalled for magnificence and boldness of design, energy of invention and austere use of colour – qualities which are related to the illustrated manuscripts and stained glass windows and stone and wooden carvings of our churches and cathedrals. Such is the power of his compositions that they stand on their own without the need of text, which is not to say we do not gain additional appreciation when we are aware of this dimension, for literature played as great a part in Blake's life as did art. He moved away, despite his admiration of Flaxman, from the dependency of his contemporaries on classical literature and history and created his own version of medieval and antique history; he investigated the emotions and thoughts of childhood; and he exploited the visions and hallucinations for which he eagerly and deliberately sought. Behind the mysterious arabesques of his art are also hidden strong republican sympathies. And with Fuseli he shared a penetrating interest in human sexuality, which he saw as a means of liberation from the chains of reason.

It would be a mistake, however, to regard Blake's genius as either insular or incomprehensible to anyone outside the British Isles. Crabb Robinson's review of his 1809 exhibition was published as far afield as the Hamburg periodical *Vaterländisches Museum*. And it must be admitted that in some ways his work was not as absolutely neglected as some of his admirers pretend. In the latter part of his life he had a circle of young patrons, the Prince Regent acquired some of his illustrations and after his death a member of the royal family offered his widow the not inconsiderable sum of £100 per annum. That Blake, with his hatred of rationalism and worship of the life of the senses, was an outstanding eccentric cannot be denied, but neither should one lose sight of the fact that he gained from the incursions into the irrational undertaken

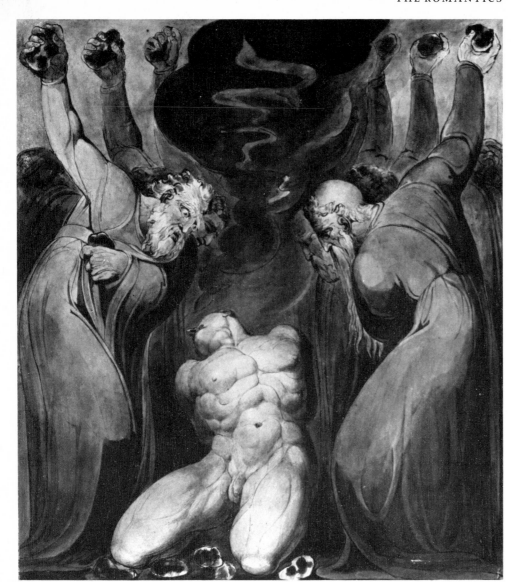

by Barry (whose lectures he may have attended and on whom he began an admiring poem), Flaxman, Fuseli, Mortimer and Romney. Nor was a distrust of empiricism confined to Britain; the careers of the Danish-German artist, Asmus Jakob Carstens, and the German, Philipp Otto Runge, show that Blake was not alone in his rejection of oils in favour of tempera and watercolours, in the holding of private exhibitions and in his hatred of the art establishment. He was not even alone in his attempt to create a private and mystical symbolism in which Michelangelesque figures soar in or struggle through a strangely flat cosmos in which every detail, however decorative, carries a spiritual significance.

For a brief while it must have seemed to Blake's young followers – to Linnell, Richmond, Calvert and Palmer – that they had fulfilled the hopes of so many Utopians from Rousseau down to Shelley and Coleridge and actually established an Eden in what remained of England's green and pleasant land. Palmer (1805–81) was by no means a simple artist: a visionary he may have been but a very cold eye had carefully scrutinized Durer, Breughel, Van Leyden, Elsheimer and Claude. In 1824, he wrote, 'Look for Van Leydenish qualities in real landscape, and look hard, long and continuously.' Like other artists whose chief interest lay in landscape he wished to elevate it above the comparatively low grade assigned to it by Reynolds. This he attempted by detailed studies of grass, leaves, branches and landscape formation (and we should remember that Palmer was a youthful prodigy who had works accepted at both the Royal Academy and the British Institution when he was fourteen), disdaining the generalized breadth of conception adopted by Constable and Turner. As a result his sketches show a curiously moving absorption in the minutiae of nature and also awe before the mystery of creation. Like Van Gogh he seemed as much stirred by the merest trembling of the smallest leaf as by the frenzied and prodigious fertility of fruit trees, gardens and cornfields. During the years 1825 to 1830, when he was living with his artist friends at Shoreham and reading Virgil and Milton, Fletcher's *The Faithful Shepherdess* and Flavel's *Husbandry Spiritualized*, his own pictorial eye ordered the creation of some landscape scenes which are more enchanted than representational.

His flocks of sheep, chapels, sheaves of corn, reapers and ploughmen, harvest moons and fruit-laden trees belong to a golden and Virgilian garden of Paradise. This vision was shared by his friends. Too soon, alas, the visionary gleam was gone. The Reform Bill descended, to prove (so they felt) that they lived in a world of increasing industrialization, in which the prosaic commonplace was elevated and the bonds of society cruelly broken. Wordsworth's words of 1817 sum up their last reactions: 'I see clearly that the principal ties which kept the different classes of society in a vital and harmonious dependence upon each other have, within these thirty years, either been greatly impaired or wholly dissolved. Everything has been put up to market and sold for the highest price it would buy'.

The group of artists who seemed content to record the changing face of Britain were the watercolourists: Alexander and John Robert Cozens, Sandby, Towne, Payne, Girtin, Cotman, Cox, Crome and De Wint. Their work was encouraged neither by the Academy nor the art patrons of the time, whose taste was summed up by

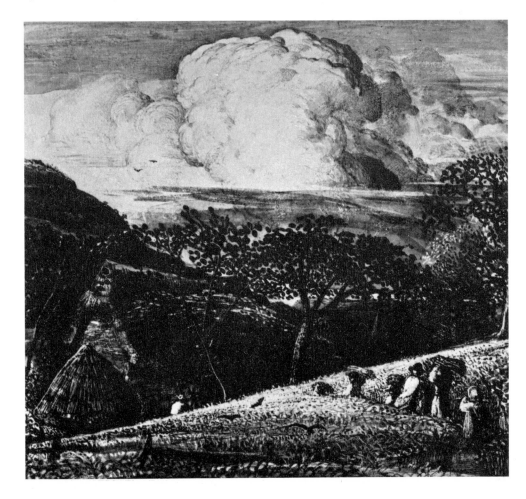

SAMUEL PALMER, *A Valley thick with Corn*, 1825.
Ashmolean Museum, Oxford.

223

Fuseli in 1805 when he said, 'Views if not assisted by nature, dictated by taste, or chosen for character, may delight the owner of the acres they enclose, perhaps the antiquary or traveller, but to every other eye they are little more than topography.' These strictures against landscape applied equally to Constable and Turner as to Cotman and Crome. Consequently, the watercolourists fell back on writing books of advice for artistic amateurs, taking up employment with private families as drawing masters, illustrating the books of topographers and antiquarians, or selling picturesque views of cottages, cascades, castles, ruins, mountains, heaths, cows and donkeys.

It must be admitted that from the turn of the century a growing number of patrons began to collect these works. It would be wrong to despise topographical work, for it did encourage the accurate depiction of form (a weakness with many of the Romantic artists) and foster the development of a style better suited to watercolour than that afforded by Canaletto, Claude or Poussin. Watercolour, which was portable and uncomplicated in use and ideally suited for quick effects, for the recording of spontaneous reactions to Nature and the sensitive depiction of a green landscape, was a godsend for the Romantic temperament. Its charm could be effectively transferred to lithography and aquatint and used to illustrate the numerous albums of picturesque views of British and Continental scenery with which the name of Samuel Prout is associated.

It could be argued that of all the areas of Romantic painting it was the watercolour which showed the greatest developments, not only in technical progress but also in the variety of treatment and the range and depth of subjects treated. Throughout the eighteenth century watercolour had been used largely for topographical and colouring purposes. Often enough, as in the lively scenes of Rowlandson and the cartoons of Gillray, watercolour was used merely for tinting and even then in a monochromatic fashion. Alexander Cozens (c. 1717–86) and his son John Robert Cozens, Sandby and Towne were among the artists who investigated its varied possibilities. Alexander Cozens has considerable importance since, in addition to an unusual sensitivity to the effects of weather, of clouds and sunshine, he invented a method of creating landscape from blots, so that the resulting scene was a projection of the artist's concern with mountains, rocks and trees as elements of his own sensibility.

The simplicity of his landscapes in which he particularly exploited the pattern of light and shade is justly famed and his series of aquatints, in which cloud formations are carefully studied and categorized, was copied by Constable, who made good use of them in his own work. The emptiness of Cozens' landscapes, the absence of any human life and the lack of reference to any specific locality means that the viewer reads into them his own interests and sentiments. His son, John Robert (1752–97), inherited a sensitivity to clouds and to the mood of landscape, utilized his father's discoveries of the value of simplifications in natural form and added a responsiveness to Alpine scenery which anticipated the obsession which was experienced by Turner from 1802 onwards.

As young men Thomas Girtin (1775–1802) and Turner had been employed to make copies of sketches by John Robert Cozens, an activity which was to have a determining effect on the development of Girtin's mature style. From 1796 he was drawn to the landscape of northern England, of Yorkshire in particular, but soon widened his interests and style to include mountain and moorland scenery. His views of Paris show not only technical command of perspective but also a responsiveness to urban landscape. But perhaps Girtin's greatest technical achievement is his pioneering employment of the brighter hues of watercolour in preference to the limited tints and monochrome of eighteenth-century topographical drawings. He frequently used a rough cartridge paper, the imperfections of which gave a depth and strength to his landscapes. He ignored the conventional methods of composition which had been in

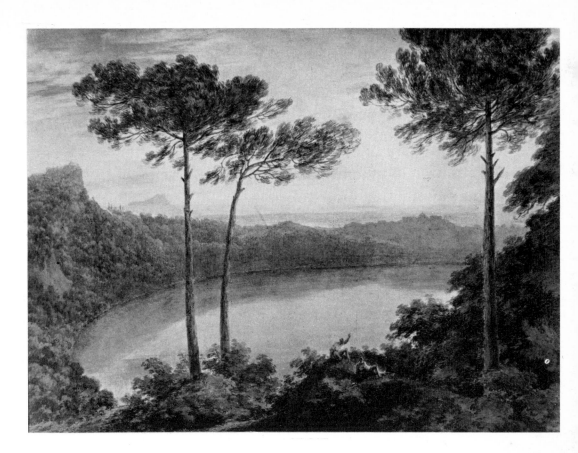

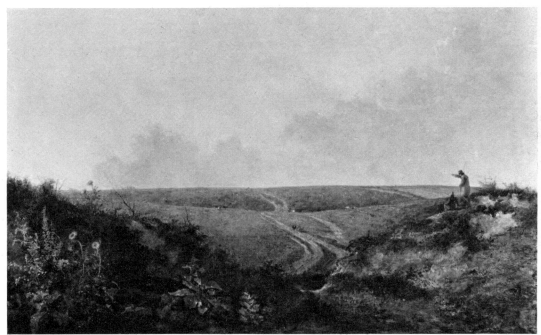

JOHN ROBERT COZENS, *Lake Albano and Castel Gandolfo*, c. 1770–80 (watercolour). Collection of Leeds City Art Galleries.

JOHN CROME, *Mousehold Heath, Norwich*, 1818–20 (watercolour).
The Tate Gallery, London.

use for over a century and worked with a direct response to nature. Cotman (1782–1842) and Crome (1768–1821) and the other painters associated with Norwich were responsible for introducing a wider degree of sophistication into the medium; and for all the decorative and austere beauty of Cotman's work in which a dignified sense of balance and pattern are evident there are dismaying signs that watercolour was being overtaxed. Paper is scraped, body colour added to the tints, underpainting employed and countless other tricks elaborated to give the resulting pictures something of the substance and permanence of oils. In fact, Crome and Cox (1783–1859) turned away from watercolour in their latter years. Turner somehow reversed the

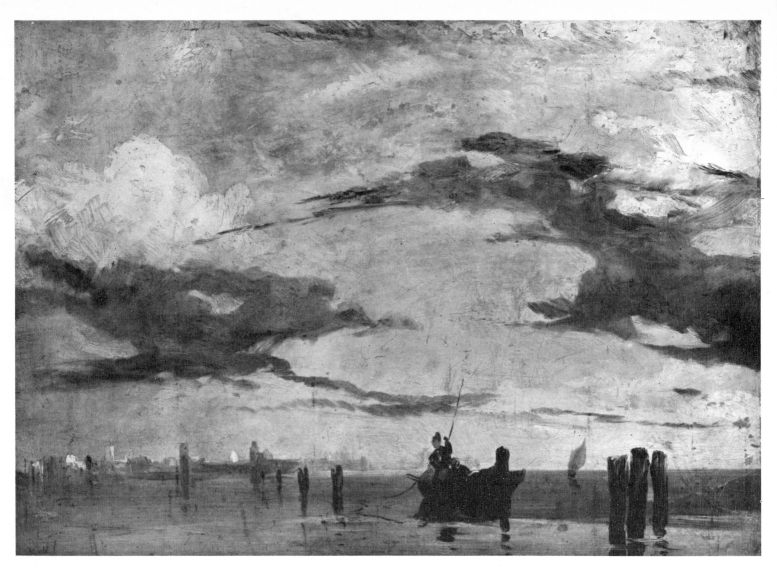

RICHARD PARKES BONINGTON,
On the Adriatic, c. 1826.
The Louvre, Paris.

process by taking into oils the ephemeral effects he had evolved in watercolour, thus anticipating the achievements of Monet's *Water-lilies* and the abstract painters of this century.

Although Bonington (1801–28), one of art's great casualties, spent much of his life in France, where for a time he shared a studio with Delacroix, he was in the direct tradition of English watercolourists. In fact, he studied under Louis Francia, a native of Calais, who had lived in England and been a friend of Girtin. A freedom and ease of handling both in oils and watercolour (criticized oddly enough by Constable and Delacroix) may have resulted from this early training. Like Cozens and Constable and Turner he tried to capture the fleeting effects of cloud formations with pencil, colour and wash. Bonington used watercolour with a freshness and vivid sense of the open air that recall Constable; but his scenes of the Venetian lagoons and French canals have about them a tender melancholy to which Turner was no stranger in his early days. He was as sensitive to the decaying market towns of Northern France as to its wind-blown heaths.

It cannot be claimed that Paul Sandby (1725–1809) had much to offer in the realm of the pictorial but he introduced several technical improvements. He was, for instance, one of the first artists to develop aquatint engraving, to utilize gouache and exploit the use of white paper to express sky, light and air. On his sketching tours through the British Isles he explored a wide range of landscape views which were to catch the imagination and extend the range of subjects of the artists who followed him. Sandby, whose lively mind was always on the look-out for new ideas, frequently

226

introduced animated groups of people into his compositions and had the happy knack of capturing the spirit of public events as well as of landscapes. Endearingly honest and touchingly humble before Nature, the watercolourists produced pictures which are among the best-loved products of the Romantic age in painting.

However diverse the elements of Romanticism, an appreciation of industrialization is not to be found among them. After the paintings of iron foundries, blacksmiths' shops and spinning factories by Joseph Wright in the 1770s (and these may have been occasioned by his interest in light rather than in industrial development), there were few other such scenes. A little later De Loutherbourg (who was also interested in the effects of light although for theatrical purposes) painted a few pictures of the foundries in Coalbrookdale. John Bourne (1814–96) was one of the few artists who depicted the world of the railways and is said to have done for the railways what Piranesi did for the architecture of ancient Rome. Constable and Turner painted a few pictures of factories and foundries which were only remotely concerned with the destinies of iron masters, worker inmates and the devastation of the countryside. Turner had not escaped from the slums of Maiden Lane to paint grim factories and the grimy towns of Northern England; and Constable turned his back on the family mills and the sources of his wealth and chose instead . . . 'The sound of water escaping from mill-dams, willows, old rotten planks, slimy posts, and brickwork . . .'

In general the public shared the prejudices of these major artists and placed strict limits on its own appreciation of realism. An accurate and detailed oil by Mulready (1786–1863) of the *Gravel Pits and Houses in the Mall at Kensington*, a charming scene which is indebted to Hubert Robert and to the seventeenth-century Dutch land-scapists, was refused by the patron who had commissioned it as being too literal. What the public wanted were pictures which were reminiscent of Canaletto, Lorrain, Salvator Rosa, Vernet and Hubert Robert, Berghem and Wouvermans – in much the same way as the musical public called for the souvenirs, reminiscences and para-phrases of operas and symphonies which were so popular at the time. They did not care, perhaps, for classical scenes, which were a little beyond their comprehension, but rather fancied escapist landscapes and scenes which were not of an excessively historical or poetical character.

Luckily there were a number of artists who had no wish to emulate their more important contemporaries, who did not use faulty pigments and bitumen, and whose craftsmanship and skill were of a high level. De Loutherbourg (1740–1812) was among the first artists to cater for this taste and by carefully adapting his memories of Dutch compositions to British scenes scored successes which he followed up by the invention of the Eidophusicon, a kind of magic lantern show for which he painted foreign ports, volcanoes, moonlit scenes, etc. Gainsborough and Girtin were other painters who experimented with these sensational devices, which entranced a nation avid for startling experiences. De Loutherbourg was also partly responsible for the pictures of domestic rusticity which were to be George Morland's speciality (p. 228). Morland (1763–1804) suffered much during his life from the rapacious attentions of art dealers and copyists; and it is certainly true that he had rather too much of the Romantic disposition to drink and dissipation which is one reason why the best of his productions – charming and good humoured scenes of gypsy encampments, decayed forges, ale houses, farms and sea coasts – have received only patronizing attention. His pictures, popularized in engravings, many of them executed by his brother-in-law William Ward, are, despite their sentimental gloss, a fairly true picture of the wretched state of the English peasantry towards the end of the eighteenth century. Ibbetson (1759–1817), perhaps a more versatile artist than Morland, carried on the same tradition and like other artists of the day was perfectly willing to copy the works of his contemporaries or those of the Dutch masters.

Even a minor artist like George Samuel (d. 1823), of whom little is known except

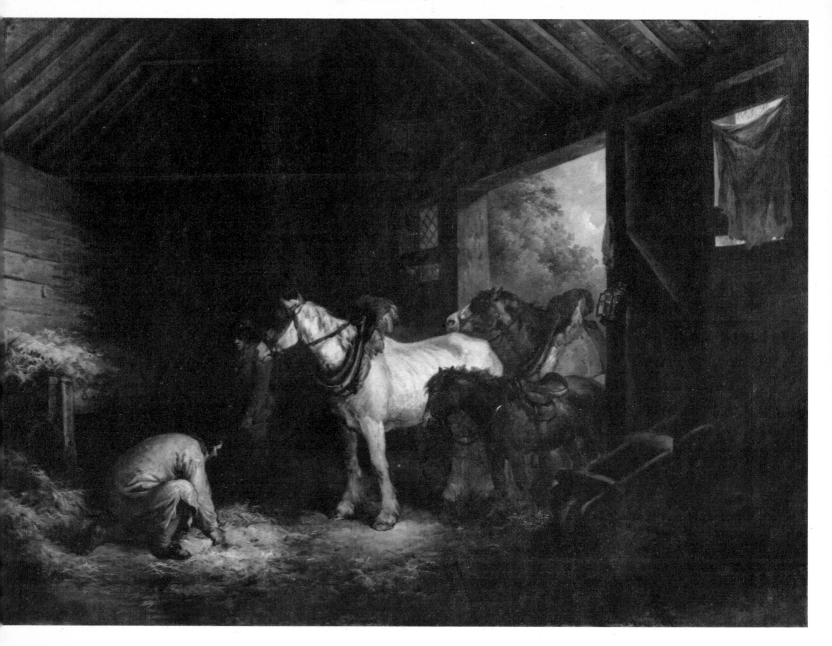

GEORGE MORLAND, *Inside a Stable*, 1791.
The Tate Gallery, London.

that he was an acquaintance of Girtin, could paint topographical views which, without showing any marked individuality, maintained the high general level of landscape painting during the Romantic period. A few artists tended to specialize in less homely scenes; one such in an earlier generation was William Marlow (1740–1813), who experimented with the juxtaposition of landscapes as in his picture of St Paul's, in which a Venetian canal takes the place of Ludgate Hill. Robert Freebairn (1765–1808) made his name with views of Italian scenery, although after his death his son published a volume of engravings of Lancashire scenery which were taken from his father's sketches. Freebairn's was a refined and sensitive talent with an elegiac and poetic quality.

Improvements in communication and in means of travel in Europe, particularly after 1815, brought about a new attitude to distant lands. It was no longer the custom to visit the European cities to complete one's education, classical or otherwise, but it became part of one's 'sentimental' education to visit Venice and Florence, Rome and Naples, and other towns which were attractive either in themselves or because of their past. There grew up, too, an intense curiosity about the remoter regions of the

WILLIAM MARLOW, *Capriccio: St Paul's and a Venetian Canal*, c. 1770–80. The Tate Gallery, London.

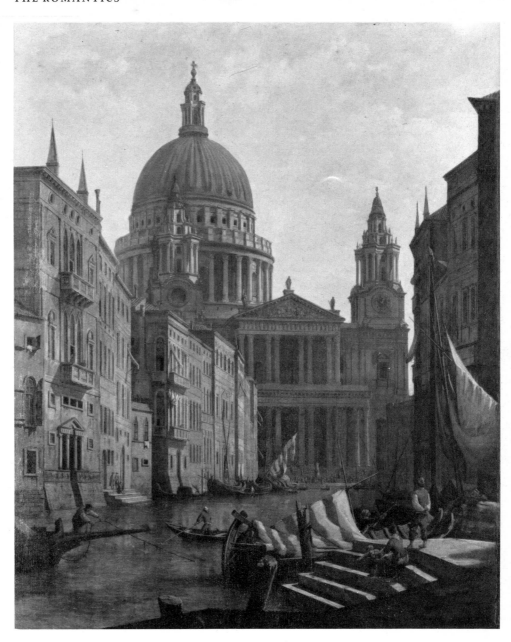

earth, which was partly satisfied by the issue of large illustrated volumes and albums of sketches.

When Captain Cook went to the South Seas he took with him William Hodges (1744–97), to record the novel and picturesque landscapes in a style which was far better suited to depict classical antiquities. John Webber (1752–93), who accompanied Cook in his third and last voyage, seemed to record the Pacific as if it were an extension of North Italy. Chinnery (1774–1852) and others investigated India and the Far East and found them remarkably pleasant and rather more picturesque in their way than the street scenes painted by Wheatley or the rustic episodes of Morland and Rowlandson. Zoffany was one of the few who ended this innocent dream when he painted *The Death of Captain Cook* (p. 230) in which the savages – certainly noble enough in their classical poses – are nevertheless hostile and murderous. The quest of the exotic continued in the numerous folios of costumes and habits of the less-well-known peoples of the earth. It was only necessary to take the high road that led to Scotland to find oneself in a romantic and savage land.

When, after the Napoleonic Wars, it became possible to cross the Channel once

229

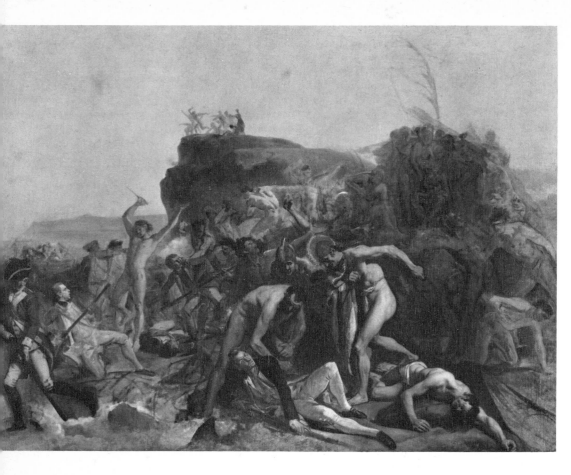

more, a generation of painters, watercolourists in particular, headed by Turner and Prout, both of them idols of the young Ruskin, introduced the British public to Picturesque Europe. Here they shared an interest with the theatre which revelled in ballets such as *Napoli*, operas such as *Masaniello* and a host of plays dealing with the hot-blooded South. Joseph Severn, Charles Eastlake and David Scott were a few of the painters who lost their hearts to Italy. Tourists who did not care to venture so far (like the Ruskins on their first trip abroad) or were afraid of the activities of the Italian brigands were happily content with the Low Countries, the Rhineland and northern France, where they found themselves in an atmosphere of decaying towns dignified by crumbling Gothic cathedrals and picturesque markets, especially in Normandy and Belgium.

In fact, 'Change and decay in all around I see' was the motto to which the saintly Samuel Prout (1783–1851) owed his considerable success and which, when exemplified in his views of the older neglected towns of Europe, earned him the adoration of Ruskin and the admiration of the public. Large annuals of engraved and lithographed plates of his work found a ready market. His pictures, which are uneven in quality, coincided with the tremendous interest in medieval life and national history and folk lore which followed the Revolutionary wars. In general his scenes are beguiling rather than accurate and the figures which crowd his market squares and cathedrals are weakly drawn. On the other hand he was a cunning master of crumbling stonework and picturesque houses enlivened by highlights, often in the form of improbably draped bedsheets or newly washed garments of gargantuan proportions. It might be said that Prout was – and still is – responsible for the Romantic tourist's view of a Europe as yet untouched by the industry which was devastating and still continues to ravage northern England.

Through Romantic painting runs a tide of uneasiness, a sense of inevitable disaster only temporarily postponed. Artist after artist gave expression to a genuine sense of anticipation of a doom that would spare neither man nor civilization. Nature seemed

230

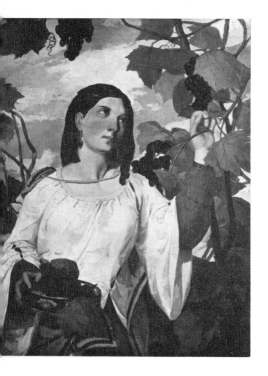

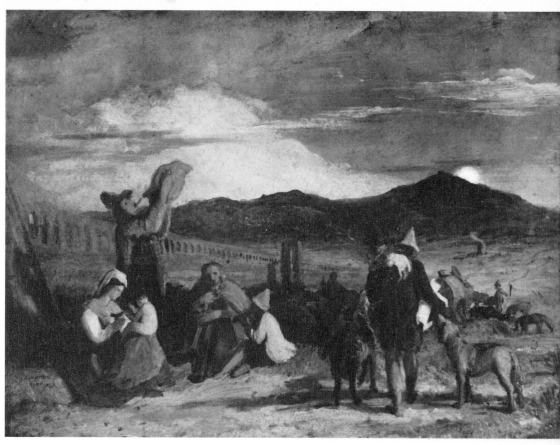

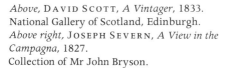

Above, DAVID SCOTT, *A Vintager*, 1833.
National Gallery of Scotland, Edinburgh.
Above right, JOSEPH SEVERN, *A View in the Campagna*, 1827.
Collection of Mr John Bryson.

to threaten everywhere in deluges and snowstorms, in tempestuous seas and oceans, in the form of lurking and savage animals. Long before Darwin had spelled out the meaning of evolution the Romantic age had sensed that life was rarely innocent or carefree. Man was subject to the blind fury of the elements; he was also subject to the hostility of wild life which preyed on itself as man was seen to prey on man in that age of ruthless industrial exploitation. As early as 1778 Copley (1738–1815) showed his age a sensational (but not heroic) episode in which an ordinary man, a poor, bare, forked animal, innocent of all lendings, is attacked by a shark (p. 232). Ten years later in his studies for *The Siege of Gibraltar* he moved away from the comparatively static poses of Watson's friends to tortured and tortuous groups of male nudes engaged in a desperate struggle for survival against the enraged and relentless sea.

Such scenes recall the terrible intensity of Michelangelo's *Last Judgement* and anticipate Géricault's *Raft of the Medusa*. Among his other scenes of disaster Turner showed a whole shipload of slaves flung out on to the waves by the inhumanity of the slave-traders and unable, because of their shackles, to defend themselves against the shoals of predatory fish-like creatures. While the early animal painters were content to depict the horses and dogs which were the pride of country gentlemen their successors showed these animals attacked by other ruthless creatures, as in the versions made by James Ward of bulls fighting one another (p. 234) or by Stubbs of a lion savaging a horse. Frequently these creatures (and humans, too) are seen against a wild and rugged landscape of rocks, gnarled trees, stormy skies and raging waters. One has only to compare such scenes with Pietro Longhi's *The Exhibition of the Rhinoceros* to see how original was the work of Stubbs and his followers and how percipient was their understanding of animal behaviour. The lions, tigers, panthers and zebras behave naturally as if at home in their own environments.

There is, moreover, the ability to see in the incidents of their daily life an emotional significance which partakes of an hallucinatory quality. Something of this intensity seems to have found its way into Blake's design of Nebuchadnezzar, which may owe

231

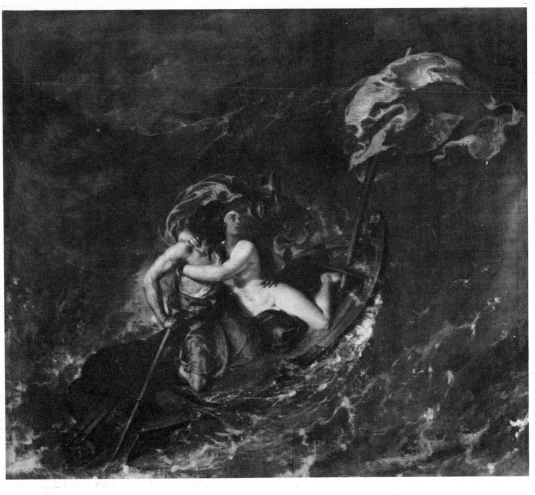

WILLIAM ETTY, *The Storm*, 1830.
Manchester City Art Gallery.

JOHN SINGLETON COPLEY, *Watson and the Shark*, 1778.
Courtesy Museum of Fine Arts, Boston.
Gift of Mrs George von Lengerte Meyer.

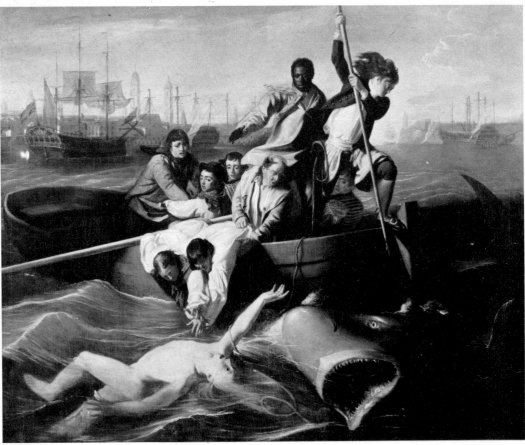

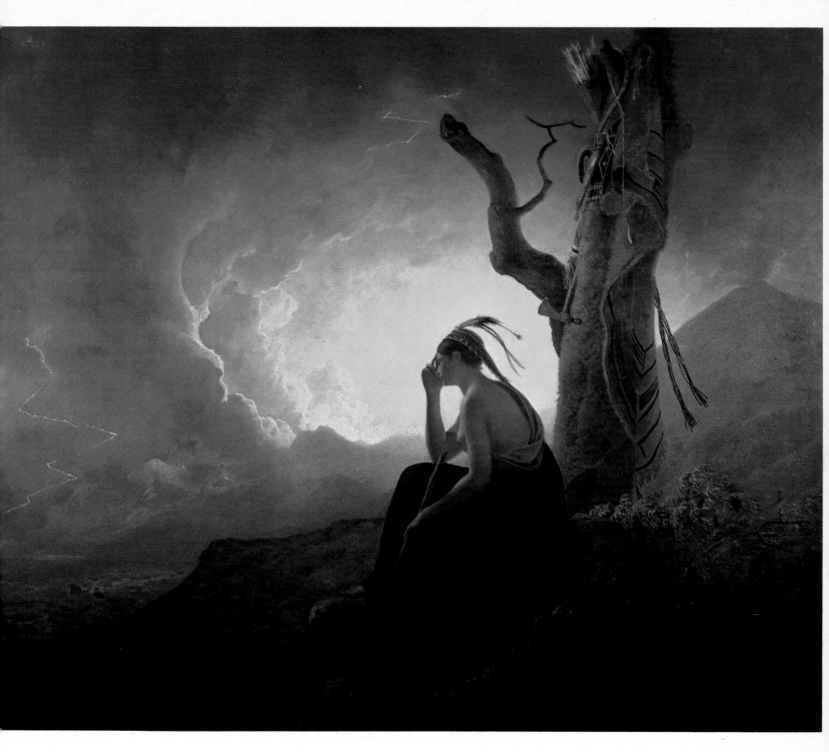

JOSEPH WRIGHT, *The Indian Widow*, 1785.
Derby Art Gallery.

a little to one of Stubbs' engravings. It was the exactness of their study, their compulsive investigation of the animal's skeleton, muscles, fur and flesh which gave distinction to the work of these highly original artists. One of the most ingenious and sympathetic of them was Thomas Bewick (1753–1828), famous for his woodcuts, particularly the vignettes which often appear to have been designed as pictorial accompaniments to Wordsworth's poems of man and nature, and for his dedicated examination of wild life in the fields and woods of his native Northumberland. He dispensed with stuffed animals and, working out-of-doors or using newly killed animals, painted brilliant watercolours, recording with an absolute and meticulous accuracy the individual features of his subjects.

This is equally true of Jacques-Laurent Agasse (1767–1849), whose interest in painting the Nubian giraffe presented to George IV was entirely pictorial. Here an

233

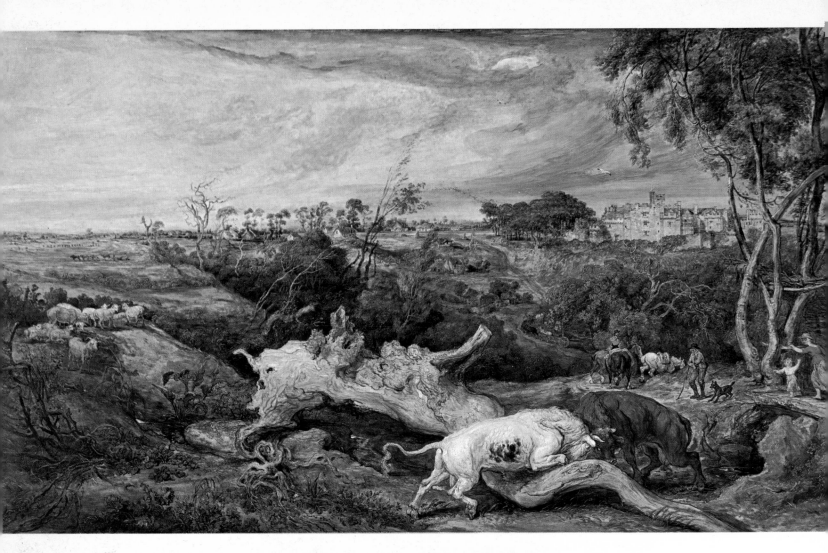

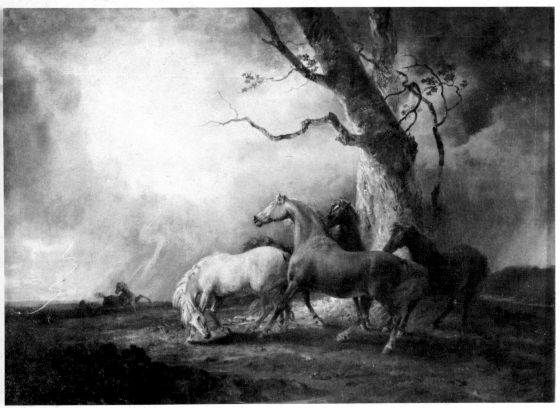

Above, JAMES WARD, *Bulls Fighting,* 1800.
Victoria and Albert Museum, London.
Left, SAWREY GILPIN, *Horses in
a Thunderstorm,* 1798.
The Royal Academy of Arts, London.

Right, above, JAMES BARRY, *Lear and
the Dead Cordelia, c.*1785.
The Tate Gallery, London.
Right, DAVID WILKIE,
Peep O'Day Boy's Cabin, 1836.
The Tate Gallery, London.

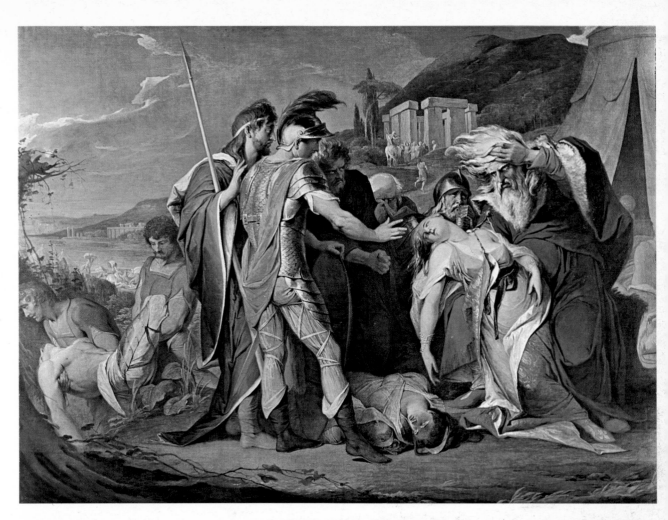

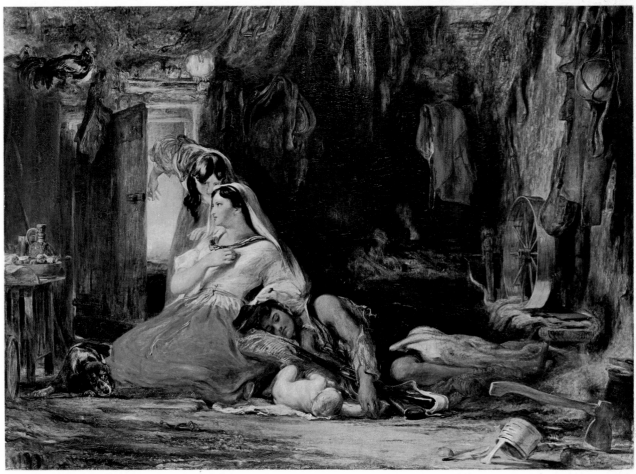

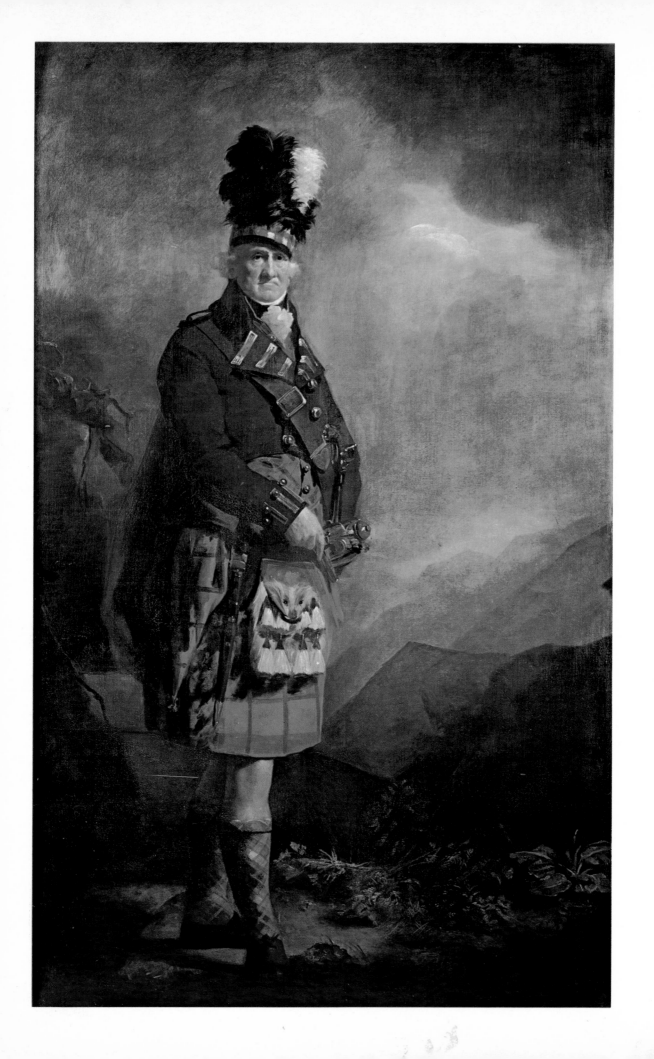

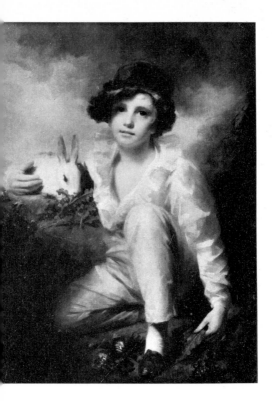

Above, HENRY RAEBURN, *Master Henry Raeburn Inglis,* 1816.
The Royal Academy of Arts, London.
Left, HENRY RAEBURN, *The McNab,* 1803–12.
By permission of John Dewar & Sons Ltd, London.

indebtedness to Stubbs is obvious. There is a sad falling off from Sawrey Gilpin's thoroughbreds, Garrard's frantic horses, Ward's vigorous cattle and maddened bulls and Stubbs, with his exact knowledge of animal anatomy and his dignified empathy with the passions of horses, lions, dogs and monkeys, when one comes to the sadistic antics of Landseer's performing monkeys and the melancholy stances of his stags and sheepdogs. If the sense of impending disaster has gone, so, too, has a quiet dignity and respect for nature: sentimental narration enters upon the scene together with an assertion of man's omnipotence over the animal kingdom. Neither Stubbs' recreation in paint of the haunting legend of a horse attacked by a lion at Ceuta and an antique sculptural group of the same subject seen at Rome nor the noble stags of Robert Hills (1769–1844) earned the praise which Ruskin lavished on Landseer's *The Old Shepherd's Chief Mourner* of his remark that it was not by a study of Raphael that Landseer earned his eminent success but 'by a healthy love of Scotch terriers'.

The contrast between Romantic toughness and Victorian sentimentality is nowhere more obvious than in the realm of sport and politics. James Gillray (1757–1815), the caricaturist, is a case in point. Not only did he specialize in political satire but he also displayed a remarkable genius as a social commentator. He produced some fifteen-hundred works, which were mostly issued as prints by Mrs Humphreys from her shop in Piccadilly. About 1811, partly obsessed by failing eyesight, he went off his head, tried to commit suicide and once startled the customers by walking into the shop naked. In order to express the intentions and traits of his subjects he exaggerated their physical characteristics, lampooning their dress, faces, hairstyles and moral behaviour without the least consideration for any sensitivity which they may (improbably) have possessed. Their vices and weaknesses find embodiment in contorted and malformed faces and physiques.

He did not spare himself, as is proved by the drawing entitled *Pray Pity the Sorrows of a Poor Blind Man* in which he portrays himself as a blind and toothless beggar. There is an unmistakable element of romantic wilfulness in Gillray's work; and the violence of his caricatures as well as the fanciful distortions of clothing, hats, trees and furnishings suggest a fetishist mentality. The astonishment provoked by the crudity, sexual and otherwise, of his treatment of social and personal relationships has deflected attention from the freedom with which he treated conventional and illusionist perspective.

Like Blake, Gillray showed a remarkable gift for working in frontal planes and for a near-surrealist displacement of objects, a trick which he may have learnt from Pier Leone Ghezzi. Rowlandson (1756–1827), whose work has remained popular with collectors of prints, drawings and watercolours, was a satirist of a different order (p. 237). Like Gillray he learned from Hogarth and Mortimer but was influenced by the French illustrators, so that although his caricatures have an overall vitality and extravagance that seem wholly English his style is basically linear – in fact sinuously Rococo. Much of the pleasure we gain from Rowlandson, quite apart from the insight he gives us into all ranks of society, lies in the contrast between the delicate rhythm of his calligraphy and the farcical excesses of the comic catastrophes which were his favourite subject matter. In addition to his breezy drawings for the various *Tours of Dr Syntax* he illustrated Goldsmith, Smollett, Sterne and other authors and also the *Microcosm of London,* for which Augustus Charles Pugin supplied the topographical backgrounds.

But while he delighted in the absurdity and folly of mankind he also showed a sympathetic appreciation of Nature. His rural scenes, in which the abundance and riotous fertility of Nature are evident, come close to the pictures of his friend Morland. There is little bitterness in Rowlandson, more romantic sensibility than is usually recognized, and an enormous amount of fun, so that (in a limited sense) his pictures are equivalents of Byron's comic epics.

237

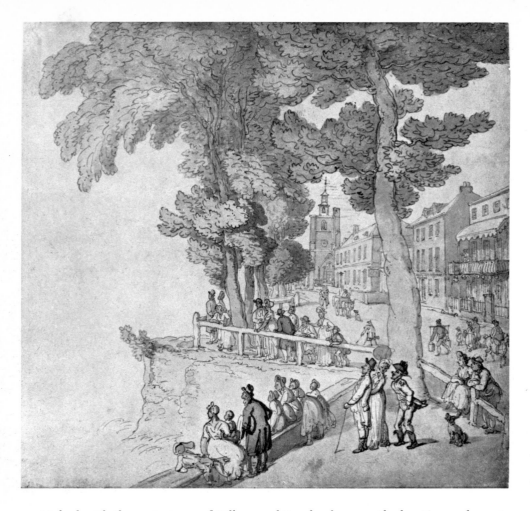

THOMAS ROWLANDSON, *A Scene in
Cheyne Walk, c.* 1810–15 (pen, ink and wash).
The London Museum.

Linked with the caricatures of Gillray and Rowlandson are the hunting and sporting scenes so popular in the Romantic age. The technique was often comparatively
crude and simplified, lending itself easily to reproduction. Of course, nothing tended
to separate landowners, aristocracy and gentry from the new industrialists so much
as days spent on the racecourse, hunting in the countryside or watching exhibitions
of pugilism in smoke-filled taverns. Benjamin Marshall (1767–1835) produced
numerous hunting and racing scenes; and his sketch of the celebrated pugilist John
Jackson became well-known in engravings. His pictures of blood horses, often with
trainers, jockeys and grooms set against stormy and dramatic skies, were much sought
after. They were typical of many such scenes turned out by competent artists
who were content to seek a fairly humble living in the provinces and of whom
Charles Towne (1763–1840) of Liverpool is representative. Scenes of sporting life in
which the elegance of horses, equipage and sportsmen are well matched responded
to the taste of the Regency bloods, who fancied themselves as boxers and jockeys. It
would be a mistake, however, to regard these sporting artists as insignificant, for
they shared common experiences, ideas and techniques – Towne, for instance, mixed
with Morland, imitated Stubbs, copied elements from the Dutch Italianate scenes of
the seventeenth century, borrowed from De Loutherbourg and derived ideas from the
Flemish paintings of wild animals at bay – and regarded their work with a high
seriousness, bringing to it a sense of craftsmanship which is lacking in the canvases
of their more distinguished fellow-painters.

Portraiture was, by and large, a secondary preoccupation of the Romantic painters.
It could hardly hope to equal the triumphs of Reynolds and Gainsborough in an
earlier generation nor could it expect a similar success, for a feature of Romanticism
was neglect of social rank, an indifference which was neither radical nor permanent
and which forced the portraitist into an uneasy position – for he was never quite sure

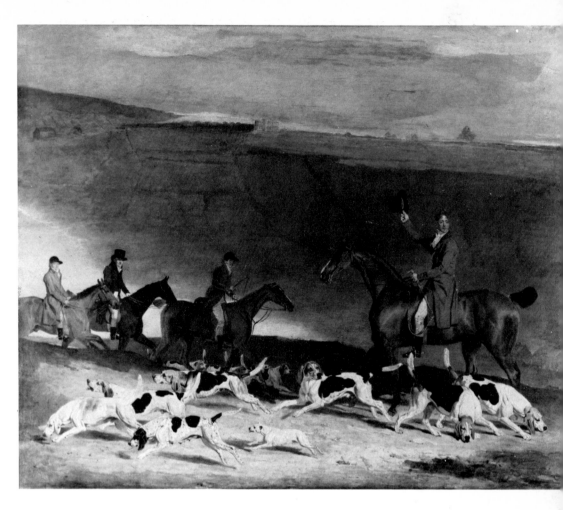

whether he was intended to paint a noble lord who had temporarily strayed into fancy dress or whether the fancy dress was, in fact, a basic element in the noble lord's character. Reynolds had evolved a type of allegorical portrait, the elucidation and full appreciation of which depended on a knowledge of classical mythology, emblem books, famous compositions by the Old Masters and a fondness for fancy dress. The intention had been to give portrait painting the dignity and stature of history painting: the result had been the creation of rather clumsy episodes which certainly did not show men and women as they were, either in their official or private lives.

But Horace Walpole was correct in pointing out that the exuberance of Reynolds' invention would be 'the grammar of future painters of the portrait'. In his different style Gainsborough, too, prepared the way for informal portraiture, for in his case there was always the willingness to create a pictorial image which corresponded in some degree to the sitter's conception of his own character. In the late seventies he wrote that nothing could be more absurd 'than the foolish custom of painters dressing people like Scaramouches, and expecting the likeness to appear'. Yet that is exactly what he himself had done when he dressed his sitters in Van Dyck costumes, a fashion which continued through the Romantic period, the apotheosis of masquerade and fancy dress. Romney (1734–1802) painted Lady Hamilton as a Bacchante (which, in a manner of speaking, she was); and Thomas Phillips (1770–1845) depicted Lady Caroline Lamb in her favourite guise, as a page, the role in which she tempted Byron.

There was room within the Romantic movement for portraiture of an informal kind. With the *Portrait of Sir Brooke Boothby* (1781) by Joseph Wright there seems to have been inaugurated in England a manner of portraiture which is related to those pictures of landowning gentry out of doors, among trees or fields, their freshly remodelled country house seen in the distance, which were popular throughout the

239

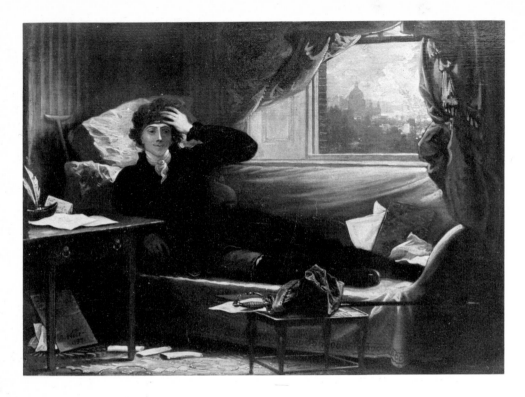

BENJAMIN WEST, *General Kosciusko*, 1797.
Allen Memorial Art Museum,
Oberlin College, Ohio.

latter half of the eighteenth century and of which Gainsborough's *Mr and Mrs Andrews* was an early and celebrated example. But Wright went further and showed his subject alone in a leafy glade, at ease on the ground, holding an open book. The spirit of Rousseau and, above all, his worship of nature breathes through this picture. It was an example which seems to have served for Copley's *Thomas Lane and his Sister* (1792), Benjamin West's *General Kosciusko* (1797) and Wallis's piece of belated Romanticism, *The Death of Chatterton* (1856). Of course, Rousseau's influence had been felt as early as 1761 with the publication of his *Julie ou La Nouvelle Héloïse* or (as it should be known) *Lettres de Deux Amants, Habitants D'Une Petite Ville au Pied des Alpes*; and the mock-pastoral had been a lively part of the Rococo movement – Marie Antoinette and her ladies, as is well known, had played at milkmaids in the Petit Hameau at Versailles.

But the Romantics actually saw men and women as part of the natural landscape and, more important, taught them to enjoy such a simple and enriching pleasure as a walk in the countryside. James Thomson, whose *The Seasons* is a key work in the history of Romantic sensibility, hailed Nature as 'all-sufficient! over all!' and begged that she might enrich him with knowledge of her works and transport him (in more senses than one) to Heaven or, at the least, whisper to his dreams. One of the finest portraits of the Romantic period is Raeburn's *Sir John and Lady Clerk of Penicuik* (c. 1790) in which his characters are seen out of doors, silhouetted in three-quarter length against the evening sky, Sir John pointing to a distant prospect with a gesture reminiscent of that of the Creator in Michelangelo's Sistine Chapel fresco, as though he were bringing a new world of shadow and light and landscape into existence. No less understanding of man and his place in Nature is the delightful picture of *The Reverend Robert Walker Skating*. Such were the attempts to find a new mode of informal portraiture in which man might be seen at home in the natural world around him.

Not unnaturally, as in literature, there was a marked interest in childhood and adolescence. Reynolds had painted portraits of children which are not without their charm even if memories of Italian *putti* and groups of St John and the infant Christ are too strongly evoked. One might have expected Gainsborough to have shown a deeper understanding of young people but too often, as in his *Pink Boy*, he was

Opposite, JOHN HOPPNER, *Princess Mary*, 1785.
Royal Collection.
By gracious permission of
Her Majesty the Queen.

content to depict an elegant pose and costume derived from Van Dyck and to place his youthful sitters in a conventional landscape or against the pillars and draperies of his studio. The Romantics were more aware, although not quite as deeply as might have been expected, of the depths of the young soul. Raeburn's offering to the Royal Academy was a portrait of the deaf and dumb son of his stepdaughter Anne Leslie, one of his finest and sweetest studies of boyhood (p. 237).

Raeburn learned something of his style from Lawrence who, whilst not the most penetrating painter of children or young people, had invaluable assets for success in this particular area: a love of elegance, an admiring appreciation of the clothes, hairstyles, carriage and elegance of his sitters, a susceptibility to the dashing looks and costumes and uniforms of his carefree and insouciantly arrogant young adolescents, as well as his own rather unhappy and unsettled character. Hence the rapid and somewhat dramatic ability to seize upon the 'style' of his sitters, especially when they were youthful and handsome, and his success as a Romantic portraitist. Opie (1761–1807) with *The Schoolmistress* and Wilkie (1785–1841) with his *Blind-man's Buff* both contributed scenes of childhood which, although not specifically original in subject and closely related to the village scenes of the Dutch seventeenth-century masters, show a happy insight into the playful life of peasant children.

But the taste for portraits of men, women and children in moments of informality was only one aspect of Romanticism, for there was also a love of pictures of the heroes of the time at their most flamboyant. It would be idle to pretend that there had not been precedents in the flamboyant portraits of Napoleon by David and Gros, but it was not militarism or martial glory which moved the British Romantic portraitists so much as the man behind the uniform. Here Romantic British portraiture was, perhaps, outstanding, and set an example for decades. Manet, for one, must have learned from the portraits by Lawrence to be found in France and elsewhere.

Particularly susceptible to the elements of make-believe and pose in Regency society, Lawrence was able to match the flamboyance of his sitters with striking poses derived from Michelangelo and Van Dyck, filling in the backgrounds with landscapes which were sometimes unreasonably and unaccountably agitated. During his triumphal tour of Europe in 1815 he created a gallery of dashing generals, wise statesmen and shrewd prelates, whose stupidity, short-sighted egotism and cowardice were concealed by his seductive panache. The element of the theatre is never far away in Lawrence's portraits and rarely to their detriment. There were other portraitists of merit: William Beechey (1755–1839), who began life as a house-painter (which may, as in the case of Braque, account for the excellent condition of his pictures), confined himself to portraiture in which he showed a dull but effective skill as in his *Wilkie*; George Dawe (1781–1829), who was a pupil of Lawrence and learnt from him a flashy but Romantic manner which stood him in good stead when, in 1819, he was commissioned by Alexander I of Russia to paint the higher Russian officers who had fought against Napoleon; and Harlow (1787–1819), equally indebted to Lawrence, whose early death cut short a promising career especially in the area of theatrical portraits. Among other portraitists, Owen, Phillips and Ibbetson showed considerable penetration when faced with the personalities of the age. Hoppner (c. 1758–1810) was among the most successful, probably because he managed to combine the styles of Reynolds, Gainsborough, Romney, Raeburn and Lawrence and yet retain a personal and pleasing quality of his own.

Hoppner's modest art is a triumph of eclecticism. Something of the status of the portraitist in Regency times is illustrated by the story of the city gentleman who with his wife, five sons and seven daughters presented themselves on Hoppner's doorstep and asked 'all to be touched off in one piece as large as life, all seated upon our lawn at Clapham, and all singing *God Save the King* – with prompt payment for discount'. Such a state of affairs was unknown to Raeburn (1756–1823) in distant Edinburgh,

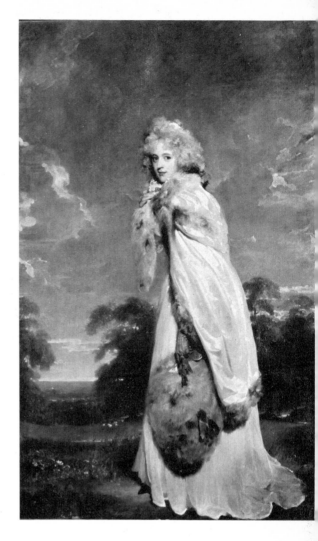

Above, THOMAS LAWRENCE, *Elizabeth Farren, Countess of Derby*, 1790.
The Metropolitan Museum of Art, New York. Bequest of Edward S. Harkness, 1940.

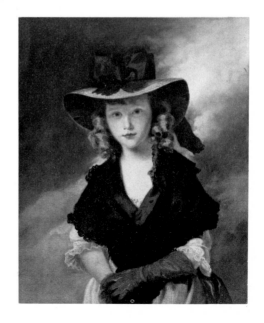

241

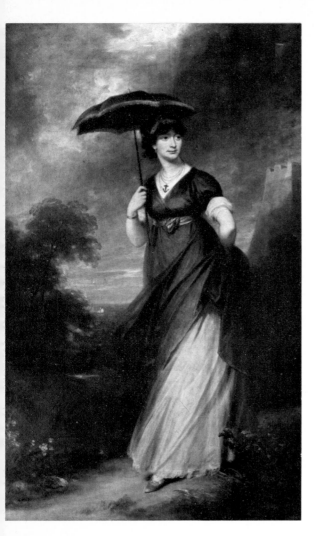

WILLIAM BEECHEY,
Princess Augusta, 1802.
Royal Collection.
By gracious permission of
Her Majesty the Queen.

where his life was that of a respectable, respected and well-to-do burgher. Nevertheless, he now seems the only serious rival to Lawrence, whose romantic gallery he complemented with his own clear-eyed portraits in which an obsession with light (and, it must be confessed, inefficient draughtsmanship) threatens the solidity and personalities of his sitters. These had no need of fancy dress: legal attire, kilts and all the appendages of Highland costumes worn without the slightest self-consciousness were more than sufficient. Raeburn was decorated by George IV, by North Carolina and Florence; he had many followers who paid him the ultimate compliment of imitating his style; and we recognize that his exploration of new and dramatic means of expression, delight in the robust personalities of his sitters and a sober joy in the exploitation of paint, colour and chiaroscuro win him the highest of places in the pantheon of Romantic painting.

Regency society was addicted to remembrances and keepsakes of all kinds among which miniatures were strongly favoured. The leading artist in this sphere was Cosway (1740–1821). Like Reynolds he selected from the repertoire of poses and gestures afforded by the Old Masters and like his contemporaries frequently painted his sitters in Van Dyck costumes, possibly to suggest a connection between the court of the art-loving Prince of Wales and that of Charles I. A happy and appealing gift of holding up a particularly flattering mirror to Nature enabled Cosway to become a distinguished and prosperous member of society. His travels and work abroad after his marriage in 1781 are insufficiently recorded but there are indications that through his wife he must have been aware of David among other artists.

Something of a fop and a typical Regency dandy, Cosway is said to have become eccentric in later life: by conversing with the Trinity he went one better than Blake, whose visitations were mostly limited to angels, and he enjoyed the honour, probably unique in the annals of modern art, of several visits from the Virgin Mary, who was keen to be painted in half-length.

Just as cheerfulness kept breaking in on Dr Johnson's would-be philosopher friend, so among the works of those artists who despised portraiture and attacked it in their critical writings one finds a secret addiction to depicting their own features. There are at least six self-portraits by Barry, showing him as a young man (but painted late in his career), as an old man and as a Greek artist. This self-probing investigation of one's own personality is a marked trait among the Romantics, for whom the question 'Who am I?' was never an idle one. There were few artists, however grandly classical their pretensions, who did not strike out a memorable self-portrait. One can forgive Wilkie much of his sentimentality when confronted with the honesty of his own self-portraits, in which nothing of the man's inner misery is ever hidden.

One does not immediately think of John Flaxman as Romantic but his self-portraits, too, reveal a fascination with fancy dress and self-scrutiny. His work was a potent force in Romanticism although this has not yet been fully admitted.*

Flaxman's linear illustrations to Dante and Homer were sold all over Europe from 1793, those to Aeschylus from 1795 and the last series dedicated to Hesiod from 1817. They were ransacked by David, Goya, Ingres and Runge, who exclaimed at their noble simplicity, directness of style and sensitive arabesques, owing much to the less erotic Greek vase paintings. These continental artists were quick to perceive, if not to understand, that Flaxman had created a new style of decorative illustration (and one wonders whether Beardsley ever came under their spell?) in which the bare areas of the designs are balanced by the significant, linear elements and in which there is no attempt at enclosed pictorial illusionism. Undoubtedly Blake profited by

*It was appropriate that the Russian designer Sophie Fedorovich should have used his designs in the ballet which Frederick Ashton based on Liszt's *Dante Sonata.*

this innovation, which may have been inspired in Flaxman by his study of Gothic art. For all his apparent Classicism Flaxman had a good deal of Romantic enthusiasm: he planned a 250-feet-high figure of Britannia to be erected on the hillside at Greenwich as a memorial to the Battle of the Nile, wrote poetry to which he supplied illustrations, and his wild sketch of *Thomas Chatterton Taking the Bowl of Poison from the Spirit of Despair* not only betrays his friendship with Romney but also the fundamentally Romantic and revolutionary strength behind his elegant designs.

In connection with Flaxman it is appropriate to return to that characteristic of Romantic painting, which is perhaps its outstanding and idiosyncratic quality – its excessively literary nature. This takes several forms: the illustration of works of literature both classical and contemporary, the illustration of literary themes and ideas and the illustration of incidents from legend and history. Unfortunately the heroes and heroines of the Romantic world are now lost in oblivion, a fact which presents difficulties in the adequate appreciation and understanding of the paintings in which they appeared. Belisarius, Numa Pompilius, Regulus, Atala, Darius, Rienzi, Sardanapalus, Tasso, Doge Marino Faliero and Jane Shore are barely remembered and certainly not with any interest. We can hardly imagine what associations and ideas these names aroused for the Romantic age! For instance, Thomas Barker of Bath (1769–1847) illustrated the *Discovery of Mazeppa*; Géricault, Delacroix, and Louis Boulanger also treated the theme, as did Horace Vernet whose versions were copied by J.F.Herring; Byron and Victor Hugo wrote poems about Mazeppa; and he was the subject of a symphonic poem by Liszt and an opera by Tchaikovsky. Yet what meaning has the legend now for a public whose ancestors flocked to see it translated into action in the music halls and circuses of the early nineteenth century? Perhaps the Romantic artists themselves overestimated the public's interest in literature.

In 1786, at great expense, the philanthropic Alderman Boydell commissioned illustrations to Shakespeare but, following his financial failure and death in 1805, the gallery of 170 items by celebrated artists went for only £6,128.16.0. Many of these pictures, in the academic and grandiose style approved by Sir Joshua Reynolds, who himself contributed three works, were, it is true, incongruously comic because of their unhistorical costumes and settings. Boydell had realized the difficulties of illustrating the national bard, 'Though I believe it will be readily admitted, that no subject seems so proper to form an English School of Historical Paintings, as the scenes of the immortal Shakespeare; yet it must always be remembered, that he possessed powers which no pencil can reach; for such was the force of his creative imagination, that though he frequently goes beyond nature, he still continues to be natural, and seems only to do that which nature would have done, had she o'erstepped her usual limits – it must not, then, be expected, that the art of the Painter can ever equal the sublimity of our Poet.'

Shakespeare was mined ruthlessly (Constable even painted a *Jaques and the Wounded Stag*) and unsuccessfully. The only effective picture inspired by Shakespeare is the excellent *King Lear in the Storm* (p. 244) painted by John Runciman at Rome in 1767 and apparently owing nothing to any stage presentation of the play. After 1815 it was not the terrifying pages of literature but the sentimental ones which caught the attention of British painters: there were no Don Juans or Fausts or Cains – and only John Martin (whose work was to inspire Gustave Doré) dared to attempt a Manfred.

Mary Shelley's *Frankenstein* (1818) found no illustrator although Samuel Rogers' *Italy* (1822) attracted Turner and the delicate charm of Stothard. Molière and Cervantes were also popular in translation. Literature in the person of Sir Walter Scott provided inspiration to painters not only in England but all over Europe, so that in 1840 Thackeray could write: 'Walter Scott, from his Castle of Abbotsford, sent out a troop of gallant young Scotch adventurers, merry outlaws, valiant knights,

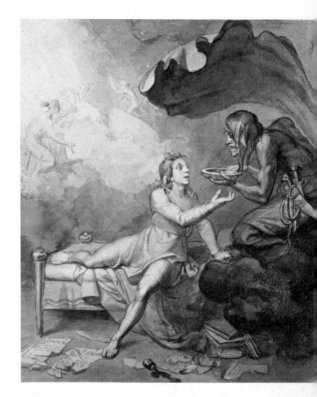

JOHN FLAXMAN, *Thomas Chatterton taking the Bowl of Poison from the Spirit of Despair, c.*1790.
British Library, London (Iolo Williams Collection).

243

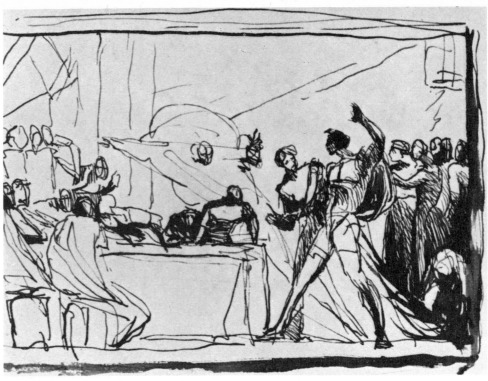

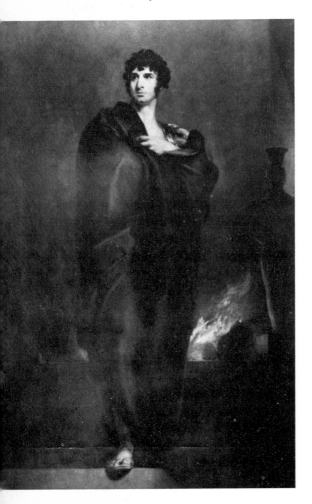

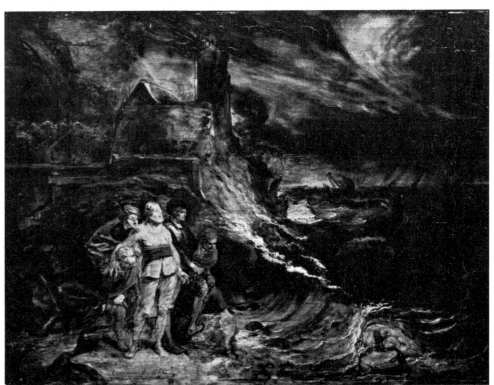

and savage Highlanders, who with trunk hosen and buff jerkins, fierce two-handled swords, and harness on their backs did challenge, combat and overcome the heroes and demi-gods of Greece and Rome.' Scotland seemed the land where Romantic qualities were found in abundance – an unspoiled countryside, a feudal way of life, a strong sense of national identity and wildly theatrical emotions which ranged from exquisite pathos to swashbuckling defiance. And all this on England's doorstep!

With his *The Assassination of David Rizzio* (1787), Opie was one of the first Romantics to pioneer interest in Scottish history, a subject which was to prove

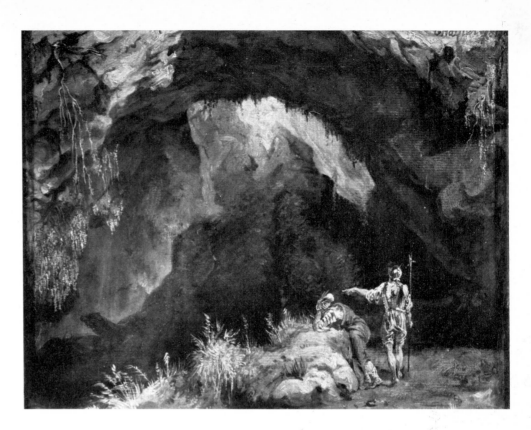

GEORGE HAYTER, *Banditti at the Mouth of a Cavern, c.*1818.
Collection of Mr Brinsley Ford.

irresistible to foreign artists, an important proof being Daguerre's large picture of *The Ruined Chapel at Holyrood seen by Moonlight* (1824). It is true that Raeburn had for long painted the Scottish lairds in their extravagant costumes but his vision was, in general, a sober one, with a restricted insight into the Romantic possibilities inherent in his subjects. A nation which had lately rediscovered medieval literature in the vital pastiches of Chatterton and Percy's doctored versions of the ballads began to call for romantic pictures in which 'old' costumes, armour and customs were employed. Aged *pompiers* of the classical-historical school were retired in favour of dashing young troubadours who plucked the strings of a mandoline while serenading a young lady vapidly reclined on a Venetian balcony. Titian, Rubens and Watteau were the artistic models of the *style troubadour*; and their influence is apparent in works by Bonington, Eastlake, Hayter, Stothard and Wilkie. Delaroche, who spread the taste throughout the Continent, began his costume works with *The Death of Queen Elizabeth* in 1827, presumably influenced by the English school.

A few last points in connection with Romantic painting in Britain should be made, among them the extent to which it was appreciated abroad and its links with European art. Flaxman was, perhaps, the most significant artist in this respect, partly because his engravings were easily transportable in a Europe at war, but also because the revolutionary nature of his linear art exerted such a wide and varied influence on artists in France, Spain, Germany and Italy. In 1801, during the brief spell of peace, the French turned aside from the rapturous study of the looted Italian masterpieces assembled in Paris by Vivant Denon to pay homage to Benjamin West (1738–1820), who was acclaimed as the Vien of the Thames, as an artistic reformer and as the creator of *Death on a Pale Horse* (1783, 1802, 1817) which was triumphantly exhibited at the Salon (p. 246).

From the recommencement of hostilities until the French defeat at Waterloo in 1815 Britain and the Continent were isolated from each other. But in the following quarter-century innumerable contacts took place. Géricault came in 1820 and spent twenty months here, during which time he arranged for his *Raft of the Medusa* to be shown in a travelling exhibition. Delacroix stayed in England from May to August of 1825. In London, with Bonington and Thales Fielding (to whose studio in Paris he

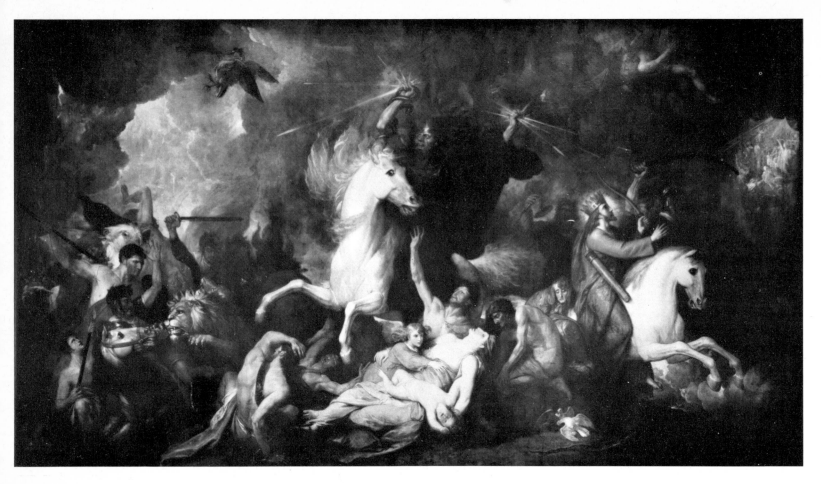

BENJAMIN WEST, *Death on a Pale Horse*, 1817. Courtesy of the Pennsylvania Academy of the Fine Arts.

had moved in 1823) he visited the galleries, met Etty, Wilkie and Lawrence, saw Shakespeare acted and read Byron and the English poets. The influence of British Romantic painting and literature was to dominate his work for some ten years. It is evident in the freshness and gloss of his colours, which he often heightened by glazing; the large *Portrait of Baron Schwiter* is a bravura performance in the style of Lawrence on whom he wrote a critical essay stating that 'His sitters assume ... that noble air and distinguished manner that he knows how to impart to almost everything', and that, 'He seizes the most delicate shade of melancholy or of gaiety in the features.' In 1828 he exhibited two works at the British Institution: *Greece on the Ruins of Missolonghi* and *The Execution of the Doge Marino Falieri*, both of which pay tribute to the life and work of Byron; and his far-spread literary sympathies are also revealed by *Milton and his Daughters* and a self-portrait as *Ravenswood*.

It was natural after decades of painting which, if not thoroughly militaristic in spirit, was, at least, dedicated to the glorification of the Emperor and Empire, that the French should have been astonished by the naturalistic and unrhetorical nature of British painting, as for instance the animals of Ward and Landseer, Wilkie's genre scenes, the honesty of Constable's landscapes and the sweep of Bonington's views of the Normandy countryside. The famous Paris Salon of 1824, in which there were three landscapes by Constable (including the *Hay Wain*, with which Géricault was happily familiar) and works by Bonington, the Fielding brothers and Harding, inspired French artists to undertake research into new pictorial techniques with which to capture the fleeting moods of Nature and the joyous sparkle and spacious atmosphere of the open countryside. It is a matter of historical knowledge that the painters of the Barbizon school were to fall upon the work of Constable and to follow his example in their scrutiny of the remoter countryside around Paris. Romantic portraiture in the person of Sir Thomas Lawrence also made its impact. Lawrence visited France several times, exhibited his portrait of the Duc de Richelieu at the Salon of 1825, and was invited the following year to paint King Charles and the Dauphin. The style of portrait he had evolved by the end of the eighteenth century of a standing figure emotionally linked to a wild or disturbed landscape found echoes in the work, not only of Delacroix, but also Gerard, Gros and Ingres. Nor was his influence confined to France. His portraits found their way all over Europe and further spread his Romantic manner.

Animal paintings, historical episodes and scenes of disaster were also influential. Géricault copied three prints after Stubbs before his visit to London in 1820; and it is likely that the intense fascination shown by Stubbs in his paintings of ferocious beasts locked in combat or gazing balefully at the viewer anticipated the wild struggles and animal studies of Delacroix. The fact that Stubbs' prints were so widely disseminated abroad is not without importance. The nightmarish fantasies of Martin made a peculiar appeal to the French by whom they were enthusiastically received. Charles x awarded him a Gold Medal in 1829 and his works were accepted in the Salons of 1827–28 and 1834. A nation which had supped full of the horrors of war and revolution was as receptive of Martin's *Fall of Nineveh*, dedicated in 1830 to the French King, as it was of its own Delacroix's *Death of Sardanapalus*, painted in 1828 and partly inspired by Byron. With his *Death of Queen Elizabeth* (1827), Delaroche opened up a new field of British subjects which were as popular for their political significance as their Romantic overtones.

It is almost certain that British Romantic painters were influenced by aspects of art on the Continent once they were able to travel there again after 1815, but the extent to which they actually came into contact with foreign artists is as yet a matter of surmise. What, for instance, did Ker Porter or Dawe or Atkinson learn during their stay in Russia? And did Francis Danby meet contemporary Swiss artists during his stay in Geneva from 1832 to 1836? How many influences – certainly those of Hackert, Carstens, Koch and Ducros – went to the formation of Georg Augustus Wallis (1770–1847), whose international fame was partly responsible for the spread of the more naturalistic styles of English landscape painting? Did Wilkie, whose admiration of the old Spanish masters was well in advance of the taste of his day, learn anything of Goya on his travels in Spain and on the Continent between 1825 and 1828? Such are the questions that constantly occur to students of British Romantic painting.

What is sure is that our artists were as much (and sometimes more) admired on the Continent as they were in Britain; and that their work which played such a large and distinctive part in the evolution of European painting compares honourably with the richness of British literature during the same period.

A clue to the nature of much Romantic painting in Britain (and to its degeneration from 1840) rests, paradoxically enough, in its basic realism. Hawksworth Fawke, son of a country gentleman, with whom Turner once spent some time in Yorkshire, watched the artist record on the back of a letter the progress of a thunderstorm as it rolled across the Yorkshire hills. Two years later, in 1818, the young man saw it translated into *Snowstorm: Hannibal and His Army crossing the Alps*.

When *Rain, Steam and Speed* (1843) was exhibited at the Academy there was open scoffing at its improbabilities until a Mrs Simon told how she had been fascinated by the eccentric but kindly looking old gentleman sitting opposite her in the train who during a thunderstorm had put his head out of the window and kept it there for nine minutes before returning to his seat where he sat, the rain streaming down his head, with closed eyes, for a quarter of an hour. Devoured with curiosity, Mrs Simon followed his example, suffered a similar soaking, and witnessed the scene exactly as the painter had later recaptured it in his studio. Constable refused to paint in a bird unless an actual bird flew across the scene he was sketching. He explained that he was prepared to sit no matter how long, 'till I see some living thing; because if any such appears, it is sure to be appropriate to the place. If no living thing shows itself, I put none in my picture'. His friend Leslie reported that a curious proof of the stillness with which he sat while painting in the open air was the discovery one day of a field mouse in his coat pocket. Constable himself insisted that painting was a science and 'should be pursued as an inquiry into the laws of nature'. He also said – and how Victorian the statement seems at first – 'In an age such as this, painting should be understood, not looked on with blind wonder, nor considered only as a poetic inspiration, but as a pursuit, *legitimate, scientific* and *mechanical*'.

It was to give his landscapes greater veracity that he abandoned the false tonalities and brown varnishes current in his day and struggled to capture the actual colour and atmospheric unity of areas of landscape by means of his famous touches of white paint flicked on with a palette knife. It is a matter of art history that when the *Hay-Wain* and *The View on the Stour near Dedham* were exhibited in the Paris Salon of 1824 the younger French artists were immensely impressed and Delacroix rushed away to make changes in the background of his *Massacres at Chios* (which background had been partly painted for him by the English artist Thales Fielding (1793–1837)) to bring it into line with Constable's technical innovations in the presentation of light and colour. Nor should we forget that behind these landscapes lies the long and sober tradition of realistic Dutch landscape to which both Turner and Constable were heavily indebted at the beginnings of their careers. Moreover, those romantic scenes of animals locked in furious combat may seem as spontaneous as Blake's lyrics but just as we know of the numerous revisions which went into 'Tyger, Tyger, burning bright', we know, too, of the weary hours of dissection and patient recording behind the pictures of Stubbs and Garrard.

As for Thomas Bewick, whose precision captures for us vignettes of pastoral life and the palpitating life of the birds and animals he studied with such unclouded vision, we realize from his own accounts the underlying realism that makes the poetry of his work. 'With an old friend I went to Chillingham park where a splendid bull wheeled about and then confronted us. The creature became so threatening a hasty retreat was necessary. I was, therefore, obliged to endeavour to see one, which had been conquered by a rival and driven to seek shelter along in the quarry hole or wood and in order to get a good look at one of this description I was under the necessity of creeping on hands and knees to leeward, out of sight and thus I got my sketch.' In the most sentimental of Morland's rustic scenes the cattle and horses and pigs are painted as lean, diseased and weak – which they were before the improvements in livestock breeding which came in the middle of the nineteenth century. Although this accuracy, this realism, this concern with the particular seems to be a distinctive and enduring feature of British Romantic art, one wonders whether it did not contain within itself the seeds of the commonplace sentimentality and striving after photographic veracity which are among the worst features of Victorian painting.

Romantic painting defies analysis or definition; and one can only point to various works of art or the careers of significant painters in an attempt to indicate its nature and essence. The range and power of our Romantic poetry has always been recognized in Europe, but that our painting should have so fully expressed 'the image of man and nature' in a 'spontaneous overflow of powerful feelings ...' and that it should as dramatically 'illustrate the manner in which our feelings and ideas are associated in a state of excitement' is still only grudgingly admitted. Nor has its importance in the history of European art been fully acknowledged. Indeed, we are in the process of discovering for ourselves how (to paraphrase Constable) it showed the world the hidden stores and beauties, and revealed what existed in Nature and the imaginative life but had not been known before its time.

6

THE VICTORIANS

Alan Bowness

T he general pattern of Victoria's reign is closely reflected in the history of its painting. Constable died in the year of accession, and although Turner was to live until 1851 and paint many of his most remarkable pictures, he belongs in spirit to an earlier age. *The Fighting Temeraire* was shown at the Royal Academy summer exhibition in 1839 with tremendous popular success, but at the end of his life, Turner's younger contemporaries could regard his exhibited works only with an admiring incomprehension. Like Constable, Turner left no followers of any consequence. Their discovery of landscape seems to have been a passing moment: the inspiration which Nature provided for so many English painters, in oil and water-colour alike, had not lasted. Rather, as we shall see, it changed character under the influence of Ruskin, and became a somewhat less grand and ennobling concept.

The personality of Wilkie dominates the first years of Victoria's reign, until his death at sea, returning from the Holy Land, in 1841. Yet he too, like Constable and Turner, belongs essentially to the pre-Victorian period. His great contribution had been to explore the possibilities of genre painting, and lead a whole group of his contemporaries – William Collins, William Mulready, Thomas Webster, C.R.Leslie – into specializing in figure compositions with an anecdotal interest. Shakespeare, Scott and Goldsmith continued to provide the favourite sources, but already in the 1840s there was a general feeling that this kind of literary genre was in decline. A general dissatisfaction with contemporary art can indeed be clearly distinguished in the critical reactions to Royal Academy summer exhibitions from Victoria's accession until the late 1840s, when things began to change.

Yet it would be quite wrong to accept that estimation of themselves which the Pre-Raphaelites (and especially Holman Hunt) fostered, as springing, unaided, out of the mediocrity of early Victorian art. As we learn more about this period, we appreciate how close were the links that bound the younger generation to the old – in choice of subject, attitude to art and technique.

249

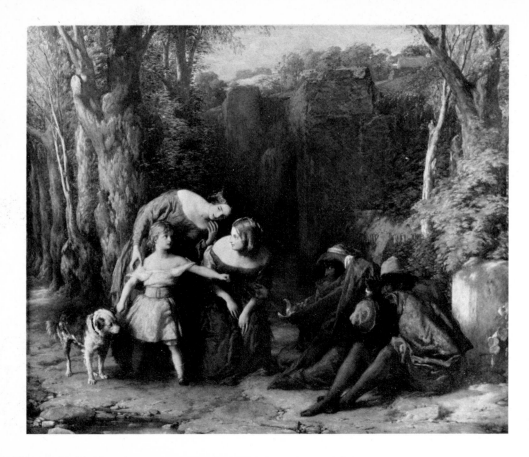

WILLIAM MULREADY, *Train up a child the way it should go,* R.A. 1841. Collection of Mr John Avery.

EDWIN LANDSEER, *The Challenge,* R.A. 1844. By permission of the Duke of Northumberland.

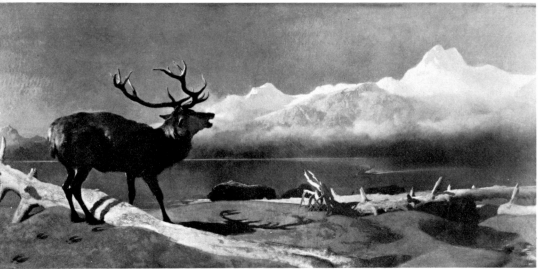

To demonstrate this, let us consider three paintings by the artists who were perhaps the most generally admired of the early 1840s: Mulready, Etty and Landseer. William Mulready (1786–1863) was a follower and rival of Wilkie who liked painting small ragged boys and pretty country girls, sometimes drawing on the reading matter popular with the rising middle class for his subject. Mulready's *Train up a child the way it should go* was one of the best-received pictures at the Academy exhibition of 1841. Taking its text from Proverbs, it offered a gentle lesson in moral behaviour: be charitable to those less fortunate than yourself. Charles West Cope's *Board of Guardians* picture in the same Academy shows a similar interest in a charity subject. In Cope's case genuine public concern about the Poor Laws is more directly reflected. Mulready's technique, however, is more original; he has already begun to use a white ground rather than the tinted kind universally preferred, and this made

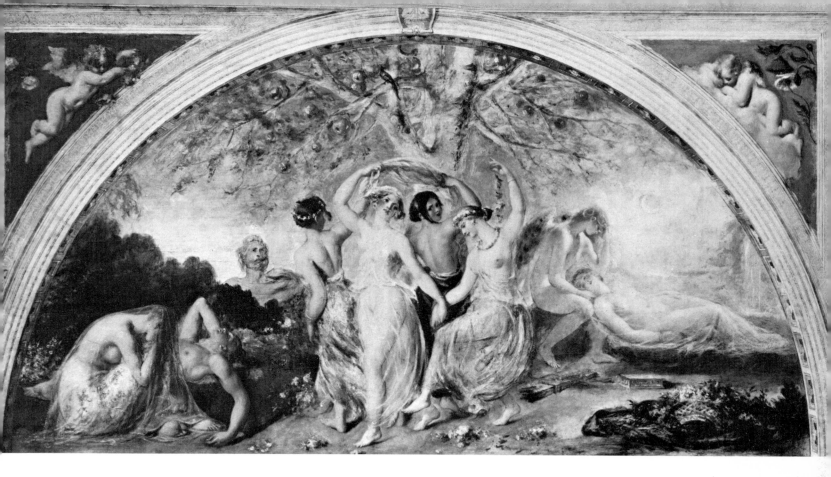

WILLIAM ETTY, *The Hesperides,* R.A. 1844.
The Lady Lever Art Gallery,
Port Sunlight, Cheshire.

his pictures look lighter and brighter in colour than almost everything else in the
exhibitions of the time. It was a lesson that Hunt and Millais observed and learned.

These two young men first met in 1844 at the Royal Academy Schools, and they
must both have been impressed by two pictures that dominated the 1844 Academy
exhibition – Etty's *The Hesperides* and Landseer's *The Challenge. The Hesperides* is a
typical Etty painting: there is a vaguely Venetian quality in subject and style that
helps explain his contemporary reputation without justifying it. William Etty
(1787–1849) seemed to represent the central tradition of great painting; his last
major work, the now lost *Joan of Arc* triptych, was the sensation of the 1847 Academy
and at £2,500 by far the most expensive work yet exhibited in Victoria's reign.

Edwin Landseer (1802–73) was a more popular artist than Etty, though not every
painter and critic was prepared to accept the overwhelming acclamation that he was
given. His precocious Rubensian paintings of the early 1820s can, not unreasonably,
be compared to work by Géricault and Delacroix: but this is almost the last point at
which English painting is in fruitful contact with French until Whistler's arrival in
London in 1860. In the 1840s, Landseer was at the height of his powers: he could
accommodate Prince Albert's misguided attempts to make him adopt a high degree
of finish in the current German manner, paint the comic animal pictures the public
demanded, and at the same time indulge his more individual taste for implying
allegorical meaning to his animal subjects, as in such paintings as *The Challenge, The
Stag at Bay* (R.A. 1846) and *The Monarch of the Glen* (R.A. 1851). There is already
evidence of that surprising liking for gratuitous violence and cruelty that helps
explain Landseer's mental and physical collapse in later life.

The Challenge – '*Coming Events cast their Shadow before',* to give it its proper title
at the 1844 Academy exhibition – is a very obvious source for Holman Hunt's
The Scapegoat (R.A. 1856) (p. 255), and in the same way *War and Peace* at the 1846
Academy provides what was surely the germinal idea for Hunt's *Strayed Sheep.* One
makes these connections not to belittle Hunt but to demonstrate the way in which he
belongs to his time, and to ask for a revaluation of Landseer, not as the artist of

251

charming landscape watercolours, but as an ambitious subject painter, a flawed genius but a genius in his own right.

Prince Albert's advocacy of German art has already been noted in connection with Winterhalter and Landseer: it can be seen at its strongest and most deleterious in the ill-fated attempt to revive monumental painting in England in the 1840s. After the destruction by fire of the old Palace of Westminster in 1834, Barry's new Parliament buildings offered an opportunity for a series of grand mural paintings celebrating the history of Britain. The problem was, who was to do them, and in what style and technique? No tradition of monumental decoration existed in England. A royal commission was established under the presidency of Prince Albert with Charles Eastlake as Secretary. Both men were of the opinion that modern German painting, and in particular that of the German Nazarenes, Friedrich Overbeck and Pieter Cornelius, provided the best model, but as it was manifestly inappropriate to employ German artists, either one would have to look for English artists already trained in Germany or under the Nazarenes in Rome, or one would have to find young English artists and award them scholarships for study abroad.

Between 1843 and 1847 a series of competitions was held, and from 1845 onwards commissions were given for specific sites in the new Houses of Parliament. One of the first prize-winners was the brilliant and delicate George Frederick Watts (1817–1904); he used his prize money to go to Italy in 1843, but made no contribution to the actual decoration. The first commissions went mainly to Daniel Maclise (1806–70) and William Dyce (1806–64), and these two men were responsible for much of the work that exists in Parliament today.

They were very different characters. Maclise was a versatile Irishman, who was prepared to turn his hand to anything – portraiture, Shakespearean illustration, allegory, historical genre. He was as open to French influence (Delaroche) as he was to German (Cornelius). Although certain details of his work at Westminster – in the *Death of Nelson*, for example – have quality, he could not manage the complexities of a multifigure composition, and his panoramic scenes leave a negative impression.

Dyce was an Aberdonian, who, as a young man, had travelled to Rome and been influenced by Friedrich Overbeck, the founder of the German Nazarene community. He seems to have been sponsored by Cornelius before the Royal Commission, and certainly the style of his early paintings is entirely within the then fashionable, approved German manner. Holman Hunt called him 'the most profoundly trained and cultured of all the painters of the time'; a man of many parts, he was a gifted administrator who declined the presidency of the Academy of 1850 to concentrate on the re-organization of the Government schools of art and design.

Dyce's *Jacob and Rachel* is the 1853 version of a picture first shown at the 1850 Academy. It marks the softening of the asperities of Dyce's early figure style, probably as a result of the influence of Hunt and Millais. Dyce had painted Arthurian subjects at Westminster, inappropriately using as models such Italian *quattrocento* painters as Pinturicchio and Perugino, whose work the Nazarenes so admired. Biblical subjects suited him better: not for nothing was he labelled an Early Christian artist by his contemporaries. He was associated with John Rogers Herbert (1810–90), a friend of Pugin's and a convert to Roman Catholicism who went around long-haired and bearded like some ancient prophet before such an appearance had become socially acceptable. Herbert's *The Youth of Our Lord* (p. 257), though later repainted, was originally shown at the Academy of 1847 where it must certainly have impressed Millais, whose *Christ in the House of his Parents* is its direct successor. Doubtless other examples of this kind of painting have disappeared from sight.

As is so often the case, a new movement in modern art – the Early Christian style – went hand in hand with a revaluation of the past. Taste was shifting towards an earlier period than had hitherto been fashionable. The long-accepted superiority of

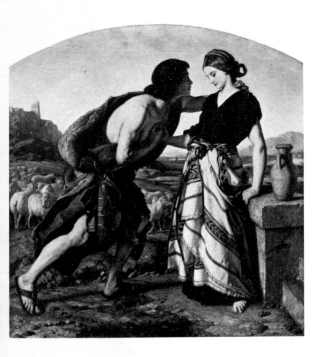

WILLIAM DYCE, *Jacob and Rachel*, 1853. Kunsthalle, Hamburg.

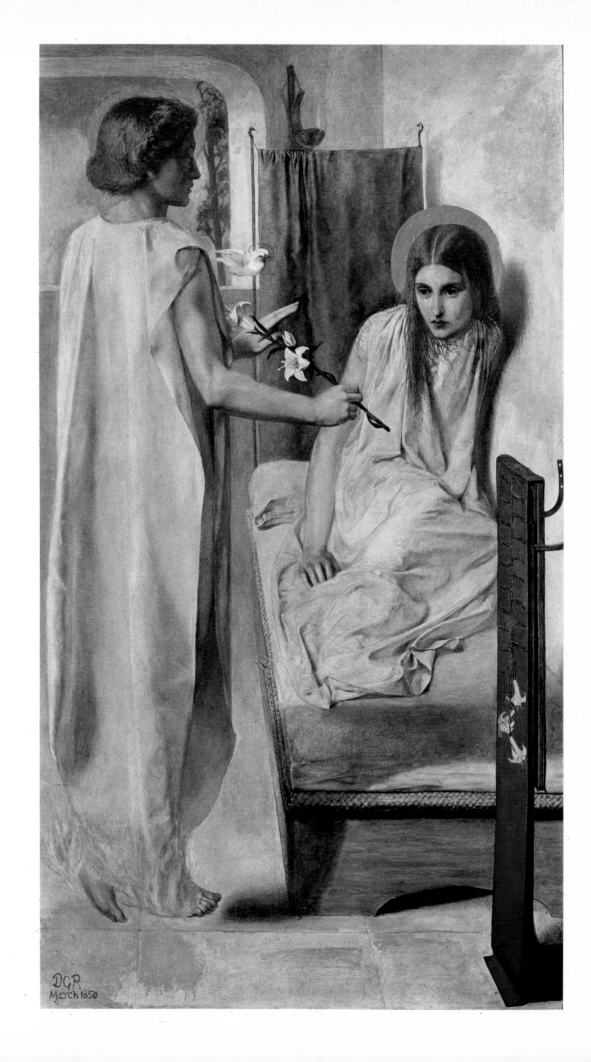

DANTE GABRIEL ROSSETTI,
The Annunciation, 1850.
The Tate Gallery, London.

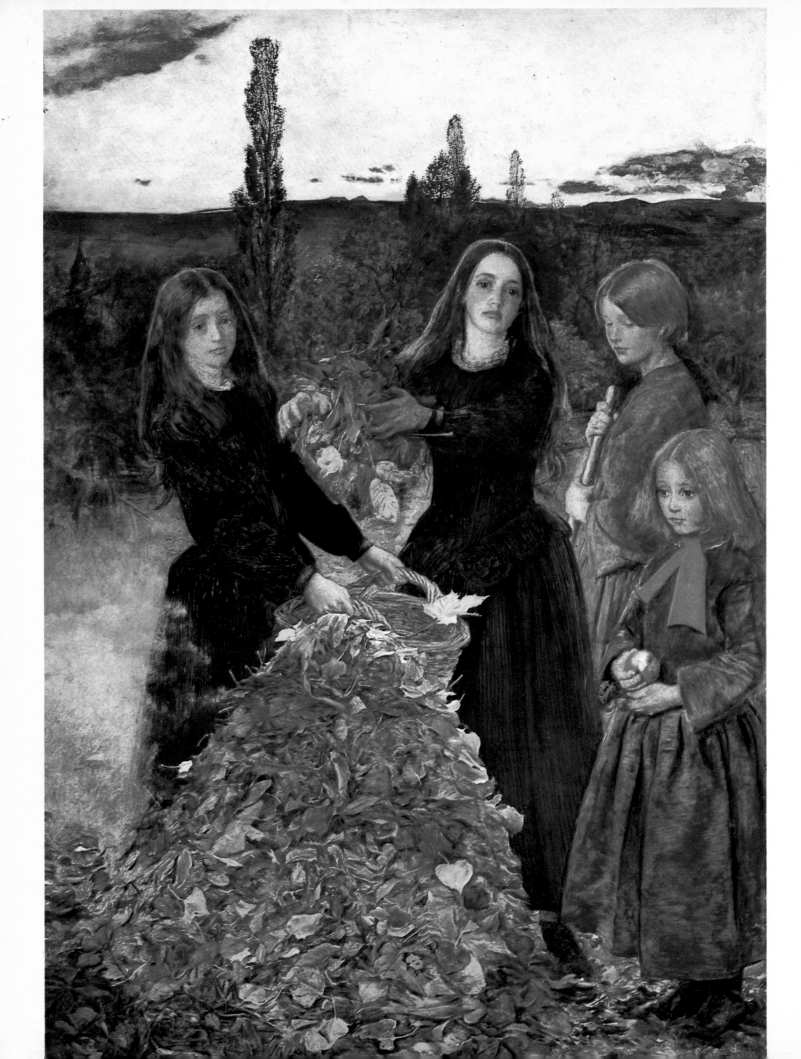

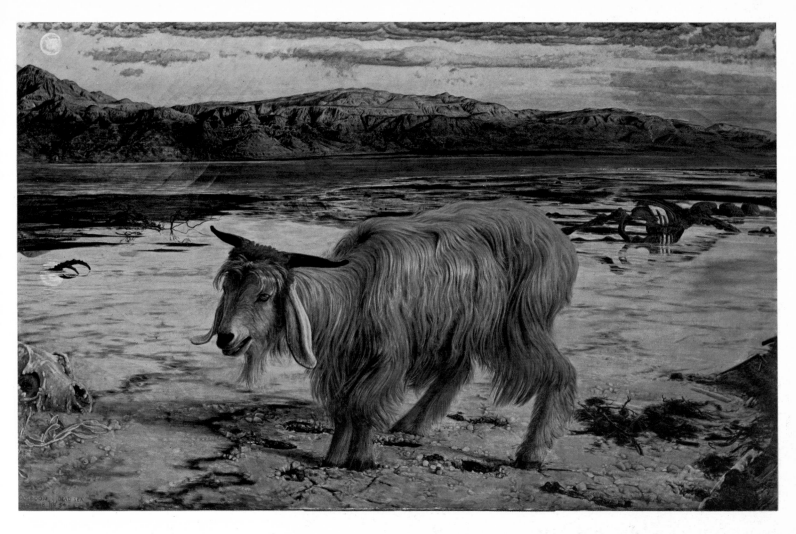

Above, WILLIAM HOLMAN HUNT,
The Scapegoat, R.A. 1856.
Lady Lever Art Gallery, Port Sunlight, Cheshire.
JOHN EVERETT MILLAIS,
Left, Autumn Leaves, R.A. 1856.
Manchester City Art Gallery.
Right, JOHN EVERETT MILLAIS,
Chill October, 1870.
Private collection.

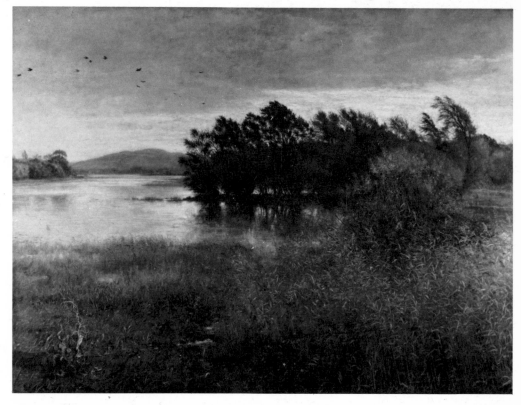

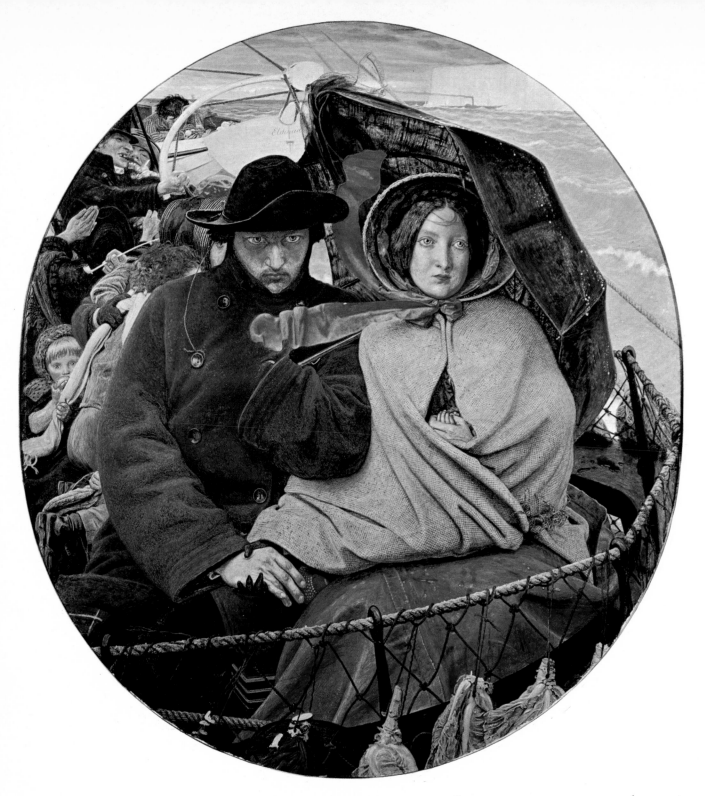

FORD MADOX BROWN, *The Last of England*
1852–5.
Birmingham City Art Gallery.

High Renaissance and seventeenth-century painting was now being challenged by a group of connoisseurs who preferred the art of the fifteenth century and before. It was seen to have a purity, a directness, a simplicity that made later painting look conventional and insincere. Prince Albert was a prominent enthusiast for these Italian and Flemish primitives, and it was in the 1840s that Van Eyck's Arnolfini portrait and the Wilton Diptych first appeared on the walls of the still new and growing National Gallery.

Such is the background to the formation of the Pre-Raphaelite Brotherhood one evening in September 1848, at Millais's family house in Gower Street, London. It can hardly have been the momentous occasion it now seems: simply a meeting of several

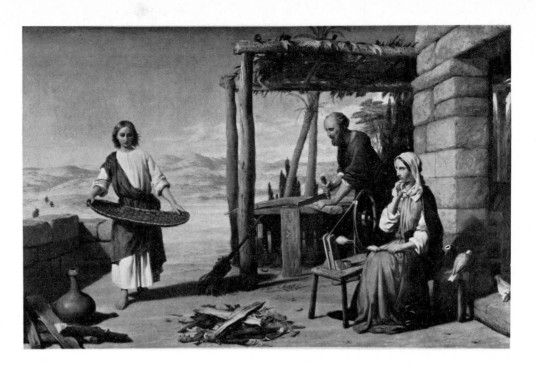

JOHN ROGERS HERBERT, *The Youth of Our Lord*,
R.A. 1847, altered later.
The Guildhall Art Gallery, London.

very young men, ambitious, and determined to do something about the low state of
British art. They were originally seven in number, but only three need concern us –
William Holman Hunt (1827–1910), John Everett Millais (1829–96) and Dante
Gabriel Rossetti (1828–82). Rossetti's younger brother, William Michael, acted as
secretary to the group. He defined the aims of the Brotherhood: '(1) to have genuine
ideas to express; (2) to study Nature attentively, so as to know how to express
them; (3) to sympathize with what is direct and serious and heartfelt in previous art,
to the exclusion of what is conventional and self-parading and learned by rote; and
(4), most indispensable of all, to produce thoroughly good pictures and statues.'

Such a naive and innocuous programme will hardly provide us with a definition
of Pre-Raphaelitism, but the fact is that there was no such thing. There never was a
group style, and only if this is accepted can one do justice to the three great indi-
vidualists who banded together as a means of establishing themselves as painters.
Hunt, Millais and Rossetti had little in common except age: each had an influence
and following that is clearly distinguishable and often mutually antagonistic.

Rossetti would have brought Ford Madox Brown (1821–93) into the Pre-
Raphaelite Brotherhood, had this not met with the disapproval of Hunt and Millais.
Brown was only a little older in years, but he was infinitely more experienced. Born
in Calais of British parentage, he had studied art in Belgium and in Paris. At first
attracted by the modern French school of Delaroche and Delacroix, he returned to
England in 1844 only because of the splendid new opportunities which the Houses
of Parliament competitions seemed to offer. Brown was never a prize-winner, and
attracted little notice; but he was quick to conclude that only artists working in the
Nazarene style were likely to be successful in England, and in 1845 he set off to spend
the winter in Rome. There he met both Overbeck and Cornelius. He had already
begun work on his first major painting: *A vision of Chaucer reading his poems to
knights and ladies fair, to king and court, amid air and sunshine*. This was to illustrate
The Origin of our Native Tongue, and the scheme was elaborated over the next months
into a triptych expressing *The Seeds and Fruits of English Poetry*, with Chaucer in the
centre, and Spenser, Shakespeare, Milton, Pope, Burns, Byron and others in the wings.

Such an over-ambitious project, in subject so typical of the times, was beyond
Brown's capacities. For years he struggled with the *Chaucer*, which was not ready
for public exhibition until the Academy of 1851; even so, as we see it now (p. 258), it is
difficult to know how much remains of the original composition and how much was

257

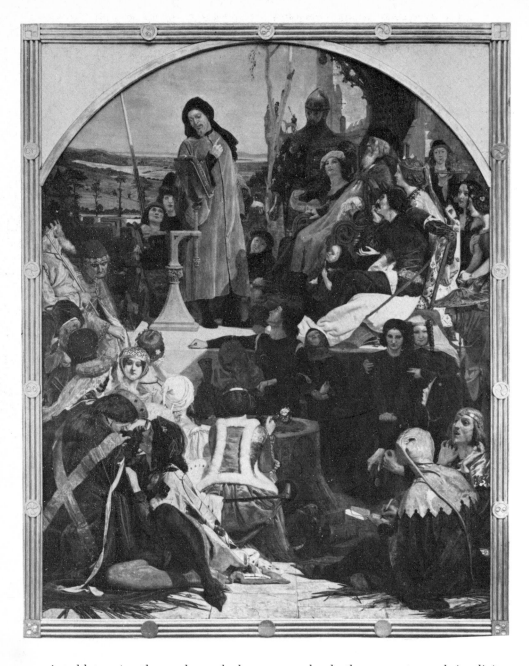

FORD MADOX BROWN, *Chaucer at the Court
of Edward III*, R.A. 1851, altered later.
Art Gallery of New South Wales, Sydney.

repainted later. Another early work shows more clearly the symmetry and simplicity
of Nazarene painting: *Wycliffe reading his Translation of the Bible to John of Gaunt,
in the Presence of Chaucer and Gower: of the first Translation of the Bible into English*.
This is clearly in the Early Christian style, but the subject is, by implication, anti-
catholic. The light tonality, partly the consequence of white underpainting, made the
picture look like a design for a fresco when it was exhibited at the Free exhibition
of 1848: Rossetti noticed it there, and as he thought it exactly the kind of picture he
would like to have painted he asked Brown for lessons.

Rossetti's enthusiasm for Brown was shortlived: he found him a pedantic and
unimaginative teacher, and switched his allegiance to Holman Hunt, whose *Eve of
St Agnes* Rossetti considered quite the most exciting thing at the 1848 Academy
exhibition. The originality of Hunt's picture rested largely in its choice of subject.
Keats had been almost forgotten since his death, and it is from the re-publication of
his poems in 1848 that his modern reputation derives. Rossetti also discovered that
Hunt had begun work on another subject, drawn from literature as were all his early
pictures: *Rienzi vowing to obtain justice for the death of his young brother* (p. 260). The
subject was taken from Bulwer Lytton's novel, published 1835, but reissued in 1848.

258

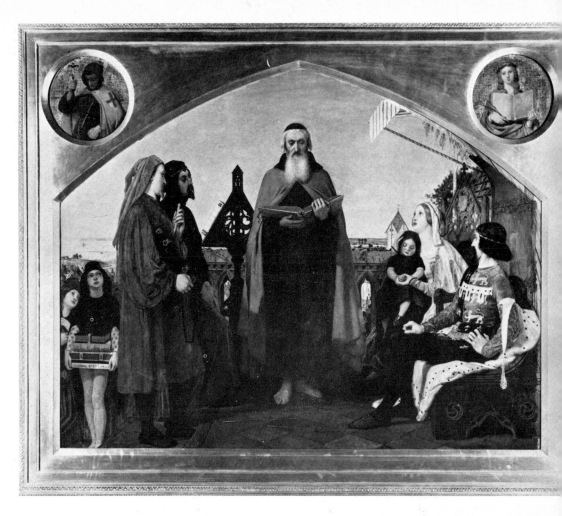

Rienzi marked a major breakthrough for Hunt, and for Victorian painting as a whole. The true originality of the picture lies in the way that Hunt tried to rid himself of all the pictorial conventions then in force and to paint 'in direct application to Nature'. He rejected the academic 'law that all figures in a picture should have their places on a line describing the letter S', a convention said to derive from Raphael and celebrated by Hogarth. He asked himself why 'should the several parts of the compositions always be apexed in pyramids? Why make one corner of the picture always in shade? For what reason is the sky in a daylight picture made as black as night? ... And then about colour, why should the gradation go from the principal white, through yellow and pink and red, and so on to stronger colours?' thus ignoring green and violet and purple and a whole range of colours newly available to the artist.

So in *Rienzi* Hunt used a white ground and let light fill his picture. He arranged the main figures in what he thought was a casual, natural arrangement, and instead of going to professional models who would have adopted conventional, artifical postures, asked his friends to pose instead. He was particularly proud of the foreground area: 'instead of the meaningless spread of whitey brown which usually served for the near ground, I represented gravelly variations and pebbles, all diverse in tints and shapes as found in nature.'

While Hunt worked on *Rienzi* his friends Millais and Rossetti also began ambitious paintings, designed for exhibition in 1849. Millais had been choosing his subjects from popular literatue and English history, but now, following Hunt's example, he adopted the new style and turned to Keats, to illustrate the opening lines of *Isabella, or the Pot of Basil*. Millais had a facility and a feeling for paint and colour that Hunt totally lacked. He painted *Lorenzo and Isabella* very quickly, on a wet white ground, to the admiration of the friends whom he used as models – Rossetti for the man

259

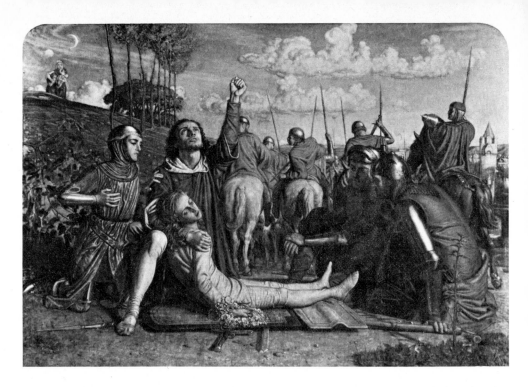

WILLIAM HOLMAN HUNT, *Rienzi vowing to obtain justice for the death of his young brother*, R.A. 1849. Private collection.

drinking; Rossetti's brother, William Michael, for Lorenzo; Millais's father for the man wiping his beard; his sister-in-law for Isabella; and so on.

There is no suggestion here of a moral precept to be discovered in the painting, as with *Rienzi*: Millais is interested in the human situation of the unhappy, doomed lovers. He pays attention to detail, but not to demonstrate a reverence for Nature, as Hunt does. We notice instead the salt spilled on the table, the divided blood orange, the passion flowers and pot of basil. These are all consciously introduced symbolic details – of a kind that have not before appeared in Millais's work, and their presence is, I believe, due to Rossetti's influence.

This is apparent if we look at the painting Rossetti was working on at this time, *The Girlhood of Mary Virgin*, certainly started before Millais began *Lorenzo*. Rossetti's admiration for the Early Christian style is evident, both in the subject and in the simplicity of composition. Like Hunt, he avoided all conventional practices, but this was partly because he had never learned them. For Rossetti had never completed his training at the Royal Academy Schools; he was temperamentally impatient and impetuous and this accounts both for his very real inadequacies as a painter and for some of his genuinely original qualities.

Rossetti painted *The Girlhood* in Hunt's studio, and in certain respects he followed Hunt's example. His sister Christina, a poet like her brother, posed with her mother for the figures of the saints, and that close attention to Nature's minutiae that we observe in *Rienzi* is equally present here. But Rossetti, aware of the way the Italian primitives had introduced detail only when there could be a justifiable reason for it, wished to do the same, and as a consequence gave every object in his picture a symbolic role. To make this plain, he wrote a pair of sonnets about this picture and its successor, *The Annunciation* (p. 253), in which he explained the significance of everything that we see:

> These are the symbols. On that cloth of red
> I' the centre is the Tripoint: perfect each,
> Except the second of its points, to teach
> That Christ is not yet born. The books – whose head
> Is golden Charity, as Paul hath said –
> Those virtues are wherein the soul is rich:
> Therefore on them the lily standeth, which
> Is Innocence, being interpreted. . . .

260

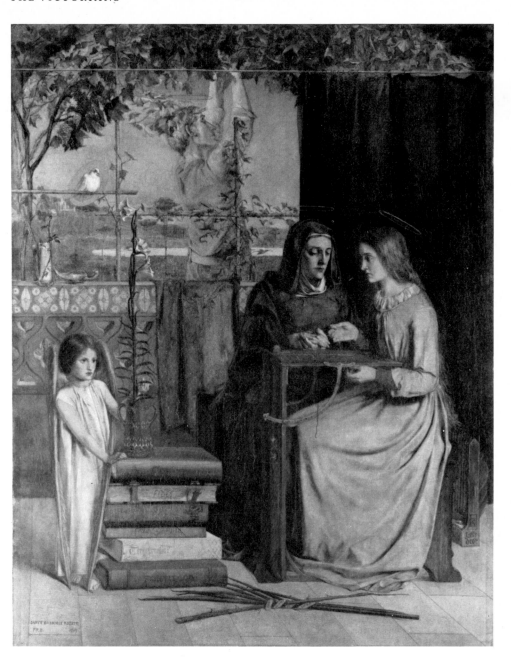

DANTE GABRIEL ROSSETTI,
The Girlhood of Mary Virgin, 1849.
The Tate Gallery, London.

Rossetti did not risk submitting *The Girlhood* to the Academy of 1849, so it was shown at the Free exhibition, where nobody seems to have noticed it. *Rienzi* and *Isabella* were hung as pendants in the Academy: they were greeted with a mixture of praise and suspicion, but both were sold for substantial sums – 100 guineas and £150 respectively. There was no hostility to innovation, and Hunt and Millais were widely regarded as very promising young men – perhaps, at last, the new generation so anxiously awaited since Victoria's accession. The violence of public reaction to their paintings in 1850 was partly the result of these expectations being rudely and quickly disappointed.

It was Millais who met the full force of popular disapproval with *Christ in the House of his Parents* (p. 262). There was a veritable storm of abuse: the picture was considered blasphemous, with hideously ugly figures. In *Household Words*, Dickens let loose a torrent of vituperation, so absurd today as to appear the criticism of somebody who had never looked at a picture. In more measured tones *The Times'* critic complained: 'Mr Millais' principal picture is, to speak plainly, revolting. The attempt

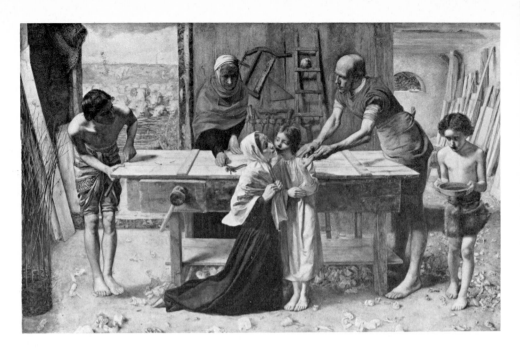

to associate the holy family with the meanest details of a carpenter's shop, with no conceivable omission of misery, of dirt, or even disease, all finished with the same loathsome minuteness, is disgusting; and with a surprising power of imitation, this picture shows how far mere imitation may fall short, by dryness and conceit, of all dignity and truth.'

Millais must have been astonished and deeply hurt. For the first time he was attempting a more serious subject than literary genre, and no one appreciated his ambitions. He had illustrated a text from Zachariah: 'And one shall say unto Him: What are these wounds in thine hands? Then He shall answer: Those with which I was wounded in the house of My friends.' Millais may have ruefully pondered on the damaging contribution of his friends, which was leading him to martyrdom, for in the choice of subject and in the carefully worked out symbolism of realistic details he was heavily indebted to Rossetti.

Rossetti's *Annunciation* (p. 253), or *Ecce Ancilla Domini*, to give it its proper title, escaped too much hostile comment, because it was exhibited at the Portland Gallery, and not at the Royal Academy, in the spring of 1850. It remained unsold at £50, and this indicates that Rossetti was regarded as a less important artist than Millais or Hunt. Yet this painting is one of the most original and forward-looking in the whole of the nineteenth century, a work which at last breaks the insularity of English art.

The revolutionary importance of *The Annunciation* lies in the way in which Rossetti expressed the symbolism of his subject primarily by abstract formal means, and in his readiness to abandon every pictorial convention of the day. The meaning of the picture is conveyed less by symbolic details, as in *The Girlhood*, than by the stark purity and simplicity of form and colour. It is essentially a white painting; the only colours that Rossetti introduces are the three primaries, blue, red and yellow, the last turning to a magical gold. The expected perspective construction for a scene taking place in a small room is deliberately rejected (it is impossible to believe that Rossetti could not have got it right had he tried) in favour of a very much flatter conception of space. This flattening enhances the picture's iconic quality: we are more aware of it as an object in its own right, less as some sort of illusionistic rendering of Nature.

In interpreting *The Annunciation* in this way we are displaying the hindsight that passing time alone brings. In 1850 the picture must have been incomprehensible. It is in direct contradiction to the contemporary work of Hunt in every respect: to label both artists Pre-Raphaelite is meaningless and can only obscure their intentions. Not that we should expect Rossetti to have realized all the revolutionary implications of *The Annunciation*. For from the way he wrote about his painting it seemed to become something of a puzzling embarrassment – 'the blessed white eyesore' – and it was another decade and more before he could take up the ideas adumbrated in it. Rossetti was in fact deeply discouraged by the public reception of his work. He vowed not to exhibit again, leaving Hunt and Millais to carry on the battle for popular recognition. In any case was he not a poet as much as a painter? Rossetti always showed a dangerous tendency to switch to the other art when one became too difficult.

Feeling, no doubt, that they had burned their fingers by attempting the Christian subjects rashly advocated by Rossetti, Hunt and Millais abandoned their attempt to revive religious art. Millais had been working on an ambitious, multifigure *Deluge* composition, meant to remind his audience of the uncertainty of life and inevitability of death, but such a subject was probably suggested by well-meaning friends and signified little to the painter. It is entirely characteristic that Millais should have whittled the composition away to a pretty girl with a pet bird, albeit entitled *The Return of the Dove to the Ark* (R.A. 1851).

Millais returned to literary genre, but he chose his subjects from contemporary poets with whom he felt a temperamental affinity. Coventry Patmore's *Tale of Poor Maud* provided the inspiration for *The Woodman's Daughter* (R.A. 1851); Tennyson, created laureate in 1850, for *Mariana* (R.A. 1851). In the first Millais comes close to painting his characters in modern dress, and the landscape setting is, for the first time, of real importance; the subject – incipient passion cutting across class distinctions – hints at real social problems rather than mindless anecdotes. In *Mariana*, Millais turns to the Middle Ages, but this is of superficial importance compared with Rossetti's experiments in medieval subject matter. What interests Millais is the *mood* of the picture – the weariness, the lassitude, the dissatisfaction with her own existence that Mariana feels. It is an attempt to capture poetry in painting, not by any kind of literal description, though this can be utilized, but by subordinating every element to an overall poetic sentiment. There is a strong parallel here with Tennyson's poetic methods, and this helps to explain the remarkable personal success that Millais won in the 1850s.

After the failure of their Christian subjects, Hunt had chosen to illustrate Shakespeare, taking a subject from *Two Gentlemen of Verona*, which Augustus Egg had used at the 1849 Academy. It was a cautious return to safe literary genre: Hunt still needed to establish his reputation. Millais was following his example when he painted *Ophelia* for the 1852 Academy. By this time, however, Ruskin had come to the support of the two young painters, whom he felt had been unjustly attacked in 1851 for their past transgressions, rather than for their present behaviour. Ruskin's advocacy certainly helped Hunt and Millais. The critic could rightly feel that they had heeded the attention he had demanded for 'the inexhaustible perfection of Nature's details'. The painting of the waterweeds and the 'weeping brook' in *Ophelia* is miraculous, never had bright daylight been rendered with such faithful accuracy. Intense local colours and an unnaturally sharp focus give the picture a hallucinatory quality that perfectly matches its subject. The image is an unforgettable one.

Ruskin also demanded that art should be a great moral teacher, yet what is the lesson of *Ophelia*? The irony of the situation in which Ruskin unconsciously found himself was that while he could see that Millais's painterly talents were superior, it was Hunt and not Millais who shared his aesthetic. Millais could claim that his other picture at the 1852 Academy, *A Huguenot*, 'contains the highest moral', but nobody was deluded. Millais was interested in the poetry of his subjects, not in any moral precepts that might be drawn. Hunt however, like Ruskin, could not accept art for its own sake, but expected it to have a grand missionary purpose. While Millais was at work on *Ophelia*, he was painting *The Hireling Shepherd*, exhibited in 1852 with a quotation from *King Lear*, but evidently not a piece of Shakespearean illustration.

Many years later, Hunt wrote about the *Hireling Shepherd* to the Corporation of Manchester, which had bought the picture:

> Shakespeare's song represents a shepherd who is neglecting his real duty of guarding the sheep ... He was the type of muddle-headed pastors, who, instead of performing their services to the flock – which is in constant peril – discuss vain questions of no value to any human soul ... I did not wish to force the moral, and I never explained it till now. For its meaning was only in reserve for those who might be led to work it out. My first object as an artist was to paint, not Dresden china bergers, but a real shepherdess, and a landscape full of sunlight, with all the colour of luscious summer, without the faintest fear of the precedents of any landscape painters who had rendered Nature before.

The 'moral suggestiveness' of Hunt's picture, to use William Michael Rossetti's phrase, was recognized by his contemporaries, who enjoyed arguing about its exact meaning. Is it not a death's head moth that the idle shepherd holds up? Does not the silly shepherdess feed sour apples to the lamb? Have not the sheep escaped into the cornfield? Hunt was now using symbolic detail to great effect: it suited the extreme realism of his style, with its scrupulous regard for the detail of Nature.

Hunt's main work of 1851–3 was his most famous picture, *The Light of the World*. This illustrates a text from Revelations, which is inscribed in gold on the frame: 'Behold I stand at the door and knock; if any man hear my voice, and open the door, I will come to him, and will sup with him, and he with me'. It is a mystical subject, conceived in highly literal terms. Hunt chose to paint it as a night scene 'to accentuate the point of his meaning': no more faithful rendering of moonlight and candlelight could be found. He later wrote that 'the closed door was the obstinately shut mind, the weeds the cumber of daily neglect, the accumulated hindrances of sloth, the orchard the garden of delectable fruit for the dainty feast of the soul. The music of the still small voice was the summons to the sluggard to awaken and become a zealous labourer under the divine master'.

The Light of the World was not an immediate public success when shown at the 1854 Academy, and Ruskin sprang to its defence in a letter to *The Times*: 'I think it is one of the very noblest works of sacred art ever produced in this or any other age', an opinion that the Victorians were soon to endorse. Twentieth-century taste, however, has preferred Hunt's companion piece, also exhibited in 1854, *The Awakening Conscience*. This was inspired by a text in Proverbs: 'As he that taketh away a garment in cold weather, so is he that singeth songs to a heavy heart'. Hunt had probably read *David Copperfield*, and with the outcast Little Emily in mind gave a contemporary relevance to his subject. 'My desire was to show how the still small voice speaks to a human soul in the turmoil of life', he wrote, finding a lesson in every detail – the pictures on the wall, the tapestry, the music on the piano, the hem of the dress, the cat and bird. 'Painting taking its proper place beside literature' wrote the admiring Ruskin.

When the two 'still small voice' pictures were on exhibition, Hunt was already in Palestine, at work on the shores of the Dead Sea, with a rifle tucked under his left arm as a precaution against bandits. He was painting *The Scapegoat* (p. 255). The conception was grandiose. The scapegoat had been driven into the wilderness by the Jews, a scarlet fillet bound to its horns as a token of sin. Hunt saw it as a symbol of the Christian faith, hated by the unconverted world; perhaps also as a symbol of the artist, scorned and neglected by a philistine public. Again, Ruskin apart, the initial reception was dismissive: 'a mere goat, with no more interest for us than the sheep which furnished yesterday's dinner'. Yet, like the drowning *Ophelia*, Courbet's *Stonebreakers* and Millet's *Angelus* – all painted within a year or so of one another –

The Scapegoat is one of the most memorable images of art. The harsh, eccentric colouring, and manic, obsessive treatment of detail perfectly suit the lunatic magnificence of the picture. We now see *The Scapegoat* as a proto-surrealist masterpiece, emanating from and appealing to unconscious levels of experience.

Hunt lived until 1910, but he painted few pictures, making each composition last a very long time. The *Lady of Shalott* subject is perhaps the most unencumbered and satisfying of his late works (p. 267); it goes back to a drawing of 1850 and an illustration for Moxon's Tennyson of 1857, but Hunt was still working on it in 1905. Although Hunt's painting seems to embody the Victorian virtues of patience, concentration and hard work, one senses a certain boredom, even idleness in his later career. The tension, sprung by ambition, has gone.

With Millais, a very similar development is visible. Ruskin's patronage led to intimacy, and then, as everyone knows, Millais fell in love with the unhappily married Mrs Ruskin. This involvement, arousing his deepest emotions, forced Millais to consider modern moral problems, and, in particular, what Hunt had called 'unconsecrated passion in modern life', and had painted in *The Awakening Conscience*.

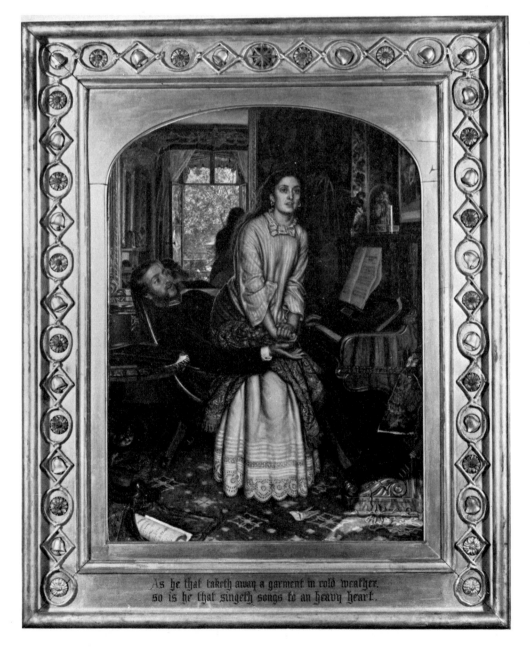

WILLIAM HOLMAN HUNT, *The Awakening Conscience*, R.A. 1854.
Trustees of Sir Colin Anderson, London.

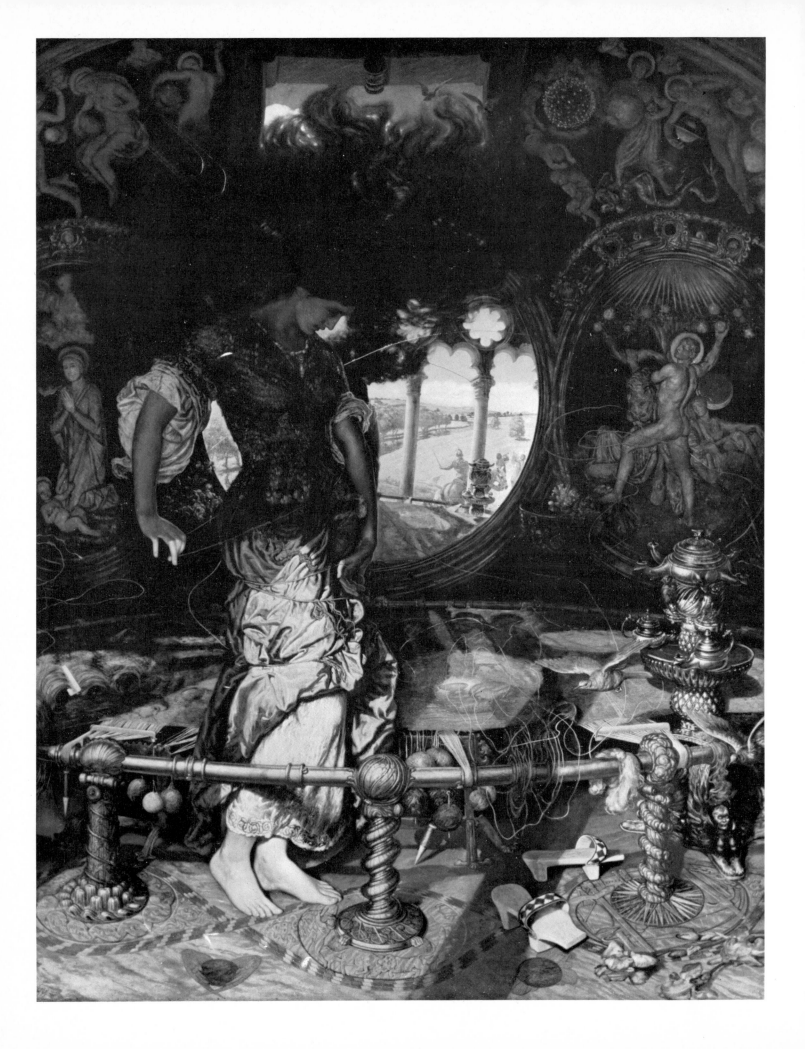

Millais treated this subject matter in a remarkable series of drawings, some personal, some socially oriented; it scarcely impinges upon his oil painting, except perhaps when he portrays Ruskin by the waterfall at Glenfinlas, or paints *The Order of Release* (R.A. 1853), with Effie Ruskin as his model. But once the nightmare was over, and Millais and Effie were safely married, Millais painted two 'honeymoon' pictures, *The Blind Girl* and *Autumn Leaves* (p. 254), that were shown at the 1856 Royal Academy exhibition.

The Blind Girl has an obvious pathos, dwelling on the simple beauties of this world – a butterfly, a rainbow – that the girl can never see. But the pervading impression is a sensuous one: it is the scent of the meadow with its fresh grass drenched by the shower of rain that mysteriously emanates from the picture. *Autumn Leaves* is even more remarkable, for here Millais conveys the sensual pleasure he experienced at the smell of burning leaves. No doubt unconsciously this is associated with the virginal girls who stare at us, the whole endowed with sadness, formally expressed in a strange colour harmony – russet against purple, orange against brown.

Autumn Leaves marks the peak of Millais's achievement. Still only twenty-seven, he was, in 1856, universally admired and immensely influential upon other painters. Ruskin, magnanimously, said with pardonable exaggeration, 'Titian himself could hardly head him now'. But the withdrawal of Ruskin's guidance on the always impressionable Millais was in part responsible for his immediate and catastophic decline. Although Millais was to live another forty years, his best work was done. Eventual presidency of the Royal Academy and an alleged income of £30,000 a year cannot hide the fact that Millais lost interest in art. Thus the melancholy of *Autumn Leaves* assumes a prophetic note, as if Millais knew what he was losing.

Not that the late Millais is contemptible. He retained that natural feeling for paint and colour that enlivens his most vacuous works: never do we suffer the harsh ugliness of Hunt, who seemed to have no colour sense at all. And when the poetic element is uppermost and anecdotal trivia are absent, Millais's quality is again apparent. This is particularly true of pure landscapes like *Chill October* of 1870 (p. 255), so unlike contemporary impressionist work, yet greatly admired by the young Van Gogh, probably because the artist was using the landscape to project a deeply felt personal emotion and not simply painting what he saw.

The appearance of Millais's painting, supported by Ruskin's exegeses, is the dominant factor in English painting of the mid-1850s, and accounts for a remarkable change of style. By 1857 and 1858 so-called Pre-Raphaelitism entirely prevailed at the Academy exhibitions, still the showcase for all new tendencies in British art, but since Hunt had little influence and Rossetti was almost unknown and never exhibited at the Academy, we should speak of Millaisian rather than of Pre-Raphaelite painting. At the 1858 exhibition Ruskin particularly admired two pictures by little known artists. One was the *Landscape, Val d'Aosta* (p. 268) by John Brett (1831–1902). He, for a short while, was Ruskin's protegé, and demonstrated better than anyone how truth to nature meant geological as well as botanical accuracy. The other was *The Stonebreaker* by Henry Wallis (1830–1916), a common enough subject, painted by Landseer and Hughes as well as by Courbet. There were many artists of this period, other than Brett and Wallis, who produced a few outstanding pictures and never painted so well again. Arthur Hughes (1830–1915) showed a curious Rossettian picture, *The Nativity*, at the 1858 Academy, but then for a few years adopted Millais's combination of detail and poetic sentiment to paint such work as *Home from the Sea* (p. 269) until he too slipped into a well-merited obscurity.

The older generation was also affected by the new style. Dyce abandoned the Early Christian, Nazarene-derived manner to paint a handful of minutely observed subjects, like *Pegwell Bay, Kent – a Recollection of October 5th, 1858* (p. 269). A slightly older generation of painters of literary and historical genre now found themselves at

WILLIAM HOLMAN HUNT,
The Lady of Shalott, 1857–1905.
Courtesy Wadsworth Atheneum,
Hartford, Connecticut.

267

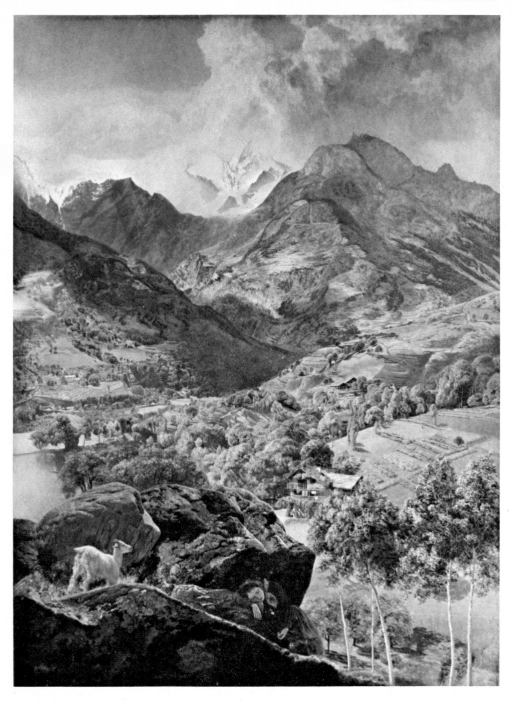

JOHN BRETT, *Landscape, Val d'Aosta*, R.A. 1858.
Collection of Sir William Cooper.

last able to paint figures in modern dress and with a consciously present-day interest.
William Powell Frith (1819–1909) who, on his own admission, sought in art 'opportunity for the display of character and variety of incident' could switch from painting scenes from the plays and novels of Shakespeare, Goldsmith, Sterne and Dickens to *Ramsgate Sands, or Life at the Seaside*. This was bought at once by Queen Victoria when it appeared at the Academy of 1854. Frith followed up this success with *Derby Day* (R.A. 1858) and *The Railway Station* (p. 270), for which he was paid £4,500, plus an extra £750 for agreeing to show it at a dealer's gallery and not at the Royal Academy. *The Railway Station* is packed with anecdotal interest, and carries with it some of the excitement of railway travel. Beneath the arches of Brunel's Paddington Station (1850–2), a criminal is arrested before making his get-away, boys are leaving for the new boarding school, a foreign visitor is arguing with a cabby. There is a self-conscious modernity about every incident, a deliberate appeal to familiar experience

268

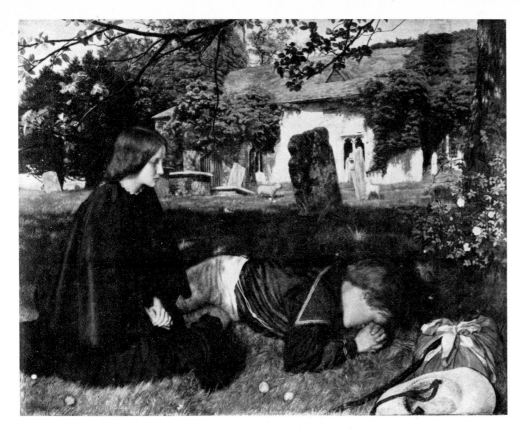

Left, ARTHUR HUGHES, *Home from the Sea,*
1856–62.
Ashmolean Museum, Oxford.
Below, WILLIAM DYCE, *Pegwell Bay, Kent –*
a Recollection of October 5th 1858, 1859–60.
The Tate Gallery, London.

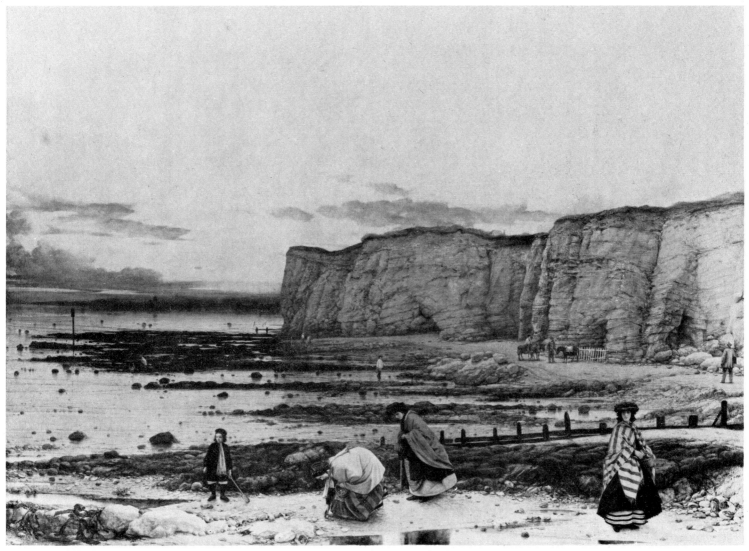

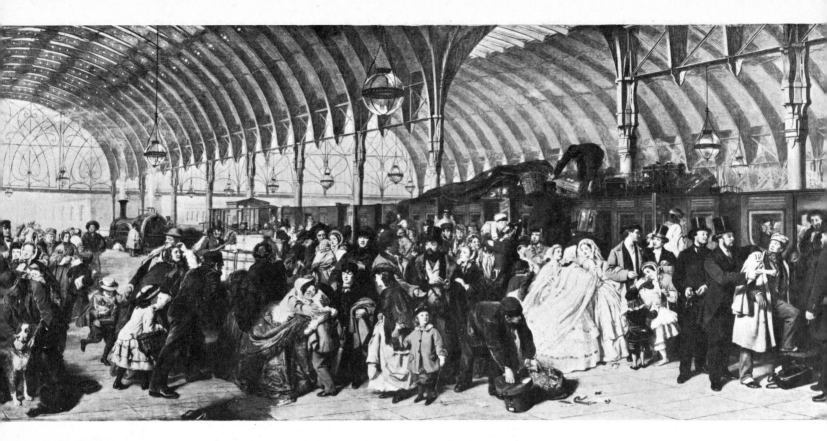

Above, WILLIAM POWELL FRITH,
The Railway Station, 1862.
Royal Holloway College, Egham, Surrey.

on the public's part. For many mid-Victorians life in the present had become so all-absorbing that this seemed to be the only possible subject for art.

Pressures were considerable, however, possibly growing worse for the artist as spectacular financial and social success became available to him. Of Frith's early associates Augustus Egg (1816–63) died comparatively young, and Richard Dadd (1817–88) murdered his father and spent most of his life in Broadmoor. Dadd is still an obscure and mysterious artist, whose work goes in several directions: in *The Fairy Feller's Master Stroke* of 1855–64 we have an odd example, perhaps the finest, of that taste for 'fairy painting' which emerges at precisely the same moment that a realism of natural detail dominates English art. Egg turned from painting Shakespearean subjects and such crucial historical moments as *Queen Elizabeth discovers that she is no longer young* (R.A. 1848) to an interest in modern problems. Thus the *Past and Present* triptych (p. 273), shown at the 1858 Academy, is a Hogarthian morality on the subject of a wife's unfaithfulness. The first picture shows the husband with a letter revealing his wife's infidelity; as in Hunt's *Awakening Conscience*, every detail of the heavily furnished room underlines the situation, a half-cut apple on the table, pictures of a shipwreck and the Fall on the walls, and so on. The second and third pictures show the same moment (note the cloud and the moon) five years later: on the one hand the disconsolate motherless daughters, on the other the fallen woman, bastard child in her arms, sheltering under the arches on which are pasted posters advertising temptation for others.

Past and Present is exceptional in Egg's work, and a comparatively late example of realist painting which conveys a strong social message. This kind of subject matter was pioneered by Richard Redgrave (1804–88), who in the 1840s drew attention, through his pictures, to the plight of the underpaid, neglected governess (R.A. 1843), to the sweated labour provided by the sempstresses (R.A. 1844), and to the problem of the fallen woman, in the now disappeared *Awakened Conscience* at the Academy of 1849.

One of the first artists to take up modern, moral subject matter was, oddly enough, G.F. Watts. We met him earlier among the young artists awarded a travelling

Right, RICHARD DADD, *The Fairy Feller's Master-Stroke,* 1855–64.
The Tate Gallery, London.

270

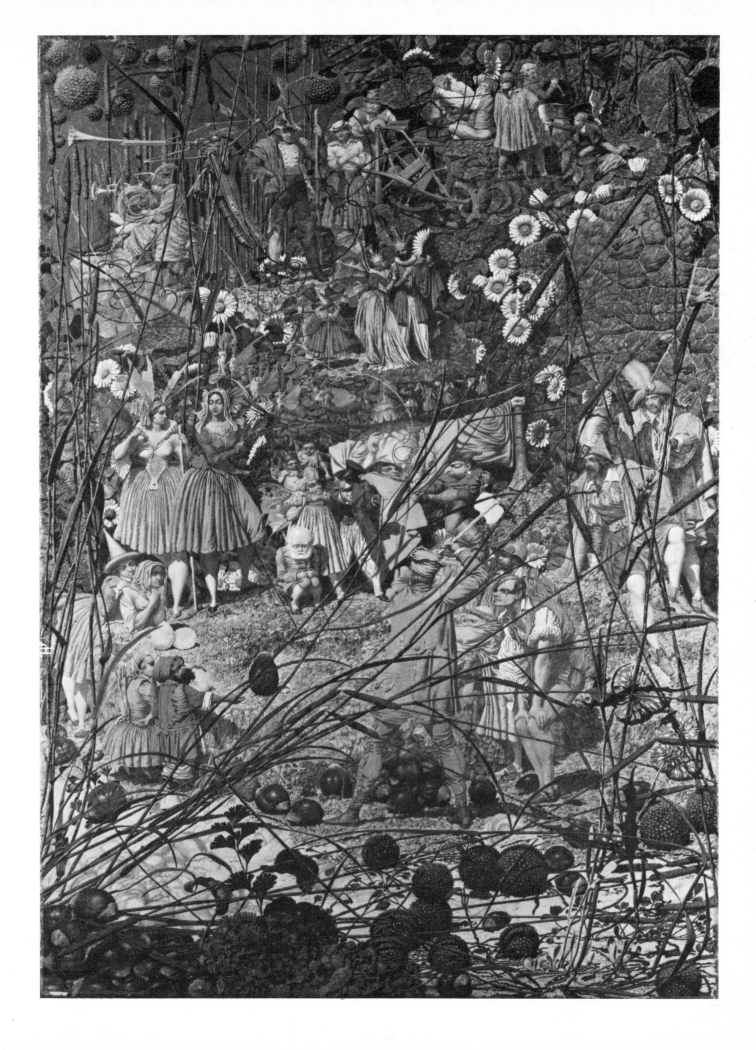

scholarship to study mural decoration, with a view to working on the Palace of Westminster. When he returned from Italy, in 1847, to the 'harsh reality' of England, Watts was, for a few depressed and miserable years, a painter uncertain of his direction. In 1849–50 he painted several pictures drawing attention to the acute social problems of the day, among them *A Seamstress, Found Drowned* and *The Irish Famine*. These were never exhibited, and remained unknown for many years, and Watts moved on to a completely different sort of painting, as we shall shortly see. Yet the pathetic figures of the *Irish Famine* have a dignity that can still be felt today, all the more because Watts could not bring himself to surround them with the telling detail that was expected of an artist in the early 1850s.

This is immediately apparent if we compare Watts' picture with the *Awakening Conscience* or with Ford Madox Brown's masterpiece, *The Last of England* of 1852–5 (p.256). Brown was never quite accepted in England – ignored by Ruskin, never really welcome at the Academy, he exists as an outsider in the English art scene, only supported by the warm friendship of Rosetti. There is also an underlying lack of sureness about his own development, as he changes abruptly from one style to another.

In 1852, however, Brown started the two pictures with a social content, *Work* and *The Last of England*. The latter is about the emigration movement, triggered off by the sculptor Woolner's departure for the Australian goldfields, but surely tinged by Brown's own despair at his continuing lack of success. 'I have [he wrote] in order to present the parting scene in its fullest tragic development, singled out a couple from the middle classes, high enough through education and refinement to appreciate all that they are now giving up. ... The husband broods bitterly over blighted hopes and severance from all he has been striving for. ...' The circumstances were common enough: in 1852 there were 65,000 British emigrants to Australia, very few of them

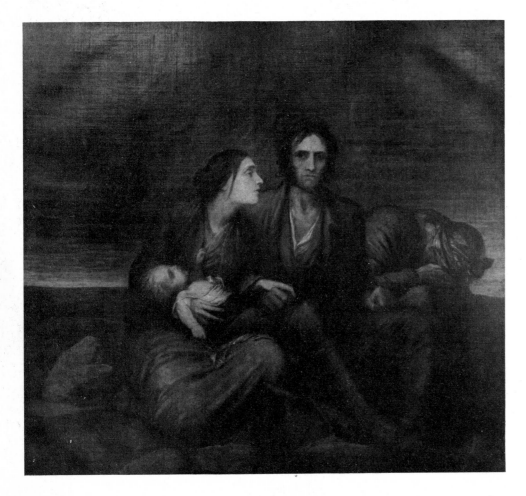

Left, GEORGE FREDERICK WATTS, *The Irish Famine*, 1849–50. Watts Gallery, Compton, Guildford.

Right, AUGUSTUS EGG, *Past and Present, I-III*, R.A. 1858. The Tate Gallery, London.

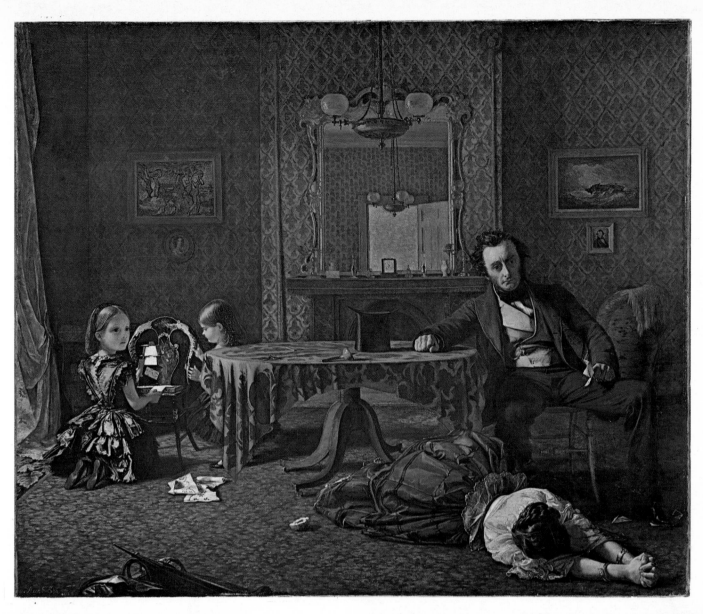

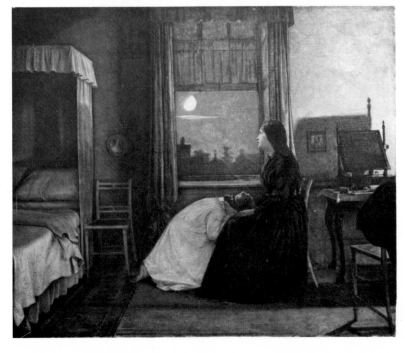

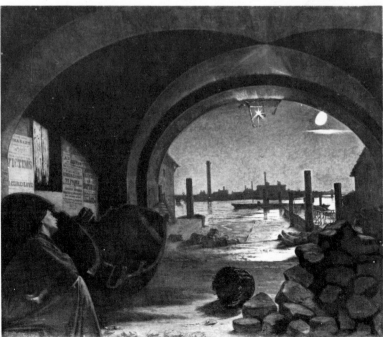

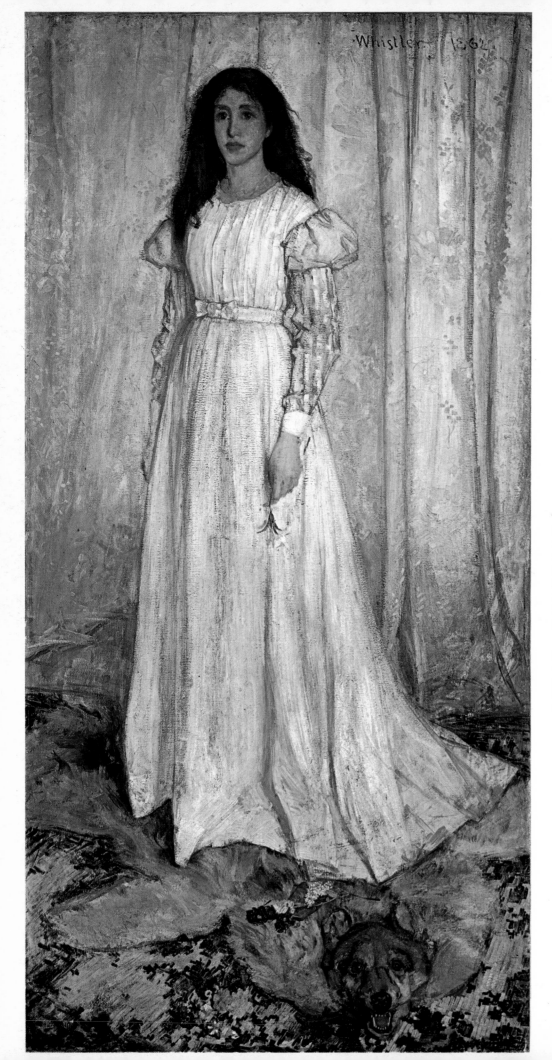

Left, James Abbott McNeill Whistler, *The White Girl,* 1862.
National Gallery of Art, Washington D.C., Harris Whittemore Collection.
Right above, Philip Wilson Steer, *Girls Running: Walberswick Pier, c.* 1889–94.
The Tate Gallery, London. Reproduced by permission of Mr W.R. Hornby Steer.

Right below, James Abbott McNeill Whistler, *Symphony in White No. 3 (Two Little Girls),* 1865–7.
Barber Institute of Fine Arts, University of Birmingham.

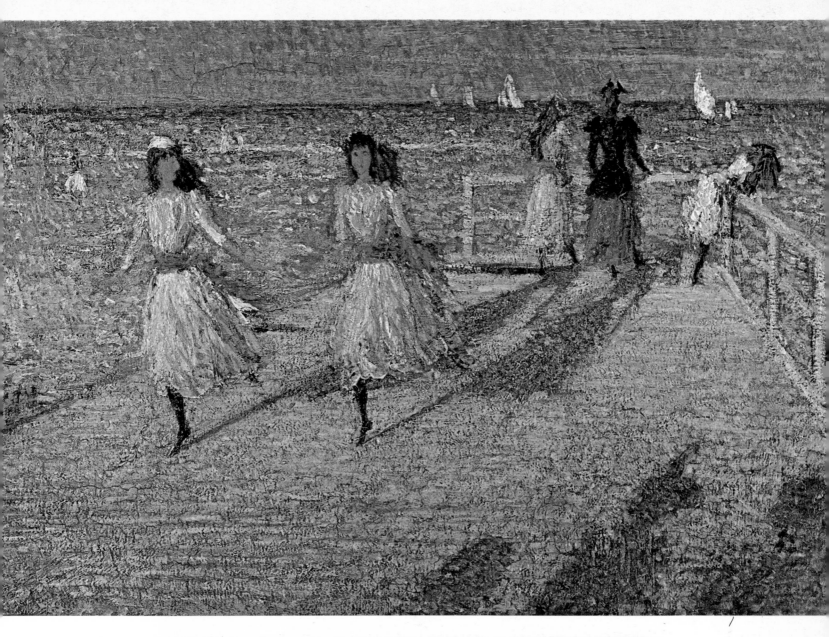

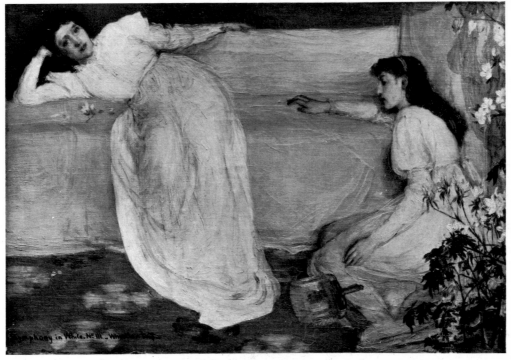

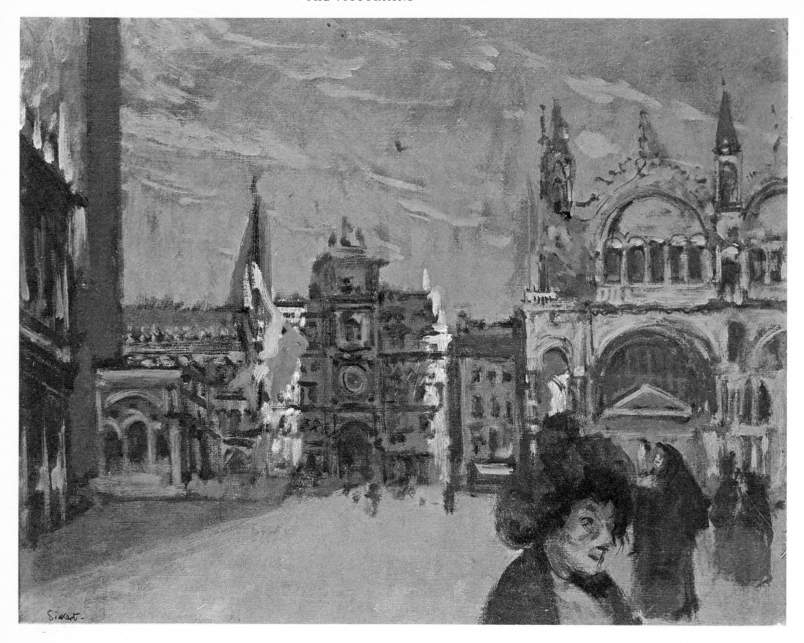

WALTER RICHARD SICKERT,
St Mark's Square, Venice, 1903.
Laing Art Gallery and Museum,
Newcastle-upon-Tyne.

ever to return. The protagonists in Brown's picture were modelled by the artist himself, with his wife and child.

This was the moment of high confidence in Victorian painting, admitting no debt to the past or to the present elsewhere, confident that the right prescript for art had been found. It was exactly parallelled at that very moment in France with Courbet's conviction that he had discovered the solution to the problem of modern art. Yet in both countries that confidence began to disappear almost immediately.

Brown became hopelessly involved in his attempt to paint 'Work as it now exists, with the British excavator for a central group, as the outward and visible type of Work' (p. 278). He crowded his composition with the rich and the poor, the young and the old, including such well-known figures as Carlyle and the Christian Socialist, F. D. Maurice – brain-workers, 'who, seeming to be idle, work, and are the cause of well-ordained work in others'. For all its incidental felicities *Work* is not a successful picture: the realism of the Hampstead setting is contradicted by a chaotic space composition which somehow exemplifies the incoherent message that Brown failed to put across.

By the time Brown was ready to exhibit *Work*, in 1865, the whole character of English painting had changed once again. The man primarily responsible for this was Rossetti, who dominates the sixties as Millais does the fifties, though in a very different way. Rossetti is the ideas man of Victorian painting, more genuinely original in his thinking than any of his contemporaries. His artistic production, however, was shaped by economic considerations: it was easier to sell watercolours than oils, and Rossetti found them easier to do, as he concentrated upon them. From 1854 until 1862 he was very dependent on the patronage of Ruskin, who turned to Rossetti when the break-up of his marriage had made support of Millais impossible. Ruskin did not want modern life pictures: he encouraged Rossetti to make highly finished watercolours with subjects from Dante, or from Malory's *Morte d'Arthur* – a new taste that coincides exactly with Tennyson's *Idylls of the King*. Rossetti had always enjoyed illustrating his favourite poems and stories, and the intensity of his vision somehow lifted literary genre painting on to an altogether higher plane: within the modest format the great issues of life and love and death were under consideration. The odd triptych form of the *Paolo and Francesca* watercolour of 1855, with Dante and Virgil in the central compartment and the lovers consigned to hell in the right, emphasizes the essentially visionary nature of Rossetti's art, far removed from the prosaic detail favoured by his contemporaries. His personal identification with Dante was so complete as to be totally convincing.

Inevitably Rossetti attracted disciples. In 1856 he met two Oxford undergraduates, Edward Burne-Jones (1833–98) and William Morris (1834–96), who became his inseparable friends and artistic associates. Together, in 1857, they decorated the Debating Hall of the new Union building at Oxford with somewhat inappropriate Arthurian subjects, frescoes so technically inept that they scarcely survived the decade. Burne-Jones made watercolours almost indistinguishable from Rossetti's, but Morris turned away from fine art to concern himself with the total artistic environment: he needed a house for himself and his bride, and everything in it had to be designed from first principles. Rossetti's influence is also discernible here: it was he who wrote the prospectus for the firm of Morris and Company when it was founded in 1861.

Rossetti's long engagement to Elizabeth Siddal and their short-lived marriage is reflected in a sequence of beautiful drawings which catch the moods of this still mysterious entanglement. After Lizzy's death in 1862 Rossetti's life-style, indeed his character, seems to change. Ruskin's support evaporates: he was always more interested in Mrs Rossetti than in Rossetti himself. And Rossetti discovers that, given the help of young friends, he can in fact produce oil paintings, and very successfully indeed. Within a year or two we find him earning £2,000–4,000 a year, and living in Cheyne Walk with the poet Swinburne, setting the tone for Bohemian life in London in the sixties.

Rossetti died in 1881, his later years troubled by chronic ill-health and his passion for Mrs Morris. He painted very little, and exhibited not at all, relying on the direct patronage of a few wealthy business men. His always severely limited subject matter was now concentrated upon iconic pictures of women, expressive of that worshipping devotion to the feminine which was Rossetti's only religion. Abandoning the Mariolatry of his earliest work, transcending the present reality of wife and mistresses that dominates the middle period, Rossetti at the end looked to the unattainable goddesses of ancient mythology – Venus and Pandora and the *Astarte Syriaca* (p. 279). There is an almost repellent sensuality about this last image, as if the destructive power of woman had finally triumphed and annihilated Rossetti.

For all the similarities, the mood of Burne-Jones's painting is a quite different one. Rossetti's personal involvement gives place to a curious detachment. Burne-Jones stands back from his subject-matter, as if it were all a beautiful dream which he

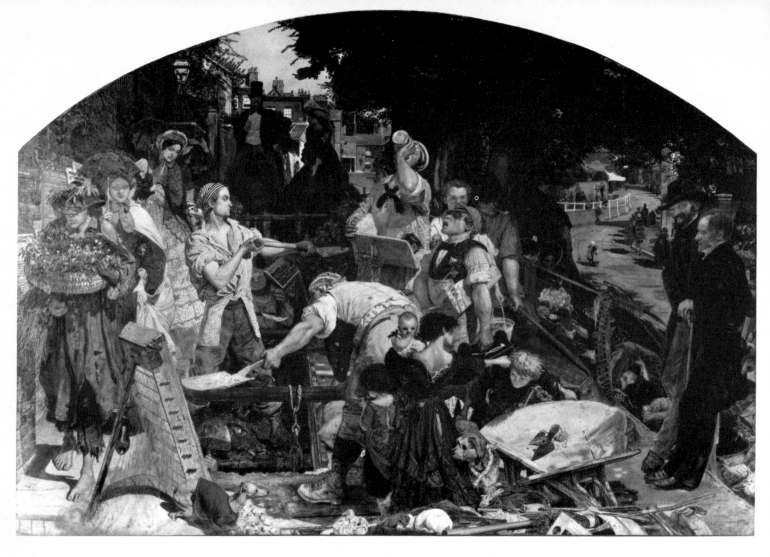

remembers clearly. It is a revelation, the meaning of which he does not question. There is no lesson to be drawn, no model to aspire to, simply the world of a golden age out of which all our myths and legends have sprung. We respond to its reality because, in Jung's term, it relates to a collective unconscious. Of course if one analyses a picture like *The Mill* one can appreciate how deliberately Burne-Jones used his knowledge of Italian Renaissance art and architecture to provide the visual data he needed. Yet neither landscape, nor buildings, nor figures are pastiche.

Burne-Jones had a natural sense of decoration, and could with ease design for large areas. His cartoons for stained-glass windows helped finance his early career, and became a major activity of the Morris workshop. Following Italian examples, he thought in terms of a narrative sequence of paintings – the story of Perseus, for example, or the Briar Rose legend. The context in which his pictures were seen was an important consideration: like others of his generation he disliked the market place atmosphere of the Academy's summer exhibitions, and it was not until the foundation of the independent Grosvenor Gallery in 1877 that Burne-Jones's work began to attract wide public attention. *King Cophetua* had a great success there in 1884: this was repeated in Paris in 1889 at the International Exhibition. For a few years Burne-Jones had a considerable European reputation, and on the Continent his painting was synonymous with Pre-Raphaelitism – an awkward extension of the term which has made its meaning even more ambiguous. Yet he was the true heir of something Rossetti had initiated and died too soon to benefit from – that decisive shift away from realism to symbolist art.

Another very long-lived artist who benefited from this change of taste was G.F. Watts, who reappears once again in this narrative. At more or less the same moment

Above, FORD MADOX BROWN, *Work,* 1852–65. Manchester City Art Gallery.

Right above, EDWARD BURNE-JONES, *The Mill,* Victoria and Albert Museum, London.
Right below, DANTE GABRIEL ROSSETTI, *Astarte Syriaca,* 1877. Manchester City Art Gallery.

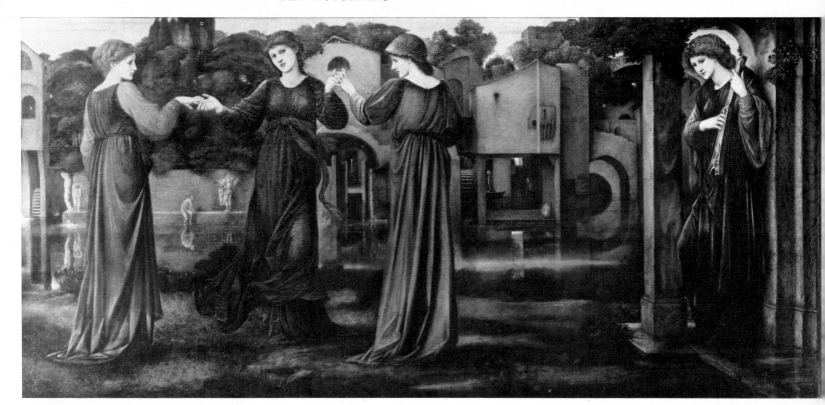

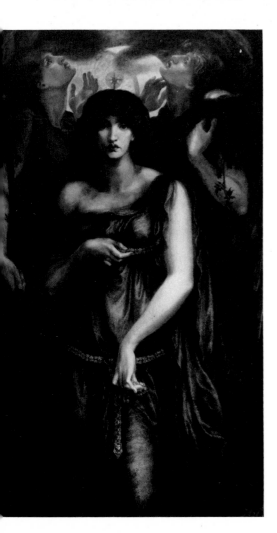

that he was painting his social realist subjects, 1850, Watts also introduced a vein of allegory, with such pictures as *Time and Oblivion* and *Life's Illusions*. Though not immediately successful, Watts was encouraged by his friends to pursue this kind of painting, which seemed so much more serious and high-minded than anything his contemporaries could offer. So he began *The House of Life*, a symbolic history of man, demonstrating all man's ambitions and tribulations – an enormous decorative scheme, existing only in the artist's imagination, into which all Watts's paintings can be loosely fitted.

'I paint ideas not objects,' Watts declared. 'My intention has not been so much to paint pictures that will please the eye, as to suggest great thoughts that will appeal to the imagination and the heart, and kindle all that is best and noblest in humanity.' Such an anti-aesthetic concept of art appears very wrong-headed in the twentieth century, yet it was sufficient to give Watts a reputation second to none in the last Victorian decades. His great public success dates from his Grosvenor Gallery exhibition of 1881–2: like Burne-Jones he had never been happy in the Royal Academy exhibitions although he had often shown there. Such pictures as *Hope*, of 1885, were immediately reproduced in thousands, to become an essential part of the furnishing of every middle class home.

For Watts, life was a mystery beyond human ken. He has been called a religious painter without a religion, for although he makes use of Christian themes he was not a believer. Subjects of sin and forgiveness fascinated him on a very personal level, and he could treat them with a lack of self-consciousness only possible before the modern growth of psychology. At the very end of his life, as we can see in *The Sower of the Systems* of 1902, his wish to illustrate philosophical abstractions brought him close to abstract art, and his aspirations were not so ridiculously different from those of Mondrian and Kandinsky.

Watts was also a great portrait painter, who has left us a remarkable record of his Victorian contemporaries. He did not work on commission, but chose his own sitters; and, adopting a uniform format, painted a *House of Fame* which he presented to the

279

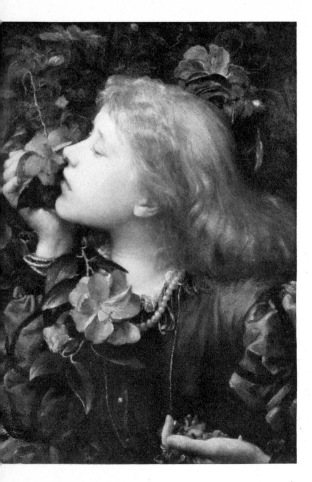

GEORGE FREDERICK WATTS, *Choosing*, 1864.
Collection of Mr Kerrison Preston.

National Portrait Gallery. Watts must have made an intensive study of portraiture: he injects into the English tradition his personal awareness of Italian art, especially of Venetian sixteenth-century painting. Yet this is not obvious in any way. Watts was able to paint portraits independent of the camera, and this became increasingly difficult in the Victorian period, as the photograph took over the function of providing an accurate record. On a more informal level, as in the portrait of his child-bride, Ellen Terry, which he called *Choosing* (1864), Watts comes close to Holman Hunt. There is the same symbolism of detail – the violets she holds are withered, the camelia she sniffs is scentless – and the wedding gown (which Hunt in fact designed) is painted with a painstaking accuracy that Watts normally eschewed.

Watt's view of art as something morally uplifting was too demanding to be widely shared by other painters, even by those practitioners of 'high art' associated with him. Frederic Leighton (1830–96), for example, did not believe that art should teach moral and religious truths: 'It is the intensification of the simple aesthetic sensation through ethic and intellectual suggestiveness that gives to the arts of Architecture, Sculpture and Painting so powerful, so deep, so mysterious a hold on the imagination,' he wrote.

Leighton had a spectacularly successful career, and he is perhaps more interesting as a social phenomenon than as a painter. Trained abroad in the modern German school, he did not settle permanently in London until 1860: eighteen years later he was President of the Royal Academy and a knight. Leighton began as an historical painter, specializing in multi-figure compositions of unimpeachable archaeological accuracy by the standards of the day. His enormous *Cimabue's Madonna carried in procession through the streets of Florence* was the sensation of the 1855 Academy, where it was bought by Queen Victoria for £600. This was in a style little known in England but popular on the continent, for in Paris and Antwerp artists were taught how to compose dozens of figures on a vast canvas, and they were encouraged to seek out unusual subjects. The Dutch-born Lawrence Alma-Tadema (1836–1912) made an early continental reputation as a painter of Merovingian history, then scored a great success with *Egyptians 3,000 Years Ago* at the Paris Salon of 1864. Edward John Poynter (1836–1919), who was born and trained in Paris, introduced this particular manner to England with *Israel in Egypt* at the Academy of 1867.

These three men – Leighton, Alma-Tadema and Poynter – form a triumvirate who came to dominate the Royal Academy from about 1870 until the end of Victoria's reign and after. Poynter in fact succeeded Leighton as President, retaining for some years his post as Director of the National Gallery. They were the establishment figures, at the time that the younger painters turned decisively away from the Royal Academy, which had lost its historical role as the meeting place for all British artists, whatever tendency they represented.

In the late Victorian public eye, Leighton, Poynter and Alma-Tadema belonged to the 'classical' school, which stood in opposition to the medievalism favoured by Rossetti and his considerable group of followers. Now, although they exploited these classical tendencies, Leighton and his friends did not invent them, as we shall shortly see. *Greek Girls picking up pebbles by the shore of the sea* was shown at the 1871 Academy: it is remarkably pure for Leighton, despite an obvious dependence on the Elgin marbles and similar classical statuary. More typical is the *Daphnephoria* of 1876, a triumphal procession of laurel-crowned Theban maidens singing a hymn to Apollo, where the sentimental anecdotal interest is strong; or the late *Garden of the Hesperides*, with the frank paganism which upset some of the more conventional members of the Victorian art-loving public.

Then there is the question of the nude, which Leighton and his friends brought back into Victorian painting after its almost complete disappearance in the fifties. As artists trained in continental academies, they accepted the nude's central role in

280

painting – a role that it had never lost in France. Admittedly there could be no place for a nude in the modern life subjects of Hunt and Millais and their followers, nor in Rossettian medieval painting. But the reappearance of classical themes was a different matter, especially when the story insisted on a naked female form. It is no accident that both Leighton and Poynter painted *Psyche* (p. 282), and the details of her story gave scope for a display of salacity only too plain today. Here, these highly respectable eminent Victorians purvey a superior pornographic art, and none more readily than Alma-Tadema. His speciality was Roman everyday existence, treated in terms that his contemporaries would understand; and what could be more attractive than the custom of public bathing, as revealed in such pictures as *In the Tepidarium* (p. 282)?

FREDERIC LEIGHTON, *Garden of the Hesperides*, 1892.
Lady Lever Art Gallery, Port Sunlight, Cheshire.

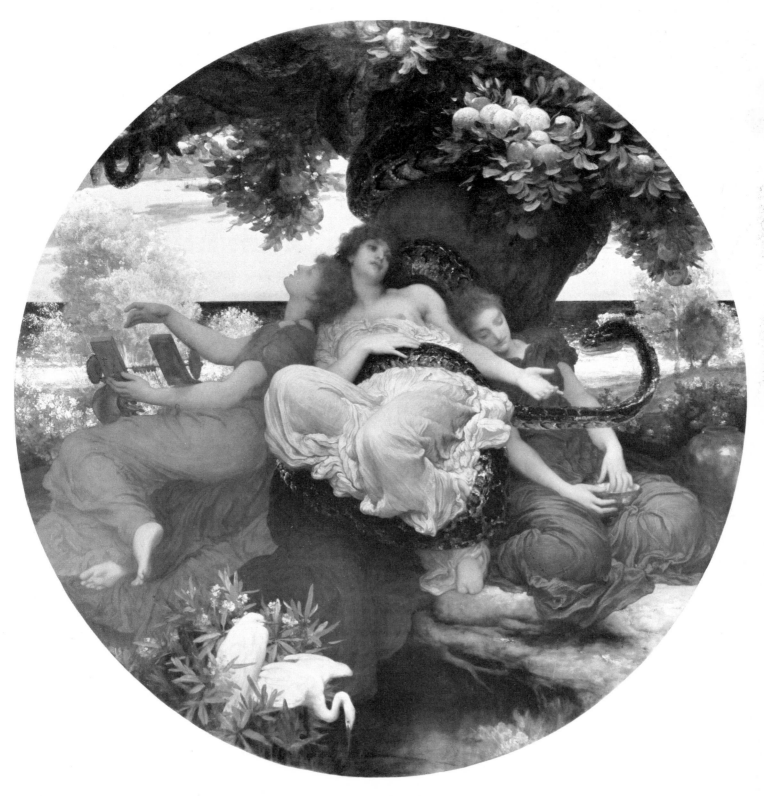

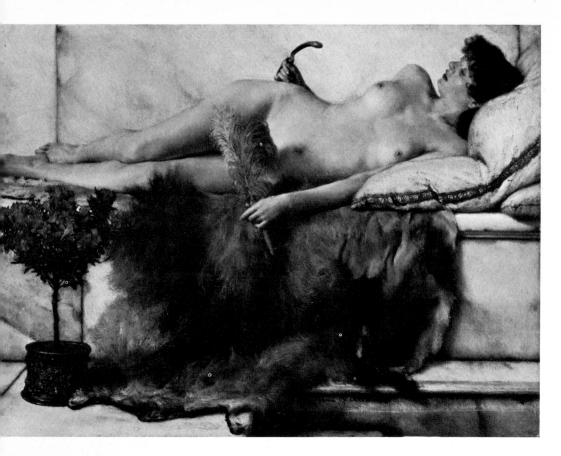

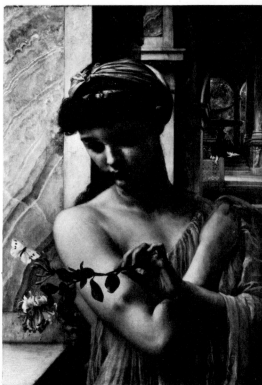

These paintings were accepted in apparent innocence, being purchased for considerable sums by respectable Northern business men, not inclined to throw their money away. Like all such unsophisticated collectors, they appreciated the high degree of finish and attention to detail showed by the artists who painted them.

To a remarkable extent, the whole of Victorian painting was dominated by men born between 1827 and 1836, and there is another member of this brilliant generation still to be considered. This was James McNeill Whistler (1834–1903). He was, of course, American, but his family connections with Britain had remained close, and he was at home in London from childhood on. Though he tended to disguise the fact, the art students he knew in Paris were mainly English, and he did his best to persuade his French painter friends, sometimes successfully, to move to England.

Whistler was quick to appreciate that not only would he find competition less intense in London than in Paris, but that the English artistic establishment was prepared to welcome new talent whereas the French was not. Whistler's first important picture, *At the Piano,* was rejected at the 1859 Salon, along with innovatory work in a similar naturalist style by Manet and Fantin. So he submitted it to the 1860 Academy, where *At the Piano* was accepted, well displayed, and discussed by artists and critics alike. It was purchased by one of the older Academicians, and Millais himself told Whistler at a party: 'I never flatter, but I will say that your picture is the finest piece of colour that has been on the walls of the Royal Academy for many years'. No wonder Whistler decided to move permanently to London.

Millais's remark about Whistler's colour needs some explanation. Like other young artists of his generation in France, Whistler was modelling himself on Velazquez and the recently rediscovered Vermeer, so far as tone, colour, composition and even subject matter were concerned. This was a new shift in taste, away from the adulation for Rembrandt, Hals and the Venetians which, for instance, Courbet's painting exemplifies. Millais was also aware of the rapidly rising reputation of Velazquez: we can see this in his painting, *The Vale of Rest,* which Whistler greatly admired at the 1859 Academy exhibition.

One of the reasons for Whistler's being able to establish himself in London so quickly comes from this connection, both personal and artistic, with Millais, still the leading modern English painter in the early 1860s. Whistler's *The White Girl* (p. 274) is a Millaisian painting – an atmospheric mood picture, in the succession of such works as *Autumn Leaves* (p. 254). In neither work is there any anecdotal content, although stories were read into both pictures. They are simply intended to convey, by formal means as well as by subject, a certain poetic, even musical feeling. That Whistler uses colour, or absence of colour, in this way, can be related beyond Millais to Rossetti, and in particular to his *Annunciation* which Whistler cannot have seen but almost certainly knew about.

Of course *The White Girl* is also an exercise in the manner of Velazquez; a portrait of Whistler's mistress, Joanna Heffernan; and too large and eccentric a picture for contemporary taste. It was rejected both at the 1862 Academy and at the 1863 Salon, but, because of the Jury's unreasonable severity at the latter, appeared in the Salon des Réfusés which the Emperor Napoleon III personally authorized. Like Manet's *Déjeuner sur l'herbe* it stood out among a great deal of very undistinguished painting at the Salon des Réfusés, and brought Whistler the Parisian reputation he so badly wanted. He was now in the unique position of acting as a go-between, bringing advanced thinking about art in London and Paris into fruitful contact. It was the English flavour of *The White Girl* that the French found so unusual and admirable.

In 1862 Whistler met Swinburne and the newly widowed Rossetti, then in Cheyne Walk, and in 1863 he settled in a neighbouring house. Thus the first true English *avant garde* was formed. Swinburne had an exceptional knowledge of modern French literature, and was in correspondence with Baudelaire: his article on *Les Fleurs du Mal* in the *Spectator* of September 1862, includes the first clear statement in England of the theory of Art for Art's sake – namely that art is concerned with truth and beauty, not with morals. All Whistler's ideas about art, summarized in the *Ten O'Clock Lecture* of 1885, must owe much to discussions with Swinburne and Rossetti in the early sixties: there is, in fact, little that is new in the later formulations, except perhaps an increased emphasis on the analogy of painting with music.

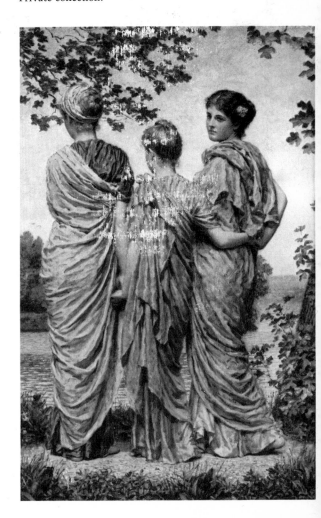

Whistler introduced Rossetti to Japanese art, of which he had first become aware in Paris. They bought kimonos, screens, fans, hangings, blue and white porcelain – many of them objects shown in the Japanese section of the 1862 international exhibition at South Kensington. For a year or two there was a Japanese craze in advanced English art circles, and Whistler's paintings are full of Japonaiserie. In *The Little White Girl* of 1864 (for which Swinburne wrote an explanatory poem) we see a fan, blue and white china, and the spring blossom motif. Other paintings of this date show Whistler influenced not only by Japanese symbolism, but by the compositional devices of Japanese wood-block prints, which he also collected. In 1864 Whistler was planning 'a group in oriental costume on a balcony', but against the landscape of the Thames with Battersea factories in the background: the subject never got beyond the study stage because, suddenly in 1865, Whistler changed his style.

The occasion was probably the appearance at the 1865 Academy of a painting now lost, *The Marble Seat*, by Albert Moore (1841–93). Moore had studied in Rome, and had made mural and ceiling paintings for the architect Nesfield. Taking the Elgin marbles as his prime source, he began painting decorative arrangements of draped female figures in vaguely classical settings. These appeared regularly at the Academy exhibitions of the later sixties: Swinburne wrote enthusiastically in 1868 that Moore's 'painting is to the artists what the verse of Théophile Gautier is to the poets: the faultless and secure expression of an exclusive worship of things beautiful'.

Whistler was immediately interested in the classicizing qualities of Moore's painting, and the two men became very closely associated, with a beneficial influence on them both. This is clear in the *Two Little Girls* (p. 275), which was certainly painted in

1865, though Whistler later altered the date to 1867, when he changed the title to *Symphony in White No. 3*, the first time he had made public use of the musical analogy to emphasize his artistic aims. In his pursuit of a musical painting, Whistler knew that he must suppress the anecdotal element, which still played a large part in the Japanese influenced works. At the very moment when he was beginning to question the assumptions of his early training in Paris, he chanced to come into close contact with Courbet again, at Trouville, where both men spent the autumn of 1865. Courbet's immediate impact was particularly destructive, and Whistler's flight to Valparaiso in 1866 was largely a retreat from the artistic scene in London and Paris. In the later sixties, Whistler found it impossible to finish a picture, and came near to creative sterility. His later close friendship with the poet Mallarmé should remind us that early in their careers the two men went through similar artistic experiences.

Around 1870 Whistler abruptly changed direction. The flirtation with classicism came to an end, and he abandoned figure subjects and imaginative compositions to paint portraits and landscapes instead. The first big portrait, that of *The Artist's Mother, Arrangement in Grey and Black No. 1*, is a conscious reversion to *At the Piano* in its Velazquez-derived composition and tonal structure. It was shown at the Academy of 1872, but with some controversy, and this was Whistler's last appearance at the R.A. Henceforth he preferred to show in environments where he was in control, and with Watts and Burne-Jones he later helped to make the Grosvenor Gallery a real alternative to the Academy, as far as the general art-going public was concerned.

Whistler could declare his independence of the Academy because he had now found wealthy patrons willing to commission pictures. W.C. Alexander asked him to paint portraits of his eight children: only one, however, was completed, that of *Miss Cicely Alexander, Harmony in Grey and Green*, because the artist's demands were so exhausting – seventy sittings, a particular dress, specially woven matting for the background, and so on. Yet, in the seventies, men and women flocked to Whistler to have their portraits painted. They also commissioned decorative schemes for the reception rooms of their town houses, always with negative, or even disastrous results. Whistler was anxious to undertake such work: his interest in a painting extended beyond the confines of the canvas to the frame, and then to the room in which it was seen. But he was not an accommodating person, and when the Liverpool ship owner, F.R. Leyland, asked him to decorate the dining-room in which an early Whistler painting had been hung, the artist grossly exceeded his patron's wishes. Nevertheless, *Harmony in Blue and Gold: the Peacock Room* can be regarded as an extension of painting into the third dimension, and, as such, a remarkably forward-looking work.

The musical titles which Whistler added to all his works are perhaps most apt for the landscapes of the river Thames at night which so fascinated him. They were not painted on the spot, but in the studio from memory, using a carefully prepared palette to ensure a very precise tonal range. Whistler was demonstrating how pictures can be built up, not by adding details, but by broad areas of tone. 'Whistler's Nocturnes make us think of Wagnerian music where the harmonies, freed from melody and rhythm, become a kind of abstraction and give only an indefinable musical impression', wrote Théodore Duret, the French critic, in 1881. That ardent Wagnerian, Claude Debussy, returned the compliment when he gave the title *Nocturnes* to the three orchestral pieces of 1897–9 that established his reputation.

It was one of Whistler's Nocturnes – *The Falling Rocket; Nocturne in Black and Gold* of 1874 that so angered Ruskin: 'I have seen and heard much of Cockney impudence before now, but never expected to hear a coxcomb ask 200 guineas for flinging a pot of paint in the public's face.' Whistler sued for libel, and at the trial in 1878 was asked to define a Nocturne: 'I have perhaps meant to indicate artistic interest alone

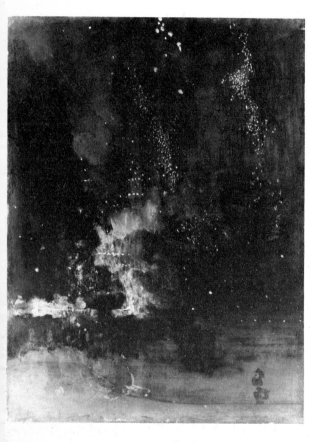

JAMES ABBOTT MCNEILL WHISTLER,
The Falling Rocket:
Nocturne in Black and Gold, c. 1874.
By courtesy of the Detroit Institute of Arts.

in the work, diverting the picture from any outside sort of interest which might have been otherwise attached to it. It is an arrangement of line, form and colour first. . . .' The outcome was that Whistler won his case against Ruskin, but was awarded only a farthing damages. The costs of the case led to his bankruptcy in 1879, and the last years of Whistler's life are a sort of sad coda, feelings of inadequacy and despair alternating with more euphoric moments of success. It might be argued that Whistler had the misfortune to live at the wrong moment: temperamentally he inclined to symbolism and abstraction, yet in the context of English painting this meant Watts and Burne-Jones. Whistler believed that Nature was the artist's servant, not his master, yet he found himself associated in the public eye with the ultra-naturalist Impressionist movement; did not his two outstanding followers in the eighties, Sickert and Steer, call themselves, in 1889, the London Impressionists? We are confronted with a confused and confusing artistic situation in the last half of Victoria's reign, where the facts, so far as one can discern them, obstinately escape the historian's generalizations.

There was also an increasing lack of confidence in the quality of English painting, a growing awareness of the superiority of French art. Whistler had introduced international standards in the sixties, but he could reasonably be regarded as an English painter, and his work was an acceptable continuation of the pioneering efforts of Millais and Rossetti. French artists who worked in England in the sixties and seventies, like the illustrators Constantin Guys and Gustave Doré, and the painters Alphonse Legros and James Tissot (1836–1902), did not upset the equilibrium, Tissot's *Ball on Shipboard*, shown at the Academy in 1874, would not have seemed in any way out of context. There was a psychological advantage in appearing in England fully armed as it were, as Leighton and Whistler had found, and as Sargent was to discover when he moved to London from Paris.

John Singer Sargent (1856–1925) was born in Florence of American parents, and trained in Paris under Carolus Duran, one of the most successful portrait painters of the later nineteenth century. An unfavourable reception at the Paris Salon of 1884 encouraged him to follow Whistler's example, and he found English patronage as welcoming as his fellow American had done. Sargent's early portraits – like that of *The Misses Vickers* of 1884 – have a style and bravura no native English painter could

Below left, JOHN SINGER SARGENT,
The Misses Vickers, 1884.
Graves Art Gallery, Sheffield.
By permission of Sheffield Corporation.
Below right, JOHN SINGER SARGENT,
*Portrait of Robert Louis Stevenson
and his Wife,* 1885.
Collection of Mr John Hay Whitney, New York.

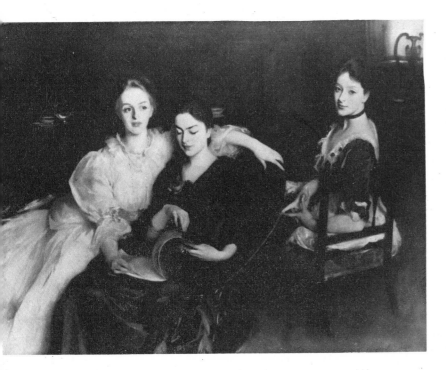

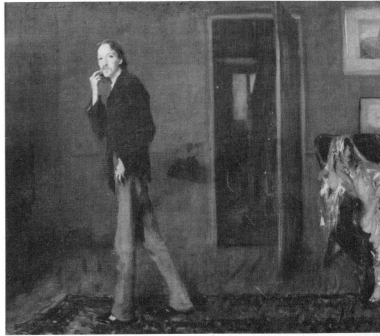

remotely rival. The Royal Academy did not want to show his work at first; it was considered too clever and too affected. Somehow Sargent had rediscovered that grand aristocratic manner which seemed to have disappeared with Lawrence's death; and he showed that he was not afraid of the photograph because there was still something the portrait painter could do. Inevitably Sargent's success bred imitation, and perhaps Sargent got bored with his own talents. He was no intellectual, simply a natural painter, at his best in such occasional portraits as *Robert Louis Stevenson* (p. 285).

Sargent was one of the young painters involved in the formation of the New English Art Club in 1886 – a focus of discontent with the Royal Academy, and the last major grouping of talents in Victoria's reign. In the early days there were several distinct factions involved, but the common ground was an acceptance of some sort of realist painting; most of the artists concerned had, moreover, studied in Paris, and were impatient with the parochialism and increasing mediocrity of the Academy.

Realism is, of course, the predominant mode of Victorian painting, and its phases merge almost imperceptibly as the century proceeds. In the sixties the poetic realism of Millais was taken up by younger painters like Fred Walker (1840–75) and Boyd Houghton (1836–75) whose premature deaths leave a gap in the story. Much of their work was in the field of illustration, which was revolutionized in the sixties by the followers of Millais and of Rossetti: these two influences can be clearly discerned, and the Rossettian style leads on directly to Walter Crane and Aubrey Beardsley, whose activities fall outside the scope of this essay.

Illustration provided another stimulus with the foundation of the weekly newspaper *The Graphic*, in 1869. Its editor wanted to draw his readers' attention to the social abuses of mid-Victorian England, especially the misery and poverty that existed in the midst of affluence. He commissioned large plates from the best young artists he could find; and in the first number appeared the *Applicants for Admission to a Casual Ward* by Luke Fildes (1844–1927). Fildes turned this somewhat Dickensian study into a large painting which he exhibited at the Academy of 1874: it was an exceptional picture whose quality he never again achieved.

Another of the social realists of *The Graphic* was Frank Holl (1845–88), a convinced socialist with a more genuine desire to paint the sorrows of the English poor than Fildes possessed. A handful of early paintings attracted attention around 1870; one of them, *No Tidings from the Sea*, of 1871, was commissioned by the Queen herself, moved by the pathos of such subject matter. Holl subsequently turned to portraiture, which was becoming the only sure way for an English artist to make a living; the amount of money available for new British art began to decline in the last two decades of the century, as the lack of confidence spread from the painters to the collectors.

From 1880 onwards almost every young painter sought part of his education in Paris: in London the near monopoly of artistic training once possessed by the Royal Academy Schools had vanished, the Royal College of Art was primarily a design school, and the newly founded Slade School at London University did not get into its stride until the middle nineties, when Fred Brown, Henry Tonks and Wilson Steer came together on the teaching staff. The Paris of the English art student in the eighties was not the Paris of the Impressionists, however: they were still little known and generally disregarded, though Monet and Renoir were beginning to make their presences felt. Jean François Millet was held to be the great modern artist, and it was his followers and, in particular, the now almost forgotten Jules Bastien Lepage, who made the strongest appeal to English artists. Bastien Lepage's death in 1884 at the age of 36 seemed a major loss for painting.

This meant that the young English painter in the 1880s could choose between Whistler's way of building up a composition with broad tonal areas, or he could adopt the more broken, loosely handled manner which sometimes gets labelled

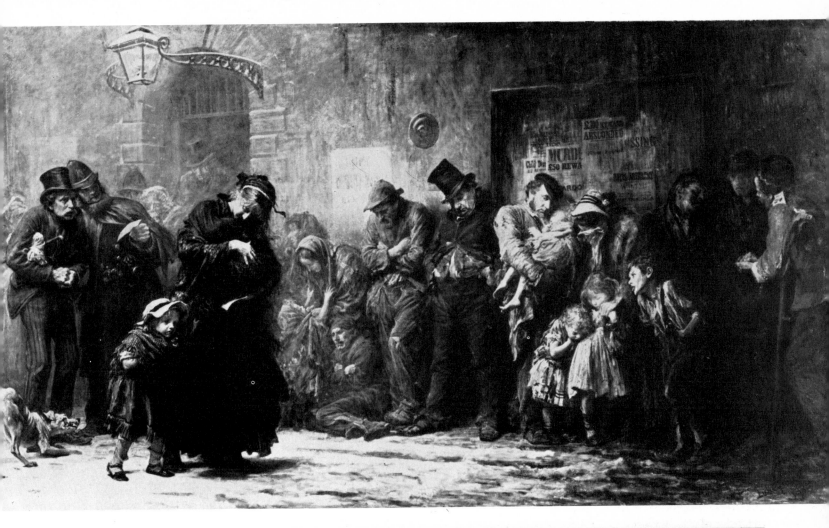

Above, LUKE FILDES, *Applicants for Admission to a Casual Ward*, 1874.
Royal Holloway College, Egham, Surrey.
Right, FRANK HOLL,
No Tidings from the Sea, 1871.
Royal Collection.
By gracious permission of
Her Majesty the Queen.

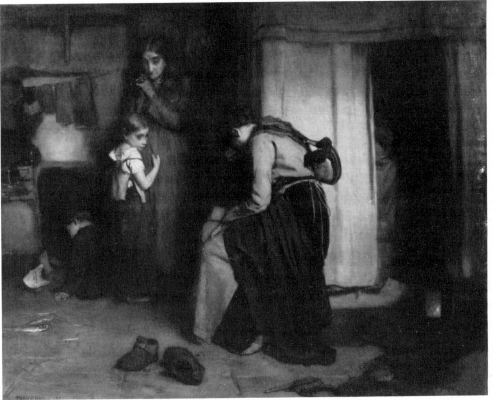

impressionistic. The colour ranges from the subdued to the bright, according to the demands of the subject – almost invariably outdoor scenes, often with people at work. There was a flight from the city into the countryside, where life seemed somehow more real and honest.

William McTaggart (1835–1910), perhaps the most interesting Scots painter of the nineteenth century, withdrew from Edinburgh in 1888 to develop a strikingly free, painterly style, entirely independent of Impressionism, about which he knew nothing. Some of the men behind the formation of the New English Art Club in 1886 began to experiment with broken colour, often in a bright high key, as we at times see in the work of George Clausen (1852–1944) and Edward Stott (1859–1918), or in William Stott of Oldham (1857–1900). *The Ferry* of 1882 is an early example of this style, where the connection with an earlier, more purely English, model is obvious.

Painters began to leave London and settle in remote places in the British Isles, a deliberate gesture in tune with a growing disillusionment about city life, and a doubting of the values of urban civilization. West Cornwall, where the climate encouraged work out of doors and the fishermen's lofts provided cheap and magnificent studio accommodation, was a magnet for young painters from the time of Whistler's visit to St Ives with the young Sickert in 1882. As at Pont Aven in Britanny, there was a mood of high seriousness and excitement as the painters dominated small rural communities. The local people and their lives and problems provided a convenient subject-matter: the village wedding in *The Health of the Bride* of 1889 by Stanhope Forbes (1857–1947) or the dangerous life of the fishermen, which is reflected in *A Hopeless Dawn* of 1888 by Frank Bramley (1857–1915). These two painters belonged to the Newlyn School, which for a year or two blew some fresh air through English painting. Even so, there is no evidence of any French influence stronger than Manet, and it was left to two slightly younger painters to put English art firmly in contact with French Impressionism and Post-Impressionism.

Walter Richard Sickert (1860–1942) and Philip Wilson Steer (1860–1942) were exact contemporaries: their working lives extended far beyond the Victorian period

WILLIAM STOTT, *The Ferry*, 1882. Collection of Mr Mark Longman, London.

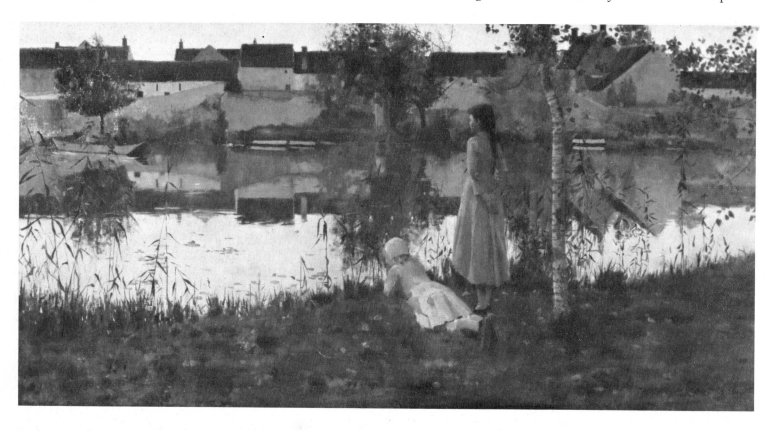

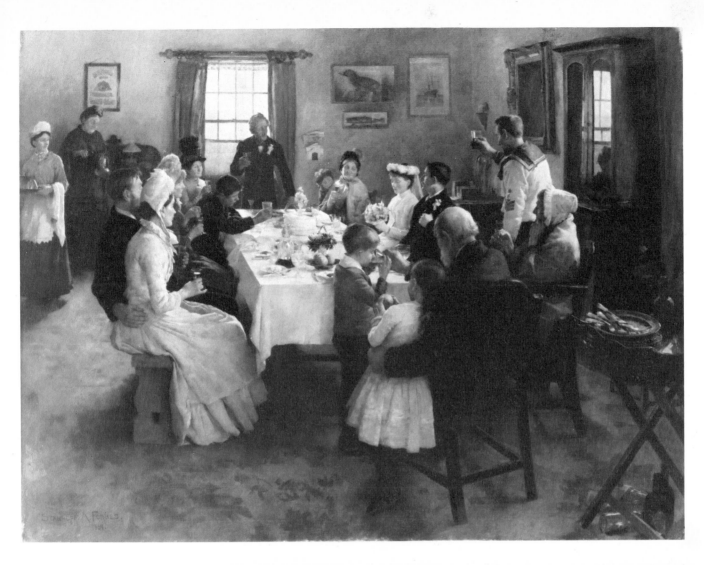

Above, STANHOPE FORBES,
the Bride, 1889. *The Health of*
The Tate Gallery, London.
Right, FRANK BRAMLEY,
A Hopeless Dawn, 1888.
The Tate Gallery, London.

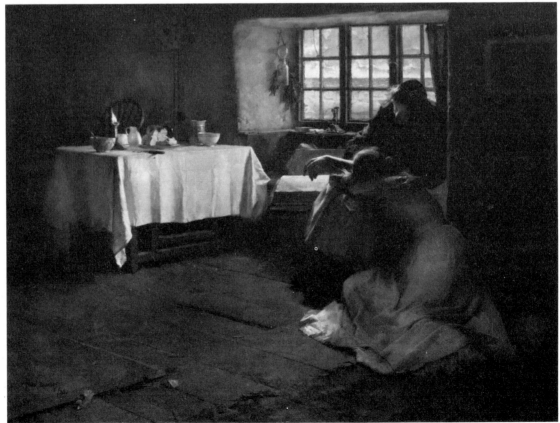

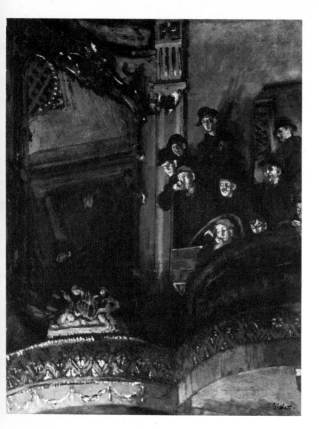

WALTER RICHARD SICKERT,
The Old Bedford, 1895.
Walker Art Gallery, Liverpool.

(and their later careers and general influence will be discussed in the next chapter). Both began in the shadow of Whistler, but broke loose. They were the most significant exhibitors at the London Impressionists exhibition in 1889, and at the New English Art Club throughout the nineties.

In the Victorian period, Sickert was much the more unsure of himself. His great period did not begin until the move to Dieppe in 1899, when he shook completely free from Whistler's influence. A tremendous admiration for Degas, whom he met in 1883, had, however, left Sickert with an ineradicable feeling of inferiority towards the French, which he transmitted to his followers. Sickert worshipped Degas, who taught him how to paint, what to paint, and what to think about other painters. Degas's insistence on the importance of drawing was totally accepted by Sickert, so was his taste for unorthodox composition. Theatre subjects, which Degas had pioneered, were taken up by Sickert, who sensibly concentrated on the English music hall, particularly *The Old Bedford* in Camden Town, to give his own work a distinctive flavour. It was, in fact, the Englishness of Sickert's work which brought him a modest artistic success in Paris in the early years of this century.

Wilson Steer is an altogether more remarkable painter than Sickert in the Victorian period, when all his best work was done. He was temperamentally an odd mixture of perspicacity and laziness, and his talents were effectively destroyed after 1894 by well-meaning friends. Although he studied in Paris in 1882–4 it was not until 1889 that he suddenly realized the importance of Impressionism, and in particular of Monet. Influenced by the high horizons, pure bright colour and broken brush strokes of Monet's seascapes and landscapes, Steer began painting in similar fashion. He experimented in his handling and choice of colours, so that at times his work is almost pointillist, although whether he knew of Seurat's work is disputable. In *Girls Running* (p. 275) and similar pictures painted around 1891, Steer flattened the pictorial space and introduced prominent figures, somewhat oddly positioned. From these young girls emanates a certain poetic quality: their presence is a consequence of Steer's private frustrations, and they charge the pictures with an emotional tension, just as in Millais's paintings of nearly forty years before.

A decade was to elapse before Victoria's death in 1901, but Steer's paintings of the 1889–93 period make an appropriate conclusion to any essay on Victorian painting. They contain that clear reference to French Impressionism and Post-Impressionism which began at this point to dominate painting everywhere. Yet their individual quality is that poetic sentiment which is very characteristic of the best Victorian art. It was a period when painting in England went its own way, because in the early nineteenth century no one country could offer a clear lead. The direction that we chose seemed by the end of the century to have been a generally unfruitful one, despite certain exceptions and promising gestures. Far too many talents never matured or went too quickly to waste. In the end the superiority of the French product had to be recognized, and this reluctant admission left us unable to contribute much to what one might call the re-invention of painting in the early twentieth century.

But if Victorian England, unlike the Romantic period, produced no major European artists, there is at least a wealth of minor figures. The incidental pleasures of Victorian painting are considerable: it is a rich and various field, full of surprises, with many opportunities for revaluation and rediscovery.

7

THE TWENTIETH CENTURY

Grey Gowrie

It is now just a hundred years since the French Impressionists gave their first exhibition and received their name. Whatever claims we may wish to make on its behalf, it is hard not to see British painting over this time in terms of a problem common to all but a few artists: how to harness energies and innovations from outside this country to individual and local ends. We cannot escape the eclecticism of British art in our era, the feeling of one glance at canvas or model to two over the shoulder. Nor altogether should we wish to. In spite of the victories of Constable and Turner, Englishmen of the late nineteenth century preferred moralizing or idealistic art to empirical or sensual. Trust in the world of felt appearances, in the ability, for instance, of scientific enquiry to determine the figures of art, was hard won. If the English artists we shall be looking at had rested safe in their own rich but incohesive tradition of portrait and poetic landscape, the power of art to cope with twentieth-century life would have been in danger. Imitation was a matter of survival.

Since the Impressionists, it is arguable that national schools of painting have been reduced to mere conveniences of geography and chronology, indicative no longer of the sensibility or feel of societies which define themselves mainly through their nationhood. The portraitists and visual chroniclers of upper class life in eighteenth-century England, and those who caught weather and district in the great Romantic era, belong to the moral and social history of this country as well as to the aesthetic. Both Stubbs and Constable built upon the English scientific enlightenment; Stubbs anatomizing horses, Constable clouds. So their empiricism and their instinct for the application of knowledge reflected a national supremacy in this arena. But after about 1850 the intellectual energies of Europe became those of 'the West'. All national sovereignties of any scale or consequence wanted to adopt industrial and highly mechanized economies, almost as a precondition of sovereignty.

From the death of Turner to the 1930s painting in this country was provincial not only by outside, particularly French standards, but by our own standards of industrial design. Artists in recent years have gained from looking back to this manufacturing tradition – as we can see in the paintings of Richard Hamilton and Bridget Riley and in the work of sculptors like Anthony Caro and Eduardo Paolozzi. A dominant theme in the steady erosion of national or 'school' considerations is the effect on painting of the whole corpus of theoretical or pure science in this century. The symbol for our century might well be, were it not perhaps too innocent, a child's building block. In language and behaviour, in the materials of the universe and the organization of society, in scientific method and the means of economic production, the prime intellectual aim has been to isolate the component parts of life. This means, in short, to *abstract* them. We are absorbed by structures. No wonder that, by comparison with the great statements on life put out by painters as different as Piero, Titian, Rembrandt, or even Turner, the subject of most modern art has been itself: what lies underneath it; its process.

Thus when Virginia Woolf wrote that in or about December 1910 the human character changed, her joke demonstrated one of the first principles of modern art: its awareness of itself as modern. Hindsight allows us to unwrap this feeling and detect a culmination as well as a beginning. There now existed, predominantly in the Western world, a sum of methods which men could call on to modify not only their sense of the external world, the workings of nature, but the workings of the human spirit itself. Henceforward, modern art was to shuttle between the artist's sense of himself, his imaginative, self-extending powers, and his desire to render Nature by imitating her own flux and process. 'That Nature is a Heraclitean Fire' is part of the title of a poem by the late-Victorian poet, Hopkins. In bowing to the ancient who saw completeness in the rhythms and movement of creation, Hopkins provides a rubric for the venturesomeness of modern civilization and for its sense of danger.

Post-Impressionism is the rather flat term assigned to the great quartet of painters who in ideas and execution embody the sources of twentieth-century painting: Cézanne, Gauguin, Van Gogh and Seurat. It was they who explored and exploited the Impressionist's pictorial naturalism and focused artistic energy on the means of its own production. Except for Seurat, and with the addition of Picasso, Matisse and Derain among others, they were introduced to the British public in November 1910. The master of ceremonies was Roger Fry who, in Kenneth Clark's phrase, taught his generation how to look.

Now that progressive art is the norm it is hard to imagine the furore which greeted *Monet and the Post-Impressionists*, as Fry's November exhibition was called. Quentin Bell has written that 'there was an outcry such as has never been heard since then in this country. The voices of good taste, of academic authority, of all the *cognoscenti*, of nearly all the 'progressive' *avant garde* painters in London, above all of the people who before this *volte face* had found Fry such a charming lecturer on nice, safe, dead painters like Piero di Cosimo and Giovanni Bellini, were raised, not simply in horror and derision, not simply in protest, but in tones of deep, savage, heartfelt personal reproach.' *The Times* found in the show a rejection of all that civilization had done, the good along with the bad. Violent as the reaction was, Fry could reassure himself that the human spirit in England had been given a fillip. And while he was bitter to find in the cultivated classes, hitherto his most eager listeners, the most inveterate enemies of the new movement, he was led to important insights into the role of art in underwriting vested social attitudes and interests.

The importance of the first Post-Impressionist exhibition (Fry organized a second in October 1912) is not simply that it introduced the founders of modern art to the English consciousness, to painters as well as the public. Its real effect was to force the various groups of professional painters to define their aims and attitudes and share in the clarity of intention, the self-directedness, which is the hope of the modern. This was an age in which artistic discovery, emanating from France,

292

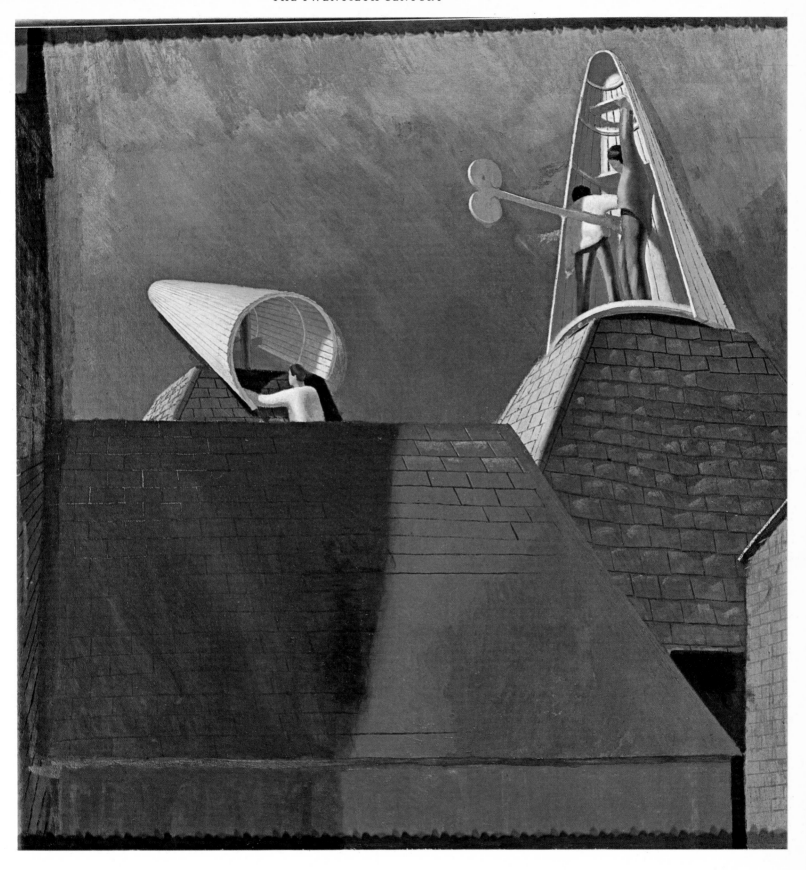

STANLEY SPENCER,
Mending Cowls, Cookham, 1914.
The Tate Gallery, London.

293

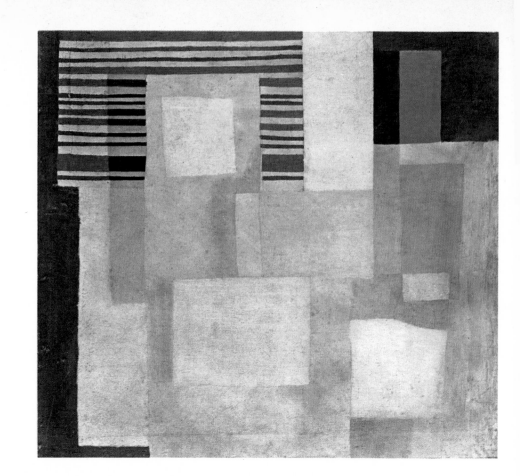

Right, BEN NICHOLSON, *Painting,* 1924.
By permission of the artist.
Below, GRAHAM SUTHERLAND, *Sun Setting between Hills,* 1938.
Collection of Lord Clark.

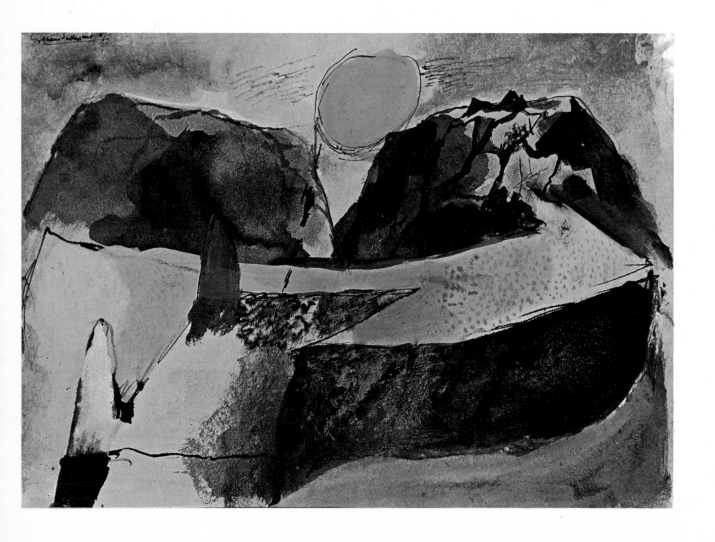

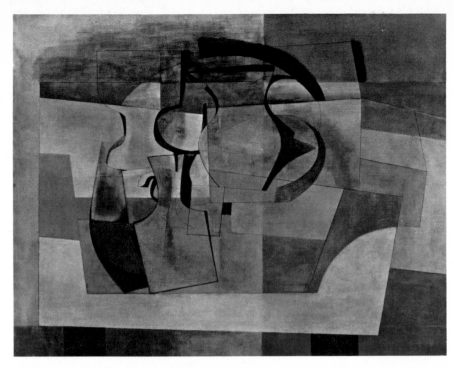

Left, BEN NICHOLSON, *December 1949
(Poisonous Yellow).*
Galleria Internazionale d'Arta Moderna, Venice.
Below, PAUL NASH, *Night Landscape,* 1938.
Manchester City Art Gallery.

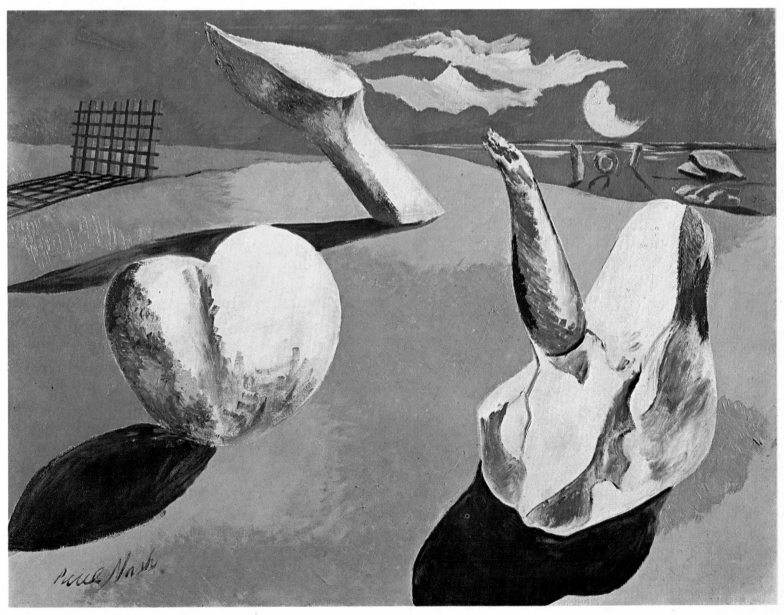

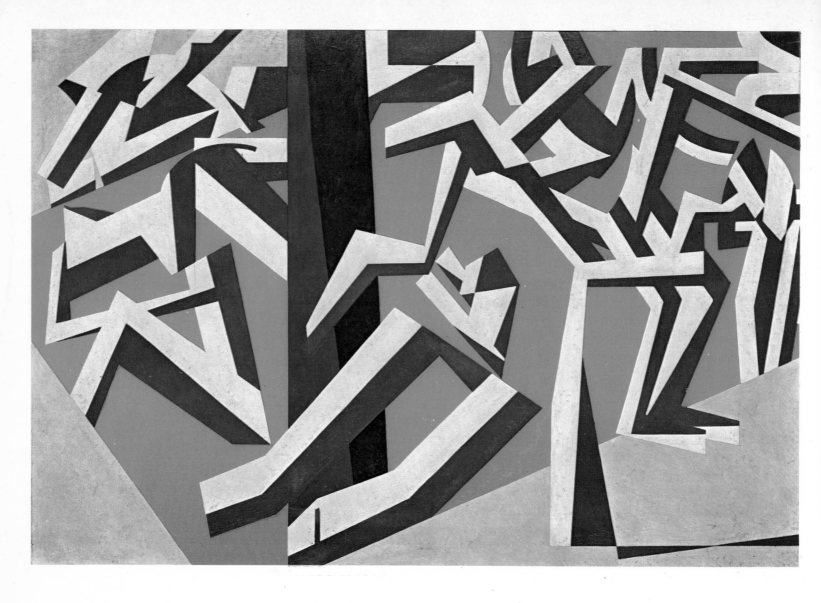

DAVID BOMBERG, *The Mud Bath*, 1913–14.
The Tate Gallery, London.

branched outward by means of the international exhibition. Fry's exhibition was not even the first of its kind in England, although it was the first to dent people's thinking about the arts in any effective way.

John Rothenstein, whose father, William Rothenstein, was an important figure in the Whistler-influenced New English Art Club, has made the point that the November show made a deep and permanent cleavage between the painters who were for it and those who were against. The politics of the London art world were riven, and this in the face of a general public which still rejected the gentle Impressionism of the New English Art Club in favour of that Victorian fixture in English life, the Royal Academy. It is true, certainly, that English artists and intellectuals are traditionally-minded in that once an imported tradition takes hold it is with difficulty put aside in favour of whatever has, at place of origin, modified or superseded it. British wrangling about the Post-Impressionist substitution of colour for tone continued long after Cubism had first shaken and then revised the foundations of modern painting.

By 1910 the New English Art Club was under mild fire from a splinter group. It had been founded in 1886 and is today chiefly remembered for its connection with Whistler and Sickert and for having provided the principal bastion against a Royal Academy given to conversation pieces, 'problem' pictures, society portraits and genteel pornography. Its main activity was housebreaking French Impressionism and adapting it to the native tradition. Sickert defined this tradition as having a moral character: seriousness of intent displayed by choice of subject. He believed that subject on the whole should reflect the reality of everyday life, particularly of life in cities. The influence of Whistler, and as time went on of Sickert himself, directed the Club towards a low-toned or dark palette. We see this in the Gwen John self-portrait of about 1900, surely the finest of all New English paintings. A lighter palette was taken up by Spencer Gore (1878–1914), who, like Robert Bevan (1865–1925) and Harold Gilman (1876–1914), was committed to a rather more French treatment of light (p. 298). Gore, indeed, had spent much of his time in France and exhibited frequently at the Paris *Salon des Indépendants*. By the time of his election to the New English Club in 1909 he was already somewhat disillusioned. Gilman and Bevan, he felt, were being kept out on reactionary grounds. The three had been meeting regularly at Sickert's studio in Fitzroy Street. Early in 1911, perhaps on Sickert's advice, they decided not to attempt to gain control of the New English Club and so the Camden Town Group was formed.

The Group remained conservative as to subject matter. Urban scenes prevailed; and what we would think of as suburban scenes, for the off-centre districts of London were still villagey and compositions could deal with a nice interplay of houses with trees and gardens. (The masterpieces of this genre did not appear, however, until thirty or so years later, in the Hammersmith-scapes of Victor Pasmore.) There were also fine portraits, with a further chance of interplay between still life and interior. Two pictures in the Tate Gallery, Spencer Gore's *North London Girl* of 1911 and Harold Gilman's Cézannesque *Mrs Mounter at the Breakfast Table* illustrate this. Robert Bevan made some remarkable compositions out of the last years of horse-transport in cities (p. 298); he is unique here and social historians will be grateful to him. Current opinion would probably rank Bevan highest among these painters. He had met the Gauguin of the Pont-Aven period in 1894 and the meeting tells, though he is less adept at colour rhythms than another Pont-Aven painter, the Scottish colourist George Henry.

If the Camden Town painters were alive to the Post-Impressionist desire to analyse ways of rendering appearance and incorporate the analysis in their paintings, their neo-realism was 'New English' enough. In fact it was akin to Sickert's original modification of Whistler's atmospherics to his own sense of lived life. Nor did the expansion of the Camden Town into the London Group, and the brief association with Wyndham Lewis, make much difference. Gore, the chairmanly or diplomatic spirit, died not long after the London's first exhibition. Wyndham Lewis became occupied with his own Rebel Art Centre and the production of the Vorticist manifesto *Blast*. The war came. The London Group survived as a semi-official body but its mildly French, mildly realist legacy was not good for much excitement in an age when excitement meant growth and development. Edward le Bas proved a notable and underestimated descendant and the Group's spirit did make a distinctive re-appearance in the late 1930s with the Euston Road School, and the work of Coldstream, Rogers, Pasmore and Bell. We must remember, too, that this spirit informed the Slade School of Art throughout the period and so gave a humanist context to the academic training of many good painters. However, we must face the fact that of all this dedicated and serious strain in English painting only Sickert, Gwen John and Bevan command much respect today, and they are internationally underestimated.

Roger Fry was not wrong in intuiting an English lack of response to plasticity, or to the presence of what his disciple Clive Bell called 'significant form'. The husband of Virginia Woolf's painter sister Vanessa Stephen, Clive Bell, was a nuclear figure of the Bloomsbury group of intellectuals, who provided England with a cultural establishment from about the middle of the First World War until the early 1930s. (Henry Lamb [1883–1960] both celebrated and caricatured this movement in his gigantic drooping portrait of another pivotal figure of the group, Lytton Strachey [p. 299].) The phrase 'significant form' denotes the aesthetic theory Bell published in his

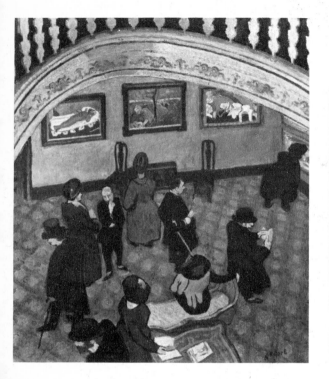

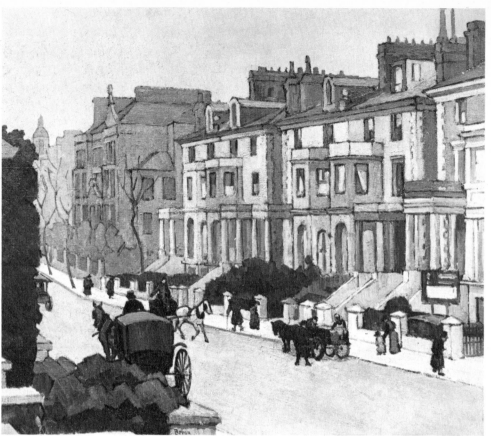

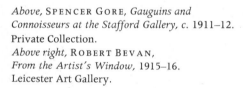

Above, SPENCER GORE, *Gauguins and
Connoisseurs at the Stafford Gallery*, c. 1911–12.
Private Collection.
Above right, ROBERT BEVAN,
From the Artist's Window, 1915–16.
Leicester Art Gallery.

book *Art*. Bell found that in every work of art lines and colours combine in a particular
way, so that 'certain forms and relations of forms stir our aesthetic emotions. These
relations and combinations of lines and colours, these aesthetically moving forms, I
call "significant form", and "significant form" is the one quality common to all forms
of visual art.'

The theory owes something to Jung's psychology and would appear to localize the
visual imprints of experience: consider what shapes, colours and lines flash before
the mind's eye at the drop of words like sun, sea, tree, building. It is close, too, to
Cézanne's insistence that Nature must be treated through a lens of forms: cylinder,
sphere, cone. As Wyndham Lewis said, any faithful discipleship of that master was
sure to be sound art. The formula looks forward to an altogether abstract painting
which in England we associate with Ben Nicholson in the 1930s, with William Scott
and Roger Hilton in the 1950s, and with Richard Smith or John Walker at the
present time. But at the beginning, no painter connected with the Bloomsbury group,
except perhaps Duncan Grant (b. 1885), the most considerable, took significant
form to any significant conclusion. In the British story of what Stephen Spender calls
the struggle of the modern, we feel the shaping spirit of restraint at work and the
presence of the responsible rather than the prodigal eye.

The Post-Impressionist revolution in England was diluted, if that word can be
used for pronouncements so astringent, by the views of Sickert (1860–1942). His
personality as wit and teacher, almost as much as his work, lours over the first two
decades of the century. Herbert Read has put the position neatly:

> Conservative critics (not to be confused with academic critics, who are not so perceptive)
> usually regard Sickert as the greatest painter we have produced in England since Turner.
> Radical critics like Roger Fry and Clive Bell, while full of appreciation for a painter who could
> so successfully transplant the art of Degas, and whose genius was always harmoniously
> evident, nevertheless had to point out that the rejection of Cézanne by Sickert and his friends
> was a decisive act of suicide.

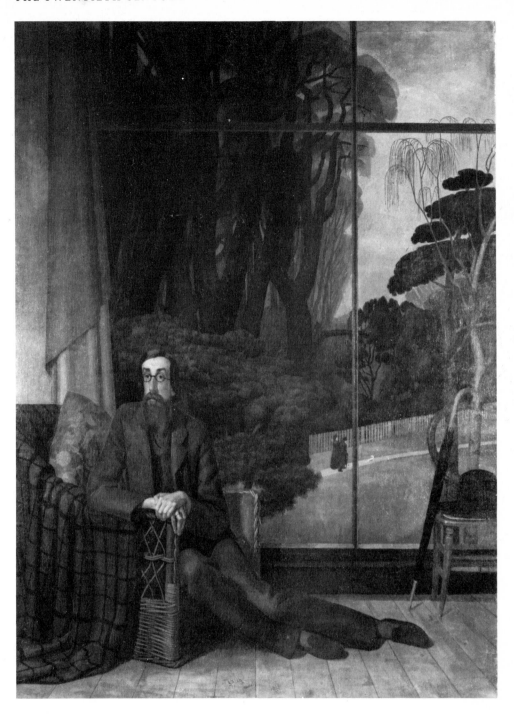

HENRY LAMB, *Lytton Strachey*, 1914.
The Tate Gallery, London.

Yet of the English painters whose careers spanned the Impressionist, Post-Impressionist and Modernist movements in France, Sickert was most European in background. He was born in Munich and his father was Danish. From 1900 to 1905, the period of the Dieppe paintings, he lived in France. He was a close friend of Degas, the painter whose achievement most powerfully claimed him. Indeed, his angle of vision on the movements of his time rather parallels that of Degas: interested, sceptical, loyal to sense as well as sensibility. It was not, for instance, that Sickert was unimpressed by Cézanne and his followers. Fry's showing of the Post-Impressionists excited him, but, as he himself pointed out, it was only six or seven years since he had, in a limited way, adapted to their predecessors. Typically, his excitement in no way modified his English, empirical idea of the social as well as the technical duties of painting. His review of the Fry exhibition aimed at making

299

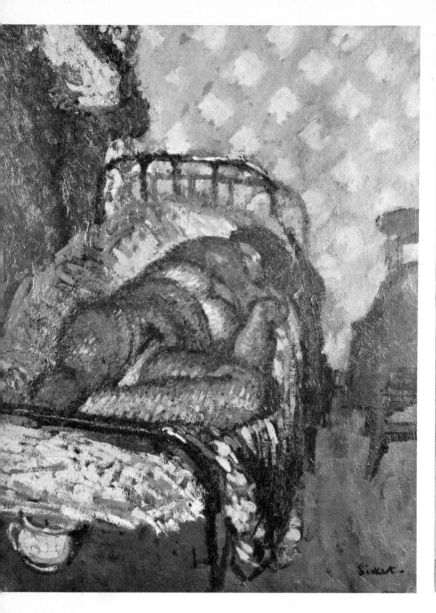

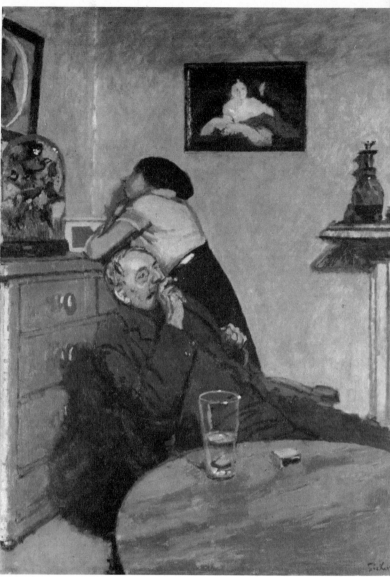

Above, WALTER RICHARD SICKERT,
L'Affaire de Camden Town.
Newcastle-upon-Tyne University.
Collection of Mr Fred Uhlman.
Above right, WALTER RICHARD SICKERT,
Ennui, c. 1913–14.
The Tate Gallery, London.

mincemeat of the colour revolution in general and Matisse in particular. Like Wyndham Lewis, Sickert was a natural writer. But with Sickert there is ambivalence between the wit and exuberance of his writings and the sobriety both of his painter's style and the judgments which stemmed from it.

Ten good years followed Sickert's return from France in 1905. Gore, Gilman, Bevan and others such as Charles Ginner were painting London scenes during this period. Moderate as were their ambitions, they did use colour in a Post-Impressionist manner: to break into the old divisions of light and dark and regroup planes and perspectives. Sickert's Camden Town interiors rank among the most important English paintings of any time, but they are dark-toned and thickly painted. An immense weight is added to Whistler's somewhat arty mistiness and to Degas's feeling for the way the human figure displaces light around it. These nudes and bedscapes are at the edge of what we call Expressionism. They have left their mark on the work of Francis Bacon, Sickert's rival for the laurels of English painting after Turner.

The culmination of Sickert's Camden Town period is the five-version *Ennui,* a work that is modern more in the direction of Sigmund Freud than of Cézanne. For the 'literary' character of the work is also the formal one. Features and gestures, furniture and clothing – all dispose themselves in room and on canvas in such a way as to make a human universal clean to the eye. The ennui and alienation of late nineteenth-century intellectuals has now taken hold of the urbanized lower middle class. This is a paint-

300

ing of statement, in the sense we have associated with Piero and Rembrandt and in the modern period with Seurat. It is literary only in this wide sense, though a recent commentator, John Raymond, has wittily suggested that it offers us a chapter of an unwritten Gissing novel. 'I have always been a literary painter, like all decent painters, do be the first to say so.' Thus Sickert, knowing her Fry affiliations, teased Virginia Woolf. Even in his last decade, when the work was in relative decline, Sickert could produce the Victor Lecour portrait and the self-portrait called *Lazarus breaks his Fast*. Ironically, both these paintings fall more in the Fry court than anything produced by an enemy of Fry like Wyndham Lewis or a friend like Duncan Grant. Indeed Grant only ever rivals Sickert in some of the early, and little known, male nudes. Sickert also survived when some of the most promising younger painters, the water-colourist J.D. Innes for example, did not. He was simply too good a painter, his personal dynamo too dynamic, for most painters who came near him to counter his judgments.

Sickert's exact contemporary, Philip Wilson Steer (1850–1942), rivalled and even surpassed him as an English impressionist in the last years of the nineteenth century. But for all the prestige he maintained, Steer fell back on a pre-Impressionist, even pre-Turner treatment of landscape, in the twentieth. (A national leaning towards nostalgia is the great enemy of art in England.) So of the generation who followed, only Gwen John had the intensity, Augustus John the range and Matthew Smith the sheer painterly application to break away.

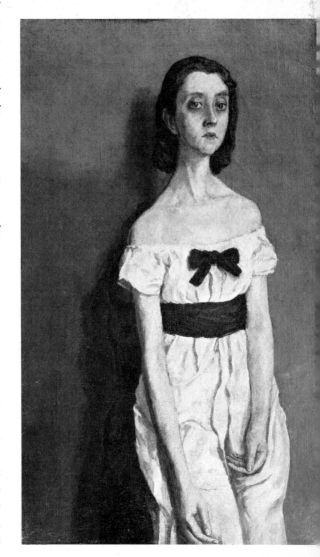

Gwen John (1876–1939) is a maverick artist and a great one, the Emily Dickinson of painting. She was somewhat isolated, both in person and reputation. She lived a great deal in France but her small output made little public mark there or in England. Like Sickert she was a pupil of Whistler, whose life classes she attended in Paris from 1898 to 1900. The draughtsmanship critical to her obsessive outlook was developed at the Slade. (Henry Tonks, who became the most notable teacher there, had the courage of his bad taste to say, at the time of Roger Fry's death, that from the point of view of British painting he felt as though Hitler and Mussolini had passed away.) Another influence on Gwen John was Rodin, whom she knew and modelled for; the move to France, effectively her home until her death in 1939, was governed by her wish to be near him. She was a friend, too, of the German poet Rilke, but her own life was generally self-contained and self-neglectful.

A fascinating account of the way Gwen John made notes for a painting has been given by Mary Taubman. She would prepare her own canvas and had a system of numbering tones. These notes

are a strange confusion of the scientific and the intuitive. A typical extract is: 'road 32, roof 13 and 23, black coats 33,' etc., and a little later: 'Harmonies of colour: *gueul de loop* and autumn leaves. Garlic (and its blue-black leaves) faded primroses and straw.' There is a sort of formula headed 'The making of the portrait'. It begins: '1. the strange form. 2. the pose and proportions. 3. the atmosphere and notes. 4. the finding of the forms'; and another: 'Method of observation: 1. the strangeness. 2. colour. 3. tones. 4. form or even Rule 1: The drawing is the discord.'

It is arguable that some aspects of Post-Impressionism – the flattening of contours, the increasing concern with surface pattern – were absorbed into Gwen John's work. But really everything she painted bears the imprint both of orthodoxy and idiosyncracy. The pleasure she gives is rather like that of the Italian master of still-life, Morandi; one sees a familiar and repeated subject and a seemingly familiar treatment continually turned to peculiar use. Now that the social role of women has, for the second time this century, been brought into high relief, it is good to record that the best modern woman painter was British. But like Emily Dickinson in poetry, Gwen John affected the course of events little. Perhaps her only contemporary follower is

301

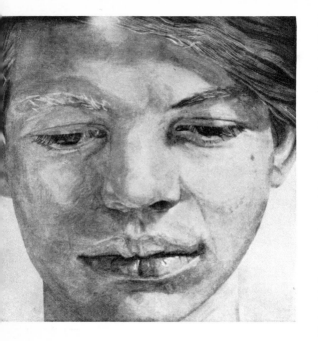

LUCIAN FREUD, *Head of a Boy*, 1954.
Collection of the Hon. Garech Browne.

MATTHEW SMITH, *Nude,
Fitzroy Street No. 1*, 1916.
The Tate Gallery, London.

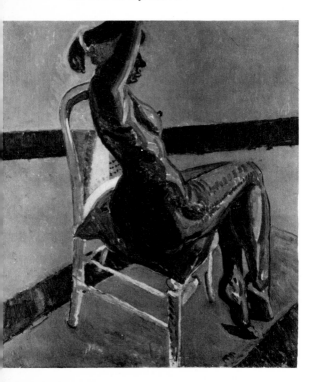

Lucian Freud (b. 1922). Freud shares some of her obsessiveness but there is not much resemblance in technique, and he owes more to Northern artists like Van der Weyden, Memling and Cranach than to anything in the French tradition. Where both these English painters are concerned, however, we may guess that consistency and intensity will guarantee their surviving the passage of successive international styles.

Gwen John's younger brother Augustus John (1878–1961) was more fashionable in their lifetime, less so now. His fluency, particularly in drawing, was in his own time legendary. But legends which grow up during a man's life, especially when, like John's, they are attached also to a flamboyant personality, can be stilled with his death. It is possible that the present low estimation of John is a quirk of our own time. He certainly added to the great English tradition of portraiture and his work before 1912 is often said to be 'Post-Impressionist without knowing it'. But John has perhaps more talent than intelligence; there is a softness to his work which compares ill with his sister's passionate logic.

North Country to her Welsh, Matthew Smith (1879–1959) followed Gwen John in spending much of his working life in France. Smith studied briefly under Matisse and he was the first English painter to follow the Fauves in making a discipline of colour freedom. Two important early paintings – the *Lilies* of 1913–14 and the first Fitzroy Street *Nude* of 1916 – establish him as the greatest colourist of the early modern period in Britain. Colour is drawing here as in no other contemporary. In the early 1920s Smith developed what Richard Morphet has called his succulent style. The paint is thickly applied and creamy; the colours are at once dark and fire-bright, like embers or velvet; the forms are written rather than drawn and have a chancy character, more Expressionist than Fauve. Francis Bacon wrote in 1953 that Smith

seems to be one of the very few English painters since Constable and Turner to be concerned with painting, that is, with attempting to make idea and technique inseparable. Painting in this sense tends towards a complete interlocking of image and paint, so that the image is the paint and vice versa. Consequently, every movement of the brush on the canvas alters the shape and implications of the image. That is why real painting is a mysterious and continuous struggle with chance – mysterious because the very substance of the paint, when used in this way, can make such a direct assault upon the nervous system; continuous, because the medium is so fluid and subtle that every change that is made loses what is already there in the hope of making a fresh gain. I think that painting today is pure intuition and luck and taking advantage of what happens when you splash the bits down, and in this game of chance Matthew Smith seems to have the gods on his side.

Perhaps Matthew Smith does not quite live up to the lucidity of this praise, for if he struggled with chance where his medium was concerned his imagination plays more safely. Flowers, fruit, the female nude, the Provençal or Cornish landscape swap visual references with each other throughout a working lifetime. While there is much to be grateful for in such zealous pursuit of sensual ease there does remain something safe about Matthew Smith – certainly by comparison with David Bomberg, say, or with Bacon himself. And although it was Sickert who first recognised the will to 'make idea and technique inseparable' in Smith's painting, he is really the Fry painter *par excellence*: the grand apostle (in Fry's phrase) of the functional as opposed to the ornamental role played by colour; a European artist who lent northern psychological expressiveness to the Parisian truth to form.

Grand apostle as he may have been, Matthew Smith was not a pathfinder in the field of colour exploration. Here the honours go to Scotland.

In the early years of the century a second wave of Scottish colourists appeared, the first being the late-Victorian Glasgow School associated with William McTaggart and George Henry. The latter was one of the most advanced artists of his day and his best work is in the style we associate with Pont-Aven, the small town in Brittany which

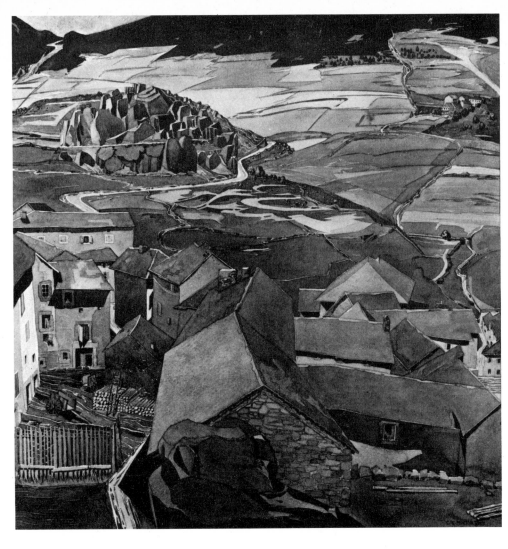

C.R. MACKINTOSH,
The Village of La Lagonne (watercolour).
Glasgow Art Gallery Collection.

attracted many artists but won its 'School' status through Gauguin's visits. Henry experimented with the influential Japanese style: rhythmic brush stroke substituted for analytic line, figures silhouetted against surfaces of pure colour. But S.J.Peploe (1871–1935), Leslie Hunter (1877–1931) and F.C.B. Cadell (1883–1937) became known as colourists on the strength of their work in the years 1910 to 1914. J.D. Ferguson (1874–1961), like Duncan Grant a Scottish-born artist working outside Scotland, impressed even the *Salon d'Automne* with his skill: Manet done over from the Fauves.

Thus while the Fry exhibition was causing its London furore, Scottish artists were producing paintings which, in terms of colour, were closely in sympathy with advanced French painting. Too closely perhaps. Cadell later embarked on a few middle-class roomscapes which show the same feeling for the oddness of the mundane as the American painter Edward Hopper say, or, in the present decade, David Hockney. The others did not make such headway, in spite of their early responsiveness to colour. Ferguson produced fine sculpture, and landscapes not unlike the excellent (and forgotten) advertising posters of the then railway companies. Peploe stayed close to the Cézanne of soup bowls and flowers but is usually less interesting on still life than his fellow Scot, Anne Redpath. Perhaps the greatest Scots artist was not a painter at all but the architectural and designing genius, C.R. Mackintosh (1868–1928).

Mention of Mackintosh brings the first phase of the struggle of the modern in Britain to an end, and on a sour note. One of the great intellectual and social failures of the Edwardian period was the missed chance of building an aesthetic on *Jugendstil*, in this country often known as *Art Nouveau*. *Jugendstil* has been criticised for the ease with which style can slide into stylisation; anyone can pick up its decorative tricks and adapt them to trivial or second-hand aims. But the same could be said of the stylistic orthodoxy which did, later on, take hold. Simplifications in concrete of the ideas informing the work of the German Bauhaus group or of Le Corbusier in France have helped to make visual wastelands of almost every city in the world. *Jugendstil* was the last tradition on a human scale, with a place for decoration as fantasy, and it is not for nothing that we still see it cropping up in the clothes and graphics of young people upset by the mechanical impersonality of modern design. Britain's contribution to the style was formative and unusual; both Aubrey Beardsley and Mackintosh used it as a milieu for their differing genius. But the impetus petered out into stylishness and illustration. We associate it often with the fairy story illustrations of Arthur Rackham and Edmund Dulac, or the less well remembered Samuel Sime. Wyndham Lewis, Fry's rival as an apostle of modern art, had nothing to say for a style which he connected exclusively with decoration. Lewis's detestation of 'the monster decoration', however, did not prevent him from being aware of the fusion that took place between *Jugendstil*'s concern for surface pattern and rhythm, and Cézanne's contriving out of Impressionism something (in his own phrase) 'solid and durable like the art of the museums'. The fusion was part accidental, part conscious creation. It is everywhere present in Cubism. Cubism, the most complete artistic revolution since the Renaissance, naturally became the most influential of twentieth-century modes of painting. Its effects in England constitute, therefore, a major episode in our artistic history.

Historically, Cubism is the art which was inaugurated by Picasso and Braque about 1908; practised by them, with many extensions and modifications, until about 1920; and which determined, as the practice was taken up in France and then internationally, a new classical or formalist art. Aesthetically, it followed Cézanne in a commitment to the painting as a tangible reality, its own subject and its own first cause. Philosophically, it provided an equivalent to that dizzying revision of procedures which was taking place in the world of science, particularly in the world of physics.

The story of this international style in Britain is complex and most versions are misleading. It is also an unlucky story, for the British contribution is often passed over. The monumental exhibition of Cubism held in Los Angeles and New York in 1971 omitted the idiosyncratic and important achievement of Wyndham Lewis (1882 –1957) and David Bomberg (1890–1957). Nor, of course, were their associates included. Frederick Etchells (b. 1886), Lawrence Atkinson (1873–1931) and Edward Wadsworth (1889–1947) could all have merited inclusion, and so particularly could the American-born Epstein, and the French exile, Henri Gaudier-Brzeska. The omissions are perhaps the posthumous fault of Wyndham Lewis (1882–1957), for if he was the mentor of Cubism in England his frequent critical attacks on the movement have created the bewilderment his difficult soul appears to have wanted.

T.S. Eliot called Lewis 'the most fascinating personality of our time'. His personality still remains, fifteen years after his death, an obstacle to his assessment: there is something of the permanent contemporary about Lewis. He lived, both as writer and artist, in the exhausting situation of being discovered, neglected, rediscovered and neglected again. Until recently his reputation was set in a niche of historical rather than aesthetic significance. He appeared condemned to lengthy paragraphs in brief surveys. But enough time has now passed to begin to see him whole. He was the champion, in works and words, of the importance of being absolutely modern and absolutely English at the same time. He was the opponent of Roger Fry who nevertheless celebrated, in immoderate and shining language, the humanist centre to the forms of art. He was a fine draughtsman, and a minor painter who found a way to transform intellect and will into rhythms as distinctive as a master's. In a last contradiction, he was a quarrelsome egotist able to trap others' personality in carbon and oil. The overriding sense in all his work is one of impatience working upon intellect – the mind racing ahead of the fingers' feel for raw materials. Whenever the crayon is at hand, his plasticity comes out. Drawings of the Vorticist period have the heavy satisfaction of woodcuts (Wadsworth, indeed, produced some of his best work in this medium). This feeling for line goes with a polemic insistence on subject. In the early and most abstract period his subject, crucial still, is the imagination of cities and all their diagram knowledge. Lewis was acutely conscious of the dichotomy between the made and the manufactured. He wrote that the

> attempt to avoid all representative element is . . . absurdity. As much of the material poetry of Nature as the plastic vessel will stand should be included. But nowadays, when Nature finds itself expressed so universally in specialized mechanical counterparts, and cities have modified our emotions, the plastic vessel, paradoxically, is more fragile. The less human it becomes, the more delicate, from this point of view.

The strength and delicacy of the ink, crayon and watercolour *Composition in Blue*, reproduced here, is a perfect equivalent to this insight. Lewis's later work – portraits and portrait drawings, forays into a surrealism contrasting natural and man-made forms – is always of interest. But his greatest work was pre-1920. The First World War affected both his humanism and his patriotism. It therefore drove him from his commitment to an English art which was to be at once modernist and nationalistic.

Wyndham Lewis first exhibited with the Camden Town Group and his *Timon of Athens* drawings were included in Roger Fry's second Post-Impressionist Exhibition. In 1913 he joined Fry's Omega workshops – 'Mr Fry's curtain and pincushion factory in Fitzroy Square' as he later referred to it, in a splenetic attack on decoration and the 'vegetable' heresy implicit in Romantic ideas of organic art. He broke away almost immediately, taking Etchells, Cuthbert Hamilton and Wadsworth with him; the next year he founded his own Rebel Art Centre in Great Ormond Street. In October 1913 he exhibited at Frank Rutter's Post-Impressionist and Futurist exhibition at the Doré galleries. It was Lewis and C.R. Nevinson (1889–1946) who welcomed the Italian Futurist leader, Marinetti, when he came to London to promote his movement. Once again, repudiation followed and there was heckling at Futurist meetings. Lewis easily uncovered in Futurism 'the Melodrama of Modernity' as he put it, and he had shrewd antennae for Marinetti's 'automobilism and Nietzsche stunt'. But in establishing Vorticism (the name came from the American expatriate poet Ezra Pound), Lewis to some extent followed the Futurist's adaptation of Cubism to urban-mechanical endeavours. He shared, too, their taste for dynamic images as against the Cubist Masters' choice of still-life.

Lewis's small mixed media compositions (many paintings of this period have been lost) and Bomberg's larger oils have the Futurist vigour of movement. But this movement looks shaped, not faked: shaped by the action of eye and arm and not, as in Futurism, by a sort of time-exposure of the subject, external to the picture itself. The drama of the vortex lies in the intersection, and occasionally the collision of compositional lines. There is always a lively clash between means and ends. We may relate this clash to the modern city, and the visual interactions of everyday experience. In a city, sky segments appear and disappear as street perspectives dictate; swaths of building are stitched together by networks of road or railway; architecture's stillness alternates with human flurry. Bomberg's great canvas of 1913–14, *The Mud Bath* (p. 296), makes a composition of just such a contrast. In the least debased sense it is a significant painting: a sign for the time. There is the age's hankering for 'Pure Form', as well as for what Bomberg himself thought of as structure in terms of colour, Cézanne's legacy. Yet a human event is also taking place, for the painting re-experiences some moment at a Jewish Steam Bath in Whitechapel. The result is an exceptional completeness, an emotional seizure rendered in the tranquillity of pure colour. Not until the great Matisses of two or three years later – *The Moroccans*, in the

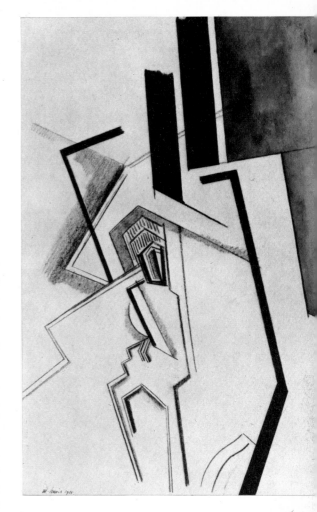

PERCY WYNDHAM LEWIS,
Composition in Blue, 1915.
Anthony d'Offay Gallery.
By courtesy of Mrs Wyndham Lewis.

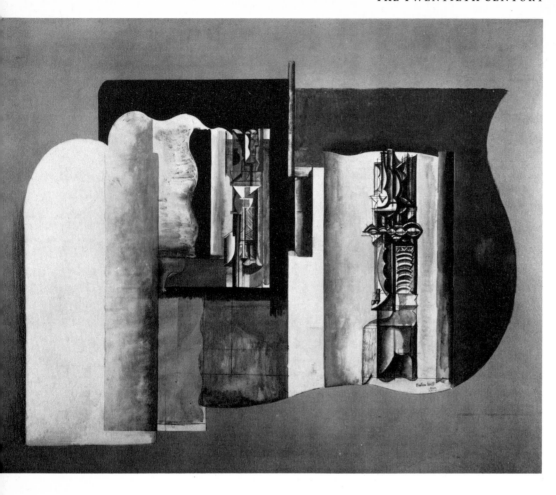

PERCY WYNDHAM LEWIS,
Abstract Composition, 1921.
Private collection.

Museum of Modern Art in New York for instance – are the colour and cubist revolutions put to such human and aesthetic use. Another Bomberg of the same period, *In the Hold,* shares with Wyndham Lewis's *The Crowd* (1914) an intuition that the twentieth-century city is agent and patient of twentieth-century war. As the Vorticist magazine *Blast* said in its second (and last) issue: 'Wars begin with this huge indefinite Internment in the cities.' Thus Bomberg and Wyndham Lewis found unique ways of pointing out the appropriateness, for modern life, of the new art.

The crux of modernity, for Lewis, was the bankruptcy of nature as subject or source and the urgent need to build, as Mondrian and Kandinsky were building, a visual language as abstract as music. But so far as the plastic arts were concerned, he spent more energy saying than doing. The interest in Marshall McLuhan's critical formulations, and McLuhan's acknowledged debt to Lewis, have alerted us to Lewis's outstanding criticism. His achievement as a painter also needs public attention.

In 1961, William Roberts (b. 1895), in one of the century's few examples of a conversation piece, painted a small watercolour called *The Vorticists at the Restaurant de la Tour Eiffel: Spring 1915.* Among those remembered were Cuthbert Hamilton, Roberts himself, Frederick Etchells, Edward Wadsworth and of course Wyndham Lewis. We may add to this list David Bomberg, Lawrence Atkinson, the work, until this point in time, of the sculptor Jacob Epstein and the drawings and pastels as well as the sculptures of Henri Gaudier-Brzeska, killed in action the same year. The cast is then complete for the most dramatic incursion into European modernism made by Englishmen in this century. It was a brief incursion but impressive: a small group of artists producing between 1905 and 1916 an abstract constructive art which, like Mondrian's work or the constructivism of Russian Revolutionary art at the end of the decade, was Cubist derived but altogether different in aim and emphasis.

306

The war put an end to the Vorticist movement by dispersing its members. English modernism became provincial again. This fact, as can be seen in the case of L.S. Lowry (b. 1887), is not in itself depressing. The provincial who either does not recognise himself as such, or does not care, may be in a position to produce great things. Danger heads for the less idiosyncratic artist: one who needs a lively atmosphere of criticism and exchange in which to flower. Without this atmosphere his work may become at once eccentric and tentative, a bad combination and unfortunately an English one. Then again, eccentricity, as in the case of William Roberts's later career, may provide a protective mannerist cover, guaranteeing survival perhaps, but allowing little in the way of exploration or development.

Had Lewis been less isolated from Europe as well as from attentive criticism, such canvases as *Archimedes Reconnoitring the Enemy Fleet* (1922), *Three Sisters* (1927), as well as the better known *Surrender of Barcelona* (1937) would have kept him in the van of the international movements which grew out of the war: Dada and Surrealism. Half-dream, half-machine men, creatures whom one could introduce to Duchamp and Max Ernst, these visually logical beings, as he called them, crowd his paintings. The English talent for line combines with Cubist lessons of spatial organisation to keep them in strict and most satisfying control. They appear to have had considerable influence on the later paintings of Sutherland. As with Sutherland, weakness lies in seldom combining the image-making, linear skill with attention, such as we find in Rouault, to the stuff of paint itself, and all that that implies for the twentieth-century achievement.

This characteristically English fault was kept at bay by David Bomberg, which makes the current international ignorance of his work hard to understand. Kept at bay only because in massiveness and contour his achievement resembles a weightlifter's dumb-bell: the thin bar between the great early and late periods supports painstaking topographical studies, particularly in and around Jerusalem. Bomberg's Jewishness

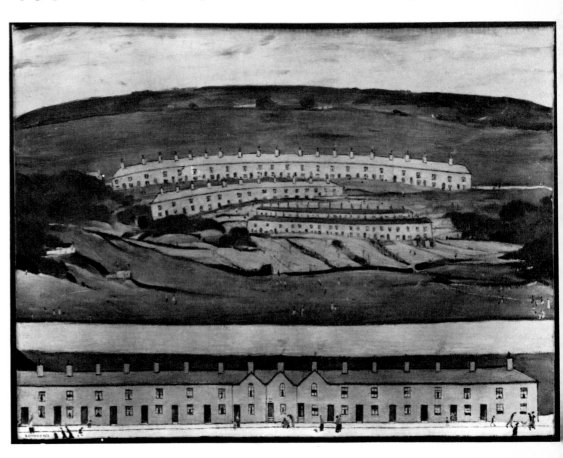

L.S. LOWRY, *Hillside in Wales*, 1962.
The Tate Gallery, London.

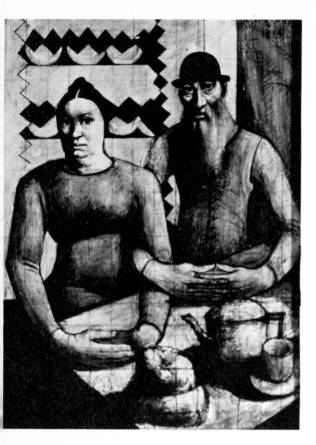

Above, MARK GERTLER, *Rabbi and Rabbitzen,* 1914.
Private collection.
Right, WILLIAM ROBERTS, *The Cinema,* 1920.
The Tate Gallery, London.

was critical to him. Here he resembles the talented but forlorn Mark Gertler (1891–1937), or more recently Bomberg's pupil Leon Kossoff. In the 1930s Bomberg painted in Spain and his style became harsher and freer. *Toledo from the Alcazar* (1929), by means of the attention it brings to the action of the brush, is as personal and emotive as El Greco's Toledo landscape. It adds to the latter that consciousness of mass which the moderns derive from Courbet. David Sylvester has written that 'the thing his early and late achievements have in common is the bigness of their form, the energy it encloses'. This gets the point of Bomberg. The fate of his reputation is part of the continuing history of English painting.

Wyndham Lewis and Bomberg were the first and last initiators in the early modern phase of British painting of this century. The experience of war with Lewis, loss of artistic nerve as well as war with Bomberg, saw to it that a distinctively British type of highly referential and symbol-employing abstraction did not take hold. Both men went their own ways and neither again in his lifetime enjoyed a critical atmosphere equal to his talent or intelligence. The war itself rearranged experience in a decisive way for most of the other English abstractionists. The stern classicism of T.E. Hulme's

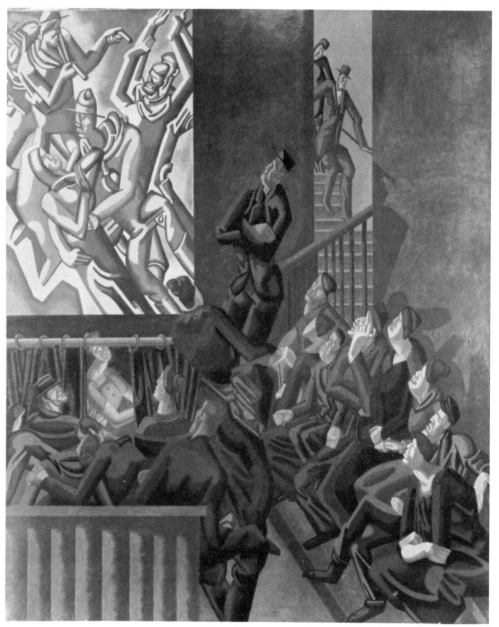

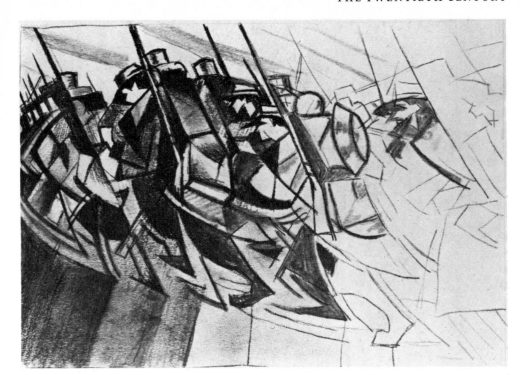

C.R.W. NEVINSON, Study for
'Returning to the Trenches', 1914–15.
The Tate Gallery, London.

guiding philosophy of forms yielded a little to the knowledge of what people were
actually going through at the Front. William Roberts has admitted that the war turned
him away from total abstraction and from the time of this conversion to the present he
has been concerned – again in considerable, if somewhat self-imposed isolation –
with exploiting tension between the spatial and social organization of his own
'visually logical' but decidedly recognisable beings. His colour sense is remarkable,
achieving a kind of sour brightness. C.R. Nevinson, who had opted for the Futurist
bandwagon, found that the angularity he had picked up from them and from Lewis,
was psychologically appropriate to the passivity and pain of men mobilised or
wounded by war. Unlike Roberts, his art did not survive the withdrawal, at the end
of the war, of a set of emotions appropriate to it. Generally, however, the war itself
was less important – in spite of important war paintings by Paul Nash and Stanley
Spencer – than the way it altogether revised the emotional climate of art.

The two artists who received most attention until the emergence of Ben Nicholson
were Paul Nash (1889–1946) and Stanley Spencer (1891–1959). Nash, as we shall see,
knowingly provided a link with the early and late phases of abstract art in England.
Spencer, although quite uninterested in the century's preoccupation with structure,
now looks the more modern – in the sense of absolutely original – of the two. A third
artist, Jack B. Yeats (1871–1951), the brother of the great Irish poet, was starting to
find his way. Like his brother, Yeats did his best work in the last decade or so of his life
and for this reason his work is usually considered alongside the painters of the 1950s.

Spencer's notorious innocence exists in odd relation to his skill at drawing. His
vision, which, like his personality, appears to have been arrested at adolescence, demanded a literal rather than an expressive outlet. This is perhaps because he remained
loyal to everything he had seen as a child and his childhood experience of art, from
reproductions only, kept to the early Flemish and Italian masters, the Pre-Raphaelites,
and the story-book graphics of Doré. He became the best draughtsman of his century
in Britain and one of the most original anywhere. In painting he is a heretic to the age,
since to him the act was essentially a chore, the hard labour needed to make larger and
more permanent things out of his sketchbook's swift intuitions. Yet he remains one
of the few English artists of any period able to work in large scale, or to suggest the

309

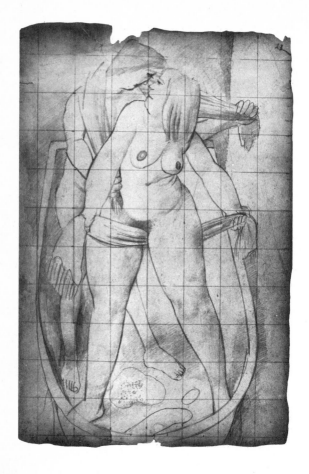

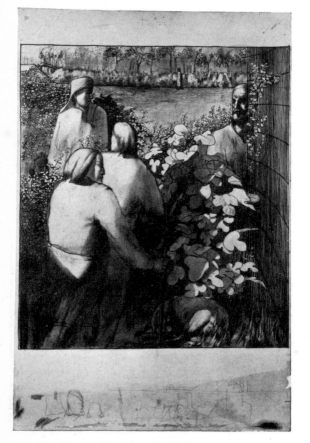

crowded complexes of society. In these elements he looks back to Hogarth and owes something to Frith and Greaves.

He grew up in Cookham, a conventionally pretty Thames-side village near Maidenhead. Until he was seventeen he had never been further than five miles from the village. He spent fifty of his sixty-eight years living there, though not consecutively. His art only interested him as a means of trapping, once and for all time, his certainty that Cookham and everything connected with it was as numinous as Jerusalem or Mecca (p. 293). Adapting George Borrow's title, we could say that Spencer painted *The Bible in Cookham*. His version is neither apostolic nor a simple transposition of sacred narrative. The religious feeling is more like Blake's, being a synthesis of sexual feeling and the imagination of place. But in Spencer both are earth-bound and utterly located. His New Jerusalem was the same thing as his Eden; even the Resurrection paintings have a kind of unexplosive gaiety, like the lower middle-class fêtes they are drawn from.

Spencer suffered money troubles and was a *de facto* bigamist. The landscapes and portraits he painted for money are as accurate and dull as he felt them to be; ironically these, with the uneven but more exciting First World War works, are the best known of his paintings. His essential work is his record of his childhood and adolescent intensity of vision, and the record of what happened to this vision when it was submitted, later in life than happens with most people, to the exigencies of his sexual nature. Because childhood and sex are lacking, the war resurrection mural at Burghclere does not have the intensity with which Spencer usually compensated for his formal deficiencies. Its best passages are those closest to his own experiences as an orderly. Spencer used drawing, as in letters and notebooks he uses writing, as the means of shaping the emotional experiences which shaped him. His complete work makes an astonishing story of what memory and desire have to do with the executive branch of the imagination.

This gives him kinship, as the Pre-Raphaelites have kinship, with the international Surrealist movement which grew up when Spencer was in mid-career. Yet in the end he is remote from it because Surrealism was essentially a deliberative movement: interested, in the modern way, in its own processes. As the Cubists had analysed the structure of painting, so the Surrealists reworked its moral and psychological components: a surreal poem about Cézanne, for instance, might have the apple gobble him up. Spencer has none of this psychic automatism. His inward eye always looked out. This may explain the over literal, gawky detail in nearly all his painting, its charm and irritation.

His achievement was too rich, however, to strait-jacket him as an English eccentric, full of nostalgia and linear ability. The great works of his early twenties, *Apple Gatherers, The Nativity, Zacharias and Elizabeth*, are modern work. It is clear, from *Swan Upping* (started 1914, completed 1919) that Spencer had learned from Cubism that displaced perspective was a legitimate compositional tool. Again, he chose to disregard this knowledge more often than to make use of it. Much depends, with Spencer, upon whether we judge him by his best work alone. If we do, he is an artist in the high sense of being in possession both of a unique vision and the means to convey it. The degree to which the uniqueness and urgency of the vision drove Spencer to neglect developing the means is the measure by which he suffers in comparison with the other great painter of Christian allegory in our era, Georges Rouault.

Spencer is paramount, in this century, in the tradition which holds that English painting is, above all, literary. In art criticism this usually denotes lack of what Bernard Berenson called 'tactile values': But it is not always useful to berate English art for not being in the French or Italian tradition. Spencer's uniqueness lies in the contrast between the private nature of his vision and the popularity lent it by his draughtsmanship. His large achievement also allowed interesting lesser painters like

Edward Burra (b. 1905) and Cecil Collins (b. 1908) to make their own idiosyncrasies available.

Literary inlay for the forms and procedures of painting is altogether different in the case of Paul Nash (p. 295). His career is a textbook of a real as well as an imagined struggle between the logic of painted forms and the dreams which underlie and underline them. Nash's work falls into obvious divisions. Before the First World War he was concerned with turning hallucinatory moments into illustrations. The symbols he chose – starry nights, foliage rhythmic and dense as Morris wallpaper, angels'

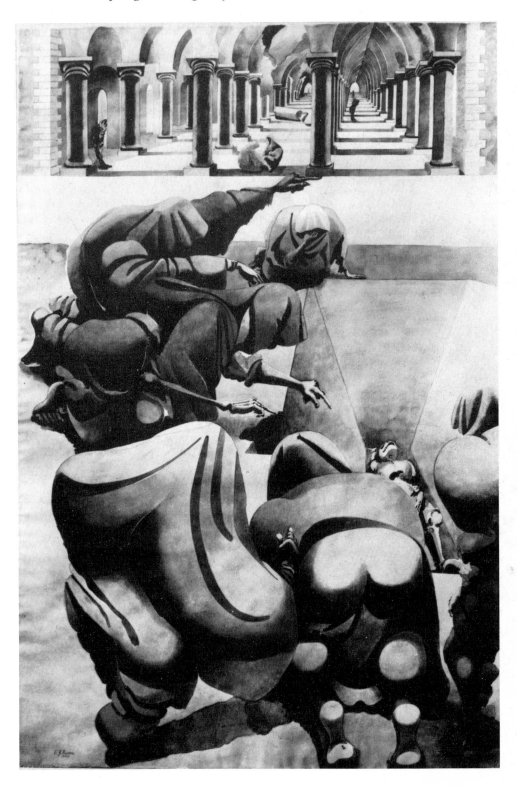

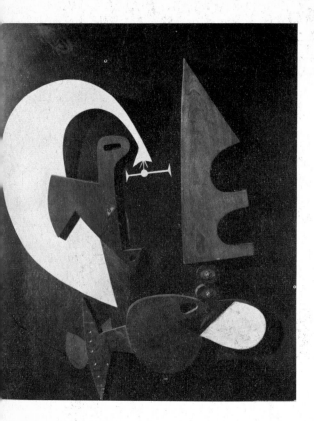

Above, CERI RICHARDS, *The Sculptor and his Model,* 1936.
Fischer Fine Art Limited.

heads from Rossetti or Burne-Jones – are *fin de siècle* and conventional enough. The gift for establishing mood right away, compositionally as much as by reference, is new and imposing. It was original, too, to resist the blandishments of neo-Impressionism at this time and, from the first, take up an English and romantic position. During the war he did a series of very rapid, mixed-media sketches of trench life and no-man's land. These establish him and point to his special gift for combining literal and symbolic accuracy without strain. Between the two wars he struggled with the post-cubist abstract-constructive movement which rivalled surrealism for the *avant-garde* laurel throughout the period. Works such as *Winter Sea* (1925–37) and *Landscape from a Dream* (1936–38) employ constructivist geometry to provide science fiction-like dislocations of time and space. There are picture-within-picture tricks, a tension between the ominous opposites of freedom and confinement. Some of these works are thinly painted and theatrical. They display that under-estimation of colour's spatial role which, except in the later landscapes, is always Nash's weakness. All the same, they are impressive. Nash was tackling a European as well as a provincial problem and he met it head on. This confrontation between the claims of ordering and ordered material, act and artefact, makes Nash a modern artist in the best sense: one who tackles his world. It also distinguishes his work from the craftsmanly but too derivative efforts of other British surrealists of the 1930s. Ceri Richards would be an admirable artist had one never encountered the work of Max Ernst; the theatre lighting of Tristram Hillier and the later Wadsworth has the monotony as well as the logic of other people's dreams.

The important thing, however, about Paul Nash's work of the middle period is that contact with the formal problems faced by constructivism and surrealism gave his late landscapes solidity as well as poetry. In our long landscape tradition, *Moon and Pillar* (1934–37) and the multi-version *Landscape of the Vernal Equinox* stand as masterpieces. 'Like Gainsborough,' Herbert Read has written, '. . . Paul Nash would collect and have about him a number of curious objects – strangely shaped stones, streaked pebbles, dried lichens, fragments of bark, crystals, pressed leaves – objects which served as stimulants to his imagination . . . . They would serve as referents of prototypes of natural forms . . .'. History, too, was a goldmine of the subconscious. Nash would contrast the relics of ancient settlements (the Avebury Circle in Wiltshire, for instance) with organic records in the form of fossils, or even with broken bulks of downed German bombers after the Battle of Britain. It is moving to remember that just at the time when Nash was mining the southern English landscape for correlatives of psychic experience, England herself was under attack. A war artist for the second time, Nash drew together Blake's poetic and Van Gogh's pictorial sunflower as a symbol for war's energetic drive towards renewal, as well as for its flaming destructiveness. These paintings rose to their occasion.

Like Nash, Jack Yeats was illustrational in his early works. Like Spencer, he illustrated a society, albeit a wider one than Cookham. Unlike either, he came to his visionary centre by means of the raw material he worked in. He is therefore the most European of the three. Yeats, though born in England, lived in Ireland nearly all his long life. He moved from reporting its fairs and sporting culture to a vision of what living at the edge of the old world might mean for life, landscape and art (p. 322). Welter of paint in a typical late work gives it the air, at first glance, of expressionism pushed to abstraction: Soutine going on Jackson Pollock. A second look shows that here colour has built landscape in the right way for the West of Ireland, all weather and movement, so that sea, sky and promontory exchange their shapes in flashes. A third and closer look reveals men and women in dancing attendance on this reality.

Yeats refused to allow his works to be seen in colour reproduction while he was alive, and this may have contributed to his not receiving in Britain the fame that went to Spencer and Nash. From the early days of the New York Armory Show (1913), how-

Opposite, ROGER HILTON, *Oi Yoi Yoi,* December 1963.
The Tate Gallery, London.

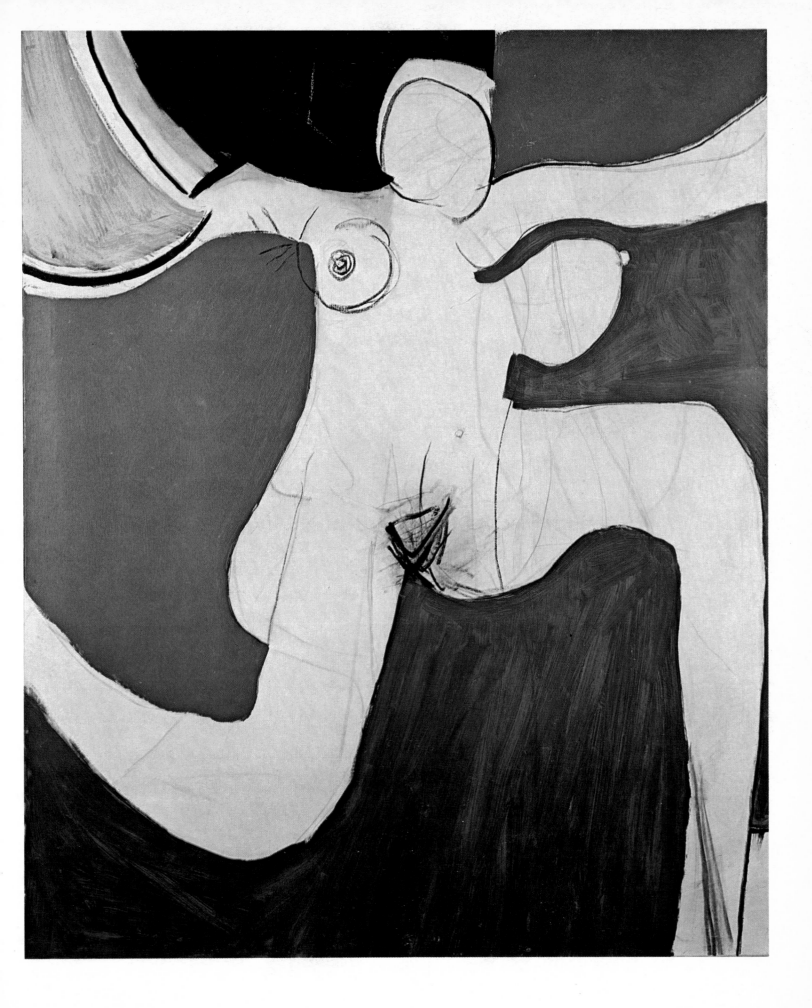

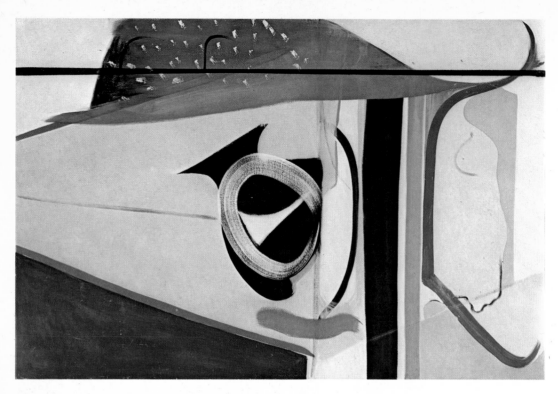

Left, PETER LANYON,
Clevedon Bandstand, 1964.
By permission of Mrs Peter Lanyon
and Gimpel Fils Ltd.
Below, VICTOR PASMORE, *Square Motif,*
Blue and Gold: the Eclipse, 1950.
The Tate Gallery, London.

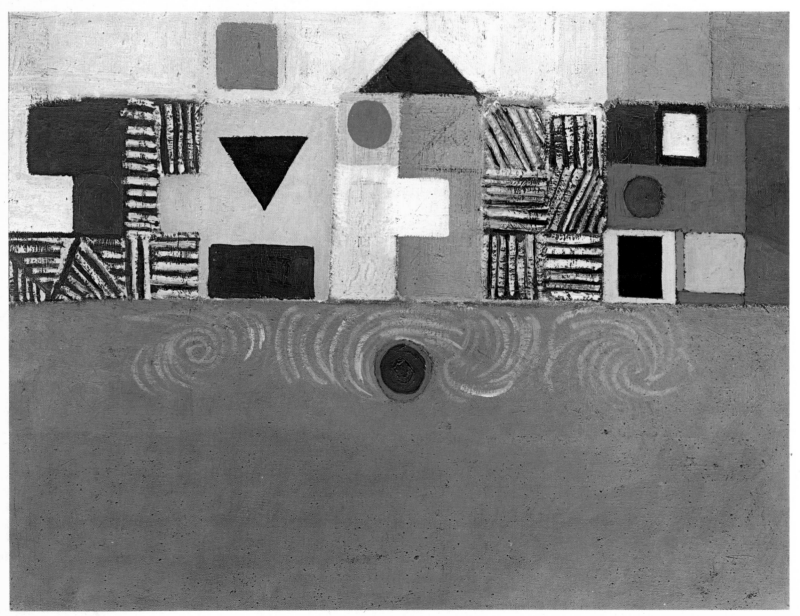

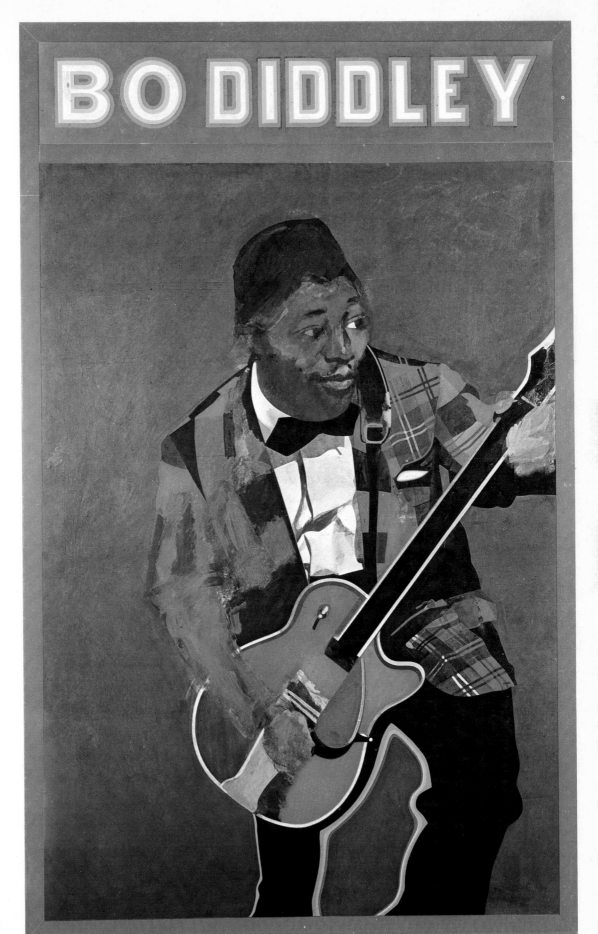

Right, PETER BLAKE, *Bo Diddley,* 1964–5.
Studio Marconi, Milan.

Overleaf, R. B. KITAJ, *ERIE SHORE*
(diptych), 1966.
By courtesy of Marlborough Fine Art
(London) Ltd.

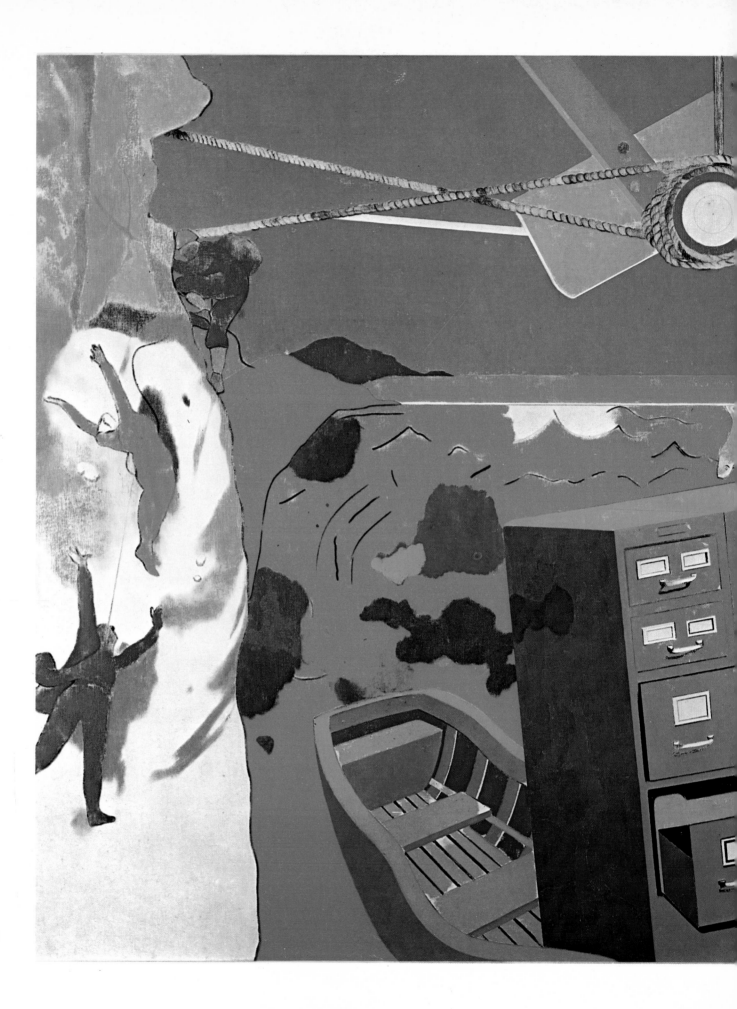

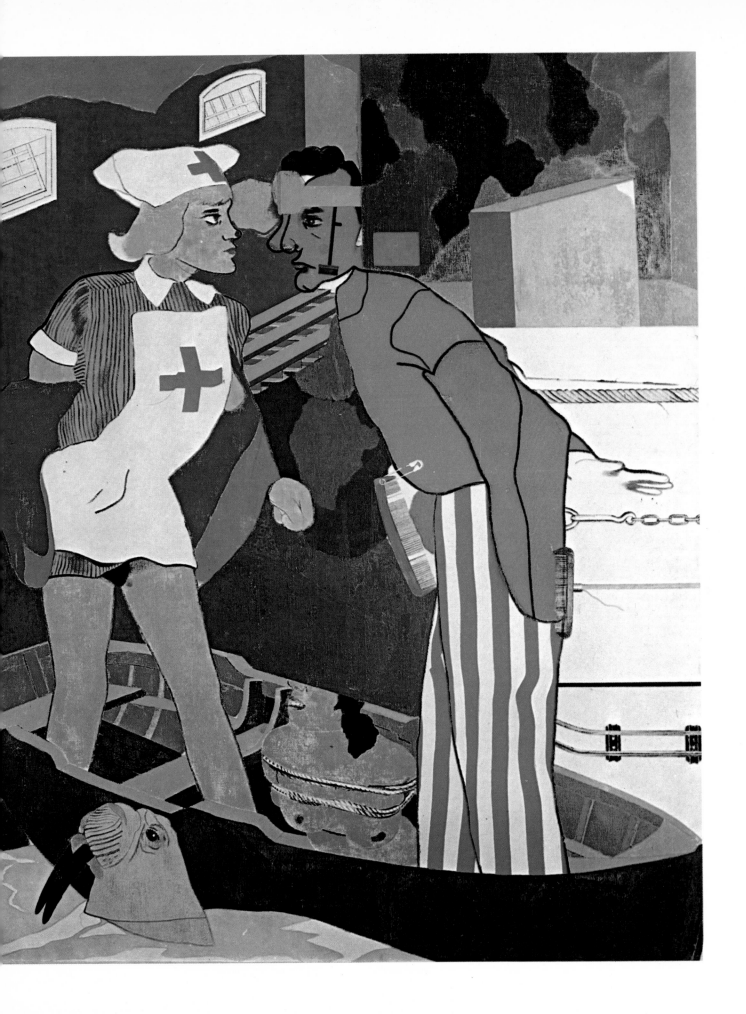

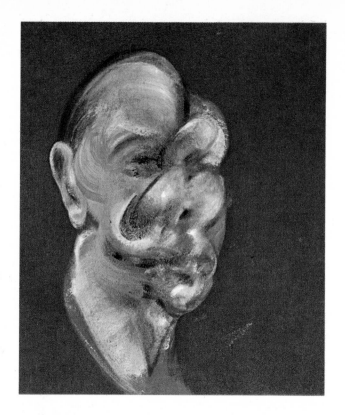
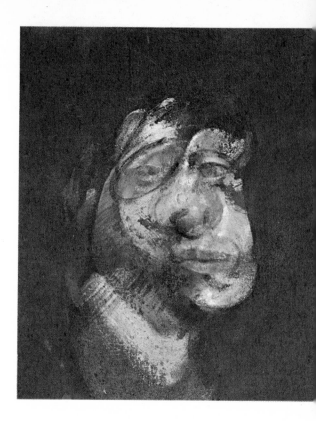
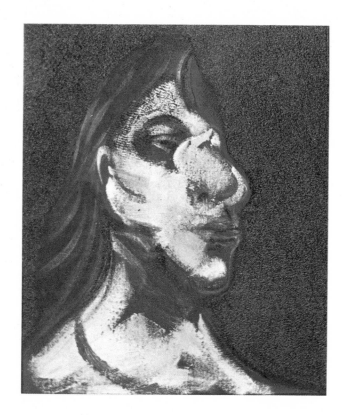
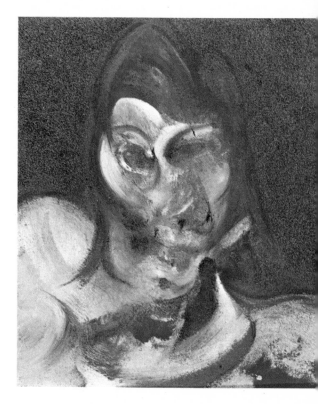

Top, FRANCIS BACON, *Study for
Three Heads,* 1962.
W. Paley Collection, New York.
Above, FRANCIS BACON, *Three Studies
for a Portrait of Henrietta Moraes,* 1963.
By courtesy of Marlborough Fine Art
(London) Ltd.

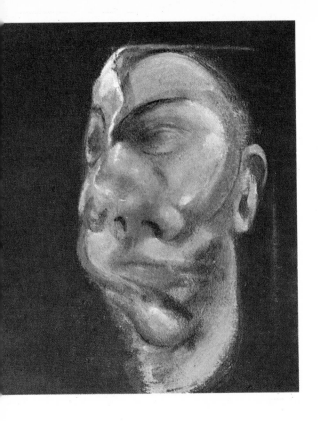

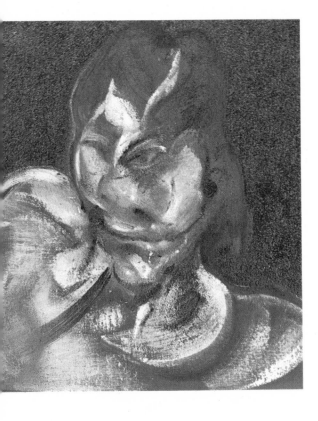

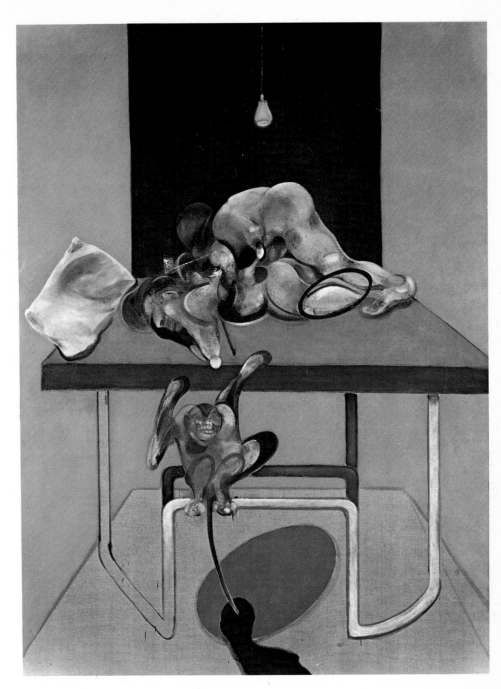

Above, FRANCIS BACON, *Two Figures with a Monkey,* 1973.
Collection of the Artist.

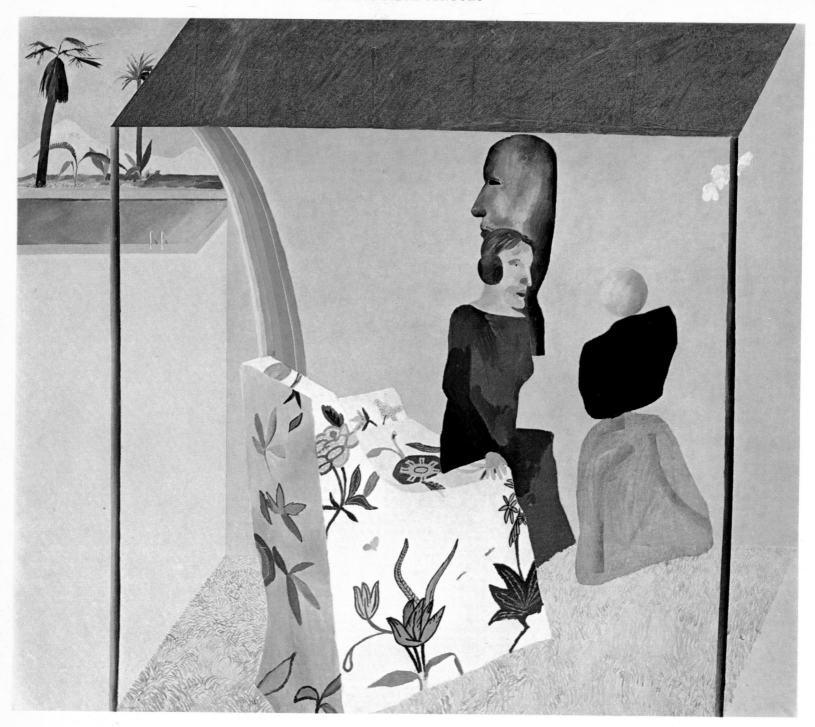

DAVID HOCKNEY, *California Art Collector*,
1964.
Collection: Mr and Mrs Denman Washington.
By courtesy of Kasmin Limited, London.

ever, he was recognized for the modern he was. In 1959 he attained the rare distinction for an artist from these islands of being created officer of the Légion d'Honneur. He appears to have had little influence, although two fine painters still maturing, Frank Auerbach (b1931) and Michael Wishart (b1928) owe something to him. And in their desire to render an isolated society both poetically and plastically, the modern Australian school shares his aim. Recent Irish painters have rejected, perhaps deliberately, Yeats's social and romantic comprehensiveness for something closer to the more classical and analytic paintings of William Orpen (1878–1931) during the First World War. Edward Maguire and Edward Plunkett are in differing ways formalist painters: Maguire building on the achievement of his teacher, Lucian Freud, to do remarkable things in portrait and still life; Plunkett, an expatriate, interested in the fruitful enduring contact between geometry and human perception. Derek Hill, also a fine portraitist, shares Yeats's fascination with the light and life of the Irish West. But Hill has gone back to pre-Impressionist French painting, Corot and Courbet especially, to render them.

Although literary and romantic Nash was alive to the move in the game which suggested that feeling was a matter for form: signs and shapes and colours being organically bound up with emotion. In 1933 he founded 'Unit One', an association of the painters, sculptors and architects, contributing, in England, to the international movement known as Constructivism. This movement was abstract in a geometric or structural way; we may associate it with a dry and tidy rather than a more liquid or messier style of painting. It held sway between the discovery of the Cubists' work, out of which it grew, and the return to an emotional and expressive abstraction just after the Second World War. (In various guises, of course, it is still very much alive. Hard-edge painting, minimal painting and sculpture, 'Op' and kinetic art all derive from it.) Through close links with architecture and design it had a tremendous effect on the appearance of the earth, perhaps more than any style in history. Locally, however, it is significant for four principal reasons. First, as we have seen, it provides a context within which to look at the brief and magnificent period of abstraction associated with Wyndham Lewis and Bomberg, Epstein and Gaudier-Brzeska. Second, it offered an alternative to the genteel survival of a post-Impressionism watered down as Impressionism had been watered down; to British academicism, in short, or the work of Sir Alfred Munnings and Paul Maze. Third, it was altogether interwoven with the achievements in the 1930s of Henry Moore, Barbara Hepworth, and of our first internationally respected painter in this century, Ben Nicholson. These three were instrumental in gaining for British artists that external attention which is necessary not just to self-esteem, but to criticism and the exchange of ideas. Finally, it provided artists and critics with coherent standards for making and judging. This provision, as the most recent decade demonstrates, still holds good.

Ben Nicholson (b1894) belongs to European history because in the 1930s he made an original contribution to abstract painting by edging it closer to sculpture than ever before. His marriage at this time to Barbara Hepworth is likely to have inspired some of his paintings in three-dimension or relief. His white paintings created space by carving entrances and exits for it. They are academic, in the sense that they demonstrate, as if in a lecture, the importance of structure, surface, balance and other concepts to the physical life of the work. But in this sense too they are modern; as we have seen, it is normal for theory to precede and inspire practice in abstract art. Because they are concerned with space, the freest form of all, their emotional effect is airy and liberated, this being in marked and marvellous contrast to the exactness with which they are made (pp. 294–5). It is the feature of interplay that is Nicholson's special talent. Interplay: not, as with Mondrian, inter-relation. For Nicholson's still-lives, with all their debt to the Cubist way of distributing forms about the surface of the canvas, are inherently playful. They are something like cartoons, in the Disney

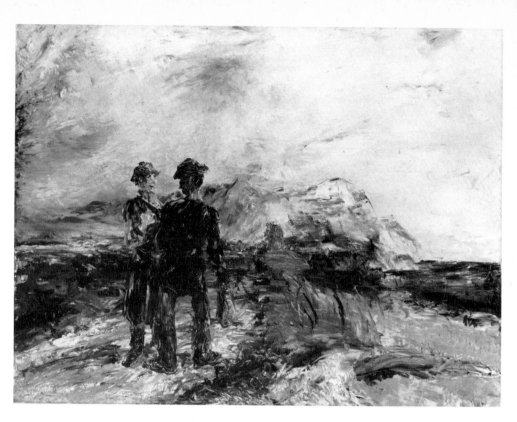

JACK YEATS, *The Two Travellers,* 1942.
The Tate Gallery, London.

meaning of the word. They do not caricature subject-material; they re-enact, rather, the processes by which material may be turned into a painting. They are records of the rules of the game. Nicholson has himself always stressed the importance of abstracting process as well as form. 'One can say that the problems dealt with in "abstract" art are related to the interplay of forces and, therefore, that any solution reached has a bearing on all interplay between forces: it is related to Arsenal v. Tottenham Hotspur quite as much as to the stars in their courses.' He is a good tennis and table-tennis player: images of bat, ball, net and table quickly supply paradigms for a Nicholson still-life. But like his father, Sir William Nicholson, a minor master of still-life who died in 1949, Ben Nicholson kept strictly within the limits he discovered in himself. The human figure appears only very occasionally in his work. It always looks rather uncomfortable, the ghost of a Braque nude.

Another facet of Nicholson's work is surface. His tactility appears two- rather than three-dimensionally, like eighteenth-century inlaid furniture. He likes to build a surface on which to draw or paint. He asks the question: which is the true Nicholson, the object or the line which encloses it? A man is in his studio, say, carving wood or cardboard into shapes. These he arranges or treats until their configuration satisfies him. What he then draws on them is conditioned by the knowledge so acquired and the finished work becomes the story of what went into it.

In the mid-1920s Ben Nicholson became friendly with Christopher Wood (1901–30). Wood was a talented painter whose death at twenty-nine was a most serious extinction of promise. He had attracted the notice and encouragement of Picasso. His work was French in its attempt to weld a naivety taken from Rousseau with the pictorial science of Braque. In some paintings he achieved this so remarkably that the synthesis is, in the long run, unsatisfying. Too artistic an aim has been too artistically accomplished. Beside Yeats's peasants, Christopher Woods's Breton fisherfolk seem assembled for a tourist photograph. His best painting, indeed, is overtly touristical. The friendship with Nicholson was fruitful for both men. Their desire to acquire an innocent eye by hard work never left them. But a stroke of luck was even more fruitful. In 1928 on a trip to St Ives in Cornwall, the two men discovered a primitive painter called Alfred Wallis (1855–1941). Wallis, an illiterate who had taken up painting when he was over 70, painted the ships and houses of his native port. What fascinated and inspired Nicholson was the way he employed any material to hand as a picture surface: old board, uneven bits of cardboard, sailcloth even, were nailed to the walls of his room, their material being incorporated in the picture. Wallis's treatment of colour was quite independent of the elastically rhythmic drawing. Years later Nicholson wrote: 'One associated with him some lively dark browns, shiny blacks, fierce greys, strange whites and a particularly pungent green.' The spontaneity of Wallis's example alerted Nicholson to the possibility of scouring painted surfaces in the interest of texture and tone. He followed Wallis too in treating colour as subject as well as device. A passage of deep blue, say, in the centre of a Nicholson table is the setting down of just such a passage of blue. It need not necessarily refer to the objects drawn all around it.

Nicholson lived in Cornwall from 1939 to 1958 and attracted many of our best artists there; during this time it rivalled London as a sphere for artistic production. His Cornish village and seascapes are pretty, toy-like even, but they lack the tension of his more abstract works. When he moves too far from the European commitment to abstraction his wit tends to veer towards whimsy. Mondrian's sojourn in England from 1938 to 1940 re-awakened the stimulus he had received at their meeting a few years earlier. But their work was only briefly complementary, Mondrian's being the fiercer and more questing spirit. After 1958 Nicholson took up permanent residence abroad. The admiration (and co-equal status in the *Association Abstraction-Création*) which he and Barbara Hepworth obtained in Paris in the early 1930s put this country on the critical map. He and Hepworth were among the reasons why, as Hitler's refugees began to trickle towards England, London briefly became the headquarters of the European movement. In 1937, when *Circle*, the international survey of constructive art was published, Gropius, Noam Gabo, Lazlo Moholy-Nagy and Mondrian were all living in Hampstead. Mondrian and Gropius moved on later to America; Gabo, an original of constructivism in its Russian and revolutionary days, stayed on until the war's end.

In the mid-1930s, it looked as though the mainstream of British art was safely channelled into abstraction. Nicholson was in control of the Seven and Five exhibiting society. David Jones and New Zealand-born Frances Hodgkins, original members in every sense, had been purged from the group – the delicate symbolism of Jones's

Below, CHRISTOPHER WOOD, *The Plage, Hotel Ty-Mad, Treboul,* 1930.
Redfern Gallery.
Below right, ALFRED WALLIS, *Land and Sea.*
Crane Arts Limited.

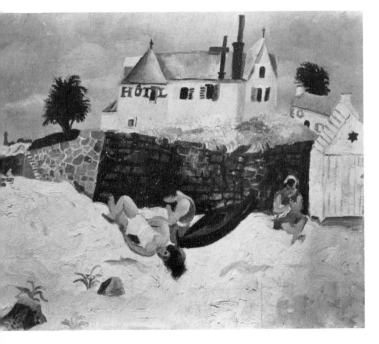

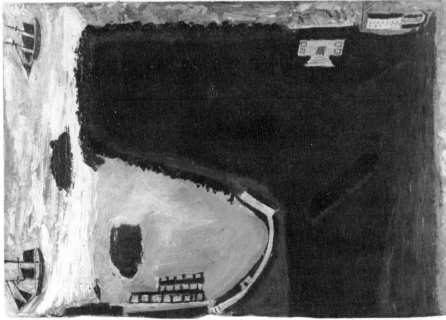

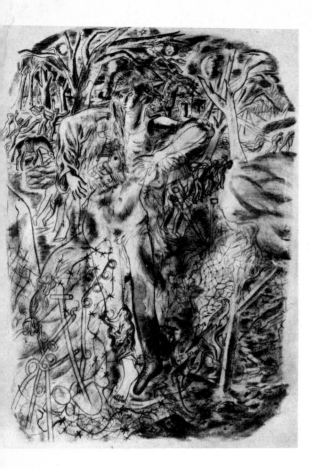

DAVID JONES, frontispiece to *In Parenthesis*
by David Jones.
By courtesy of the artist and
Faber and Faber Limited.

watercolours being, as we now know, a gloss on his very great inspiration as a poet. Even John Piper was painting geometric abstractions at this time. At the founding of Unit One Nash wrote a letter to *The Times* suggesting that design could be considered as a structural matter and imagination pursued apart from literature or metaphysics. The argument, as *Punch*'s cartoons of the time teach us, even filtered into the middlebrow imagination.

By the time *Circle* was published, however, the situation had changed. The International Surrealist Exhibition, one of the most far-reaching of all the great twentieth-century exhibitions, was held in London in 1936. The darkening political horizon was also having its effect. Fascism, indeed, must have appeared surrealistic in the nightmare of its outlook but formalist in the efficiency of its procedures. The war, when it came, interrupted any idea of art's self-sufficiency. It also cut off exchange with the Continent and made sure that a large number of powerful European artistic minds turned to America for patronage and refuge. But external circumstances, however influential, do not determine aesthetic history. England's return to her own romantic tradition can be laid at the door of four considerable artists: two established and two emerging. Nash and Henry Moore, Graham Sutherland and Victor Pasmore looked obliquely, or with some hostility, at the prevailing modes of the thirties. Pasmore concerns us here as a member of the Euston Road School; others were William Coldstream (b 1908), Graham Bell (1810–43), Claude Rogers (b 1907), and Lawrence Gowing (b 1918). The aim of this school was to cut through the argument between surreal and formalist notions. It wished to give back to the painter his craftsman's dignity as an unprejudiced examiner of the objective world. Although neither this approach nor the extreme professionalism of its application can properly be called literary, it was a deliberate move away from the Continent. Stylistic links were with the old London Group, with the New English Art Club even. Great attention to touch, however, kept the school on speaking terms with Cézanne.

Henry Moore (*b* 1898) belongs in this study because until the 1960s, when a new urban aesthetic took hold, he was almost everywhere regarded as the most powerful British artist since the death of Turner. Moore, and within a narrower definition Barbara Hepworth, provided the longed-for plasticity which most artists felt England lacked. Recently, Moore has seen his standing among current *artists* slump. But as Kokoschka once remarked, a man may live to see his reputation die and resurrect three times, and Moore is unlikely to be affected long.

The 1930s and 40s saw perhaps his greatest work outside sculpture; certainly his two-dimensional skills have never since attained the intensity of the years immediately before and during the last war. Until about 1937, his drawings were those of a sculptor foremost: their instinct is for the locus of stress. In the last twenty years they have reverted to this, although a constant decorative fluency makes them a good deal less interesting. But between 1937 and the war's end the drawings and notebook sketches make a contribution to twentieth-century art that would place Moore high had he done no sculpture. They are surreal, prophetic, celebratory. Moore saw that locating sketches for abstract sculpture in conventional landscape could make the scenery magical and frightening. The simplicity of this device in no way diminishes its force, as witness *Sculptural Object in a Landscape* (1939) and *Crowd Looking at a Tied-up Object* (1942). *Ideas for Sculpture* (1938) draws a group of working models simply, but by giving them human scale in a basement room created an entirely convincing image of totalitarianism, of the political and mental attitudes soon to lead to the huddled heaps of humanity which Moore would sketch in their subway refuge. Uncannily, the shelter drawings prophesy the Buchenwald photographs. The dignity and domesticity of Moore's early family groups stand in plastic and ironic contrast behind these sleepers threatened by extinction. In an age when patriotic art has been, with a few exceptions, synonymous with bad art, the war work of Nash and Moore

324

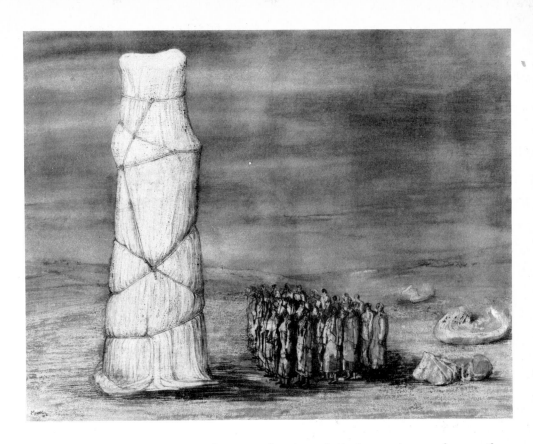

HENRY MOORE, *Crowd looking at a Tied-up Object*, 1942. Collection of Lord Clark.

celebrated England by making her travail universal. Both may be owed more than conventional aesthetics allow.

Henry Moore is a literary artist, therefore, only in the sense that he is at times a surreal and always a romantic one: he generates emotion by referring to the off-surface reality which his great formal gifts make tangible. He is also particularly English in the way of a romantic poet like Wordsworth – that is to say, his figures achieve monumentality and dignity by taking on the configurations of landscape. The best work of Graham Sutherland (b 1903) reverses this procedure, deriving a like romantic feeling from doing so, making landscapes take on emotions. His work since the war, honourable in its un-English ambition, distorts his talent by blowing it up – literally aggrandizing it in scale. His feeling for oil paint is as minimal as Spencer's. But unlike Spencer he is too knowing an artist not to appear worried by this. For in a way that at once establishes his national credentials, Sutherland works best in the romantic atmosphere of watercolour or gouache and therefore, by definition, in miniature. His Pembrokeshire landscapes are in the tradition of Blake and Samuel Palmer; his earliest work, etchings and engravings, leaned heavily to the latter. But both the formal and the emotional feel of them are altogether different. The *genius loci* of the Welsh peninsula, Celtic, pre-Christian, haphazardly settled or cultivated, inspired Sutherland to make the kind of connections between natural landscape and mental states which have been so fruitful for all Romantic art. For ten years, from 1934, Sutherland produced the bulk of his landscapes: predominantly Welsh, predominantly in watercolour or gouache, although there were a few small oils of equal intensity. The mood in the world outside was surreal and threatening and the landscapes do not 'take on' this mood so much as generate it. In essentials, Sutherland's unique gift was to apply techniques for line, atmosphere, personal rhythm, to the shapes of the observed world. Thus there is an extraordinary scrambling of detail. Topographical or botanical close-ups have the expressive generous force usually reserved for paintings of sky or sea.

In the work illustrated (p. 294), the sun weighs down on the two hills with malign accuracy. It seems out to get them. Elsewhere a leafy lane may have the superficial flatness of decorative foliage but a semi-circular twist of paint at the centre makes a

325

hungry orifice of its entrance. Shadows organize the landscape pictorially while, flame-like, they appear to devour it. More perfectly than Nash himself, Sutherland fulfilled Nash's requirements. 'We today,' the latter had written, 'must find new symbols to express our reactions to our environment. In some cases this will take the form of an abstract art, in others we will look for some different nature of imaginative research. But in whatever form, it will be a subjective art.'

The bomb-site paintings Sutherland undertook as an official war artist are understandably less subjective in outlook. Since subjective mannerisms remain, however, their effect is theatrical in a literal sense: they look like the back-cloth to an opera about the Blitz. Studies of machinery and factory-floor settings more successfully offered analogues to the vegetable forms he had mastered. They sowed the seeds of his later allegiance to surreal presences, visually logical beings, like Wyndham Lewis's later figures, which make the same contrast between the organic and the material.

This obsession with metamorphosis lours over Sutherland's post-war work, and must hail from Picasso. The same could be said with respect to all stages in their careers of Moore and Francis Bacon, but Sutherland's assimilation of the master is much more shaky. His thorns and spiked boughs, apocalyptic beasts and carnivorous birds try to make the trip between linear and emotional anguish. But the end is a kind of stylized indecision: the *Guernica* sketches crossed with *Audubon*. Nor, since he draws so finely, is Sutherland suited to the way oil paint itself can offer alternate or ambiguous images – it must be said that this is a weakness of Picasso as well. Alan Davie, who shares something of Sutherland's imaginative need for magical and totemic presences in a painting, is superior here. It is hard to avoid the harsh conclusion that Sutherland's desire to participate, once the war was over, in the general awakening of British artists to European concerns led him from his true path. In the present decade, he seems a minor meridional master; thirty years ago, he was unquestionably the greatest painter in watercolour and gouache to have come out of England since Turner, and arguably the greatest in these media in the world. Admittedly, in 1961, so large an authority as Douglas Cooper still felt able to assert that Sutherland was the leading British painter. But he did so from France and a School of Paris perspective, as if unaware that by that time France no longer provided the values with which the Western world judged painting.

During and just after the war, Sutherland's much merited prestige made him seem a

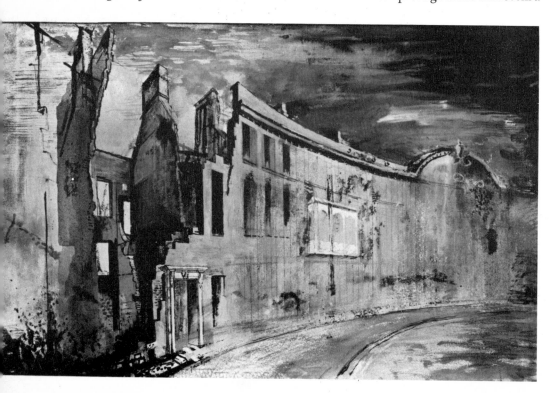

JOHN PIPER, *Somerset Place, Bath*, 1942. The Tate Gallery, London.

pivotal figure among younger painters; more so than his contemporary, John Piper (b 1903). Piper, in spite of his earlier abstract work, did not, like Sutherland, organise his picture surface in a post-Cubist way or go in for subjective distortion. In a far more traditional and English manner he provided a romantic atmosphere by sitting down and painting one: gloomy skies and haunted-looking buildings. The break with strict modernism could not have been more complete. It must have seemed hard to recall that Piper's wife, Myfanwy Evans, had founded the abstract periodical *Axis*. But Piper undeniably chose the right road for himself. He has few formal strengths; he is admired rather for versatility and the delicacy with which he handles the various media he works in.

The younger painters associated with Sutherland's wartime manner were Keith Vaughan, the Scots painters Robert Colquhoun and Robert Macbride, the Irishman Louis le Brocquy, Prunella Clough, John Minton and John Craxton. They were responsible, in the 1940s, for a particular kind of romantic handwriting: their careers (Colquhoun, Macbride and Minton all died young) draw a kind of graph of the tensions between this early illustrative allegiance and the overwhelming French tradition. At this time, the existential anxiety of the new French literary and philosophic school was also making itself felt, particularly in Minton's drawings and in the work of Lucian Freud.

Keith Vaughan (b 1912) has consistently trembled on the edge of distinction. In his early work he extended the Blake, Palmer and Sutherland tradition by making it very sensitive to the spacing of figures in landscape. He adjusted to France the hard way, junking the rare gift of an early and personal fluency for a slow painful immersion in the problems of applying oil paint. The texture of his paintings, for instance the way paint sits on and makes deep space out of canvas, is therefore as satisfying as it could possibly be. His subject is the male nude, or, more precisely, the interaction between forms suggested by the male nude and forms suggested by landscape. Under this sign he has accomplished remarkable things. It is difficult to decide what prevents him going overboard. Possibly he invites too close a comparison with his greater models. These are Cézanne of *The Bathers*, Matisse of *The Dance*, and the Russian-French painter Nicholas de Stael, whose 1952 exhibition in London had a profound effect on the next decade. Possibly Vaughan is subject-bound: he has said that he believes that a painter has only one basic idea, which probably lasts him a lifetime. If Vaughan is more respected than influential it may be because he has himself been trapped by the restrictions of previous fashions.

Two other contemporaries of Keith Vaughan, Roger Hilton (b 1911) and William Scott (b 1913), have been caught in something of the same situation. Their dilemma has been heightened by the fact that, as predominantly abstract painters who are neither constructivist nor expressionist, their work is caught in a blind spot between Ben Nicholson and Victor Pasmore on the one side, and the Everest-like international standing of the abstract expressionist New York School on the other. This is not to say that the logistics of reputation are vitally important either in life or in a short contemporary study. It is to say that international reputation, at least since the war, has become a critical referent, involved with the type, quality and quantity of an artist's output, and thus demanding to be taken into account, Where an artist is inherently idiosyncratic, out of the Western mainstream (Lowry, say, or Burra, or David Jones) his standing abroad makes little difference to his assessment. Where he works in a local version or variant of an international style, the degree to which he achieves 'breakthrough' or makes substantive addition to the style is clearly important. In the 1950s New York usurped Paris as the artistic capital of the world. It did so in terms of the factor of influence, and not necessarily of achievement, since Dubuffet and Giacometti were in the full spate of their energies. William Scott was one who had early seen what the Americans were up to. New York, like Paris before it, attracted

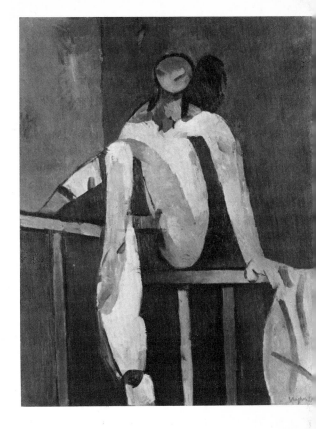

KEITH VAUGHAN, *Leaping Figure*, 1951. The Tate Gallery, London.

WILLIAM SCOTT, *Frying Basket and Eggs*. The National Gallery of Canada, Ottawa. The Massey Collection of English Painting.

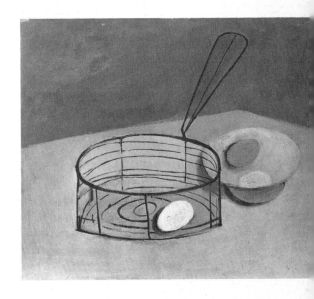

artistic immigration. Of the leading abstract expressionists – Jackson Pollock, Franz Kline, William de Kooning, Hans Hoffmann, Mark Rothko, Arshile Gorky – only the first two were native-born. Scott was awed by the intensity and horizon of their work, its overwhelming scale. But he felt that this should become neither the European nor the English horizon. He himself continued with analysing the forms of still life until the weight of his interest distended them into abstraction. In response to America, however, he did paint larger paintings, and thickened and brightened his layers of colour.

Hilton remained much closer to Paris, where he had spent many years. His originality lies, like Vaughan's, in his marvellous attention to the way paint is applied and the way in which, following Clive Bell, this offers up simultaneously the significance of a work and the psychology of its maker (p. 313). Lately he has made play with the boisterous and witty rhythms which can be achieved by combining graffiti-like nude female outlines with the disciplined concern with painted areas and their divisions; in literary terms Hilton's work is like doggerel by a good poet.

If Hilton, Vaughan and Scott, and others associated with English painterly abstraction after the last war, have something of the air of a lost generation, an older man, Ivon Hitchens, a contemporary, Victor Pasmore (b 1908), and two younger men, Peter Lanyon (1918–64) and Alan Davie (b 1920), instilled confidence with work whose collective strength is untentative and certain of its direction. Lanyon and Davie reacted early and with force to the New York abstract expressionist school and are almost unique in this study in their constant ability to compose on a large scale. The former died in 1964 as the result of a gliding accident; he was 46 and his promise was only an extension of his achievement (p. 314). 'What Lanyon did,' Alan Bowness has written, 'was to provide a wholly new vision of landscape painting, using a pictorial language familiar with the terms of cubism, constructivism and later of abstract expressionism.' In January 1957, his first exhibition in New York was very well received and he made friends with Kline, Motherwell and Mark Rothko – the latter, with Pollock, an especially admired forerunner. Yet it is unfair to remember Lanyon as an English abstract expressionist merely. His work is anchored to his native Cornwall, and the formal interchanges between land, sea, and sky to which his gliding trips accustomed him.

Just as Lanyon, who profitted from the constructivist Naum Gabo's stay in Cornwall from 1939 to 1946, made at least as much use of the French as the American tradition, so Alan Davie, exploring symbolic forms rather than symbolic gestures, is at least as

ALAN DAVIE, *White Magician*, 1956.
Peter Stuyvesant Foundation.

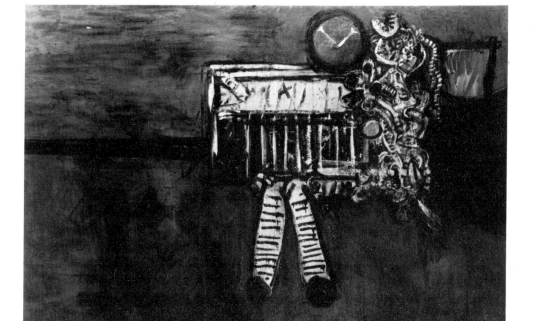

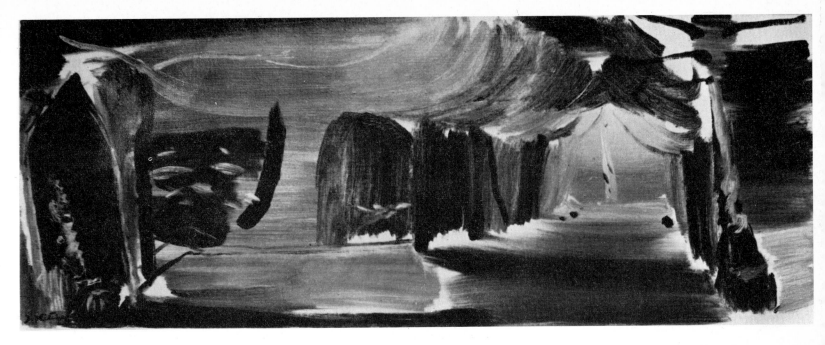

IVON HITCHENS, *Winter Walk No. 3*, 1948.
By courtesy of Mrs M. C. Hitchens.

near to Miro and Leger as to Pollock. In terms, too, of 'placing' painters within their native tradition, Lanyon operated in a Turner-like atmosphere where landscape verges on pure abstraction. Davie, a Scot, has made constant and inspired use of ancient Celtic illustrational or decorative abstraction, as in the Book of Kells. In paintings of brilliant intensity, coloured perhaps by his early experiences as a jeweller and his continuing feeling for jazz, he kaleidoscopes the past in terms of archetypal symbols and the present in terms of colour improvizations on these symbols. He is an anthropologist among action painters.

Ivon Hitchens (b 1893) belongs to the great generation born in the 1890s. (Others were Bomberg, Gaudier-Brzeska, Spencer, Gertler, Ben Nicholson, David Jones, Roberts and Moore.) He was a founding member of the Seven and Five Society in 1919 and the only one to survive the purges ten years later carried out by the (at that time) Stalin of non-figuration, Ben Nicholson. It was not until the decade after the last war, however, that he came into his own. Hitchens brought about a remarkable synthesis. Taking the long and narrow mid-period Turner landscapes (*Walton Reach* in the Tate Gallery comes to mind) as a starting point he blended what he learned from them with the lush and rhythmic brush strokes of the Fauves. Following the Cubist tradition, he is also flexible as to surface organisation. Put so briefly, it sounds like a recipe. In fact it was a personal re-enactment, no doubt of a slow and painful kind, of the essential processes which had been shaping all Western art for over a hundred years. Lush rhythms made critics connect Hitchens with Matthew Smith. But the Fauvist element of colour, in which Smith had immersed himself so early, did not take hold of Hitchens until 1953 or 1954. Until that time his landscapes were Fauve-like in the sense that they were built up by blocks of colour. But the colours remained appropriate to the English climate. Autumnal browns and khakis would meet with slimy greens, suggesting water-meadows and their look of over-cooked vegetables. The effect was oriental: a writing-down of Sussex rides and hammer ponds in broad calligraphic strokes. In the mid-1950s, he allowed colour to take over and become theme as well as a device for ordering perspective. The effect was to animate the picture surface and pull the landscape references further and further from their original context. Hitchins's paintings began to look like the airy and elegant work of the School of Paris abstractionist Hans Hartung. But the quiet and continuing presence of an English and topographical eye made them seem less vacuous, less restricted to ideograms of flight. Save for a few perhaps too infrequent forays into nude and flower studies, Hitchens has painted in this vein for nearly twenty years. His weakness is a tendency to repetitiveness, as against repetition. The distinction here is not unlike the one which applies to Keith Vaughan. Repetitiveness implies a mind becoming stuck in a groove; repetition, in the sense of Bacon's heads, or the Italian Morandi's bottles, need involve no such narrowing of psychological or perceptive powers.

W.H. Auden once wrote that the way to distinguish a major from a minor poet lay in the fact that the minor work, however notable or intense, would offer few clues as to what point in the author's career it had been written. Whereas the major was always the developing artist; impossible, for instance, to confuse his early work with his late. If this test holds good for painters, Victor Pasmore has the making of a major artist. As has been said, his was the principal talent in the Euston Road School's reassertion of objective and painterly values over the rival orthodoxies of surrealism and abstract construction. Pasmore painted nudes, flowers, a few portrait heads. But the difference, aside from date, between a Pasmore townscape and one of Spencer Gore's, a girl's head by Pasmore and one, say, by Sir John Lavery, was always the obstinate analytic intelligence overriding Pasmore's mistiness and romanticism. Winter trees against a grey Thames-side sky, factories and bridges contributing to and partaking of the smokey orchestration of tones, all reveal themselves, when the first poetic impression is over, as objects in their own right. They are neither referential nor scenic but loved and analysed for themselves. Trees, railings, street signs particularly, start to look very sculptural. Yet in spite of this, Pasmore's conversion to an almost totally non-figurative idiom came, in 1948, as a great shock to critics and admirers. His first abstract work, sometimes categorised as neo-plastic or painterly, to distinguish it from constructive, may be his best. Where Nicholson rested in the certainties of circle and square, Pasmore chose forms connected with energy and flux. In Van Gogh's sketches, and in the margins of his unprecedentedly absorbing letters, the Dutch artist would build up little landscapes, light and all, by angular ink strokes of generally uniform length. Pasmore may have adapted these strokes to the thick and grainy pigment he now employed. From Leonardo he took the spiral, W.B. Yeats's symbolic 'gyre', the Heraclitean flux at the heart of nature. Circles, squares, triangles and the like appear in the context of these permanencies almost as toys. In a composition of surpassing dignity, *Square Motif, Blue and Gold: The Eclipse* (1950), they can also make one laugh. This painting (p. 314) must be among the most sensuous abstracts ever painted. Without possessing the historical importance of a Kandinsky they have, surely, a greater emotional range.

In the mid-1950's, Pasmore made a second and even more dramatic break with his painterly past. Abstract constructions – carpentry and the use of perspex giving them the simultaneous air of being machine tooled and home made – are as adaptive as ever to his feeling for light. But their severity seems a bit wilful: forced by, rather than emerging from, an aesthetic governed by the severe. Nevertheless, Pasmore remains the most inventive constructionist in the field. In the range and experience of his interests he outdistances the others, notably the husband-and-wife artists Kenneth and Mary Martin and the much younger Anthony Hill and Joe Tilson. It may be that Pasmore is psychologically too suspicious of his own great powers of transferring emotion to paint. Whenever he returns to paint, as in the staining or decoration of his plywood panels, mystery as well as mastery returns. He is a nuclear artist of this century in England, but like Sickert he is still too little considered abroad.

Such neglect is part and parcel of the shift in European artistic opinion in the mid-1950s, when the work of the New York School became known. Abstract expressionism is one of the few aptly named or descriptive *isms* of the century. The new paintings were abstract in the classic sense of being their own first cause; expressionist in that the physical act of painting them provided a drama of impulse and self-discovery from onlooker as well as artist. For some time New York remained the political centre of the world of art.

The history of this transfer of creative and critical power from Paris to New York in the mid-1950s would require a separate essay. Here it is enough to say that England was on the whole liberated by the change since her best artists felt confident to paint as they wished, less inhibited than previously by the French-based theories of plasticity which had held sway for so long. Of course the American achievement was itself a response to ideas originally formed in France. 'I don't see why the problems of modern painting can't be solved as well here as elsewhere,' Jackson Pollock said in 1944, acknowledging in the same breath that Picasso and Miro were the artists who interested him most. But the School of Paris sensitivity to the materials and craft of painting made it oddly unaware of the external world – the made world of cities which was now, to all intents and purposes, 'Nature'. The Colour-Field and Pop Art movements reflected Anglo-American sensitivity to the technical and economic materialism which both countries had called into being or applied. In England a generation of artists, Lanyon, Davie, Hamilton, Caro and Paolozzi, tackled America much as the generation of Fry had tackled France. But they did so with far greater zest and acuteness, due to their sense that 'America' was less a school of painters than an emblem of the Western world they too had inherited and would treat with on equal terms.

What happened was a two-way exchange, a special relationship that produced healthy children. Pop Art, for instance, was born in England and may owe its name to a pun on the words *popular* and *lollipop* which Richard Hamilton employed in a 1956 collage of an American domestic interior. In the early 1950s a young group of painters, sculptors, architects and critics were meeting regularly in London at the old Institute of Contemporary Arts in Dover Street. Leading figures among them were Richard Hamilton and the sculptor Paolozzi, the writer-architect Rayner Banham and the critic Lawrence Alloway, who was subsequently influential in America and in the analysis of abstract expressionism and colour-field painting. Their discussions of the implications of popular culture were perhaps coloured by a distaste for the prominent social realist school, notably John Bratby, Jack Smith (subsequently an abstractionist in the manner of the late Kandinsky) and the Polish immigrant, Josef Herman. Such distaste need not have been technical, for the painters mentioned were all highly talented and remain so. It is more likely that the approach to ordinary life exhibited

Below, JOHN BRATBY, *Woman in Bed.*
Collection of Mr Jack Hill.
Below right, JOSEF HERMAN, *Morning,* 1951.
Middlesbrough Municipal Art Gallery.

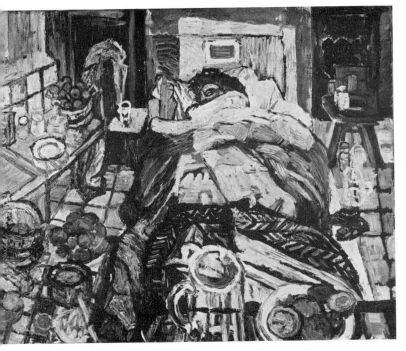

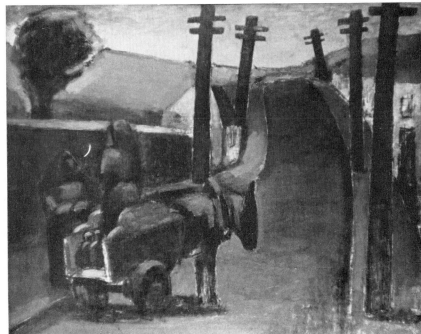

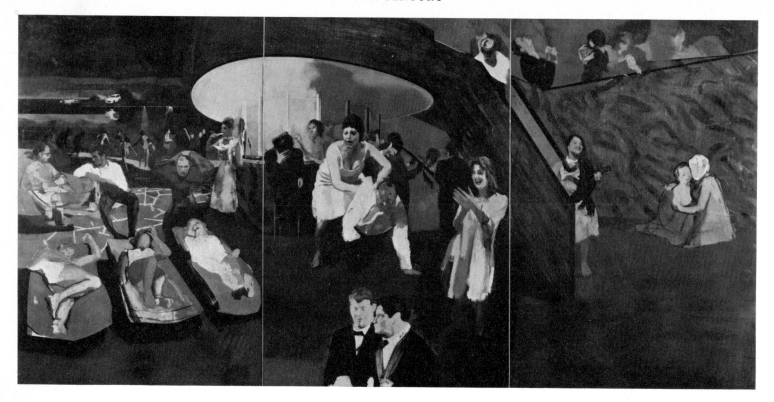

MICHAEL ANDREWS, *All Night Long*, 1963–4. National Gallery of Victoria.

RICHARD HAMILTON, *Patricia Knight*, 1964. Courtesy of Petersburg Press.

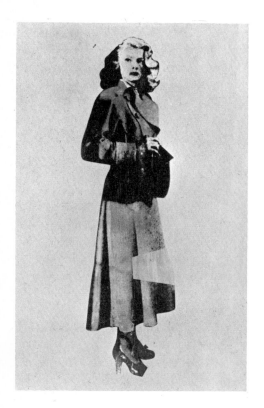

by them was old-fashionedly populist, Marxist even – as the criticism of John Berger affirmed. Pop Art was a good deal more sophisticated and analytic; insofar as it is possible to provide Pop with a family tree, the American work of the French master, Duchamp, must rank high among the ancestors. Pop, therefore, is an art inspired by artefacts; and by the fun which the Dada movement had derived from a world increasingly substituting things for ideas.

Richard Hamilton (b 1922), and the American expatriate R.B. Kitaj (b 1932), are among the very few painters connected with the Pop movement whose work is broad enough in range and intense enough in feeling to keep discussion at the aesthetic rather than the sociological level. Hamilton is one of the most intelligent painters living, expert in James Joyce's no man's land between consciousness and the way art boils down consciousness to fact. He can be enjoyed more simply as a still-life painter of the first rank, his car-fenders and toasting machines being as lovingly and precisely remade as the fruit and flowers of William Nicholson's or Allen Gwynne Jones's small masterpieces. R.B. Kitaj should not, perhaps, be treated as a Pop painter at all. His work is little concerned with consumer-good artefacts and it has none of the shiny, billboard or magazine advertisement texture of the paintings of Peter Phillips or Allen Jones. Kitaj has made intensive use of the chopped-up way visual images reach us in newspapers, instruction manuals, the particularly American form of the comic-strip (pp. 316–7). Like Paolozzi, with whom he has collaborated, Kitaj does much of his work in screen-print, a medium particularly well suited to the way his magpie intelligence rummages among 'the heap of broken images' (in T.S. Eliot's phrase) of our civilization. But this description, accurate enough as far as it goes, may belie his very extraordinary talent as a painter. On the rare occasions that his work can be seen assembled in one place it does fall into place. He appears to be putting together a gigantic and witty comic-strip of twentieth-century life as it has filtered into his consciousness through his very wide-ranging reading. Against the charge, to some degree justifiable, of remoteness, it can be said that incessant exposure to images rather than life is nowadays very much part of life.

Far more instinctive in their approach to reality, no less intelligent in their attitude

332

to painting, are three English artists who have sharply pinpointed the difference between the English wing of the Pop art movement and the American. Michael Andrews (b 1928) is not, perhaps, a Pop painter at all; indeed the term is in general more suited to the apparatus of publicity than to criticism. He is an intense, existential painter in the way of Lucian Freud or Francis Bacon. Unlike them, he is outstanding in the control of grouped figures. He can paint a Hollywood party, or one at a Soho drinking club, in such a way as to pinpoint the emotional isolation of individuals attending them without interrupting the rhythmic possibilities, for a painter, of the large group. Peter Blake (b 1932) and David Hockney (b 1937) are both graduates of the Royal College of Art, which in the early 1960s overtook the Slade School as the art academy of most influence and prestige. (The Royal College has benefited from fine painters on its staff; among them, Carel Weight, Roderigo Moynihan and Ruskin Spear.)

Blake's roots in Pop are early and marked. *On the Balcony* in the Tate Gallery, completed in 1957, was started in 1955. It is a pinboard compendium and *trompe l'oeil* collage of photographs, magazines, lapel buttons of popular (in the sense of well-known) personalities, and images which act as puns between the painting and the thing painted. Blake works in a gentle, almost a New English Art Club manner of great delicacy and skill. He is drawn to Victorian subjects, and surely the Victorians were ur-Pop in their passion for collecting and arranging the minor clutter of their productive civilization. He is also Victorian in treatment, although always scrupulous in his attention to the way paint first makes contact with canvas. With Patrick Proctor and Rory MacEwen he has revived the English watercolour tradition: Procktor putting it to new and exciting use in portraiture, MacEwen intensifying and abstracting botanical illustration. Generally, Blake exhibits affection and nostalgia rather than bite (p. 315). His paintings find equivalents in John Betjeman's poetry and indeed Blake's wife Jann Haworth has made Pop dolls by superimposing likenesses of Betjeman's head on assorted Teddy Bears. Without Blake's impeccable technique, the responses underlying his painting might well be, like these bears, a little hard to take.

David Hockney too is in danger of being whimsical: cunning-naive in the artfully childish way he locates the friends and lovers of his world in the paintings and drawings that celebrate them. This said, he is the most sheerly interesting and imaginative painter of his generation and altogether distinctive in style. He owes a little to Spencer and Bacon, a little more to the Frenchman Jean Dubuffet, quite a lot to life of the affluent American West Coast (p. 320); he is a sort of Fragonard of the swimming pools, patios and motel interiors of Los Angeles. Recently he has painted in a much drier, almost neo-classical style, as if his aim were to bring to Californian and London social life the detachment of Ingres. Since he is not Ingres, the recent paintings are perhaps more impressive in reproduction than in life; he has yet to evolve a technique which can combine the immediacy and personal bounce of his paintings of the early 1960s (such as the one shown here, p. 320) with his unique ability to transfix his leisure culture and dignify it. He is already a considerable English painter; in etching he is one of the twentieth-century masters in any country. He shares this distinction with the expatriate S. W. Hayter, creator of Atelier 17 in Paris and father-figure of all contemporary non-figurative graphics.

Richard Smith (b 1931) and Bridget Riley (b 1931) may be considered the best by rather a long way of the younger abstractionists, although John Walker (b 1900) and Keith Milow (b 1945), who has recently turned to still-life and figurative montage paintings, may be coming up fast. They have wide followings abroad, although their aims are very different. Richard Smith's ambitions are heroic. The commercial world's concern with advertisement and packaging provides him with a lily pond cruder but no less preoccupying than Monet's. He is concerned too with the architecture of the canvas; no doubt on the principle that a picture which jettisons illusion should also

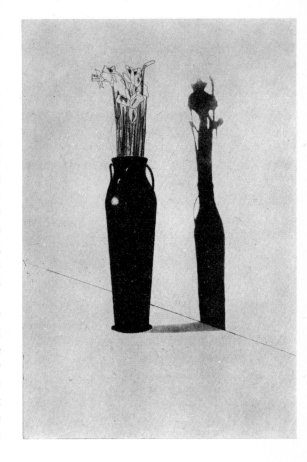

DAVID HOCKNEY, *Flowers and Vase*, 1969 (etching).
Courtesy of Petersburg Press.

jettison illusion's characteristic 'window' frame. Bridget Riley is the most internationally noted British exponent of 'Op' (for optical-illusion) art. Op is a latter-day illusionist art. Instead of tricking the eye into believing that a two-dimensional surface is a three-dimensional one, or generally ringing changes on this theme, Op puts the eye through its behavioural paces: generating movement, blind spots, the conjuring tricks of perception one finds in old fashioned books of indoor games for children. This art and its extensions into three-dimension, often involving contemporary electronic technology, has also been called 'kinetic'. But the term, which implies heat and motion, does not necessarily protect works of art from a mechanical remoteness and chill. Bridget Riley's extraordinarily professional execution saves her from coldness. So do her intuitions of the achievement of Seurat. But it must be said that such art, like the 'hard-edge' variety practised with distinction by Robyn Denny, sails close to the constantly shifting sands of contemporary design. As to electronics, Bernard Cohen,

Below left, BRIDGET RILEY, *Untitled Study,* 1963.
By courtesy of John Webb, Brompton Studio.
Below, ROBYN DENNY, *Life Line 1,* 1963.
The Tate Gallery, London.

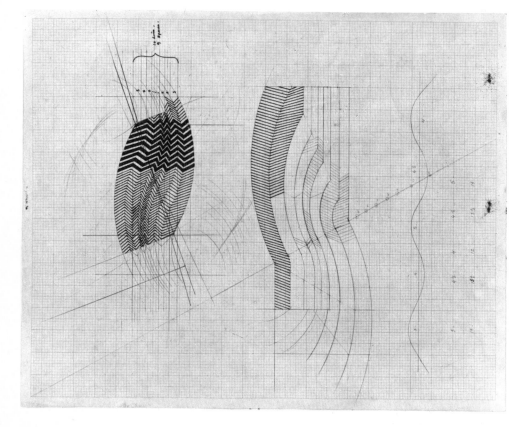

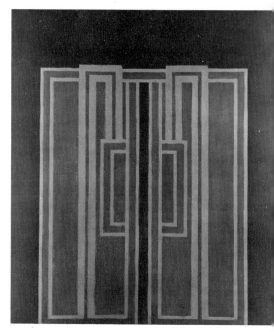

Below, RICHARD SMITH, *Riverfall,* 1969.
The Tate Gallery, London.
By courtesy of the artist.

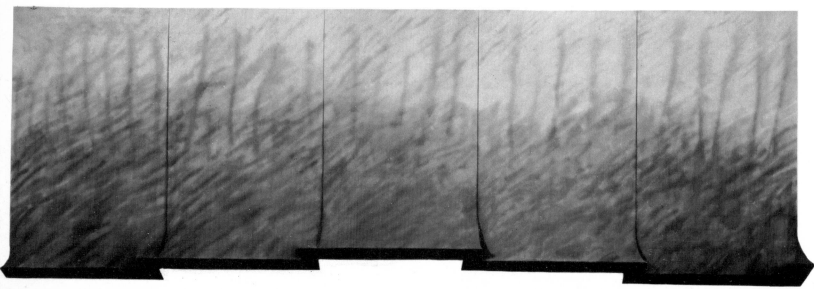

younger brother of the fine painter and teacher Harold Cohen, has made a purely painterly and inspired use of the 'print-out' patterns of computer hardware. Nor is painterly a subjective term. It is what painters as distinct in time and undertaking as Matthew and Richard Smith, Sickert and Michael Andrews are about, and it provides a constant against which can be judged the predatory habits and eclectic nature of much contemporary art, intent as it is on reflecting the technical transience of its civilization.

Once more, then, we are confronted with the argument that in the present century art movements are of more consequence than national boundaries. But of course a painter of the first rank may give his country not glory merely, but the lifehood of outside critical attention and ideas. In the last fifteen years the work of Francis Bacon, admired first by artists, then by a national audience, now internationally to a degree that acknowledges him as the foremost world painter of his time, has generated just such attention. It is fitting, therefore, that the last words of this study should be devoted to him.

Francis Bacon (b 1909) (pp. 318–9) was born and grew up in Ireland, where his father trained racehorses. He went to school in England, travelled about Europe in the late 1920s, delighting particularly in the decadent Berlin of the Weimar Republic. He made his historical debut in 1930 as an interior decorator and furniture designer; he worked in what we would call the Art Deco style, based on the Constructivism of the previous decade. He studied the art of Picasso, at that time involved in attenuated semi-geometrical figure paintings which were beginning to look haunted and surreal. Inspired, he taught himself to paint. His early work, nearly all of which he subsequently destroyed, attempted to give abstracted hominoid shapes a similarly heightened air – sometimes by little references to the Western religious tradition. His work was not successful and he was turned down for the International Surrealist Exhibition in 1936. He himself dates his career from the 1944 Tryptych *Figures at the Base of a Cross* in the Tate Gallery.

At first glance this work still owes much to Picasso. It is a study, like the paintings and sketches of the Guernica period, of how to assault the nervous system of an onlooker with formal equivalents for pain, mental stress, distortions not of art merely but of daily living and his own hold upon it. Closer acquaintance suggests that here is someone who has looked very hard and imaginatively at the whole Baroque tradition of wrenching the human figure until it is, literally, dragged towards that self-extension known as the sublime. But although the Triptych is a very strong, even a terrifying picture, one is at least as much aware of the scepticism and control underlying the element of shock. It is as if the artist were playing 'chicken' with theatrical excess and learning to paint on the dangerous Baroque margin between going very far and going too far.

Bacon then dropped the linear, attenuated style of the Triptych in favour of something much more solid. He was teaching himself oil paint's correspondence with the density of the observed world; the Courbet road to nature. *Figure Study I* (1945–6) shows a coat and hat in a landscape. This painting seems to have inaugurated the interest in clothes (no twentieth-century painter has rendered them so attentively) which reflected Bacon's preoccupation with Velasquez's *Innocent X* and led to his own robed and enthroned *Popes*. The effect of *Figure Study* is surreal, but not only on account of the garments and their location. A strong formal understanding of the kind of space clothes are designed to occupy draws shocking, and effective, attention to the absence of any owner. '"What modern man wants",' Bacon has said, quoting Valéry, '"is the grin without the cat": the sensation without the boredom of its conveyance.' Throughout his career, Bacon has attempted to combine psycholgical immediacy – his chamber of horrors side – with whatever formal mechanics are most likely to allow the viewer to retain the painted image until it moves into

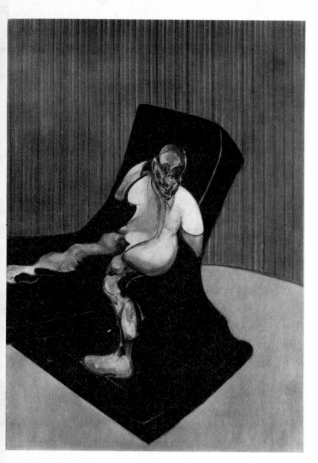

FRANCIS BACON, *Seated Figure on Couch*, 1962.
Marlborough Fine Art Ltd.

memory and becomes a way of looking at the world. In the years following the War this search led Bacon to solidity at all cost. The *Magdalene* in the Bagley Art Gallery has the poise of a Giotto figure, and so much presence that the umbrella half concealing her becomes an item of haphazard convincing detail and not the gratuitous surreal emblem for which it is sometimes mistaken.

In the following decade, Bacon's iconography juxtaposed the violent signs of our century with the gravities, hollow maybe, but socially and spiritually well anchored, of earlier epochs. His habit of working from photographs and news-clippings is in this decade everywhere apparent. It affected younger English painters like Richard Hamilton, and the new figuration of Pop Art. Himmler and Goebbels, silent or in oratorical flood; Nadar's captivating photograph of Baudelaire's sidelong look; people rushing for shelter during street fighting in Petrograd in 1917; Marius Maxwell's photograph of animals in equatorial Africa; the Screaming Nurse from Eisenstein's film *Potemkin*; a postcard of the Promenade des Anglais in Nice; a few friends or relations – all appear and reappear as visual metaphors in compositions of increasing formality and scale. Their function is to awaken the sense of the suggestive which gives painting a resonance beyond its object-life, and liberation from the confines of art. Bacon would bring technical devices out into the open and reinstate them as images. The famous boxes which circumscribe his male nudes, popes, businessmen and monkeys start life as ways of containing space and end it as prisons out of Kafka. His brush-strokes are rapid (he does no preliminary drawing) and blur into one another. So originates the suggestion of flesh poised, like that of M. Valdemar in Poe's horrifying tale, on the edge of instant putrefaction.

Apart from the gigantic *Crucifixion* (1962) in the Guggenheim Museum in New York, inspired by the Cimabue torso, crawling, in Bacon's phrase, 'like a great worm down the Cross', the work of the most recent decade has quit the public for the private realm. His originality is on as firm ground here, and slightly less susceptible to the aesthetics of shock. Memory traces of friends, nudes and the urban interiors which provide a natural setting for all but our most superficial human encounters, are re-created, hit and miss, in the very large body of work which has made his international name. Bacon is unique in this century in his ability to render the indoor, overfed, alcohol-and-tobacco-lined flesh of the average urban male. His paint is how most of us look. The translation of Edward Muybridge's wrestlers, photographed in sequence of muscular stress, to one of Bacon's homoerotic interiors, is offered as a clear statement of decline. Their flesh sags in anticipation of sexual disappointment. Bacon paints beds, platforms, chairs and sofas with the attention Courbet gave to rocks. The effect is a suffocating enclosure: the landscape of hell done as hell's hotel bedroom; the non-world of Sartre's *Huis Clos* and Beckett's *Endgame*. The implied theatricality seems to be deliberate. Compositional layout is very much like a conventional stage set; at any moment another nude, bearing hypodermic or ashtray, may enter left or right. Sofas and tables have, like flesh, puffed out and turned flabby, their Art Deco youthfulness long gone. These interiors reveal a truism of art impossible to over-emphasize. The function of any medium is to offer interchange, metamorphosis, the telescopic sliding-together of our perceptions until they are gathered back to their solitary neural source. Like Eliot's early poetry (a direct influence) Bacon's paintings are documentaries of nervous stress. They may be staged contemporarily but they are always performed with awareness of historical precedent and the shapes of tradition.

Bibliography

1 The Middle Ages

General works
Rickert,M. *Painting in Britain. The Middle Ages,* 1965.
Tristram,E.W. *English Medieval Wall Paintings. I. The Twelfth Century,* 1944.
  II. The Thirteenth Century, 1950.
  III. The Fourteenth Century, 1954.
Caiger-Smith,A. *English Medieval Mural Paintings,* 1963.
Demus,O. *Romanesque Mural Painting,* 1970
Millar,E.G. *English Illuminated Manuscripts from the Xth to the XIIIth Centuries,* 1926.
Millar,E.G. *English Illuminated Manuscripts of the XIVth and XVth Centuries,* 1928.
Pevsner,N. *The Englishness of English Art,* 1964.
Goldschmidt,A. 'English Influence on Medieval Art of the Continent', *Medieval Studies in Memory of A.Kingsley Porter,* ed. W.R.W.Koehler, vol. II, (1939), pp 709–728.
Lehmann-Brockhaus,O. *Lateinische Schriftquellen zur Kunst in England, Wales und Schottland von Jahre 901 bis zum Jahre 1307,* 5 vols, 1955–60.
Ker,N.R. *Medieval Libraries of Great Britain, A List of Surviving Books* (Royal Historical Society, London, 1964).
Ker,N.R. 'Books at St Paul's Cathedral before 1313', *Studies in London History presented to Philip Edmund Jones,* 1969, pp 43–72.
Dodwell,C.R. *Theophilus, De Diversis Artibus,* 1961.
Thompson,D.V. *The Materials and Techniques of Medieval Painting,* 1936, reprinted 1956.

Sixth to Ninth Centuries
Kendrick,T.D. *Anglo-Saxon Art to AD 900,* 1938, reprinted 1972.
Henry,F. *Irish Art. I. The Early Christian Period to AD 800,* 1965.
  II. The Viking Invasions 800–1020, 1967.
Luce,A.A. *et al., Evangeliorum quattuor Codex Durmachensis,* 1960. (Facsimile of Book of Durrow.)
Kendrick,T.D. *et al., Evangeliorum quattor Codex Lindisfarnensis,* 1956, 1960. (Facsimile and full study of the Lindisfarne Gospels.)
Alton,E.H., Meyer,P. *Evangeliorum quattuor Codex Cenannensis,* 1950. (Facsimile and study of the Book of Kells.)
Nordenfalk,C. 'An illustrated Diatessaron', *Art Bulletin,* L (1968), 119–40.
Bruce-Mitford,R.L.S. 'The Art of the Codex Amiatinus', *Journal of the Archaeological Association,* XXXII (1969), 1–25.

Tenth to Eleventh Centuries
Rice,D.T. *English Art 871–1100,* II, 1952.
Wormald,F. 'The Winchester school before St Aethelwold', *England before the Conquest. Studies in primary sources presented to Dorothy Whitelock,* ed. P.Clemoes, K.Hughes, 1971.
Homburger,O. *Die Anfänge der Malschule von Winchester im X Jahrhundert,* 1912.
Wormald,F. *The Benedictional of St Ethelwold,* 1959.
Wormald,F. *English Drawings of the 10th and 11th centuries,* 1952.
Alexander,J.J.G. *Anglo-Saxon illumination in Oxford Libraries,* 1971.
Gollancz,I. *The Caedmon Manuscript,* 1927.
Wormald,F. 'The Survival of Anglo-Saxon illumination after the Norman Conquest', *Proceedings of the British Academy, XXX* (1944), 128–45.

The Twelfth Century
Boase,T.S.R. *English Art 1100–1216,* III, 1953, 1971.
Boase,T.S.R. *English Romanesque illumination,* 1951.
Dodwell,C.R. *Thr Canterbury School of illumination, 1066–1200,* 1954.
James,M.R. *The Canterbury Psalter,* 1935.

Omont,H. *Psautier illustré (XlIle siècle)* (Bibliothèque Nationale, Paris, n.d.). Reproduies B.N., latin 8846.
The St Albans Psalter. 1. The Full Page Miniatures by Otto Pächt.
  2. The Initials by C.R.Dodwell.
  3. Preface and Description of the Manuscript by Francis Wormald (Warburg Institute, London, 1960).
Kauffmann,C.M. 'The Bury Bible', *Journal of the Warburg and Courtauld Institutes,* XXIX (1966), 60–81.
Smalley,B. 'L'exégèse biblique du 12e siècle', *Entretiens sur La Renaissance du 12e siècle,* ed. M. de Gandillac, E.Jeauneau. (Centre culturel international de Cerisy la Salle, 1965) (Paris, Mouton, 1968).
Dodwell,C.R. *The Great Lambeth Bible,* 1959.
Oakeshott,W. *The Artists of the Winchester Bible,* 1945.
  Sigena-Romanesque Paintings in Spain and the Winchester Bible artists, 1972.
The Year 1200. 1. Exhibited Catalogue.
  2. A Background Survey (Metropolitan Museum of Art, New York, 1970).

The Thirteenth Century
Jantzen,H. *High Gothic,* 1962.
Brieger,P. *English Art 1216–1307,* IV, 1957.
Turner,D.H. *Early Gothic Illuminated Manuscripts,* 1965.
Boase, T.S.R. *English Illumination of the Thirteenth and Fourteenth Centuries,* 1954.
James,M.R. *The Bestiary* (Cambridge University Library MS. Ii.4.26) (Roxburghe Club, Oxford, 1928).
Vaughan,R. *Matthew Paris,* 1958.
James,M.R. *The Apocalypse in Art,* 1931.
The Trinity College Apocalypse, colour facsimile with introduction and description by P.Brieger, 1967.
Hassall,A.G. and W.O. *The Douce Apocalypse,* 1961.
Wormald,F. 'Paintings in Westminster Abbey and contemporary paintings', *Proceedings of the British Academy,* XXXV (1949), 161–76.

The Fourteenth Century
Evans,J. *English Art 1307–1461,* V, 1949.
Warner,G.F. *Queen Mary's Psalter,* 1912.
James,M.R., Cockerell,S.C. *Two East Anglian Psalters at the Bodleian Library* (Roxburghe Club, Oxford, 1926).
Cockerell,S.C. *The Gorleston Psalter,* 1907.
Egbert,D.D. *The Tickhill Psalter and related manuscripts,* New York, 1940.
van den Gheyn,J. *Le Psautier de Peterborough,* Brussels, 1905.
Freeman Sandler,L. 'A follower of Jean Pucelle in England', *Art Bulletin,* LlI (1970), 363–372.
Millar,E.G. *The Luttrell Psalter,* 1932.
Rouse,E. Clive. *Longthorpe Tower, Peterborough, Northamptonshire* (H.M. Stationary Office, 1964).
Pächt,O. 'A Giottesque Episode in English Medieval Art', *Journal of the Warburg and Courtauld Institutes,* VI (1943), 51–70.
Wormald,F. 'The Fitzwarin Psalter and its allies', *Journal of the Warburg and Courtauld Institutes,* VI (1943), 71–79.
James,M.R., Millar,E.G. *The Bohun Manuscripts* (Roxburghe Club, Oxford, 1936).
James,M.R. 'An English Medieval Sketchbook, No. 1916 in the Pepysian Library, Magdalene College, Cambridge', *Walpole Society,* XIII (1924–5).
Rickert,M. *The Reconstructed Carmelite Missal,* 1952.

The Fifteenth Century
Wormald,F, 'The Wilton Diptych', *Journal of the Warburg and Courtauld*

Institutes, XVII (1954), 191–203.

Kuhn, C. 'Herman Scheerre and English illumination of the early fifteenth century', *Art Bulletin*, XXII (1940), 138–156.

Rickert, M. 'The so-called Beaufort Hours and York Psalter', *Burlington Magazine*, CIV (1962), 238–246.

Herbert, J. A. *The Sherborne Missal* (Roxburghe Club, Oxford, 1920).

Alexander, J. J. G. 'William Abell "Lymnour" and fifteenth century English illumination', *Kunsthistorische Forshungen Otto Pächt zu ehren*, ed. G. Weber, A. Rosenauer, Vienna, 1972.

James, M. R. *The Chaundler manuscripts* (Roxburghe Club, London, 1916).

Dillon, Viscount, Hope, W. H. St J. *Pageant of the Life and Death of Richard Beauchamp, Earl of Warwick, K.G. 1389–1439*, 1914.

James, M. R., Tristram, E. W. 'The Wall Paintings in Eton College Chapel and the Lady Chapel of Winchester Cathedral', *Walpole Society*, XVII (1928–9), 1–43.

2 Tudor and Early Stuart Painting

Auerbach, E. 'Vincent Volpe, the King's Painter', *Burl. Mag.*, XCII (1950), 222.
'Holbein's Followers in England', *id.*, XCIII (1951), 44.
Tudor Artists, 1954.
Nicholas Hilliard, 1961.

Chamberlain, A. B. *Hans Holbein the Younger*, 1913, 2 vols.

Colding, T. H. *Aspects of Miniature Painting, its Origin and Development*, Copenhagen, 1954.

Croft-Murray, E. *Catalogue of British Drawings*, British Museum, I, 1960, introduction.
Decorative Painting in England, 1537–1837, I, 1962.

Cust, Sir L. 'The Painter HE (Hans Eworth)', *Walpole Society*, II (1913).
'Marcus Gheeraerts', *id.*, III (1914).
'The Lumley Inventories', *id.*, VI (1918).

Ganz, P. *The Paintings of Hans Holbein*, 1950.

Goodison, J. W. 'George Gower, Serjeant-Painter to Queen Elizabeth', *Burl. Mag.*, XC (1948), 261.

Grossman, F., 'Holbein, Torrigiani and some Portraits of Dean Colet', *Journal of the Warburg and Courtauld Institutes*, XIII (1950), 211.
'Holbein Studies I', *Burl. Mag.* XCIII (1951), 39.

Hervey, M. 'Notes on a Tudor Painter: Gerlach Flicke', *Burl. Mag.*, XVII (1910), 71.

Hilliard, N. 'A Treatise concerning the Arts of Limning', *Walpole Society*, I (1912).

Hind, A. M. *Engraving in England in the 16th and 17th Centuries*, I, 1952; II, 1955.

Kurz, O. 'An Architectural Design for Henry VIII', *Burl. Mag.*, LXXXII (1943), 81.
'Holbein and Others in a 17th Century Collection', *id.*, LXXXIII (1943), 279.
'Rowland Lockey', *ibid.*, XCIX. (1957), 13.

Lees-Milne, J. 'Two portraits at Charlecote Park by William Larkin', *Burl. Mag.*, XCIV (1952), 352.

Long, B. *British Miniaturists*, 1929.

Mercer, E. *English Art, 1553–1625*, 1962.

Millar, O. *The Tudor, Stuart and Early Georgian Pictures in the Collection of Her Majesty the Queen*, 1963, 2 vols.
'Marcus Gheeraerts the Younger: A sequel through Inscriptions', *Burl. Mag.* CV (1965), 533.

Paget, H. 'Gerard and Lucas Hornebolt in England', *Burl. Mag.*, CI (1959), 396.

Parker, K. *Holbein Drawings at Windsor Castle*, 1945.

Piper, D. 'The 1590 Lumley Inventory: Hilliard, Segar and the Earl of Essex', *Burl. Mag.*, XCIX (1957), 224, 299.

The English Face, 1957.
'Holbein the Younger in England', *Journal of the Royal Society for the Encouragement of Arts*, CXI, (1963), 763.
'Some Portraits by Marcus Gheeraerts II and John de Critz reconsidered', *Proceedings of the Huguenot Society*, XX (1960), 210.

Pope-Hennessy, J. 'N. Hilliard and Mannerist Art-Theory', *Journal of the Warburg and Courtauld Institutes*, VI (1943), 89.
A Lecture on Nicholas Hilliard, 1949.

Popham, A. E. 'Hans Holbein's Italian Contemporaries in England', *Burl. Mag.*, LXXXIV (1944), 12.

Pouncey, P. 'Girolamo da Treviso in the service of Henry VIII', *Burl. Mag.* XCV (1953), 208.

Reynolds, A. G. *Nicholas Hilliard and Isaac Oliver*, 1947 (revised ed., 1971).
English Portrait Miniatures, 1952.
'Portraits by N. Hilliard and his Assistants of King James I and his Family', *Walpole Society*, XXXIV (1959), 14.

Saxl, F. 'Holbein and the Reformation', in *Lectures*, 1957, I, 277.

Schmid, H. A. *Hans Holbein der Jüngere*, Basle, 1948, 3 vols.

Strong, R. 'Edward VI and the Pope', *Journal of the Warburg and Courtauld Institutes*, XXIII (1960), 312.
Portraits of Queen Elizabeth I, 1963.
Hans Eworth: A Tudor Artist and his Circle, 1965.
Holbein and Henry VII, 1967.
The English Icon: Elizabethan and Jacobean Portraiture, 1969.
Tudor and Jacobean Portraits, 1969, 2 vols.

Vertue, G. 'Notebooks', *Walpole Society*, 6 vols, 1930–55.

Walpole, H. *Anecdotes of Painting in England* (ed. Wornum and Dalloway, 1862).

Waterhouse, E. K. *Painting in Britain, 1530–1790*, 1953.

The Autobiography of Thomas Whythorne, ed. J. Osborn, 1961.

Winter, C. 'Holbein's Miniatures', *Burl. Mag.*, LXXXIII (1943), 266.

Yates, F. A. 'Queen Elizabeth as Astraea', *Journal of the Warburg and Courtauld Institutes*, X (1947), 27.
'Elizabethan Chivalry: The Romance of the Accession Day Tilts', *id.*, XX (1957), 4.
The Valois Tapestries, 1959.
'The Allegorical Portraits of Sir John Luttrell', *Essays in the History of Art presented to Rudolf Wittkower*, 1967, 149.

3 Painting under the Stuarts

Auerbach, A. and Adams, C. Kingsley. *Paintings and Sculpture at Hatfield House*, 1971.

Baker, C. H. Collins. *Lely and the Stuart Portrait Painters*, 2 vols, 1912.

Beckett, R. B. *Lely*, 1951

Buckeridge, B. *An Essay towards an English School*, 1706.

Corbett, M. and Norton, M. *Engraving in England in the Sixteenth and Seventeenth Centuries*, part III, 1964.

Croft-Murray, E. *Decorative Painting in England*, vol. II, 1970.

Fokker, T. H. *Jan Siberechts*, Brussels and Paris, 1931.

Glück, G. *Van Dyck, Stuttgart*, 1931.

Goulding, R. W. 'The Welbeck Abbey Miniatures', *Walpole Soc.*, vol. IV, 1916.

Graham, R. *A Short Account of the most eminent Painters . . .*, 1695.

Herrmann, L. *British Landscape Painting of the Eighteenth Century*, 1973.

Hind, A. M. *Wenceslaus Hollar and his View of London and Windsor . . .*, 1922.

Hulton, P. H. 'Drawings of England in the Seventeenth Century by Willem Schellinks, Jacob Esselens & Lambert Doomer', *Walpole Soc.*, vol. XXXV, 2 vols., 1959.

Mayhew, E. de N. *Sketches by Thornhill*, V. & A. Museum, 1967.

Millar, O. *Rubens: The Whitehall Ceiling*, 1958. ['The Restoration Portrait'],

Journal of the Royal Society of Arts, vol. CIX, 1961, 410–33.

Van Dyck, Wenceslaus Hollar & the Miniature-Painters, Queen's Gallery, 1968.

ed. 'Abraham van der Doort's Catalogue of the Collections of Charles I', Walpole Soc., vol. XXXVII, 1960.

ed. 'The Inventories and Valuations of the King's Goods', *Walpole Soc.,* vol. XLIII, 1972.

Nisser, W. *Michael Dahl . . .,* Upsala, 1927.

Norgate, E. *Miniatura, or the Art of Limning,* ed. M. Hardie, 1919.

Ogden, H.V.S. and M.S. *English Taste in Landscape in the Seventeenth Century,* Chicago, 1955.

Palme, P. *Triumph of Peace,* 1957.

Piper, D. *The English Face,* 1957.

'The Contemporary Portraits of Oliver Cromwell', *Walpole Soc.,* vol. XXXIV, 1958, 27–41.

Catalogue of Seventeenth-Century Portraits in the National Portrait Gallery, 1963.

Poole, Mrs R.L. *Catalogue of Portraits in Oxford . . .,* 3 vols., 1912–25.

Sainsbury, W.N. *Original Unpublished Papers . . .,* 1859.

Stewart, J.D. *Sir Godfrey Kneller,* National Portrait Gallery, 1971.

Strong, R. *The Elizabethan Image,* Tate Gallery, 1969–70.

Ter Kuile, O. 'Daniel Mijtens', *Nederlands Kunsthistorisch Jaarboek,* vol. XX, 1969, 1–106.

Tyler, R. *Francis Place,* City Art Gallery, York, and Iveagh Bequest, Kenwood, 1971.

Vaughan, W. *Endymion Porter and William Dobson,* Tate Gallery, 1970.

Wark, R. *Early British Drawings in the Huntington Collection,* San Marino, 1969.

Whinney, M. and Millar, O. *English Art 1625–1714,* 1957.

Whitley, W.T. *Artists and their Friends in England,* 2 vols., 1928.

Williams, I.A. *Early English Watercolours,* 1952.

Woodward, J. *Tudor and Stuart Drawings,* 1951.

4 The Eighteenth Century

Allan, D.G.C. *William Shipley,* 1968.

Antal, F. *Hogarth and his place in European art,* 1962.

Archer, M. and W.G. *Indian Painting for the British,* 1955.

Archer, M. *British Drawings in the India Office Library,* 2 vols., 1969.

Brydall, R. *Art in Scotland; its origin and progress,* 1889.

Butlin, M. 'An eighteenth-century art scandal: Nathaniel Hone's "The Conjuror"', *The Connoisseur,* May, 1970.

Constable, W.G. *Richard Wilson,* 1953.

Canaletto, 1962.

Croft-Murray, E. *Decorative Painting in England,* II, 1970.

Dawe, G. *The Life of George Morland,* 1807.

Dobson, A. *William Hogarth,* 1907.

Edwards, E. *Anecdotes of Painters,* 1808, reprinted, with introduction by R.W. Lightbown, 1970.

Finberg, H.F. 'Gawen Hamilton, an unknown Scottish portrait painter', *Walpole Society,* VI, 1917–18, p. 51.

Fryer, E. *The Works of James Barry, Historical Painter,* 1809.

Galt, J. *The Life, studies and works of Benjamin West,* 1920.

Gaunt, W. *The great century of British Painting,* 1971.

Gowing, L. 'Hogarth, Hayman and the Vauxhall Decorations', *Burl. Mag.,* XCV, 1953. p. 4.

Graves, A. *The Royal Academy of Arts,* 1905–6.

The Society of Artists of Great Britain, 1907.

Graves, A. and Cronin, W.V. *A History of the Works of Sir Joshua Reynolds,* 1899–1901.

Hardie, M. *Water-colour painting in Britain,* ed. D. Snelgrove with J. Mayne and B. Taylor, I, 1967.

Harris, J. *Sir William Chambers,* 1970.

Hayes, J. *The drawings of Thomas Gainsborough,* 1970.

Herrmann, L. *British Landscape painting in the eighteenth century,* 1973.

Hilles, F.W. *The Literary career of Sir Joshua Reynolds,* 1936.

Hogarth, W. *The Analysis of Beauty,* ed. J. Burke, 1955.

Hutchison, S.C. *The History of the Royal Academy,* 1968.

Irwin, D. *English Neoclassical art,* 1966.

Long, B. *British Miniaturists, 1520–1820,* 1929 (reprinted, 1966).

Manners, V. and Williamson, G.C. *Angelica Kauffmann,* 1924.

John Zoffany, 1920.

Millar, O. *Tudor, Stuart and Early Georgian Pictures in the Royal Collection,* 1963.

Later Georgian Pictures in the Royal Collection, 1969.

Zoffany and his Tribuna, 1967.

Mitchell, C. 'Benjamin West's "Death of Wolfe" and the Popular History Piece', *Journal of the Warburg and Courtauld Institutes,* VII, 1944, p. 20.

Nicolson, B. *Joseph Wright of Derby,* 1968.

The Treasures of the Foundling Hospital, 1972.

Northcote, J. *Life of Sir Joshua Reynolds,* 2nd ed. 1819 reprinted with an introduction by R.W. Lightbown, 1971.

Oppé, P. *Sandby Drawings at Windsor Castle,* 1947.

'Memoirs of Thomas Jones', *Walpole Society,* XXXII, 1946–8.

Parker, C.A. *Mr Stubbs the horse painter,* 1971.

Pasquin, A. *Memoirs of the Royal Academicians,* 1796 and *Authentic History of the Professors of Painting in Ireland,* reprinted with introduction by R.W. Lightbown, 1970.

Paulson, R. *Hogarth's Graphic Works,* 1970.

Hogarth: His Life, Art, and Times, 1971.

Pavière, S.H. *The Devis Family of Painters,* 1950.

Praz, M. *Conversation Pieces,* 1971.

Pye, J. *Patronage of British Art,* 1845, reprinted with introduction by R.W. Lightbown, 1970.

Raines, R. *Marcellus Laroon,* 1966.

Rouquet, J.A. *State of the Arts in England,* 1755, reprinted with an introduction by R.W. Lightbown, 1970.

Smart, A. *The Life and Art of Allan Ramsay,* 1952.

Smith, J.T. *Nollekens and his times,* ed. W. Whitten, 1917.

Taylor, B. *Stubbs,* 1971.

Vertue, G. 'Notebooks', *Walpole Society,* 6 vols. 1934–55.

Vesme, A. de and Calabri, A. *Francesco Bartolozzi,* Milan, 1928.

Walpole, H. *Anecdotes of Painting,* 4 vols, ed. J. Dalloway, 1828.

Wark, R.R. *Sir Joshua Reynolds. Discourses on Art,* San Marino, 1959.

Waterhouse, E. *Gainsborough,* 1958.

Painting in Britain, 1969.

Reynolds, 1973.

Webster, M. *Francis Wheatley,* 1970.

Whitley, W.T. *Thomas Gainsborough,* 1915.

'An eighteenth-century art chronicler: Sir Henry Bate Dudley, Bart.', *Walpole Society,* XIII, 1925, p. 25.

Artists and their friends in England, 2 vols., 1928.

Catalogues

Introducing Francis Cotes, R.A., Nottingham University Art Gallery, 1971.

Francis Hayman, Kenwood, Iveagh Bequest, 1960.

Joseph Highmore, Kenwood, Iveagh Bequest, 1963.

Hogarth, Tate Gallery, 1971.

Irish Portraits, National Portrait Gallery, 1969.

Thomas Jones, Marble Hill House, Twickenham, 1970.

Angelika Kauffmann und ihre Zeitgenossen, Bregenz and Vienna, 1968.

George Lambert, Kenwood, Iveagh Bequest, 1970.

Philippe Jacques de Loutherbourg, R.A., Kenwood, Iveagh Bequest, 1973.

Philip Mercier, City Art Gallery York and Kenwood, Iveagh Bequest, 1969.

John Hamilton Mortimer, Towner Art Gallery Eastbourne and Kenwood, Iveagh Bequest, 1968.

Samuel Scott, Guildhall Art Gallery, 1972.

5 The Romantics

Addison, A. *Romanticism and the Gothic Revival*, New York, 1938.
Andrews, Keith. *The Nazarenes*, 1964.
Bernbaum, Ernest. *Anthology of Romanticism*, 1948.
Betjeman, John and Taylor, Geoffrey. *English, Scottish and Welsh Landscape, 1700–1860, an anthology*, 1944.
Binyon, Laurence. *The followers of William Blake*, 1925.
  English Water-Colours, 1933; 1945.
Boase, T.S.R. *English Art 1800–1870*, 1959.
Brion, Marcel *Romantic Art*, 1960.
Brydall, R. *Art in Scotland*, 1889.
Bury, A. *Two Centuries of British Water-Colour Painting*, 1950.
Clark, Sir Kenneth. *The Gothic Revival*, 1923; 1950; 1962.
  Landscape into Art, 1949; 1956.
  Moments of Vision, 1954.
  Looking at Pictures, 1960.
  Civilisation, 1969.
Collins Baker, C.H. *Windsor Castle Catalogue*, 1937.
Cursiter, Stanley. *Scottish Art*, 1949.
Dickes, W.F. *The Norwich School of Painting*, 1905.
Finberg, A.J. *English Water Colour Painters*, 1906.
Fry, Roger. *Reflections on British Painting*, 1934.
Gage, John. *Colour in Turner*, 1969.
Grigson, Geoffrey. *The Romantics: an Anthology*, 1942.
Halstead, John B. *Romanticism, Selected Documents*, 1969.
Harris, R.W. *Romanticism and the Social Order, 1780–1830*, 1969.
Hodgson, J.E. and Eason, F.A. *The Royal Academy and Its Members*, 1905.
Holme, C. *The Royal Academy from Reynolds to Millais*, 1904.
Honour, Hugh. *Chinoiserie*, 1961.
  Neo-Classicism, 1968.
Hussey, Christopher. *The Picturesque*, 1927.
Irwin, David. *English Neoclassical Art*, 1966.
Klingender, Francis D. *Hogarth and English Caricature*, 1944.
  Art and the Industrial Revolution, 1947; 1968.
Lamb, W.R.M. *The Royal Academy*, 1951.
Lemaître, Henri. *Le Paysage anglais à l'acquarelle 1760–1851*, Paris, 1955.
Low, David. *British Cartoonists, Caricaturists and Comic Artists*, 1932.
Manwaring, Elizabeth Wheeler, *Italian Landscape in Eighteenth-Century England*, New York, 1925.
Merchant, W. Moelwyn. *Shakespeare and the Artist*, 1959.
Novotny, Fritz. *Painting and Sculpture in Europe, 1780–1880*, 1960.
Piper, John. *British Romantic Artists: Aspects of British Art*, 1942; 1947.
Praz, Mario. The Romantic Agony, 1933.
Quennell, Peter. *Romantic England: Writing and Painting 1717–1851*, 1970.
Read, Herbert. *The Meaning of Art*, 1931; 1964.
Redgrave, Samuel and Richard. *A Century of Painters*, 1866; 1947, ed. Ruthven Todd.
Reynolds, Graham. *English Portrait Miniatures*, 1952.
Richardson, E.P. *American Romantic Painting*, New York, 1944.
Roget, J.L. *History of the Old Water Colour Society*, 2 vols, 1891.
Rosenblum, R. *Transformations in Late Eighteenth Century Art*, Princetown,
Steegman, John. *The Rule of Taste*, 1936.
Summers, Montague. *The Gothic Quest*, 1938.
  N.J., 1967.
Sitwell, S. *Conversation Pieces*, 1936.
  Narrative Paintings, 1937.
Smith, Bernard. *European Vision of the South Pacific 1768–1850*, 1960.
Talman, J.L. *Romanticism and Revolt*, 1967.
Waterhouse, Ellis. *Painting in Britain 1530–1780*, 1953.
Whitley, W.T. *Art in England, 1780–1820*, 1928.
  Art in England, 1821–1837, 1937.
Wilenski, R.H. *English Painting*, 1933.
Williams, I.A. *Early English Watercolour Paintings*, 1952.

Catalogues
Italian Art and Britain, Royal Academy, 1960.
Painting in Britain 1700–1850, The Collection of Mr & Mrs Paul Mellon, Virginia, USA, 1963.
The Romantic Movement, Tate Gallery, 1959.
Romantic Art in Britain 1760–1860, The Philadelphia Museum of Art & Detroit Institute of Art, USA, 1968.

6 The Victorians

Andrews, Keith. *The Nazarenes*, 1964.
Baron, Wendy. *Sickert*, 1973.
Bell, Malcolm Sir Edward Burne-Jones: a record and review, 1892, 2nd edition, 1903.
Bell, Quentin. *Victorian Artists*, 1967.
Blunt, Wilfred. *George Frederick Watts*, 1975.
Boase, T.R.S. *English Art, 1800–1870*, 1959.
Browse, Lillian *Sickert*, 1960.
Burne-Jones, G. *Memorials of Edward Burne-Jones*, 1904, o.p.
Chapman, R. *The Laurel and the Thorn – a Study of G.F. Watts*, 1945.
Doughty, O. *A Victorian Romantic: Dante Gabriel Rossetti*, 1949; 1960.
Farr, Dennis. *William Etty*, 1958.
Fildes, L.V. *Luke Fildes, R.A. – a Victorian Painter*, 1968.
Fredeman, William E. *Pre-Raphaelitism – a Bibliocritical Survey*, Harvard, 1965.
Frith, W.P. *My Autobiography and Reminiscences*, 1887, o.p.
Gaunt, W. *The Restless Century: Painting in Britain 1800–1900*, 1972.
Grylls, Rosalie Glynn. *Portrait of Rossetti*, 1964.
Henderson, Philipp. *William Morris: his life, work and friends*, 1967.
Hilton, Tim. *The Pre-Raphaelites*, 1970.
Holman Hunt, W. *Pre-Raphaelitism and the Pre-Raphaelite Brotherhood*, 1913, o.p.
Hueffer, Ford Madox. *Ford Madox Brown: a record of his life and work*, 1896.
Hunt, J.D. *The Pre-Raphaelite Imagination 1848–1900*, 1968.
Ironside, R. and Gere, J. *Pre-Raphaelite Painters*, 1948, o.p.
Klingender, Francis D. *Art and the Industrial Revolution*, 1947, edited and revised by Sir Arthur Elton, 1968.
Laughton, Bruce. *Philip Wilson Steer*, 1971.
Maas, J. *Victorian Painters*, 1969.
Millais, J.G. *The life and letters of John Everett Millais*, 1899, o.p.
Ormond, Richard. *Sargent*, 1970.
Pennell, E.R. and Reynolds, Graham. *Whistler*, 1908.
Reynolds, Graham. *Victorian Painting*, 1966, o.p.
Reynolds, Graham. *Painters of the Victorian Scene*, 1953, o.p.
Roberts, Keith. *The Pre-Raphaelites*, 1972.
Rossetti, D.G. *Letters*, ed. O. Doughty and A. Wahl, 4 vols, 1965, 1967.
Staley, Allen. *The Pre-Raphaelite Landscape*, 1973.
Surtees, V. *The Paintings and Drawings of Dante Gabriel Rossetti 1828–1882: a catalogue raisonné*, 2 vols, 1973.
Sutton, D. *James McNeill Whistler: Paintings, Etchings, Pastels and Watercolours*, 1966.
Waters, B. and Harrison, M. *Burne-Jones*, 1973.
Whistler, J.M. *The Gentle Art of Making Enemies*, 1890, o.p.
Wood, Christopher. *Dictionary of Victorian Painting*, 1972.

Catalogues
Richard Dadd, Tate Gallery, 1974.
William Holman Hunt, Walker Art Gallery, Liverpool, 1969.
Daniel Maclise 1806–1870, The Arts Council, 1972.
Dante Gabriel Rossetti, Royal Academy, 1972.

7 The Twentieth Century

Alley, R. *British Painting since 1945*, 1966.

Alley, R. *William Scott*, 1963.

Barber, N. *Conversations with Painters*, 1964.

Baxandall, D. *Ben Nicholson*, 1962.

Berger, J. *Success and Failure of Picasso*, 1965.

Bowness, A. *Alan Davie*, 1967.

   Recent British Painting, 1968.

Browse, L. *Sickert*, 1960.

Cooper, D. *The Work of Graham Sutherland*, 1961.

D'Offay, Anthony. 'The New Constructive Geometric Art in London, 1910–15', *The Avant-Garde*, New York, 1968.

Fry, R. *Vision and Design*, 1920.

Gaunt, W. *British Painting from Hogarth's Day to Ours*, 1945.

Grigson, G. *Henry Moore*, 1943.

Hendy, P. *Mathew Smith*, 1944.

Herbert, R.L. *Modern Artists on Art*, 1971.

Heron, P. *The Changing Forms of Art*, 1955.

Hughes, R. 'Machined Mosaics', *Time*, October 1971, p. 86.

Johnson, E.L. *Contemporary Painters and Sculptors as Printmakers*, New York, 1966.

Kirkpatrick, D. *Eduardo Paolozzi*, 1970.

Lucie-Smith, E. and White, P. *Art in Britain 1969–70*, 1970.

Martin, J.L. *et al. Circle*, 1971.

Melville, R. *Henry Moore*, 1970.

Michael, W. and Fox, C.J. *Wyndham Lewis on Art*, 1969.

Michel, W. *Wyndham Lewis*, 1971.

Middleton, M. *Eduardo Paolozzi*, 1963.

Neve, C. 'Jack Yeats: Rider to the Sea', *Country Life*, vol. CXLVIII No. 3823, July 1970, p. 279.

Pevsner, N. *The Englishness of English Art*, 1955.

Piper, D. *Painting in England 1500–1880*, 1960.

Read, H. *Art Now*, 1960.

Reichardt, Jasia. *Victor Pasmore*, 1962.

Robertson, B. *et al. Private View*, 1965.

Rosenthal, T.G. *Jack Yeats*, 1963.

Rothenstein, Sir John. *Autobiography in 3 Parts*, 1970.

   British Art Since 1900, 1962.

   Modern English Painters, Sickert to Smith, 1952.

Rothenstein, Sir John and Alley, R. *Francis Bacon*, 1964.

Thompson, D. *Ceri Richards*, 1963.

Sausmarez, M. de. *Bridget Riley*, 1970.

Rutherston, A. *Contemporary British Artists: Henry Lamb*, 1924.

Russel, J. *Ben Nicholson*, 1969.

Willett, J. 'Where to Stick it', *Art International*, vol. XIV/9, November 1970, p. 28.

Woolfe, V. *Roger Fry*, 1940.

Catalogues

Francis Bacon, Tate Gallery, 1962.

Vanessa Bell Memorial Exhibition, Arts Council, 1964.

David Bomberg, Arts Council Exhibition, 1967.

John Bratby, Retrospective, 1971.

William Coldstream, Arts Council, 1962.

Robert Colquhoun, The Arts Council of Great Britain, Scottish Committee, 1963.

Mark Gertler, The Minories, Colchester, 1971.

Spencer Frederick Gore, The Arts Council, 1955.

David Hockney: Paintings, Prints and Drawings 1960–1970, The Whitechapel Art Gallery, London, 1970.

Richard Hamilton, Tate Gallery, 1970.

Josef Herman, The Royal National Eisteddfod of Wales, 1962.

Gwen John, Arts Council Exhibition, 1968.

R.B. Kitaj, University of California, 1967.

Peter Lanyon, Arts Council Exhibition, 1968.

Charles Rennie Mackintosh, Scottish Arts Council, 1968.

Mary Martin, Kenneth Martin, Arts Council, 1970–71.

Modern British Pictures from the Tate Gallery, Arts Council, 1947.

Ben Nicholson, Tate Gallery, 1969.

Eduardo Paolozzi, Print Retrospective, 1968.

Victor Pasmore, Tate Gallery, 1965.

Bridget Riley, The Arts Council, The Hayward Gallery, 1971.

William Roberts A.R.A., The Arts Council, 1965.

William Rothenstein Memorial Exhibition, Arts Council, 1950.

The School of Paris, The Museum of Modern Art, New York, 1965.

Helen Sutherland Collection, Arts Council, 1970–71.

List of Illustrations

Index